THE LIFE OF ANDREW JACKSON

Other Books by Robert V. Remini

MARTIN VAN BUREN AND THE MAKING OF THE DEMOCRATIC PARTY

THE ELECTION OF ANDREW JACKSON

ANDREW JACKSON

ANDREW JACKSON AND THE BANK WAR

THE PRESIDENCY OF ANDREW JACKSON (EDITOR)

THE AGE OF JACKSON (EDITOR)

WE THE PEOPLE: A HISTORY OF THE UNITED STATES

(WITH JAMES I. CLARK)

THE REVOLUTIONARY AGE OF ANDREW JACKSON

ANDREW JACKSON AND THE COURSE OF AMERICAN EMPIRE, 1767–1821

ANDREW JACKSON AND THE COURSE OF AMERICAN FREEDOM, 1822–1832

ANDREW JACKSON AND THE COURSE OF AMERICAN

DEMOCRACY, 1833–1845

THE AMERICAN PEOPLE: A HISTORY

(WITH ARTHUR S. LINK, STANLEY COHEN,

DOUGLAS GREENBERG,

AND ROBERT C. MCMATH, JR.)

THE LIFE OF
ANDREW JACKSON

Robert V. Remini

1817

HARPER & ROW, PUBLISHERS, New York
Cambridge, Philadelphia, San Francisco, Washington
London, Mexico City, São Paulo, Singapore, Sydney

FIRST EDITION

Copyeditor: Rick Hermann

Designer: Sidney Feinberg

Index by Maro Riofrancos

Library of Congress Cataloging-in-Publication Data

Remini, Robert Vincent, 1921–
  The life of Andrew Jackson.

  Condensation of the author's three-volume biography originally published 1977–1984 under titles: Andrew Jackson and the course of American empire, 1767–1821; Andrew Jackson and the course of American freedom, 1822–1832, and Andrew Jackson and the course of American democracy, 1833–1845.
  Bibliography: p.
  Includes index.
  1. Jackson, Andrew, 1767–1845. 2. Presidents—United States—Biography. 3. United States—Politics and government—1815–1861. 4. United States—Territorial expansion. I. Title. E382.R454   1988   973.5′61′0924   [B]   87-46168 ISBN 0-06-015904-9

88 89 90 91 92 HC 10 9 8 7 6 5 4 3 2 1

For My Granddaughter,
Grace Marie

Contents

Preface   ix

Chronology of Jackson's Life, 1767–1845   xi

Genealogy of the Jackson Family   xv

1. Boy from the Waxhaw District   1
2. Frontiersman and Lawyer   14
3. Congressman Jackson   28
4. The Duel   42
5. Old Hickory   55
6. The Creek War   68
7. The Battle of New Orleans   86
8. Indian Removal   105
9. The First Seminole War   116
10. Governor Jackson   129
11. An Era of Corruption   137
12. "Jackson and Reform"   157
13. The First People's Inaugural   172
14. The Reform Begins   183
15. Political Upheaval   190
16. Return to Reform   208
17. The Bank War Begins   220
18. Jackson and the Union   233
19. The Union Preserved   244
20. "The Grand Triumphal Tour"   252
21. Panic!   261

22. The End of the Bank   272
23. The Hermitage Fire   278
24. Jacksonian Diplomacy   283
25. Jacksonian Democracy   295
26. Texas   309
27. Life in the White House   315
28. Farewell   327
29. Retirement   336
30. The Silver Jubilee   342
31. "We Must Regain Texas"   346
32. "We Will All Meet in Heaven"   354

      Notes   361

      Bibliography   397

      Index   399

      Photographs follow page 208

Maps and Floor Plans

The Creek Campaign, 1813–1814   76
Route of British Invasion   94
Battle of New Orleans, January 8, 1815   98
Indian Removal—Southern Tribes   107
First Seminole War, 1818   123
Hermitage, First Floor   300
Hermitage, Second Floor   301
The White House, 1833, Main Floor   318
The White House, 1833, Second Story   319

Preface

In 1977 the first volume of my biography of Andrew Jackson appeared in print, followed in 1981 and 1984 by the second and then the concluding volumes. When I first undertook this project I had intended to write a complete life in one volume. But it did not work out that way. One volume grew to a second and a third, and I might have gone on to produce a fourth had my editor at Harper & Row, Hugh Van Dusen, not intervened in the nick of time.

Then, at the annual meeting of the American Historical Association in December 1984 I was conversing with Aida D. Donald, executive editor of the Harvard University Press, when she broached the idea of condensing my three-volume biography into a single volume. She said that the idea had originated with her husband, David Herbert Donald, who felt that such a book would serve the needs of both students of history and the general public. I confess the idea had not occurred to me before, and later that day when I talked with David he dispelled whatever doubts I may have had.

Jackson is one of those unusual figures in history who seem to get multi-volume biographies written about them, such as my own and those of James Parton, Marquis James, and James Bassett, or he is reduced to narratives of less than two hundred pages—I've written one of these, also, I must confess—which are used almost exclusively in survey courses in American history taught in colleges and universities. Something in-between, something of more normal size for a major historical figure, something around four hundred pages or so for a biography of Jackson is almost unknown. And it was David Donald's contention that such a book was needed for an audience of both students and the general public who cannot or will not plow through two and three hefty volumes and yet cannot get enough information or analysis of men and events in the briefer studies.

By the time our conversation ended I was totally convinced. But I was not certain that Harper & Row would go along with the scheme since they had already invested a great deal in issuing a three-volume study. Fortunately, Hugh Van Dusen liked the idea very much and probably saw more value in it than I did. In any event he approved the venture and I set to work in the mistaken notion that a single volume could easily and quickly be extracted from the three-volume behemoth. I soon learned otherwise. Shrinking 1,609 pages—the total number of the three volumes—to the present 400 pages proved not simply difficult but traumatic and agonizing. Jackson had such a long, full and exciting life that he defies (and resents) abbreviation of any kind. More difficult than that was applying the surgical knife to my own prose and restating with totally new words the events and ideas that I had once felt were as exact and proper as I could make them when they were first produced in the original volumes. But once I made the initial incision and survived the awful pain, the task grew less difficult and wrenching, particularly when I found several opportunities to rethink more carefully what I had originally set down. Also, the results of recent research could be added; and the insights of monographs published in the last several years could be introduced to enrich the text. Finally, some of my rhetorical flourishes needed excision.

In this new work, then, I have not abandoned or seriously modified the major themes developed in my three-volume biography but I have tried to strengthen the arguments and clarify the language that provide support. The notes have been reduced substantially to provide space but I have made a special effort to retain all the citations that are essential for the book's principal arguments. The bibliography, too, has been cut drastically and I would refer the reader to volume III of my larger work for a more complete discussion of both primary and secondary sources.

In making this biography possible I am deeply grateful to Hugh Van Dusen, David and Aida Donald, and, as always, the Ladies' Hermitage Association in Tennessee and the University of Illinois at Chicago who have handsomely supported my research for many years.

July 1987   ROBERT V. REMINI
Wilmette, Illinois

Chronology of Jackson's Life
1767-1845

1767, March 15	Born, Waxhaw settlement, South Carolina
1775–1780	Attends schools conducted by Dr. William Humphries and James White Stephenson
1780–1781	Serves in American Revolution; captured and wounded by British officer; imprisoned in Camden and later released; contracts smallpox
1781	Death of mother, Elizabeth Hutchinson Jackson
1782	Attends school conducted by Robert McCulloch
1783–1784	Teaches school in Waxhaw
1784–1786	Moves to Salisbury, North Carolina, and reads law with Spruce McCay
1786–1787	Reads law with John Stokes
1787, September 26	Licensed as an attorney in North Carolina; practices law and tends store
1788	Appointed public prosecutor for western district of North Carolina and migrates west; fights first duel with Waightstill Avery; settles in Nashville
1790–1791	Marries Rachel Donelson Robards for the first time

1791, February 15	Appointed attorney general for the Mero District
1794, January 18	Remarries Rachel Donelson Robards
1796, January 11–February 6	Participates in Tennessee Constitutional Convention
1796, October 22	Elected to U.S. House of Representatives
1797, September 26	Elected to U.S. Senate
1798	Resigns Senate seat
1798, December 20	Elected judge of Tennessee Superior Court
1802, February 5	Elected major general of Tennessee militia
1804, April	Forms business partnership with John Coffee and John Hutchings
1804, July 24	Resigns as judge
1804, August 4	Purchases Hermitage property
1805–1807	Participates in Burr conspiracy
1806, May 30	Kills Charles Dickinson
1809	Adopts son of Elizabeth and Severn Donelson
1812–1815	Leads troops against Indians and British
1813, March	Nicknamed Old Hickory
1813, September 4	Gunfight with the Bentons
1813, November 3	"Adopts" Lyncoya
1814, March 27	Defeats Creek Indians at Horseshoe Bend
1814, August 9	Imposes Treaty of Fort Jackson on Creek Nation
1814, November 7	Captures Pensacola
1814, December 1	Arrives in New Orleans
1815, January 8	Defeats British advance toward New Orleans
1815, March 31	Fined for contempt of court
1816–1818	Signs treaties with Indian tribes
1818, March 15	Invades Spanish Florida
1818, April 6	Captures St. Marks
1818, April 29	Orders execution of Robert Ambrister and Alexander Arbuthnot

1818, May 24	Captures Pensacola
1819, February 8	Congressional censure rejected
1821	Appointed and confirmed governor of Florida Territory
1821, June 1	Resigns army commission
1821, July 17	Receives Florida from Spanish
1821, November 13	Resigns as Florida governor
1822, July 20	Nominated for President by Tennessee legislature
1823, October 1	Elected U.S. Senator
1823	Builds church on Hermitage property
1825, February 9	Defeated for President in House election
1825, February 14	Accuses Clay of "corrupt bargain"
1825, May 5	Entertains Lafayette at Hermitage
1825, October 12	Resigns Senate seat
1825, October 14	Nominated for President by Tennessee legislature
1828, June 1	Death of Lyncoya
1828, November	Elected President
1828, December 22	Death of Rachel
1829, March 4	Inaugurated seventh President
1830, April 13	Attends Jefferson birthday dinner
1830, May 27	Vetoes Maysville Road bill
1830, May 28	Signs Indian Removal bill
1830, June	Exercises first pocket veto
1830, October	Assists establishment of Washington *Globe*
1830, October 5	Reopens American ports to British West Indian trade
1831, April	Accepts cabinet resignations and appoints new cabinet
1831, November 24	Andrew Jackson, Jr., and Sarah Yorke marry
1832, January	Operated on for removal of bullet
1832, January 25	Van Buren's nomination as minister rejected
1832, March 27	Accused of maintaining a "Kitchen Cabinet"
1832, July 10	Vetoes Bank bill
1832, July 14	Signs Tariff of 1832
1832, November 1	Granddaughter, Rachel Jackson, born
1832, November	Reelected President
1832, December 10	Issues Proclamation to people of South Carolina
1833, March 2	Signs Force Bill and Compromise Tariff

1833, March 4	Pocket vetoes distribution bill
1833, March 4	Inaugurated for second term
1833, May 6	Assaulted by Robert B. Randolph
1833, June 6–July 4	Tours New England and Middle Atlantic states
1833, September 23	Dismisses Duane
1834, March 28	Censured by Senate
1834, April 4	Grandson, Andrew Jackson III, born
1834, April 15	Protests censure
1834, May	Threatens action against France
1834, June 30	Signs Coinage Act
1834, October 13	Hermitage burns
1835, January	Announces nation free of debt
1835, January 30	Escapes assassination attempt
1835, May 29	Refuses to apologize to France
1835, December 18	Second Seminole War begins
1835, December 28	Nominates Taney as chief justice
1836, February	Crisis with France resolved
1836, June 23	Signs Deposit bill
1836, July 2	Signs Post Office bill
1836, July 11	Issues Specie Circular
1836, August 2	Rebuilding of Hermitage completed
1836, November 19	Suffers severe hemorrhage attack
1837, January 16	Senate censure expunged
1837, March 3	Recognizes Texas' independence
1837, March 4	Issues Farewell Address
1837, March 7	Leaves White House for Hermitage
1837, June 9	Grandson, Samuel Jackson, born
1838, July 15	Joins Presbyterian Church
1840, January 8	Attends silver jubilee of victory at New Orleans
1842, September 1	Writes last will and testament
1843, February 14	Restitution of New Orleans fine authorized by Congress
1844, May 13	Endorses Polk for President
1844, December	Urges Texas' annexation
1845, May	Suffers massive edema
1845, June 8	Dies at Hermitage
1845, June 10	Buried in Hermitage garden

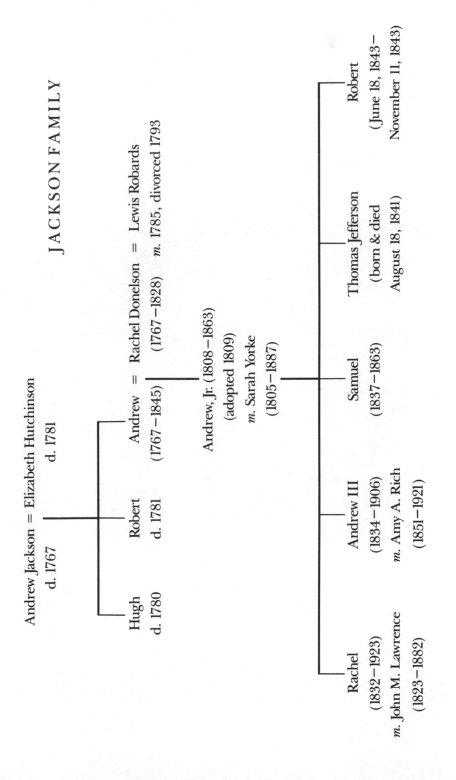

JACKSON FAMILY

Andrew Jackson = Elizabeth Hutchinson
d. 1767   d. 1781

Hugh
d. 1780

Robert
d. 1781

Andrew = Rachel Donelson = Lewis Robards
(1767–1845) (1767–1828)   *m.* 1785, divorced 1793

Andrew, Jr. (1808–1863)
(adopted 1809)
m. Sarah Yorke
(1805–1887)

Rachel
(1832–1923)
m. John M. Lawrence
(1823–1882)

Andrew III
(1834–1906)
m. Amy A. Rich
(1851–1921)

Samuel
(1837–1863)

Thomas Jefferson
(born & died
August 18, 1841)

Robert
(June 18, 1843 –
November 11, 1843)

CHAPTER 1

Boy from the Waxhaw District

IT WAS NOT HALF AN HOUR BEFORE DAWN, January 8, 1815. A thick mist rolled from the murky waters of the Mississippi River and covered the ground separating two armies facing each other. Slowly, as the light of the new day spread across the plain, the mist gradually thinned and drifted away, revealing the British army, in magnificent array, stretched across two-thirds of the open field. A short distance in front of them and crouched behind an open ditch, American militiamen, sharpshooters, frontiersmen, pirates, blacks, army regulars, and others, waited for the attack to begin, their guns pointed straight ahead.

Then, with a screech, a Congreve rocket rose from one flank of the British army, followed by a second that ascended from the other flank. They signaled the beginning of the Battle of New Orleans.

Displaying superb military discipline, the army of redcoats charged forward. The Americans saw them and cheered. They had been waiting for hours for this moment and could scarcely contain their excitement and joy. Their guns trained on the brightly colored targets before them. Trigger fingers tensed. Suddenly the entire American line was illuminated with a devastating blaze of fire. A battalion band in the background struck up "Yankee Doodle" as artillery, rifles, and small arms emptied into the faces of the oncoming British. The initial roar of defiance no sooner echoed away than another thundering rebuke smashed into the scarlet ranks. And with each volley, dozens of redcoats crumbled to the ground.

The commanding officer of the American forces, General Andrew Jackson of Tennessee, stood behind the ditch in a central position and surveyed his line with rapid glances to the left and right. His soldiers loved him and had already dubbed him "Old Hickory" in recognition of his strength, tenacity, and courage. At the moment he looked calm and resolute. He stood ramrod straight, surrounded by his aides, when suddenly he raised his voice in a single command. "Give it to them, my boys," he called to his men. "Let us finish the business to-day."[1]

"Fire! Fire!" ordered General William Carroll to the Tennessee and Kentucky sharpshooters. And it was executed with deadly precision. Not hurriedly or excitedly but calmly and deliberately. Hardly a shot was wasted by the skilled marksmen as row after row of American riflemen shattered the advancing column. One British officer said he never saw a more destructive fire poured upon a single line of men. Every shot seemed to find its mark; scores of soldiers pitched to the ground, many of them falling on top of one another.[2]

Then it happened. The advancing troops lost their nerve and the column halted. "The horror before them was too great to be withstood." They could no longer face the "flashing and roaring hell" in front of them. They recoiled and began a general retreat.[3]

The commanding officer of the British army, Lieutenant General Sir Edward Michael Pakenham, saw his men halt and turn around and he rode forward from his position in the rear to stop them. "For shame, for shame," he screamed at them, "recollect that you are British soldiers. *This* is the road you ought to take," he admonished as he pointed to the fiery furnaces before them.[4]

A shower of lead balls from the sharpshooters behind the ditch greeted Pakenham's call to advance. One shattered his right arm, another killed his horse. Mounting an aide's pony, Pakenham pursued the retreating column with cries to halt and reform their line.

They heard him. Once out of range of the fierce American rifles their spirits surged again. They advanced once more. At the same time a column of 900 Highlanders off to the left side of the line were ordered to cross the field and help their comrades. The tartan-trousered Highlanders followed an oblique route to the right while the once-fleeing column headed back toward the ditch.

But the ditch saw what was happening and responded instantly. Round, grape, musketry, rifle, and buckshot raked the entire length of the Highlanders' line. The carnage was frightful. And once the British column returned within rifle range the mud ditch barked its command to halt. Round after round smashed into the British ranks. One thirty-two-pounder, loaded to the muzzle with musket balls, crashed into the head of the column at point-blank range and leveled it to the ground, some 200 men killed or wounded in this single salvo. In the fire General Pakenham was struck several times. One bullet ripped open his thigh, killed his horse, and threw both to the ground. As his aides started to lift him, a second shot struck him in the groin and Pakenham instantly lost consciousness. He was carried to the rear out of gun range and propped up under an oak tree in the center of the field. Within minutes Lieutenant General Sir Edward Pakenham died.[5]

The brave Highlanders halted not one hundred yards from the ditch, taking round after round from the Americans until more than 500 of them lay on the ground. At last they too turned and fled in horror and dismay.[6] The British army lay shattered on the field.

The Americans stopped firing when the redcoats retreated out of range. Then word was passed down the line to cease fire. The men rested on their arms. The entire assault had taken hardly more than two hours, the principal attack lasting only thirty minutes.

General Jackson walked slowly down the line with his staff, stopping at the center of each command to congratulate the men on their bravery and skill. Then, the entire line suddenly burst forth with loud and prolonged cheers for their General. Jackson nodded and gestured his appreciation. The cheering continued for many minutes.

But when the Americans scaled the parapet they had built behind their ditch and wandered around the battlefield, their smiles and happy countenances vanished as they gazed upon the horror stretched out before them. The ground, one observer reported, was "covered with dead and wounded laying in heaps, the field was completely red." The ground immediately in front of the ditch was so strewn with the dead, the dying, and the horribly wounded that "you could have walked a quarter of a mile to the front of the bodies of the killed and disabled." Many of the mortally wounded pitched and tumbled about in the agonies of death. "Some had their heads shot off, some their legs, some their arms. Some were laughing, some crying, some groaning, and some screaming."[7]

General Jackson stared at the scene in front of him in disbelief. "I never had so grand and awful an idea of the resurrection as on that day," he later wrote. "After the smoke of the battle had cleared off somewhat, I saw in the distance more than five hundred Britons emerging from the heaps of their dead comrades, all over the plain, rising up, and still more distinctly visible as the field became clearer, coming forward and surrendering as prisoners of war to our soldiers. They had fallen at our first fire upon them, without having received so much as a scratch, and lay prostrate, as if dead, until the close of the action."[8] The British later admitted to casualties totaling 2,037. Jackson received a report which claimed a total of 13 Americans killed, 39 wounded, and 19 missing in action.[9]

It was a stupendous victory. It was the greatest feat of American arms up to that time. It was a splendid climax to a not-so-splendid war, the War of 1812, a war that had provided not victories but one American defeat after another.

Until New Orleans. *"Who would not be an American?"* demanded one newspaper after the victory had been announced. *"Long Live the republic!"*[10]

Andrew Jackson's role in bringing honor and glory to the nation made him a popular and beloved hero for the remainder of his life. The American people could never do enough to repay him for the overwhelming victory he had won for them. The country had entered this war against Great Britain with a desperate need to prove its right to independence and not until New Orleans had it demonstrated that it had both the will and the strength to defend its freedom. "The last six months is the proudest period in the history of the republic," asserted one newspaper.[11]

By this victory, General Andrew Jackson restored to the American people their pride and self-confidence, and they never forgot it. Indeed, "from that time on the Union had less of the character of a temporary experiment," something momentary and likely to disappear in a stroke. "The country had also won respect abroad," thanks to Andrew Jackson, "and was recognized in the family of nations as it had not been before."[12]

The Battle of New Orleans created the nation's first authentic military hero. And because of that victory and what it produced, the history of the American nation was permanently altered. Andrew Jackson did more than assist a nation in proving its worth and the strength of its institutions. He reshaped those institutions and breathed a new life into them.

The Jackson clan that produced this Hero of New Orleans, as he was subsequently called, originated from Castlereagh on the eastern coast of Northern Ireland, approximately 125 miles from Carrickfergus. They were Scotch-Irish and had left Ireland like so many of their compatriots to flee the miseries of their homeland and seek a better life in America.

Andrew Jackson, father of the future President, sailed to America in 1765 accompanied by his wife, the former Elizabeth Hutchinson, and his two sons, Hugh and Robert, aged two years and six months respectively. It is probable, but not absolutely certain because of the sparseness of documentary evidence, that they landed in Pennsylvania and then moved slowly southward, following a route taken by several of Elizabeth's sisters who had preceded the Jacksons to America by a year or two.

Eventually the Jacksons settled in the Waxhaw region which straddled North and South Carolina. The Waxhaw Creek, a branch of the Catawba River, gently watered the area but the soil was blood red from iron deposits and produced little more than scrub pine. Still the region supported small game animals, turkeys and deer, and because the Catawba Indians to the north were friendly this area (which subsequently became Lancaster District in South Carolina) proved attractive to new settlers. By the time the Jacksons arrived in the district there was a meetinghouse and a newly formed Presbyterian Church with a graduate of the University of Glasgow as minister. In a few more years this frontier area would also boast an academy where the classics were taught.

One especially attractive feature of the Waxhaws for the Jacksons was the knowledge that they would find family and former neighbors from Ireland already established in the region. The Crawford and McCamie families were related and helped the Jacksons get located once they arrived. Indeed, Elizabeth had several sisters living with their husbands and families in the district, so the struggle for survival was not as difficult as it might have been without their support. Even so the Jacksons arrived with little money and were forced to settle on less fertile land around Twelve Mile Creek, another branch of the Catawba. Whether the elder Andrew Jackson was a squatter or not is unclear, but some early writers have claimed that he "never *owned* in America one acre of land."[13]

Jackson labored for two long years over this red clay to make it yield. He built a small log house and produced enough crops to feed his family adequately. But his efforts apparently wore him down. He died suddenly of unknown causes in March 1767 at a time when his wife was pregnant with their third child. A wagon bore the body to the Waxhaw churchyard, and there is a traditional tale in Lancaster that the body slipped off the wagon on the way to the cemetery. When they discovered their loss, the mourners retraced their steps, found the missing corpse, and brought it to the churchyard where it was finally buried.[14] Following the interment, Elizabeth went to the home of her sister, Jane Crawford, and there, on March 15, 1767, in the Lancaster District, South Carolina, she gave birth to her third son and named him Andrew in memory of her late husband.[15] She apparently abandoned the farm her husband had struggled with, took up residence with the Crawfords, and acted as housekeeper and nurse to her ailing sister. Elizabeth was a remarkable woman of enormous strength and courage. Her life was nearly as heroic as her famous son. She lived in hope that her third child would someday become a Presbyterian minister but she slowly abandoned that hope as she watched him grow into a hot-tempered young man who frequently unleashed a torrent of foul language whenever his passions were aroused. Young Andrew could flood a room with bloodcurdling oaths that frightened his listeners half to death. Indeed, he was so good at terrorizing those around him by his language and actions that throughout his life he frequently exploded in rage to scare his victims into doing what he wanted, even though his rage was completely feigned.

For the first dozen years of his life, or thereabouts, young Andrew Jackson lived at the Crawfords' home with his mother and brothers. It is impossible to say whether he felt like an outsider or not, although his lively temper might indicate a degree of unhappiness. In any event he enjoyed a few advantages, including attendance at the academy conducted by Dr. William Humphries. Later he attended a school run by the Presbyterian minister, Mr. James White Stephenson, perhaps because his mother still nurtured the slowly fading hope that he would someday enter the ministry. At Humphries's academy he learned to read, write, and "cast accounts." Later he said he also studied the "dead languages," by which he presumably meant Latin and possibly Greek.[16] But Jackson never acquired an adequate education, even for the late eighteenth century, and this severely hampered his efforts as President to achieve some of his most cherished goals. Still, despite problems with grammar, syntax, and spelling—he was really indifferent to spelling and could write a single word or name four different ways on the same page—President Jackson frequently wrote and spoke with great clarity and power. Indeed, some of his utterances convey enormous fire and passion, even on the printed page. It is intriguing to imagine what he might have accomplished had he enjoyed a proper education.

Of history and political science, Jackson knew next to nothing. His own political sense later on seems to have been intuitive and formed out of his own personal experiences. In time he grew to appreciate the value of history and once recommended to one of his wards "the history of the Scottish chiefs" as useful and instructive. He always regarded Sir William Wallace as "the best model for a young man. . . . We find in him the truly undaunted courage, always ready to brave any dangers, for the relief of his country or his friend." Small wonder he admired Wallace. The virtues Jackson ascribed to Wallace were precisely his own.[17]

Nor did Jackson know anything about mathematics or science. He was fascinated by the new inventions of the age but that is about as far as it went. Literature had no particular attraction for him, although he could and did quote Shakespeare on occasion and was said to have read *The Vicar of Wakefield* from cover to cover. In fact that book was reportedly the only "secular" book he ever read from start to finish. He did read the Bible many times, particularly toward the end of his life. He also read other religious tracts throughout his life, no doubt the result of his mother's and, more importantly, his wife's influence. He became in time a deeply religious man. Late in life he formally joined the Presbyterian Church, albeit his acceptance of the Presbyterian creed came with a number of reservations.

As a youth, Andrew gained a reputation as a "wild, frolicsome, willful, mischievous, daring, reckless boy."[18] He was self-willed, overbearing, and difficult to get along with. Sometimes he bullied; then again sometimes he could be a generous protector. As noted by an early writer, Andrew Jackson was a fighting cock all his life who was very kind to hens who clucked about him for protection and sustenance; but he would savage with beak and spur any other cock who dared to challenge him or question his word. Undoubtedly these unpleasant traits resulted in some measure from his living with the Crawfords as a poor relation; he also lacked the guidance of a strong father figure who could ween him from his inclination to bully. There was anger deep inside young Andrew and it appeared at a very early age. The years of deprivation in several forms (a missing father, possible humiliation in accepting charity from relatives, and the subsequent deaths of his brothers and mother leaving him orphaned at the age of thirteen, to mention only the most obvious) probably provoked this hostility. It never totally left him. Until the day he died he could suddenly explode in rage over some slight or offense and then go to infinite pains to seek revenge against the offender.

Some boys once gave young Andrew a gun loaded to the muzzle and dared him to fire it. They wanted to see the bully boy knocked to the ground by the discharge. Never one to refuse a challenge, he grabbed the gun and fired it. The recoil sent him sprawling. Infuriated, Andrew jumped to his feet. "By G——d, if one of you laughs, I'll kill him," he threatened. And the other boys had the good sense not to call him on it.[19]

Still, there was a far brighter side to Andrew's early life. With all his sudden outbursts of anger and rage, he also liked to play games and have fun. He was not morose or antisocial. True, many of his games involved practical jokes, but he also loved sports, such as wrestling, footraces, horse races, and jumping matches. "Frolic . . . not fight, was the ruling interest of Jackson's childhood," wrote an early biographer.[20] And this interest carried forward into his young adult life. He soon discovered dancing and the joy of prancing around a room with a charming girl in hand. "No boy ever lived who liked fun better than he," said one, "and his fun . . . was of an innocent and rustic character, such as . . . gives a cheery tone to the feelings ever after."[21]

At the time Andrew attended school he was a tall and extremely slender boy. He eventually grew to six feet and he remained slender—even cadaverous—all his life. Until the very end of his life when he became unnaturally bloated from his various diseases, Andrew Jackson never weighed more than 145 pounds. What remains of his clothing show his arms and legs to be extremely thin. He was sinewy and, as a youth, very agile. His face was long and narrow with a strong and pronounced jaw. His sandy-colored hair was long and bushy, and sometimes it appeared to stand straight up as though at attention. But perhaps his most distinguishing feature was his bright, intensely blue eyes which blazed whenever a passion seized him. More than anything else his eyes, when ignited, had a powerful effect on those around him. They riveted attention; they commanded obedience; and they could terrorize.

Andrew Jackson's education took a different and very radical turn with the outbreak of war between the American colonies and the British Crown. He was nine years of age when delegates in Philadelphia signed a Declaration of Independence from Great Britain in 1776. The war did not reach the Waxhaw settlement until a few years later when the British suddenly burst into South Carolina and captured both Savannah and Charleston. Following the fall of Charleston on May 12, 1780, bands of redcoats and Tories roamed the countryside, killing and looting. A force of 300 British soldiers, commanded by Lieutenant Colonel Banastre Tarleton, ravaged the Waxhaws, slaughtering 113 and wounding 150. It was rightly called a barbarous massacre because so many bodies were mangled in the fighting, with a dozen or more wounds inflicted on each corpse.

Then tragedy again struck the Jackson family. The eldest son, Hugh, joined the regiment of Colonel William Richardson Davie when hostilities reached South Carolina. He fought at the Battle of Stono Ferry and died immediately thereafter from the "excessive heat of the weather, and the fatigues of the day."[22] He was barely sixteen years of age.

With the Tories rampaging throughout the Waxsaw settlement, a constant call for help echoed over the South Carolinian countryside. And it was answered by Colonel Davie and Colonel Thomas Sumter who came down from the north seeking revenge for the Tarleton massacre. At the Battle of Hanging Rock on August 1, 1780, the Americans almost won the day but lost it when they celebrated prematurely by drinking captured rum. In their inebriated condition they panicked and rode off in wild confusion when the enemy suddenly turned and fired at them.

The Battle of Hanging Rock was Andrew Jackson's "first field."[23] Although thirteen years of age he had joined the patriot cause and rode with Colonel Davie but probably did no more than carry messages. The experience made quite an impression on the boy and it is possible that insofar as General Jackson had any model for soldiering, or so his early biographers claimed, that model was Colonel William R. Davie.

Following the Battle of Hanging Rock, Andrew and his brother Robert rejoined their mother at the Waxhaw settlement. Fighting in the region was continuous and pitted Whig against Tory, neighbor against neighbor, and even father against son in a vicious civil war. During one particularly bloody engagement Andrew and his brother took refuge in the home of their cousin, Lieutenant Thomas Crawford, but the boys were soon discovered by British dragoons and taken prisoner. At one point the officer in command of the dragoons ordered Andrew to clean his boots, an order the lad instantly rejected. "Sir," he supposedly cried, "I am a prisoner of war, and claim to be treated as such."[24] Outraged, the officer lifted his sword and aimed it straight at Andrew's head. The boy instinctively ducked and threw up his left hand in time to break the full force of the blow. Even so, he received a deep gash on his head and fingers, the marks of which he carried through life.[25]

Andrew and Robert, along with twenty other patriot prisoners, were taken on horseback to Camden, a distance of forty miles, where they were thrown into a jail along with 250 other prisoners. They had no beds, no medicine, no dressing for their wounds. The boys were separated, robbed, and exposed to smallpox which they both subsequently contracted. Fortunately their mother arrived just as an exchange of prisoners was being arranged between the American and British commanders, and she persuaded the British to include her sons in the exchange, along with five Waxhaw neighbors.

Of the two sick boys, Robert was clearly critical. He could neither stand nor sit on horseback without support. So Elizabeth procured two horses, strapped the dying Robert on one and rode the other herself. Poor Andrew had to walk the forty-five miles home barefoot and without a jacket. On the last leg of the journey a driving rain drenched them. Somehow, with a will born of desperation, Elizabeth got her children home. Two days later Robert was dead and Andrew in mortal danger.

For days the boy was delirious. But the devotion and nursing skill of his mother eventually brought him around, although it was a slow recovery and stretched over several months. Then, when Andrew seemed finally out of danger, Elizabeth decided to go to Charleston, a distance of 160 miles, to nurse prisoners of war held in prison ships in the harbor, among whom were two of her nephews. She contracted cholera in Charleston while tending the sick aboard the prison ships and died shortly after her arrival. She was buried in an unmarked grave in the suburbs of Charleston and a small bundle of her possessions was sent to her fifteen-year-old son at the Waxhaws. Elizabeth Hutchinson Jackson was an extraordinary woman, of great courage, high purpose, and enormous interior strength. Many of these attributes were inherited by her son.

The American Revolution was one long agony for Andrew Jackson. Perhaps there were moments when he felt like a patriot and hero, but most of the time he experienced hardship, pain, disease, multiple wounds of the head and fingers, and grief arising from the annihilation of his immediate family. He emerged from the Revolution burdened with sorrow and a deep-seated depression. He saw himself as a participant "in the struggle for our liberties" and he never forgot the price that he and others had paid to secure them.[26] He also emerged marked with deep patriotic and nationalistic convictions, which remained with him for the remainder of his life.

The war ended about the time Elizabeth died. The surrender of Lord Cornwallis at Yorktown had just occurred. Young Andrew was sent to live at the home of Thomas Crawford until he could decide upon his future. He later moved to the home of Joseph White, an uncle of Mrs. Crawford, and found work at a saddler's shop which helped lift him from his profound sense of depression. He also found release in the company of a number of socially prominent young bucks from Charleston whose families had fled to the Waxhaws while awaiting British evacuation of the city. Andrew immediately fell in with their wild ways, drinking, cockfighting, gambling, mischiefmaking. His energies found release in all sorts of devilment that virtually alienated him from his disapproving relatives. When the British finally evacuated Charleston in December 1782 and his companions returned home, Andrew followed along. In Charleston, he led a life of almost complete abandonment with no one to exercise control over his behavior. And he was all of fifteen. He dissipated a small inheritance from his grandfather in gambling, and when he had lost it all he packed what few belongings he had and returned to the Waxhaws.[27]

Andrew finished his education at a school run by Robert McCulloch and then taught school himself for a year or two near the Waxhaw Methodist Episcopal Church in South Carolina. Finally, in 1784, he decided to pursue the practice of law. With the Revolution ended, a peace treaty signed, and a new nation launched, Andrew reckoned that the legal profession offered the brightest prospects. Since he was young and extremely ambitious he decided to become a lawyer. So, at the age of seventeen, he bade farewell to the Waxhaws for the last time and rode north to Salisbury, the seat of Rowan County in North Carolina, some seventy-five miles away. He was accepted as a law student by Spruce McCay, an eminent attorney and later a judge of some distinction. Andrew found quarters in the town's modest tavern, the Rowan House, where he was joined by several other law students, one of them a bright and engaging fellow by the name of John McNairy.[28]

For two years Andrew studied the law by reading law books, copying documents and legal papers, running errands, sweeping out the office, and attending to McCay's instruction and advice. How much law Andrew actually learned is questionable. But he did apply himself. That was his nature. Since he had determined to become a lawyer he undoubtedly diligently performed all the tasks assigned to him by his instructor.

But he acquired an unsavory reputation in Salisbury, a reputation as the leader of a hooligan gang. Almost every night after finishing his business at McCay's, Andrew would join his friends in an evening of wild abandon. It was a rollicking life he led, full of fun and high spirits. But this time he was not acting out some inner rage, as he had done previously in the Waxhaws. This was simply adolescent exuberance, a letting off of steam after a long and probably monotonous day at the law office. But he could be rambunctious. Residents of the town later remembered that "Andrew Jackson was the most roaring, rollicking, game-cocking, horse-racing, card-playing, mischievous fellow that ever lived in Salisbury."[29] He did not trouble himself with devouring law books, it was said, because he "was more in the stable than in the office." He was often away on "parties of pleasure" and was considered "quite a beau in the town." Between horses and parties, Andrew had quite a time for himself. He indulged in drunken sprees and practical jokes. One of his favorite tricks was moving outhouses to far-off places. Others included stealing signposts.[30]

There was a dancing school in Salisbury, and of course Andrew attended it regularly. So constant was his attendance that he was asked to manage the Christmas ball. As a joke—and a particularly ugly one at that—he sent invitations to Molly Wood and her daughter, the town's notorious prostitutes. Not realizing it was a joke, the women appeared at the ball dressed in their fineries. When they entered the room the dancers jolted to a halt, appalled at their presence. The women were quickly escorted outside and Andrew was tongue-lashed for his cruel and vicious joke.

On another occasion he and his comrades-in-mischief were celebrating in a tavern and suddenly decided that the glasses used in their celebration should never be profaned by future use. So, with a flourish, they smashed them on the floor. And if the glasses, why not the table? Away went the table, shattered beyond repair. Next the chairs were demolished, then the bed. Finally the curtains were torn and piled into a heap. To conclude the ceremonies the entire mess was set ablaze. Oh, it was a night to remember and cherish forever. Indeed, it *was* remembered, especially by the disapproving townsfolk. Years later, when it was reported that Andrew Jackson was running for President of the United States, some people in Salisbury could scarcely believe it. "What!" exclaimed one lady. "Jackson up for President? *Jackson? Andrew* Jackson? The Jackson that used to live in Salisbury? Why, when he was here, he was such a rake that my husband would not bring him into the house! It is true, he *might* have taken him out to the stable to weigh horses for a race, and might drink a glass of whiskey with him *there.* Well, if Andrew Jackson can be President, anybody can!"[31]

For all his wildness and practical jokes, Andrew was a relatively popular figure in Salisbury. His exuberance was appealing and most of his escapades were relatively harmless. More important, at the age of twenty, he had begun to show distinct signs of a charismatic presence. There was a quality about him that commanded attention, respect, and occasionally fear. Whenever something happened in which he was involved, Andrew was invariably the prime mover. His leadership of the law students in Salisbury on their nightly prowls was only one example. His presence signaled authority. Because of his height he tended to look down at people, his eyes gripping them in the process. People were flattered by this, clutched as they were by the intensity of his gaze and his apparent absorption in what they were saying to him. He was one of those men, wrote an early biographer, "who convey to strangers the impression that they are 'somebody.' " And this was true long before he became a distinguished and important man.[32]

Tension and tremendous energy also seemed tightly wound within that spindly frame. He was an uneasy coil that might suddenly release an explosion of anger. Yet the anger that lurked just below the surface was not an unbridled force. Indeed it was observed many times that he more often than not feigned anger for the paralyzing effect he knew it had upon his victims. Rarely was his temper out of control. *"No man,"* said one, *"knew better than Andrew Jackson when to get into a passion and when not."*[33]

Besides, Jackson was to a large extent a very cautious and prudent man. "If there ever lived a *prudent* man," commented his biographer, "Andrew Jackson was that individual."[34] He dared a great deal during his long and exciting life but never what his keen intelligence warned him was excessively dangerous or beyond his grasp. He did not court danger; he did not take risks for no purpose. Basically, he was a conservative and deliberate man whose ambition and determination to succeed conditioned everything he did.

Andrew remained with McCay until 1786 when he moved into the office of Colonel John Stokes, a brave revolutionary officer who was one of the best lawyers practicing before the North Carolina bar. For the next six months Andrew completed his legal training under Stokes's excellent guidance and on September 26, 1787, he appeared for examination before Samuel Ashe and John F. Williams, two judges of the Superior Court of Law and Equity of North Carolina. Since these judges found him a man of "unblemished moral character" and competent in the knowledge of the law, they authorized the young man to practice as an attorney in the several courts of pleas and quarter sessions within the state.[35]

For a year after his admission to the bar young Jackson drifted around North Carolina practicing law, helping two friends run a store, and getting himself arrested. The circumstances of his arrest are unknown, but he and four friends—all young attorneys from Salisbury—were charged with trespassing. All were "held and firmly bound unto Lewis Beard Sheriff" and put up a recognizance bond of one thousand pounds by which they guaranteed to appear in court. The record does not reveal what occurred in court, but presumably the case was settled to everyone's satisfaction.[36] This was another low point in his early career. Obviously Jackson was getting nowhere in North Carolina. His practice did not grow and he seemed bored and restive.

At this point Jackson heard that John McNairy, his old gaming companion and fellow student at McCay's, had just been elected by the legislature to serve as Superior Court judge for the Western District of North Carolina. The district stretched to the Mississippi River and included the present state of Tennessee. McNairy had the authority to appoint the public prosecutor for the district, and he offered the post to Jackson. It was a thankless job, certainly an unpopular one as practiced in the wilderness, but Jackson felt frustrated in the east and saw, or thought he saw, a future in the west. So he accepted the offer. Life in the wilderness would be exciting and rewarding, he reckoned. His law practice—which he would continue while serving as public prosecutor—was sure to become more lucrative now that a great many people were heading over the mountains. They would need law and government and assistance in conducting their business affairs. There would be few lawyers on the frontier and Jackson no doubt believed that here was a challenge in which he might make a contribution and improve his fortune. In the spring of 1788 he, McNairy, and Bennett Searcy—another fellow student at McCay's who had been appointed clerk of the court—along with several others, agreed to rendezvous at Morgantown and then move together as a band across the mountains into what is now eastern Tennessee.

The country the group planned to enter was undergoing settlement in two general areas: the eastern section around the Watauga, Holston, Nolichucky, and French Broad rivers and extending as far as Knoxville; and the western section located in the Cumberland River valley and centered around the town of Nashville. Between the two settlements was a wilderness infested with hostile Indians that tended to divide the two communities and make them suspicious of one another.

The colony around Nashville was settled in 1779 by explorers commanded by Captain James Robertson. They were followed by the families of these explorers guided by Colonel John Donelson. The Donelson family, therefore, constituted one of the important first families of Tennessee. At one point, settlers in the eastern end of this wilderness declared their independence of North Carolina and created a new state which they called "Franklin," and elected John Sevier, the great hero of the Battle of King's Mountain during the Revolution, as governor. But North Carolina would not tolerate this "treason" and after much persuasion convinced the settlers to return to their former allegiance. In August 1788 the North Carolina legislature consolidated the settlements around the Cumberland to form the district of Mero (an incorrect spelling of Miró), the name of the Spanish governor of New Orleans. James Robertson had insisted on the name in the hope of flattering the governor into granting commercial privileges to the Cumberland settlers as well as prod him into discouraging the Indians from attacking the settlers. It was at approximately this moment, or a few months earlier, that McNairy was selected by the North Carolina legislature to help bring law and order into the western counties. He, Jackson, and the others headed west in the spring of 1788 along the Wilderness Trace that stretched over the Allegheny Mountains. Besides a horse and a gun and a few personal belongings, they each carried letters of introduction from distinguished citizens of the old community to the settlers of the new. As it turned out, they would all play a significant role in the development of Tennessee. And Andrew Jackson, of course, would reach far beyond this place and time to alter the course of American history.

CHAPTER 2

Frontiersman and Lawyer

THERE IS A TRADITION that when Andrew Jackson rode into Jonesborough, the principal town of East Tennessee, he trailed behind him a second horse and a pack of hound dogs. He made a grand entrance. The entrance suggested the style and manner that Jackson would display to the end of his life. He adopted all the attributes of a gentleman, someone of importance, a man of substance, a person to be reckoned with. Shortly after he arrived in Jonesborough he purchased a female slave, Nancy, aged eighteen or twenty. This, too, signified the position he wished to assume in his new life in the west. He obviously considered himself a gentleman.[1]

A gentleman of honor, let it be understood. For no sooner did Jackson arrive in Jonesborough than he got caught up in a dispute that prompted him to issue a challenge and fight his first known duel. And he fought the duel against Waightstill Avery, a man Jackson had once thought might instruct him in the law, that is, before he decided on McCay.

Avery, like McCay, made frequent court visits to Jonesborough, where he served as attorney for the state. After his arrival in Jonesborough Jackson obtained a license to practice in the county just to occupy his time during the interval before departing for Nashville. While trying a case of no particular significance he came up against Avery as his legal opponent. It is not certain what happened to prompt the duel, but at one point Avery resorted to sarcasm to rebut Jackson's argument and the young man flew into a rage. Tearing a blank sheet from a law book, Andrew scribbled a few lines on it and hurled it at Avery. It is not certain what he wrote but the next day he issued a formal challenge and it is the earliest known letter written by Jackson.

Agust 12th 1788

Sir: When a man's feelings and charector are injured he ought to seek a speedy redress; you recd. a few lines from me yesterday and undoubtedly you understand me. My charector you have injured; and further you have

14

Insulted me in the presence of a court and larg audianc. I therefore call
upon you as a gentleman to give me satisfaction for the Same; and I further
call upon you to give Me an answer immediately without Equivocation and
I hope you can do without dinner untill the business done; for it is consistent with the character of a gentleman when he Injures a man to make a
spedy reparation; therefore I hope you will not fail in meeting me this day,
from yr obt st

Andw. Jackson

Collo. Avery
P.S. This Evening after court adjourned[2]

Although no duelist, Avery was not about to get himself killed by a
young upstart acting out some inflated notion about his honor. Still, this
was the frontier and he could not dismiss a formal challenge without
risking his own reputation. Reluctantly, then, he agreed to meet Jackson
in a hollow north of the town just a little after sundown. The duelists took
their positions, the signal was given, and both men fired simultaneously—
into the air! Neither man had any intention of getting hurt, so they (or
their seconds) had worked out a satisfactory solution before the duel. By
the agreement Jackson's honor was technically restored. He therefore
strode up to Avery, announced he had nothing further to settle, shook
hands, and walked away.

This first known duel says something important about Andrew Jackson.
Obviously he was a hothead, and sensitive about his honor and reputation. As a gentleman, ambitious for recognition and acceptance, he understood his duty when he considered himself insulted. At the same time
he was not trigger-happy, oblivious to the possibility that he might get
himself killed or severely wounded. He was not an expert shot by any
means, nor could he discount Avery's shooting ability. Thus, when a
sensible solution was proposed by which his honor could be repaired and
a possible danger avoided, Jackson quickly accepted it. Despite his temper and hotheadedness, he was always a cautious man, open to any
legitimate compromise when it suited his interest. Not that he was incapable of a genuine duel with intent to kill, but the circumstances and his
self-interest would have to be of greater concern than his testy verbal
exchange with Avery.

A few months later Jackson and his friends, along with a number of
settlers, left Jonesborough and headed for Nashville. As they well knew,
they traveled through dangerous frontier country. One night the company was asleep except for the sentinels and Andrew Jackson. He sat on
the ground, his back against a tree, smoking a corncob pipe. At about ten
o'clock he began to doze off, barely conscious of the hooting of owls in
the black woods surrounding them. Owls! Strange to hear them call to
one another in this country, he thought. Instantly he understood. He
grabbed his rifle, bolted to his feet, and ran to where his friends were
sleeping.

"Searcy," he hissed, "raise your head and make no noise."

"What's the matter," his friend asked.

"The Owls—listen—there—there again. Isn't that a little *too* natural?"

"Do you think so?" said Searcy.

"I know it," Jackson replied. "There are Indians all around us. I have heard them in every direction. They mean to attack before daybreak."

The rest of the company were quickly awakened and Jackson urged them to break camp immediately. No one questioned his advice; everyone responded speedily to his direction. The party fled the camp and plunged deeper into the forest, neither hearing nor seeing a sign of Indians for the remainder of the night. A few hours later, unfortunately, a company of hunters happened upon the abandoned camp and decided it was a good place to spend the night. Before daybreak the Indians attacked and killed all but one of their number.[3]

This incident is one of many told by early biographers to demonstrate Jackson's emergence as a leader of men under frontier conditions. Despite the presence in the company of older and perhaps more experienced guides, it was Jackson who was credited with recognizing the danger and having the presence of mind to take charge and speed the party to safety.

The remainder of their journey to Nashville was relatively uneventful, and they arrived on October 26, 1788. As they neared the town, they paused on the bluff overlooking the settlement and saw stretched out in front of them a gently undulating, fertile country watered by the great Cumberland River. The original settlers of Nashville numbered 120 men, women, and children, among whom were John Donelson and his wife and eleven children—the youngest a thirteen-year-old girl named Rachel. Despite constant attack by Indians, the settlers planted their colony and sustained it. Still the Indians would not yield this fertile valley and for many years the pioneers were forced to live in fortified "stations" scattered along the Cumberland River.

In 1785, after a particularly long and difficult winter in which an unexpectedly large number of settlers arrived without warning and placed a heavy strain on the community supply of corn, John Donelson moved his family to Kentucky and remained there until the corn reserves had been replenished. During the Donelson sojourn in Kentucky young Rachel married Lewis Robards. When the Donelsons returned to Tennessee Rachel was left behind with her husband. Not long after John Donelson's return to Nashville he was murdered while surveying in the woods. Two men who were with him found his body near a creek, but it was never officially determined whether the murderers were white or red men.

It was eight years after the Nashville settlement had been established that Jackson, McNairy, and party arrived on the scene. The town now boasted a courthouse, two stores, two taverns, a distillery, and a number of houses, cabins, and tents. The Indian menace still kept the community in a state of alert, and several more years would pass before the people of Nashville could safely roam the countryside and build separate cabins for themselves.

In seeking a place to live, Jackson chose the best he could find. The widow Donelson was living in a blockhouse, and since she was a woman of property as well as a notable housekeeper, Jackson decided to move in as a boarder. The widow was happy to have him because of the added protection he could provide against the Indians. Several other friends joined the Donelson household, occupying one cabin while the family resided in the blockhouse just a few steps away. One of the boarders Jackson met at this time was John Overton, another lawyer. They soon became fast friends.[4]

The widow's daughter, Rachel Donelson Robards, had also come back to live with the family. Her stay in Kentucky had been an agony, her marriage shattered in a storm of violent quarrels. Although of good family and much in love with Rachel, Robards was neurotically suspicious of her coquettish ways and began to believe all manner of improprieties about her. The marriage was a mistake from the very beginning, for Rachel was a lively, vivacious girl, "the best story-teller, the best dancer, the sprightliest companion, the most dashing horsewoman in the western country,"[5] all of which frequently drove Robards into fits of jealous rage. She was a high-spirited, frivolous charmer and probably should have been more circumspect in her behavior. Moreover, she refused to be cowed by her husband's irrational behavior. The break in the marriage came in Kentucky when Robards "caught" Rachel talking with a Mr. Short in a manner he felt was improper. The ensuing quarrel ended with Robards demanding that the Donelsons take Rachel back because he could no longer live with her. Shortly thereafter her brother Samuel fetched her home to Nashville.

But Robards soon regretted his hasty decision. He found he could not live without his wife and so begged her to take him back. Whatever doubts Rachel may have had about resuming their marriage she soon suppressed, no doubt at the urging of her family and in light of her own understanding of her situation, given the social mores of the 1780s. The couple was reunited in Tennessee and they bought property in the vicinity but continued to live with Rachel's mother until such time as the Indians had been sufficiently subdued to permit them to move to their own home.

It was at this momentous juncture that the frolicking, rollicking, girl-chasing Andrew Jackson came on the scene. This redheaded, sharp-featured shaft of fun and excitement had just the temperament to insinuate himself into Rachel's affections. Naturally chivalrous and always the gallant in the approved western and southern fashion that was the mark of a true gentleman, Jackson quickly ingratiated himself with the entire Donelson household. All, that is, except Robards. For here was Rachel, a frisky young girl brimming with a sense of gaiety who loved to dance and ride horses and tell amusing stories to anyone who could appreciate them, married to a jealous and suspicious neurotic, and here was Jackson of commanding presence and personality who could match Rachel's high spirits and spice them with a little wildness of his own—all living together in a single domicile. Surely all the ingredients were present for an explosive domestic quarrel.

It came soon enough. A group of women went to a blackberry patch under guard one day to pick blackberries when Robards, who accompanied them, remarked to one of the guards that he believed Jackson was "too intimate with his wife." The guard, who liked Jackson, reported to his friend what Robards had said, and Jackson, in a quarrelsome mood, confronted Robards and warned him that if he ever again linked his name "in any way" with Rachel, "he would cut his ears out of his head, and that he was tempted to do it any how." Infuriated, if not frightened by the threat, Robards went directly to the nearest magistrate and swore out a peace warrant. Jackson was arrested and ordered to appear in court. Guards were summoned from the blockhouse to make certain the troublemaker obeyed the arrest order. Robards trailed behind them. As they went, Jackson suddenly asked one of the guards for his butcher knife. It was given him after he pledged his honor to do no harm with it. Whereupon Jackson ran his finger along the cutting edge of the weapon and lightly touched the sharp point, periodically glancing at Robards as he stroked the knife to see if the husband understood his meaning. In a flash Robards dashed for the canebrake, Jackson at his heels. After a few moments the prisoner reappeared alone and proceeded with his guard to the magistrate. But, since the complainant had failed to appear, the warrant was dismissed.[6]

There were several other incidents which worsened the situation. Indeed, Robards became more and more hostile, more and more surly and vicious. "I resided in the family," recalled one boarder who was also Jackson's friend, and Robards's behavior toward Rachel "was cruel, unmanly & unkind in the extreme." Specifically, "Lewis Robards was in the habit within my knowledge of leaving his wife's bed, & spending the night with the negro women." Robards's sister-in-law "fully corroborates all I have said. She states . . . that the breach arose from Robards own cruel & improper conduct."[7] Apparently guilty himself of adultery, Robards suspected his wife of his own misdeeds.

In view of all that had happened because of his presence, Jackson at last moved out of the Donelson home and found new quarters at Kasper Mansker's station. Robards remained a short time with his wife, then he too packed up and returned to Kentucky, leaving the field wide open to the smitten Jackson. In no time the young lawyer was deeply—indeed, passionately—in love with Rachel Donelson Robards. And she with him.

If Jackson's personal life in Tennessee began on very shaky grounds, his professional life, by comparison, got off to an auspicious start. Almost immediately he acquired a license to practice law in Nashville and his friend McNairy appointed him an attorney for the entire Mero District, which included the counties of Davidson (of which Nashville was the county seat), Sumner, and Tennessee. He therefore functioned as both public prosecutor and licensed lawyer.

When Jackson arrived in Nashville in 1788 he discovered a mountain of work awaiting him as prosecutor. Debtors had refused to pay legitimate obligations and had bribed the only licensed attorney in western Tennessee. Besides, the sheriff was incompetent. Merchants and other creditors immediately deluged Jackson with petitions to help them collect their just bills. He quickly set to work. Within a month he enforced seventy writs against the debtors. Naturally, demand for his services soared and his practice got off to a flying financial start. So rapidly did it grow that Jackson dismissed any lingering doubts he may have had about moving on and decided to settle permanently in this western wilderness.

Some debtors had moved to Sumner County and simply presumed that they were outside the jurisdiction of Davidson County and therefore no longer need pay their obligations. Jackson pursued them with a vengeance. His persistence so infuriated these men that one of them walked up to him one day and to vent his anger deliberately stepped on Jackson's foot. Without batting an eye, Jackson picked up a piece of wood and calmly knocked the man out cold.[8] Respect for the law, Jackson-style, had arrived in Tennessee.

Early court records of Davidson County show that Jackson handled between one-fourth and one-half of all cases on the docket during the first years of his tenure, which was an extraordinary record.[9] During a single session in April 1789 a total of thirteen suits were argued, principally for debt, and Andrew Jackson was counsel in every one of them. Most of his business involved land titles, debts, sales, and assault, and in trying these cases he traveled regularly, principally between Nashville and Jonesborough. In the first seven years of his residence in Tennessee, Jackson shuttled the 200 miles between the two towns a total of twenty-two times—and this despite the serious Indian menace.[10]

Like all frontiersmen, Jackson was called upon to protect the community from Indian attack. Within six months of his arrival he was conscripted into an expedition to punish the hostiles following their bold attack on Robertson's station. A twenty-man team pursued the Indians to their camp on the south side of Duck River. Most of the "savages" escaped, but the team captured sixteen guns, nineteen shot pouches, and all the Indian baggage consisting of moccasins, leggins, blankets, and skins.[11] This was Jackson's first formal expedition against the tribes in the Nashville District and he held the rank of private. Nevertheless, he was cited by his comrades as "bold, dashing, fearless, and *mad upon his enemies.*" He impressed everyone with his "great ambition for encounters with the savages" and over the next several years won a notable reputation as an Indian fighter.[12]

The presence of the Indians and the danger they constituted shaped in very large measure the early political policy of Tennessee. The Cumberland settlers even stooped to intrigue to protect themselves. They courted the Spanish who were ranged along their southern border, slyly intimating secession from the United States as an inducement to the Spanish governor in New Orleans to discourage Indian attacks.[13]

They courted the Spanish for economic reasons as well. Spain controlled a vast empire that stretched from Florida to Louisiana and Texas, up the west bank of the Mississippi River to some indefinite point close to Canada, and westward to the Pacific Ocean north of California. The peace treaty ending the American Revolution fixed the southern boundary of the United States at the thirty-first parallel from the Atlantic to the Mississippi River, but Spain did not recognize this boundary. Spanish troops and officials continued to administer a wide stretch of territory north of Baton Rouge that included Natchez on the east bank of the Mississippi. The expansion of the United States to the west and south was therefore blocked by the Spanish. Expansion to the north was blocked by the British in Canada.

For Tennesseans the worst aspect of this situation was the presence of the Spanish at the mouth of the Mississippi River. If they wanted to sell their produce at Natchez or New Orleans, or ship it east via the Gulf of Mexico, they first had to have Spanish approval to enter the territory south of the thirty-first parallel. And if the Spanish refused, as they sometimes did, these Tennesseans found themselves in a financial death grip. Between the economic obstacle presented by the Spanish presence in the Mississippi Valley and the constant complaints by such leading westerners as James Robertson and John Sevier that Indian attacks on American settlements were instigated by the Spanish in Florida and Louisiana, a situation quickly developed that invited conspiracy, intrigue, and even treason.

As a gesture of goodwill and a means of encouraging the Americans to secede from the United States, the Spanish offered handsome land grants in Louisiana and a measure of religious freedom, provided they took an oath of allegiance to Spain. As an additional inducement to immigrate to Louisiana, it was decreed that Americans could ply the full length of the Mississippi River subject to a 15 percent duty—unless they migrated to Louisiana, in which case the duty was rescinded.[14]

But westerners had no real desire to become citizens of Spain, except as a last resort. Americans played a dishonest game with the Spanish to gain immediate objectives. They intrigued either to win a change in Indian policy or to force the opening of the Mississippi River. They schemed with the Spanish in order to frighten North Carolina into first ratifying the federal Constitution, which had recently been written and submitted to the states for their approval, and then ceding the western territory to the United States.[15] Eventually most of these intrigues improved conditions for the western settlers. Governor Miró succeeded in inducing the Indians, especially the Creeks and Chickamaugas, to lessen the intensity of their attacks; the Mississippi was partially opened; and North Carolina both ratified the Constitution and ceded her western lands to the new Union.

Within six months the United States Congress organized the North Carolina cession into the Southwest Territory. William Blount of North Carolina was appointed governor by President George Washington, Daniel Smith of the Mero District was chosen secretary, and John McNairy, David Campbell, and Joseph Anderson were selected as territorial judges. Blount was an original, an early version of the sharp-nosed manipulator, land jobber, politician, and financier—and never mind ethical standards or moral considerations. He campaigned for the governorship for the simple reason, he baldly admitted to his brother, that it was of "great Importance to our Western Speculations."[16] Blount snagged the appointment because he knew how to bring maximum political pressure on the right people, something Jackson quickly learned after he met Blount.

To establish the territorial government, Blount received extensive appointive powers that helped him initiate personal rule in the territory. These appointments included justices, sheriffs, constables, clerks, registrars, and militia officers of every rank below general. His two private secretaries—Willie Blount, his half brother, and Hugh Lawson White, a young, energetic, and intensely loyal young lawyer—assisted him in establishing control. Archibald Roane and David Allison, both friends of Jackson who may have traveled with him to Tennessee, won important posts that helped reinforce Blount's position. Roane became attorney general of the Washington District and Allison served as the governor's business manager. For the positions of brigadier general in the territorial militia, Blount recommended James Robertson and John Sevier, and their commissions were duly approved by the federal government in 1791.[17]

All Blount's appointments guaranteed his absolute control of the Southwest Territory. And that control attracted to his cause all ambitious men within the territory, including Andrew Jackson. Without Blount's approval, career advancement in Tennessee was virtually impossible. Jackson appreciated this fact and acted accordingly. He had several friends who could have introduced him to Blount or mentioned his name to the governor, including McNairy, Smith, and Allison. Moreover, since Jackson had an excellent record as a successful and hard-driving prosecutor it behooved the governor to enlist the support of such an obviously talented and ambitious young lawyer. Both stood to gain by an association. Accordingly, on February 15, 1791, the position of attorney general of the Mero District was offered to Jackson and accepted. Thus began a long and fruitful association between the two men.

The duties of this office were not unlike those Jackson had discharged as prosecuting attorney, but Blount had additional responsibilities for the young man in terms of the ever-present Indian problem. He told General Robertson that he wanted a recent treaty with the Cherokees "preserved inviolate and if this can not be done I beg you to make examples of the first violators of it. It will be the duty of the Attorney of the District Mr. Jackson to prosecute on Information in all such cases and I have no doubt that he will readily do it." When Blount heard that a number of white settlers had violated the treaty he showed he meant what he said, at the same time indicating further confidence in his newest appointee. "Let the District Attorney Mr. Jackson, be informed," he said; "he will be certain to do his duty, and the offenders will be prosecuted."[18] A year and a half later, on September 10, 1792, Blount named Jackson judge advocate for the Davidson County cavalry regiment commanded by Lieutenant Colonel Robert Hays. This was Jackson's first military appointment, and although it was conferred solely because of his legal skills, it was the beginning of a long and significant association with the Tennessee militia.

James Robertson was another loyal Blount partisan and the major political force in the Cumberland region. He too appreciated Jackson's obvious energy and determination to get ahead, and he unstintingly encouraged the young man. This double-barreled support further advanced Jackson's career. And Andrew was also making money—slowly at first, then more quickly as his reputation spread. Like all westerners he acquired land as quickly and as avidly as possible. Land acquisition was the quickest route to financial success and social advance—both of which Jackson was determined to have.

His social standing took a decided swing when he made up his mind—the exact time of which is unknown—to take as his wife the youngest girl of one of the first families of Tennessee: Rachel Donelson, daughter of the late John Donelson and wife of Lewis Robards. Rachel and Robards were separated, but in the fall of 1790 a rumor of unknown origins began to spread that Robards intended to return to Nashville and take his wife back to Kentucky—and by force if necessary. On hearing this rumor, Rachel became extremely agitated since she knew it was "impossible to live" with her husband. She therefore decided to flee to Spanish-occupied Natchez on the Mississippi River where she may have owned property and where she could find devoted friends and relatives and protection from her husband.[19]

When Jackson learned of Rachel's decision to flee Nashville he announced that he would accompany her to Natchez. Colonel Robert Stark, "a venerable and highly esteemed old man and friend of Mrs. Robards," had already agreed to escort her to her destination, but because the route was perilous and liable to Indian attack—especially if taken overland—

Stark supposedly prevailed upon Jackson to accompany them and serve as escort; at least that was the story later concocted.[20] It is extremely odd that Stark would invite Jackson, the third party of this marital triangle, when any number of male Donelsons—brothers, brothers-in-law, cousins—could have obliged. By this time Jackson was clearly a suitor and may have explained his intention to marry Rachel once she obtained a divorce, thereby winning the Donelsons' consent. It is hardly likely that they would agree to anything that might further humiliate Rachel and embarrass the family.

Jackson's decision to accompany the Stark party to Natchez was absolute calculation. It confirmed Robards's worst suspicions and provided him with the evidence necessary to commence divorce proceedings—proceedings which would charge Rachel with adultery and desertion. Both Jackson and Rachel were responsible for what happened. They deliberately chose to defy the conventions of society, and they both paid a very high price. As she grew older, Rachel became extremely pious. Not an ordinary piety that may result with advancing age, but a rousing, evangelical, near-fanatical piety that permeated her entire life. It is possible that Rachel later suffered great torment and remorse over her youthful and illicit love for Andrew Jackson. It is possible her later life constituted one long act of atonement.

According to the official Jacksonian version of what happened, written by John Overton in 1827 and issued by the Nashville Central Committee, Rachel's decision to flee to Natchez occurred in January 1791. This date and subsequent dates involving the marriage are important because Overton later offered them as proof that Jackson and Rachel were morally innocent of the charges of adultery and bigamy brought by Robards. According to Overton, it was "in the winter or spring of 1791," almost six months after Rachel first heard the rumor of Robards's intentions, that Rachel, Jackson, and Stark and his family floated downriver from Nashville to Natchez. After delivering his charge, Jackson returned to Nashville in time to attend superior court in May 1791. Meanwhile Rachel resided with the families of Colonel Thomas Green and Colonel Bruin in Natchez.

Hardly had Jackson returned to Tennessee than word reached Nashville that Robards had obtained a divorce in Virginia (he was living in a district of Kentucky which was then a part of Virginia) through the good offices of his brother-in-law, Major John Jouett, a member of the Virginia legislature. But Robards had no divorce. All he had was an enabling act, dated December 20, 1790, permitting him to bring suit against his wife in the Supreme Court of the District of Kentucky. The act specifically declared: "A jury shall be summoned . . . and shall find a verdict according to the usual mode; and if the jury . . . shall find for the plaintiff . . . that the defendant hath deserted the plaintiff, and that she hath lived in adultery with another man since such desertion, the said verdict shall be recorded, and thereupon the marriage between the said *Lewis Roberts* [*sic*] and *Rachel* shall be totally dissolved."[21]

When word of the so-called divorce reached Nashville, according to Overton, Jackson, a lawyer, made no attempt to determine its veracity. He had no documentary or legal proof of a divorce. Nonetheless, he hastened back to Natchez as soon as his business permitted—"in the Summer of 1791," according to Overton—and married the woman he had "innocently & unintentionally" caused much "loss of peace & happiness."[22]

Who performed the marriage is unknown. Overton does not say. And no record of the marriage survives.[23] Overton merely says, "In the Summer of 1791, Genl. Jackson returned to Natchez, & as I understand, married Mrs. Robards."[24] Natchez was under Spanish rule in 1791, which meant that all legal marriages had to be performed by the Catholic Church under the supervision of a duly ordained Catholic priest. The Catholic Diocese of Baton Rouge did a thorough inventory of all records held in the parishes founded prior to 1870 and published a *Guide to Archival Materials.* There is no record of a marriage between Jackson and Rachel.

But they were Protestant, and it is possible that a Protestant minister in Natchez did in fact marry them. A theory has been advanced that Colonel Thomas Green, acting as a magistrate of Georgia, married them at the home of his son, Thomas Marston Green. If he did so, no record or document regarding a marriage exists.[25]

The couple probably lived for a short time at Bayou Pierre, after their "marriage," possibly on property owned by Rachel.[26] They then returned to Nashville in the fall of 1791, according to Overton, where they began a respectable life together that won the admiration of their neighbors.

Two years later they learned the awful truth. There was no divorce, at least not in 1791. It was on September 27, 1793, that Robards finally received a divorce decree from the Court of Quarter Sessions of Mercer County at the courthouse of Harrodsburgh. Since Rachel and Andrew had been living together for more than two years there was no problem in convincing the jury that "Rachel Robards, hath deserted the plaintiff, Lewis Robards, and hath, and doth, Still live in adultery with another man." Accordingly, "it is therefore considered by the Court that the Marriage between the Plaintiff and the Defendant be disolved."[27]

It is difficult to explain why Robards waited so long to exact his revenge. Perhaps he hoped for a reconciliation, as unlikely as that was; perhaps he sought to share the estate of Rachel's late father;[28] perhaps it was his way of getting even, of punishing Jackson and Rachel for offending his honor and pride.

The shocking news of the delayed divorce reached Jackson in December 1793. His friends convinced him of the propriety of obtaining a marriage certificate and going through with another wedding ceremony.

On January 17, 1794, he obtained a license and the following day they were married by the justice of the peace of Davidson County, Robert Hays, Rachel's brother-in-law.[29]

Such are the "facts" surrounding the marriage that were presented to the American people in 1827 when Jackson ran for the presidency. They constitute a plausible account if one wants to believe that Rachel and Jackson were innocent of any deliberate wrongdoing and is willing to overlook the fact that Jackson, a lawyer, did not bother to obtain legal proof of divorce before "marrying" Rachel, that no record of the 1791 "marriage" or who performed it exists, and that it took two years for the couple to learn that no divorce had been granted despite the fact that on February 4, 11, 18, and 25 and March 3, 10, 17, and 24, 1792, the Kentucky *Gazette,* in accordance with instructions of the Virginia legislature, formally summoned Rachel to appear before the court to answer the charge of adultery.[30]

Even more damaging is the fact that Overton's account cannot be reconciled with several pieces of evidence that contradict his story in significant ways. The first of these concerns the time of arrival of the Stark party in Natchez. The Spanish kept precise records. Upon entry to Natchez all foreign subjects were required to take an oath of loyalty to the Spanish Crown if they wished to remain. According to Spanish records, Stark arrived in Natchez on January 12, 1790—not 1791.[31]

The second piece of evidence is a letter written by George Cochran in Natchez to Jackson, dated November 3, 1790, which he concludes, "My best respects Wait of Mrs. Jackson."[32] Could Jackson have been "married" in the fall of 1790? But Robards did not obtain legislative approval to begin divorce proceedings until December 20, 1790. Did Jackson "marry" even before the Virginia legislature acted?

A second letter from Cochran to Jackson, dated October 21, 1791, states that Jackson's letter of the previous April was the only communication Cochran had received from him since his "departure from this country." If the "marriage" had taken place in Natchez in the summer of 1791, as Overton contended, why would Cochran, who lived in Natchez, say in October that since April he had had no communication from Jackson since his "departure from this place"?[33]

Another piece of evidence indicating that Andrew and Rachel "married" a full year earlier than was later claimed, "married" even before Robards received legislative approval to initiate divorce proceedings, is an inventory of the estate of John Donelson, Rachel's father. The July and October 1790 terms of the Davidson County court list Rachel as "Rachel Donelson," but the January 1791 term lists her as "Rachel Jackson."[34] (There is no mistaking the date; it is given twice: January 28, 1791.) Thus, at the approximate time Overton said she fled to Natchez, she was already officially referred to as "Rachel Jackson."

It would appear that Overton's dates are off by one year. Instead of marrying *after* Robards received legislative approval for the divorce proceedings, as alleged in 1827, Andrew and Rachel were "married" months before, earlier than November 3, 1790, when Cochran referred to Rachel as "Mrs. Jackson," and probably sometime in late October 1790. If this is true, they "married" when Rachel was still legally bound to another man—unless, of course, they did not marry at all (which would explain the absence of any documentation) and simply lived together as common-law husband and wife.

Such behavior seems quite untypical of Jackson, considering his ambition and his desire for social status. But it is possible that he was forced to pretend because he wished to protect Rachel's reputation and because it was required of him as a gentleman and a man of honor.

One thing is certain. Whatever Rachel and Andrew did, and whenever they did it, their actions did not outrage the community. This in itself is an important consideration in determining what happened. Community acceptance of their behavior is proven in the fact that within the next few years the people of the state conferred a number of honors on Jackson that they would never have given had they believed him guilty of moral impropriety. As William B. Lewis, Jackson's neighbor, later wrote, "I would ask how it is possible that any man could have been held in such high estimation by a whole community if he had acted as has been alleged? Could any man, so destitute of moral virtue, and even setting at defiance the common dreams of life, no matter what his talents, and acquirements might be, maintain so high a standing? The thing is impossible and the mere supposition of its possibility is a vile slander upon the whole population of this State." In another letter Lewis wrote, "The Genl and Mrs. Jackson both perhaps acted imprudently but no one believed they acted criminally—the whole course of their lives contradicts such an idea."[35]

Because they were in love and trapped in an impossible situation, Andrew and Rachel handled the problem badly—even Lewis admitted that. For the very reason that they were not criminals they were forced to cover up the questionable start of their marriage in order to live a respectable life together. When Jackson ran for the presidency it was imperative that they move the date of the first "marriage" forward a year (although it is entirely possible that after thirty-seven years—from 1790 to 1827—they honestly confused the dates).

Whatever the circumstances of this marriage, the union of these two remarkable people sobered their lives. The wildness in each dissipated. Jackson's ferocious temper was considerably subdued; he became more tender and considerate of Rachel, and, if possible, more chivalric. She in turn became extremely pious. Religion became a near-obsession with her. But the bitterness and the quarrels that had disfigured her marriage to Robards were absent from her marriage to Jackson. The love Rachel and Andrew bore each other matured over the years, tested by his long absences and strengthened no doubt by the villainy of those who pricked them with vicious taunts about the origins of their union.

When the couple returned to Tennessee after their sojourn in Natchez, they established their home on a small plantation called Poplar Grove, located on a hairpin turn of the Cumberland River, with the house nestled at the center of the turn. As Jackson's law practice grew he gradually laid the foundation for a large estate, acquiring a lovely plantation, Hunter's Hill, about thirteen miles from Nashville. And his marriage automatically promoted Jackson's social standing despite the divorce and the charge of adultery. He was now linked to the Donelsons—and, after the Robertsons, no family held higher distinction in western Tennessee. Rachel brought stability and order and social distinction to Jackson. She also proved indispensable in the management of his growing estate. Andrew Jackson owed a great deal to Rachel Donelson in many different ways and more than he could ever possibly acknowledge. But he loved her with a devotion and intensity that compensated for many of his deficiencies. He loved her and thought of her almost every day for the remainder of his life.

CHAPTER 3

―――――◦◦――――――

Congressman Jackson

THE INDIAN MENACE PERSISTED in Tennessee, and over the next few years Jackson developed into a fire-breathing frontiersman obsessed with the Indian presence and the need to obliterate it. He railed against the Indians and against Congress. Because of the indifference of Congress, he said, innocent settlers were murdered, treaties violated, the frontier splashed with blood. "What Motives Congress are governed by with Respect to their pacific Disposition towards Indians I know not; some say humanity dictates it; but Certainly she ought to Extend an Equal share of humanity to her own Citizens; in doing this Congress would act Justly and Punish the Barbarians for Murdering her innocent Citizens."[1]

Blount, too, was aware of the problem and aware of the federal government's unwillingness or inability to resolve it. Recognizing that his own political fortunes were in jeopardy, he decided that some bold course of action was essential. Forthwith he proposed the admission of Tennessee as a new state into the Union. Once a full-fledged state, Tennessee could manage the Indian problem any way it saw fit. Blount also appreciated the fact that this action would strengthen his own political position at home and assist his land schemes as well.

Moving with incredible speed, Blount nudged the General Assembly of the territory into planning a census, calling for a plebiscite on the question of statehood, arranging a constitutional convention, and preparing a financial report to the people that would prove fiscal solvency. It was a stupendous performance, for Blount was acting pretty much without direction, having only the guidelines provided by the Northwest Ordinance of 1787 and what friends in Congress advised as to procedure for a territory to become a state.

The Ordinance mentioned one qualification precisely: there had to be 60,000 people in the territory before it could apply for admission to the Union. So the census was conducted with extreme care, and Blount officially reported the results in November 1795. The territory had an aggregate population of 77,263, he said, of which 65,776 were free white males and females, 10,613 were slaves, and 973 were free Negroes. The eight eastern counties of the territory had a population of over 65,000 while the three western counties totaled slightly less than 12,000.[2]

In the plebiscite for statehood, 6,504 voted for statehood and 2,562 against, a ratio of 13 to 5 in favor.[3] Davidson County voted overwhelmingly against statehood, 96 to 517. The domination by the eastern counties probably explains the lopsided vote.[4] It can be assumed that Jackson was one of the 96, responding to the advice and expectation of his mentor, William Blount.

Following the plebiscite, Blount called for the election of delegates to a constitutional convention to meet in Knoxville on January 11, 1796. Each county would elect five delegates for a total of fifty-five. The election was held on December 18 and 19, 1795, and the five members designated by Davidson County were John McNairy, James Robertson, Thomas Hardeman, Joel Lewis, and Andrew Jackson.

The delegates met in a small building on the outskirts of Knoxville. They spent $10.00 for seats, $2.62 for an oilcloth to cover the president's table, and $22.50 for candles, firewood, and stands. The legislature had allowed each member $2.50 per diem expenses, which the delegates voted to reduce to $1.50. Obviously, they were men of republican virtue. The difference, they agreed, should be given to the secretary, the printer, and the reading and "engrossing clerk," who had not been provided for by the legislature.

As soon as the convention was organized, the delegates voted to appoint two members from each county to draft a preliminary constitution, each county naming its own members. Most of the delegations chose their brightest and most energetic colleagues. The Davidson County members chose McNairy and Jackson.

The entire session of the convention lasted twenty-seven days. Unfortunately, none of the debates were recorded. From what can be learned about the convention Jackson took an active though not an important part in the proceedings. He seconded the motion to establish a bicameral legislature. He opposed a profession of faith to be required of all officeholders—belief in God, the afterlife, and the divine authority of the Bible—and played a prominent role in defeating it. In addition, he seconded a motion to exclude clergymen from the legislature. (The original draft excluded them from all civil or military office or positions of trust within the state.) He also supported a property qualification of 200 acres and a three-year state residency requirement to hold a seat in the General Assembly and a one-year county residency to represent a county. Finally, he won the right of judges of inferior courts to issue writs of certiorari to bring evidence into their own court.[5]

Like many western frontiersmen, Jackson had ideas about government that varied according to the issue. He would be very conservative with respect to property rights and slavery, and he would resent (if not resist) any interference by government in these matters. On the question of Indians, however, he would take the opposite view and demand full government participation in eliminating the Indian presence.

In the matter of suffrage, Jackson was consistently democratic all his life—like most westerners. He advocated simple residency for all freemen as the sole condition for the franchise. If men were to be bound by laws and subject to punishment under them, he later said, then they "ought to be entitled to a voice in making them." For officeholders, however, he supported a property qualification.[6]

There is a tradition—totally mistaken in fact—that Jackson suggested the name of the state, Tennessee, which was derived from Tinnase or Tenase, the name of a Cherokee chief. But the name was already in general use at the time of the convention as a result of General Daniel Smith's *Short Description of Tennessee Government,* published in 1793, and was adopted by the delegates because they liked its ring. It sounded American!—not at all like Carolina, Virginia, or Georgia, all of which were English in origin.

The final document approved by the convention was a workable and democratic instrument. Any white man could vote after six months' residence in the state, while a freeholder could vote as soon as he entered a county. In effect the delegates adopted universal manhood suffrage that included free Negroes. Those who owned 200 acres of land could be elected to the legislature but only those who possessed 500 acres could serve as governor. A bill of rights proclaimed that "all power" resided in the people. Religious freedom, trial by jury, and freedom of speech, press, and assembly were guaranteed.[7]

Their work done—work that would last until 1834 without significant amendment—the convention adjourned on February 6, 1796. Jackson received $53.16 in salary and expenses for his efforts. His modest but respectable role in the convention unquestionably helped his reputation and advanced his image as a leading figure of the western community. He certainly improved his standing within the Blount clique; they knew he could be relied upon as a valued lieutenant on the Cumberland. Several times during the convention proceedings Jackson led or participated in a fight for something Blount and his friends advocated. All of which indicated that he was developing steadily as a credible politician and one of the more important men in western Tennessee.

One reason the Blount faction appreciated Jackson was that the young man had strong western views, just the sort of views that the Cumberland settlers liked to hear and would redound to the credit of the Blount crowd. On the questions of Indians, the Spanish, and the English, for example, Jackson regularly thundered imprecations for their many offenses. He had a reputation as a forceful, vigorous spokesman. "You have loud speach," one man told him bluntly.[8] They especially liked it when he lambasted Congress. Thus, when Jackson heard of the treaty signed by John Jay with Great Britain opening West Indian ports to American shipping (provided certain severe restrictions were enforced), he erupted into a torrent of passionate, almost incomprehensible language to Nathaniel Macon, the able and conservative congressman from North Carolina.

> What an alarming Situation; has the late Negociation of Mr. Jay with Lord Greenvill, and that Negociation (for a Treaty of Commerce it cannot be properly Called, as it wants reciprocity) being ratified by the Two third of the senate & president has plunged our Country in; will it End in a Civil warr; or will our Country be relieved from its present ignominy by the firmness of our representatives in the Congress (by impeachments for the Daring infringements of our Constitutional rights) have the insulting Cringing and ignominious Child of aristocratic Secracy removed Erased and obliterated from the archives of the Grand republick of the united States.[9]

Here is the wild, threatening, supernationalist Jackson, slamming around the frontier in hot temper, glibly invoking the menace of civil war, shouting impeachment, posturing defiantly. Sensitive to the point of violence when it came to what he interpreted as the rights and dignity of the "Grand republick," Jackson fearlessly (and sometimes recklessly) demanded appropriate action, however extreme, to assert national pride. As a vocal and active force on the frontier, poised close to the "hated Spanish Dons" and their allies, the "savage hostiles," he could become an exceedingly dangerous man.

But there is much to be learned about Andrew Jackson in this long, angry, inchoate, confused, frequently wrongheaded letter. This outburst by a western lawyer and politician who was contemptuous of Congress for failing to protect the dignity and honor of the country, and who, at one point, sneered at "the 20 aristocratic neebobs of the Senate," bespoke the essential character and ideology of Andrew Jackson. Fundamentally, he argued a narrow interpretation of the federal Constitution. He believed in states' rights and invariably suspected mischief by the central government. Frontiersmen of the southwest naturally tended toward a strong states' rights philosophy as a result of their being left to their own devices when it came to safeguarding their economic and political interests. It is significant that Jackson always wrote *states* with a capital *S* but invariably wrote *united* (referring to the United States) with a small *u*. Too much can be made of this, of course, in view of his haphazard spelling and punctuation. Still it does provide a small clue to his thinking. For Jackson, as for many others on the frontier, the state was the important thing. The federal government in Philadelphia was a remote, impersonal operation that not only failed to assist the beleaguered westerners in coping with the Indian problem but frequently disgraced itself abroad by consenting to treaties that negated

American commercial rights or land claims, thereby humiliating a proud and free people.

Thus, Jackson understood the necessity of statehood for Tennessee in terms of community self-interest. To what extent he actively participated in generating support for the new state constitution and in providing for its implementation after he returned home from the convention in Knox-ville is not clear. What is known is the haste with which the constitution was put into operation. Without approval from Congress—or anyone else—Tennessee immediately commenced to function as a state. March 28, 1796, was fixed as the day for the territorial government to go out of business. John Sevier, the popular Indian fighter and revolutionary war hero and fast becoming the leader of a faction separate from Blount's, was elected governor. The General Assembly was elected and the members began their first session toward the end of March. It was all arbitrary and illegal yet it said something about western temper and style.

Congress took exception to these high-handed tactics but after several snorts of disapproval, especially by members of the Federalist party, finally passed an enabling act which President Washington signed on June 1, 1796, making Tennessee the sixteenth state to be admitted to the Union. William Blount of Knox County and William Cocke of Hawkins County were elected to the United States Senate. Then without apparent warning or prior arrangement Blount decided that the time had come to advance the career of Andrew Jackson in a very significant way. He determined to run the young man for Tennessee's single seat in the United States House of Representatives.[10]

There were compelling reasons for this decision. Since Blount and Cocke were both from the eastern part of the state, it made a great deal of political sense to select the third member to Congress from the west. Furthermore, Jackson had impeccable connections with the Cumberland settlers as well as strong ties to the Blount operation. Blount wanted someone in Congress who would speak up for the rights of the frontiersmen, especially in their continuing war with Indians, and he was confident that Jackson would be "loud" enough to be heard in the furthest parts of Tennessee. Also, Blount wanted someone his faction could depend upon, someone who understood the importance of party loyalty. And they knew they could count on Jackson. Only three years before, the young man had written: "Any Transaction of . . . Governor Blount with Respect to My Business will be perfectly pleasing to me as I know from experience that My Interest will be attended to."[11] Finally, Blount wanted a popular candidate who could win. When Jackson's nomination was announced, John Overton conceded that election was a foregone conclusion. "I must beg leave to congratulate you on your interest and popularity in this country," wrote Overton to Jackson. "Your election is certain and I believe that there is scarcely a man in this part of the Territory that could be elected before you."[12] So, in the fall of 1796, with little serious opposition, Jackson was elected to Congress as Tennessee's first (and sole) representative in the lower house. He was twenty-nine years of age.

When Jackson arrived in Philadelphia, the nation's capital, in the late fall of 1796 to participate in the deliberations of the Fourth Congress, second session, it was not his first trip to the great city. In March 1795 he had come to Philadelphia to sell 50,000 acres of land he held jointly with John Overton and another 18,750 acres on commission for the estate of the late Joel Rice. And here began the strangest, most convoluted, most potentially dangerous sequence of events in Jackson's long, complicated, and sometimes hidden personal history. This is the story of Jackson as land speculator. And it nearly landed him in prison.

From the moment he arrived in Tennessee Jackson had immersed himself in land speculation, for land was the surest and quickest way to wealth and security in the west. It is by no means improbable that by the time he journeyed to Philadelphia to sell land he was speculating in tens (maybe hundreds) of thousands of acres.[13] After twenty-two days of what Jackson called "difficulties such as I have never experienced before" he found a buyer in David Allison, a Blount appointee and business manager for the family who had taken up residence in Philadelphia where he became a partner of the mercantile firm of John B. Evans and Company, an establishment that conducted a substantial amount of business with the settlers of the Cumberland.[14] Under the circumstances, when Allison offered Jackson a fifth of a dollar per acre for his land, the young man accepted, taking three promissory notes in exchange.

Jackson had been running a trading operation in Tennessee north to Kentucky and south to Natchez, Mississippi, and he planned to open a regular store on the Cumberland River to consolidate these activities. In preparation for this he took his brother-in-law, Samuel Donelson, as a partner.[15] To stock his store Jackson made purchases from Meeker, Cochran and Company, a Philadelphia firm, and he presented Allison's notes, which he endorsed, in payment. Allison also took Jackson to John B. Evans and Company, where Allison was a partner, to purchase additional supplies. Upon Allison's recommendation Jackson was permitted to "have goods to any amount I thought proper to take out."[16] When the invoice was presented, Jackson again offered Allison's notes, which Evans accepted after they were properly endorsed. Later Jackson admitted he did not realize at the time that in signing the notes he "stood security for the payment" of them.[17]

A remarkable admission. What businessman or lawyer enters financial transactions involving thousands of dollars without knowing his responsibilities and the degree of his involvement? He lamely excused himself to Overton by declaring that he "was placed in the Dam'st situation ever man was placed in."[18] Nevertheless, Evans warned him as a matter of course that the notes must be redeemed or he would bring suit. Jackson returned to Tennessee deeply depressed by the experience, "fatigued even almost unto death," he wrote.[19]

But the real blow came two months later when Meeker, Cochran and Company notified him that Allison had defaulted and that he, Jackson, was liable for the notes he had endorsed. A few months later a similar notice came from John B. Evans and Company.[20] To cover himself Jackson sold his store for 33,000 acres of land. Then he dashed over to Knoxville and sold this land to James Stuart for twenty-five cents per acre. This happened at the time Jackson was attending the Tennessee constitutional convention and he probably offered the land to Stuart through William Blount, who served as Stuart's agent.[21]

In February 1796 Jackson and Overton revalidated their partnership and took protective action against their liability by agreeing to bear an equal share in any loss incurred in the Allison transaction "under penalty of $100,000 each."[22] The following month Jackson began acquiring large parcels of land all over Tennessee with the idea of selling it for a profit in Philadelphia to pay off the notes. At this time he also purchased the Hunter's Hill plot, 640 acres on the south side of the Cumberland River, which became his home for a number of years. Over a period of two months in the spring of 1796 Jackson obtained 29,228 acres of land for sale in Philadelphia.[23]

When Jackson reached Philadelphia in 1796 to begin his congressional term, he again had trouble finding a buyer for his land, and again— incredibly—he turned to Allison and Blount. He sold 28,810 acres to them, accepting two notes from Allison and one from Blount. Blount promised the money plus interest within two years.[24] With the Blount security Jackson was out of immediate danger, but the Allison problem remained. Allison owed him over $20,000 and there was nothing the young congressman could do to collect his money except wait and hope for the best. The affair dragged on for several more years and almost sent Jackson to debtor's prison.[25]

Heading for Philadelphia in the fall of 1796 to take up his duties as a congressman, Jackson was beginning a period of long absences from home. These absences would be very difficult for him—and more so for Rachel. Frequently he wrote her long, loving letters that show a side of the man infrequently seen. So many of their letters to each other were lost in the Hermitage fire of 1834 that it is often forgotten how much tenderness and affection he showed toward his loved ones. One of the earliest letters to survive was written in 1796 and is reproduced here in full.

My Dearest Heart

It is with the greatest pleasure I sit down to write you. Tho I am absent My heart rests with you. With what pleasing hopes I view the future period when I shall be restored to your arms there to spend My days in Demestic

Sweetness with you the Dear Companion of my life, never to be separated from you again during this Transitory and fluctuating life.

I mean to retire from the Buss of publick life, and Spend My Time with you alone in Sweet Retirement, which is My only ambition and ultimate wish.

I have this moment finished My business here which I have got in good Train and hope to wind it up this Touer, and will leave this tomorrow Morning for Jonesborough where I hope to finish it, and tho it is now half after ten o'clock, could not think of going to bed without writing you. May it give you pleasure to Receive it. May it add to your Contentment until I return. May you be blessed with health. May the Goddess of Slumber every evening light on your eyebrows and gently lull you to sleep, and conduct you through the night with pleasing thoughts and pleasant dreams. Could I only know you were contented and enjoyed Peace of Mind, what satisfaction it would afford me whilst travelling the loanly and tiresome road. It would relieve My anxious breast and shorten the way—May the great "I am" bless and protect you until that happy and wished for moment arrives when I am restored to your sweet embrace which is the Nightly prayer of your affectionate husband,

Andrew Jackson

P.S. My compliments to my good old Mother Mrs. Donelson, that best of friends. Tell her with what pain I reflect upon leaving home without shaking her by the hand and asking her blessings.

A.J.[26]

Though painful—increasingly so over the years—the separations necessitated by "publick life" could not be avoided, and late in 1796 Jackson began his new career as a member of Congress in Philadelphia.

Philadelphia! The nation's capital. A city of 65,000 people, and the center of all that was elegant and civilized in American society. It was a rare opportunity for a young westerner to spend a season in this splendid city and Jackson made the most of it. Since he was on very close personal terms with Blount, who had extensive connections in Philadelphia, Jackson probably enjoyed a rich social life in the capital. In any event he took up lodgings with a man named Hardy.

Albert Gallatin, Swiss born and French accented, remembered seeing Jackson on his arrival in the city and later described him as "a tall, lank, uncouth-looking personage, with long locks of hair hanging over his face, and a queue down his back tied in an eel skin; his dress singular, his manners and deportment those of a rough backwoodsman."[27] Albert Gallatin never could abide this western upstart, and his description of the young congressman is a gross distortion. To depict Jackson as uncouth, ill-mannered, and dressed in a bizarre costume is more bad memory and wishful thinking than reality, more malice than truth. As a matter of fact Jackson had a Philadelphia tailor, Charles C. Watson, who provided him before the start of the congressional session with a black cloth coat with velvet collar, a pair of florentine breeches, and sundry other fashionable items of apparel.[28] As one of the first men of Tennessee and the state's single representative, he would no more walk into Congress outlandishly dressed than he would deliberately outrage southern honor. As an early biographer noted, Gallatin's baleful description was unrecognizable to Jackson's friends.[29]

Unlike many congressmen, Jackson was present on the opening day of Congress and found himself in the company of such distinguished American statesmen as James Madison of Virginia, Frederick Muhlenberg of Pennsylvania, Nathaniel Macon of North Carolina, Edward Livingston of New York, Fisher Ames of Massachusetts, Roger Griswold of Connecticut, Abraham Baldwin of Georgia, and Robert Goodloe Harper of South Carolina, many of them so-called Founding Fathers. Not until the third day of the session, when the Senate finally had a quorum, were both houses of Congress ready to begin business.

Just a few months earlier, President Washington had issued his Farewell Address. Now a committee of the House of Representatives was appointed to write a formal reply to the address. It was expected to be full of extravagant praise as an appropriate farewell to the "Father of His Country." On December 11, the reply, a glowing tribute, was formally reported out of committee and debated for two days. Then a vote was called for its adoption. Edward Livingston, Nathaniel Macon, and Andrew Jackson voted nay.[30] Years later, this vote was remembered and used against Jackson when he ran for the presidency. He was rebuked for daring such disrespect toward the great Washington. The vote took courage and independence, even if it showed a lack of courtesy and judgment. Jackson believed that the Jay treaty with Great Britain, concluded by the Washington administration, stained the honor of the "Grand republick." For that offense Washington deserved no thanks, according to Jackson. Then, too, the present administration had been impossibly tolerant of Indian massacres in Tennessee. To repeated pleas for help, the administration had responded with a thundering silence. And Jackson did not especially care for the administration's sympathy with England against France. His anglophobia had less to do with the attitude of Thomas Jefferson and his Republican friends (whose ideology and sentiment favored France) than it did with his revolutionary experiences and his western antagonism (and suspicion) of both England and Spain. The British and Spanish surrounded the United States and thwarted further American expansion. And they constantly fomented Indian attacks along the frontier.[31]

In voting against the tribute to Washington, Jackson teamed with several other congressmen committed to a conservative philosophy of government. All of them interpreted the Constitution narrowly; they feared a strong central government; they were concerned for the privileges of the states; and they opposed all but the most necessary appropriations by the federal government. In identifying himself with these men—men like Nathaniel Macon of North Carolina and Henry Tazewell of Virginia— Jackson reinforced his own native conservative bent which reflected western concern for the rights and sovereignty of the states. The conservatives of Congress welcomed him into their ranks and several of them corresponded with him regularly and became his intellectual mentors.[32]

Of more immediate importance to Jackson, and to his political career, was his response to a petition from Hugh Lawson White of Tennessee asking compensation for his services in an offensive attack against the Indians led by General Sevier in 1793. President Washington had steadfastly refused to honor the petition, claiming it required congressional approval. When the petition came to the House it carried a negative committee endorsement because the Tennesseans had initiated the attack without presidential approval and in defiance of general orders from the War Department against waging war against Indians without provocation.

The committee's reaction brought Jackson to his feet, fury etched clearly on his face.[33] In a "loud" voice he conveyed to his colleagues some of the horror of tomahawk warfare, especially as waged against women and children. "When it was seen that war was waged upon the State," he cried, "that the knife and the tomahawk were held over the heads of women and children, that peaceable citizens were murdered, it was time to make resistance." The expedition was defensive, he declared, one entirely just and necessary. It was involved in peacekeeping efforts, yet some 1,200 Indians suddenly assaulted them, drove them off, and "threatened to carry the Seat of Government."[34]

For a freshman congressman it was a strong speech and earned Jackson the attention and respect of his colleagues at the very outset of his brief career in Congress. A long debate followed, in the course of which James Madison added his voice in support of Jackson's position. At length the House approved the claim of the petition and awarded $22,816.[35]

By the time his first session in Congress ended, Jackson's performance could be summed up as modestly successful—nothing extraordinary, nothing outstanding, but solid nonetheless. He served on five committees, chaired one, presented two petitions, introduced one resolution, made five speeches, and voted twenty-four times with the majority out of a total of thirty-nine roll calls. He proved himself a diligent and hardworking representative, devoted to the interests of his state and his constituents, and although he was committed to the rights of the states in principle, his voting pattern demonstrated a pragmatic concern for the needs of Tennesseans. As a politician, Jackson was developing rapidly.

Congress adjourned on March 3, 1797, and Jackson was happy to quit the hectic capital and return home. Not that politics ceased to engage his attention. Now that the Sevier clique was becoming more and more active as a faction separate from the Blount crowd, he was drawn inevitably into the political conflicts developing within his state. Jackson had to be careful of Governor Sevier because of the older man's popularity throughout Tennessee; and it was only by a hair that an open and serious quarrel between the two was avoided in 1797. It all began with Jackson's decision to seek election as major general of the militia in 1796, an office that could rapidly advance his name, reputation, and political ambitions, for there was no surer way of gaining popularity with Tennesseans than military success—particularly against the Indians.

The operation of the militia and the selection of the commanding officers were essentially democratic processes. Regimental and company officers were elected by members of the militia regardless of rank; brigadier generals were elected by the field officers of each of the three militia districts within Tennessee; and the field officers of all three districts plus the brigadier generals elected a major general who commanded the militia of the entire state. In the event of a tie vote in the selection of the major general, the governor cast the deciding vote. Thus Jackson's decision to seek the post of major general—the highest military rank in the state—when he was not yet thirty years of age indicates the gargantuan size of his ambition.

But Governor Sevier decided to thwart Jackson's ambition, probably because of Jackson's youth and inexperience. After all, commanding troops to combat the Indians required more than legal training and political ambition. And Sevier may have been jealous of Jackson's new popularity in the state and fearful of what he might accomplish as general.

When Jackson learned of the governor's opposition he burst out in a long diatribe against Sevier, accusing him of attempting to control what should be untainted by executive interference. The governor took exception to these "scurelous" remarks and the implication of wrongdoing. But what did he, a man of achievement and distinction, he wrote, care about the language of a *"poor pitiful petty fogging Lawyer"*? The "voice of calumny has more than once been busied in trying to effect my political Distruction."[36] The danger of an open split between the two men was now very real, and such a rupture, if it occurred, could surely damage Jackson's reputation throughout the state.

Jackson lost the election for major general of the militia to George Conway, whom Governor Sevier supported, but the defeat taught the young man an important lesson: he must prepare his way, he must increase his personal strength within the militia before announcing another candidacy.[37] Thereafter Jackson took keen interest and active participation in the militia elections, and slowly over the years built his political strength within the organization.

Tension between Sevier and Jackson eased considerably. Six months after the militia election both men had calmed down. Eventually, mutual friends, among them General Robertson, intervened with soothing words. Both were reminded that a public quarrel was self-defeating. Soon Sevier was saying that "I never was nor am I yet, either your private or political enemy," and Jackson, matching these words, said that it was "with pleasure sir that I now remark to you that I think you had no *malicious* design to injure my reputation."[38]

The Blount people, of course, were extremely pleased with Jackson and his behavior over the past year, not simply because he had dared to take on the popular Sevier but because his fine performance in Congress justified their faith in him and signaled the beginning of an important new political career within their clique. Blount himself, who had been constantly promoting Jackson's interests for the past five years, broadly hinted that he would support the young man for the United States Senate in the next election.[39]

The opportunity came sooner than expected. It developed because of a conspiracy in which Blount himself was expelled from the Senate for scheming to help the British in an attack upon Spanish Florida in order to prevent the possible closing of the Mississippi River. Some of Blount's friends at home deserted him or expressed their loyalty to him very cautiously. But not Jackson. Committed mind and will to the entire conspiratorial design against the Spanish in Florida and Louisiana, and fiercely loyal to his friends as a matter of principle, he stoutly defended his political mentor at every opportunity and sought to explain and justify the conspiracy in terms of its advantages to westerners.[40] Blount never had a better friend.

The election in 1797 to the United States Senate by the Tennessee legislature involved a six-year term, and when the votes were counted Jackson had received 20 of them as against 13 for William Cocke. Blount was delighted. "Jackson Ele[ction] had my most hearty Concurrence," he wrote.[41] William C. C. Claiborne was chosen as Jackson's replacement in the House of Representatives. But this victory was not achieved without another public row. Jackson and Cocke got into a vicious quarrel over the election and it almost ended in a duel. Fortunately both men agreed to have the dispute arbitrated by a panel of men they both respected and in this way a bloody encounter was avoided. The tone of Jackson's correspondence during this dispute and his seeming readiness to shoot a man over what can only be described as a ridiculous peeve give some indication of his intensely unhappy mood during the winter of 1797–1798.[42] When he departed Tennessee to begin his duties as a United States senator—a post to which he was singularly unsuited—he left a wife distressed by his absence and resentful of his willingness to go. The "Situation in which I left her—*(Bathed in Tears)*," he wrote his brother-in-law, "fills me with woe. Indeed Sir, It has given me more pain than any Event in my life."[43]

In Philadelphia Jackson was one of the walking wounded. His generally angry mood and depression prevailed throughout the entire senatorial term, brief as it was. The Vice President and presiding officer of the Senate, Thomas Jefferson, later recalled the young senator's arrival in the chamber to take his seat. He particularly remembered the anger. "His passions are terrible," Jefferson said. "When I was President of the Senate, he was Senator, and he could never speak on account of the rashness of his feelings. I have seen him attempt it repeatedly, and as often choke with rage. His passions are, no doubt, cooler now; he has been much tried since I knew him, but he is a dangerous man."[44]

There was something terribly wrong with Jackson that winter, and it showed. One of his agonies was certainly financial. Every few years his involvement with David Allison came back to haunt him. Jackson complained and threatened, but it did him little good. Finally Allison was thrown into debtor's prison in Philadelphia where he died a little over a year later, on September 30, 1798. Still Jackson fumed, despite the poor man's incarceration. "On the Subject of Mr. Allison," he wrote John Overton, "I can assure you there are no hopes of Payment. . . . If he was only Possessed of honesty. . . . Judmt. last court has passed against me as his Bail for upwards of Two Hundred Dollars, and D——n the Rascal, he will not Evan convay me land in the amount. This Shews the Principle of the man."[45]

Another sign of Jackson's distress at this time was his inactivity in the Senate. His senatorial record is nearly blank. Although he responded to a number of roll calls, his participation in debate was nil. He chaired one committee, introduced one bill, and twice called for the yeas and nays. As something of a sign of his disaffection, he voted with the majority only thirteen times out of a total of thirty-four votes.

Clearly he did not belong in the Senate, and he probably knew it. He was too young, too inexperienced. Sitting in that quiet chamber, hearing men of considerable experience and national distinction discuss momentous issues of war and peace, freedom and liberty, Jackson may have been intimidated. And if Jefferson was correct in his recollection that Jackson tried repeatedly to express himself on the floor and failed because of emotional turmoil, it is small wonder that his participation dwindled to nothing. It must have been very disheartening, very frustrating, very depressing.

Everything considered, Jackson failed completely as senator. He was moody and angry, plagued by debts, inarticulate in debate, and in February 1798 he fell on the ice and injured his left knee, which incapacitated him for many days. He spent the "best hours of every day for seven successive months quiescent in a red morocco chair."[46] And what with being bored and concerned about Rachel and disgusted with the administration of President John Adams[47] he was in no mood to pay close attention to his senatorial duties. Indeed, one session of the Senate was about all he could stomach, and so in April 1798 he asked for and obtained a leave of absence for the remainder of the session. On his return to Nashville he resigned his seat without apology or explanation. It was a flat rejection of a job he could not handle.[48] It was another low point in Jackson's early life. He had assumed responsibilities far beyond his reach and he virtually made a fool of himself.

CHAPTER 4

The Duel

O NE REASON FOR JACKSON'S DECISION to resign from the Senate was the likelihood of another office, one that would keep him close to his interests in Tennessee without requiring him to leave the state for months on end and thereby agitate Rachel, one that would pay more than any other office in the state with the exception of the governorship, and one that would advance his political and military ambitions by taking him to all parts of Tennessee and bringing him into contact with the people and the leaders of the various sections of the state. He set his sights on election by the legislature to a seat on the bench of the state superior court, often called the supreme court because its judges sitting together comprised Tennessee's highest tribunal. The post carried an annual salary of $600, which was $150 less than the salary of the governor.

It is not clear whether Jackson initiated the move toward a judgeship or whether he was first approached by a friend or a member of the Blount faction. Whatever the circumstances, he was elected without opposition to the bench in 1798 at the age of thirty-one, shortly after his return to Tennessee. With his distinguished reputation and standing in the state, his affiliation with the Blount organization, and his large circle of friends, there was no difficulty in arranging his election by the legislature.

Jackson's commission as justice, signed by the governor, was dated September 20, 1798, but the formal election by the legislature took place on December 20.[1] He served on the bench for six years, holding his court principally in Knoxville, Jonesborough, and Nashville. Considering how little law Jackson actually knew to qualify as a jurist, he nonetheless earned a respectable reputation and record.

There were several reasons for Jackson's subsequent success. He was a man of the highest integrity; his decisions were swift and devoid of prejudice or discrimination; he was courageous and he spoke without fear or hesitation. Moreover, he had a fierce sense of justice, however wrongheaded it might be at times. It was this sense that sustained his impartiality under most circumstances. "Tradition reports," an early biographer said, "that he maintained the dignity and authority of the bench, while he was *on* the bench; and that his decisions were short, untechnical, unlearned, sometimes ungrammatical, and generally right."[2] If his decisions were indeed generally right, then surely justice and the people of Tennessee were well served—with or without the supporting niceties of legal scholarship.

Recorded decisions did not become general practice in Tennessee until after Jackson left the bench in 1804. Consequently, only five of his written decisions survive, each signed by Jackson and the other members of the superior court.[3] Judicial proceedings in Tennessee during this period were neither primitive nor makeshift. Early judges were careful to establish proper courtroom practice and decorum, and they insisted on strict compliance with accepted procedures. Disrespect for the law, rowdy behavior, and legal highjinks brought severe penalties. Jackson knew what was proper and what was expected of him. He wore a judicial gown in court and conducted himself with appropriate dignity. It was widely believed that no backlog ever clogged the Jackson court. Cases were dispatched with a swiftness that would stagger more learned jurists. In fifteen days he went through fifty cases!

On one occasion Jackson was holding court in a small village when a great, hulking fellow named Russell Bean, who had been indicted for cutting off the ears of his infant child in a "drunken frolic," paraded before the court, cursed judge, jury, and all assembled, and then marched out the door.

"Sheriff," Judge Jackson intoned in his most solemn voice, "arrest that man for contempt of court and confine him."

The sheriff trailed after Bean to collar him, but soon returned empty-handed with the excuse that it was impossible to apprehend the culprit.

"Summon a posse, then," the judge commanded, "and bring him before me."

Off the sheriff went again, and again he returned without his prisoner. It seemed that no one dared lay a hand on the armed man. Bean threatened to shoot the "first skunk that came within ten feet of him."

Jackson exploded. "Mr. Sheriff," he stormed, "since you can not obey my orders, summon me; yes, sir, summon me."

"Well, judge, if you say so, though I don't like to do it; but if you will try, why I suppose I must summon you."

"Very well," Jackson said, rising and walking toward the door, "I adjourn this court ten minutes."

Bean was standing a short distance from the court, in the center of a crowd, cursing and flourishing his weapons and vowing death to all who might attempt to arrest him.

Mr. Justice Jackson walked straight toward the man, a pistol in each hand. "Now," he roared, staring into the eyes of the ruffian, "surrender, you infernal villain, this very instant, or I'll blow you through."

Bean stared into Jackson's blazing eyes. Then, as though reading something terrible in those eyes, he quietly surrendered his weapons. "There, judge," he said, "it's no use, I give in." And he surrendered meekly.

Several days later while sitting in prison Bean was asked why he gave up to Jackson after holding off an entire posse. "Why," he said, "when he came up, I looked him in the eye, and I saw shoot, and there wasn't shoot in nary other eye in the crowd; and so I says to myself, says I, hoss, it's about time to sing small, and so I did."[4]

For a backwoods judge, Jackson performed exceedingly well. There was no nonsense with him. There was "shoot" in his eyes, and sane men did not trifle with that.

As Jackson moved about Tennessee dispensing justice with a stern hand, he observed many transformations that had occurred in the state since his arrival in 1788, some dozen years earlier. New towns dotted the landscape almost to the Mississippi River; frame houses replaced rude log cabins; dancing masters, dressmakers, and other artisans were setting up shop in the leading settlements; stores carried silks and brocades as well as homespun and buckskin. Civilized society had arrived, and the frontier was moving on—although vestiges of it would linger for many years.

During his tenure as a superior court judge, Jackson helped organize a lodge of the Order of Freemasons in Tennessee. The grand lodge of North Carolina on September 5, 1801, provided the necessary dispensation to "open the Lodge in due form on the first Degree of Masonry." Jackson, George W. Campbell, Jenkin Whiteside, John Rhea, and others met at the home of Daniel Harrison where the lodge was formally opened. Jackson was named senior warden *pro tem*, and on his motion a committee was formed to prepare the bylaws for the governance of the lodge.[5]

It also developed during Jackson's judicial career that his long-smoldering feud with Governor John Sevier broke out into violent conflict. And it could only happen in the west that the governor of the state and a justice of the supreme court would end up shooting at one another. It began when Jackson learned of a remarkable land fraud in which a company of speculators in Tennessee were forging North Carolina land warrants and selling Tennessee land to which they held no right. Jackson turned over his evidence to the governor of North Carolina who, in turn, asked Governor Sevier to extradite the accused conspirators.[6] Sevier refused. Then a letter was found that seemed to implicate Sevier himself in the fraud. But Jackson did something extraordinary when he submitted his evidence to the governor of North Carolina. He failed to name Sevier. He had the makings of political blackmail and probably planned to use it. For Jackson still desperately desired the rank of major general of the militia and the one man who could successfully block him, as proved in the last election, was John Sevier. Perhaps the next time the election came around, if Sevier did not interfere, Jackson could win that election.

But time worked differently than Jackson expected. When Sevier ran out his constitutional limit of three successive terms as governor of the state and could run again only after the interval of another term, he was succeeded by Archibald Roane, a member of the Blount faction and Jackson's good friend. Then Major General Conway died and the election of his successor was scheduled for February 5, 1802. Sevier, out of a job, decided to take over the militia again and therefore announced his candidacy. But Jackson also expected to take the post and for years had been working diligently to cultivate the necessary votes to win it. So successful had he been in these efforts that the officers of the militia not only put him forward enthusiastically but made it appear that his nomination was "unsolicited."[7]

Sevier was shocked to learn that he had been challenged for the post by a lawyer with no appreciable military experience. His shock turned to outrage when the results of the election, held on February 5, 1802, were announced. Both he and Jackson received seventeen votes each, while Brigadier General James Winchester got three. That Jackson could achieve such a feat against an immensely popular war hero demonstrates how far his political skills had developed and how well he had used them. Over the previous few years he had assiduously cultivated the friendship of many of the officers of the militia. He became particularly popular with the young officers. They liked his style and, indeed, many of them imitated it. No doubt Jackson would have won overwhelmingly in the election had he not been running against someone as popular and powerful as John Sevier.

Since a tie existed, the final selection lay with the new governor. And Governor Roane broke the tie in favor of his good friend, Andrew Jackson. The commission signed by the governor was dated April 1, 1803.[8] Thus, at the age of thirty-five, Mr. Justice Jackson became Major General Andrew Jackson of the Tennessee militia. It was one of the most important and decisive events of his entire life.

According to some historians, Jackson then presented his evidence of fraud against Sevier to Governor Roane.[9] Since Roane intended to seek reelection as governor the following year, and since Sevier would undoubtedly challenge him, this evidence proved highly useful to Roane in damaging Sevier's reputation within the state. And Jackson, by providing the evidence and challenging the great revolutionary war hero, claimed in effect political preeminence in West Tennessee. Since William Blount had died suddenly on March 21, 1800, leadership of the Blount faction in the west was now assumed by Andrew Jackson.[10]

The following year Sevier announced his candidacy for governor, whereupon Roane released the information he had received from Jackson. Naturally Jackson had to substantiate the charges, and on July 27, 1803, he authored a communication published in the Knoxville *Gazette* charging Sevier with fraud and citing his evidence.

Sevier was livid. That a "petty fogging Lawyer," as he had called Jackson, would dare to compete with a Revolutionary War hero for military office was bad enough; that he would accuse him of fraud was monstrous. Furious at the outcome of the military election and seething with indignation over the fraud charges, Sevier's friends in the legislature rushed through a bill on November 5, 1803, to wreak at least some degree of revenge on the "petty fogging Lawyer." Their bill, which passed, divided the military command of the state into an eastern district and a western district, and Jackson was allowed to retain command only over the western district.

Sevier himself responded to Jackson's newspaper attack on August 8, 1803, insisting in the *Gazette* that he had committed no crime in his land dealings. Obviously, he said, the charges were politically motivated in an attempt to discredit him and bring about his defeat in the gubernatorial election.

As the controversy intensified the danger of violence also increased. Then, on the first day of October, 1803, Mr. Justice Jackson arrived in Knoxville to hold court and ran into Sevier in the public square. It was a dramatic moment. Seeing the cause of his present embarrassment, Sevier lashed Jackson with stinging words about daring to challenge and humiliate a great man. Who did Jackson, a pitiful nothing of a lawyer, think he was? Sevier sneered at him and his "pretensions." Poor Jackson could hardly answer, so shocked was he by the suddenness and intensity of this abuse. He stammered a defense by citing his many services to the state.

"Services?" Sevier laughed. "I know of no great service you have rendered the country, except taking a trip to Natchez with another man's wife."

Jackson went wild. "Great God!" he screamed, "do you mention *her* sacred name?"

"Draw!" roared Sevier. The crowd scattered. Shots rang out and one bystander was grazed by a bullet.[11] Fortunately the two men were separated before a general melee could begin; but thereafter the expression "Great God" became a favorite saying with the young men of Knoxville.[12]

As soon as he could lay hands on pen and paper Jackson scratched out a challenge.

Knoxville, October 2, 1803

Sir, The ungentlemanly expressions, and gasgonading conduct of yours, relative to me on yesterday was in true character of yourself, and unmask you to the world, and plainly shews that they were the ebulitions of a base mind goaded with stuborn proof of fraud, and flowing from a source devoid of every refined sentiment, or delicate sensation. But Sir the voice of the people has made you a Governor, this alone makes you worthy of my notice, or the notice of any Gentleman. For the Office I have respect, and as such I only deign to notice you, and call upon you for that satisfaction and explanation that your ungentlemanly conduct and expressions require, for this purpose I request an interview, and my friend who will hand you this will point out the time and place, when and where I shall expect to see you with your friend and no other person. my friend [Captain Andrew White] and myself will be armed with pistols—you cannot mistake me or my meaning.

I am etc etc.

Andrew Jackson[13]

Sevier accepted the challenge to meet at any time and place, provided it was not on the sacred soil of Tennessee.[14] To Jackson that was "a mere subterfuge. Your attack was in the Town of Knoxville," he wrote Sevier. "Did you take the name of a lady into your polluted lips in the Town of Knoxville? Did you challeng me to draw, when you were armed with a cutlass and I with a cane, and now sir in the neighborhood of Knoxville you shall atone for it or I will publish you as a coward and a poltroon. . . . I shall expect an answer in the space of one hour."[15]

Sevier did not respond.

Jackson wrote again, and now he was willing to fight in Georgia, Virginia, North Carolina, or the "Indian boundary line" if necessary. Anywhere. To prod Sevier to a response, Jackson added: "I have spoke for a place in the paper [Gazette] for the following advertisement . . . as follows, To all who shall see these presents Greeting. Know ye that I Andrew Jackson, do pronounce, publish, and declare to the world, that his excellency John Sevier, Captain General and commander in chief of the land and naval forces of the state of Tennessee, is a base coward and poltroon. He will basely insult, but has not courage to repair the wound. *Andrew Jackson.*"[16]

Sevier shot right back. "Your conduct . . . Shews you to be a pitiful poltroon. . . . I shall not receive another letter from you, as I deem you a Coward."[17]

When Jackson's "advertisement" appeared in the *Gazette* on Monday, October 10, 1803, it produced what Jackson had demanded. The two men agreed to meet on Wednesday in the Indian territory in the neighborhood of South West Point.

Jackson got to the designated spot on time—and waited. No Sevier. Not a sign. Finally, Jackson started back to Knoxville to force a showdown. He had not gone a mile when he sighted his man riding toward him in the company of mounted men. Jackson drew a pistol, dismounted, and drew a second pistol. Seeing the armed judge before him, Sevier leaped from his horse, a pistol in each hand.

The two men immediately began to curse one another. This verbal assault was so therapeutic that for a moment they put away their pistols.

Then Jackson lunged at Sevier, threatening to cane him. Sevier drew his sword which "frightened his horse and he ran away with the Governor's Pistols." Not to lose an opportunity, Jackson drew a pistol, whereupon Sevier ducked behind a tree. At that point Sevier's son drew on Jackson and Jackson's second drew on the son.

It was all quite ridiculous. Even the antagonists must have recognized the absurdity of it all. Finally members of Sevier's party rushed forward making friendly signs, and soon the two men, still cursing each other, were persuaded to end their murderous feud. The entire party rode together peaceably to Knoxville. Although Jackson and Sevier did not reconcile, their disagreement never flared again into open combat.[18]

Sevier won election to the governorship despite the accusations of wrongdoing. The people of Tennessee simply could not believe the charges leveled against their hero. To them, Sevier was synonymous with Tennessee, and they could no more vote against Sevier than vote against their own state.

The quarrel between Sevier and Jackson marked the beginning of political sectionalism between East and West Tennessee. After Blount's death in 1800 Jackson assumed political leadership of the Cumberland region and Sevier that of the eastern counties of the state. However, Blount's half-brother, Willie Blount, assumed nominal leadership of the Blount faction around the state. Sevier had no trouble winning a second series of three terms as governor, from 1803 to 1809, after which Willie Blount succeeded him. Fortunately for Jackson, the two events most critical to his military career—his election as major general of the militia and the outbreak of the War of 1812—came at times when Sevier was out of office and the administration of the state was in the hands of Jackson's political friends. And while there is no question that Jackson was a man of considerable ability, ambition, and connections, yet there is much to be said in ascribing his subsequent fame as a soldier and politician to just plain luck.

During the period of Jackson's early military career he received few calls for action from the federal government. The earliest alert came in 1803 immediately following the purchase of Louisiana from France. In selling Louisiana to the United States, Napoleon violated an earlier treaty obligation never to alienate the territory except to return it to Spain, who held it previously. The French had never actually reoccupied the territory but permitted the Spanish to administer it on their behalf. So the question immediately arose: would Spain respect the purchase by the United States or declare it a violation of her treaty rights with Napoleon and refuse to surrender the territory? The fear worried President Thomas Jefferson and he therefore sent an alert to the command in western Tennessee to stand ready to march in case it became necessary to expel the Spanish from Louisiana.

Jackson responded immediately. He issued a general order to the militia to prepare themselves in the event of a national crisis. The presence of the Spanish, he said, was "degrading to our national Character" and if "impelled by the most cogant necessity of defending our national dignity and liberties" we will provide "prompt satisfaction."[19]

Fortunately, the treaty of cession between Napoleon and the American government was respected by the Spanish, and it was unnecessary to prod them out of Louisiana with a show of military force. Jackson clearly regretted missing a chance of humiliating the "hated Dons." The expulsion of foreign control from the Mississippi was a mighty deed in the minds of westerners, one that further endeared their new President to them. General Jackson told President Jefferson, "all the Western Hemisphere rejoices at the Joyfull news of the cession of Louisiana, an event which places the peace happiness and liberty of our country on a lasting basis, an event which generations yet unborn on each revolving year, will hail the day, and with it the causes that give it birth."[20] Later in the year General James Wilkinson and a detachment of regular army troops floated down the Mississippi and hoisted the American flag over the city of New Orleans. W. C. C. Claiborne, who had accompanied Wilkinson to New Orleans to receive the transfer, was appointed governor of Louisiana, a post Jackson tried to win for himself and which prompted deep resentment against Jefferson when he failed to obtain it. It truly galled Jackson to lose the post. He had used considerable political influence to gain the office and it humiliated him to be passed over. Relations between Jefferson and Jackson—what little there was—collapsed. In the following years Jackson became increasingly anti-Jefferson. He veered closer to the more extreme states' rights wing of the Republican party, taking his political direction from such conservative and doctrinaire Republicans as John Randolph of Roanoke and Nathaniel Macon of North Carolina.[21]

On July 24, 1804, shortly after losing the Louisiana post, Jackson resigned his judicial office because of bad health—or so he said.[22] But there were other reasons. For one, he could no longer afford the luxury of judicial life with its limited salary and its enormous demands on his time. His financial situation had deteriorated considerably in the last few years and he needed to devote more time and energy to his personal affairs if he hoped to escape the possibility of bankruptcy.

The principal problem was the wretched Allison business. On January 1, 1795, Allison mortgaged 85,000 acres of land on the three forks of the Duck River to Norton Pryor, a Philadelphia merchant, for $21,-800. After Allison's death, Pryor engaged Jackson to bring suit to foreclose the mortgage and gain clear title to the property. Since Jackson had just been elevated to the superior court, he asked John Overton to prosecute the foreclosure for him. Overton agreed and the suit was brought in the United States District Court on October 27, 1801, to satisfy Allison's indebtedness of $21,800 to Pryor. The land was ordered sold and the sale took place on April 14, 1802, with Jackson acting for Pryor in purchasing three land parcels, one of which (10,000 acres) constituted Jackson's fee for the transaction. Shortly thereafter the marshal of West Tennessee issued deeds to the property and Jackson proceeded to sell his share in small sections. So certain was he of the deed that he offered warranted titles to those who bought the land from him, thereby binding himself to buy back the land if the title proved defective—and to buy it back at the current value of the land, not the original price. "I never once thought on the subject," Jackson moaned at a later date.[23]

Years passed and the land quadrupled in value. In 1808 Andrew Erwin bought Pryor's land and went to Tennessee to sell it to individual purchasers. After receiving assurances from Jackson that the title was good, Erwin took possession and initiated suit against squatters. Then in 1810 or 1811—Jackson could not remember the exact date—George W. Campbell told him that he had been examining the proceedings of the original suit in 1801 and had found that the decision was invalid because it had been handed down by a federal court that did not have jurisdiction. If Campbell was correct Jackson faced ruin, since the property was now worth hundreds of thousands of dollars. With a desperation born of panic, Jackson galloped through the Indian wilderness into Georgia in search of the Allison heirs. He found them in Wilkes County and begged them to sign over to him "all their right to any property within the state of Tennessee." In exchange, he was willing to give up their father's notes to him and make a small cash settlement of $500. The heirs agreed and executed a deed in his favor.[24]

Now the situation was reversed. Jackson held the single legal deed not only to the land he had sold himself but to the entire 85,000 acres originally mortgaged to Pryor. He returned to Tennessee, gave clear title to those who had purchased from him, and then tried to negotiate with Andrew Erwin for the land Erwin had purchased from Pryor. Erwin absolutely refused. He felt he had legitimately purchased the land from Pryor and would not agree to any further negotiation. So Jackson bided his time. Later, when he had won fame as a General, he filed suit against Erwin and asked the court to grant him the land by virtue of the Allison deed. The case dragged on for ten years, and not until 1824 was it settled when Erwin agreed to pay Jackson $10,000 and Jackson conveyed to Erwin a deed of release for all of Allison's lands.[25]

When it came time to pay Jackson the $10,000, Mrs. Erwin went to the General and begged him to forgive the debt. She said her husband faced ruin as a result of the judgments that had piled up against him over the last few years. And without another consideration Jackson did as she asked. Having won his case, he graciously and generously waived payment. It was typically Jackson, vindictive one minute and forgiving the next.[26]

The thirty-year history of the Allison land deal scarred Jackson for life with fearful marks of fiscal conservatism. He hated debt; paper money represented the instruments of dishonest land and stock jobbers; banks that manipulated debts and loans were an abomination.

Having resigned his judgeship, Jackson returned full-time to his business interests in 1804. He sold his plantation at Hunter's Hill and moved with his wife and slaves to a 420-acre place about ten miles from Nashville which he came to call the Hermitage. Rebuilding his personal fortune took time, effort, and considerable sacrifice. Fortunately, he had the help of Rachel and the Donelsons. Curiously, he did not resume his law practice. As far as can be determined, he ceased practicing law in 1796 when he went to Congress.

The first thing he did to get back on his financial feet was to expand his mercantile interests. On February 16, 1802, he formed a partnership with Thomas Watson and John Hutchings, one of Rachel's many nephews. Together the three men operated a cotton gin and distillery as well as mercantile stores in Gallatin, Lebanon, and Hunter's Hill. A dispute between Watson and Jackson later dissolved the partnership, and in April 1804 Jackson and Hutchings formed a new partnership with John Coffee, a local businessman who would soon marry Rachel's niece, Mary (Polly) Donelson. The firm, called Jackson, Coffee and Hutchings, was established at Clover Bottom, the site of a racecourse, four miles from the Hermitage and included a store, boatyard, a tavern, and a racetrack.[27] They sold dry goods for the most part—blankets, calico, cowbells, grindstones—and coffee, rum, gunpowder, salt, and whatever else their neighbors wanted and they could obtain. The company prospered and soon expanded into Sumner County and at the Cantonment on the Tennessee River close to Muscle Shoals.

While Jackson tended store his farm was cultivated by slaves supervised by Rachel. Over a period of years Jackson had accumulated many slaves. In 1794, according to a list of his taxable property, he owned 10 slaves. The Davidson County tax books show that the number rose to 15 in 1798. The 1820 census reported that he held 44 slaves, of whom 27 were male and 17 female. By the time Jackson became President of the United States there were 95 slaves at the Hermitage. A few years later that number totaled 150.[28]

For the most part Jackson treated his slaves decently and tried to make certain they were not abused by overseers.[29] But he could also be very severe. If he felt punishment merited he had his slaves whipped and on occasion chained. With runaway slaves he had little mercy. His behavior on occasion can only be described as barbaric. The worst example of his cruelty toward his slaves occurred when he advertised in the Nashville *Tennessee Gazette* on September 26, 1804 (and succeeding issues), for a runaway.

STOP THE RUNAWAY

FIFTY DOLLARS REWARD.

Eloped from the subscriber, living near Nashville, on the 25th of June last, a Mulatto Man Slave, about thirty years old, six feet and an inch high, stout made and active, talks sensible, stoops in his walk, and have a remarkable large foot. . . . The above reward will be given any person that will take him, and deliver him to me, or secure him to jail, so that I can get him. If taken out of the state, the above reward, and all reasonable expenses paid—and ten dollars extra, for every hundred lashes any person will give him, to the amount of three hundred.

ANDREW JACKSON
Near Nashville,
State of Tennessee

Under the watchful eye of Rachel the slaves at the Hermitage produced a variety of crops, the most profitable of which were cotton, corn, and wheat. Jackson was one of twenty-four men in the county who boasted a cotton gin with which he de-seeded his own crop and that of his neighbors as well, for which he received a fee in goods. He had had a distillery, but it burned in 1801 together with the copperware, stills, caps, worms, and the rest of the equipment.[30] Jackson also bred horses, cows, and mules. He raced horses and sometimes won thousands of dollars. Shortly after he resigned from the bench, he took a long tour of Virginia in an effort to find an improved breed. He returned from that trip with Truxton, a stallion fifteen hands three inches high, which he bought for $1,500, one of the greatest racehorses Jackson ever owned.

In the autumn of 1805 a spectacular race was arranged between Jackson's five-year-old Truxton and Captain Joseph Ervin's mighty stallion, Plowboy. The stakes were $2,000, payable on the day of the race, and an $800 forfeit payable in a list of specified notes should the race be canceled by one side or the other. Just before the day of the race Plowboy went lame, the race was canceled, and Ervin paid the forfeit. Ervin at first offered a variety of notes which Jackson refused to accept. The notes were supposed to be due on demand, but Ervin offered notes which were not due and therefore not according to the list agreed upon. Eventually proper notes were produced and the affair presumably settled.

But a short time later Captain Patten Anderson, a friend of Jackson's, gossiped in a Nashville store about Ervin's attempt to pass off improper notes. The gossip was relayed to Charles Dickinson, the son-in-law of Ervin, who took exception to the clear implication of impropriety. Various rumors and reports were bandied back and forth, and the intensity of feeling heightened with each new round of interpretation about the forfeit. Jackson, of course, became involved and at length Dickinson posted a letter to the General calling him a coward and an equivocator.[31]

It was also later reported that Dickinson, when drinking, had taken the "sacred name" of Rachel Jackson into his "polluted mouth" by referring indecorously to the curious circumstances of Jackson's marriage. There was a wild side to Dickinson—like Jackson in his youth—that occasionally erupted into reckless boasts and drunken heroics. But Dickinson was well connected, charming, affluent, something of a dandy, and known to be one of the best shots—if not the *best* shot—in Tennessee.

It would be preferable to explain the duel that eventually followed as a consequence of Dickinson's vile and vulgar insult, but the fact of the matter is otherwise. The duel resulted from a horserace bet, not the need of an outraged husband to defend the name of his beloved wife.[32]

In time, as the misunderstandings and misinterpretations multiplied, Dickinson published a statement in the Nashville *Review* on May 24, 1806, in which he called Jackson "a worthless scoundrel," "a poltroon and a coward."[33]

Within an hour after reading these words Jackson issued a formal challenge to a duel. The letter read in part: "Your conduct and expressions, relative to me of late have been of such a nature and so insulting, that it requires and shall have my notice. . . . I hope, sir, your courage will be ample security to me that I will obtain speedily that satisfaction due me for the insults offered, and in the way my friend who hands you this will point out. he waits upon you for that purpose, and with your friend will enter into immediate arrangements for this purpose."[34]

The two men agreed to meet on Friday, May 30, at Harrison's Mills on the Red River in Logan County, Kentucky, which was just beyond the state border north of Nashville. Eight paces (twenty-four feet) were measured off. The duelists took their positions.

"Are you ready?" asked General Thomas Overton, Jackson's second and the brother of John Overton.

"I am ready," said Dickinson.

"I am ready," replied Jackson.

"Fere!" cried Overton in his old-country accent.

Dickinson quickly raised his pistol and fired. The ball struck Jackson in the chest. As it hit, a puff of dust rose from the breast of his coat and Jackson slowly raised his left arm and placed it tightly against his throbbing chest. He stood very still, "his teeth clenched."

Horrified to see Jackson still standing after his dead-aim shot, Dickinson drew back a step. "Great God!" he cried, "have I missed him?"

"Back to the MARK, sir," shouted Overton as he aimed his pistol at the dumbstruck man.[35]

Dickinson returned to the mark and waited for Jackson's fire. He was at the General's mercy. Jackson could have been magnanimous and refused the shot or fired into the air, but he had promised to kill Dickinson and nothing could dissuade him. "I should have hit him," he reportedly said, "if he had shot me through the brain."[36]

Slowly Jackson raised his pistol and took aim. He squeezed the trigger. There was a "click" as the hammer stopped at half cock. Dickinson waited. Jackson drew back the hammer, aimed again, and fired.

The bullet struck Dickinson just below the ribs. He reeled. His friends rushed forward and caught him as he fell. They tried to stop the flow of blood but there was nothing they could do. The bullet had passed clean through his body, leaving a gaping hole. The twenty-seven-year-old man bled to death.

Overton looked quickly at the prostrate Dickinson and then walked over to Jackson. "He won't want anything more of you, General," Overton said, and with that he led Jackson away. About a hundred yards on, it was noticed that one of Jackson's shoes was soaked with blood. The General opened his coat. The bullet had shattered two of his ribs and buried itself in his chest.

Jackson's life may have been saved because of the loose-fitting coat he wore. Because of it, Dickinson misjudged his target and instead of piercing Jackson's heart he buried a bullet next to it that remained in place for the remainder of Jackson's life. More than a month passed before the General could move around without difficulty. The wound never properly healed and caused Jackson considerable discomfort thereafter. The fact that he lived for nearly forty years with this foreign object next to his heart says something extraordinary about the strength, will, and character of Andrew Jackson.

Townspeople in Nashville were aghast at what had happened, particularly when they learned how poor Dickinson was made to stand defenseless while a wrathful man took his time to slaughter him. Many men said the duel was a scandal, a brutal, cold-blooded killing. Coming on the heels of his quarrel with Sevier, the duel did Jackson great harm and saddled him with a reputation as a violent and vengeful man. For the next few months Andrew Jackson was virtually a social outcast in western Tennessee.

CHAPTER 5

Old Hickory

For several years following the infamous duel with Dickinson, Jackson took particular pains to recoup his political and financial losses. Most of his attention was given to developing his plantation and increasing his landholdings. He and Rachel lived in a square two-story blockhouse of three rooms, one room on the ground floor and two upstairs. Later he built a second house, smaller than the first and standing approximately twenty feet from it, and connected the two with a covered passageway. This was their home until he built the stately Hermitage mansion in 1819.

In May 1805 Jackson and his wife received into their unostentatious frontier home a very distinguished visitor who stayed with them for several days. It was none other than Aaron Burr, former Vice President of the United States. Burr had tried to slip past Thomas Jefferson to snatch the presidency in the House election of 1801 but he failed in his outrageous scheme and was subsequently read out of the Republican party. Westerners overlooked his vaulting ambition because he had generally favored their interests and had been particularly powerful in advocating the admission of Tennessee into the Union. His killing of Alexander Hamilton in a duel at Weehawken, New Jersey, in 1804 reinstated him in the Republican party, as far as westerners were concerned, because Hamilton had long been identified with the Federalist party and eastern interests.

Out of office and out of favor in the east, Burr sought new opportunities for his clever and ingenious mind beyond the Appalachian Mountains. In 1805 he began to sport himself among the western gentry, enjoying their hospitality and dropping hints that some delectable misfortune might soon engulf the hated Spanish in the southwest. The fact that this agreeable and delightful man stayed with the Jacksons during his five-day visit to Nashville helped repair the damaged social standing of the Jackson family in the community.

Three months later Burr returned to Nashville with plans to expel the Spanish from the southwest and colonize the region with Americans.

55

Whether he was plotting the establishment of a personal empire at the expense of both Spanish and American territory, as later reported, can probably never be determined with certainty. In any event Jackson found him utterly charming, and Burr, for his part, acknowledged his host as "a man of intelligence and one of those prompt, frank, ardent souls whom I love to meet."[1] At one point Jackson arranged a splendid ball in Burr's honor, and for years afterward many in Nashville remembered "the hush and thrill attending the entrance of Colonel Burr, accompanied by General Jackson in the uniform of a Major General." The invited company lined the sides of the room and looked on intently "while the two courtliest men in the world" circuited the room. Jackson introduced his guest "with singular grace and emphasis. It was a question with the ladies which of the two was the finer gentleman."[2]

Fully aware of Jackson's fire-breathing nationalism and intense hatred of the Spanish, Burr cleverly drew his host deeper into his schemes. He finally asked Jackson to provide him with a list of officers for one or two regiments who were fit for the business of war and could be trusted. He also asked him to build five large boats on Stone's River at Clover Bottom, to be used for descending the river, and to purchase a large quantity of provisions to be transported in these boats. The orders were accompanied by $3,500 in Kentucky banknotes which Jackson gladly accepted.

Jackson was now an accomplice in whatever Burr was plotting. He knew the purpose of the five boat orders—or thought he did. Jackson never revealed precisely what Burr said to him (other than to insist it did not involve treason in any shape or fashion), but he clearly believed the orders for the boats and provisions were intended for an assault on the Spanish both in Florida and beyond the Louisiana Territory in Mexico. "I love my Country and Government," he wrote. "I hate the Dons. I would delight to see Mexico reduced, but I will die in the last Ditch before I would yield a foot to the Dons or see the Union disunited."[3]

On October 4, 1806, as the conspiracy took shape, Jackson issued a proclamation to the officers of the second division of the Tennessee militia. "The late conduct of the Spanish government," the proclamation began, "added to the hostile appearance and menacing attitude of their armed forces . . . make it necessary that the militia . . . should be in complete order and at a moment's warning ready to march."[4] He sent a copy of this proclamation to Brigadier General James Winchester along with a letter that cited the "Hostile and menacing attitude of Spain" as the reason for issuing the proclamation. "You no doubt have seen from the late papers," he said to Winchester, "that the negotiation for the purchase of the Floridas has failed," a negotiation in which President Jefferson had offered $2 million. "The certain consequence is war," Jackson declared, "and no doubt but less than 2 millions can conquer not only the Floridas, but all Spanish North America."

All Spanish North America! Here, then, was Jackson's dream of an American empire, stretching from coast to coast, a dream he never significantly altered. "I have a hope," he revealed, that with 2,000 volunteers commanded "by firm officers and men of enterprise—I think could look into Santa Fe and Mexico, give freedom and commerce to those provinces and establish peace, and a permanent barrier against the inroads and attacks of foreign powers on our interior, which will be the case so long as Spain holds that large country on our borders."

His hope extended from the Floridas to Mexico! And war would bring other delights. "Should there be a war," Jackson enthused, "it will be a handsome theatre for our enterprising young men, and a source of acquiring fame."[5]

The immediate cause of Jackson's issuing the new alert was the reappearance of Aaron Burr in Nashville the week before. Again a sumptuous banquet was given him at Talbot's Hotel. A local newspaper reminded its readers that Colonel Burr was "the steady and firm friend, of the state of Tennessee."[6] If it ever crossed Jackson's mind that a conspiracy against the United States might be in train, he blanked it out. Not until November 10, 1806, did the unthinkable finally command his attention. A week or so after Jackson accepted Burr's money, a young man, Captain John Fort, called at the Hermitage with an introductory letter and casually mentioned that one of Burr's plans included the seizure of New Orleans.

New Orleans! Fort had spoken incautiously and realized it immediately. When Jackson questioned him, Fort "attempted to take [me in]," Jackson wrote, "to explain etc., etc., but from circumstances I was in Possession of, it flashed upon my mind that plans had been named of settling new countries, of Punishing the Dons, and adding Mexico to the united states etc., etc., [that] were only mere coverings to the real designs." Now it dawned on him that perhaps the "real design" was the dismemberment of the Union.[7]

How was it to be done, Jackson asked? Well, replied Fort, the bank would be captured, then the port closed, Mexico conquered, and the western part of the United States joined to the conquered territory to form a great southwestern empire.

As he listened, Jackson could scarcely believe his ears. How would this conquering come about? he asked. Federal troops, said Fort, led by General Wilkinson.

Ah, General James Wilkinson, the same villainous Wilkinson who commanded the U.S. army in the lower Mississippi Valley. Although it was not known by Americans at the time, Wilkinson was a double agent. He spied for the Spanish, accepting their gold while commanding American forces in the southwest.[8] And now he had apparently gotten himself involved with Burr in a conspiracy to seize New Orleans. But Jackson knew Wilkinson was a scoundrel ever since his good friend Colonel Thomas Butler, who served under Wilkinson, had been dismissed from the army for refusing to cut the queue of his long hair.

Although Jackson was alarmed at the possibility of a conspiracy to divide the Union, he was cautious enough to refrain from accusing anyone directly or mentioning the name of the chief conspirator or the source of his information. He dared not risk embarrassment until he had more evidence than Fort had provided. To protect himself he wrote a carefully worded letter to President Jefferson in which he offered the services of his militia in the event of "insult or aggression made on our government and country FROM ANY QUARTER."[9] It was a puzzling, ambiguous letter and Jefferson responded by informing the General that he was a man of peace but that whenever the country was endangered by hostile aggression "we must meet our duty, and convince the world that we are just friends and brave enemies."[10] Obviously, Jefferson missed what Jackson was getting at, and assumed that he was simply talking about an attack by Spain.

Meanwhile, Burr was picked up in Kentucky and arraigned before a grand jury in Frankfort on charges of raising troops for illegal purposes. He was defended by a young lawyer named Henry Clay, and the charges were eventually dismissed for lack of evidence. Burr then hurried to Nashville and convinced Jackson that he had no objectives save those sanctioned by legal authority. And Jackson believed him. Jackson desperately needed to believe him in view of his own involvement. Moreover, he wanted the Spanish expelled from the continent and Mexico reduced. Also his name had been closely linked to Burr's from the moment the two men met in Tennessee, and Jackson could ill afford Burr's disgrace, particularly in the aftermath of the Sevier and Dickinson fiascoes. Most important, Jackson always judged other men's integrity according to their personal commitment to him. Since Burr had always been supportive, Jackson summarily cleared him of suspicion.

The General delivered the boats and provisions that Burr had ordered. Since the order had been reduced to two boats, a balance of $1,725.62 was returned in the same banknotes the partners had received. On December 22, 1806, Burr left Clover Bottom with the two boats and a few followers, expecting to rendezvous at the mouth of the Cumberland River with a flotilla of boats and men coming from an island in the Ohio River owned by Harman Blennerhassett, one of his chief lieutenants. The entire expedition, when it finally assembled, numbered approximately sixty men. Not long after Burr's departure from Clover Bottom, word reached Nashville that President Jefferson had just issued a proclamation declaring a military conspiracy in progress in the west and calling for the apprehension of those involved.

General James Wilkinson, who began having doubts about the ultimate success of Burr's schemes and fearful of the consequences, informed

Jefferson that a conspiracy existed to seize New Orleans, revolutionize the Louisiana Territory, and invade Mexico. With this evidence before him, and predisposed to believe anything detrimental about Burr, Jefferson called for the arrest of the conspirators.[11] On January 1, 1807, Jackson received orders from the President and Secretary of War Henry Dearborn to hold his command in readiness and be prepared to march to frustrate the conspiracy. He immediately summoned the militia to duty and notified Dearborn that twelve companies would be mustered and ready to move within a few days. "Nothing on my part," he assured the secretary, "shall be wanted to promote the interest of the government, and quell the conspiracy." Having helped to launch Burr's expedition, Jackson was now arranging to scuttle it.[12]

As soon as Burr got wind of what was happening around him he deserted his men and fled into the Mississippi wilderness. Shortly thereafter he was captured in disguise just a few miles from the frontier of Spanish West Florida. Charged with treason, he was taken to Richmond, Virginia, for trial in the United States Circuit Court, presided over by Chief Justice John Marshall.

The conspiracy (or whatever it was) at an end, Jackson sent his soldiers back to their homes "with the best wishes of your General." Then, loyal and reckless, he journeyed to Richmond to testify on Burr's behalf. "I am more convinced than ever that treason never was intended by Burr," he said, "but if ever it was you know my wishes that he may be hung."[13] Given his own involvement it is not surprising that he felt solicitous about Burr. But his sense of loyalty also compelled him to testify on his friend's behalf. It was one of his most striking personal characteristics. He was examined by a grand jury after he arrived in Richmond, along with approximately fifty other witnesses.[14] But his appearance before the grand jury did not have the impact of the wild speeches he delivered on the steps of the capitol building before a stunned audience. His remarks were so provocative and his rage so uncontrolled that the defense counsel decided against placing him on the witness stand in the trial that was scheduled to begin several months later. It was feared his violent outbursts would offend the jury and injure Burr's case.

The decision to dispense with his presence before the jury infuriated Jackson, who had hoped to use the witness box as a platform from which to accuse Wilkinson of conspiracy and treason. "I have no doubt," he wrote to his friend, Senator Daniel Smith, "nor have I had of the guilt of Wilkingson; from the proofs I see exhibited against him at Richmond," which included evidence that he was "a pensioner of Spain." Jackson wrote to Smith because the senator was a "real friend of mr Jefferson and the republican cause." The President should "shake off this viper," he wrote, for the honor of the nation. "I have loved Mr Jefferson as a man, and adored him as a president," he protested, but if the President continues to "support such a base man with his present knowledge of his corruption and infamy, I would withdraw that confidence I once reposed in him and regret that I had been deceived in his virtue."[15]

Jackson's public pillorying of the administration offended not only Jefferson but his secretary of state, James Madison, who did not forget this rudeness later when, as President, he sought generals to fight the war against Great Britain. Disgusted, Jackson returned home, still maligning Jefferson, still labeling Wilkinson a traitor, still demanding that the administration brand Wilkinson a "Spanish hireling." Later it was generally understood that because of his outspoken criticisms Jackson represented the anti-Jefferson, anti-Madison faction in Tennessee and that he would not support Madison's candidacy for the presidency in 1808.

Burr was eventually acquitted of treason when the trial degenerated into a political duel between the presiding judge and the President. Marshall's ruling on what constituted treasonable acts virtually guaranteed an acquittal. Jackson never totally escaped the suspicion that he had helped Burr in his scheme to divide the Union, and that suspicion hounded him for years. In providing boats and provisions, Jackson clearly had participated in the conspiracy. He justified it as a legitimate enterprise to expel the Spanish from the continent and reduce Mexico. But the charge that he intended to divide the Union or injure his country is patently ridiculous. What Jackson failed to realize was that error of judgment can sometimes produce the same effect, intended or not.

His hope for military glory extinguished for the moment, Jackson retired to his farm for the next several years and generally tended his crops, bought and sold land and slaves, and improved his racing stable. Truxton won more than $20,000 in prize money over the next several years and his stud fee of $30 in ginned cotton brought additional revenue. With careful and attentive management of the farm, enterprising land speculations that netted handsome returns, and a series of excellent cotton crops, Jackson completely recovered from the Allison debacle and began living the life of a well-to-do southern planter. He entertained often and became known as the most public private man in the state. "His house was the seat of hospitality," wrote Thomas Hart Benton, a young officer in his militia, "the resort of friends and acquaintances, and of all strangers visiting the State."[16]

The General also maintained close rapport with his militia, which he boasted came out in full quota whenever he called. "My pride," he said, "is that my soldiers has confidence in me, and on the event of a war I will lead them on, to victory and conquest. Should we be blest with peace, I will resign, my military office, and spend my days, in the sweet calm of rural retirement."[17]

Jackson was now living a handsome life on a "delightful farm" with his wife and several wards. The General and Rachel had no children of their own, although they undoubtedly tried to have them. However, at frequent intervals, they were asked by friends and Rachel's relatives to act as guardians for children whose fathers had died. Among many, two of his wards deserve special mention. One was Andrew Jackson Donelson, the son of Samuel Donelson, who later served as Jackson's secretary; and the other was Andrew Jackson Hutchings, the son of Jackson's business partner, with whom the General had a long and close relationship. Then, in 1809, through legal adoption, Rachel and Andrew finally obtained a child of their own. They were permitted to have one of the twin boys born December 4, 1809, to Severn Donelson and his wife, Elizabeth. The natural mother was in poor health and could not nurse two children, so she willingly allowed Rachel to take one of them three days after his birth.[18] The child was legally adopted and christened Andrew Jackson, Jr.

For the next several years, despite a momentary and rash impulse to move to Mississippi, Jackson continued to prosper and consolidate his position of prominence in the community and state. He was living quietly with his family at the Hermitage, where he now owned 640 acres of land,[19] when his placid and comfortable life was suddenly shattered by news of a declaration of war against Great Britain in 1812. He was forty-five years of age at the time. The causes of the war were many, but the most important one without question was psychological. Although Britain, over a period of many years, had seized American ships, impressed American sailors, tampered with American trade, and encouraged Indian raids along the northern frontier and thus provided any number of good reasons for combat, perhaps the most compelling reason driving the United States into war was the urgent need to prove its inalienable right to liberty and independence. Since winning its freedom from England the country had been subjected to a series of humiliations in one form or another. For many Americans there had grown an overpowering need to prove to the world once again that they had a right to be free and that they could successfully defend their independence against even their most powerful adversary.

And there was another reason, almost as important and far more pragmatic: American expansion. For years Americans dreamed of taking Canada from England. They tried to do it during the Revolution and failed. For one thing, the acquisition of Canada would terminate British provocation of the Indians along the border. War with Britain also meant probable hostilities with her ally, Spain, and a successful war with Spain could provide the Floridas. In terms of geographic expansion, therefore, war could mean the creation of a tremendous American empire stretching from ocean to ocean.

Within Congress there was a contingent of young militants who actively urged a declaration of war against Great Britain. These War Hawks, as they were called, included some of the best young talent in the country, north and south, men like John C. Calhoun of South Carolina, Henry Clay and Richard M. Johnson of Kentucky, Peter B. Porter of New York, and Felix Grundy of Tennessee. This second generation of Americans since the founding of the Republic were anxious to prove their mettle as worthy successors to their illustrious forebears. They demanded the restoration of American honor through the chastisement of war. They plotted and eventually succeeded in forcing President James Madison to ask Congress for a declaration which was provided on June 18, 1812.

Jackson was overjoyed. At last, he said, the nation's honor had been restored. Immediately he offered the President the 2,500 Tennessee volunteers under his command. Naturally he expected a prompt reply, praising him for his patriotism and calling him and his troops to duty. Instead he received a polite if perfunctory acceptance of his offer but no summons. It was a shock. Months passed, and still no call. At first he could scarcely believe or understand it. Then the truth slowly dawned on him: the administration remembered his involvement with Burr and therefore had no wish to favor him with an active command. Henry Dearborn was sent against Quebec and Brigadier General James Winchester, along with two of Jackson's regiments, was ordered to assist General Harrison in the north. But nothing for Jackson. Nothing for the old friend of Aaron Burr.

Meanwhile, once actual fighting began, General William Hull was forced to surrender Detroit to a combined force of British soldiers and Indians. The invasion of Canada to advance American territorial expansion northward began with supreme confidence and ended in supreme disaster. Along the northern frontier one defeat followed another. No general of any ability emerged. No general of any merit was summoned. The only good general sat idle in Tennessee, and no one knew it but Andrew Jackson.

He raged at home against the "old grannies" in Washington who risked the safety of the nation by failing to recognize him. He talked publicly of conquering Florida and of raining death and destruction upon the Indians.[20] But there was nothing he could really do but wait and see what happened. Not until October 1812 when Governor Willie Blount, who had succeeded Sevier, was asked to provide 1,500 volunteers to support General Wilkinson in the defense of New Orleans did the situation change for Jackson. In requesting these volunteers the administration not only wished to protect the country against the possibility of a southern invasion but build a strike force that would seize eastern Florida and keep it after the war as reparation.

In requesting volunteers for the New Orleans expedition, the administration indicated to Blount that it could do without Andrew Jackson, but it did not impose this sentiment as an obligation. Blount, who was politically allied to Jackson and had received his principal support in West Tennessee from the Jackson forces, hesitated only briefly before deciding to disregard the administration's hint. He felt authorized to appoint whomever he believed best qualified to command the expedition, and after obtaining legal support for his interpretation he filled in Jackson's name on one of the seventy blank commissions that Washington had forwarded. Henceforth Andrew Jackson was a major general of *United States* volunteers. Blount forwarded the commission to Jackson along with the general order directing the volunteers to New Orleans.[21]

Now, at last, Jackson had an active command. Now, he might begin his search for military glory. But he had a problem. The troops had been called to support General Wilkinson. It was bitter medicine to serve under a "villain" whom he had publicly denounced, but it was that or nothing. Jackson had no choice. "At a period like the present," he wrote to Blount, ". . . it is the duty of every citizen to do something for his country." Still, there was "a sting to my feelings" in knowing that the intention of the administration "was either to exclude me from the command, or if I did command by an apparent willingness and condesension on my part to place me under the command of Genl Wilkinson." Nevertheless "I will sacrifice my feelings, and lead my brave volunteers to any point your excellency may please to order."[22]

Blount instructed Jackson to call out two divisions and have them ready in Nashville on December 10, 1812. But the winter of 1812–1813 proved particularly brutal, and the day set for the rendezvous saw snow a foot deep on the ground. The quartermaster, William B. Lewis, had obtained a large quantity of wood, but every stick of it was burned on the first night to keep the men from freezing. Jackson and Lewis roamed among the troops from dusk to morning that first night, checking on the condition of the men. At about six o'clock in the morning Jackson entered the local tavern to rest. As he walked in he overheard a civilian comment on the stupidity of the authorities for having massed troops without providing adequate shelter. It was monstrous, the critic said, that the men should be outside in the cold while the officers had the best accommodations in town. The unwary civilian had barely gotten the words out of his mouth when Jackson slammed him against the wall with a fiery verbal blast. "You d——d infernal scoundrel," he cried, "sowing disaffection among the troops. Why, the quartermaster and I have been up all night, making the men comfortable. Let me hear no more such talk, or I'm d——d if I don't ram that red hot handiron down your throat."[23]

It was a mark of Jackson's leadership that he personally supervised the care of his men and concerned himself with every detail of their physical well-being. He had great pride in them, as he had in himself, and was extremely solicitous of their welfare. Over the years the men had come to know this, and they reciprocated with respect and devotion. They realized he could be tough and unyielding, arbitrary and rigid; they knew his anger could be a terrible burden to them; but they also knew that he sincerely cared about their comfort more than his own and would tend to their needs as his first priority.

A few days later the cold spell broke and the troops were organized into an army and readied to march. For the general staff, William Berkeley

Lewis, the General's friend and neighbor, was named assistant deputy quartermaster; William Carroll, a bright and energetic young man from Pennsylvania, was appointed brigade inspector; Thomas Hart Benton, the clever young lawyer whom Jackson had met on the circuit and recognized as a man of talent and industry, was chosen first aide-de-camp; and John Reid, who came from Virginia and was probably recommended to Jackson by Benton, was named second aide and secretary to the General. Reid later wrote an early narrative of Jackson's military career that was completed after Reid's death and converted into a campaign biography by John H. Eaton. It is unquestionably the best of the several books written on Jackson's early life. John Coffee, a simple, brave, and modest man, who was Jackson's former business partner and totally devoted to him, received command of the cavalry. A giant, Coffee stood well over six feet. His round face framed in a helmet of black hair, his prominent nose, and his firm jaw projected a physical presence of enormous strength and stamina. He proved a superb field commander and Jackson's ablest military associate.

Colonel William Hall and Benton received command of two regiments of infantry comprising 1,400 men. The troops came from every station and from every corner of the state. They were businessmen, planters, and yeomen, most them descendants of revolutionary war veterans. Finally, on January 7, 1813, the army was ready to move in defense of the lower country. On orders from Governor Blount the infantry and riflemen were to be transported by boat (via Natchez) to New Orleans and the cavalry and mounted infantry were to proceed by land. On his arrival in New Orleans, Jackson was instructed to await the orders of President Madison.

In sending him off, Blount congratulated Jackson on his skill and energy in raising and organizing the volunteers. The General demurred. It was my duty, he said. I was "brought up under the tyranny of Britain," and although very young I "embarked in the struggle for our liberties, in which I lost every thing that was dear to me, *my brothers and my fortune.*" But "I have been amply repaid by living under the mild administration of a republican government." To maintain that government and the independent rights of the nation "is a duty I have ever owed to my Country to myself & to posterity, and when I do all I can . . . I have only done my duty."

Duty to his country and its republican government! That, more than anything else, bespeaks the quintessential Jackson at the outset of his military career. Indeed, a sense of duty was one of the strongest and most important characteristics of his entire life. Duty to protect a free society. Duty to preserve its "independent rights." Duty to safeguard its "republican government." He concluded his letter by "praying that the God of Battles may be with us, and that high Heaven may bestow its Choice Benedictions on all engaged in this Expedition."[24]

With a few taps of a drum, the firing of a cannon, and a burst of huzzas from a crowd standing on the wharf, the fleet moved away from its mooring and headed down the Cumberland toward the Ohio and Mississippi rivers. His army finally in motion, Jackson notified the secretary of war that he was under way at the head of 2,071 volunteers and if the government so ordered they would rejoice at the opportunity of placing the American eagle over the Spanish towns of Mobile, Pensacola, and St. Augustine.[25]

Ice clogged the Ohio River. Earlier a series of earthquakes along the Mississippi had changed the course of the river. Three men and a boat were lost during the long voyage, but thirty-nine days later and one thousand miles downriver from Nashville the expedition arrived in Natchez, where Coffee and the cavalry awaited them. It was a well-executed operation.

There were several communications from General Wilkinson awaiting General Jackson when he arrived, and each one reiterated a single command: Halt! Do not come any closer. Jackson and his volunteers were ordered to remain in Natchez. Several reasons were given for this abrupt and rude command: no provisions in New Orleans to share and no instructions from Washington about what to do with these volunteers. There was also the matter that Jackson had "not done me the honor to communicate with me" about "your command." In any event Wilkinson wanted one thing clear: "I . . . must repeat my desire, that you should halt in the vicinity of Natchez."[26]

So Jackson halted. Weeks passed without further instructions. Then, on March 15, he received an order from the new secretary of war, John Armstrong, ordering him to dismiss his troops and return home. Jackson could scarcely believe his eyes. Dismissed! Here he was with over two thousand men, five hundred miles from home, cast loose in the wilderness, without pay, without transport, without medicine, and told to return home. Dissolving an army in Indian country! The order was insane. At length Jackson decided that Wilkinson was responsible for this madness. Since his troops were without food and far from home, they would probably join Wilkinson once they were dismissed. Thus Wilkinson and the "imbeciles" in Washington would get rid of him, take his army, and humiliate him by forcing him to return alone to Nashville.[27]

Well, they would soon learn differently. Snorting his fury, Jackson called in Colonel Benton and told him he would not obey Armstrong's order. He would not dismiss his volunteers; instead he would lead them all back to Tennessee himself, at his own expense if necessary. Since he had no transports at this juncture he would march them home. Still burning with anger he then penned a blistering letter to the secretary of war. At the call of their country, he wrote to Armstrong, his men "voluntarily rallied round its insulted standard. They followed me to the field; I shall carefully march them back to their homes."[28] If you reject me, he said in effect, you reject my army as well.

Actually the administration had decided to abandon the project against East Florida to avoid international complications, and consequently Armstrong dismissed the intended strike force—none of which Jackson knew. But Congress did authorize the seizure of what was left of West Florida, and in the spring of 1813 American forces easily captured Mobile and forced the Spanish to withdraw to Pensacola.

Ironically, the disastrous journey from Nashville to Natchez and back again proved a personal triumph for Jackson. All the things the volunteers admired about their General, all the masterful qualities of his leadership, were amplified before their eyes: the fortitude, the personal courage, the strength of character, the heroic presence, the personal identity with their small successes and many hardships, the consideration, patience, and understanding. What it all added up to was the fact that they admired, trusted, and loved him, and so if he said they would walk from Natchez to Nashville, then, by God, they would do it.

But something else emerged on that painful road back home. It was a quality in Jackson's character that is essential to an understanding of his subsequent military successes. The quality had probably always been there but now it suddenly billowed out into full view. That quality was willpower. Not the ordinary kind. Nothing normal or even natural. This was superhuman. This was virtually demonic. This was sheer, total, concentrated determination to achieve his ends. So if he determined to march his men back to Nashville he would get them there even if it meant carrying every last one of them on his back.

Andrew Jackson was not a great general. He was better than most of the commanders available in 1812, but that hardly does him credit. What distinguished him and basically made the difference between victory and defeat on the battlefield for him was his absolute determination to win—at whatever cost. As a consequence he was capable of extraordinary feats of courage and daring, feats of perseverance in the face of incredible odds. Nothing less than victory was acceptable to him. Defeat was unthinkable.

This fierce exercise of will, supported by supreme self-confidence and genuine (though unexceptional) military talent, shaped repeated triumphs over the Indians, the British, and the Spanish. Starting with the overland journey from Natchez to Nashville a Jackson emerged whose whole existence and purpose in life was to achieve military victory. His men recognized it and were awed by it. On occasion they rebelled when his demands upon them transcended human capability. But most times they realized that such a commander wins battles and carries his men to victory and undying fame and so they respected him and obeyed him and fought hard for him.

At his command the Tennessee volunteers marched back to Nashville. And it was an agony. In organizing the march Jackson had to accommodate 150 men on the sicklist, of whom 56 could not sit upright or raise their heads from their pillows. And there were only eleven wagons to convey the sick back home. For many, therefore, it was a long, difficult, painful journey that they would never forget. Jackson ordered his officers to turn their horses over to the sick, and he himself surrendered his own three horses for this duty. Trudging alongside his men day after day, never showing weariness or fatigue, he cheered his men with a word, a gesture, a sign of his pride in them. His concern for their safety and comfort was instinctive; it was rooted in his sense of leadership. "It is . . . my duty," he told his wife, "to act as a father to the sick and to the well and stay with them untill I march into Nashville."[29]

Once it began, the march moved quite rapidly, averaging eighteen miles a day. Jackson prodded the men along in the gentlest possible way. When a delirious invalid lifted himself in a wagon and asked where he was, Jackson responded: "On your way *home!*" whereupon all the soldiers cheered.[30] As the army lurched forward, Jackson was everywhere, moving up and down the column, watching for any incident that needed his attention, overseeing the distribution of rations, encouraging his men to keep going. As a leader there was only one word to describe Andrew Jackson: indomitable. His men said he was "tough," tougher than most anything imaginable. Tough as hickory, someone ventured, which was about as hard as anyone could suggest. Soon his men started calling him Hickory. And because they deeply admired him as a commander they added the prefix "old," thereby giving him his everlasting nickname: Old Hickory.

Within a month the army had pulled itself back to Tennessee. And when the troops arrived in Nashville, word was soon spread about Jackson's heroic conduct and how the men had knighted him. Some of the stories were exaggerations, but all repeated the strength and quality of his character and leadership: his toughness and perseverance, his regard for the comfort and safety of his men, his pride in their accomplishment, his total command of the entire operation. "Long will their General live in the memory of his volunteers of West Tennessee," the Nashville *Whig* pronounced, "for his benevolence, humane, and fatherly treatment of his soldiers; if gratitude and love can reward him, General Jackson has them. It affords us pleasure to say, that we believe there is not a man belonging to the detachment but what loves him."[31] At the age of forty-six Andrew Jackson had become "the most beloved and esteemed of private citizens in western Tennessee." He had become a father figure, a beloved general, the guardian of the people of the frontier.[32]

CHAPTER 6

The Creek War

ALTHOUGH JACKSON'S CHARACTER FLAWS —the savage hatreds and readiness to violence—seemed to vanish from the minds of frontier Americans following his return from Natchez, he periodically battered his image by involving himself in some outrageous behavior that tried the patience and understanding of his friends and neighbors. Even now, with his newly acquired reputation, he allowed himself to be drawn into an unseemly affair of honor that had people shaking their heads in wonder over the fearful, conflicting qualities fused within his singular personality.

The origins of the affair are a bit cloudy, but they apparently developed during the homeward march of the volunteers from Natchez. In any event a man by the name of Littleton Johnston quarreled with William Carroll, Jackson's brigade inspector. The matter was serious enough for Johnston to challenge Billy Carroll to a duel, but Billy haughtily refused to fight on the ground that Johnston was no gentleman. Johnston tried again, this time asking Jesse Benton, the brother of Thomas Hart Benton, to carry the challenge. Billy still refused. Thereupon Jesse offered himself as Johnston's surrogate, and his social standing was such that Billy could not again refuse without being labeled a coward.[1]

By this time the army had arrived in Nashville. The duel was set and Billy needed a second, but he soon discovered that no one would oblige him. So he rode out to the Hermitage and asked Jackson to act as his second. Old Hickory properly refused. "I am too old," he said. But Billy persisted and argued that a conspiracy existed to run him out of the country. At that, Jackson reacted sharply. "Well Carroll," he said, "you may make your mind easy on *one* point: they sha'n't run you out of the country as long as Andrew Jackson lives in it."

Initially, Jackson hoped to talk the two men out of their quarrel. And at first he succeeded. Jesse was a hothead—like his more talented brother—and prone to get himself into awkward situations that he later regretted. Thus a few soothing words from Jackson were enough to bring Jesse around and get him to forget the whole affair.

68

But the junior officers, who were rather jealous of Billy's excellent standing with Jackson, itched to see him called to account and they prevailed on Jesse to renew the quarrel. Disgusted, Jackson agreed to act as Billy's second, and what took place was one of the strangest duels ever recorded in Tennessee history. Because Billy had "never shot much" and Jesse was a "first rate marksman," Billy insisted that the firing distance between them be reduced to ten feet (rather than thirty) to eliminate Jesse's advantage and "equalize" their situations. It was further agreed that they would take a back-to-back position—which meant they had to wheel around and face each other in order to fire.

The duel took place on Monday, June 14, 1813, at six o'clock in the morning.

"Prepare!" called John W. Armstrong, the other second.

"Fire!"

Jesse wheeled "with great quickness" but "came round to a very low squatting position with his body considerably prostrated." He fired and hit Carroll in the thumb.

Billy also fired. And the bullet caught Jesse in the act of squatting. It inflicted a long, raking wound across both cheeks of his buttocks. Though not lethal, the wound proved very painful and extremely embarrassing. Poor Jesse became the object of much laughter in Nashville.[2]

When Colonel Thomas Hart Benton heard that General Jackson had been party to his brother's humiliation he exploded in rage and wrote his commanding officer a hot-tempered letter, accusing him of conducting the duel in "a savage, unequal, unfair, and base manner." It was, he continued, "very poor business in a man of your age and standing to be conducting a duel about nothing between young men who had no harm against each."[3]

Benton's accusations were bad enough, but what really infuriated Old Hickory was the fact that they were repeated in public places, over and over, in every major town in Tennessee. Jackson had just regained popular favor and he was not about to see his reputation endangered by Benton's reckless charges. The trouble with Benton, Jackson said, was his inability to keep his mouth shut, and Old Hickory promised to horsewhip Thomas the first time he saw him.[4]

The opportunity came early in September, when Jackson, John Coffee, and Jackson's nephew, Stockley Hays, rode into Nashville and put up at the Old Nashville Inn. The next morning Jackson and Coffee walked to the post office to pick up their mail, both of them armed and Jackson carrying a riding whip. Suddenly, Coffee spotted Thomas standing in the doorway of the City Hotel, "looking daggers" at them.

"Do you see that fellow?" Coffee asked Jackson in tones barely above a whisper.

"Oh yes," replied Jackson, "I have my eye on him."

As always in such circumstances the General was in full control of himself. He did not impulsively rush at Benton to make good his threat. Instead, he continued on to the post office where he collected his mail. Returning, he and Coffee walked along the sidewalk that would bring them to the door of the City Hotel. Both Bentons were waiting, their pistols loaded with two shots each. As Jackson came abreast of Thomas he suddenly turned toward him, brandished his whip, and cried, "Now, you d——d rascal, I am going to punish you. Defend yourself."[5]

Benton reached into his pocket for what Jackson believed was a pistol. Old Hickory drew his own gun and backed Thomas into the hotel. Jesse, meanwhile, ducked through the barroom to a door that opened into a hallway that led to the rear porch overlooking the river. From that position he raised his pistol and fired at Jackson, hitting him in the arm and shoulder with a slug and a ball. The General pitched forward, firing at Thomas as he fell. The shot missed. Thomas then fired twice at the prostrate figure, and Jesse faced forward to shoot again but was interrupted by a bystander, James Sitler.[6]

Now Coffee rushed into the room, joined by Stockley Hays and two others. Stockley carried a sword cane, the others, knives. Stockley tried to run Jesse through with his sword cane but the point of the weapon struck a button and broke. He then wrestled Jesse to the ground and repeatedly stabbed him in both arms with a dirk. Meanwhile Coffee fired at Thomas and missed; he then tried to club Benton with his pistol but Thomas retreated quickly and in his haste fell backward down a flight of stairs at the rear of the hotel. And with that, the gunfight ended.[7]

Half-unconscious from the loss of blood, Jackson was lifted and carried to the Nashville Inn, his shoulder shattered by the slug and his arm pierced by a ball which lay embedded against the upper bone of his left arm. He soaked through two mattresses before the doctors could stanch the flow of blood. Every physician in Nashville worked over the wounded General, and all but one recommended the amputation of the shattered arm.

"I'll keep my arm," ordered Old Hickory, and with that, he slipped into unconsciousness. The doctors did not dare to contradict him and they made no effort to remove the shrapnel which remained in his arm for nearly twenty years. Both wounds were dressed with poultices of elm and other wood cuttings, as prescribed by the Indians. Jackson was utterly prostrate from the great loss of blood. It was three weeks before he could leave his bed.

Down in the street the Bentons remained for an hour or more, recounting to the crowd what happened and denouncing Jackson as an assassin. Thomas recovered a small sword that Jackson had dropped in the hotel and after brandishing it in the public square broke it in two, shouting defiance in his booming voice as he paraded back and forth across the plaza.

Jackson's many friends appreciated neither the defeat of the General nor the accompanying theatrics. It soon became obvious that Nashville was not a safe place for the Bentons. "I am literally in hell here," wrote Thomas; "the meanest wretches under heaven to contend with—liars, affidavit-makers, and shameless cowards. All the puppies of Jackson are at work on me. . . . I am in the middle of hell, and see no alternative but to kill or be killed; for I will not crouch to Jackson; and the fact that I and my brother defeated him and his tribe, and broke his small sword in the public square, will for ever rankle in his bosom and make him thirst for vengeance. My life is in danger . . . for it is a settled plan to turn out puppy after puppy to bully me, and when I have got into a scrape, to have me killed somehow in the scuffle."[8] To escape the vengeance of Jackson's puppies, Thomas returned to his home in Franklin and, after the war, resigned his commission in the army and headed west to Missouri.

Thomas Benton and Jackson never saw one another again until 1823, when both men became United States senators and both realized it was to their mutual political benefit to forget their ancient quarrel. A handshake dissolved the ten-year hatred and signaled the beginning of an eventful political alliance. But Jesse never forgave. He went to his grave cursing Andrew Jackson.

While Old Hickory was recovering from this disgraceful affair, tended by the faithful Rachel, news reached Tennessee that the Creek Indians had massacred white settlers at Fort Mims in Alabama, then a part of the Mississippi Territory. William Weatherford, known as Chief Red Eagle, led the attack—and with it commenced the Creek War that finally placed Jackson on the road to national fame.

Red Eagle, leader of the militant Red Sticks (so called because they painted their war clubs a bright red color), a faction of the Creek Nation, was a remarkable chief. The son of a Scot trader, he preferred his mother's people, she being the half sister of the great Creek chieftain Alexander McGillivray, himself a mixed blood. Red Eagle fell under the sway of another extraordinary Indian chief, Tecumseh, a Shawnee, who conceived a plan to organize the Northern and Southern tribes from the Great Lakes to the Gulf of Mexico into a great confederation and with it hurl the white man back into the sea from whence he had come.[9]

The Creek Nation split over cooperating with Tecumseh, the Red Sticks actively pursuing a policy of war against white settlers. Thus, it needs to be remembered that from start to finish the Creek War, as it developed, was essentially an Indian civil war. And, most important of all, that it was General Andrew Jackson who took supreme advantage of this internal strife and used it to advance the interests of his country.

The massacre at Fort Mims occurred on August 30, 1813, and resulted in the deaths of almost 250 whites who "were butchered in the quickest manner. . . . The children were seized by the legs, and killed by batting their heads against the stockading. The women were scalped, and those who were pregnant were opened, while they were alive, and the embryo infants let out of the womb."[10] Red Eagle tried to stop the savagery, but many clubs were raised over his head and he was forced to withdraw to save his own life.

News of the massacre burst like a thunderclap over Tennessee. The Tennessee legislature promptly empowered the governor to summon 5,000 volunteers for a three-month tour of duty. Blount responded immediately and ordered Jackson to "call out organize rendezvous and march without delay" 2,500 volunteers and militia "to repel an approaching invasion . . . and to afford aid and relief to the suffering citizens of the Mississippi Territory."[11] A similar force of 2,500 men from eastern Tennessee, commanded by Major General John Cocke, was also ordered against the Creeks. Fortunately, John Sevier was safely entombed in Congress or there might have been a popular cry to give him supreme command of the operation.

Still recovering from his wounds and still too weak to lead a campaign, Jackson recognized nonetheless that his moment for military glory had arrived and that if he failed to assume leadership now he might not get another chance. To his mind, he had no choice. He had to lead the campaign even if it meant dragging himself from his bed and tying himself on his horse. So he issued the appropriate orders to his militia to rendezvous at Fayetteville for immediate duty against the Creeks. "The late attack of the Creek Indians," he said in his orders, ". . . call a loud for retaliatory vengeance. Those distressed citizens of that frontier . . . implored the brave Tennesseans for aid. They must not ask in vain." Since everyone knew he had been gunned down in Nashville by the Bentons, he felt obliged to mention his physical condition. "The health of your general is restored," he said; "he will command in person."[12]

Jackson planned to slice through the Creek Nation, hewing a road through the wilderness as he marched, until he reached Mobile on the coast. Such a march from Tennessee to the Gulf would provide a magnificent highway across the southwestern heartland for future American settlers, at the same time shredding Creek power in the area and reducing the Nation to immediate military impotency. After that he would "strike at the root of the disseas" by invading Spanish Florida. He would capture Pensacola and thereby exterminate any future Creek potential to make war.[13] There was no question in Jackson's mind that the removal of Spanish and British influence in the area (and British influence was known to exist in the south) was essential to the final solution of the Indian problem.[14]

On October 7, 1813, still pale and weak, with his arm in a sling, Jackson took command of his West Tennessee army at Fayetteville. Three days later he broke camp and headed south to link up with Coffee's cavalry, which he had sent ahead to Huntsville to prepare a camp for the main army.[15] Clipping along at the astounding speed of 36 miles a day, the army joined Coffee's cavalry, moved into Creek country, and arrived at the southernmost tip of the Tennessee River, where Jackson built Fort Deposit as a depot for supplies at the mouth of Thompson's Creek. After waiting several days for supplies and reinforcements from Tennessee that never came, the impatient Jackson decided to move ahead. He pushed south to the Coosa River, cutting a road over the mountains as he went, and established a base at Fort Strother that became his advance supply depot. He had barely a week's rations, but he expected to be joined momentarily by General Cocke from East Tennessee.

At Fort Strother, Jackson came within striking distance of the Red Sticks. Thirteen miles to the east lay the hostile village of Tallushatchee with its nearly 200 warriors. Jackson ordered General Coffee and his cavalry and mounted riflemen to destroy it. On the morning of November 3, 1813, a thousand men encircled Tallushatchee and systematically slaughtered most of the warriors. "We shot them like dogs," reported Davy Crockett.[16] Coffee lost 5 men killed and 41 wounded in the attack; he slew 186 braves (every man in the village) and brought back to Jackson's camp 84 women and children as captives. "We have retaliated for the destruction of Fort Mims," Jackson wrote triumphantly to Governor Blount.[17]

On the bloody battlefield a dead Indian mother was found still clutching her living ten-month-old infant. The child was brought to Jackson's camp along with the other captives, and the General asked some of the Indian women to care for the child and give him nourishment. They refused. "No," they said, "all his relations are dead, kill him too." As they spoke the words "all his relations are dead," something responded inside Jackson. He was reminded of his own early life, his family wiped out by war, himself an orphan. Brusquely, he dismissed the women and had the child taken to his tent where he dissolved a little brown sugar and coaxed the boy to drink. Afterward the General sent him to Huntsville to be nursed, clothed, and housed at his own expense until the end of the campaign, when the infant was sent to the Hermitage. The child was named Lyncoya, and when he arrived at the Hermitage Jackson gave explicit orders how he should be treated. Not like a servant nor an orphan, he said. "I therefore want him well taken care of," the General told Rachel, "he may have been given to me for some valuable purpose—in fact when I reflect that he as to his relations is so much like myself I feel an unusual sympathy for him."[18]

After the Tallushatchee victory, many hostile Indian villages wisely switched their allegiance to Jackson. One of these was Talladega, a small community of 154 people which lay thirty miles south of Fort Strother across the Coosa River. When he learned of this treachery, Red Eagle surrounded the town with a thousand braves and planned to burn it to the ground. Old Hickory now had his chance to destroy a relatively large hostile force and so at midnight he set his men in motion. Invariably, he moved his army in three parallel columns. He had 1,200 infantry and 800 cavalry, just double the number of Weatherford's warriors besieging Talladega. At dawn on Tuesday, November 9, 1813, the army deployed for battle. The infantry advanced in two lines, militia on the left and volunteers on the right. The cavalry formed two extreme wings on the flanks and were ordered to advance in a crescent-shaped "curve," the points thrown toward the town and the rear connected to the advance lines of infantry. A mounted reserve was stationed behind the main line. Jackson's plan directed that an advance guard move ahead to contact the enemy and initiate an engagement; then they would fall back and join the main force, drawing the Indians into the curved outstretched arms of Jackson's army.

The maneuver began beautifully. The vanguard moved out. Suddenly Red Sticks came "screaming and yelling" from cover and took four or five rounds of shot.[19] The guard fell back. The Indians, nearly a thousand of them, swarmed into the trap and the two curving arms of troops snapped shut around them. The Tennesseans fired at the Red Sticks at point-blank range. The destruction would have been complete had not a portion of the infantry on the right, for some unaccountable reason—perhaps a confusion of orders—suddenly retreated instead of advancing. The line broke, a hole widened, and the Indians poured through it by the hundreds to escape the withering fire. The reserves were quickly dismounted and thrown into the gap, once again closing the ring. The Indians trapped within the circle were shot to death in a steady rain of fire. Later, Coffee's cavalry pursued the fleeing Red Sticks for three or four miles, killing and wounding them as they ran. Unfortunately for Jackson, some 700 Indians escaped to renew the war at a later time. This "faux pas of the militia," he reported, which forced him to dismount the reserves, prevented total destruction of the Red Sticks.[20] Nevertheless, 300 Indians lay dead on the battleground. Jackson's losses amounted to 15 dead and 85 wounded.[21]

After burying his dead, providing litters for the wounded, and gathering what food was available, Jackson swung his army back to Fort Strother, hoping to find there the long-awaited supplies from Nashville. But he found nothing. Not only had the provisions failed to come, but the sick had eaten what little remained of Jackson's private stores bought at his own expense. Now, returned to the fort, the army had only a few dozen biscuits and a small supply of meat. So the remaining cattle were slaughtered and distributed among the troops.

Days passed. Still no supplies. The troops grew angry and mutinous. Field officers held a meeting and presented Jackson with a petition requesting that the army be permitted to return home. Old Hickory rejected the plea with haughty disdain, reminding his men what was expected of them as soldiers and frontiersmen. The situation collapsed altogether when the militia broke camp and started home anyway. But they did not get far. Jackson drew up the volunteers in front of them and forced them back to the camp. The next day the roles were reversed; the volunteers attempted to march off and were halted by the militia.[22] It was one of the lunacies of war.

But the rebellion was worse than Jackson realized. An entire brigade formed and prepared to march back to Tennessee, threatening all who attempted to stop them. It was mass desertion and the supreme challenge to his leadership. Snatching a musket and resting it on the neck of his horse (his left arm was still useless), Jackson positioned himself in front of the brigade. Slowly, deliberately, he aimed his gun directly at the mutineers. There was "shoot" in his eyes, just as there had been when, as a judge, he had arrested Russell Bean. General Coffee and Major Reid galloped forward and placed themselves beside him. The troops, sullen and silent, stared at the trio. His voice hoarse with emotion, Old Hickory croaked out an oath. The first man who advanced toward Tennessee would get a bullet through the brain.

Minutes passed. No one moved. No man had the courage to tempt the "shoot" in Jackson's eyes. Then a few loyal companies formed behind their General to block the road. And that did it. Several mutineers peeled off and returned to their posts. More followed. Then others. Finally the remainder of the brigade saw the hopelessness of their situation and backed away. The rebellion ended. And it ended with Jackson in even greater command of his troops.[23]

He thought the worst was over. Supplies began to arrive at the camp, thanks to Major Lewis, and Jackson expected General Cocke to join him momentarily. Then they would move swiftly against Weatherford and the Red Sticks and annihilate them. But his army had other ideas. They hated the deprivation and suffering and discipline expected of them. The possibility of sudden Indian attack only added to their misery. The volunteers made no secret of their determination to break camp on December 10, 1813, when their one-year enlistment expired. They counted as part of that year the time they had spent at home where they were at the call of the government. Jackson, on the other hand, held the view that a year's enlistment meant 365 days of actual service.

On the evening of December 9 General Hall went to Jackson's tent to report that his entire brigade planned to slip away during the night. Instantly Old Hickory wrote out an order commanding the brigade to parade on the west side of the fort. At the same time he posted the artillery company fore and aft of the rebellious troops, their two small fieldpieces trained on the mutineers. The loyal militia were strung along an adjacent "eminence" commanding the road to Tennessee and ordered to prevent by any means necessary the departure of the brigade.[24] Then Jackson mounted his horse and rode along the line of the mutinous volunteers. He spoke to them, quietly at first, almost pleadingly. He begged them not to desert. Reinforcements were expected at any moment and when they arrived he would let them go. He gave them his

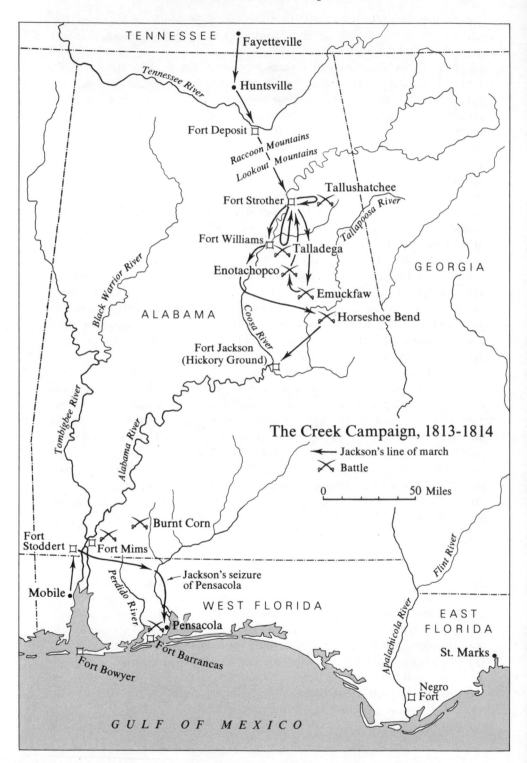

TENNESSEE

• Fayetteville

• Huntsville

Tennessee River

Fort Deposit ⊡

Raccoon Mountains

Lookout Mountains

Tallushatchee

Fort Strother ⊡

Tallapoosa River

Fort Williams ⊡

Talladega

Enotachopco ✗

GEORGIA

Emuckfaw ✗

ALABAMA

Black Warrior River

Coosa River

Horseshoe Bend ✗

Fort Jackson
(Hickory Ground) ⊡

The Creek Campaign, 1813-1814

⟵ Jackson's line of march

✗ Battle

Tombigbee River

Alabama River

0   50 Miles

Burnt Corn ✗

Fort
Stoddert ⊡ ⊡ Fort Mims

Perdido River

Jackson's seizure
of Pensacola

WEST FLORIDA

Flint River

• Mobile

EAST
FLORIDA

Pensacola •

St. Marks •

Fort Barrancas ⊡

Apalachicola River

Fort Bowyer ⊡

Negro
Fort ⊡

GULF   OF   MEXICO

word. "It was a scene," Jackson later told his wife, "that created feelings better to be Judged of than expressed . . . a whole Brigade whose patriotism was once the boast of their Genl and their country . . . turning their backs on an enemy fifty miles in advance."[25]

No one stirred. Finally Old Hickory ordered the artillery gunners to light their matches, he himself remaining motionless before the brigade, within the line of fire. The men had seen enough of Andrew Jackson to know that he would give the order to fire without flinching. Suddenly, officers stepped forward and pledged themselves and their men to remain at the fort until the arrival of reinforcements. The men nodded their agreement, and with that the attempt at mass desertion ended. They were all dismissed to their quarters. My volunteers, Jackson sadly informed his wife, had sunk from the "highest elevation of patriots—to mere, wining, complaining Seditioners and mutineers—to keep whom from open acts of mutiny I have been compelled to point my cannon against, with a lighted match to destroy them."[26]

On December 12, 1813, General Cocke and 1,500 men arrived at Fort Strother. With these replacements Jackson had no choice but to keep his pledge and allow the First Brigade to return home. They no sooner left than he learned that the term of service for a majority of Cocke's men would also expire within a few days—and a few weeks later for the remainder of them. Disgusted, Jackson ordered Cocke to march his troops back home and discharge them; even though it severely weakened his position.

Then disaster struck—again. No sooner had Cocke and his men left camp than Jackson received a letter from Coffee, who had returned to Tennessee with his men to recruit horses and procure clothing, informing him that the cavalry had deserted. Coffee had been ill at the time and could do nothing to prevent the desertion.[27] Following hard on the heels of this misfortune, Jackson was told by Governor Blount that he sided with the militia in their interpretation of their term of service and advised Old Hickory to abandon Fort Strother and retreat to the Tennessee frontier.[28]

Jackson was devastated. There was nothing he could do but inform his troops of the governor's recommendation and give them the choice of staying with him and completing the campaign or returning home. To his dismay, they chose to return. As they streamed away, Old Hickory wished them each "a smoke tail in their teeth, with a Peticoat as a coat of mail to hand down to there offspring."[29]

The fort was now practically deserted. Only one regiment separated Jackson from the ferocious Red Sticks a few miles away. On January 14, 1814, the term of service for this regiment would also expire. Then he would be alone.

But Governor Blount suddenly came to his rescue. He ordered a new levy of 2,500 troops—and was surprised and delighted to find not only popular support for his call but approval by the War Department in

Washington.[30] He gambled on popular resentment against the Indians and won. Even some officers of the disbanded companies who had served under General Jackson now began to raise new companies in this burst of patriotic fervor. By the middle of March 1814 several thousand men were available to Old Hickory.

But that was March. In January all Fort Strother could muster against the Indians was a handful of men and the indomitable will of their commander. Then, on January 14, 800 raw recruits marched into the fort. Their unannounced and unexpected arrival actually startled Jackson. He could scarcely believe his eyes. But he accepted his blessing joyfully and then he spun into action. Before any of them could discover the hazards of life in the wilderness with Old Hickory or the ordeal of fighting Red Sticks under his command, the recruits were marched into Creek country. The action verged on rashness, and Jackson nearly paid a dreadful price for it.

Jackson headed directly for the important and heavily fortified encampment of Tohopeka, or the Horseshoe Bend, a 100-acre peninsula formed by the looping action of the Tallapoosa River. On January 21 he camped at Emuckfaw Creek, three miles from the fortification, and dispatched his spies (Jackson always placed great value on his spies). About midnight they returned with a report that the Indians were encamped some three miles distant; their whooping and dancing indicated that they knew of Jackson's presence and were planning an attack.

At dawn the Red Sticks struck. Jackson was ready. The action raged for an hour, with the heaviest fighting on the left wing. After the Creeks had been repulsed Jackson sent Coffee, who had rejoined him, together with 400 men and some friendly Creeks, to destroy the Indian encampment. But Coffee found it too strongly fortified to risk an assault and returned to Jackson's camp. On his return the Red Sticks struck again, this time on the right wing. With great difficulty the Indians were repulsed. During the action Coffee was wounded and Jackson's brother-in-law and aide, Major Alexander Donelson, was killed. Then came the main attack, again on the left side, where Jackson expected it. The Creeks peppered the army with "quick irregular firing, from behind logs, trees, shrubbery, and whatever could afford concealment."[31] Lying prone behind logs the Indians loaded their guns, rose, fired, and then ducked down again to reload. To dislodge them Jackson ordered a charge led by Billy Carroll which "broke in on them, threw them into confusion," and eventually drove them off.[32]

The Creeks had devised an excellent plan of attack—hitting three different points of the American line at once—but the execution faltered when one of the attacking parties designated to strike the front line decided instead to retire to their village. Jackson barely escaped being cut to pieces.[33] It was a close call, and Jackson decided against taking further chances with his raw recruits and wisely ordered a retreat to Fort Strother.

As Jackson pulled back, the Red Sticks followed stealthfully. When he reached Enotachopco Creek and started across, the Indians attacked just as the artillery was entering the water behind the front guard and the flank column. Jackson immediately ordered the rear guard to engage the hostiles; at the same time he called for the left and right columns to wheel around, recross the creek above and below the Red Sticks, and surround them—in imitation of the Talladega strategy. "But to my astonishment and mortification," Jackson later reported to General Thomas Pinckney, ". . . I beheld . . . the rear guard precipitately give way. This shameful retreat was disastrous in the extreme." The raw troops plunged back into the creek in their effort to escape the withering fire. Jackson, screaming orders, managed to reform his columns and throw them hard against the Indians. He landed a solid blow. Detachments were hurried across the creek in strength, and after several minutes of intense fighting they drove off the Indians. In the action the Tennesseans proved themselves men of courage and fortitude despite their inexperience, and they earned their commander's highest praise.[34]

During the engagement Jackson was described later by a friendly observer as a "rallying point," even for the brave. "Firm and energetic . . . his example and his authority alike contributed to arrest the flying, and give confidence to those who maintained their ground. . . . In the midst of a shower of balls . . . he was seen . . . rallying the alarmed, halting them in their flight, forming his columns, and inspiriting them by his example."[35] In the engagement 20 Americans were killed and 75 wounded, some of whom died afterward; approximately 200 dead Indians were counted on the ground and in the creek. Jackson's gallantry and skill succeeded in extricating the army from the depths of Creek country and the danger of annihilation had they remained.

Old Hickory pulled himself back to Fort Strother where in early February he received word that 2,000 East Tennesseans would soon join him. On February 6 the Thirty-ninth Regiment of U.S. Infantry, commanded by Colonel John Williams, arrived at Fort Strother. By March Jackson had nearly 5,000 men under his command, a force large enough to attempt the complete destruction of the Red Sticks.

But discipline was essential, and so Jackson began a rigid program to train his men and make them an effective fighting unit. He banned the transportation of whiskey, and he put his troops to work improving the road between Forts Strother and Deposit. The strictest discipline was imposed, and mutiny severely dealt with. It was during this period that an incident occurred which would haunt Jackson for the rest of his life, an incident that convinced some people that he was a ruthless, pitiless killer. John Woods was hardly eighteen years of age when he enlisted in the militia. He belonged to a company that had caused considerable disciplinary problems. He was standing guard one cold, rainy February morning and left his post, after first receiving permission from an officer, to go to his tent for a blanket. There he found that his comrades had left him his breakfast and so he sat down and ate it. A few minutes later another officer discovered him and told him to get back to his post. Woods refused, an argument ensued, and the officer ordered the young soldier's arrest. Then Woods lost control of himself. He grabbed his gun and swore he would shoot the first man to lay a hand on him. As the quarreling intensified, someone informed Jackson that a "mutiny" was in progress. The cry "mutiny" was electrifying and reminiscent of many similar incidents in the recent past. Jackson bolted from his tent. "Which is the ———— rascal?" "Shoot him! Shoot him! Blow ten balls through the ———— rascal's body!"[36] Meanwhile, Woods had been persuaded to give up his gun and submit to arrest.

Most soldiers believed the incident would be forgotten, but Jackson was determined to make an example of Woods. He insisted on a court-martial on the charge of mutiny. The young man pleaded not guilty, the court found against him and ordered his execution. Several efforts were made to win clemency for Woods, but the stern commander turned a deaf ear to all of them. On March 14, two days after the trial, John Woods was shot to death by a firing squad in the presence of the entire army.[37]

Many years later, when Jackson sought the presidency, this "bloody deed" was recounted in detail in the newspapers to prove that Old Hickory was a butcher who could have imposed a milder sentence but chose instead to snuff out a young man's life. The punishment was indeed harsh. Under different circumstances Jackson might have been more lenient—although he was most unpredictable—but his experiences of the previous December and January left his mood and temper strict and unyielding in matters of discipline. He had kept a force in the field despite massive desertions and the worst possible hardships. The experience toughened him. As far as he was concerned, the troops must be made to understand their duty whatever the circumstances—even if it meant the sacrifice of a young man's life.

A rocklike and determined General had been formed by painful experience. If possible Jackson's already cold and steely will was strengthened. He became a relentless, driving, indefatigable machine devoted to one solitary purpose—the destruction of his country's enemies. Jackson forged an army in the early months of 1814. Now he could get on with the war.

The same day Woods was executed Jackson commenced the campaign that he passionately believed would annihilate the Red Sticks and end the Creek War. His plan, now that his army numbered several thousand men who behaved like disciplined soldiers, called for him to move southward along the banks of the Coosa River, then eastward toward Emuckfaw in the vicinity of Horseshoe Bend, where he knew many tribes of the Creeks were gathering for self-protection. After destroying this "confederacy" he would march to the Holy Ground, at the junction of the Coosa and Tallapoosa rivers, which was the sacred meeting place of the Indians. The Creeks believed that it was protected by the deities and that no white man could violate it and live.[38] General Jackson saw himself as the appropriate white man to smash that Indian superstition.

On March 14, 1814, Jackson moved. He left 450 men behind to guard Fort Strother and sent Colonel John Williams and his regiment downriver to establish an advance post thirty miles to the south. After a slow start Jackson gained momentum and briskly headed toward the strong encampment of Indians at Horseshoe Bend. He now commanded a force of nearly 4,000 men, including many Creek allies. According to his intelligence, 1,000 hostiles and nearly 300 women and children were congregated inside the Bend.

The stronghold at Horseshoe Bend was a 100-acre wooded peninsula almost completely surrounded by water and with a stout breastwork running across its 350-yard neck. The breastwork was made of "large timbers and trunks of trees" laid "horizontally on each other, leaving but a single place of entrance."[39] It ran five to eight feet high and had a double row of portholes "artfully arranged" to give the defenders "complete direction of their fire." Because of the curvature of the breastwork no army could advance upon it without being exposed to a deadly cross fire. It was "a place well formed by Nature for defence & rendered more secure by Art," said Jackson.[40]

At ten o'clock on the morning of March 27 Jackson arrived at the Bend. He was dumbfounded by what he saw. "It is impossible to conceive a situation more eligible for defence than the one they had chosen," he reported to General Pinckney; "and the skill which they manifested in their breast work, was really astonishing."[41] Several hours earlier Jackson had detailed Coffee and his cavalry, along with the entire force of friendly Cherokees and the companies of spies, to occupy the side of the river opposite the Bend in order to prevent the Red Sticks from escaping. In addition, Coffee was told to make some feint to divert the enemy from the principal point of attack. The plan was simply to contain the Creeks inside the fortress where Jackson would smash through the breastwork to overpower and destroy them.

Jackson stationed his artillery, one six-pounder and one three-pounder, on a small eminence about 80 yards from the closest and 250 yards from the furthest points of the breastwork. At 10:30 A.M. he opened fire. The balls thudded harmlessly into the thick logs or whistled through "the works without shaking the wall." Whenever the Indians peeked over the breastwork to pepper the gun crews, Jackson raked them with musket and rifle fire. For two hours the firing continued, the artillery pounding the defenses without inflicting appreciable damage.

Meanwhile Coffee sent a group of swimmers across the river to cut loose the Creek canoes and bring them back to be used to ferry soldiers in an assault on the rear position of the encampment. Then a party of soldiers crossed the river to set fire to the huts clustered at the turn of the Bend and to attack the Indians within the compound. When Jackson saw the smoke from the burning huts and realized it was the diversion he had directed, he ordered his troops to storm the breastwork.

The order brought a shout from Jackson's men. The Thirty-ninth Regiment charged forward under a withering fire of Indian bullets and arrows. The soldiers reached the rampart and thrust their rifles through the portholes. For a time it was point-blank shooting, muzzle to muzzle, "in which many of the enemy's balls were welded to the bayonets of our musquets." Major Lemuel P. Montgomery was the first to reach the breastwork. Leaping on the wall, he called to his men to follow, but no sooner had he spoken than a bullet struck him in the head, and he fell lifeless to the ground. Ensign Sam Houston mounted the wall and renewed Montgomery's cry. An arrow pierced his thigh but Houston jumped into the compound followed by a large contingent of regulars who poured over the wall. The breastwork was breached; the troops scaled the rampart in force.[42]

The Red Sticks, stunned and frightened, backed away to conceal themselves in the thick brush that covered the ground. But the troops pursued them and gave no quarter. The killing became savage. "The *carnage* was *dreadful,*" Jackson reported.[43] Some headed for their canoes to escape, splashing across the river when they found them gone, only to run headlong into Coffee's troops. Others leaped down the river bluff and concealed themselves among the cliffs that were covered with brush and fallen trees. Hour after hour throughout the afternoon the fighting continued, the troops flushing the Indians from their hiding places and shooting them when they frantically sought new cover. Now the Red Sticks were in total disarray, scampering wildly from place to place. The soldiers systematically slaughtered them. A few Indians, under cover of darkness, managed to cross the river and escape.

The next day Jackson ordered a count of the dead. Some 557 Indians were found on the ground; Coffee estimated as many as 300 Creeks dead in the river; and a few dozen bodies were later discovered in the woods—a total of approximately 900 Red Sticks killed. Few warriors escaped the carnage; Jackson figured that no more than fifteen or twenty braves got away, but the number may have been higher. Three hundred captives were taken, all but four of them women and children. His own casualties amounted to 47 dead and 159 wounded, along with an additional 23 friendly Creeks and Cherokees killed and 47 wounded.[44]

Jackson was not satisfied with his incomparable victory. William Weatherford, Chief Red Eagle, had escaped him. The chief was away from the Bend on the day of battle, and Menewa ("Great Warrior"), a mixed-blood, commanded the fighting.[45] Menewa was wounded seven times and lay unconscious among the dead, but he revived, crawled to the river, found a canoe, and made his escape. Despite the disappointment of the loss of Weatherford the power of the Red Sticks was irreparably broken.

The Battle of Horseshoe Bend was one of the major engagements of the War of 1812. Apart from the incredible number of men killed, it crushed the Indian will and capacity to wage war just when the British were about to land troops from the Gulf and provide the hostiles with an enormous supply of arms and ammunition. Had the Creeks not been defeated so decisively they would have become a force of incalculable danger to the entire southern half of the United States.

Jackson sank his dead in the river, collected his wounded, and after allowing his soldiers a short respite set out on April 5 for the Holy Ground at the juncture of the Coosa and Tallapoosa rivers, burning and destroying Indian villages as he went. On April 18 he raised the American flag over the old Toulouse French Fort, which was rebuilt and renamed Fort Jackson. Here many Creek chiefs surrendered to Old Hickory. A few days later Weatherford himself walked into Jackson's camp and calmly claimed the protection that had been extended to the other chiefs, at the same time expressing his desire for peace for himself and his people. Old Hickory was astounded at Red Eagle's audacity.

"I am in your power—do with me what you please," said Weatherford. "I am a soldier. I have done the white people all the harm I could; I have fought them, and fought them bravely: if I had an army, I would yet fight, and contend to the last: but I have none; my people are all gone. I can now do no more than weep over the misfortunes of my nation."

Jackson marveled at this heroic man. He could not help but feel deep admiration for such a great leader. There was a long pause after Red Eagle finished speaking and then Old Hickory told the chief that he would not take advantage of his desperate situation and therefore gave him permission to return to his home. "But if," said Jackson, "you choose to try the fate of arms once more, and I take you prisoner, your life shall pay the forfeit of your crimes. But if you really wish for peace, stay where you are, and I will protect you."[46]

So ended the interview. Weatherford accepted his defeat, and Jackson, although awed by Red Eagle's courage, made it clear that the Creeks could find safety only in submitting unconditionally to his authority. Weatherford agreed to do what he could to convince any holdouts that they should surrender. A few days later he left the camp to fulfill his pledge. But his career as a Creek leader was over; when the War of 1812 ended he retired to a farm and occasionally (or so it was reported) visited Old Hickory at the Hermitage.[47]

Apart from Jackson's admiration of the chief, which was genuine, the General had more need of Red Eagle alive than dead or locked in a stockade. Whatever the chief could do to immobilize hostiles would be advantageous to him, for greater enemies still needed to be reckoned with: the British and Spanish.

Not that Jackson relied on Weatherford to end the Creek War. The mopping-up operations belonged to his army and they went about it efficiently and with considerable enthusiasm. So thorough was this operation that Jackson reported to Governor Blount on April 18 that the Creek War was virtually ended.[48]

Jackson's reputation as general, as westerner, as frontiersman, as symbol, was made by the Creek War. He mirrored in splendid excess the westerner's yearning for heroics, drama, storm. After 1814 he was altogether unique and special to frontiersmen—their *beau idéal*—and that feeling never changed appreciably for the rest of Jackson's life.

But the war did something more to him. It permanently shattered his health. In the relatively short space of eight months his constitution had been devastated by chronic diarrhea and dysentery brought on by wilderness conditions, lack of adequate food and medicine, and his own indifference to his physical suffering. When he began the campaign he was still recovering from the gunfight with the Bentons. For months he could barely move his arm because of the shattered bone. Then pieces of the bone "came out of my arm" and he sent them to Rachel as a souvenir. "I hope all the loose pieces of bone is out," he wrote her, "and I will not be longer pained with it."[49] Throughout the war he suffered many days of pure agony when he thought he would collapse because of the pain. Yet he forced himself to keep going. He would not indulge his body. It, too, must respond to the demands of his sovereign will. By the end of the war his constitution was half wrecked, but his willpower had grown to monumental proportions.

In recognition of his services the government begrudgingly awarded him the rank of major general in the United States Army and command of the Seventh Military District, which included Louisiana, Tennessee, the Mississippi Territory, and the Creek Nation. The offer went forward on May 28, and on June 18, 1814, Jackson accepted it. The government then directed him to proceed without delay to Fort Jackson and arrange the peace treaty with the Creek Nation. He was given guidelines to assist him in his negotiations, but Jackson needed no assistance when it came to dealing with hostile Indians.

He arrived at Fort Jackson on July 10, 1814, and immediately summoned the Creek chiefs—friendly and hostile—to a general meeting. When they assembled he hardly acknowledged the help he had received during the war from friendly Creeks. He treated all the Indians in the same manner. For their crime, he told them, the entire Creek Nation must pay. He demanded the equivalent of all expenses incurred by the United States in the war, which by his calculation came to 23 million acres of land. He wanted roughly three-fifths of the present state of Alabama and one-fifth of Georgia! In addition, the Creeks must cease all communication with the British and Spanish. They must acknowledge the right of the United States to open roads through Creek country and to establish military and trading posts wherever necessary, and they must surrender the instigators of the war.[50]

When the interpreters finished translating Jackson's words, the chiefs retired to a private council to discuss the monstrous terms imposed on them by the man they now called Sharp Knife.[51] The following day they tried to convince Sharp Knife that his terms were harsh and unjust, but they spoke to a stone wall. They reminded him that the chiefs there present had been friendly, that most of the Red Sticks had fled to Florida and the protection of the Spanish. Sharp Knife just stared at them. The Creek Nation, he growled, must be cut off from the "mischief-makers from the lakes. . . . Until this is done, your nation cannot expect happiness, nor mine security. . . . This evening must determine whether or not you are disposed to become friendly. Your rejecting the treaty will show you to be the enemies of the United States—enemies even to yourself."[52]

The chiefs withdrew to council. Unjust as Jackson's treaty was in crushing the power of the Creek Nation and divesting them of their lands, the alternative to submission was renewal of the war. Sharp Knife's overwhelming military strength and their own weakness necessarily dictated their decision. On August 9, 1814, the chiefs surrendered themselves to his vengeance. Thirty-five chiefs (only *one* of whom was a Red Stick), under protest, signed the treaty at 2:00 P.M. They then withdrew from the fort to carry the word of their disgrace and ruin to the other members of the tribe.[53]

What Jackson had done had the touch of genius. He had ended the war by signing a peace treaty with his Indian allies! Most of the surviving Red Sticks had fled to Florida and planned to continue their warfare. Thus Jackson converted the Creek civil war into an enormous land grab. Moreover, he insured the ultimate destruction of the entire Creek Nation. All the other southern tribes would one day experience the same melancholy fate at the hands of General Andrew Jackson.

CHAPTER 7

———◆———

The Battle of New Orleans

GENERAL JACKSON'S DISTINCTION at this stage of the War of 1812 was his proven ability to command an army, maintain it in the field, and deploy it effectively to pacify the frontier. He was not a great tactician, nor were his battles brilliantly executed; but he commanded the confidence of his officers and the obedience of his men, even under terrible adversity. When necessary he moved his army rapidly, and he understood and could evaluate the importance of intelligence reports. And welding all of this together was his titanic determination, his stupendous will to overcome the enemy and achieve total victory.

"Retaliation and vengeance" had characterized his treatment of the Creeks. The Europeans deserved no less. "I owe to Britain a debt of retaliatory vengeance," he told Rachel; "should our forces meet I trust I shall pay the debt—she is in conjunction with Spain arming the hostile Indians to butcher our women & children."[1] But in administering this vengeance, Jackson had one problem. Although an armed attack against the British was quite in order in view of Congress's declaration of hostilities against that nation, the United States was not at war with Spain. Indeed, the Madison administration had indicated a willingness to respond favorably to Spain's desire to maintain peaceful relations between the two countries. Even so, Jackson felt no compunction against attacking the Spanish, operating on the broad principle later approved by the administration that if Spain cooperated with the British and Indians, then the United States must take appropriate countermeasures.[2] So General Jackson took it upon himself to write to the Spanish governor of Pensacola, Don Matteo Gonzáles Manrique, and instruct him in the terror he could expect if Jackson's complaints were not immediately and satisfactorily redressed. There were "refugee banditti from the creek nation" crowding into Florida, Old Hickory informed Manrique, and "drawing rations from your government and under the drill of a British officer." Josiah Francis (Hidlis Hadjo), Peter McQueen, and other leaders of the hostile Creeks had formed a "matricidical band for whom your christian

86

bowels seem to sympathise and bleed so freely." They should be arrested, confined, and tried for their crimes. The United States had retaliated against enemy atrocities and would do so again if further provoked. Be warned of my creed, said Sharp Knife. "An Eye for an Eye, Toothe for Toothe and Scalp for Scalp."[3]

As Jackson headed south from Fort Jackson to instruct the Spanish on proper behavior toward the United States and its Indian foes, the British prepared to launch a mighty assault in the Gulf of Mexico to drive the Americans out of West Florida and Louisiana. The war in Europe was over. Napoleon had been captured, and the British were now free to concentrate their military forces in America and deliver the final blow that would bring the United States to heel.

Already the offensive had begun. British troops under the command of Sir George Cockburn invaded the Chesapeake, marched on Washington, burned the President's mansion and the Capitol, and then shelled Baltimore. Another army plunged into New York from Quebec but failed to secure Lake Champlain and dared not advance until its rear could be protected. Meanwhile Vice Admiral Sir Alexander Cochrane, commander of the North American station, recommended to his government an expedition to invade the United States from the Gulf. Only a few thousand troops were necessary, he contended, for they would be joined by Indians and Spanish in routing the Americans and driving them back from the coast and up the Mississippi Valley. Control of the valley would produce a linkup with Canada that at the very least would reduce the United States to an island surrounded and contained by Great Britain in the north, west, and south.[4]

Cochrane's excellent plan persuaded the Admiralty. It was approved along with the use of troops from the Chesapeake area which would be supplemented by more than 2,000 additional men to be sent from Europe. These troops could be expected in Jamaica by mid-November 1814.

While the British developed their plans for a massive invasion of the United States from the Gulf of Mexico, General Jackson hurriedly moved his army from Fort Jackson down the Coosa and Alabama rivers to Mobile, where he arrived on August 22. This splendid strategic move thwarted British intentions of reaching the Mississippi River via Mobile— clearly the most feasible plan for invasion because it facilitated the linking up with Indians and Spanish in the area before pushing on to the Mississippi. When he learned of Jackson's move, Cochrane decided to strike instead at New Orleans directly. It was his first big mistake.

Because of Jackson's threats, the Spanish governor, González Manrique, invited the British to land at Pensacola—a clear and palpable violation of Spanish neutrality.[5] He acted on his own, feeling compelled to respond to what he believed was the immediate danger of an American invasion.[6]

At first the British hoped to drive Jackson from Mobile, and on September 12 Admiral Sir William Percy, commanding four ships, the *Hermes, Carron, Sophie,* and *Childers,* reached Mobile Bay with a total of 78 guns. Three days later this fleet opened up on the fort occupied by Jackson's troops. The battle raged for hours and ended when the *Hermes* blew up and the British disengaged and withdrew. As a consequence, Cochran revised his invasion plan and eliminated any idea of capturing Mobile and the surrounding country.

At this point Jackson decided to invade Florida. By doing so he could not only carry the offensive to the British but also dismantle their spy system, which he believed—correctly—was centered in Florida. Moreover, he could punish the Spanish for violating their neutrality. "This will put an end to the Indian war in the south," he told James Monroe, the secretary of war, "as it will cut off all foreign influence."[7]

Jackson left Mobile on October 25 and reached Pensacola on the afternoon of November 6, 1814. Pensacola was hardly more than a village dominated by two small forts, St. Rose and St. Michael; its real strength lay in Fort Barrancas, which guarded the entrance to the bay. Under a flag of truce, Jackson demanded possession of Barrancas along with its munitions "until Spain can preserve unimpaired her neutral character."[8]

Governor González Manrique never got Jackson's demands because the flag of truce was fired on, probably by the British, as it neared the town. Thereupon, Old Hickory attacked immediately, sending one column of 500 mounted men on the west side of the town to make a noisy attack, while he led the main force from the east side. After a sharp exchange of fire, the Americans poured into the town, driving the Spanish soldiers from houses and gardens. The assault was so swift that resistance collapsed within minutes. Governor González Manrique tottered forward with a white flag and surrendered the town and its fortifications. The British, together with hundreds of their Indian allies, retreated to their ships and sailed off into the Gulf. "I had the Satisfaction to see the whole British force leave the port and their friends at our Mercy," gloated General Jackson. American casualties included 7 dead and 11 wounded. The Spanish suffered 14 killed and 6 wounded. No document records British or Indian losses.[9]

Jackson felt he had seriously disrupted the British plan of operations against the southern section of the nation.[10] Indeed, the invasion of Florida and the capture of Pensacola was a strategically wise move. His action sealed off potential avenues of invasion, avenues that made more military sense than a frontal assault up the Mississippi River to New Orleans.

Still, worried that Mobile was the real invasion site, Jackson returned Pensacola to González Manrique—"the enemy having disappeared and the hostile creeks fled to the Forest, I retire from your Town, and leave you again at liberty to occupy your Fort," he told the governor[11]—and sped back to Mobile. Once back, he waited ten days for the British to appear, and when they failed to show up he concluded that New Orleans, not Mobile, was the focal point of the invasion. Promptly, he ordered General Coffee with 2,000 men to cover New Orleans by riding to Baton Rouge and link up with the newly mustered militia said to be on its way from Tennessee and Kentucky. He also dispatched Colonel Arthur P. Hayne to the mouth of the Mississippi to discover sites on which batteries might be erected that would command the river and prevent the British from crossing the bar. After completing these arrangements, he turned over command of Mobile to Brigadier General James Winchester, and on November 22, 1814, with 2,000 troops, he finally set out for New Orleans himself.

Jackson also summoned Rachel to New Orleans. He told her to bring beds, tables, carriage, servants, and Andrew Jr. He needed her desperately because he was close to total physical collapse. Before leaving Pensacola "I was taken verry ill," he said; "the Doctor gave me a dose of Jallap and camemel, which salavated me, and there was Eight days on the march that I never broke bread. My health is restored but I am still verry weak."[12] Debilitated, but nonetheless determined to throw back the invasion, Jackson struggled to his horse and headed west to New Orleans, arriving early in the morning of December 1. Just a few days before his arrival, an armada of sixty British ships—frigates, sloops, gunboats, and various other transports—carrying 14,000 troops left Jamaica under the command of Admiral Cochrane and headed directly for New Orleans.[13]

By the time Jackson reached New Orleans he was beginning to show the effects of many long months of campaigning, to say nothing of his most recent illness. His frame was long and gaunt, indeed emaciated. His complexion was sallow but his carriage was very erect, and the strength— if not the fierceness—of his countenance bespoke a spirit that willed mastery over his damaged body. Steely determination lay coiled within that emaciated shell. He was forty-seven years of age, his hair iron gray, but in his manner he radiated confidence, stern decision, and enormous energy. One observer described him at the time as "erect, composed, perfectly self possessed, with martial bearing. . . . One whom nature had stamped a gentleman."[14]

The city of New Orleans lies slightly more than 100 miles from the mouth of the winding Mississippi and curves along the eastern bank of the river in an area of swamps and bayous and great trees festooned with Spanish moss. Because the river is broad and almost unfordable, the city is virtually invulnerable to attack from the west. Consequently invasion must come from the south or the east.

An attack up the long river was difficult but possible, although the route was protected by Fort St. Philip, a military post sixty-five miles downstream that was garrisoned by regular troops manning twenty-eight twenty-four-pounders. Further up the river, approximately twenty-five miles below New Orleans, Fort St. Leon was situated at a sharp looping bend in the river, known as the English Turn. Sailing vessels were obliged to stop here to wait for a change in wind direction in order to navigate the bend. Invading ships that stopped at the bend were sitting ducks; the guns of the fort could easily pick them off.

Clearly, invasion from the south would be extremely difficult. That left two eastern approaches: the land route through Mobile (which Jackson always feared because it made more military sense than any other) and the water route from the Gulf into Lake Borgne and Lake Pontchartrain. The lakes were connected by a narrow, shallow strait called the Rigolets, situated only a few miles to the north and east of New Orleans. Bayou St. John flows out of Pontchartrain and comes within two miles of the city limits, but Fort St. John—a small brick fort in a rather bad state of repair—guarded the entrance to the bayou. The land between the lakes and the city was generally swampy, flat, dotted with bayous, and virtually roadless. Sweeping northeastward from the city, however, was a narrow ridge of dry land called the Plains of Gentilly; a road, Chef Menteur, followed this ground and connected the Rigolets with the city. Most citizens of New Orleans believed the invasion would come along this route.

Jackson was greeted on his arrival by the governor, W.C.C. Claiborne—whose tenure was troubled by a running quarrel with the legislature, fears of a slave revolt, and the charged emotions of a city about to be invaded—along with Commodore Daniel T. Patterson, the commandant of the naval district, and Edward Livingston, chairman of the New Orleans committee of public defense and the sharpest legal talent in the city who quickly won Jackson's admiration for his intelligence and good judgment. Livingston soon became the General's secretary, translator, confidential adviser, and aide-de-camp. After the greetings, Livingston invited Jackson to his home for dinner. Livingston's wife, Louise, a beautiful Creole lady and a leader of New Orleans society, was a trifle distressed when she learned of the imminent arrival of her husband's guest. At the time she was giving a dinner party for a small group of ladies. "What shall we do with this wild General from Tennessee?" they whispered among themselves. Then, as they fluttered with apprehension, he entered the room. Dressed in a uniform of coarse blue cloth and yellow buckskin, his high dragoon boots badly in need of polishing, he nonetheless appeared "the very picture of a war-worn noble warrior and commander."

Jackson bowed to the ladies seated around the room. It was done gracefully despite the awkward need to acknowledge those sitting in distant corners and in widely separated groups. He turned to Mrs. Livingston, escorted her back to her sofa, and sat conversing with her for several minutes. The ladies were astonished at his poise and gratified by his grand manner. At dinner the General continued his conversation in a free and relaxed style, discussing the invasion, assuring the ladies he would save the city, and urging them not to trouble themselves about the matter. When he finally rose from the table and left the house with Livingston, the ladies descended on their hostess. "Is *this* your back woods-man? Why, madam, he is a prince."[15]

Once he established his headquarters at 106 Royal Street, the General took a number of defensive actions. He called a conference with engineers to learn the best way to seal the city against invasion. Next, he sent squads of men to fell the huge trees in the bayous and so clog the streams and creeks and other small water routes that finger their way toward New Orleans and which might serve as corridors for the invasion. But this excellent idea was totally negated by Jackson's failure to inspect the completed task, or assign some responsible official with the responsibility of checking every important bayou and making certain they were closed. Then he ordered additional batteries of cannon erected at Fort St. Philip. A fleet of five small gunboats, commanded by Lieutenant Thomas Ap Catesby Jones, was also stationed on Lake Borgne to protect the city from that quarter, although by now Jackson was certain that it would be used only as a feint to throw him off his guard. The main attack, he convinced himself, would come at Chef Menteur on Lake Pontchartrain, approximately fifteen miles east of the city.

Within the city itself the defensive force on paper totaled only 700 men, of which about 200 were absent from duty. Moreover, there were justified fears about the loyalty of the French and Spanish inhabitants. Another problem was the pirates who operated out of Barataria Bay, a large body of water some seventy miles southwest of New Orleans. The chief of the pirates was Jean Lafitte, who with his brothers Pierre and Dominique and a corps of freebooters lived on the island of Grand Terre in the bay, and engaged in the lucrative if unlawful practice of privateering and smuggling, much of it at the expense of the Spanish in Mexico and Florida.

Lafitte was a shrewd operator. Fluent in English, Spanish, French, and Italian, he was an energetic and efficient businessman who calculated his advantages before committing himself or undertaking a financial venture. Formerly a New Orleans blacksmith, Haitian born, and a man of great courage, he was adventurous, cunning, totally unnautical, but highly successful as a practicing pirate. Since he was so practical and skillful as a man of business, he first offered his services to the British, who laid down two conditions for an alliance: the pirates must cease their attacks on Spanish shipping and they must return English booty already seized.[16] That ended that. Lafitte next turned to the Americans, and after some hesitation Jackson yielded to the appeals of Livingston and a committee of the city's leading citizens to accept the services of these "hellish banditti," as the General called them.[17] The pirates later proved very useful in manning two batteries during the British main attack against New Orleans.

Jackson also accepted the aid of free blacks in the city. They numbered about 600 and sent their offer of help through Governor Claiborne. Jackson responded enthusiastically. "Our country," he wrote in reply, "has been invaded and threatened with destruction. She wants Soldiers to fight her battles. The free men of colour . . . would make excellent Soldiers. They will not remain quiet spectators of the coming contest."[18] Jackson directed that they be officered by white men and treated identically with other volunteers. Pierre Lacoste was placed in command of the black battalion, and later, when a second battalion of refugee Santo Domingo blacks was formed, the General assigned Major Jean Daquin to command it.

Many Louisianians were not happy with this decision, fearing a bloody revolt if guns were placed in the hands of blacks. When an assistant paymaster questioned the General's right to enlist "men of colour" into the service, Jackson cut him down. "Be pleased to keep to yourself your opinions upon the policy of making payments of the troops with the necessary muster rolls without inquiring whether the troops are white, black or tea."[19]

Nearly two weeks after Jackson arrived in New Orleans—on December 13, 1814, to be exact—the British armada was sighted off Cat Island at the entrance to Lake Borgne. American gunboats on the lake had been ordered to avoid a contest, but as they drew back the wind died, and the British, with forty-five barges equipped with forty-two cannons and manned by 1,000 sailors and Marines, opened fire on the Americans and forced their surrender. On the American side 6 were killed during the engagement, 35 wounded, including Lieutenant Jones, and 86 captured; on the British, 17 were killed and 77 wounded.[20] The lake was now free of any American force.

The British victory was an American disaster. It extinguished Jackson's watch on the lakes and prepared the way for the invasion of the mainland.[21] Yet it did have one salutary effect. The American sailors taken prisoner all swore that Jackson's army numbered four times its actual size. And that gave the British pause. Consequently, Cochrane decided to move all troops to Pea Island, just to the east of the Rigolets, and then transport them to the mainland. It was a tedious and difficult operation—and it took time.

The exact size of Jackson's army was probably unknown to anyone, including the General himself. Perhaps 3,500 to 4,000 Americans is the best approximation of his strength at the start of the invasion. And time worked to his advantage, in that each additional day swelled his ranks with arriving volunteers. Time was what Jackson needed to hurry his troops into the city once he learned of the landing and had some sense of its location and the general movement of the invading forces. One of his first orders after hearing of Cochrane's arrival was to General Coffee. "You must not sleep until you arrive within striking distance," he commanded; furthermore, Coffee must send an express to General Carroll and order his presence in New Orleans by the fastest route possible.[22] Coffee reached New Orleans early in the morning of December 20, and he was joined the following day by Carroll and almost 3,000 Tennessee recruits, along with Colonel Thomas Hinds and a regiment of Mississippi dragoons.

When the news of the sighting of the British first reached New Orleans the inhabitants panicked. Although by this time they had acquired enormous confidence in Jackson, the alarm produced a shock wave that left confusion and terror in its wake. In these circumstances Jackson felt he must *take* control of New Orleans. If he was to defend the city, halt the invasion, and throw the British back into the sea, he had no alternative. So, on December 16, he proclaimed martial law throughout New Orleans, turning it into an armed camp and making all citizens potential soldiers. The proclamation directed that every citizen entering the city must report to the adjutant general's office and that no person might leave without permission in writing signed by the commanding General or one of his staff. Ships must have passports to clear the port, and a curfew was ordered for nine o'clock. Any unauthorized person found in the streets after that hour would be arrested as a spy.[23]

At nine o'clock on the morning of December 22, having completed their landing operation, the British headed toward New Orleans via Bayou Bienvenue. An advance attack force of 1,800 soldiers under Colonel William Thornton began the assault. Major General John Keane, who would make all the wrong decisions for the expedition, accompanied the advance, and the flotilla moved with perfect order into the wide, flat expanse of swamp. As they moved inland the ground became firmer, the path more distinct. The troops debarked in single file as gradually the swamp gave way to stunted cypress trees, then canebrakes, and finally the open, cultivated fields that formed the plantation of General Jacques Villeré of the Louisiana militia.

Major Gabriel Villeré, son of the general, was sitting on the porch of the main house when he suddenly spotted redcoats flashing through the orange grove as they headed toward the river. He jumped from his chair and ran into the house to escape by a rear door—and was captured by several armed men. In desperation, he suddenly sprang from his captors and leaped through a window. Dashing across the yard, he hurdled a picket fence and plunged into the cypress forest that fringed the swamp before the British could catch him.[24] With the help of a neighbor he eventually got to the city with the horrifying news that the British were now drawn up alongside the Mississippi.

What happened should have been prevented. The British had stumbled upon an unclogged water passage, barged into it, and marched to

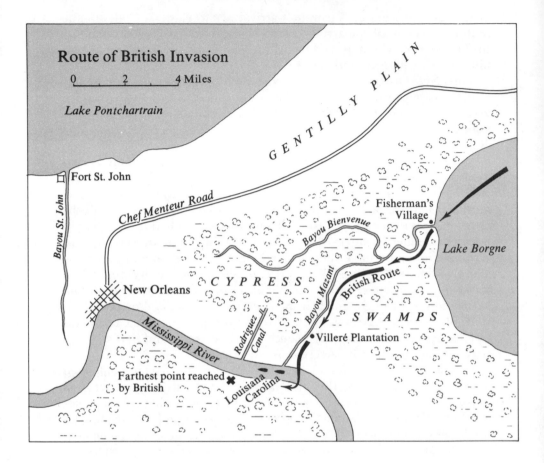

Route of British Invasion

0   2   4 Miles

Lake Pontchartrain

GENTILLY PLAIN

Fort St. John

Bayou St. John

Chef Menteur Road

Fisherman's Village

Bayou Bienvenue

Lake Borgne

CYPRESS

Bayou Mazant

British Route

New Orleans

Mississippi River

Rodriguez Canal

SWAMPS

• Villeré Plantation

Farthest point reached by British

Louisiana

Carolina

the river, hardly a dozen miles south of New Orleans. Since the felling of trees in the Bienvenue area was the responsibility of Villeré, he was later court-martialed for negligence. But ultimate responsibility rested with Jackson, who should have made certain the bayou was blocked, so justice was probably served when the major was eventually acquitted.

When General Keane joined the column at Villeré's house he ordered the troops into battalion formation and marched them to the upper line of the plantation, where they halted in a position between the river and a cypress swamp. He was urged by other officers to continue the march and seize the apparently defenseless city. Since the troops had moved without opposition, without even the knowledge of the Americans, it seemed a safe bet that New Orleans could be taken with the troops at hand—rather than wait for reinforcements from the main contingent.

And they were undoubtedly right. At the time of their arrival at Villeré's plantation, Jackson had no notion of the exact British location, nor did he have adequate defenses to stop a surprise attack. He would have been reduced to street fighting, guerrilla fashion, which would have had a devastating effect on the city and its population.

But Keane was a cautious man. Captured pickets and sailors had told him that the city was crawling with soldiers, maybe as many as 20,000; and he feared his lines of supply and communication with the fleet were too tenuous. So he decided to wait until the main body of his command caught up with the advance column. His timid decision may well have saved the city from capture.[25]

When Gabriel Villeré finally reached Jackson and reported the British position at his father's plantation, the General supposedly reacted with an "emphatic blow upon the table with his clenched fist." He cried out: "By the Eternal, they shall not sleep on our soil!" Then he summoned his secretary and aides. "Gentlemen," he said as they entered the room, "the British are below; we must fight them to-night."[26]

Jackson understood the urgency of making immediate contact with the enemy and keeping them from moving directly into the city. No Keane, he. Old Hickory could scarcely contain his need to rush to combat. "I will smash them," he allegedly said, "so help me God!"[27] Hurriedly, orders were dispatched to assemble the regulars, battalions of city guards, the Mississippi dragoons, the free black battalions, and Coffee's cavalry and rush them downriver. Carroll's Tennesseans and the Louisiana militia were left behind to guard the Chef Menteur in case Jackson's original hunch was correct and the British were only feinting as they moved up the Mississippi.

The General ordered Coffee to move along the cypress swamp on the left and hit the British on the flank while he commanded the main force which would strike along the river. He also directed the USS *Carolina* to drop down the Mississippi to a point opposite the British camp and open fire at half past seven o'clock. And that would be the signal for a general attack.

At the start of this attack Jackson had a little better than 2,000 men to throw against the invaders, slightly more than Keane's force by a few hundred. It was pitch black when the Americans took their position but the enemy campfires, blazing brightly and fiercely on account of the cold, beautifully silhouetted the British and made them splendid targets for the American gunners.

At half past seven the *Carolina* erupted with a broadside that roared over the delta and took the British completely by surprise. For ten minutes or so Keane's men stumbled about in confusion as they scrambled for their guns and extinguished the roaring fires. Then Jackson ordered a frontal assault. For two hours the fighting was a confused tangle of men frequently fighting hand to hand. By nine-thirty a thick fog had come up from the river and "occasioned some confusion among the different [American] Corps," Jackson reported. "Fearing the consequences, under this circumstance, of the further prosecution of a night attack with troops then acting together for the first time," he disengaged, pulled his men back several hundred yards away from the enemy, straddled the road leading to the city, and waited for daylight. The Americans suffered 24 killed, 115 wounded, and 74 missing or captured; the British admitted to 46 killed, 167 wounded, and 64 missing or captured.[28]

Jackson made a wise decision, for shortly after eight o'clock Keane began receiving reinforcements. Fresh, disciplined troops would have given Jackson's unseasoned men a bad time of it. The Americans would have been outnumbered in short order.

At best Jackson got away with a draw, although in a real sense the British could—and did—claim victory, for the Americans had failed to destroy their advance guard. Still, Jackson had taken the offensive, turned a surprise invasion into a surprise counterattack and frightened the British into staying where they were. Always aggressive, Old Hickory brought the invasion to an abrupt halt. Indeed his action saved New Orleans; for had he not attacked so quickly and with such "impetuosity," the British would have immediately marched against the city after the arrival of reinforcements. They undoubtedly would have taken it.[29]

The following day, Christmas Eve, 1814, the very day American and British ministers in Ghent, Belgium, signed a treaty of peace ending the war, Jackson decided to move his army back another mile and set up his defense behind an old millrace called Rodriguez Canal, a ditch four feet deep and ten feet wide that ran from the eastern bank of the Mississippi to a cypress swamp about three-quarters of a mile inland. Earthen ramparts were thrown up at the northern rim of the canal (that closest to the city), and artillery pieces were installed at regular intervals. Meanwhile, the *Carolina,* joined by the USS *Louisiana,* regularly lobbed cannonballs into the enemy camp.

For their part, the British strengthened their position by completing the transfer of troops from the fleet to the advanced position alongside the river. According to the American estimate they now had 7,000 troops "against our 3,000."[30] Then, on Christmas day, the new British general to assume command of the invasion arrived. Not the Duke of Wellington, as many Americans feared, but his wife's brother, Lieutenant General Sir Edward Michael Pakenham. Soldiering since the age of sixteen, he achieved military distinction during the Peninsula War against Napoleon when he broke open the French line in a daring but costly attack. Now thirty-seven years old, Pakenham was given command of this army when its previous general, Sir Robert Ross, was killed at Baltimore.

As his first action, Pakenham decided he must silence the *Carolina* and *Louisiana* or drive them away. At his command, on the night of December 26, nine fieldpieces were dragged to the riverbank along with furnaces for heating shot. The following morning the battery opened up on the *Carolina* in a devastatingly accurate display of firepower. On the second round the ship caught fire and soon raged out of control. The crew tumbled over the sides. And none too soon. The *Carolina* suddenly blew up with a tremendous roar, shaking the ground for miles. Jackson, from his command post at the Macarté house 200 yards behind the mud rampart, ordered the *Louisiana* out of range. It was the heavier and better-armed vessel and it now took station across the river in a position to rake any column of troops that advanced on Jackson's barricade. Except for 1 killed and 6 wounded, the *Carolina* crew were saved to join the American line where they helped man the artillery.

The following day Pakenham ordered a general advance of his army. It was formed into two columns. But the American batteries immediately opened up with a stupendous cannonading, supported by the deadly fire of the *Louisiana,* and forced the invaders to retreat. Pakenham then decided to treat the American position as a fortification and erect breaching batteries to knock out their guns. For the next three days he had heavy naval cannons dragged to his position rather than wait for the siege train of field artillery that was still somewhere at sea. It was a horrendous task and involved moving four twenty-four-pound carronades and ten eighteen-pounders through the swamp. Beginning at a point about 700 yards south of the American position and working inland from the water's edge, Pakenham constructed five batteries (seventeen guns) which were capable of hurling a broadside of over 300 pounds of lead per salvo. (The American artillery could heave 224 pounds per salvo.) The first battery faced across the river to a gun position set up by Jackson on the west bank and commanded by General David Morgan and Commodore Daniel T. Patterson. Pakenham's other batteries were strung out across the line, behind which two columns of troops were formed, with fusiliers on the right and grenadiers on the left.

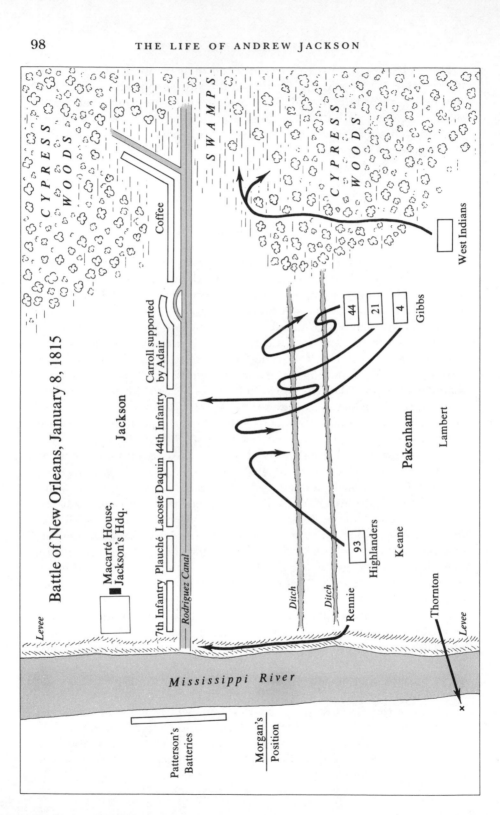

Battle of New Orleans, January 8, 1815

Meanwhile Jackson strengthened his own defenses, extending the line into the swamp, digging the ditch deeper, and mounding the mud rampart higher. By this time he knew that the invasion was before him, not a mere ruse to distract him from Chef Menteur. So he summoned Carroll and his Tennessee division and repositioned them on the defensive line. He also increased the number of gun emplacements along the ditch from five to twelve.

On New Year's morning, 1815, having completed his preparations for bombarding and assaulting the American position, Pakenham ordered the commencement of a general bombardment. It began at ten o'clock with Congreve rockets. These screaming balls of fire frequently terrorized an army and threw it into wild confusion even before the main cannonading began.

"Don't mind these rockets," cried Jackson to his men, as he scurried to the rampart, "they are mere toys to amuse children." Later the British acknowledged, reported John Reid, one of Old Hickory's aides, "that ours is the first . . . army that was not thrown into confusion by their rockets."[31]

For two hours the bombardment was continuous, the entire delta shaking from the impact of the explosions. The Americans responded in kind and steadily improved their aim as the morning wore on. Patterson's naval batteries located the British artillery mounted on the levee and knocked it out. "Too much praise," Jackson later informed Monroe, "cannot be bestowed on those who managed my artillery."[32] Indeed they had battered the British position into a "formless mass of soil and broken guns." Once formidable batteries were now totally destroyed and useless. Moreover, the British had failed in their objective. They could not breach the American line.

By noon the invaders slackened their fire. By three the firing ceased altogether. British casualties included 44 killed and 55 wounded; Americans suffered 11 dead and 23 wounded.[33]

Pakenham cursed the imbecility that confined him to this narrow plain between the river and the swamp. One thing now struck him as crystal clear: since he could not maneuver he must punch his way straight ahead through Jackson's fortification. That necessitated massive power hurled directly forward, committing thousands of men to a frontal assault in such depth that the Americans would be overwhelmed by sheer numbers. So Pakenham decided to wait for reinforcements under Major General John Lambert that were expected daily. In fact they had already arrived at the fleet anchorage and reached Pakenham's position on January 6.

To lessen the burden of the frontal assault and to support his soldiers in their attack, Pakenham planned to catch Jackson in a cross fire. He proposed to ferry 1,500 troops, under the brilliant Colonel William Thornton, to the west bank, capture Patterson's guns, and turn them on Jackson. This enfilade, timed to coincide with an assault by the main force on the east bank, would rake Jackson's position and wipe him out. There was only one problem: boats. Boats to ferry the men across the river. Barges were available, but they lay moored in Bayou Bienvenue. To haul them to the Mississippi meant widening a small canal, the Villeré, that ran to the bayou. So the British started digging, while Jackson bravely ignored the grave danger now facing his army if the enemy succeeded in setting up a cross fire. Instead he prepared three lines of defense—all on the same side of the river! The first was the rampart at Rodriguez Canal; the second was erected two miles closer to the city; and the third still closer by a mile and a quarter. Obviously, the General expected to fall back from one position to the next if the battle turned against him.

At the Rodriguez Canal the rampart averaged five feet in height; it was twenty feet thick in some places but so thin in others that cannonballs could easily puncture it. Along this line Jackson formed 4,000 men with another 1,000 in reserve.[34] Besides the artillery—set up in three groups, river, center, and swamp—the line consisted of the Seventh Regiment, commanded by Colonel George Ross, alongside the Mississippi; Plauché's battalion of city militiamen; Lacoste's and Daquin's battalions of black soldiers; the Forty-fourth Regiment; the Tennesseans under Carroll, supported by General John Adair's Kentuckians; and Coffee's cavalry on the left, with Choctaw Indians scouting in the swamp.

Against this impregnable line Pakenham planned to send a column of 2,200 men under Major General Sir Samuel Gibbs to hit the American position left of center, accompanied by a second column of 1,200 men under Major General Keane to strike Jackson's right along the river. Simultaneously, a West Indian regiment of 520 men would skirmish in the swamp to distract Coffee and slice through his line if possible, while Thornton, having crossed the river, would capture Morgan's batteries as Gibbs and Keane moved up and then turn the batteries against Jackson. A third column of 1,500 men under Major General Lambert was held in reserve near the center of the field.[35]

On January 7, Commodore Patterson walked along the western side of the Mississippi to a point directly opposite the British position and there watched the enemy's movements for several hours. What he saw revealed the British plans. Pakenham had deepened and widened the Villeré Canal and had brought fifty barges to the river, which were to be used to ferry troops to the west bank at nightfall. Jackson was immediately notified, and he sent 500 Kentuckians across the river, only 250 of whom were armed. But it was too little, too late. The American force on the west bank was undermanned and underarmed. It was totally inadequate to its task. The Battle of New Orleans was about to begin, and the Americans were dangerously exposed to a possible cross fire.

At 4:00 A.M., January 8, 1815, a column of redcoats stole to within half a mile of the mud rampart. This was the Forty-fourth Regiment, ordered out in advance of Gibbs's column and instructed to carry fascines and ladders with them. The fascines were bundles of sugarcane to be thrown into the ditch in front of Jackson's line to fill it up. The sixteen ladders assigned for the operation were needed to scale the rampart. The fascines and ladders had to be in place in order for the advance to move forward smoothly once the attack began.

The Forty-fourth Regiment moved rapidly but quietly. They were almost in position when they realized their blunder.

They had forgotten the fascines and ladders!

Quickly they raced to the rear to pick up this equipment. Then they tried to dash back into position before the signal to attack.

Too late. The battle had commenced.[36]

It was Sunday morning, and at six o'clock two Congreve rockets rose with a screech on either side of the British line and signaled the start of battle, a battle that decisively changed the course of American history.

Immediately, Gibbs's column charged forward, directed at Jackson's left in order to have the cover of the woods. Drums beat a steady rhythm to accompany the advancing column.

Jackson surveyed his line and ordered all troops resting in the rear to move quickly to the rampart. Gun crews at the batteries tensed for action. The climactic moment of Britain's determination to seize and occupy the American southwest had arrived.

The army of redcoats came within range of the defenders. Suddenly the entire ditch responded with a blast of fire that virtually leveled the front ranks of the onrushing invaders. This was followed by another round and then another. The American ranks rotated, line after line: the first line delivered its destruction and stepped back to reload; the second line jumped forward, aimed, fired, and retreated as the third line took its place. There was not a moment's intermission in the musketfire.[37]

The initial confusion of the British offensive, occasioned by the failure of the Forty-fourth Regiment to have the ladders and fascines ready, spread among Gibbs's men as they neared to within a hundred yards of the American line. Instead of rushing the rampart, as planned, they paused instinctively at the first blast of shot and returned the fire. That action proved fatal. In imitation, the Forty-fourth also halted, threw down their ladders and fascines and started shooting too. And this hesitation of both the column and the Forty-fourth made them easy targets for the American marksmen as volley after volley thundered from the rampart into their ranks. Within moments the entire advance deteriorated into a reeling, confused army, verging on total disarray.

Soon the British officers barked out commands to advance, and the disciplined column began to move again. Some of the men scrambled into the ditch, but they had no means of scaling the rampart. There was no sign of the ladders and fascines. They panicked and cried out their distress.

From the rampart the fire poured directly into the faces of the advancing column. It was so withering that the troops recoiled. General Gibbs screamed at the men to reform and advance, but his commands went unheeded. The troops began a general retreat.

Pakenham rode forward from his position in the rear to halt the retreat and was killed. Gibbs too was struck down in the devastating fire. He was carried from the field, writhing in agony. He lingered for another day before death released him from his torment. General Keane was also painfully wounded in the groin and was borne to the rear. Now not a single senior officer remained in the forward position to assume command and rally the dispirited troops.

The destruction of the high command in one blow "caused a wavering in the column which in such a situation became irreparable," General Lambert later reported.[38] The brave Highlanders who crossed the field from the left to help their comrades came within 100 yards of the rampart, taking round after round from the Americans until more than 500 of them lay on the ground. At last they too turned and fled in horror and dismay.[39] "Before they reached our small arms, our grape and canister mowed down whole columns," said General Coffee, "but that was nothing to the carnage of our Rifles and muskets."[40]

When the attack began General Jackson hurried back and forth behind his line, particularly on the left side, to assure himself that all necessary precautions had been taken. He called words of encouragement to his men. Those not occupied with loading or firing cheered him as he went by. Once the battle became a general engagement, Jackson took a position on slightly elevated ground near the center of the line in order to have a good sweep of the line and a general view of the entire scene. He looked absolutely calm and composed as he watched, as though he had no doubt about the ultimate outcome of the battle. Few spoke to him, unwilling to disturb his concentration or flow of thought.

When the British columns broke, Thomas Hinds, whose Mississippi dragoons were positioned slightly to the rear, dashed up to Jackson and requested permission to pursue the fleeing troops. It was a terrible temptation, one Jackson no doubt ached to indulge. But it had hazard written all over it. Reluctantly, he shook his head.

Far to the rear of the British attacking force, General Lambert waited with his reserves. When he learned of Pakenham's death and the wounding of Gibbs and Keane he assumed command. He ordered the reserve troops forward. But he moved slowly and cautiously, expecting the Americans to counterattack. Pakenham had earlier ordered up the reserves, but the bugler was struck in the arm in the act of sounding the advance and dropped his bugle. The charge never sounded. Now the reserves could do no more than cover the retreat of the fleeing column. Fortunately Jackson decided against pursuit. His men would have run headlong into a powerful British reserve unit.[41]

Successful as the Americans were in the center and left side of their line, the situation on the right—the side nearest the river—was completely different. Keane's brigade, commanded by Colonel Robert Rennie, crept up on the Americans so quickly and so suddenly after the signal rocket exploded that the sentries at the American outposts had to scramble for their lives. Rennie's men pursued them and soon the troops of both sides were so intermingled that the American commander, Captain Humphrey, had to withhold his fire for fear of hitting his own men. At last the Americans managed to escape by racing over a plank stretched across the ditch to the rampart. Then Humphrey's batteries opened up. Rennie and two of his men reached the top of the rampart but were immediately cut down by the New Orleans sharpshooters, Rennie catching a ball in "one of his eyes." Had the entire British column followed quickly behind Rennie's successful advance, Keane might have breached Jackson's line. But Pakenham ordered him to support Gibbs instead of Rennie. It was a costly mistake. Keane led his men across the field to their subsequent destruction.[42]

At the extreme left of Jackson's line, where Coffee and his men guarded the cypress swamps, a detachment of British West Indian troops skirmished in the woods. Some succeeded in getting close to Coffee's position but then became mired and were drowned or captured.

As the British beat a retreat and Jackson's officers surrounded and congratulated him on their astounding victory, Old Hickory seemed a trifle apprehensive. He cast an anxious glance across the river. Why no movement? Why such silence? The quiet distressed him.

Then, suddenly, General Morgan's guns spoke. Jackson sighed with relief. He mounted the breastwork and turned to his men. "Take off your hats and give them three cheers!" he commanded. The army obeyed as it tried to discern what was happening nearly a mile and a half away.

What was happening was disaster. Disaster for the Americans. The defeat on the west side of the Mississippi was as total as the victory on the east side. Jackson had been oblivious to the needs and danger of his position across the river. He did not adequately reinforce it with troops, and so Thornton—despite a delay in getting into position because the Mississippi's currents had swept his flotilla downstream a mile and a half from the scheduled landing position—had little trouble in defeating the Americans. Morgan and Patterson only had time to spike their long-range guns before retiring. As the Americans fled in confusion and panic, an adjutant ran after them crying, "Shame, shame! Boys, stand by your general." But they would not listen, they would not stop, and General Morgan dejectedly followed them on horseback.[43]

Thornton and his men had just repaired many of Patterson's guns and were about to enfilade Jackson's line when news arrived of the disaster on the east bank, along with orders to retire, recross the river, and join the main army. All of Thornton's successful efforts went for nothing, and he reluctantly obeyed his orders. It was then late morning.

Hours earlier the battle in front of the Rodriguez Canal had ended. The entire assault had taken hardly more than two hours, the principal attack lasting only thirty minutes. When the grim business of counting the dead was done, the figures showed 13 American dead, 39 wounded, and 19 missing in action on January 8. British casualties amounted to 2,037, of which 291 were killed, 1,262 wounded, and 484 captured or missing.[44]

It was an incredible victory. A magnificent victory. Never again would Americans feel that they had to prove by force of arms that they could defend themselves. Never again did they lack confidence in their ability to protect their liberty and command the respect of the rest of the world.

The victory was shaped by the many advantages Jackson enjoyed in fighting the battle where he did. Most importantly, he was able to mass tremendous firepower behind the rampart and send it crashing into the faces of the onrushing enemy. The expert marksmanship of the defenders, especially the riflemen, was another factor in determining the magnitude of this victory. And Jackson had luck. It began when Keane decided to halt at the river, rather than head immediately for the city, and ended with the delays that stalled Thornton's attack on the west bank until after it was too late.

Jackson always said he was lucky. The luck of the Scotch-Irish.

CHAPTER 8

---◆◇---

Indian Removal

For the next ten days both armies watched each other, not certain as to their next move. General Lambert's first communication to Jackson asked for a truce to bury the dead and attend the wounded. The truce was readily agreed upon, and the dead were quickly interred, although Pakenham's body was reportedly encased in a hogshead of rum and shipped to Havana for reshipment to London. Then, at midnight, January 18, with fires still ablaze to fool the watchful Americans, the once proud British army silently decamped. The soldiers retired to their ships and sailed away.

Not until January 21 did Jackson find it prudent to remove the major portion of his army from behind the Rodriguez Canal. Two days earlier he had indicated to the Abbé Guillaume Dubourg, apostolic administrator of the diocese of Louisiana and the Floridas, that the return of the army to the city should occasion a public act of thanksgiving. "The signal interposition of heaven," Jackson wrote, "in giving success to our arms against the Enemy . . . while it must excite in every bosome attatched to the happy Government under which we live, emotions of the liveliest gratitude, requires at the same time some manifestation of those feelings. Permit me therefore to entreat that you will cause the service of public thanksgiving to be performed in the Cathedral." The abbé heartily approved the idea and said he would begin immediately to "make the dispositions for the ceremony, the brightest ornament of which, will certainly be *yourself*, General, surrounded by your brave army."[1]

On the morning of January 21 Jackson ordered the army drawn up behind the rampart for the last time. After reading an address to the troops which praised them for their bravery and skill, the General marched them back to New Orleans. It was the first time he had visited the city since the attack began.

The old and the infirm, women and children, all turned out to hail the noble rescuers of their city. "Every countenance was expressive of gratitude—joy sparkled in every feature on beholding fathers, brothers, hus-

105

bands, sons, who had so recently saved the lives, fortunes and honor of their families."[2]

On Tuesday, January 23, the day the abbé had decided to hold the religious service of thanksgiving, the streets were jammed with sight-seers, the balconies and rooftops alive with spectators. People gathered everywhere: in the great square opposite the cathedral that fronted the river, in the streets leading to the square, along the levee. The uniformed companies of Plauché's battalion formed two lines from the entrance of the square (by the river) to the church. A temporary arch was erected in the middle of the square, opposite the main entrance of the cathedral. The arch was supported by six Corinthian columns, and on each side of it stood a young lady—one represented Justice, the other Liberty. Under the arch, standing on a pedestal, were two children holding a laurel crown. Between the arch and the cathedral a number of lovely young girls took positions at regular intervals, each representing a different state or territory of the Union, all dressed in white with transparent blue veils and a silver star on their foreheads. Each held in her right hand a flag in-scribed with the name of the state she represented and in her left hand a basket of flowers. A lance embedded in the ground behind each young lady carried a shield with the name of a state or territory. The shields, linked together with a garland of evergreens and flowers, filled the dis-tance from the arch to the cathedral.[3]

Then, through the gate of the plaza strode the Hero of the Battle of New Orleans—a title almost instantly conferred on Jackson and one he would carry throughout his lifetime and beyond. He was accompanied by his staff. An enormous cheer burst from the crowd. People waved to him and called him by name. Repeated salvos of artillery announced his presence and saluted his magnificent achievement. Entering the square, the Hero was requested to proceed to the cathedral by the walk prepared for him. As he passed under the arch the two children lowered the laurel crown on his head.[4] The eight-year-old daughter of Dr. David Kerr stepped forward and congratulated the General on his victory in the name of the people of Louisiana. A ballad was sung to the tune of "Yankee Doodle." As he continued toward the church the young ladies strewed flowers in front of him and recited an ode especially written for the occasion.

At the porch of the cathedral the abbé, resplendent in his ecclesiastical robes, welcomed Jackson with a speech glowing with praise to the Al-mighty for having sent the country such a sublime "saviour." The crowd hushed to hear the response. "Reverend Sir," Jackson began, "I receive with gratitude and pleasure the symbolical crown which piety has pre-pared; I receive it in the name of the brave men who have so effectually seconded my exertions for the preservation of their country—they well deserve the laurels which their country will bestow. For myself, to have been instrumental in the deliverance of such a country is the greatest

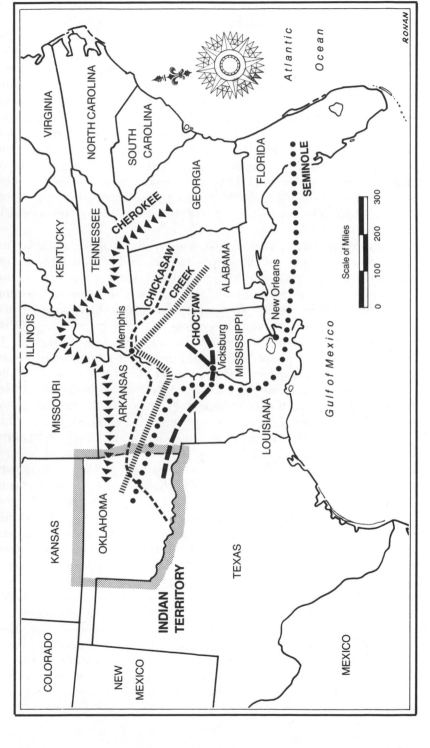

blessing that heaven could confer."[5] Jackson was then escorted into the cathedral to attend the *Te Deum,* after which he returned to his quarters accompanied by a guard of honor.

In Washington, at the beginning of the New Year, gloom and despair locked the nation's capital in hushed fear and anxiety. For months Washingtonians were unhappily conscious of the nation's shame and disgrace. From the very start the war had gone badly; now the capital lay in ruins, burnt by the enemy, and the government humiliated by its flight from the British invaders. Congress indulged itself with ill-tempered accusations of blame for the war's misfortune. Worse, rumors abounded that representatives from the Hartford Convention in Connecticut, which adjourned on January 5, 1815, were headed for Washington bearing constitutional revisions as the price of their continued acceptance of the Union.

Then, on February 4, in the midst of this frightful gloom and apprehension, came the report of the stupendous victory at New Orleans—and Washington went "wild with delight." The capital erupted in one long cheer of happiness and gratitude. The city was illuminated, the President's mansion thronged. Newspapers broke out their largest type to announce: "ALMOST INCREDIBLE VICTORY!!! Enemy . . . beaten and repulsed by Jackson and his brave associates with great slaughter. The Glorious News . . . has spread around a general joy, commensurate with the brilliance of this event, and the magnitude of our Victory."[6]

"Glory be to God that the barbarians have been defeated," shouted *Niles' Weekly Register.* "Glory to Jackson . . . Glory to the militia . . . Sons of Freedom . . . benefactors of your country . . . all hail."[7]

The news shot further north as fast as it could be carried, "kindling everywhere the maddest enthusiasm." Parades were organized, speeches extolled the bravery of the American militia, and Jackson was lauded as the "saviour of his country." "This day shall ne'er go by, from this day to the ending of the world, but He, in it, shall be remembered."[8]

Then, nine days later, and certainly before Americans could catch their breath over this ecstatic event, came the announcement that the commissioners in Ghent, Belgium had signed a treaty of peace with their British counterparts that ended the War of 1812. Men rushed through the streets screaming, "Peace! Peace! Peace!" And in Washington the delegates from the Hartford Convention, embarrassed and dismayed, slipped quietly out of town before anyone could remember their mission.

Jackson's role in bringing honor and glory to the nation made him a popular hero for the remainder of his life. In the public mind, the victory over the British was all associated with Andrew Jackson. Old Hickory! The Hero of New Orleans. He restored the nation's confidence in itself and its ability to maintain its freedom and independence against impossible odds.

Jackson was voted the thanks of the Congress and had bestowed upon him a gold medal. James Monroe sent him the congratulations of the President. "History records no example," he wrote, "of so glorious a victory, obtained, with so little bloodshed on the part of the victorious. . . . By these important services you have merited in an eminent degree the approbation of the Government and the gratitude of your fellow citizens."[9] Even Jackson now knew he had ascended to the ranks of the Immortals. The "morning of the 8th of January," he wrote, ". . . will be ever recollected by the British nation, and always hailed by every true american."[10]

Jackson's role in the War of 1812 was also crucial to the future course of American expansion. Not only did he spare the nation an almost certain amputation of territory in the southwest if the British invasion had succeeded, but he prepared the way for the immediate future growth of the American nation.[11]

At the moment he remained in New Orleans, where he lifted martial law only after he officially learned of the signing of the peace treaty. His stubborn refusal to end martial law until officially authorized to do so, even though everyone knew the war had ended, needlessly antagonized the people of New Orleans. Their gratitude toward him turned to resentment. As a consequence the Louisiana Senate purposely omitted his name from a list of officers to whom it extended its appreciation for saving the city.

One incident that particularly rankled was Jackson's arrest of a federal district judge, Dominick Augustine Hall, for issuing a writ of habeas corpus freeing a legislator named Louis Louailler, who had been jailed for writing a newspaper article that criticized the city's military authority. His imprisonment occurred prior to the lifting of martial law. Like everyone else in New Orleans, Judge Hall felt that martial law must end and he chose the manner of a writ of habeas corpus to express that belief. When the writ was handed to him, Jackson responded with an order of his own. "Having recd information that Domanic A Hall has been engaged in aiding abetting and exciting mutiny within my camp," he wrote Colonel Mathew Arbuckle, "You will forthwith . . . arrest and [confine] him, and make report of the same to head Quarters."[12] The order was immediately carried out, and by evening Hall was locked in the same barracks with Louailler.

Eventually, on March 13, 1815, official notification of the ratification of the peace treaty arrived in New Orleans. Almost instantly, Jackson lifted martial law. Louailler was released—he had been court-martialed and acquitted, but Jackson refused to free him—and Hall was permitted to resume his role as federal district judge. No sooner was he restored to office than Hall issued an order on March 21 for Jackson to show cause why he should not be held in contempt for refusing to obey the court order to release Louailler.

On Friday, March 24, 1815, at 10:00 A.M., the celebrated trial, *United States* v. *Major General Andrew Jackson,* began. The Hero appeared at the trial but Hall refused to allow him to read a prepared statement explaining why the complaint against him was invalid. The judge proceeded to find him guilty and imposed a fine of $1,000. "The only question," Hall said, "was whether the Law should bend to the General or the General to the Law."[13] But Jackson never claimed that the law should bend to his will. Under martial law he was the law, and he believed himself justified in what he had done.

The Hero of New Orleans paid the fine, much as it may have distressed him to do so. He was not prepared to defy Hall; he was unwilling to blemish his victory with a quarrel he was certain to lose. In a final display of spirit, he refused to accept $1,000 raised by popular subscription and requested that the sum be distributed among the families of soldiers who died in defense of the city.

The General's final days in New Orleans, prior to his return home, were spent quietly in the relaxed company of his family. A few days after the announcement of peace, Rachel and their adopted son, Andrew, finally arrived in New Orleans. Rachel was now an extremely stout, dark-complexioned, forty-seven-year-old woman, religious to the point of fanaticism yet warm and gently beguiling.

At a grand ball given in the Hero's honor, one complete with transparencies, flowers, colored lamps, a sumptuous dinner, and dancing, Rachel could scarcely believe such splendor possible this side of the heavenly throne. At supper she was placed opposite a transparency that read, "Jackson and Victory: They are but one." When the meal ended, Jackson and his lady led the way to the ballroom and there treated the guests to "a most delicious *pas de deux,*" country-style. "To see these two figures, the General, a long, haggard man, with limbs like a skeleton, and Madame la Generale, a short, fat dumpling, bobbing opposite each other like half-drunken Indians, to the wild melody of *'Possum up de Gum Tree,'* and endeavoring to make a spring into the air, was very remarkable, and far more edifying a spectacle than any European ballet could possibly have furnished."[14]

These final days in New Orleans were relatively happy ones for Jackson. He could enjoy playing the role of Hero and Savior. The old animosities toward him had dissipated with hardly a trace. On April 6, 1815, he finally departed the city for home after turning over his command to Edmund P. Gaines.

The trip north was one long, exhilarating ovation. "He is everywhere hailed as the saviour of this Country," reported John Reid. He has been "feasted, caressed & I may say idolized. They look upon him as a strange prodigy; & women, children, & old men line the road to look at him as they would at the Elephant. This is the sort of business in which he feels very awkwardly. . . . He pulls off his hat—bows graciously but as tho his spirit were humbled & abashed by the attention which is shown him."[15] Everyone in Nashville turned out to welcome the Hero when he arrived on May 15. A procession escorted him into town in a wild, enthusiastic demonstration. "I am at a loss to express my feelings," said Jackson in response to a welcoming speech given by Felix Grundy, the great War Hawk. "The approbation of my fellow-citizens is to me the richest reward."[16]

In the months immediately following his return to the Hermitage Jackson relaxed at home and tried to readjust to the relative calm of plantation life in a quiet southern community. And, as a matter of fact, the transition went well. The United States Army was reorganized in the spring of 1815 into the northern and southern divisions, with Jackson commanding the southern and Jacob Brown the northern, and the government allowed the Hero to name the Hermitage his headquarters, thus permitting him the luxury of attending to military business while managing his plantation and generally enjoying the life of a country gentleman. Moreover, a major general's pay of $2,400 a year, together with $1,652 in allowances, gave him a dependable income that substantially eased his life-style. He had achieved the good life in every possible way.

The General's staff lived with him, becoming practically part of his family. At various times they included Sam Houston, Richard Keith Call, Andrew Jackson Donelson, Robert Butler, James Gadsden, John and Samuel Overton, Dr. James C. Bronaugh (his personal physician), and John H. Eaton. One of Jackson's principal duties during this period was visiting the various Indian tribes (Creeks, Cherokees, Chickasaws, and Choctaws) in the area, holding ceremonial talks with them, and arranging land settlements in accordance with the several treaties that had been agreed upon. For one thing he was directed by the administration to execute Article IX of the Treaty of Ghent. This article stated that all possessions taken from the Indians subsequent to 1811 must be returned. Automatically that required Jackson to return approximately 23 million acres of land he tore from the Creek Nation at the conclusion of the Creek War. But Sharp Knife had no intention of returning the land. He blithely ignored Article IX and simply continued his policy of removing the Indians from the surrendered lands. And nobody stopped him, nobody dared.

The Cherokees protested that a section of the Creek cession belonged to them. They appealed to the administration in Washington, and William H. Crawford, the new secretary of war, accepted their argument and in a treaty signed on March 22, 1816, returned 4 million acres of land that the Treaty of Fort Jackson claimed for the United States.

Jackson raged. And he was not timid about sounding off to the secretary of war—or the President of the United States. "On the principle of right and justice," Jackson lectured Crawford, "the surrender ought never to have been made."[17] Crawford was shocked at the reaction he received to his treaty, not only from the Hero but from westerners generally who threatened him with political retaliation. Under the circumstances he decided to appoint a commission of three men to talk with the Indians and, if possible, conclude amicable treaties with the Cherokees, Choctaws, and Chickasaws. He naturally named Jackson to head the group and included General David Meriwether of Georgia and Jesse Franklin of North Carolina.

One of the principal tasks assigned to the commission was the necessity of fixing land boundaries between the various tribes and the United States. By this time Jackson had certain definite ideas about how the government should treat the Indians. They had developed over many years, especially when the Creek War seriously jeopardized American efforts to combat the invasion of British troops from the Gulf of Mexico. "The lower country is of too great importance to the Union," Jackson wrote to President James Monroe, "for its safety to be jeopordized."[18] Later Jackson particularized many of his ideas about the Indians and how they should be treated. For one thing, "I have long viewed treaties with the Indians an absurdity," he said, "not to be reconciled to the principles of our Government. The Indians are the subjects of the United States. . . . I have always thought, that Congress had as much right to regulate by acts of Legislation, all Indian concerns as they had of Territories." In short, Indians had no rights if they conflicted with the security of the United States. "The Indians live within the Territory of the United States," he declared, "and are subject to its sovereignty and . . . subject to its laws."[19]

After much haggling and with the help of a little bribery, the commissioners signed a treaty with the Cherokees on September 14, 1816. In addition to forcing the surrender of an enormous tract of Cherokee land to the south of the Tennessee River, the agreement promised peace and friendship between the United States and the Cherokee Nation. Furthermore, as payment for the removal of these Indians, the United States granted $6,000 annually for ten years to the tribe and $5,000 to be paid sixty days after the treaty was ratified.[20]

The Chickasaws proved a bit more difficult to convince, since Jackson insisted that they cede all their land on the north and south side of the Tennessee River and down the west bank of the Tombigbee River to the Choctaw boundary in Mississippi. In effect this would provide land for white settlers from Tennessee to the Gulf of Mexico.[21] As compensation the United States offered a grant of $12,000 per annum for ten years and $4,500 in sixty days for any improvements on the lands surrendered. When the Chickasaws resisted these terms, Sharp Knife again resorted to bribery—"a few presents," he liked to call them—and again, they convinced the chiefs to accede to his demands. It was a formidable purchase.[22]

Almost immediately, settlers poured into "this fertile country."[23] General Coffee and a number of other Tennessee cronies invested heavily in the area, forming the Cypress Land Company and purchasing excellent land at the foot of Muscle Shoals. Jackson himself speculated in the schemes, although his motive had less to do with economic gain than promoting the country's defense through white immigration into the area.

Early in 1817 the administration authorized Jackson to "extinguish the Indian titles" made in a treaty with the Cherokees in 1806.[24] This authorization was later broadened to permit Jackson to arrange an "exchange" of land with the Cherokees in accordance with an agreement concluded in 1808. It seems that the Cherokees had agreed in 1808 to surrender territory on the east side of the Mississippi River in return for land in Arkansas. In subsequent years several thousand Cherokees had moved to Arkansas but failed to cede a corresponding amount of land in the east. Jackson was now given the task of convincing the eastern Cherokees that they must provide a compensatory cession. He was also authorized to grant additional lands to those eastern Cherokees who would remove to the Arkansas River and the area immediately adjoining the Osage boundary line. With these negotiations Jackson became directly involved for the first time in implementing a policy he would convince himself was the best—if not the *only*—policy for the government to pursue toward the Indians, namely, their removal west of the Mississippi, beyond the states and organized territories of the United States.[25] And, as he always insisted, Congress had full authority to carry out this policy.

Naturally, the Cherokees contested the white man's version of what happened in 1808. They insisted that no exchange had been authorized by the Nation and that those Cherokees who moved to the Arkansas River did so on their own initiative without obligating the Nation in any way. All of which infuriated Jackson. He accused the chiefs, when they assembled before him, of calling him a liar. But then Andrew Jackson never liked to be contradicted—and certainly not by Indians. So he resorted to threats. "Look around and recollect what had happened to our brothers the Creeks," he warned. A similar fate awaited the Cherokees, he predicted, if they persisted in their "unfriendly & hostile" attitude.[26]

Justifiably frightened of what Sharp Knife might do, the eastern Cherokees signed the treaty prepared for them on July 8, 1817. They ceded 2 million acres of land in Georgia, Alabama, and Tennessee and received in return an equivalent amount of land on the west side of the Mississippi with the understanding that the United States reserved the right to build military roads and posts in the area if necessary. Those who removed—approximately 6,000 Cherokees over the next two years—received a rifle and ammunition, one blanket, and one brass kettle or a beaver trap. In addition, the United States agreed to provide flat-bottomed boats and provisions to assist in the removal.[27]

By the time Jackson had completed these negotiations, if not a few months earlier, he had definitely worked out in his mind the principal parts of his removal policy—a policy he would officially institute after he became President. The main thrust of the policy came from other statesmen, including past Presidents starting with Thomas Jefferson.[28] By the summer of 1817 he was reciting it to his good friend and fellow commissioner John Coffee, and parts of it showed up in his correspondence with the secretary of war and the new President, James Monroe. Jackson believed that the steady increase and movement of the white population was slowly surrounding and pressuring the Indians into adopting one of two possible courses of action: either "to become industrious Citizens" and accept the sovereignty of the states in which they lived; or "remove to a Country *where* they can retain their ancient customs, so dear to them, that they cannot give them up in exchange for regular society." In other words, he told John Coffee, they may stay put if they are "prepared for agricultural persuits, civil life, and a government of laws." They will become citizens of the United States, their property will be protected by law, and they will mingle with the rest of "civilized" society. For those Indians who preferred to retain "their ancient customs and habits," they must remove to a place beyond the states and territories in the vicinity of the Arkansas River. No other possibility existed except eventual extinction as a race. Removal of the Indians, he finally decided, was "the only means we have in preserving them as nations, and of protecting them."[29]

Jackson's commitment to the principle of removal resulted primarily from his concern for the integrity and safety of the American nation. It was not greed or racism that motivated him. He was not intent on genocide. He was not involved in a gigantic land grab for the benefit of his Tennessee cronies—or anyone else. After living with the Indian problem for many years and experiencing any number of encounters with the various tribes, friendly and hostile, he came to the unshakable conclusion that the only policy that benefited both peoples, white and red, was removal. The extinction of the Indian, in his mind, was inevitable unless removal was officially adopted by the American government.

Jackson got an opportunity to implement his ideas in the fall of 1820 when he was directed by the Monroe administration to negotiate a land-cession treaty with the Choctaw tribe. To Sharp Knife this was an invitation to achieve removal, and he told the secretary of state, John Quincy Adams, that the foreign policy of the United States must take into account the fact that "we are [presently engaged in] removing [the Indians] west of the Mississippi."[30]

He met the Choctaws at a place called Doak's Stand in Mississippi and there he told them that they must remove if they wished to remain Indians. If not, he said, "you must cultivate the earth like your white brothers. You must also, in time, become citizens of the United States, and subject to its laws."[31] It meant that they must be subject not only to the laws of the United States but the laws of the states in which they resided. It was that latter submission that troubled many Indians. Submission to state laws would slowly rob them of everything precious in their culture and society.

The Choctaws tried to resist Jackson's arguments, but he was determined to make them yield. Eventually, he threatened them—"If you refuse . . . the nation will be destroyed"—and they reluctantly capitulated. It was, they said, impossible to resist him. They ceded some of the finest land in the United States, according to one Mississippi newspaper. It was the heart of the Delta.[32]

The Treaty of Doak's Stand, signed on October 18, 1820, was a model of Indian removal. It disposed of an "alien" people and obtained rich lands in the delta of west central Mississippi. It is not surprising, therefore, that the state of Mississippi named its new capital after Andrew Jackson. It was a fitting tribute for his contribution to the state's growth and prosperity. It also marked the continuing destruction of the southern tribes as a presence within the boundaries of the sovereign states. Worse, it was the harbinger of what was to come for the Indian when Jackson became President of the United States.

CHAPTER 9

———————◇———————

The First Seminole War

WHEN THE REPUBLICAN PARTY in 1816 nominated James Monroe for the presidency over his nearest rival, William H. Crawford, General Jackson was doubly pleased because he detested Crawford (on account of the return of Indian land acquired in the Treaty of Fort Jackson) and admired Monroe. For a number of years he had supported Monroe's political ambitions, and during the late war he believed he enjoyed the Virginian's favor and assistance. Now he expected even greater deference—in particular, a free hand to deal with military problems in the south.

The appointment of John C. Calhoun as secretary of war was a good beginning, as far as the Hero was concerned. Calhoun told him that he participated "in those feelings of respect, which any lover of his country has towards you. In any effort to add greater perfection to our military establishment, I must mainly rely for support on your weight of character and information."[1] Even the President acknowledged the continuing debt the nation owed Jackson, as his recent success with the Indians amply documented. "The advantage of the late treaties with the Indians is incalculable," wrote Monroe.[2] Yet that advantage needed to be augmented, as both the President and Jackson knew full well. The southern frontier was unsafe as long as the Spanish occupied Florida and provided a haven for rampaging Indians.

The Spanish position in Florida was totally untenable after the War of 1812. Deserted by the British and incapable of defending—much less administering—the Florida province, the Spanish played a waiting game. They had long since identified the man intent on their expulsion. Andrew Jackson was only the latest in a long series of conspirators who lusted after Spanish possessions. And Spanish officials were quite convinced—correctly so—that he was prepared to sweep across the Gulf from Florida to Texas and then to Mexico. Other Americans had had such dreams of empire, but Jackson, with his demonstrated military skills, was the man who could most probably realize them.

One immediate problem for the Spanish was the so-called Negro fort.

116

This outrage stood alongside the Apalachicola River in Florida, some sixty miles from the American border. Fugitive American slaves occupied the fort and—by its very existence—encouraged other slaves to flee their servitude and join them. Every American slaveholder along the southern frontier reckoned the fort a threat to his safety and his property. Like other slaveholders, Jackson worried about the problem, and in his usual aggressive manner he attempted to solve it. In the spring of 1816 he wrote to Mauricio de Zuniga, the commandant of Pensacola, to warn him of the consequence if the situation did not improve. A "negro fort erected during our late war with Britain . . . is now occupied by upwards of two hundred and fifty negros many of whom have been enticed away from the service of their masters—citizens of the United States," he wrote. Their conduct "will not be tolerated by our government, and if not put down by Spanish Authority will compel us in self Defence to destroy them."[3]

That meant an invasion of Florida. The Spanish were as agitated by the presence of the fort as the Americans and just as anxious to destroy it, but they lacked the military strength to do so. Astoundingly, Zuniga told Jackson that he was willing to cooperate in the fort's removal and that if the renowned General "Andres" Jackson would care to assist in reducing the fort, he, the Spanish governor, would be proud to serve under him.[4] Not much later, in the spring of 1816, General Edmund P. Gaines, who constructed Fort Scott near the mouth of the Flint River north of the Florida border, sent an expedition across the border that blew up the Negro fort, killing 270 persons.[5] So much for the Negro menace.

Another American concern—and a pretext for intervention—was the marauding tactics of the Seminole Indians, who along with their Creek allies residing in Florida periodically raided Georgia settlements and then retired to the protection of villages inside the Florida border. During 1816 and 1817 a number of Seminoles refused to acknowledge American claims to lands acquired as a result of the Creek War and resisted all efforts to force their removal from those lands. This applied particularly to a small party of Seminoles living in Fowltown, just north of the Florida border, on land claimed by the United States under the Treaty of Fort Jackson. Neamathla, chief of the Seminoles in Fowltown, notified General Gaines that he could expect a bloody encounter if attempts were made to dislodge them. The challenge was irresistible. Forthwith, an expedition marched out of Fort Scott, reached Fowltown on November 12, 1817, and burned the town and drove off the warriors and women.[6] Nine days later the Seminoles took revenge by ambushing a large open boat conveying forty soldiers, seven women, and four children as it floated up the Apalachicola River toward Fort Scott. In one swift, horrible blood-bath the men and women were butchered—all but one woman, who was taken captive, and four men, who escaped by jumping overboard and swimming to shore.

Thus began the First Seminole War. Within weeks Gaines was authorized by the secretary of war to pursue the Indians and, if necessary, to cross the Florida line and "attack them within its limits . . . unless they should shelter themselves under a Spanish post. In the last event, you will immediately notify this Department."[7]

Intervention was one thing, but seizure quite another. And unquestionably seizure was the administration's real intention. So, within ten days of authorizing the invasion of Spanish territory in pursuit of Indians, the administration ordered General Jackson to Fort Scott to take command of the expedition. The action was appropriate in view of the General's overall command of the southern district. But the administration would have to be out of its mind if it expected Jackson to content himself solely with pursuing Indians. Designating him commander of the expedition was certain to embroil the Spanish—as it had before—and the administration had no reason to think otherwise. And in no way was Jackson cautioned about provoking a confrontation with the Spanish or creating a situation that could have international repercussions. Rather, his instructions were very broad. "Adopt the necessary measure," he was instructed by the secretary of war, "to terminate a conflict which it has ever been the desire of the President, from considerations of humanity, to avoid; but which is now made necessary by their Settled hostilities."[8]

Jackson thought the best way to terminate the conflict was outright seizure of Florida. But would Monroe authorize it? And was the President prepared to accept the consequences of expelling the Spanish from Florida? So Jackson put the question to him directly. "Let it be signified to me through any channel (say Mr. J Rhea) [a Congressman from Tennessee] that the possession of the Floridas would be desirable to the United States, and in sixty days it will be accomplished."[9]

Monroe later claimed that he was ill when the letter reached him and that he never spoke to Rhea. But Jackson actually did receive a letter from Rhea which gave him all the assurances he needed. "I expected you would receive the letter you allude to," Rhea wrote Jackson, "and it gives me pleasure to know you have it, for I was certain it would be satisfactory to you. You see by it the sentiments of the President respecting you are the same."[10] The letter seemed to approve Jackson's request—but it was dated January 12, whereas Jackson's letter to Monroe was dated January 6. Obviously Rhea's letter was written before Monroe received Jackson's; the mail could never have traversed a route from Nashville to Washington and back and left time for Monroe to signal acceptance of the proposal through Rhea.

In his own mind Jackson always believed he had permission to seize Florida and that the permission came straight from Monroe. And indeed it had. On December 28, 1817, Monroe wrote Jackson a very provocative letter. "This days mail will convey to you an order to repair to the command of the troops now acting against the Seminoles, a tribe which has long violated our rights, & insulted our national character. The mov'-

ment will bring you, on a theatre, when possibly you may have other services to perform depending on the conduct of the banditti at Amelia Island, and Galvestown."

Since the invasion in pursuit of the Indians had already been approved, what "other services" did Monroe have in mind if not the seizure of Florida? Naturally, the President had to be careful what he put on paper in case his letter should fall into the wrong hands; still, to make his point abundantly clear, he added: "This is not a time for you to think of repose. Great interests are at issue, and until our course is carried through triumphantly & every species of danger to which it is exposed is settled on the most solid foundation, you ought not to withdraw your active support from it."[11]

Jackson had always understood Monroe's true position with respect to Florida—as secretary of state under Madison, for example, Monroe had encouraged General George Mathews in 1811 to seize East Florida only to "disavow him when the action became embarrassing"[12]—just as the President understood his. So when his commander-in-chief spoke of "great interests" and settling every species of danger on "the most solid foundation," Jackson naturally believed he was being instructed to seize Florida.

In any event, once ordered to Florida, Jackson gathered his available troops, who numbered some 1,000 men, and on January 22, 1818, departed for Fort Scott. They covered the distance of 450 miles in forty-six days despite heavy rains that turned bad roads into ditches and greatly slowed the movement of the baggage wagons. He reached Fort Scott on March 9.

Jackson always had a good spy network from which he obtained excellent information throughout his military campaigns. On this occasion, he wrote, "it is reported to me that Francis, or Hillis Hago, and Peter McQueen, prophets, who excited the Red Sticks in their late war against the United States, and are now exciting the Seminoles to similar acts of hostility, are at or in the neighborhood of St. Marks. United with them . . . [are] Arbuthnot and other foreigners."[13]

Alexander Arbuthnot! A name that would later haunt Jackson's reputation long after the man had been hanged from the yardarm of his own ship. A Scot by birth, now seventy years of age, he had come to Florida from the Bahamas in 1817 to trade with the Seminoles and the Spanish. He exchanged knives, guns, powder, and blankets for skins, beeswax, and corn. He was so decent in his dealings with the Indians that the Seminoles invariably heeded his counsel and the Creeks conferred on him power of attorney to act on their behalf.[14] He in turn urged them to keep the peace and avoid the provocations that lead to war. Totally committed to the Indians and their interests, Arbuthnot believed they had been cynically used and then abandoned by the English as well as robbed and murdered by the Americans.

Soon Arbuthnot was joined by another British subject, the swaggering, roistering braggadocio Robert Ambrister, a former lieutenant of the Royal Marines. Like Arbuthnot, whom he despised as a weak and feckless man, Ambrister championed the Indian cause, but unlike Arbuthnot, he counseled the Seminoles to war against the Americans in defense of their rights and property. He strutted before them in his brightly colored uniform, barking orders and assuming the posture of command—all of which the younger Indians found irresistible. And he encouraged a war to which he one day forfeited his life.

After Jackson reached Fort Scott and fed his near-starving men three meat rations and one quart of corn, the General wheeled his army out of the fort and headed straight into Florida. He now commanded 3,000 troops, both regulars and volunteers, and an additional force of 2,000 Indian allies—most of whom, ironically, were Creeks.[15] From the site of the demolished Negro fort on the Apalachicola, he headed straight for St. Marks in Spanish territory which lay approximately seventy miles to the southeast of Fort Scott and ten miles from the coast. "The Spanish government is bound by treaty to keep her Indians at peace with us," Jackson wrote the secretary of war on March 25. "They have acknowledged their incompetency to do this, and are consequently bound, by the law of nations, to yield us all facilities to reduce them."[16]

On April 6, Jackson reached St. Marks and notified the Spanish commandant that he had come to garrison the fortress in order to "chastise" the Indians and the black brigands who were warring against the United States. His action, he said, was totally justifiable on the grounds of self-defense. The unfortunate commandant, who lacked a force with which to contest Jackson's demand, readily capitulated. The Americans occupied the fort; the Spanish flag was unceremoniously lowered, and the Stars and Stripes was run up the flagstaff in its place.[17]

Jackson found St. Marks empty of hostiles, but he did capture that "noted Scotch villain Arbuthnot who has not only excited but fomented a continuance of the war. I hold him for trial."[18] At the same time Captain Isaac McKeever, a naval commander cooperating with Jackson's expedition, captured Francis the Prophet (sometimes called Josiah Francis or Hillis Hadjo) and Himollemico, two Creek chieftains. McKeever lured them aboard his ship by flying the English flag. The unlucky Indians thought they had discovered allies and expected to find ammunition and powder.

"I had Francis the prophet & HoemalleeMecko hung on [April] the 8th," Jackson informed Rachel. "They will foment war no more."[19] Two days after the seizure of St. Marks, Jackson resumed his march. He swung his army toward the town of Chief Billy Bowlegs, on the Suwannee River, a hundred miles to the east. The town was a refuge for runaway slaves, and Jackson believed it also sheltered a strong contingent of Indians. The capture of this town and its inhabitants would speed Jackson's determination to crush all Indian resistance to the American presence in the south.

The route to Bowlegs's town lay through a flat and swampy wilderness, and in many places the army waded through extensive sheets of water. On April 16, after two brief skirmishes with some hostiles, Jackson reached the vicinity of Bowlegs's town. Without pausing he formed his lines of attack and sent his men into the Seminole town. But the Indians had been warned of his approach and had escaped across the Suwannee River.[20]

A few nights later the swaggering former Marine, Robert Ambrister, along with a white attendant, Peter B. Cook, blundered into Bowlegs's town unaware that their Indian friends had decamped and that Jackson and his army now occupied the village. They discovered their mistake soon enough. But something worse followed. On the person of one of the black prisoners a letter was found from Arbuthnot to his son, warning him of Jackson's approach.[21] Now Sharp Knife understood how the Indians had managed to escape him, how they had even contrived to slip away with their families and much of their supplies. "I hope the execution of these two unprincipled villains [Arbuthnot and Ambrister] will prove an awfull example to the world," he wrote to Secretary Calhoun.[22]

After putting more than 300 houses to the torch, Jackson turned around and headed for St. Marks, completing the march in five days. Almost immediately Old Hickory convened a court of twelve officers, presided over by General Gaines, to try Arbuthnot and Ambrister. After hearing the evidence, the court found the seventy-year-old Arbuthnot guilty of exciting the Indians to war and acting as a spy for them. He was sentenced to be hanged.

Ambrister was charged with aiding the enemy and assuming command of the Seminoles to wage war against the United States. The evidence against him was so strong that Ambrister pleaded guilty and threw himself on the mercy of the court. Nevertheless, he was found guilty and sentenced to be shot.[23]

On April 29, 1818, the sentences were carried out. As Arbuthnot was jerked up the yardarm of his own ship a group of Indians stared at him, scarcely understanding how so powerful a friend could be summarily executed by a foreign intruder. The executions made a deep and profound impression. General Andrew Jackson was a terrible, vindictive enemy against whom the Indians found only their graves and the confiscation of their property.[24]

Jackson did not witness the executions. To his mind, the two British subjects were guilty of inexcusable crimes and their punishments obligatory. He hoped that the executions would "convince the Government of Great Britain . . . that certain, if slow retribution awaits those unchristian wretches who . . . excite a Indian tribe to all the horrid deeds of savage war."[25] On the day of the executions he resumed his military campaign by marching toward Pensacola. "Pensacola must be occupied with an American force," he declared, "The Governor treated according to his deserts or as policy may dictate."[26]

While St. Marks was an inadequately defended garrison, Pensacola was the center of Spanish rule in Florida—and Jackson calmly informed the secretary of war of his intention to extinguish that rule. No doubt this decision was shaped by the information he received early in May that hundreds of Indians were assembling at Pensacola and with Spanish assistance were planning to attack American settlements.[27] On May 24, 1818, the General and his army arrived at Pensacola, easily sweeping aside a token Spanish force and capturing the town. The Spanish governor, Colonel José Masot, retreated to Fort Carlos de Barrancas outside the town, where he hoped to make a stand. Jackson went right after him and demanded his surrender. Masot refused. "Your Excy. has violated the territory of Spain by taking possession of the post of the Appelachy, and lowering the Spanish colours," he shrilled. "If your Excelly. will persist in your intentions to occupy this fortrass, I am resolved to defend it to the last extremity, opposing force to force."[28]

Jackson responded to this protest by dragging forward his single nine-pound piece and five eight-inch howitzers and aiming them at the fort. There was a slight puff of resistance that lasted only a few moments and then a white flag broke out over the fort. Masot had demonstrated his loyalty to his king by making at least one small gesture of defiance. Anything more was lunacy. So he meekly surrendered and marched his troops out of the fort. "All I regret," Jackson later wrote, "is that I had not stormed the works, captured the Governor, put him on his trial for the murder of [an American family recently killed in an Indian raid] . . . and hung him for the deed."[29]

Thus, with very little show of military might, Jackson had virtually annihilated the Spanish presence in Florida. In a proclamation issued immediately after taking possession of Pensacola, Jackson justified his actions by invoking the "immutable laws of self defence." The proclamation then announced the establishment of a provisional government for the Florida province. William King, colonel of the Fourth Infantry, was appointed civil and military governor of Pensacola, and Captain James Gadsden was appointed collector of the revenue.[30] The arrogance of the proclamation was positively colossal. In one stroke Jackson redirected governmental authority under powers he assumed by virtue of military conquest. It was worthy of the great Napoleon, whom Jackson himself greatly admired.

On June 2 Jackson notified President Monroe that the Seminole War was over now that St. Marks, Fort Gadsden (the old Negro fort), and the Barrancas were in American hands. "These were the hot beds," he wrote; the "possession of these points" was "essential to the peace and security of our frontier." Now if Monroe would spare him the Fifth Infantry and

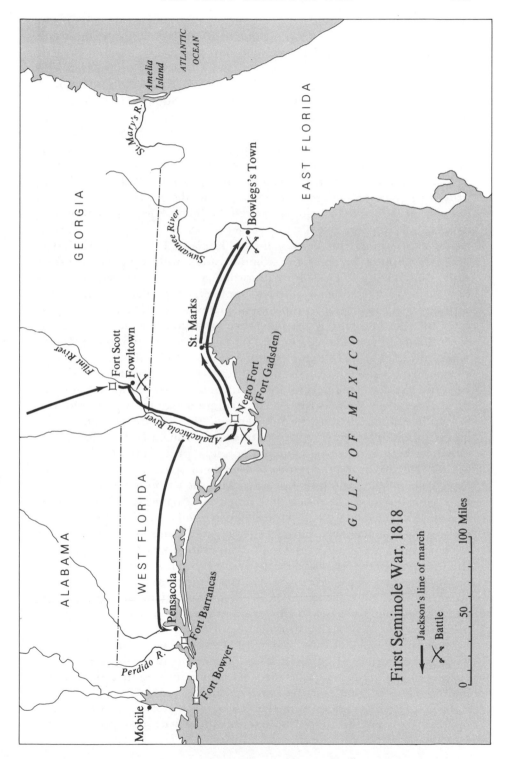

First Seminole War, 1818

Jackson's line of march

Battle

0   50   100 Miles

additional guns, he "would insure Ft St Augustine add another Regt. and one Frigate and I will insure you Cuba in a few days." But, he informed Monroe wearily, the war had crippled him physically. "I am at present worn down with fatigue and by a bad cough with a pain in my left side which produced a spitting of blood, have reduced me to a skelleton. I must have rest . . . so I must tender my resignation." He said he was returning to Nashville immediately.[31] Jackson was aching to capture Cuba but his health drove him home. His broken, bleeding body rebelled; he seriously considered resigning his commission.

At the beginning of this Florida adventure Monroe probably thought he could intimidate Spain into yielding this province by applying a little pressure.[32] Jackson, sent to do the job, provided more pressure than was needed: he had seized Florida, removed the Spanish government in residence, and executed two British subjects—all of which invited formal declarations of war from both Spain and England. Don Luis de Onís, the Spanish minister, battered the administration with indignant protests when official word of Jackson's extraordinary exploits reached Washington. At the very least he expected an apology, a repudiation of Jackson's action, and the General's punishment. The feckless President tried to duck his responsibility by leaving town, an action that the secretary of state, John Quincy Adams, interpreted as procrastination in the face of a "rapidly thickening" storm.[33] Upon his return to Washington, Monroe summoned his cabinet to assist him in resolving the embarrassment that he himself had created. His cabinet, it turned out, was divided. Calhoun, furious because Jackson's Rhea letter had gone over his head to Monroe for authorization to seize Florida, argued for censure and an official investigation. The secretary of the treasury, William H. Crawford, who may have begun to fear Jackson as a potential presidential rival in 1824, agreed. He also urged the return of Florida to Spain. The attorney general, William Wirt, said little but sided with the Calhoun-Crawford position. Only the dour, tough-minded, pragmatic Adams defended Jackson, arguing that the military action was defensive and necessitated by circumstances. Jackson had been authorized to invade Spanish Florida in pursuit of Seminoles; the object of the military operation was the submission of the Indians, not the Spanish, and therefore Jackson was perfectly justified in what he had done. To prevent further problems with the Indians, Adams argued, St. Marks and Pensacola must be retained.[34] Characteristically, Monroe saw a way to slip between the alternatives presented by his cabinet, a way of taking diplomatic advantage of what the Hero had accomplished while refusing to defend Jackson or take responsibility for what had occurred. He drafted a note to the Spanish minister that accused Jackson of exceeding his instructions but insisted that the General had been guided by military necessity in seizing St. Marks and Pensacola.

To John Quincy Adams went the delicate task of facing down an irate Spanish minister. Spain demanded the immediate restoration of St.

Marks and Pensacola, the disavowal of the military action, and "suitable punishment" for General Andrew Jackson.[35] Adams's reply was a masterful display of diplomatic skill in explaining the administration's position. The General would not be censured or punished, he said, because he was acting in self-defense. Moreover, Adams continued, if the Spanish commanders in St. Marks and Pensacola cannot police their provinces to prevent Indian outrages against innocent people, then "Spain must immediately make her election, either to place a force in Florida adequate at once to the protection of her territory . . . or cede to the United States a province, of which she retains nothing but the nominal possession, but which is, in fact, a derelict, . . . a post of annoyance to them."[36] It was a powerful argument, clearly and succinctly articulated, and it proved persuasive to the ministry in Madrid in view of Spain's recent loss of colonies in Central and South America.

Naturally, Jackson was shocked by the administration's obvious embarrassment and dilemma. He believed he had executed the presidential will. The General immediately reduced the problem to one of personalities, suspecting some enemy at work to tarnish the luster of his victory. He did not have far to look. There he was, big and hulking, sitting in the chair of the secretary of the treasury: none other than William H. Crawford, who had returned Indian lands in violation (said Jackson) of the Treaty of Fort Jackson.

But the General soon found that he had other enemies. As negotiations for the acquisition of Florida commenced, Congress reconvened in Washington in a feisty mood because its authority had been circumvented by the waging of an undeclared war with Spain. Moreover, there were those with political ambitions who now saw General Jackson as a dangerous threat to their future plans. It was obvious to everyone that Jackson commanded enormous popular support. He could easily rival the former War Hawk, Henry Clay of Kentucky, for western votes and Crawford for southern votes. Because of this, Old Hickory invited the kind of surgical stroke by master politicians that would cut him down to size. Both Clay and Crawford were skillful surgeons and with the beginning of the new congressional session privately announced that the operation would begin immediately.

Congressmen who supported the move to punish or censure Jackson did so for a wide variety of reasons: some regarded the Florida operation as a clear violation of the Constitution; some worried about Jackson's possible emergence as a "man on horseback," like Napoleon, who was a very recent and frightening example; others hated Monroe and wanted to damage his administration; and still others, who were committed to a states rights' philosophy, regarded the Florida expedition as a fearful extension of federal—and particularly executive—authority.

With pressure mounting in the capital for his censure, Old Hickory darted across the mountains, despite his many and lingering infirmities, and entered Washington on January 23, 1819. Already the House Committee on Military Affairs had brought out a report condemning the executions of Ambrister and Arbuthnot, probably the most vulnerable and troublesome of Jackson's actions in Florida. These "hellish machinations" were the work of "Mr Wm. H. Crawford and Mr Speaker Clay," the General wrote, and "I shall await the 4th of march next when mr Clay has no congressional privileges to plead."[37]

So one of the first "great debates" in Congress began when Henry Clay rose in the House of Representatives to do battle. Always a gut fighter, he enjoyed a verbal brawl. Mind and tongue honed to a sharp edge, he cut up opponents with a precision and speed unrivaled in either house. His long, cadaverous body, his lancing eyes, and his wide mouth outlined by thin, bloodless lips added dramatic tension to his appearance. His performances invariably stampeded the gallery and won shouts, whistles, and applause. Now, about to shred the great Hero of New Orleans, he stood in the well of the House and savored every moment of the drama. A slight smile flickered across his face. Then he began. He denied any personal animosity toward Jackson or the administration and insisted he was acting from principle. First he attacked the Treaty of Fort Jackson and cited it as the direct cause of the Seminole War. He then pilloried Jackson for the execution of Arbuthnot, subtly alluding to Alexander the Great, Caesar, and Napoleon and yet denying that Jackson had any designs on the liberty of the American people. The representatives, he said, "may bear down all opposition . . . even vote the general the public thanks; they may carry him triumphantly through this House. But, if they do . . . it will be a triumph of the principle of insubordination—a triumph of the military over the civil authority—a triumph over the powers of this house—a triumph over the constitution of the land. And I pray most devoutly to Heaven that it may not prove, in its ultimate effects and consequences, a triumph over the liberties of the people."[38]

From the moment he read this speech, Andrew Jackson conceived a full-blown and lasting hatred for Henry Clay. "The hypocracy & baseness of Clay," he told his friend and neighbor Major William B. Lewis, "in pretending friendship to me, & endeavouring to crush the executive through me, make me despise the Villain. . . . I hope the western people will appreciate his conduct accordingly," he added. "You will see him skinned here, & I hope you will roast him in the West."[39] On the other hand, because John Quincy Adams had defended him so ably in his dealings with the Spanish, Jackson further requested that the western newspapers give the secretary a "proper ulogium." Monroe, too, deserved praise because his message to the Congress at the beginning of the session reported the Florida expedition to the General's full satisfaction. The only question mark was Calhoun; but the President had assured Jackson of the war secretary's "liberality." Besides, said Old Hickory, Calhoun "has professed to be my friend, approves my conduct and that of the President." So Jackson anointed him a friend who had defended him in the cabinet—a false impression the secretary assiduously cultivated as the General gained political visibility.[40]

Despite the best efforts of Clay, Crawford, and their friends, the members of Congress decided against jeopardizing their position by offending the American people through the censure of its great war hero. On February 8, 1818, four resolutions condemning Jackson's actions in Florida were voted down by healthy margins.[41] Jackson exulted. He felt fully vindicated. His spirits soared so high that he even deigned to attend a presidential reception. And what a personal triumph that was! "From the earnestness with which the company pressed round him," wrote the observant Secretary Adams, "the eagerness with which multitudes pushed to obtain personal introductions to him, and the eye of respect and gratitude which from every quarter beamed upon him, it has as much the appearance of being his drawing-room as the President's."[42]

A few days later Clay called at Jackson's hotel to assure the General there had been nothing personal intended in his speech in the House. A superb politician, Clay always tried to divorce personal rancor from public disagreement. Unfortunately, Jackson had already left for New York to visit his godson at West Point. But he never reached his destination because he was mobbed everywhere he appeared. In Philadelphia it became a four-day celebration. In New York, "whenever the General went into the streets it was difficult to find a passage through them, so great was the desire of the people to see him." When he appeared at a reception, an orchestra invariably struck up *See the Conquering Hero Comes.* "Among the people," one newspaper said, ". . . his popularity is unbounded—old and young speak of him with rapture."[43]

The final disposition of Florida was skillfully handled by Adams. After considerable negotiations, Spain recognized that in view of her great losses in South America, and the ease with which the Americans could retake Florida, it made sense to sell this "derelict," as Adams had called it. The Spanish were particularly fearful of Andrew Jackson, or "the Napoleon of the woods," as they dubbed him. His latest incursion was known as the "Pensacola outrage." They were literally terrified of him, and that terror paralyzed their will to resist. In their minds they had created a monster capable of committing every affront they dreaded, including now an invasion of Cuba.[44] Adams realized the strength of his bargaining position and the Jackson "magic" that had withered the nerve of Madrid. Andrew Jackson was his unspoken advantage; the slightest hint of bringing him into military operation threw the Spanish into a paroxysm of alarm. So Adams informed Onís that the western boundary of the United States must be traced by a line from the source of the Colorado River in Texas—some Americans insisted that Texas was part of the Louisiana Purchase—to the source of the Missouri River and *"thence straight to the Pacific Ocean."* In effect, Adams demanded a continent, and ultimately the Spanish capitulated. On February 22, 1819, the Adams-Onís, or Transcontinental, Treaty was signed. Spain ceded to the United States all territories east of the Mississippi River known as East and West Florida at a cost to the United States of $5 million in assumed claims against Spain. The western boundary of the United States was fixed at the Sabine, Red, and Arkansas rivers and thence westward to the Pacific Ocean along the forty-second parallel. It was a magnificent achievement. Both sides claimed satisfaction. Spain retained Texas. The Americans gained a continent.[45]

A Washington newspaper hailed the acquisition of Florida as "an event among the most important in the annals of our history since 1803."[46] More than anything else, John Quincy Adams's diplomatic accomplishment was the triumph of an idea, the idea of continentalism. It was Adams who insisted that the boundary of the United States extend across the plains and mountains and touch the Pacific. But where Adams offered the transcontinental vision, Jackson provided the means by which that vision could be translated into reality. Without taking anything away from Adams in negotiating the treaty, the presence of Andrew Jackson, long schooled in the belief that all foreigners in the southwest must be expelled and, more importantly, encapsulating that belief with demonic determination, provided the essential military conquests to realize the dream. Without Andrew Jackson, or someone of his temperament, talents, and determination, the leap across a continent was unlikely, if not impossible.

CHAPTER 10

Governor Jackson

THE EXPANSION OF THE UNITED STATES, as represented in the Adams-Onís treaty, occurred at almost the same time that another question arose to distress and frighten the nation: slavery. It arose in the form of an application by Missouri for admission to the Union as a slave state. After a prolonged and acrimonious debate, a compromise was arranged by which Missouri entered the Union as a slave state while Maine was detached from Massachusetts and entered the Union as a free state—thereby preserving the balance between slave and free states—and, except for Missouri, slavery was restricted north of the parallel 36°30' within the territory acquired by the Louisiana Purchase. Many southerners complained about the compromise, and Jackson, too, was troubled. He clearly worried over the nation's future.

> The Missouri question so called, has agitated the public mind, and that I sincerely regret and never expected, but that now I see, will be the entering wedge to seperate the union. It is even more wicked, it will excite those who is the subject of discussion to insurrection and masacre. It is a question of political ascendency, and power, and the Eastern interests are determined to succeed regardless of the consequences, the constitution or our national happiness. They will find the southern and western states equally resolved to support their constitutional rights. I hope I may not live to see the evills that must grow out of this wicked design of demagogues, who talk about humanity, but whose sole object is self agrandisement regardless of the happiness of the nation.[1]

As the nation breathed a sigh of relief at having avoided internal conflict over the Missouri question, confirmation arrived from abroad that Spain had finally accepted the treaty and that Florida at long last belonged to the United States. And no sooner did the President receive this information than he wrote to Jackson and renewed a previous offer to him to assume the governorship of the newly acquired territory. Will you take it, he asked? "The climate will suit you," he purred, "and it will give me pleasure to place you in that trust." Monroe pressed Jackson to make his decision quickly because Congress would adjourn on March 3, and he wanted confirmation before the end of the session.[2]

Jackson's many friends in Washington and Nashville saw the advantages of his becoming governor. Patronage was one; land acquisition was another. But such motives held no interest for the General. Rather, what operated powerfully on Jackson was the fact that the appointment tended to vindicate his entire course of action throughout the Seminole War. He had taken considerable criticism over his invasion. Perhaps if he accepted the post for a short term he could establish the territorial government on a firm basis, take care of his friends, win a measure of vindication, and then return home. Also, he could savor the delight of presiding over the formal ouster of Spanish rule from Florida. So, on February 11, he replied to Monroe and said he was willing to accept the appointment provided the President permitted him to resign it as soon as the territorial government was organized and in full operation.[3] He was commissioned in March, 1821, received a salary of $5,000 plus expenses—the same he received as general of the army—and given authority not only as governor but as captain-general of Cuba, which meant complete military command throughout the territory. He also had authority to suspend officials not appointed by the President, but he was forbidden to lay new taxes or grant public lands.

Shortly after accepting his commission as territorial governor, Jackson resigned from the army effective June 1, 1821. His illustrious military career now concluded, he was about to embark on a new career in search of even greater fame. Together with his wife and the "two Andrews," as he called his adopted son, Andrew Jackson, Jr., and his ward, Andrew Jackson Hutchings, he took passage down the Mississippi River and eight days later, on April 22, arrived at New Orleans. Rachel was aghast by what she saw along the route, especially in New Orleans. "Great Babylon is come up before me," she gasped. "Oh, the wickedness, the idolatry of the place! unspeakable the riches and splendor." But at least she had the consolation of her religion. "I know I never was so tried before, tempted, proved in all things. I know that my Redeemer liveth, and that I am his by covenant promised."[4]

From the beginning of the negotiations to transfer Florida, the Spanish behaved rather badly. They virtually invited Jackson's wrath. And they got it. Colonel José Callava, the Spanish governor, treated the Jacksons contemptuously when they arrived in Pensacola. He steadfastly refused to meet with the General and work out details for the transferral until he received explicit (and written) orders from the governor of Cuba. Incendiary words shot back and forth between Callava and Jackson for several weeks before the difficulties were finally smoothed over and the date for the delivery of the Floridas agreed upon: July 17, 1821.[5]

On Tuesday, July 17, 1821, at 7:00 A.M., American ceremonial soldiers marched into Pensacola, a band blaring their arrival. The whole town seemed agitated and in motion, excited by what was about to happen. A crowd lined the square in front of Government House, where the ceremony would take place. But there was no shout of joy as the American troops marched in. If anything there was a sense of apprehension. The largely Spanish population had only a vague idea of what life would be like under American rule.

The American troops took their position in front of Government House opposite a small Spanish garrison retained for the ceremony of transition. General Jackson and his staff rode in on horseback. Callava stepped forward and the two men greeted each other in formal terms. It was now 10:00 A.M. Jackson handed the Spaniard the instruments of his authority to take possession of the territory, and Callava then declared that by virtue of the special mandate dated May 5, 1821, at Havana he herewith surrendered West Florida to the American general. Then, slowly, solemnly, the Spanish flag was lowered and the American ensign hoisted 100 feet into the air while the band struck up "the tune of 'long may it wave, o'er the land of the free and the home of the brave.'" An American war vessel anchored in the bay boomed a salute, and Spanish Floridians standing in the square "burst into tears to see the last ray of hope departed of their devoted city and country."[6]

On June 6, 1821, a similar ceremony at St. Augustine had transferred East Florida to the United States. Colonel Robert Butler, adjutant general for the southern district, acted for Jackson in the transfer, receiving it from Don José Coppinger.

From the very beginning of his tenure as governor, Jackson was forced to work against impossible odds. To begin with, Callava remained on hand as a diplomatic agent finishing up the king's business, and he created all manner of trivial difficulties. First it was the ownership of cannons at the forts, then provisions for the Spanish garrisons during their journey from Florida to Cuba; thereafter, it was a dispute over documents involving property of a deceased landowner. Far worse, however, was Jackson's treatment by the Monroe administration. Not only had the most important officials of the territory—judges, district attorneys, secretaries, collectors—been appointed in Washington, but the President made his selections without consulting Jackson. "Not one of those I recommended is appointed," complained Jackson.[7] While the General was given extraordinary authority as governor, his real power was strictly limited. For example, he had no right to grant or confirm titles or claims to land to any person, nor could he impose or collect new or additional taxes.

Despite these problems, Jackson set to work at once to establish a workable American government for Florida. One of his first decrees organized the territory into two counties: Escambia, the area between the Perdido and Suwannee rivers, and Saint Johns, the area east of the

Suwannee. Three revenue districts were established: Pensacola, St. Marks, and St. Augustine. Jackson created a civil government for each county by appointing mayors and aldermen for the principal towns and commissioning justices of the peace. He also empowered the mayors and aldermen, acting as the town councils, to levy the taxes needed to support the town governments—an action later criticized as a violation of Jackson's authority. In judicial matters the Governor served as the court of highest appeal, and no capital punishment was permitted without his express consent. Five of the ten justices of the peace in each county constituted the county court. In civil proceedings Spanish laws were to be followed, but in criminal proceedings, common law. Thus trial by jury was assured in all criminal cases. For each county the Governor appointed a clerk, sheriff, and a prosecuting attorney.[8]

The indisputably statesmanlike reform of the governmental system of Florida[9] was accompanied by other decrees touching a wide range of problems. Jackson established a board of health under the direction of Dr. James Bronaugh and ordered repairs for the several hospital buildings in the Pensacola vicinity. There were ordinances—published in Spanish and English—for the "preservation of health," community protection, establishment of rates of pilotage, and registration of all inhabitants who wished to become American citizens.[10]

At Rachel's urging, Jackson also cracked down on such ungodly activities as she pointed out to him. Sabbath breaking seemed the worst in her eyes, and Jackson issued a decree to put an end to it. Violation meant a $200 fine and the posting of a $500 good-behavior bond. And within a few days an incredible change settled over the community—or so she said. "What, what has been done in one week!" Rachel exclaimed. "Great order was observed; the doors kept shut; the gambling houses demolished; fiddling and dancing not heard any more on the Lord's day; cursing not to be heard."[11]

One of the first of the President's appointees to arrive in Florida was Eligius Fromentin, an ex-Jesuit who had been expelled from France during the Revolution and had come to America and married a fortune. Monroe named him federal judge for West Florida. Wily, conspiratorial, suave, urbane, and well educated, though not especially competent as a jurist, he soon took up with Callava, with whom he had much in common. Callava himself was a handsome, dignified, exquisitely mannered Castilian who had won rapid promotion during the peninsula campaign and had been appointed colonel and governor before he reached the age of forty. The two men quickly developed a close relationship and were soon joined by another ambitious entrepreneur, John Innerarity, the Pensacola representative of the trading house of Forbes and Company.

The first in a series of explosions that rocked Florida, and involved Jackson, Fromentin, and Callava, among others, occurred in mid-August 1821, when Henry Brackenridge, the *alcalde* (mayor) of Pensacola, brought to Jackson the plight of one Mercedes Vidal, a free quadroon who was the illegitimate daughter of the late Nicholas Maria Vidal. Vidal, who died in 1806, left large landholdings to his several half-caste children. Forbes and Company were designated executors of the will but failed to do anything about arranging a settlement. The surviving Vidals went to court for an accounting, but John Innerarity disregarded the court's ruling or the Spanish governor's directives that the papers relevant to the case be delivered.[12] Mercedes Vidal, one of the children, managed to obtain copies of enough documents to substantiate her claim for her inheritance and raise serious questions about the activities of the company and the reasons for delaying a settlement. She retained Brackenridge and Richard Call as attorneys and demanded immediate action because of her suspicion that the records had recently been transferred to the residence of Lieutenant Domingo Sousa, one of Callava's clerks, prior to their intended removal to Havana.[13] The pathetic story of this unfortunate woman, cheated of her inheritance for the past fifteen years, sent Brackenridge scurrying to Jackson rather than Judge Fromentin because the Governor exercised supreme judicial authority. Jackson demanded proof of the charge. Brackenridge showed him the documents. Hauled before the glowering Jackson, the terrified Sousa admitted conveying the papers to the house of Callava, whereupon Jackson sent a guard to Callava's house to demand the papers.

When the guard caught up with Callava, dining with Fromentin, Innerarity, and others, the guard was told in response that a royal commissioner was not subject to such demands. Whereupon Callava was taken into custody and dragged before Jackson. For two hours the two men screamed and ranted at one another, Jackson demanding the papers and Callava refusing to give them up. The shouting, banging, and gesticulating must have been horrendous. At last Jackson could stand it no longer and remanded Callava to prison. The Spanish officers who witnessed this last scene stood dumbfounded. "The Governor, Don Andrew Jackson," one of them wrote, "with turbulent and violent actions, with disjointed reasonings, blows on the table, his mouth foaming, and possessed with the furies," ordered the imprisonment of His Catholic Majesty's Royal Commissioner and Governor.[14] Callava was summarily carted off to the calaboose, a small, dirty, uncomfortable building erected by the Spanish many years before. As he entered the jail, accompanied by a large contingent of Spanish officers, Callava was suddenly struck by the insanity of it all. He reared back and roared with laughter. Soon chairs, cots, and beds were brought in, along with food, cigars, claret, and champagne. The Spaniards amused themselves by performing uproariously funny imitations of "Don Andrew Jackson, Governor of Florida." They made a night of it.

The next morning Jackson issued a writ to have the Vidal papers removed from Callava's house. Once the papers were obtained the Governor signed an order discharging the prisoners. In fact he emptied the entire calaboose.[15]

Meanwhile Fromentin had issued a writ of habeas corpus for Callava's release, and Jackson was obliged to summon the judge to instruct him on the proper use of his authority. Jackson had acted well within his judicial powers, and Fromentin's "interference," he told the judge, only encouraged the Spanish in their "mischief-making." In reporting the matter to John Quincy Adams, the Governor said that "the lecture I gave the Judge when he came before me will, I trust, for the future, cause him to obey the spirit of his commission, aid in the execution of the laws, and administration of the Government, instead of attempting to oppose me, under Spanish influence." In effect, Fromentin had encouraged civil disobedience and insubordination, Jackson declared. Then, mindful of the Vidal family and their plight, he expressed a deeply felt conviction. "I did believe, and ever will believe, that just laws can make no distinction of privilege between the rich and poor, and that when men of high standing attempt to trample upon the rights of the weak, they are the fitest objects for example and punishment. In general, the great can protect themselves, but the poor and humble, require the arm and shield of the law."[16]

This was one of Jackson's abiding principles. Long before he became President of the United States he articulated the fundamental doctrine of Jacksonian Democracy: the obligation of the government to grant no privilege that aids one class over another, to act as honest broker between classes, and to protect the weak and defenseless against the abuses of the rich and powerful.

Jackson then proceeded to hear the Vidal case, and not unexpectedly he ruled in favor of the heirs. But there were many subsequent appeals before the case was finally adjudicated. Some congressmen thought of demanding an investigation into the affair but, after recollecting Jackson's popularity and the outcome of the last such inquiry, dropped the idea.

Almost immediately upon his release from prison, Callava bolted to Washington to protest his treatment. As in the past Secretary Adams defended Jackson and placed much of the blame for what happened on the Spanish because of their procrastination in handing over Florida to the United States. He even justified the imprisonment of Callava.[17]

But blame for the incident belonged in both camps. Callava's conduct was clearly provocative, but Jackson could have prevented the unseemly outcome of the affair. His official position demanded tact, generosity, and consideration of a defeated foe, the more so in view of Spanish sensitivity about honor and pride and outward appearance. Jackson need not have imprisoned Callava. It served no purpose except to worsen the situation and make the Governor look ridiculous.

All of which convinced Jackson that he must leave Florida as soon as possible and return home. He hated every moment of his term as governor, and some of his actions proved it. The governorship had been a mistake from the first. Monroe never trusted him enough to accord him complete freedom. The presidential appointments also rankled. And then to suffer the defiance of Spanish officials aided and abetted by their American allies was more than duty required. It was time to go home.

Still, Jackson had served most creditably. A government had been established with legal processes that got Florida off to an excellent institutional start. In addition, Old Hickory proved remarkably effective in placing able men in sensitive slots so that the territory's interests and needs were honestly and wisely handled. Moreover, Jackson encouraged many cultural activities to assist the "Americanization" of Florida. On the day he arrived in Pensacola the process began with the opening of the Commonwealth Theatre. In August a printing press arrived and soon there was a circulating library with a reading room that boasted fifty newspapers and other periodicals.[18]

As long as Jackson represented the United States government in Florida and administered its laws he insisted that there would be "no distinction between the rich and poor the great and ignoble," that the government would be run for the benefit of all.[19] To guarantee a democratic process, he believed that the franchise must be extended to every freeman. "All freemen residents will be bound by your laws," he wrote to Bronaugh, ". . . and of right, ought to be entitled to a voice in making them." His broad definition of the franchise did not exclude free blacks or, presumably, Indians who remained in Florida and became citizens, as his treaty with the Cherokees in 1817 suggested.[20]

Jackson served as governor of the Florida Territory for slightly more than eleven weeks. It was longer than he ever intended. As early as October he had alerted Monroe of his desire to return to Tennessee. In arguing his need to go home he pleaded the poor health of his wife, never mentioning that his own was far worse. His formal letter of resignation, dated November 13, 1821, was hand-delivered to the President by Dr. Bronaugh, and Monroe accepted it officially on December 1, 1821.[21]

On balance Jackson's tenure was more successful than contemporaries or historians have allowed. Of course it was needlessly turbulent. True, he acted like a despot at times. But he understood the importance of uniting East and West Florida and providing democratic rule—which had been his primary goals. More than anything else, he desired the immediate integration of the territory into the United States, culturally as well as politically. As he told President Monroe, "Congress ought to provide an energetic code of law for its government, that may as far as possible . . . Americanize the Floridas."[22]

On the night of October 4 a farewell dinner was tendered the Jacksons by the military officers and citizens of Pensacola. "I have made no discrimination of persons," Jackson declared in a prepared speech to them. "My house has been surrounded by no guards, . . . all have had free admittance . . . when they required my aid for the protection of their rights."[23] Three days later a fine carriage drawn by four gray horses departed Government House with the Jacksons aboard, and after a leisurely trip they arrived in Nashville on November 7 and were given a handsome and brilliant reception.

An embarrassed administration in Washington was happy to see him go. But not the American people. They saw his tenure as another outstanding accomplishment; in their eyes his struggles reflected once more his democratic commitment to all the people, his patriotic purpose. He had defended the weak against the powerful, the poor against the mighty. A man of his accomplishments and democratic principles, they said, did not belong on a farm, rusticating in Tennessee. Such a man was needed in Washington. Such a man belonged in the White House.

CHAPTER 11

---◁▷---

An Era of Corruption

AT THE AGE OF FIFTY-FIVE and fresh from the swamps and horrendous squabbling of Florida, Andrew Jackson returned to the Hermitage a sick and exhausted old man. He verged on physical collapse. He suffered bodily discomfort that was constant and frequently unbearable. From 1821 until his death in 1845 Jackson endured physical pain practically every day of his life. There were two bullets lodged in his body, one of which regularly formed abscesses and produced spasms of coughing resulting in massive hemorrhages. He had also contracted dysentery and malaria for which he periodically poisoned himself by taking large doses of mercury and lead in the form of calomel and sugar of lead. Still, Andrew Jackson would not yield to the infirmities of his pain-wracked body. It, too, must bend to his imperious will.

Shortly after his return to Tennessee from Florida, the General suffered a severe physical breakdown. For four months, he wrote, "I have been oppressed with a violent cough, and costiveness." This was followed by an excruciating attack of dysentery that totally immobilized him. And, for the first time, he began to complain of the "great quantities" of phlegm he brought up with each coughing spell. His lungs, irritated by perpetual inflammation on account of the bullet wound, had finally produced the characteristic bronchiectasis—which means he would be tormented by excessive phlegm for the remainder of his life.[1]

When his health cracked in the spring of 1822 and he realized he must rest or face the prospect of imminent death, Jackson began to take stock of his life. He pondered the welfare of his children and how he had neglected them in the past few years. "I have my little sons including Lyncoya, at school, and their education has been greatly neglected in my absence. Justice to them, require my attention when I have health to give it." The "two Andrews," as Jackson called his children, included his adopted son Andrew Jackson, Jr., and his ward, Andrew Jackson Hutchings. Andrew Jr. turned fourteen on December 4, 1822, and would soon begin elementary classes at Cumberland College, formerly Davidson

137

Academy, in Nashville. The other Andrew, the son of John Hutchings, Jackson's onetime business partner, came to live with the Jacksons in 1817 when his father died and designated the General his guardian. Just a lad of eleven, young Hutchings caused Jackson countless emotional headaches. Yet the General loved these two boys very deeply and never withdrew his affection or support despite the many problems they both visited upon him.

In a different way, Lyncoya was another problem. The young Creek, now ten years of age, had been raised by Jackson from infancy, and although accustomed to a white society, he retained some "Indian habits." At the age of five he fashioned a bow "after the manner of the Indians," and with his face smeared with warpaint he would jump out from behind bushes to frighten other children. Still, Jackson hoped to enroll him in West Point when he grew older because he believed it was the best school in the country.[2]

In addition to the "two Andrews" and Lyncoya, there were numerous wards in the Jackson household, both male and female, whose natural parents, for one reason or another, could not raise them. Inevitably the Jacksons were asked to assume the responsibility, and almost without exception they agreed. Unquestionably, the General's favorite was his nephew, Andrew Jackson Donelson, the son of Samuel Donelson, who became Old Hickory's ward in 1805. He showered the young man with every possible favor and attended carefully to his education, as he did all his wards. He was gratified when young Donelson elected to enter West Point as a cadet in 1817 and supremely pleased when he learned that the young man had graduated second in his class. After Donelson graduated he served in the army for two years under Jackson as aide-de-camp before entering Transylvania University in Lexington, Kentucky, in 1822 to study law. Later he served his uncle as private secretary.

His children and wards gave Jackson much pleasure during his months of convalescence. But he was absolutely dependent upon his wife, Rachel. "Aunt Jackson," as her many nieces and nephews called her, or "Sister Rachel," as her brothers and sisters referred to her, had become almost saintlike in her patience, devotion, understanding, and good works. She was known by all as an extremely pious and religious woman whose greatest pleasure was churchgoing and listening to sermons about her Redeemer. Every clergyman to pass through Nashville was invited to the Hermitage. In 1823 Jackson built a church for his wife on the Hermitage grounds, just a short distance from their home. In one of her few surviving letters—most of them were destroyed in the Hermitage fire of 1834—written to her brother John during a particularly trying period in Florida, she said that she yearned to return home, and only her unshakable religious faith gave her the courage to endure her homesickness.

Tell our friends and all I hope to see them againe in our own Country and to know it is the best I Ever seen— What a pitty that some do not know when theay ar well of in this world theay not only hurt themselves but those that is innocent—But stop say to Sister Mary I have Herd but one sermon sinc I herd Mr Hodge he promised me to Come to this place in june but no he never came . . . Mr J has been very unwell & no wonder my health is Delicate—The Lord is my help in him will I trust & I will praise him with joyful lips remember me to all my Dear friends The young ones how I want hear them Tell that Jesus the hope of glory is formed in them tell Brother Sanday I have maney things to say to him—farewell my Dear Brother & may you say as pious job I know that my redeemer Liveth[3]

Jackson's recovery after his return home was hastened not only by Rachel's devoted care but the many friends and relatives who regularly visited him and buoyed his spirits. Both Rachel and Andrew loved to entertain and, of course, they had the means to do it lavishly. Their home, the Hermitage, provided the necessary setting. Plain, commodious, solid, and built of brick, it stood two stories high. The front faced south, and a guest entered the house through a porch into a spacious hall at the end of which an airy and well-lighted staircase ascended in a spiral to the second floor. There were four rooms leading off the central passageway on the ground floor; the northwest room was the dining room; the southeast and southwest rooms were sitting rooms; and the northeast room was the Jacksons' bedroom, which had a door leading into the garden.

In entertaining visitors, Jackson rarely sat at the head of the table, but preferred to sit between two ladies, "seeking a chair between different ones at various times." He was "very easy and graceful in his attentions," always free, sometimes playful, but never undignified or forward. He had great powers of attention and concentration without appearing gossipy. He had developed into a skillful conversationalist but at times mispronounced words or used them incorrectly; "and it was remarkable, too, that when he did so it was with emphasis on the error of speech, and he would give a marked prominence in diction."[4]

Rachel matched Jackson's graciousness and warm hospitality, exuding "the very personification of affable kindness." She spoke low but quick, with short and wheezing breaths. She "was once a form of rotund and rubicund beauty, but now was very plethoric and obese, and seemingly suffered from what was called phthisis." Because of her supposed "phthisis" her doctor prescribed a pipe, so she often rose from her bed at night to smoke for relief. Sometimes she smoked cigars, which startled easterners unaccustomed to such habits among females.[5]

On one occasion the Jacksons entertained a wedding party and included among the guests Judge John Overton, Jackson's longtime friend; the Reverend Dr. O. Jennings, the Jacksons' local Presbyterian pastor, whose daughter was the bride; and Henry Baldwin, one of the groomsmen. The ceremony concluded, the guests streamed into the spacious hall of the Hermitage and after several hours of eating and drinking, a small knot of guests sat down with Jackson and his wife in one of the rooms for an evening of conversation. Judge Overton, a "queer-looking little old man," came in first. Small, sharp-featured, with a gourdlike bald head and peaked Roman nose, "he had lost his teeth and swallowed his lips." Since his narrow, prominent jaw curved slightly upward, observers claimed there was always a danger that nose and chin would collide when he talked. As he sat in the Hermitage this day, a bandanna thrown over his bald head, he kept "mounching, mounching, mounching" on his toothless gums, looking for all the world like the "Witch of Endor." Next to him sat Jackson, his gray hair always standing straight up and out. Extremely slender and slightly round-shouldered, he stood six feet tall and had strong cheekbones, a lantern jaw, a long, straight nose, and a mouth which "showed rocklike firmness." His teeth were long and loose "and gave an ugly ghastly expression to his nasal muscle." As he conversed, Jackson spoke volubly and with animation, sometimes a bit vehemently and with much declamation, but never without "perfect dignity and self-possession." Next to Jackson sat Dr. Jennings and beside him the smiling Rachel with young Baldwin close by.[6]

In no time the conversation turned to religion and Jackson ventured to defend the "soo-blime" (as he pronounced it) concepts of Swedenborgianism. Jennings challenged his remarks and the General began a harangue which got more animated by the minute. His eyes flashed, hair stood at attention, and his clenched right hand gestured for emphasis.

The group was delighted to see the General in such splendid form. Back and forth went the argument, and even the Witch of Endor joined in. "Crunch, crunch, crunch," went his chin and nose as they whacked away at each other. "Mumble, mumble, mumble," was all that could be heard. Finally he let out an oath as he tried to win the attention of the group. "By God!" he shouted. Then he realized his mistake. He turned to Rachel, sheepishly. "By Jupiter!" he corrected himself.

Rachel looked at her husband, his face flushed with the excitement of the dispute. She lowered her head a trifle, then reached across and touched Baldwin on the knee.

"Mr. Baldwin, dear," she said in her low soft voice, "you are sleepy!"

The startled Baldwin protested that he was not sleepy at all but wide awake and enjoying the discussion. But his protests were all in vain. Rachel rose, rang for a servant to bring a "candle to light the dear child to bed." When Rachel rose everyone else in the room got to their feet. That ended the discussion and the group then dispersed.[7]

Jackson's "affectionate regard and devotedness to his wife, and his ready submission to her soothing voice," wrote one observer, "even when in his most excited and revengeful moods, were beautiful and commendable traits in his character." Moreover, the observer went on, "it is strong proof of her excellent judgment, self-control, mild temper, and ardent affection for him, that she had such a controlling influence over him."[8]

During Jackson's physical breakdown in 1822 she was particularly solicitous and she assumed many additional responsibilities in running the Hermitage. This respite afforded the General considerable time to engage in some serious thinking, not only about his family but his own future and the future of the country. His thoughts almost automatically turned to conditions within the Republic, and he could not shake a terrible sense of fear and foreboding. The nation was still recovering from an economic panic precipitated in large measure by the Second Bank of the United States when it reverted to a policy of tight money and credit. That panic created misery across the nation and for several more years would have a serious economic and political impact, particularly in the western states.

Jackson's growing agitation over conditions in the country did not focus solely on the financial. His mind ranged across many areas and the more he pondered what was happening throughout the nation the more agitated he became. His concern reached such an emotional pitch that he started to prepare what he called "memorandoms" in an effort to organized his thoughts and pinpoint the things that were particularly troublesome. The newspapers fed his tormented mind the details of many corrupt practices by elected officials that were repeated in one city after another throughout 1822. "That scandalous defalcations in our public pecuniary agents, gross misapplications of public money, and an unprecedented laxity in official responsibilities occurred and been suffered under our government for the past six or eight years are faults not to be concealed," declared the New York *Statesman* in one edition.[9] "Enormous defalcation," trumpeted a headline in the Baltimore *Federal Republican* in the fall of 1822, involving naval agents, marine paymasters, pursers, and others. And these, said the journal, constitute only "one of the innumerable instances of corruption in Washington."[10]

The entire nation seemed lost to morality and lofty ethical standards, grumbled Jackson as he scratched out his concerns over several sheets of paper. The public commentators worried over the collapse of civic and private virtue. "Scarcely is there a large city, or indeed a small one where there is a Bank—that has not had cause to bewail the aberration from rectitude of some man of (before) unsuspected honesty," recorded one man, "& one whom the people have delighted to honor—Even now as I passed thro' Richmond a trial was pending against the state Treas^r as defaulter for $120,000."[11]

"Charges . . . of . . . swindling the Govrt out of 25,500 . . . violating the consti . . . perfidious conduct . . . intrigue . . . interfering with the state elections," scribbled Jackson in his "memorandoms." And on and on he went, venting the frustration and anger pent up inside him, alternating between serious charges of corruption in government and the malice he suffered from Washington officials during his Florida tenure.[12] Much of his venom was directed at William H. Crawford, the secretary of the Treasury, but in time he came to believe that the entire administration in Washington was corrupt, from top to bottom.[13] The years 1816–1828 are generally called the Era of Good Feelings because it was a period in which one party, the Republican party, ruled the nation and supposedly brought political peace and good will to the country; but as everyone knew there was considerable quarreling and factious bickering within that party, and Jackson now feared that it was also riddled with corruption.

Granted much of what Jackson heard or read was nothing but rumor with little hard evidence to support it—although a great deal of "corruption in government" did in fact exist[14]—nevertheless what is important is Jackson's own personal belief that widespread corruption was rampant in Washington and needed to be eradicated. And it should be remembered that to the American of the early nineteenth century public corruption was not simply a matter of bribery or stealing government money. There were other—far worse—forms of corruption, such as subverting the constitutional system, lusting after political power, and placing private interests ahead of the public good. To use one's public office to acquire power or a higher office, such as Jackson accused Crawford of doing,[15] was far more vicious and destructive and dangerous than mere thievery.

A clear case in point was the determination of certain congressmen—in particular the friends of Crawford—to hold the traditional caucus to nominate the next Republican presidential candidate. Such a nomination was tantamount to election since the Republican party had no rival at the national level. (The Federalist party had been slowly dying on account of its presumed connection with the Hartford Convention.) In other words, a mere handful of congressmen meeting in caucus would elect the President of the United States. Although a congressional caucus was not unusual and had been practiced for decades, at least in the past a political contest between two parties had ensued. Now there was only one party. That fact rendered a congressional caucus totally improper and dangerous. It negated the idea of free elections. For congressmen to decide the presidential question, rather than the American people, was a gross violation of the constitutional system. And for congressmen to insist that a caucus be held to nominate the Republican candidate served as one more indication, as least to Jackson, of the prevailing "corruption in Washington."[16]

Moreover, everyone knew that the decision of the caucus was preordained and that William H. Crawford would receive the nomination because of his popularity with congressmen and the efficiency of his political apparatus in Washington, particularly in the awarding of the patronage. It appeared to many people, therefore, that Congress was about to "steal" the presidency from the control of the American electorate. This

suspicion became an absolute certainty when Crawford suffered a paralyzing stroke a little later that left him immobile, speechless, and almost
blind, and yet congressmen continued to plan their caucus for him anyway. They had the audacity to presume that they could lift into the
executive mansion a man who could not perform his duties. The next
President of the United States, if Congress had its way, would be paralyzed, sightless, and dumb.

Each day letters came to the Hermitage from Washington citing additional instances of "corruption" and misbehavior. The Vice President,
Daniel D. Tompkins, repeatedly disgraced himself. "I dont think he was
perfectly sober during his stay" in Washington, wrote Dr. James C. Bronaugh to Jackson. "He was several times so drunk in the chair that he
could with difficulty put the question. I understand he will never return
here."[17]

Even more horrendous to Jackson's mind were the revelations of fraud
by the Second Bank of the United States and the role the Bank had played
in triggering the Panic of 1819. Soon states enacted legislation to penal-
ize the Bank and prevent it from collecting its debts. In Kentucky—and
Kentucky deserves special mention because events in that state would
play a significant role in determining Jackson's bank policy after he was
elected President—stay laws forbade foreclosures and abolished imprisonment for debt.

The dramatic economic collapse of the nation at the start of a new
decade, coupled with the revelations of fraud by the Second Bank of the
United States (BUS) and its involvement in political elections, provoked
a howl of protest from the American people along with a serious and
sustained reaction against increased government rule in Washington.
The American electorate did not require much government from the
nation's capital, but what little came out of it was expected to be honest
and efficient.

This demand for limited government had been preached by conservatives for decades. Almost from the foundation of the Republic under the
Constitution they had been arguing the doctrine of minimal government
and urging the necessity of frugality. The central administration can only
be kept honest, they claimed, by restricting it. Unwarranted assumption
of power brings corruption and threatens freedom. When the party system began during the presidency of George Washington, the Federalists,
under the leadership of Alexander Hamilton, attempted to centralize
authority, award the national government increased powers, and allow
the executive full discretion in the administration of government. The
Republicans, on the other hand, under the direction of Thomas Jefferson
and James Madison, opposed centralized government, argued the rights
of the states, and sought to reduce national expenditures.

Basic to this ongoing disagreement between parties was their differing
views of the meaning of "republicanism." This was the ideology of the

revolutionary generation which contended, among other things, that those who exercised power were naturally inclined to diminish liberty and that they therefore regularly devised means to limit if not abrogate the rights of the people. This ideology also viewed "corruption" as power's greatest weapon and "virtue" as freedom's greatest defense. The struggle between liberty and power during the colonial age produced the Revolution. But the dangers to freedom persisted even after independence from the British Crown had been won. They persisted as long as power could be concentrated and the operation of government corrupted. The only defense rested upon the virtue of the American people.[18]

The events that transpired during the administration of James Monroe—especially after the Panic of 1819—revealed anew that the old tensions between liberty and power had not lessened. The exercise of increased authority by the central government, the large expenditures of money on internal improvements, the rechartering of the Bank of the United States in 1816, the rising demand for greater tariff protection, the revelations of corruption within the government, the abuse of the federal patronage, the demand for a congressional caucus—all these sounded alarm bells in the minds of those familiar with the ideology of "republicanism," and that included Andrew Jackson. His correspondence throughout the 1820s echoed the philosophy of the Founding Fathers. "I weep for the liberty of my country," he wrote, "when I see . . . the rights of the people . . . bartered [by congressmen] for promises of office." "My fervent prayers are that our republican government may be perpetual, and the people alone by their Virtue, and independent exercise of their free suffrage can make it perpetual." He hoped that the congressional caucus could be put "to sleep forever"; if not, "a central power will arise here; who under patronage of a corrupt, and venal administration, will deprive the people of their liberties."[19] Jackson always emphasized free elections as the panacea for all governmental ills. "The great constitutional corrective in the hands of the people against usurpation of power . . . is the right of suffrage," he said.[20]

Realistically, Jackson knew that the most efficient way to check the growing power of the central government was through the states. But this involved a delicate balance—one must not overpower the other. "To keep the sovereignty of the States and the general govt properly and harmoniously poised," he declared in 1824, "is the pivot on which must rest the freedom and happiness of this Country."[21]

Jackson's political thought, therefore, embraced the Revolution's most "republican" ideals. As a first principle he affirmed the conservative doctrine of limited government. He opposed a broad definition of constitutional power. He advocated states' rights, but the states must never regard themselves as superior to the general government. Nor did they possess the right of secession. Jackson also stressed debt reduction as an important article of faith. He regarded the national debt as a national curse and a danger to free government. For Jackson, therefore, the total elimination of the national debt became a very real objective. As President it was one of his major achievements.[22]

As he sat in his study in the Hermitage brooding over the state of the nation and the activities of its leaders, Jackson scribbled out his worry over the corruption and intrigue and departure from principle that he felt were eroding American institutions and threatening the freedom of every citizen. "If intrigue, management and corruption can avail," he wrote, ". . . nothing but the virtue of the people can prevail."[23] Later when he visited Washington his worst fears were all confirmed. "How can a republic last long under such scenes of corruption?" he moaned.[24]

Jackson was not the only one to express concern over conditions in the Republic. His correspondence demonstrated that his concerns were shared by other men. Soon they were telling him that he must permit his name to be brought forward for the office of President in order "that the great principles of the constitution upon which our republican government rests might be preserved, and our liberties perpetuated."[25] To these increasing suggestions that he run for the presidency, Old Hickory did not refuse. But he said he would not seek the office. It must come to him. To every application that he enter the race, "I gave the same answer that I have never been a candidate for any office. I never will. But the people have a right to choose whom they will to perform their constitutional duties, and when the people call, the Citizen is bound to render the service required."[26]

Naturally it was in Tennessee where the drive began to lift Jackson into the presidential chair. The Nashville Junto, consisting of Judge Overton, John H. Eaton, William B. Lewis, Felix Grundy, and others, had inherited the old Blount faction and were doing splendidly with it when the economic panic of 1819 struck. Because so many of the banks in Tennessee were owned and operated by the Junto, it suffered a mauling at the polls in the next election by the John Sevier faction, now led by Colonel Andrew Erwin and Senator John Williams. To recoup their loss, the Junto turned to Jackson and asked him to run for President, even though some of the members were fearful of the Hero's prejudices against banks and against paper money issued by banks. Still, they needed to rally from their defeat and so Grundy wrote to Old Hickory and asked permission to put his name before the General Assembly on September 22, 1822, as Tennessee's favorite son. "Let the people do as it seemth good unto them," was Jackson's response.[27]

Initially most of the Nashville Junto preferred John Quincy Adams or, as a second choice, John C. Calhoun. Then when Henry Clay announced his candidacy, a few of them switched to the Kentuckian, including Judge Overton. But when it became obvious that Jackson would agree to run, Overton abandoned Clay and together with Grundy, Eaton, William B.

Lewis, Pleasant M. Miller, and others arranged to get Jackson nominated for the presidency by the Tennessee legislature.[28] The resolutions submitted "the name of major general ANDREW JACKSON . . . to the consideration of the people of the United States, at the approaching election for the chief magistracy" and were passed unanimously on July 20, 1822.[29]

In their political maneuvering to place Jackson's name in nomination the Junto felt obliged to run him for a seat in the United States Senate. If nothing else it would strengthen his credentials for high office and improve his candidacy throughout the country.[30] In addition, his election would mean the defeat of John Williams, a leader of the Sevier faction who was then standing for reelection. A victory would also afford Jackson personal satisfaction because Williams had supported the attempt in Congress to censure him for the invasion of Florida. Still, it was a risky business. Williams was not without powerful friends in the Tennessee legislature, and if he defeated Jackson he would rub out the Hero's presidential plans in a single stroke. The Junto braved the risk, however, and through careful attention to the details of politics squeezed out a victory in the legislature on October 1, 1823, by a vote of 35 to 25.

Once elected, Jackson was obliged to serve in that sewer of corruption, Washington. "I am a senator against my wishes and feelings," he groaned, "which I regret more than any other of my life . . . but from my political creed . . . I am compelled to accept."[31] "He was a soldier," commented his friend Major Lewis, "and knew how to obey as well as command!"[32] So Jackson packed his bags and headed for Washington, arriving on the morning of December 3, 1823. He took lodgings at William O'Neal's boardinghouse along with his colleague in the Senate, John H. Eaton, and their friend Captain Richard Keith Call.

Meanwhile the Junto began organizing his presidential campaign by scheduling Jackson meetings all over the state. But what came as a complete surprise to them was the unprecedented outpouring of support that was instantly generated throughout the entire country by the announcement of Jackson's candidacy. They were flabbergasted. That Jackson was popular in the country no one doubted, but that he could be wildly popular as a presidential candidate vying with such distinguished statesmen as John Quincy Adams, John C. Calhoun, William H. Crawford, and Henry Clay (the other announced candidates) came as quite a shock.

Nevertheless, they quickly recovered and set about taking full advantage of this unexpected windfall. Perhaps the most important and wisest thing they did was to prepare a campaign document known as *The Letters of Wyoming*. First published as a series of eleven letters signed by "Wyoming" appearing in the Philadelphia *Columbian Observer* in June and July 1823 and authored principally by John H. Eaton, they were reprinted in pamphlet form in 1824 and widely circulated. The letters had such appeal that they were reprinted in other newspapers around the nation, for they seemed to catch the mood in the country that something was terribly wrong and needed repair. The theme of the work was the lamentable fact that the nation had plunged into an era of intrigue and misrule. Virtue and morality, so characteristic of the revolutionary generation, had vanished. Corruption—the word was repeated over and over throughout the text—ruled in Washington. "Look to the city of Washington, and let the virtuous patriots of the country weep at the spectacle. There corruption is springing into existence, and fast flourishing." Worse, it permeated the nation as a whole. Only by returning to the principles of the Revolution through the election of Andrew Jackson to the "chief magistracy" could the nation recover and regain its virtue. "Remember, he was of the Revolution!" He "is the last of those valiant establishers of the liberty of our Republic, who can succeed to the highest office known to our Constitution."[33]

The Letters of Wyoming forcefully reasserted the ideology of republicanism, the ideology which posited the belief in a perpetual struggle between liberty and power and between their respective instruments of support, virtue and corruption. Republics exist as long as the people "adhere to principles and virtue," said *Wyoming.* We can "sustain our republican principles . . . by calling to the Presidential Chair . . . ANDREW JACKSON."[34]

The Letters of Wyoming was an important political document not only as a campaign statement but in the continuing discussion of how to preserve liberty in a democratic society. It was part of an ongoing process to educate the American people to the idea that the appearance of Andrew Jackson in public life and his elevation to the presidency meant the reestablishment of a republican ideology that had its origins in the Revolution and was the only basis for the maintenance and perpetuation of American freedom.

The *Letters of Wyoming* also provided a blueprint of the ideological intentions of the developing Jacksonian movement. It was a statement of what Jackson's drive for the presidency was all about. It committed an age that would soon bear the General's name to the preservation of liberty as handed down by "our revolutionary fathers." Through Andrew Jackson the progress of American freedom was assured.

Although Jackson undoubtedly had a hand in writing the *Letters of Wyoming*—several phrases seem to come straight from his "memorandoms"—he could not openly participate in the campaign. Instead he attended his duties as senator, painful though they might be, and hoped to convince his colleagues in the upper house that he merited serious consideration as a contender for the presidency.

With the opening of the first session of the Eighteenth Congress in December 1823, the corridors naturally buzzed with talk about the approaching presidential election. Only the Radicals, the most conservative branch of the Republican party and the most organizational-minded, trumpeted the need for a congressional caucus to choose the party's candidate. Needless to add, they expected Crawford to get the nod, for he was their favorite. The present leader of the Radicals in Congress was the junior senator from New York, Martin Van Buren. A skillful organizer and political broker, he had created a statewide machine in New York called the Albany Regency to run the state in his absence. Known as the "Little Magician" or "Red Fox of Kinderhook," Van Buren had a reputation for intrigue and expert political management. At the age of forty-two, he exuded charm and total self-possession. Short, stocky, elegantly dressed in the latest fashion, fair-complexioned with light yellowish-red thinning hair and small brilliant eyes under a bulging forehead, he possessed the most exquisitely developed manners of anyone in Congress. The "compleat" politician, he expected to win nomination for Crawford in the caucus and then sit this broken man in the White House.

Jackson came to admire Van Buren despite his support of Crawford and his reputation as a "Magician." He found him thoughtful, honest, attentive to duty, and full of useful and sage advice. Both Jackson and Van Buren later agreed that their earlier and unfavorable opinions of one another underwent sharp revision. Initially Van Buren regarded Jackson as a "military chieftain" without presidential stature. Within three years he would salute him as the nation's greatest politician and statesman. For his part Jackson was deeply impressed by Van Buren's performance as a senator. Van Buren took his duties seriously and acted responsibly. Slowly, the two men formed a degree of grudging respect toward one another that eventually blossomed into a firm friendship.[35]

Jackson also ran into Colonel Thomas Hart Benton when he arrived in Washington. Benton was now the senator from Missouri and the two men occupied adjoining chairs. Not unexpectedly, both men were assigned to the Committee on Military Affairs. Constantly thrown together, the Colonel and the General were forced to speak to one another. Benton was an army in himself in terms of legislative skill and political astuteness. Big, powerful-looking, with an ego to match, he also sounded powerful whenever he spoke. Regaining Benton's friendship made enormous good sense, so, one day, Jackson approached him and inquired about the health of his wife. He followed through a few days later by calling at Benton's lodgings. The next time they met, Benton stepped up to Jackson and bowed. The General immediately shot out his hand, and the two men shook hands and wiped away the enmity of ten years.[36]

Unquestionably, the most controversial event of this session was the convocation of a congressional caucus to select the Republican party's nominee for President. On February 7, 1824, the Washington *National Intelligencer* carried a notice signed by eleven congressmen from as many states calling on their colleagues to join with them on Saturday, February 14, to recommend a candidate to the people of the United States. Despite the many cries that "King Caucus" should be knocked in the head, the organizers held their meeting on the appointed day. Only 68 out of a possible 261 members acknowledged the summons, 48 of whom represented four states: New York, Georgia, North Carolina, and Virginia. When the balloting ended the chair announced to "heavy groans in the Gallery" that William H. Crawford had received 64 votes, 2 of which were proxies, John Quincy Adams received 2 votes, and 1 each was awarded to Jackson and Nathaniel Macon of North Carolina. The caucus then selected Albert Gallatin for the vice presidency and issued an address to the people arguing the tradition and regularity of its action.[37]

Jackson shook his head in disgust. "Everything is carried by intrigue and management," he ranted at his friend, John Coffee. "It is now a contest between a few demagogues and the people; and it is to be seen whether a minority less than one fourth of the whole members of congress, can coerce the people to follow them; or whether the people will assume their constitutional rights and put down these demagogues."[38]

The caucus was actually an exercise in futility. As many Crawfordites realized, particularly Van Buren, the Republican party was falling apart, given its many conflicting personalities all vying for the presidential chair, and it would take superhuman effort after the election to pull it back together again. One of Van Buren's principal reasons for insisting on the caucus was his belief that it served the necessary purpose of binding the party together. Without it an important instrument of party discipline was lost.

The same month that the last congressional nominating caucus plummeted out of existence, John C. Calhoun decided against running for the presidency, since his northern support had weakened appreciably after Jackson entered the contest. He chose instead to stand for the vice presidency. What resulted, then, was a contest with four candidates for the presidential election: Crawford, Jackson, John Quincy Adams, and Henry Clay. Presumably Crawford was the southern candidate, Adams the New England candidate, and both Jackson and Clay the western candidates.

Quite understandably, the Radicals tried to discredit Jackson because they saw him as Crawford's most serious rival. In Congress they tried to prod him into "some act of violence" to destroy his candidacy, but in this, Jackson wrote, "they have much mistaken my charector."[39] They had not realized that he exercised total control over his emotions when it suited his purpose. They assumed he was a hotheaded frontiersman. They expected him to behave like Sam Houston, who sometimes appeared in Washington dressed in Indian clothes. They thought Jackson would show up carrying "a scalping knife in one hand and a tomahawk in the other, allways ready to knock down, and scalp any and every person who differed with me in opinion." But he surprised them. Instead of a war-whooping savage as the new senator from Tennessee they "found a man of even temper, firm in his opinions advanced, and allways allowing others to enjoy theirs, untill reason convinced them that they were in error."[40]

Scrupulous in his conduct, avoiding quarrels of any kind, repairing old ones, and making every effort to impress his colleagues with his statesmanlike deportment and demeanor, Jackson completed his first senatorial session with notable gains to his political reputation. A few times the Radicals baited him, but he never threw the "gantlette" back at them, he said. If there had been any doubt about whether his presidential candidacy would be taken seriously by the potentates of Washington, those doubts evaporated completely during the winter of 1823–1824. By the time the session ended and the members returned home they all knew that Andrew Jackson was a political force to be reckoned with.

And the presidential election of 1824 proved it. Old Hickory was the outstanding candidate in the election, and only John Quincy Adams approached him as a serious threat. Crawford had suffered a serious stroke and nothing Van Buren attempted could shore up his crumbling campaign. Clay, to his great misfortune, competed with Jackson for votes in the west and south, but he calculated that if the election went to the House of Representatives because no candidate had a majority of electoral votes, then he would be chosen President because of his personal strength in the lower house. His mistake came in thinking that he would be one of the three candidates with the highest number of electoral votes to go into the House election, as stipulated by the Twelfth Amendment to the Constitution.

Although the election of 1824 marked the first presidential election in American history in which popular voting figured in the outcome, that in no way changed the fact that the President was (and still is) selected by electors, all named according to the constitutions of their respective states. In six states the electors were chosen by the legislatures; everywhere else they were selected by popular vote. The several states voted at different times during the fall of 1824, and when all the votes were counted it was revealed that Jackson topped the other candidates, both in popular and electoral votes. But he failed to obtain the requisite majority of electoral votes and so the final choice of President belonged to the House of Representatives. Of a needed majority of 131 votes, Jackson fell shy by 32. He won a plurality of 99, followed by Adams with 84, Crawford with 41, and Clay with 37. In the vice presidential contest Calhoun was elected with little real opposition.

As expected, Adams took all 51 of New England's electoral votes. Then he picked up votes in New York, Delaware, Maryland, Louisiana, and Illinois. Crawford won votes in New York, Delaware, Maryland, Virginia, and Georgia. Clay took Kentucky, Missouri, and Ohio and a few votes in New York. Jackson swept the south—almost *in toto.* He performed less notably in the west. He lost Kentucky, Ohio, and Missouri but took Indiana, Tennessee, and Illinois. He won New Jersey and Pennsylvania but received only one vote in New York.

The final results of the popular vote around the country showed a clear preference for Andrew Jackson. He polled 152,901 votes against 114,023 for Adams, 47,217 for Clay, and 46,979 for Crawford. Jackson's plurality left no doubt about the people's choice, but it should be remembered that his popular vote was less than the combined tally of his opponents.[41] In any event the American people under the operating rules of 1824 had expressed their preference. They wanted Andrew Jackson in the White House. The next move belonged to the House of Representatives.

According to the Twelfth Amendment to the Constitution, when no candidate receives a majority of electoral votes the House selects the President from among the three persons with the highest count, each state having one vote determined by its delegation. A majority of states is necessary for election. Unfortunately for Clay he had the lowest vote of the four candidates and was therefore excluded from House consideration. Since he was a powerful figure in the House and exercised much influence among its members he would have a great deal to say about the final outcome. He could have decided it in his own favor had he been among the top three; now he must decide it for someone else.

Henry Clay was born in Virginia in 1777, studied law, and later moved to Kentucky where he won election to the United States House of Representatives in 1810 and assumed leadership of the War Hawks and became Speaker. A tall, bony, sharp-featured man, he had developed into a most effective public speaker. Combining sarcasm and humor with large amounts of loosely reasoned argumentation, Clay easily dominated the lower house and won its leadership through outstanding political and theatrical skills.

Jackson thoroughly disliked him. In large measure, Clay's attack on the General for his incursion into Florida in 1818 destroyed any possibility of friendship. And both men were westerners and therefore rivals for the same constituency. Clay saw Jackson as a threat to his main ambition in life. Jackson, on the other hand, pronounced Clay a typical western gambler, out to succeed at any cost.[42]

In choosing the candidate he would support in the House election, Clay started off by rejecting Jackson almost out of hand. The Hero was a "military chieftain," according to the Kentuckian, unsuited by temperament and ability to fill the office of President. Clay also dismissed the shattered secretary of the Treasury, not only on account of his health but because of his Radical principles. Clay was a nationalist to the marrow and believed that the central government should assist the country's economic growth. In a program termed the "American System" he argued in favor of protective tariffs, internal improvements, and a centralized banking system.

That left John Quincy Adams as the only remaining possibility. In terms of education, intellectual endowments, and experience in public service, Adams was ideally suited to occupy the presidential chair. Born in Braintree, Massachusetts, in 1767 (the same year as Jackson) and educated in the United States, France, and the Netherlands, he was admitted to the bar and began the practice of law in Boston at the age of twenty-three. Appointed minister to the Netherlands by President Washington, he later served as minister to Prussia, Russia, and Great Britain. His spectacular rise as a diplomat won him the post of secretary of state in the Monroe administration in 1817. Yet he was a cold, forbidding, sanctimonious man. He abhorred partisan politics and managed to alienate both Federalists and Republicans. But intellectually, though certainly not temperamentally, he and Clay complemented each other. For one thing, he was committed to a nationalistic program of public works. Thus, it made considerable sense to Clay to help advance Adams to the presidency, especially if he hoped to obtain immediate action on his American System proposals.

When Jackson returned to Washington after the fall election for the start of the new congressional session in December 1824, he heard nothing but the loud, raucous sounds of intense politicking. Once it became certain that the House would make the final presidential selection the Washington scene erupted in rumors of intrigue, plots, deals, and arrangements. "Rumors say that deep intrigue is on foot," Jackson relayed back to his Tennessee henchmen, "that Mr Clay is trying to wield his influence with Ohio, Kentucky, Missouri & Elonois in favour of Adams—others say the plan is to prevent an election all together This last I do not believe."[43]

There was in fact much talk about "bargain & sale." Said Jackson: "I envy not the man who may climb into the presidential chair in any other way, but by the free suffrage of the people. *The great whore of babylon being prostrated, by the fall of the caucus,* the liberty of our country is safe, & will be perpetuated, and I have the proud consolation to believe, that my name aided in its downfall."[44]

As the new year, 1825, commenced and the time for the House election drew closer rumors of "bargain & sale" grew louder and the pressures on Clay mounted. Several congressmen sought out the Kentuckian to see what could be arranged. Others offered to play go-between. Representative James Buchanan of Pennsylvania, a born busybody and a Jackson supporter, had heard that Clay's friends were disturbed over the rumor that the General, if elected, would "punish" the Kentuckian by excluding him and his cronies from the cabinet. Concerned that these friends of Clay's would go over to Adams, Buchanan took his information to John Eaton and afterward to Jackson himself. As he stood before the wary General repeating what he had heard, he could not control the nervous affliction that troubled one eye. He kept winking at Old Hickory as he spoke. Clay's friends, said Buchanan after a barrage of winks, gave assurances that they would "end the presidential election within the hour" if the General would first declare his intention of dismissing Adams as secretary of state.[45]

Jackson stared in disbelief at the winking, fidgeting little busybody. Everything he had heard about intrigues and plots now stood twitching before him. In return for his support, Clay obviously wanted to become secretary of state (because it was the fastest and the traditional road to the White House) and so Buchanan had been sent to sound him out with winks and blinks. Jackson responded by quietly repeating his resolution to remain clear of the contest. Actually Clay never authorized anyone to approach Buchanan, nor had he proposed a possible deal. By the time Buchanan spoke to Jackson, the Kentuckian had already made up his mind to swing his support to Adams. The fateful decision came on January 9, 1825. A meeting was arranged between Adams and Clay for an evening's conversation. "Mr. Clay came at six," Adams confided to his journal, "and spent the evening with me in a long conversation." In the course of the conversation Clay asked the New Englander "to satisfy him with regard to some principles of great public importance, but without any personal considerations for himself."[46] Nothing crude or vulgar, like declaring the terms of their political deal, passed their lips. No need. Both men understood one another's purposes. Both knew what was expected of them when their conversation ended. Surely they both realized that in exchange for House support Adams would designate Clay as his secretary of state.

On January 24 the Kentucky delegation in Congress announced its decision to swing behind Adams. In view of the fact that the Kentucky legislature had instructed the delegation to cast the state's vote for the western candidate (Jackson) in the House election since Adams had not received a *single* popular vote in the state, the representatives were risking more than they knew when they decided to listen to Clay rather than the legislature. On the same day the Ohio delegation also declared for Adams. Obviously Clay had powerful influence with both delegations.

The public announcement of Clay's decision came like a thunderclap. "We are all in commotion," wrote Robert Y. Hayne of South Carolina, "about the monstrous union between Clay & Adams, for the purpose of depriving Jackson of the votes of the Western States where nine tenths of the people are decidedly in his favor."[47] Many Congressmen agreed that the union was indeed "monstrous," if not grotesque. The west did not want John Quincy Adams. They had voted for Old Hickory. For Clay singlehandedly to overrule this judgment made a mockery of representative government. Martin Van Buren was aghast at the stupidity of the action. If you do this thing, he told a Kentucky colleague, "you sign Mr. Clay's political death warrant."[48]

Clay's reputation sank rapidly after his announcement. Everybody loved him, but nobody trusted him. Once he seemed destined for the highest office. No more. His "monstrous union" with Adams—or "coalition," as it was more elegantly called—"is so unnatural & preposterous," wrote Louis McLane of Delaware, "that the reports of no committees, nay all the waters of the sweet Heavens cannot remove the iota of corruption."[49]

Whether Jackson might have taken some action to block the "coalition's" grab for the presidency can never be known because he suffered a serious physical collapse from a bad fall at this time that kept him in bed for weeks. Hemorrhage followed hemorrhage. Weak, frequently unconscious, he seemed to be slipping closer and closer to death. Yet he rallied. Somewhere, somehow he found the strength to recover. He willed to survive. Hereafter to the end of his life, the hemorrhages became regular occurrences. How he survived these bloody episodes no one could say. To his friends he seemed superhuman.

While Jackson lay on his bed politically bleeding to death, the House of Representatives met at noon on February 9, 1825, to choose the sixth President. It was a cold and snowy day, but a large crowd of spectators jammed their way into the galleries to watch the proceedings. A majority of thirteen states—each state having one vote determined by its delegation—was necessary for a choice. According to advance calculations by the shrewdest politicians, the Adams-Clay coalition had twelve states; Jackson seven, and Crawford four. The strategy of the Crawford men, led by Van Buren, required them to keep Adams from winning the thirteenth state and maintain a deadlock over a protracted period of time. That way, the delegations might be talked into switching to Crawford to break the deadlock. Obviously the key to the scheme lay in holding the thirteenth state in abeyance, and that state turned out to be Van Buren's own state of New York. But try as he might, Van Buren could not keep his state split.[50] On the first ballot New York chose to jump on the bandwagon and declare for Adams, thereby giving him the majority. The final count showed Adams with thirteen states, Jackson with seven, and Crawford with four. Of the eleven states that had voted for Jackson in the electoral college, four—Louisiana, Maryland, Illinois, and North Carolina—deserted him in the House election. Clay probably converted Louisiana, and Daniel Webster of Massachusetts won over Maryland. Illinois dumped Jackson, thanks to Daniel Cook and his personal friendship for Adams. The people later defeated Cook for reelection in 1826, but Adams paid him off with a "diplomatic junket" to Cuba.[51] North Carolina deserted to Crawford, probably because of his conservative principles. Missouri's vote was cast by its single delegate, John Scott. Even though "nine tenths of the people" in the west preferred Jackson over Adams, Scott cast Missouri's vote for the New Englander. He was bought off when Adams assured him his brother would be retained in office even though it violated the law to do so.[52] Scott was subsequently defeated for reelection in 1826 and never returned to public office.

"I weep for the Liberty of my country," moaned Jackson, who by this time was recovering from his recent illness. The "rights of the people have been bartered for promises of office."[53] Publicly, Jackson took his defeat with dignity and grace. But privately he continued to express his concern over the corruption that seemed to encompass the entire country. "The Election is over," he wrote his friend John Overton, "and Mr Adams prevailed on the first Ballot." The western states were bartered away by Clay, he added, and together with Maryland they decided the outcome. "Thus you see here, the voice of the people of the west have been disregarded, and demagogues barter them as sheep in the shambles, for their own views, and personal agrandisement." He expected to leave Washington in March and reach the Hermitage in April. He looked forward to returning home, he said. It would be good to be among decent folk again.[54]

Five days after the election President-elect Adams offered the "gamester" from Kentucky the post of secretary of state. Adams had no choice in making the offer, but Clay should have rejected it. He was too good a politician not to see the danger. He knew the risk in accepting. He had heard all the rumors of a corrupt bargain. But like a gambler, he decided to chance it. He wanted the office with a passion because it historically led straight to the presidency. For a week he deliberated. He agonized. Then, despite the clear signals of what would happen, despite his own awareness of the risk, he accepted the offer. And in that moment he destroyed forever his presidential chances.

As soon as he heard Clay's decision, Jackson started bellowing. "So you see," he raged, "the *Judas* of the West has closed the contract and will receive the thirty pieces of silver. His end will be the same. Was there ever witnessed such a bare faced corruption in any country before?" Clay's acceptance, according to Old Hickory, proved beyond question that "a secrete understanding" to thwart the will of the people had been reached. "When we behold two men political enemies, and as different in political sentiment as any men can be, so suddenly unite, there must be some unseen cause to produce this political phenomenon." Many congressmen agreed. A "corrupt bargain" between Adams and Clay had been arranged to deprive the people of their right to free elections. "Oh," Jackson wailed, I "shudder for the liberty of my country."[55]

The election of John Quincy Adams to the presidency in 1825 and the appointment of Henry Clay as secretary of state confirmed in Jackson's mind the need for reform and the restoration of republican principles and practices in the operation of government. It set in motion a movement that changed the course of American political history, a movement that historians would later call "Jacksonian Democracy." The cry of "corrupt bargain" announced to the nation that the campaign for the presidency in 1828 had already begun.

CHAPTER 12

"Jackson and Reform"

THE THEFT OF THE GOVERNMENT —for that was the way Jackson and his friends regarded the House election of 1825—was in their minds the ultimate corruption. Denying Jackson's right to the presidency was so blatantly scornful of the popular will, especially the will of westerners, that some politicians worried for the safety of the constitutional system. If the presidency could be stolen through a "corrupt bargain" and power seized by a small cabal of ambitious and ruthlesss men, then liberty itself was in jeopardy.[1]

But the Jacksonian movement, as it developed, was more than a crusade to restore popular government and root out corruption. It was a recognition that the old divisions between the ideals of Jefferson and the goals of Hamilton had not vanished. It reaffirmed the principles of republicanism, principles which had been overthrown, according to the Jacksonians, by the election of John Quincy Adams. The determination of some men to steal the government in order to reassert Federalist (Hamiltonian) doctrines seemed obvious, particularly by those who wanted to believe this interpretation of the election. The struggle launched in the eighteenth century and continued into the nineteenth, they argued, still raged. It seemed perpetual: liberty versus power; virtue versus corruption; the people versus an elite.

"An issue has been fairly made, as it seems to me," wrote Vice President John C. Calhoun to Jackson at this time, "between *power* and *liberty.*"[2]

Thus, at the very beginning of the Jacksonian movement it was recognized by its leaders that they were struggling to advance republicanism, that they were engaged in a *moral* conflict between an aristocracy intent on further aggrandizement and the people concerned for the preservation of their liberty and property rights. Thus, the Democratic party, when it finally emerged, rested fundamentally on a moral base, which gave the Jacksonians an enormous advantage over their enemies.

The great fear among those men who coalesced around Jackson follow-

157

ing the election of 1825 was the loss of the government to men who lusted after money and power before everything else and would even sacrifice liberty to attain them.[3] The "honorable men in this great republic," wrote Henry Lee to Jackson in 1828, "hope by electing you to preserve our liberty."[4]

Immediately upon the announcement of the results of the House election, rumors began circulating that a new political alliance had been formed to put down the Adams-Clay coalition. Senator Rufus King of New York reported a Jackson-Calhoun combination in train. A "Party is forming itself here to oppose Mr. Adams' administration," he declared. "South Carolina is headquarters, and I understand that a Dinner takes place today [at] the Quarters of this Delegation, when Gen'l Jackson, Mr. Calhoun . . . and others are to be guests. . . . This first step may serve to combine the malcontents."[5]

An alliance between Jackson and Calhoun was natural enough. As secretary of war, Calhoun had always catered to Jackson's desires and temperament—except during the Seminole incident. Now that Clay had a clear shot at the presidency after Adams, Calhoun recognized that his future belonged with Old Hickory. As for the General, a union with the South Carolinian was not unthinkable. An alliance was a logical step if Jackson intended to coalesce his forces for the 1828 contest, turn the rascals out of office, and restore the government to the people from whom it had been stolen.

So the work of fashioning opposition to the Adams administration began almost at once. And the Jacksonian forces had an issue that would reverberate around the country for decades, and in the process shred Henry Clay's presidential ambitions. The "corrupt bargain" charge summarized succinctly everything the Jacksonians believed and preached. It was a rallying cry. It entered political discourse immediately and never left. Over and over it was repeated for the next three years. It reminded Americans of the moral failures of their age.

Once Jackson had reached an understanding with Calhoun he returned home to prepare for the next election. The Tennessee legislature obligingly renominated him for President in October 1825, and with that action the General began a serious campaign to organize his forces. He resigned from the Senate in order to give more attention to his presidential quest and immediately undertook the supervision and direction of what became the Nashville Central Committee, which would map strategy for defeating the Adams-Clay coalition. This committee included such worthies as John Overton, Hugh Lawson White, William B. Lewis, John H. Eaton, and, to some extent, Felix Grundy, Sam Houston, and G. W. Campbell. These men functioned in several capacities. They prepared statements for the newspapers, they corresponded with a wide network of politicians around the country, and they sometimes traveled to other states to visit local committees supporting Jackson. They established communication with state and local committees and later with a central committee in Washington. They provided much of the propaganda and campaign material for the election of 1828.

The full emergence of this new party—which named itself the Democratic party—took several years and the combined efforts of many politicians from every section of the country. Eventually they nailed together an organization structured for the advancement of Andrew Jackson and the restoration of republicanism. "What a pleasure it is to see that party almost unbroken rising in almost every part of the Union to put down the men who have corrupted and betrayed it," said one politician.[6]

The most important work of organization took place in Washington, and that phase of the operation began when Congress reconvened in December 1825. The Jacksonians began their assault on the administration almost immediately, pressuring fence sitters to recognize that a two-sided contest was developing and that they must take sides. They had a powerful weapon in their arsenal right from the beginning: the bargain. And they wielded it with gusto. John Randolph of Roanoke, the eccentric if not addled senator from Virginia, lambasted the coalition in a speech in the upper chamber by calling it "the coalition of Blifill and Black George [quoting Henry Fielding's *Tom Jones*] . . . the Puritan and the black-leg." Outraged by these remarks, Clay challenged Randolph to a duel and they shot it out on the southern shore of the Potomac River. Both men escaped injury but Clay drilled a hole through Randolph's coat.[7]

President Adams unwittingly assisted in the initial stages of the organization of the Democratic party. In rapid succession he committed a series of blunders that reinforced the notion that his administration favored the elite over the people. His first important blunder came on December 6, 1825, when he submitted his State of the Union message to Congress. In a bold, courageous, statesmanlike, and politically inept assertion of the government's responsibilities to advance the intellectual and economic well-being of the country, Adams laid before Congress a program of public works of breathtaking magnitude, a program immediately denounced by the conservative (Radical) followers of Crawford and Jacksonians as unconstitutional and visionary. Drawing principally from Clay's American System, the message offered a wide range of proposals that left the Radicals and Jacksonians gasping in disbelief. "The great object of the institution of civil government," the President averred, "is the improvement of the condition of those who are parties to the social compact." To accomplish his program of building roads and canals, establishing a national university, and exploring the western territories, said Adams in the most appalling statement of the message, the Congress must not give the rest of the world the impression "that we are palsied by the will of our constituents."[8]

An incredible blunder. He invited the Congress to disregard the will of the people—just as he himself had done a few months before. The Jacksonians guffawed. What further proof did anyone need that Adams and his crew were plundering buccaneers in illegal possession of the government? Soon friendly politicians around the country were agreeing that "the approaching contest is, I think, more now than at any former period considered by the sound planters, farmers & mechanics of the country, as a great contest between the *aristocracy* and democracy of America."[9]

Jackson naturally agreed. To those politicians who wrote of their outrage he responded sympathetically. He also stated his own position:

> When I view the splendor & magnificence of the government embraced in the recommendation of the late message, with the powers enumerated, which may be rightfully exercised by congress to lead to this magnificence, together with the declaration that it would be criminal for the agents of our government to be palsied by the will of their constituents, I shudder for the consequence—if not checked by the voice of the people, it must end in consolidation, & then in despotism—Yet, I have great confidence in the intelligence, and virtue, of the great body of the american people,—they never will abandon the constitutional ship,—their voice will be roused, & must be heard—Instead of building lighthouses in the skies, establishing national universities, and making explorations round the globe—their language will be, pay the national debt—prepare for national independence, & defense—then apportion the surplus revenue amongst the several states for the education of the poor—leaving the superintendence of education to the states respectively. This will be the safe course to perpetuate our happy government.[10]

Probably as a group, the politicians most horrified by what Adams had said in his message were the Radicals. "The message of the President," sputtered Nathaniel Macon of North Carolina, "seems to claim all the power to the federal Government."[11] As a consequence, these Radicals, led by Martin Van Buren, edged closer to the Jacksonians over the next several months and began to put out feelers for a political alliance.

Not much later Van Buren personally decided to go over to Jackson. It was a cold and crafty decision. He recognized the Hero's popularity. More importantly, he appreciated the need of the Radicals to reassert their conservative doctrines of limited government and strict economy in any reordering of political ties. Jackson was the single answer to all Radical needs and aspirations. Van Buren also appreciated the mood of the American people. Old Hickory was *their* candidate, cheated of his rights by corrupt and designing politicians.

Van Buren's move into the ranks of the Jacksonians also represented a deliberate attempt to revive the two-party system in American politics. Unlike the Founding Fathers, who cursed parties as divisive and destructive, the Magician regarded the party system as essential for representative government. Modern, efficient government, he argued, demanded well-functioning political parties openly arrayed against each other. Without parties, a democracy cannot function. A well-defined two-party system provides a balance of power between opposing forces, and this in turn safeguards liberty and the institutions of republicanism. The era of a one-party system under James Monroe produced a concentration of power in Washington that necessarily generated corruption and led inexorably to the fraudulent election of John Quincy Adams. Only a revival of the two-party system, said Van Buren, could restore the healthy interplay between opposing interests and insure order, legitimacy, and stability.[12]

Since Jackson had resigned his Senate seat and was not readily available, Van Buren decided to go to the Vice President and see if they could agree to an alliance that would serve their respective goals and interests. The two men met late in December 1826 at the home of William H. Fitzhugh of Virginia. Coming straight to the point, Van Buren offered his own support and presumably the support of a large contingent of Radicals for the election of Jackson in 1828. He emphasized the need for a reinvigorated party structured around Jackson and dedicated to pure republicanism. Such a party, he said, would unite the north and the south and forge an alliance between what he later termed "the planters of the South and the plain Republicans of the North." A Jackson victory, he went on, "as the result of his military services without reference to party . . . would be one thing. His election as the result of a combined and concerted effort of a political party, holding, in the main, to certain tenets and opposed to certain prevailing principles, might be another and far different thing."[13]

To initiate their "combination" and gain the support of other Radicals, Van Buren told Calhoun that he would write to Thomas Ritchie, editor of the Richmond *Enquirer* and a leader of the Richmond Junto, the political machine controlling Virginia. A New York–Virginia axis would appeal to all Jeffersonians, no matter their geographical location. It might be difficult for some Radicals to accept Calhoun in organizing this new party because of a long-standing feud between Calhoun and Crawford, just as it might be difficult for Jackson to accept Crawford, but the good of the country dictated the termination of these petty animosities. The ticket would be Jackson and Calhoun to be nominated by the several states.

All the while Van Buren spoke, the Vice President stared at the little man, his magnetic eyes fixed on the New Yorker. Finally the Magician finished his presentation and waited for a response. There was a moment's pause, then Calhoun rose from his chair and stretched out his hand. With a smile, Van Buren grasped it eagerly.[14]

In the ongoing development of the Democratic party, Jackson's role was central. Not that he campaigned in any active and public way, although he carefully observed and sometimes directed the activities of the Nashville Central Committee. Quite naturally, he regarded the movement to place him at the head of the government as one of "reform." An era of reform, he declared, must succeed this era of corruption. His first responsibility once he became President, he declared, would be to "reform the Government" and "purify the Departments" by removing every corrupt agent who had obtained his position through "political considerations or against the will of the people."[15]

As for specific issues, Jackson had some decided ideas. On banks, for example, he linked them to the general corruption of the times—indeed he regarded them as a major cause—and condemned them as dangerous to the safety of free institutions. On the money question—hard or soft—he entertained very extreme views. Hard money—specie—had his whole-hearted endorsement, but paper money he regarded as the instruments of banks to spread their corruption. "Ragg money," as he regularly called it, weakened the fabric of society and enabled the rich to fatten themselves at the expense of the poor.[16] On the tariff and internal improvements Jackson could be flexible, depending on their relations to the national interest in areas such as defense, but on the Indians he was resolved to remove them west of the Mississippi River.[17]

Although Jackson's understanding and appreciation of the major issues of the 1820s matured and moderated somewhat from earlier stands—despite the claims of some politicians that he lacked conviction on any national issue—he became extremely cautious and circumspect in giving them voice. There was always the danger of entrapment. The opposition was seen by him as malevolent and vindictive, necessitating the exercise of every precaution against unwittingly assisting them in their treachery.

As the presidential campaign gained momentum in 1827 and as a swelling army of political managers appeared on the scene to direct a vigorous demonstration of support for Old Hickory, Jackson was hard pressed to meet all the obligations they placed on him: their call for information; the plea for clarification; the necessity of explaining his behavior in connection with one event or another. Why had he voted against George Washington in the House of Representatives in 1796? What part did he play in the Burr conspiracy? How did he justify jailing Judge Hall in New Orleans? The execution of a number of militiamen brought a particularly aggressive propaganda campaign by the opposition that required Jackson's assistance in answering. The executions of Ambrister and Arbuthnot, the killing of Charles Dickinson, the tavern brawl with the Bentons—all demanded explanations or justifications. But perhaps the most devastating charge leveled at Jackson, as the campaign swung into full operation, involved the circumstances of his marriage to Rachel. Since General Jackson had taken a high moral position in this campaign and decried the corruption in Washington and around the country, the friends of the administration revived the charge that his was an adulterous and bigamous marriage and challenged him to explain his own reprehensible behavior in running off with another man's wife.[18]

The extraordinary circumstances of the Jackson marriage received widespread notoriety when Charles Hammond, editor of the Cincinnati *Gazette,* made an astounding charge. "In the summer of 1790," he wrote, "Gen. Jackson prevailed upon the wife of Lewis Roberts [*sic*] of Mercer county, Kentucky, to desert her husband, and live with himself, in the character of a wife." Starting with the March 23, 1827, issue of the *Gazette* Hammond presented his case, which he later serialized in a pamphlet called *Truth's Advocate and Monthly Anti-Jackson Expositor.* This publication prompted the Nashville Central Committee to issue a full account of the "true facts" surrounding the marriage, most of which was written by John Overton.[19]

Jackson was visibly shaken by the widespread broadcast in the newspapers of the circumstances of his marriage. But he thought he understood what had brought it about. Henry Clay, charged with corruption in the fraudulent election of a President the people did not want, had responded to the charge by resorting to gutter tactics. Jackson had been informed that Hammond visited Clay in Kentucky and had obtained all the information that later appeared in the *Gazette.* He therefore asked Senator Eaton to look into it. Eaton confronted Clay and demanded an explanation. Clay denied involvement, although he admitted seeing Hammond. Still Jackson suspected him. Where else could it originate? Who other than Clay had the opportunity, the access, or the need for this information? In a letter to Sam Houston, Old Hickory released all the fury of his pent-up anger and frustration.

> I am determined to unmask such part of the Executive council, as has entered into the combination to slander and revile me; and I trust, in due time to effect it, and lay the perfidy, meaness, and wickedness, of Clay, naked before the american people. I have lately got an intimation of some of his secrete movements, which, if I can reach with possitive and responsible proof, I will wield to his political, and perhaps, his actual destruction. he is certainly the bases[t], meanest, scoundrel, that ever disgraced the image of his god—nothing too mean or low for him to condescend to, *secretely* to carry his cowardly and base purpose of slander into effect; even the aged and virtuous female, is not free from his secrete combination of base slander—but *anough, you know me,* I will curb my feelings until it becomes proper to act, when retributive *Justice will vissit him and his pander heads.* [20]

The contemptible sewer tactics of the coalition, stormed Jackson, in dredging up the details of his marriage in this campaign was another example of their moral and political bankruptcy. Legitimately charged with corruption for stealing the government, the administration men answered the charge by slinging filth. To Jackson, it confirmed all he had suspected and known about how Adams and Clay had come to power.

Other criticisms assailed him. His military career took much abuse, something the General never tolerated—not from anybody. A handbill was issued by the opposition entitled, "Some Account of Some of the Bloody Deeds of GENERAL JACKSON," or "The death of Jacob Webb, David Morrow, John Harris, Henry Lewis, David Hunt, and Edward Lindsey—six militia men, who were condemned to die, the sentence approved by Major General Jackson, and his order the whole six shot." The handbill was bordered in black and at the top showed six black coffins over which were affixed the names of the "murdered" militiamen. This "Coffin Hand Bill" described how the six men wanted to return to their homes during the Creek War at the conclusion of their enlistment, but were charged instead with desertion and then executed by command of the pitiless Jackson. John Binns, editor of the Philadelphia *Democratic Press,* conceived the Coffin Hand Bill and enlivened it with a poem entitled "Mournful Tragedy."

Democrats countered by accusing Adams of pimping for the Czar of Russia when he was the United States minister to that country. This charge appeared in a campaign biography of Old Hickory published by Isaac Hill of New Hampshire and entitled *Brief Sketch of the Life, Character and Services of Major General Andrew Jackson.* Unfortunately this vile canard was widely believed and circulated. In the west the Democrats mocked the President as "The Pimp of the Coalition" whose fabulous success as a diplomat had at last been explained.[21] In addition, the Jacksonians charged the President with recklessly spending public money for gambling furniture in the White House, in particular a pool table, cues, and balls. His lordly and aristocratic manner was projected in the press to emboss their image of a President who was hostile to the aspirations of the majority of the American people.

Adams remained aloof from these gutter attacks, but Jackson became more deeply involved in the campaign as the assaults on his private history and public career intensified. For one thing he opened a correspondence with Duff Green, the new editor of the leading Jackson newspaper in Washington. Green had bought out the old Washington *Gazette* with the financial backing of Jackson and his friends and changed the paper's name to the *United States Telegraph.* Once the newspaper began publication the General contacted Green and indicated some of the guidelines he wanted his propagandist to follow. "Should the administration continue their systematic course of slander," he said, "it will be well now and then to throw a fire brand into their camp by the statement of a few facts." However, "female character never should be introduced or touched by my friends, unless a continuation of attack should continue to be made against Mrs. J. and then only, by way of *Just retaliation* upon the *known guilty.*"[22]

Another publicist with whom Jackson began a correspondence at this time was Amos Kendall of Kentucky, editor of the *Argus of Western America.* Kendall had been a friend of Clay's but broke with him on ideological and personal grounds and joined the ranks of the Democrats. He violently opposed the Bank of the United States and wrote many scathing attacks against that institution in his newspaper. His arrival into the Jackson camp was nearly as significant—although in a completely different way— as the arrival of Calhoun and Van Buren. He and his associate in the running of the *Argus,* Francis P. Blair, not only brought enormous vitality to the Jacksonian cause by virtue of their journalistic skills but they also added immeasurable strength to the party in a state dominated by Henry Clay. Moreover, as westerners, they soon won Jackson's confidence and ear. Together they provided more energy, ideas, and issues than any two other men in the entire Democratic party.

Other important journalists also joined the Jackson ranks. Thomas Ritchie of the Richmond *Enquirer* and Edwin Croswell of the Albany *Argus,* the mouthpiece of the Albany Regency, followed Van Buren's lead. Isaac Hill's New Hampshire *Patriot,* James Gordon Bennett's New York *Enquirer,* and Nathaniel Greene's Boston *Statesman* contributed valuable support to the Jacksonian movement. Soon the friends of the administration—now called "National Republicans" to distinguish them from the Democratic-Republicans as well as indicate their ideological commitment—complained that the Democrats had established a "chain of newspaper posts, from the New England States to Louisiana, and branching off through Lexington to the Western States."[23]

Among many Jacksonians, especially journalists, there was genuine concern for what Kendall had called "the principles for which we are all contending." Theirs was no simple drive to oust a maladroit administration. They contended that misrule and abuse of power existed within the government. They also feared that Hamiltonian men of business controlled and directed the government to advance their economic interests. "Contending as we are against wealth and power," said a future member of Jackson's cabinet, "we look for success in numbers combined by intelligence & impelled by patriotism."[24] Thus, Jackson's election would not only expel a corrupt administration from office but create a new party based on mass support dedicated to the restoration of the constitutional safeguards of liberty. Jackson himself seemed to understand the larger implications of his candidacy. In his many letters to party leaders around the country he emphasized the ideology of republicanism and slowly began to formulate the outline of a reform program. "When the constitution will be so amended as to preserve to the people their rightful sovereignty," he told John Branch of North Carolina, "& restore in practice the proper checks and ballances; when the public debt will be paid, and the executive department of our government freed from the corrupting influence of a monied aristocracy; when Congress will regulate with an eye single to the public weal, and limit by special veto all appropriations, and compel every officer in the government annually to account to congress how the funds entrusted to his care have been applied. Then, and not until then, will our national character be freed from the charges of corruption which is now imputed to it—keep our officers free from temptation, & they will be honest."[25]

By 1828 many party leaders were thoroughly aware of Jackson's ideological creed and the ultimate purpose of his election. On the very afternoon that he died, De Witt Clinton of New York wrote to Caleb Atwater, his political ally in Ohio, and instructed him on the meaning of Old Hickory's election. "If you wish not to see a second reign of terror—support Gen. Jackson," he wrote, "—if you wish for the restoration of pure, republican principles, support him." In sum, declared the Democratic press, "the parties are Jackson and Adams, democracy and aristocracy."[26]

"Scarce a doubt remains of Ohio's vote being for Jackson & reform at the next election," said Atwater. "We are making it a text at this election, for members of our Legislature. We shall succeed too, without a doubt."[27] Clearly, the managers of the Democratic party in the several states succeeded brilliantly in fixing the campaign slogan "Jackson and Reform" in the public conscience. The Hero of New Orleans who had saved the nation from military defeat in 1815 would now save it from the corruption and misrule brought on by an aristocratic and illegitimate administration.

Because of the excitement of the contest, an unprecedented number of demonstrations for Old Hickory occurred during this election. Much of this ballyhoo was conceived and organized by the new breed of politicians who had appeared in the last ten years. They encouraged the public to feats of organized mayhem. Parades, barbecues, dinners, street rallies, tree plantings, and patriotic displays of every variety occurred throughout the nation. Said one: "the *Hurra Boys* were for Jackson and . . . all the noisey *Turbulent Boisterous* Politicians are with him." The Hurra Boys distributed hickory brooms, hickory canes, and hickory sticks. They stuck them on steeples, on steamboats, on signposts. Poles made of hickory were erected "in every village, as well as upon the corners of many city streets." "Planting hickory trees!" snorted the National Republicans. "Odds nuts and drumsticks! What have hickory trees to do with republicanism and the great contest?"[28]

With all the talk about freedom and misrule by an elite, it is not difficult to understand why an anti-Masonic outburst of violence occurred at this time. It all started in 1826 with the disappearance and apparent murder of William Morgan, a stonemason from Batavia, New York. Morgan belonged to a local Masonic lodge and because of a dispute with his lodge brothers he wrote a book disclosing Masonic secrets. When efforts to dissuade him from this betrayal failed, Morgan was arrested for indebtedness. His bail was paid, but as he left the jail he was seized and probably taken to the Niagara River, where he was drowned. His disappearance immediately engulfed the western districts of New York in wild excitement. Masons were denounced for their membership in an organization committed to kidnapping and murder to protect its hidden purposes. Soon the excitement was intensified by religious and psychological forces, and by economic grievances. The frustrated, the angry, the malcontent in society convinced themselves that Masons were entrenched in business, politics, and the courts—indeed, every important position within the power structure of the state—and were preventing non-Masons from getting ahead. Perceptive politicians like Thaddeus Stevens of Pennsylvania and Thurlow Weed of New York quickly recognized the value of the uproar and began to direct it into the electoral field. At the height of the disturbance someone discovered that Andrew Jackson was a "grand king" of the Masonic Order, and it severely damaged his candidacy in New York.[29]

To some this anti-Masonic outbreak reflected a democratic surge to terminate the alleged privileges of an elite class. Many feared that the rich and powerful were ordering society for their personal profit. The theft of the presidency to restore Hamiltonian men of business to government provided ample proof that conspiracies existed. If the government could be stolen, nothing was safe.

Fortunately for Jackson this potential danger to his candidacy was localized in 1828. The political strength of the anti-Masonic movement had only begun to mount. By the late summer of 1828 its threat seemed minuscule, and a great many Democrats declared their confidence that Jackson would win, and maybe win big.[30]

One reason for this optimism was the stunning success the Democrats achieved in the off-year elections of 1827. They now controlled both houses of Congress and were planning to tailor their legislative business almost exclusively to ensure the General's election to the presidency in 1828. Led by Senator Van Buren, the Democrats in Congress concocted a tariff bill aimed at attracting electoral votes in both the northeast and northwest by hiking the protective rates on items favored in those areas, such as raw wool, flax, molasses, distilled spirits, and hemp. Southerners generally opposed protective tariffs and believed them unconstitutional because they favored northern economic interests to the detriment of southern economic interests. After a bruising fight, in which accusations of subterfuge and deceit figured prominently, the tariff passed, and President Adams signed it. Although dubbed a "Tariff of Abominations" in some quarters, especially in the south, the bill helped Jackson find votes in those states where he needed them most: Kentucky, Illinois, Indiana, Missouri, Pennsylvania, Ohio, and New York.[31]

And find them he did. By the thousands, people crowded to the polls, guided by the Democratic party. Local Jackson organizations had given much attention to turning out the vote. Not a few central committees brought the electorate to the polls in companies of fifty or sixty marching behind a banner blazoned with the motto "JACKSON AND REFORM." Elsewhere Hickory Clubs distributed flags and bunting to encourage the party faithful to troop to the polls and register their demand for the restoration of virtue and republicanism.

"To the Polls!" commanded the *United States Telegraph*. "To the Polls! The faithful sentinel must not sleep—Let no one stay home—Let every man go to the Polls . . . and all will triumph in the success of

JACKSON, CALHOUN and LIBERTY"[32]

Voting procedures in 1828 varied widely throughout the twenty-four states. State legislatures chose the electors in both South Carolina and Delaware; everywhere else the electors were selected from a general or district ticket by an electorate that was roughly equivalent—except in Virginia, Louisiana, and Rhode Island—to the adult white male population. New York, Tennessee, Illinois, Maine, and Maryland utilized the districting system (which meant that the state's electoral vote could be split), while the others used the general ticket, which awarded all the state's electoral votes to the candidate with the highest popular total. Between 1824 and 1828, four states—New York, Vermont, Georgia, and Louisiana—changed their electoral laws to permit, for the first time, popular selection of presidential electors. This single reform increased the total number of voters participating directly in American presidential elections by several hundred thousand.

Balloting began in September and ended in November. In each state voting occurred over several days and the polls opened at various times even within a single state. When the final returns were tabulated in the late fall, Jackson had won 647,276 popular and 178 electoral votes to Adams's 508,064 popular and 83 electoral votes. In the electoral college Adams suffered a crushing defeat. In addition to New England he won New Jersey, Delaware, a majority of electoral votes in Maryland, 16 of New York's 36 votes, and a single vote from Illinois. Jackson took all the rest.[33]

A "great revolution has taken place," moaned one National Republican. "It was the howl of raving Democracy," sneered another. Jackson's "triumphant majority," wrote Hezekiah Niles, a journalist of the opposition, resulted from the "ardor of thousands." The coalition of Adams and Clay, said Edward Everett to his brother, was defeated "by a majority of more than *two* to *one,* an event astounding to the friends of the Administration and unexpected by the General himself and his friends. . . . [They] are embarrassed with the vastness of their triumph and the numbers of their party."[34]

But Jackson's victory did not actually register a "vast" outpouring of voters. It just looked that way. In a country of nearly 13 million, some 1,155,340 white males participated in the election, which is statistically rather small. Even so, that small number represented an increase of more than 800,000 over the previous presidential election, so it appeared at the time to signal a far-ranging awakening of public interest in the election of the chief executive.

It was, in fact, an outstanding showing and several factors shaped it. First and foremost was the Hero's enormous popularity among all classes of Americans in all sections of the country. Second was the conviction that Adams had obtained his office by a cynical and flagrant disregard of the will of the people. And third was the superior organization of the Democratic party. Through the work of local and state committees and newspapers a "concentrated effort," as Van Buren termed it, scored large majorities for Jackson in certain key states in the west and Middle Atlantic area. "Organization is the secret of victory," pronounced one newspaper friendly to Adams. "By the want of it we have been overthrown."[35]

When the news of Old Hickory's victory finally arrived at the Hermitage it created no great sensation. Rachel looked a little wistful when she heard it, for she realized what it meant in terms of public exposure and comment. "Well, for Mr. Jackson's sake, I am glad," she said; "for my own part, I never wished it." Rachel was still recovering from the shock of the death of her Indian son, Lyncoya, who had died on June 1, 1828. He was only sixteen years of age and probably died of tuberculosis. Rachel had nursed him diligently, tending to his diet and a regimen of exercise, but in vain. After "very severe sufferings" Lyncoya "expired under the roof of the hero who had conquered his nation but who followed his remains to a decent grave."[36]

Early in December, after the final results of the election were known, Rachel forced herself to go to Nashville to buy the clothes she would need for her new position as First Lady. As she shopped she soon grew weary and retreated to the private office of a newspaper editor in town—one of her many relatives—and while waiting to regain her strength happened to see a campaign pamphlet that defended her behavior prior to her marriage to Jackson. What she read staggered her. Never before had she known the full range of the slander leveled against her. The language, the implications, the outright accusation of adultery and bigamy. Now she understood it all. Overwhelmed, she slumped to the floor and wept hysterically. From that moment on Rachel Jackson began a slow mental and physical decline. The beginning of the end came on Wednesday, December 18, when she contracted a cold and "pleuritic symptoms" set in. Then, as she went about her household chores with her servant, Hannah, she suddenly felt a stabbing pain in her chest and left arm. She screamed as she clutched her heart. Sinking into a chair, she struggled for breath and fell forward into Hannah's arms. Servants came running at the sound of her cry. They gently carried her to her bed.[37]

Jackson was seated at his writing desk when he heard his wife's scream. Dropping his pen he raced to her aid. He knelt at her bedside and offered words of comfort. A rider sped into town to summon medical assistance.

Over the next sixty hours General Jackson watched her closely, rarely leaving her side. She rallied somewhat and begged her husband to get some rest. Finally he consented to lie on the sofa in an adjoining room. Dr. Henry Lee Heiskell, visiting from Virginia, and Dr. Samuel Hogg, the Jacksons' regular physician, agreed to remain in the house.

It was then nine o'clock, Sunday, the 22nd of December. The General bade his wife goodnight and retired to the next room. He was gone only five minutes. At her bidding the servants lifted Rachel from her bed for the first time so that the sheets might be arranged for the night. While sitting in the chair, supported by Hannah, Rachel suffered another severe attack. She let out a long, loud cry. There was a "rattling sound in her throat." Her head fell forward onto Hannah's shoulder. Rachel died at that moment.[38]

Jackson bolted through the door when he heard the cry. Servants and relatives also rushed in and immediately set up a prolonged and mournful wail. The doctor and Jackson lifted her from the chair and gently placed her back on her bed.

"Bleed her," commanded Jackson.

The doctor sliced into her arm but no blood flowed.

Jackson froze.

"Try the temple, Doctor," he begged.

The doctor obeyed. Two drops oozed from the incision and stained her cap. Nothing more.

The husband searched her face for any sign of life. He stood by her side for hours, hoping to see some indication of returning life. Only when her hands and feet grew cold did Andrew Jackson accept the fact that his beloved was dead.

In the morning Major Lewis arrived and found Jackson still sitting by his wife's side, grieving, his face in his hands. The General was wholly inconsolable and had quite lost his voice. He remained in the room nearly all the next day, "the picture of despair."[39]

Rachel was buried on Christmas Eve in the garden of the Hermitage. Old Hannah collapsed at the gravesite. During the rites Jackson himself broke down. For the first time since her death tears ran freely down his cheeks. One mourner stepped up to him to convey his sympathy. The Hero caught the gentleman's hand and squeezed it three times. He started to speak but all he could utter was, "Philadelphia." The gentleman was overcome with sadness. "I never shall forget the look of grief," he said.[40]

Jackson shielded his wife's grave with a wooden cover until he could arrange a suitable monument. What he ordered before leaving for Washington was a small, round, white domed roof supported by pillars of white marble resembling a Greek temple. Later a tablet was placed directly over the grave.

"My heart is nearly broke," the old soldier wept, as he prepared to leave for Washington. To the day he died, Andrew Jackson grieved over the loss of his wife. Becoming President meant little to him at this moment. "A loss so great," he said, ". . . can be compensated by no earthly gift."[41]

CHAPTER 13

The First People's Inaugural

SLOWLY, OVER THE NEXT SEVERAL WEEKS, Jackson forced his mind to attend to his new responsibilities. On Sunday, January 18, 1829, the steamboat that would begin his journey to Washington arrived on the Cumberland. The trip from the Hermitage to the capital began on January 19 and took a little more than three weeks. Jackson was accompanied by an entourage that included his nephew, Andrew Jackson Donelson, who would serve as his private secretary; Donelson's wife, Emily; William B. Lewis; Andrew Jackson, Jr.; Henry Lee; and Jackson's ward, Mary Eastin.

When at last Jackson appeared in public he was of course dressed in deep mourning—and he remained in deep mourning for many years. He dressed in a black suit, white shirt, and black tie. Usually he wore a black band on his arm and another black band around his tall beaver hat, a portion of which hung down the back of his neck and was called a weeper. He appeared terribly grave on his first public appearance, but observers noted that he still looked every inch the gentleman and soldier. Indeed, commentators declared that he was the most presidential-looking figure to head the nation since George Washington.[1]

Through the Democratic press the General let it be known that he wanted no "public shows and receptions" during his journey.[2] But the public could not resist assembling to catch a view of him when they heard of his presence in the neighborhood. Apart from everything else, they needed to reassure themselves that he was well and ready to assume command of the government.

The Jackson party arrived in Washington very quietly on February 11 about midmorning, riding in a plain carriage drawn by two horses and accompanied by a single black servant. He was "preceded by perhaps 10 horsemen."[3] The General took up residence in the National Hotel, the newest and most fashionable hotel located at the northeast corner of Pennsylvania Avenue and Sixth Street.

Jackson's first concern for his administration was the formation of a cabinet. Almost immediately Van Buren's name came up and no one seriously questioned his preeminent position within the Jackson organization and the need to recognize and make use of it. The fact that he had just been elected governor of New York hardly mattered. When, after extensive consultation with his immediate advisers, Jackson found that the Magician's appointment elicited no strong opposition, he wrote to Van Buren on February 14 and invited him to take the post of secretary of state. No other offer was suitable in view of his stature and rank in the party. The appointment troubled Calhoun and his friends because the position was considered next in line to the presidency, but there was nothing they could do about it given the South Carolinian's situation as Vice President.[4]

To placate the Calhoun wing of the party the President-elect handed over the Treasury Department—the second most important position in the cabinet—to Samuel D. Ingham of Pennsylvania. Moreover, Pennsylvania's important role in the election, the size of Jackson's majority in the state, and her "keystone" position in the Union and in the party all necessitated a major appointment. A "considerable majority" of the state's congressional delegation came to Jackson after his arrival in Washington and "presented Ingham as the candidate of the Democracy of that state. The General immediately assured them that he should have the Treasury."[5] He himself preferred Henry Baldwin but yielded to the wishes of the delegation.

Then Jackson did something exceedingly foolish. He decided he must have a close personal friend in the cabinet with whom he could talk freely and openly, someone he could trust, someone loyal, someone he could rely on. Which is a dubious way to fashion a cabinet where needs more important than loyalty must be served. Jackson had two possibilities in mind: John Henry Eaton and Hugh Lawson White, both old friends and associates from Tennessee. White had the edge in terms of intellectual ability and dedication, Eaton in terms of friendship and service. White was the soul of rectitude and a man of uncommonly good judgment. His selection would have been preferable. But Eaton had a special claim on Jackson, not only as biographer but as longtime aide and associate. Indeed, Jackson once told Rachel that Eaton "is more like a son to me than anything else; I shall as long as I live estimate his worth and friendship with a grateful heart."[6] What complicated the matter was Eaton's recent marriage to Margaret (Peggy) O'Neal Timberlake on January 1, 1829.

Eaton was a middle-aged widower and Peggy a twenty-nine-year-old beauty when they married. The daughter of a local Washington innkeeper, the lady was winsome, witty, saucy at times, and distinctly forward, sometimes overstepping the bounds of society's limits on young matrons. She liked to exercise influence. She needed to feel important. After the death of her first husband, Lieutenant John Timberlake, a naval purser who may have committed suicide because he had defrauded the government to cover his wife's debts, Peggy turned over her affairs to Eaton, "and scandal says they slept together," reported Amos Kendall. "I believe the tale is a lie," Kendall went on, "but it is rife among the ladies here." "Eaton has just married his mistress," laughed one gossipy politician, "and the mistress of eleven doz. others!"[7]

Before marrying Peggy, Eaton consulted Jackson about his intended action. He felt he must do what was "right & proper" in terms of "honor" and "justice," and Jackson agreed. Thus it was not the Hero who told Eaton to marry Peggy. Eaton reached that conclusion himself. He simply asked Jackson if he approved, and, he said, "it was a matter of infinite satisfaction to me, to find, that your advice & opinions accorded with my own."[8]

But why Jackson would consider Eaton for a cabinet position, knowing the sort of gossip and abuse it would engender, raises questions about his judgment. Perhaps he felt he owed him something. Perhaps he did it as a gesture, believing that Eaton would refuse the post rather than subject himself and his wife to vicious slander. If that is what Jackson thought, he thought wrong. Eaton desperately wanted the position. So he told White that he would step aside if White really wanted the job himself, even though White had already informed him that he would decline any offer. Naturally White refused to compete, and with his refusal Jackson lost his one opportunity to have not only a close and loyal friend in his cabinet but a man of integrity and superior intellect. That Jackson let the appointment slip from his control demonstrated poor leadership. It would not be his last such mistake. Jackson's appointments on the whole ran from poor to wretched—with a few notable exceptions.

Jackson fumbled again when he appointed John Branch, senator from North Carolina and former governor of the state, to head the Navy Department. "By what interest that miserable old woman, Branch, was ever dreamed of no one can tell," said Louis McLane. According to Kendall, "Branch was selected, because North Carolina is a plain, unambitious state, which has thrust forward no claims to high offices although in merit she is not inferior to her more showy neighbors." Which if true is even more senseless than the reason for appointing Eaton. Branch was an old friend and an early supporter of the new President. He owned land in Tennessee and had frequently visited Jackson at the Hermitage. In addition, he was a strong states' rights man and a vocal critic of banks— two strong points in his favor as far as Old Hickory was concerned. Someone mentioned that Branch was noted for his splendid dinners and impeccable manners and therefore might "promote the social prestige of the new party." The way Jackson was headed he needed all the social prestige he could get, but placing one man of impeccable manners in the cabinet with another whose wife was suspected of sleeping around town with "eleven doz." men guaranteed a free-for-all among Washington gossips and troublemakers.[9]

Another mistake was the appointment of John McPherson Berrien of Georgia as attorney general. "Berrien is a Georgia Crawford man of fine talents," acknowledged Kendall, "but was a federalist until since the last war. I know not what would have induced the General to take him unless it was to satisfy the friends of Crawford." Naturally the Radicals wanted a "strong constitutional Attorney General," but Jackson appointed him because he advocated Indian removal and that was an important consideration. Jackson was determined to initiate Indian removal, and it was essential to his plans to have a supportive attorney general at his side.[10]

The President-elect erred yet again with the appointment of William T. Barry of Kentucky as postmaster general. At first Jackson decided to continue John McLean in the office in appreciation of his disloyal behavior toward John Quincy Adams. But McLean wanted the seat on the Supreme Court that had recently become available and Jackson let him have it. Barry, the recently defeated Democratic candidate for governor of Kentucky, was initially intended for the bench but readily agreed to switch with McLean when it was proposed to him. Barry proved to be incompetent, indolent, and obtuse, and totally unequal to the assignment. Jackson had already decided on the reform principles to guide the operation of the Post Office and therefore he needed someone in charge of the department who would work closely with the President and who understood what the reform was all about. Barry hardly measured up to the requirements and his tenure became a near disaster.

Indeed, as was quickly pointed out when the appointments were announced by Duff Green in his newspaper, the cabinet was uniformly second-rate, with the single exception of Martin Van Buren. "The Millennium of the Minnows!" commented one man; and surely it ranked among the worst cabinets in the nineteenth century. For an administration intent on restoring republicanism through a vigorous program of reform, this list of its executive officers hardly inspired confidence. That it collapsed within two years is not surprising.

By hobbling the cabinet with inferior appointments, Jackson only increased his own burden. Since he needed skilled administrators to implement his policies once he indicated their general direction, several newspapermen would have been better choices than those he finally selected. A large number of journalists descended on Jackson in February and offered him their talents and advice. Duff Green, Isaac Hill, and Amos Kendall were among the first to show up. Later, Thomas Ritchie of Virginia, Dabney Carr, Gideon Welles, and Nathaniel Greene paid their respects. Of the group, Amos Kendall made the best impression. Talented, indefatigable, western, a smashing writer, and devoted to "Jackson and Reform," he impressed the President-elect with his wide knowledge, keen perceptions, and quiet humor. Kendall was rabid about the Bank of the United States (BUS) and the need to reform the government. "That there are horrible abuses in the government," he said, "admits of no doubt." And "if I get established here in an independent situation," he remarked, "the country shall know a few secrets, should not Old Hickory contrive to bring them out sooner."[11] Jackson was so taken with Kendall that he appointed him fourth auditor of the Treasury. Bringing Kendall into the government was one of Jackson's better and most significant appointments.

Kendall carried the good news of Jackson's reform program—as far as he understood it from their discussions—to a group of fellow journalists who met regularly at the home of the Reverend Obadiah Brown. Brown served as clerk in the Post Office Department during the week and as pastor of the First Baptist Church in Washington on Sunday. In the parlor of Brown's home congregated such Jacksonian literary lights as the acerbic Isaac Hill, the bluff Nathaniel Greene, the tall, spare Duff Green. Later Gideon Welles of Connecticut and Mordecai M. Noah of New York joined the group. All of them were immediately concerned with patronage. Kendall assured them all that "rewards will invariably take place" but warned that they must serve Jackson's reform intentions. Only those who "have been violent in their opposition, or made the best use of their status to injure the cause of Jackson" would be removed. The publicists paid no heed to the reform aspect and spoke only of dismissing all who belonged to the opposition. Patronage quickly devolved into spoils, and the spoils went solely to the victors.[12]

Once the main business of naming his cabinet had been accomplished, Jackson turned to completing a final draft of his inaugural address. In his collection of papers Jackson left a document entitled "Rough Draft of the Inaugural Address." It is in his hand and appears to have been composed by him alone. The paper is remarkable for its ideas and language. He had been called to office, he wrote, by the "voluntary suffrages of my country." A "government whose vital principle is the right of the people to controul its measures, and whose only object and glory are the equal happiness and freedom of all the members of the confederacy, cannot but perpetuate me with the most powerful and mingled emotions of thanks, on the one hand, for the honor conferred on me, and on the other, of solemn apprehensions for the safety of the great and important interests committed to my charge."

He then outlined his reform program. First, he wished to observe the strictest economy in governmental disbursements; then liquidate the national debt; provide a "judicious" tariff; and distribute the surplus on the basis of representation for the purpose of promoting education and internal improvements within the states. Most important, he would rid the departments of corrupt officials, and he would adhere to "a Just respect for state rights and the maintenance of state sovereignty as the best check of the tendencies to consolidation."[13]

His friends were not terribly happy with these efforts—they were far too specific—and got him to allow a number of alterations. Unfortunately the alterations sapped the original address of its vitality and strength. What was most notable in the final, printed version of Jackson's inaugural was the mention of the Indians and his desire to pursue a "just and liberal policy" toward them. Removal is what he had in mind, of course, but it was stated with delicacy and a certain degree of ambiguity. Also, the final version spoke of the need for *"reform."* The word *reform* is underscored. In this regard he said he wished to correct those "abuses that have brought the patronage of the Federal Government into conflict with the freedom of elections." In addition, he would correct the "causes which have disturbed the rightful course of appointment" and placed power in "unfaithful or incompetent hands."[14]

Once the address had everyone's approval the Tennesseans prepared for the inauguration on March 4. The town already swarmed with tourists, all anxious to witness the beginning of the "people's government" when their Hero would stand before them and take the oath of office. "I never saw such a crowd here before," commented Daniel Webster, senator from Massachusetts. "Persons have come five hundred miles to see General Jackson, *and they really seem to think that the country is rescued from some dreadful danger!"*[15] Soon every hotel room and lodging house was packed with hordes of people who came from every "point on the compass." It reminded some of the "inundation of the northern barbarians into Rome." Only the White House had available sleeping quarters. John Quincy Adams and his family departed the mansion at around nine o'clock the night before the inaugural and moved into Commodore David Porter's house on Meridian Hill, which Adams rented. Because Jackson had shamefully snubbed him by not calling on him after his arrival in Washington, Adams decided to boycott his successor's inaugural. It was bad form on the part of both men. Jackson certainly should have shown the President the courtesy of a brief, formal call. But he blamed Adams for the slanderous articles about his marriage that appeared in the Washington newspapers, and for failing to put a stop to them. Jackson owed Adams a great deal for his strong support in the past; and it was ridiculous to think the President could control his partisan press. Jackson should have suppressed his anger and performed what courtesy dictated. But he felt it would be a betrayal of his beloved, and he therefore refused.[16]

Wednesday, March 4, 1829, the day of the inauguration, dawned bright and sunny, a day made to order for an outdoor celebration. After a long season of cold and rainy weather it was "as if nature was willing to lend her aid towards contributing to the happiness of the thousands that crowded to behold the great ceremony."[17] This was the first election in which the inaugural ceremony was planned for the east portico of the Capitol, and thereafter it became the traditional setting for these rituals. An open-air ceremony was scheduled because of the vast numbers of people jammed into the city and the necessity of giving them an opportunity to witness their Hero's final triumph as he took the oath of office. By 10:00 A.M. the open area in front of the east portico was thronged with people, as well as the main streets leading to it. They even swarmed up the steps leading to the portico, so that a ship's cable had to be stretched about two-thirds of the way up the flight of stairs to hold them back. Francis Scott Key stared in wonder at the incredible spectacle of this surging, pulsating sea of humanity. "It is beautiful," he gasped, "it is sublime."[18]

At 11:00 A.M. Jackson emerged from his quarters at Gadsby's Hotel and was met by "an immense concourse of people." A group of soldiers of the revolutionary army formed a procession around him, along with officers who had served at New Orleans in 1815 and members of the Washington Central Committee. Jackson was dressed in a plain black suit, black tie, and long black coat, and because of his height he was plainly visible along the route to the crowds who lined both sides of Pennsylvania Avenue.[19]

As the procession moved along Jackson was soon flanked by "hacks, gigs, sulkies, wood-carts and a Dutch wagon." The General walked eastward along the avenue and with each burst of cheering he waved to the crowd and nodded his head in appreciation. When he reached the Capitol Jackson headed first for the Senate chamber to witness the swearing-in of the Vice President, John C. Calhoun. At 11:30 A.M. he arrived in the chamber and was immediately conducted to a chair in front of the secretary's desk. A seat had also been provided for the retiring President but it remained vacant throughout the proceedings.[20]

At high noon, after Calhoun's swearing-in by the president *pro tem* of the Senate, a procession formed in the chamber and slowly made its way to the east portico for the principal ceremony. Fifteen to twenty thousand people (the *Telegraph* claimed thirty thousand) swarmed around the Capitol. As the massive rotunda doors swung open, marshals marched out, followed by the justices of the Supreme Court. A Marine band took up a position to the right of the steps and other uniformed soldiers stood at attention around the groups.

The screaming and shouting of the crowd reached its pitch when General Jackson strode into view. Cries of "huzza" split the air—again and again. The noise "still resounds in my ears," recorded Margaret Bayard Smith, the wife of the Maryland senator, a week later. "Never can I forget the spectacle," said another, "nor the electrifying moment when the eager, expectant eyes of that vast and motley multitude caught sight . . . of their adored leader." In an instant, as if by "magic," the color of the whole mass changed—"all hats were off at once, and the dark tint which usually pervades a mixed map of men was turned . . . into the bright hue of ten thousand upturned and exultant human faces, radiant with sudden joy."[21]

For a moment Jackson just stared at the spectacle before him. Then in a motion that thrilled the crowd, he bowed low before this enormous congregation. He bowed to the "majesty of the people."[22]

A table covered with scarlet velvet had been positioned between the central columns of the portico with chairs for Jackson, Calhoun, and the chief justice. After bowing, Jackson took his seat and then adjusted two pairs of eyeglasses, one "thrown up on the top of his head, and the other before his eyes."[23] Once the applause and cheers abated, Jackson rose to read his inaugural address. Unlike modern inaugurals, the address preceded the taking of the oath of office.

"Fellow-Citizens," he began, "about to undertake the arduous duties that I have been appointed to perform by the choice of a free people, I avail myself of this . . . solemn occasion to express [my] gratitude . . ." The crowd grew very quiet in order to hear him. There was an "almost breathless silence," but "not a word reached their eager ears." They were grateful that the address lasted no longer than ten minutes. It was one of the shortest inaugural addresses in the history of the presidency and nearly set a record. Later, when it was published, it met with general approval. "The address itself is excellent chaste patriotic sententious and dignified," James Hamilton, Jr., senator from South Carolina, told Van Buren. "As far as I have heard . . . it has given universal satisfaction."[24]

When Jackson finished his address the crowd again roared its delight in him. He "stood for some minutes amid the shouts of thousands," gestured his thanks, and sat down. "There was a stateliness and elegance in the General's manner that charmed everybody."[25]

Chief Justice John Marshall then rose to administer the oath of office. A Bible was held by one of the attendants. Jackson approached the chief justice, placed one hand on the Bible, and raised the other. Repeating after Marshall the words prescribed by the Constitution, Jackson pronounced each word with great force. He then raised the Bible to his lips and kissed it reverently. The President shook hands with Marshall, as the crowd erupted with screams and cheers. Again, Jackson turned to them and bowed. "Yes," said Mrs. Smith ecstatically, watching from an upper floor of her house, "to the people in all their majesty."[26]

The crowd was now beside itself and could no longer hold back. In one great surge the people charged forward, broke the chain barring their way, and swarmed around their Hero as he received the congratulations of the guests on the portico. It took no little effort by the marshals to free the President from this unruly mob. He found temporary refuge inside the Capitol, but since a public reception was scheduled in the White House following the swearing-in, Jackson was obliged to retrace his steps up Pennsylvania Avenue.

He exited from the west entrance of the Capitol, walked down the hill to the gate, and found a handsome white horse waiting for him to take him to his new home. As the Hero mounted, a waiting crowd let out a shout. By this time the avenue was again jammed with people. "As far as the eye could reach," reported Amos Kendall, "the side-walks of the Avenue were covered with people on foot and the centre with innumerable carriages and persons on horseback moving in the same direction. For a full half hour, I stood waiting for the stream to run by; but like a never failing fountain the Capitol continued pouring its torrents."[27] Slowly, gesturing his appreciation to the people who cheered and waved to him, Jackson headed for the White House, and oh, said the disapproving Mrs. Smith, "such a cortege as followed him! Country men, farmers, gentlemen, mounted and dismounted, boys, women and children, black and white. Carriages, wagons and carts all pursuing him to the President's house."[28]

By the time the President arrived at the mansion all the rooms on the lower floor were filled to capacity by a mixture of every conceivable race, color, and social standing. People from the "highest and most polished," said Joseph Story, an associate justice of the Supreme Court, "down to the most vulgar and gross in the nation" poured into the White House. "I never saw such a mixture," he moaned. "The reign of KING MOB seemed triumphant," he added. "I was glad to escape from the scene as soon as possible."[29]

A modest White House reception had been planned. What took place verged on public disorder. It became a wild, near-riotous scene. Barrels of orange punch had been prepared, but as the waiters opened the doors to carry them out, the mob spotted them and rushed forward to seize them. Pails of liquor splashed to the floor, glasses fell and were smashed, and such mayhem ensued "that wine and ice-creams could not be brought out to the ladies." Several thousand dollars in smashed china and glassware were lost during the pandemonium. To add to the general melee, men with "boots heavy with mud" stood on the "damask satin-covered chairs" in order to get a better look at their President. It was a "regular Saturnalia," laughed Senator Hamilton. "The mob broke in, in thousands—Spirits black yellow and grey, poured in in one uninterrupted stream of mud and filth, among the throngs many fit subjects for the penitentiary."[30]

When Mrs. Smith and her family arrived at the mansion they were aghast at the spectacle in progress. "What a scene did we witness!" she gasped. *"The Majesty of the People"* had disappeared, and a rabble, a mob, of boys, negros, women, children, scrambling, fighting, romping. What a pity what a pity."[31]

Poor Jackson. They nearly suffocated him with their display of affection. Everyone wanted to shake his hand. Finally the pressure got so bad and the danger of actually injuring the President so real that a number of friends formed a ring around him as "a kind of barrier of their own bodies." The President, reported Mrs. Smith, was "*literally* nearly pressed to death and almost suffocated and torn to pieces in their eagerness to shake hands with Old Hickory." Happily, he made his escape from his well-wishers and returned to his temporary quarters at Gadsby's. It was then 4:00 P.M.[32]

The flight of the President did not dampen the spirits of the mob, however. If anything, the mayhem got worse. Indeed, it now looked as though the mansion itself was in danger and might collapse around them. To relieve the pressure inside the building, tubs of punch and pails of liquor were transferred to the lawn outside and all the windows were thrown open to provide additional exits for those anxious to keep up with the refreshments. The strategy worked. The "rabble" bolted after the liquor, using the fastest means of exit, including jumping out the windows.

It was wild. For persons of refinement it was an awful commentary on American life and customs. But not everyone agreed. Senator James Hamilton, Jr., declared it a great success. "Notwithstanding the row Demos kicked up," he told Van Buren, "the whole matter went off very well."[33]

Jackson, meanwhile, rested in his rooms at Gadsby's. Later he dined with Calhoun and some friends on sirloin steak cut from a prize ox roasted for the occasion. Not that Jackson was a big eater. On the contrary, he usually ate very little, for he had no interest and took no delight in eating for its own sake. He loved the sociability that dining allowed, but normally he just picked at his food. He planned to retire early since he had no intention of attending the inaugural ball to be held at the Washington Assembly Rooms. He was still in deep mourning for his wife.

Inauguration Day, 1829, proved so lusty in its display of the American spirit at its most boisterous, exuberant, and vulgar that its essential ingredients became traditional. It was the first "people's inaugural." The people—not politicians or Washington society or a central committee—made it uniquely their own. "It was a proud day for the people," reported the *Argus of Western America* on March 18, 1829. "General Jackson is *their own* President. Plain in his dress, venerable in his appearance, unaffected and familiar in his manners, he was greeted by them with an enthusiasm which bespoke him the Hero of a popular triumph."

Speaking from a different point of view, Mrs. Smith had to agree, despite many reservations. But she tempered her comments with a small warning. "It was the People's day, and the People's President and the People would rule. God grant that one day or other, the People do not pull down all rule and rules."[34]

The inauguration of General Andrew Jackson of Tennessee, despite the vulgarity and animal spirits unleashed by the occasion, was one of the great moments in American history. And the reason for this, as everyone agreed, was that it represented in a symbolic way a significant advance in representative government for the American people.[35] Andrew Jackson was the people's own president—the first such—and that was something wonderful and exciting. Seeing the crowds and hearing them cheer a government that they themselves had called into existence augured well for the future of a democratic society.

CHAPTER 14

———⟨◦⟩———

The Reform Begins

Not until march 10, after the "ravages of the mob" had been "repaired and the building prepared . . . for his residence," did President Andrew Jackson move into the White House. And like most everything else he touched, Old Hickory radically altered the structure and appearance of the executive mansion almost immediately. For it was Andrew Jackson who had the wit and imagination (along with the political skill) to muster from Congress the means to complete the building of the White House and finish its interior decoration. At his direction, the north portico was constructed in 1829, having been designed twenty-two years before by Benjamin Latrobe. In addition, single-story wings were extended east and west from the main building as offices and housing for horses and carriages. And in 1833 iron pipes were laid to bring running water from Franklin Park to the White House. Previously two pumps had provided water via wooden troughs. The first formal garden around the White House was also laid out, and the President himself planted several magnolia trees in memory of his beloved Rachel.[1]

When Jackson moved into the White House he gathered as much family around him as possible. The Donelsons—Andrew and Emily (who served as the President's official hostess) and their nearly three-year-old son, Andrew Jackson Donelson, Jr.—formed a solid core. Jackson's own twenty-year-old son joined his father in the executive mansion but soon returned to Tennessee to supervise the running of the plantation and the Hermitage, and only periodically returned to Washington to visit. Mary Eastin, the daughter of William and Rachel (Donelson) Eastin, one of Jackson's many wards and the friend and confidante of Emily Donelson, also moved into the White House. Later in the spring, Ralph Earl, the painter, joined the White House entourage. Married to Rachel Jackson's niece, Jane Caffery (who died shortly after their marriage), Earl had often been Jackson's traveling companion. After Rachel's death the new President found Earl's presence very comforting, so he installed the painter in the White House and gave him a private studio where he could work undisturbed. Over a number of years Earl produced many striking and authentic portraits of Old Hickory.

William B. Lewis, who accompanied the Jackson party from Tennessee to Washington, followed the General into the executive mansion, and when he started to make preparations to return home the President— according to Lewis's account—begged him to stay. So it was arranged for him to take an auditorship in the Treasury Department and live at the White House. Lewis provided many services for Jackson, not the least of which was writing to political friends to explain the President's thinking on the major issues facing the administration.

In the arrangement of living quarters, Jackson chose the two rooms at the end of the corridor on the southwest side of the building, with his office at the other end of the hall. The Donelsons occupied the northwest corner room facing Pennsylvania Avenue and used the room next to it as a nursery. At the other end of the corridor rooms were set aside for Earl and Lewis, with Donelson occupying a corner office which he always kept locked. Jackson seemed very pleased with this arrangement, at least in the beginning, and the presence of his family so close to him made life much easier all around.[2]

The first and most pressing matter facing President Jackson upon the inauguration of his administration was the necessity of expelling from office those men whose corrupting practices he believed had scarred the operation of the American government for the past ten years. It was the perpetuation of American liberty that Jackson wished to safeguard and which explains his decision to make his appointments an essential component of his reform program. He also feared the emergence of an "official aristocracy" that would presume to act without any regard for the popular will. After a few years in office they tended to view their positions as a matter of right, and even to anticipate bequeathing their tenure to their offspring.

Prior to his inauguration Jackson prepared an "Outline of principles" respecting his intended reform program which he submitted to the heads of the various departments. The document was dated February 23, 1829. In it he directed his cabinet to undertake immediately "a strict examination" into the operation of their respective departments and to report to him directly on "what retrenchments can be made without injury to the public service, what offices can be dispensed with, and what improvements made in the economy and dispatch of business." As much as possible they must limit the operation of government, he said. Because of the "widespread corruption," he expected removals. But, he added, these removals must emanate from principle. He therefore directed that *only* those who had been "appointed against the manifest will of the people" or whose official station "was made to operate against the freedom of state elections" would be replaced. The appointment power must serve the cause of freedom, or, as Jackson put it, "to perpetuate our

liberty." In addition, he expected all new appointees to help restore
virtue and morality to government. They must conform to a strict moral
code. "Connected with the character of the administration are the moral
habits of those who may be entrusted with its various subordinate duties.
Officers in their private and public relations should be examples of
fidelity & honesty; otherwise . . . they will have to be removed." A rigid
adherence to this principle, he declared, will both "elevate the character
of the government, and purify the morals of the country. This principle
will be regarded as a fundamental one by the President."[3]

Jackson called his policy "rotation in office." But hungry politicians,
avid for wholesale removals, called it something else. "To the victor
belong the spoils of the enemy," intoned the stentorian Senator William
L. Marcy of New York, one of Van Buren's closest allies. That bald-faced
and arrogant statement put a different light on Jackson's intended program of rotation. Instead of reform, declared his enemies, Jackson had
introduced one of the worst political practices imaginable: the "spoils"
system. "The government," asserted one man after the President had
inaugurated rotation, "formerly served by the *elite* of the nation, is now
served, to a very considerable extent, by its refuse."[4]

Needless to say, Andrew Jackson did not introduce the spoils system
to American government. Nor did he dismiss thousands of officeholders,
despite the assertions of his opponents. He removed only 919 persons
out of 10,093 during the first eighteen months of his administration. For
the entire eight years of his presidency he only removed 9 percent of all
officeholders, which is approximately one in ten. This is hardly the record
of a spoilsman, particularly when the figures are considered in the light
of normal replacements due to death and resignation, plus those dismissed for incompetence and dishonesty.

Still Jackson was determined to establish an important democratic principle of government, and in his first message to Congress, delivered on
December 8, 1829, he explained his principle and the reasons for advancing it.

> Office is considered as a species of property, and government rather as
> a means of promoting individual interests than as an instrument created
> solely for the service of the people. Corruption in some and in others a
> perversion of correct feelings and principles divert government from its
> legitimate ends and make it an engine for the support of the few at the
> expense of the many. The duties of all public officers are, or at least admit
> of being made, so plain and simple that men of intelligence may readily
> qualify themselves for their performance; and I can not but believe that
> more is lost by the long continuance of men in office than is generally to
> be gained by their experience. I submit, therefore, to your consideration
> when the efficiency of the Government would not be promoted and official
> industry and integrity better secured by a general extension of the law
> which limits appointments to four years.

In a country where offices are created solely for the benefit of the people no one man has any more intrinsic right to official station than another. Offices were not established to give support to particular men at the public expense. No individual wrong is, therefore, done by removal, since neither appointment to nor continuance in office is matter of right. . . . It is the people, and they alone, who have a right to complain when a bad officer is substituted for a good one. He who is removed has the same means of obtaining a living that are enjoyed by the millions who never held office. The proposed limitation would destroy the idea of property now so generally connected with official station, and although individual distress may be sometimes produced, it would, by promoting that rotation which constitutes a leading principle in the republican creed, give healthful action to the system.[5]

The argument Jackson advanced for rotation was the argument of democracy. Offices exist for the benefit of the people. No one has an intrinsic right to them; they are open to all. Removal, therefore, does not in itself constitute a wrong. What Jackson advanced was the contention that a popular government had been established with his election and any vestige of elitism in the operation of government was contrary to the popular will.

Acceptance of rotation came simply and naturally. It found favor with the American people because it did indeed seem appropriate to democratic government. Instead of Congress legislating acceptance of the principle, it simply recognized the right of each new administration to choose the personnel most congenial to its approach to government. When properly controlled the system of rotation provided fast response to the changing demands of the American people as expressed through the ballot box. And that, after all, is what democracy is all about.

Skeptics then and later questioned the extent of the corruption that Jackson claimed existed prior to his inauguration. It was fashionable to regard rotation as a euphemism for spoils. The truth seems to be that Jackson was correct in his contention that corruption had been rampant for over ten years.[6] Nearly half a million dollars was discovered stolen from the Treasury alone, and when combined with the thefts involving Indians, army and navy contracts, and the operations of the BUS, these facts gave substance to Jackson's insistence that the so-called Era of Good Feelings had been in fact an Era of Corruption.

Sensitive to the "great noise" generated by his reform efforts, Jackson proceeded very carefully with his removals. He became even more circumspect when Martin Van Buren, the "voice of caution" himself, arrived in Washington to take up his duties as secretary of state. The coach carrying Van Buren clattered into Washington on March 22. As he stepped out of his carriage and entered the hotel, a crowd of office-seekers surrounded him. They pursued him to his room and swarmed around him as he dropped to the sofa. He told them he expected to pay his respects to the President within an hour and would therefore listen to them until he had to leave. An hour later he entered the White House to meet President Jackson. It was their first meeting since they had become political allies. A single lamp lighted the vestibule of the White House and a solitary candle flickered in the President's office as the Magician entered the room.

Major Lewis stood by Jackson's side. Van Buren worried about this meeting but the President immediately dispelled his fears with a warm greeting and signs of his obvious pleasure at having his first secretary in Washington at last. In fact the President startled Van Buren by the "affectionate eagerness" with which he greeted the New Yorker. More than that, once their conversation began, Van Buren was struck by the quickness and sharpness of his mind. Like Webster, Benton, Kendall, and dozens of others, he immediately caught Jackson's intellectual strengths. "The character of his mind was that of judgment," commented Thomas Hart Benton, "with a rapid and almost intuitive perception, followed by an instant and decisive action."[7] Like his writing style, Jackson's conversation had "a vigorous flowing current . . . and [was] always impressive."[8] On this occasion it really dazzled Van Buren—perhaps because it was so unexpected. And Van Buren needed to get a sharp fix on Jackson's ability right from the start lest he presume an attitude that could have wrecked their relationship. Years later he recorded in his *Autobiography* what his association with Jackson had been like. It started, he said, at the moment he entered the White House. "From that night to the day of his death the relations, sometimes official, always political and personal, were inviolably maintained between that noble man and myself, the cordial and confidential character of which can never have been surpassed among public men."[9]

Temperamentally, physically, and in every other way, the two men seemed quite dissimilar. The long, cadaverous, sharp-featured, excitable Jackson stood in sharp contrast to the short, stoutish, ever-cautious Van Buren. But these obvious differences masked many similarities. Both men were widowers, a kind of mutual loss that put them in a special category. Although Jackson's loss was recent, Van Buren, with four young sons to raise since his wife's death ten years before, still appreciated what the President suffered. More importantly, both men were practical politicians. Different perhaps, but both effective, successful, and attuned to a modern (popular) approach to politics. Also, both were committed to a states' rights philosophy and both tended to a laissez-faire notion of economic theory. Both were Jeffersonian in their approach to government and rather regarded themselves as heirs of Jefferson's political philosophy, although neither was a theoretician. Both believed in limited government. Both understood the need for reform.[10]

In their first meeting in the White House the two men talked for several hours. And not only was Van Buren impressed by his chief but the

President came to a real awareness of the Magician's many talents. Jackson especially liked the zeal, the near-fervor with which his secretary spoke in recommending ministers to England, France, Spain, and the other important European capitals. If indeed Van Buren could run his department with this same enthusiasm and determination for success, then they were off to an excellent start. By the time they finished their talk an initial bond had been established that grew stronger with each subsequent meeting. From their first conversation Van Buren proved he could be relied upon for sound, honest advice. Later he provided repeated evidence of his good judgment, wide knowledge, and unswerving loyalty. In time Jackson found him an excellent sounding board for ideas, and he appreciated his constant presence—the Magician had no wife to consume his time—the ease with which he could converse with him, and the small courtesies the little man frequently bestowed on the members of his family.

As much as he relied on Van Buren over the next several years, the President never surrendered control of his administration on any issue— not to him or to anyone else. "I have found the President affectionate, confidential and kind to the last degree," Van Buren wrote shortly after his arrival in Washington. "He has, however, his own wishes and favorite views upon points which it is not my province to attempt to controul."[11] Because the New Yorker learned from the outset that Jackson was master in his own house, he survived several brushes with catastrophe. Because he never forgot this fact he eventually won the right to succeed the Hero into the White House.

One bit of advice Van Buren offered concerned the appointment of the collector of the Port of New York. This was a very sensitive and important position. Some $15 million annually passed through the collector's hands. If any post needed a man of the highest integrity it was this one. And when Van Buren learned that Jackson intended to appoint Samuel Swartwout to the office he almost collapsed. Not only did Swartwout have criminal tendencies but the Regency detested him. Van Buren alerted the President immediately and warned him that Swartwout's appointment would "not be in accordance with public sentiment, the interest of the Country or the credit of the administration." Unfortunately, Jackson refused to listen. He liked Swartwout because he had been an early supporter—unlike Van Buren—and so he went ahead with the appointment. In time, of course, Swartwout absconded with $1,222,705.09. It was a monumental theft. And when his peculations were finally uncovered a few years later, the criminal fled to Europe. Jackson was mortified. "Can he live after this?" the President cried, "or will he cut his throat?" Between Jackson and Van Buren the subject was never mentioned again. "I was too sensible of the extent of his disappointment and mortification to do so myself," Van Buren later wrote.[12]

When the scandal broke, Jackson's opponents doubled over with laughter. All the talk about rooting out corruption in government, they said, and here the greatest theft in the history of the Republic occurred in the General's own administration. All the talk about restoring virtue to government, and this single miscreant stole more money than all the defaulters in Adams's administration put together. Here, then, was the bitter fruit of rotation, hooted the President's critics. Here the dreadful consequence of denying the government the service of an elite bureaucracy in order to serve some idealistic democratic principle. Perhaps this appalling incident taught Jackson a valuable lesson. Perhaps he learned that it takes more than the personal integrity of the President himself to insure an administration free of corruption. Whatever the lesson, he clearly suffered from the derision he so richly deserved.

But rotation was not Jackson's only reform. It was only part of a larger program, which applied to both foreign and domestic affairs, a program he eventually called "reform retrenchment and economy." It consisted mainly of the following: the reduction of the size and operation of the government; the limitation of government expenditures in order to pay off the national debt; the alteration of the structure of the Bank of the United States, the "greatest corrupter" in the country; the "judicious" adjustment of the tariff schedule so that harmony between the sections might be restored; the extension of the western boundary to protect the southwestern frontier; the rearrangement of "our affairs" with England and France to win commercial access to the West Indies from the former and to settle spoliation claims with the latter; the introduction of a constitutional amendment governing the election of the President and Vice President, to prevent voiding the popular will as had happened in 1825; and the removal of Indian tribes beyond the Mississippi River so as to "protect and preserve them as nations."[13]

As he prepared to initiate these reforms as well as write his first message to Congress to invite their implementation into law, Jackson suddenly lost control of his household and administration. Through his own folly he created a major public scandal that sent his reforms temporarily into limbo. It also disrupted his family and caused the Donelsons to return home to Tennessee. It produced a constitutional crisis that shook the country to its foundations.

CHAPTER 15

Political Upheaval

In A CHARMINGLY NAIVE, if quaintly expressed, comment on the course of American affairs in the nineteenth century, one of Jackson's earliest biographers wrote in 1860 that "the political history of the United States, for the last thirty years, dates from the moment when the soft hand of Mr. Van Buren touched Mrs. Eaton's knocker."[1] Supposedly it was the Magician's manipulation of an unsavory social scandal that produced the political shocks that rocked the nation and ultimately hurled John C. Calhoun into political oblivion and elevated Van Buren to the highest office in the land. This version of the "Eaton malaria," as Van Buren called it, won immediate acceptance if for no other reason than that it added the suspicion of sordidness to an already tawdry affair.

The Eaton marriage was a messy business from the very beginning, considering Peggy's unsavory reputation. It then triggered events which immediately flew out of control. The situation worsened because of Jackson's sense of loyalty, his single-minded determination to have his own way, Peggy Eaton's overbearing presumption of her rights, the meddling by sanctimonious hypocrites, and the self-serving ploys of ambitious politicians.

The political ramifications were the most intriguing. From the earliest stirrings of the new Democratic party two men (aside from Jackson) emerged as its principal architects: Martin Van Buren and John C. Calhoun. A natural rivalry between them and their cohorts seemed inevitable, but it was generally understood that Calhoun would succeed Jackson at the end of his presidential term—probably after four years, given the state of the General's health. But Van Buren had several things going for him. First, he had staunch friends among the Nashville Central Committee, several of whom actively disliked Calhoun. They heard rumors that the South Carolinian had criticized the Hero's supposedly "unauthorized" invasion of Florida in 1818 and had urged his censure in Monroe's cabinet. None of this sat well with men like Sam Houston and Major Lewis, both of whom tried unsuccessfully to obtain hard evidence of

190

Calhoun's actual recommendation in the cabinet. Lewis himself preferred Van Buren for personal reasons. He had more to gain by the New Yorker's advance toward the throne, particularly if he served as king-maker. Since Lewis was Eaton's brother-in-law, a powerful alliance soon developed between the three men once they gathered in Washington to launch the Jackson administration.

A counterbalance to this influence was the presence in the White House of Andrew Jackson Donelson. He resented Lewis's position of trust and especially his obvious intent to play a key role as presidential adviser. As a consequence Donelson took an immediate dislike to Van Buren. His wife, Emily, naturally sided with her husband and contributed to the unpleasantness by refusing to socialize with Peggy Eaton.

The situation grew worse through the meddling action of two clergy-men, the Reverend J. M. Campbell, pastor of the Presbyterian Church in Washington, where both the General and Rachel had worshipped, and the Reverend Ezra Stiles Ely of Philadelphia, who had known Jackson since the young Tennessean first began to travel east on business in the 1790s. Convinced he was acting in the best interests of the new adminis-tration, Ely wrote Jackson a long letter early in 1829 in which he recited all the whispered charges reported against Peggy.[2]

Jackson reacted with characteristic vehemence when he received the letter, denying the charges and tongue-lashing his erstwhile friend for his "dark and sly insinuations."[3] Whether Jackson consciously or uncon-sciously equated Peggy's plight with Rachel's hardly matters. His natural sympathy for women in distress, buttressed by his long friendship with Eaton, strengthened by a conviction that these rumors were circulated by "the minions of Mr. Clay" to injure the Eatons and "through the Eatons to injure me," drove Jackson to heroic lengths to defend and protect the couple. He risked his presidency to defend this ostracized lady. He defied social custom—not for the first time—to protect a female. But as many said at the time, he would no longer be Andrew Jackson had he acted otherwise.[4]

Ely's meddling was followed by that of Campbell when he called on the President in the White House to convey the information which he had taken upon himself to gather about Mrs. Eaton. Jackson favored him with one of his greatest and most passionate performances. No sooner did Campbell finish his *"vile tale"* than Old Hickory pounced on him. He raged and gestured and threatened and spoke with such conviction and emotional intensity that he reduced the poor clergyman to virtual si-lence.[5]

For the next several days the President spent all his time debating with Campbell about specifics of the gossip. He even invited him back to the White House for another go-around. This ghastly business reached an absurd height when Jackson decided to call a cabinet meeting on Septem-ber 10 to examine the evidence relative to Eaton's alleged "criminal intercourse with Mrs. Timberlake," as though the cabinet constituted some sort of moral and judicial body. In addition to Van Buren, Ingham, Branch, Barry, and Berrien, the President asked Lewis and Donelson to attend, along with the Reverends Ely and Campbell. Eaton was conspicuous by his absence.[6]

Jackson began the meeting by reviewing the evidence provided by Campbell, after which he called on Ely to present the results of his own inquiries. By this time Ely was anxious to extricate himself from this unholy mess and regain his good standing with the President and he declared that he had found no evidence of misconduct on the part of Eaton.

"Nor Mrs. Eaton either," snapped Jackson.

"On that point," Ely replied, "I would rather not give an opinion."

"She is as chaste as a virgin!" thundered the President.[7]

The cabinet sat stony-faced as they heard these incredible words. Finally Campbell asked to speak and Jackson nodded his consent. The clergyman said he had simply tried to spare the administration embarrassment and the country from grief.

Jackson interrupted. Campbell had been summoned to present evidence, he snapped, not give a sermon.

"I perceive that I have mistaken the object of the invitation to come," Campbell replied; "that it was not to give me an opportunity of saying any thing in my justification." With that, he bowed to the cabinet and left the room. Shortly thereafter the meeting broke up.[8]

What a farce! The cabinet of the American government sitting in solemn council to hear evidence about the alleged sexual misconduct of one of its members. The President was engaged in a lunatic crusade in which he had absolutely no business.

When the cabinet adjourned Jackson thought that Peggy had been completely vindicated. He should have known better. In his own household he could not make a convincing case. His niece and official hostess, Emily Donelson, agreed to receive Mrs. Eaton as her uncle's guest in the White House, but she absolutely refused to pay the lady the courtesy of calling on her at her own home. Wives of several cabinet officers felt the same way. "The ladies here with one voice have determined not to visit her," Emily told a friend.[9] Other critics began referring to Mrs. Eaton as "Bellona," the Roman goddess of war, and the Eaton affair as the "petticoat war." For some it was all terribly amusing.

The matter of the Eatons' place in society was certain to cause problems as the Washington social season neared. Normally the President gives the first formal dinner for his official family, followed by all the other cabinet members beginning with the secretary of state. Jackson's party brought a complete turnout, but so much bad feeling showed on the faces of several cabinet wives that the evening was a dismal failure. When it ended Old Hickory retired to his bedroom mortified and humiliated.

As next in line to give a formal dinner, Van Buren tried to add glamour to his guest list by inviting the widow of Governor Thomas Mann Randolph of Virginia, the sole surviving child of Thomas Jefferson. Yet he received a note from John Branch almost immediately accepting the invitation for himself but declining for Mrs. Branch and his daughter and offering the transparent excuse of "circumstances unnecessary to detail." John McPherson Berrien, a widower, also declined. He had a "conditional engagement" out of town, and his daughter's "state of health" precluded her attendance. Although Samuel Ingham attended, his wife did not. Nor did the wives of Eaton and William Barry, who decided "to remain behind their batteries."[10]

A few weeks later Van Buren gave another party. (He seemed to be courting trouble.) The *Washington Journal* thereupon accused him and his ally in crime, Sir Charles Vaughan, the British minister and a bachelor, of attempting to force an "unworthy person" upon Washington society. It urged everyone invited to demonstrate their outrage by not showing up. Naturally this insured a record turnout. Wild beasts could not hold back the matrons of Washington—except, of course, the Mesdames Ingham and Branch and Mlle. Berrien. They were all indisposed. But the party was reportedly a sensation.[11]

Another of Van Buren's diplomatic friends, who was also a bachelor, gave a ball soon afterward, on December 23, 1829. The host was the Russian minister, Baron Krudener. Since Mrs. Ingham was again indisposed, the host conducted Peggy to the dinner table, as next in rank. Eaton was assigned to Madame Huygens, the wife of the Dutch envoy. The Madame was not happy with this arrangement and at one point supposedly announced that she would give a party to which Mrs. Eaton would not be invited and that her example would be followed by the wives of the cabinet members—which would put the Eatons out of society with a vengeance.

While Van Buren stirred and seasoned this cauldron of female venom, busy reporters transmitted the details of Madame Huygens's remarks to President Jackson. Not long afterward Van Buren received a summons to the White House. He was told by Jackson to hand the Huygenses their passports if what he heard proved to be true. Jackson regarded the entire matter as a "conspiracy" ultimately aimed at himself. But the lady denied saying the things attributed to her. She protested that "she had been too long connected with diplomatic life, and understood too well what belonged to her position, to meddle in such matters." So strong was her disavowal that the President received it with "unaffected pleasure." The Huygenses were absolved.[12]

Not the cabinet officers, however. The President summoned the three offending gentlemen (Ingham, Branch, and Berrien) to a meeting and read them a memorandum in which he denounced the "combination" formed to drive Eaton and his family out of society and thereby "coerce me" into dismissing him from the cabinet. "I will not part with major Eaton from my cabinet," declared the President, "and those of my cabinet who cannot harmonise with him had better withdraw for harmony I must and will have."[13]

At first Jackson placed the blame for the "combination" on "Clay and his minions," and later on "females with clergymen at their head." At no time did he consider a larger plot having to do with the presidential succession. That came soon enough.[14]

But at least the Eaton affair revealed one loyal friend to Jackson. Martin Van Buren had assiduously taken great pains to demonstrate his total loyalty and dependability. And, except for the dinners he and his friends gave, he manipulated nothing. He just watched events develop on their own and then he acted with prudence and political astuteness, providing the President with thoughtful and sage advice on the conduct of public affairs. Everything simply fell into place, and all in his favor.

Jackson watched with growing pleasure the conduct of his friend. "I have found him every thing that I could desire him to be," Old Hickory wrote John Overton. "Instead of his being selfish and intriguing, as has been represented by some of his opponents, I have ever found him frank, open, candid, and manly. As a Counsellor he is *able* and *prudent*, Republican in his principles and one of the most pleasant men to do business with I ever saw.

"I wish I could say as much for Mr. Calhoun and some of his friends," Jackson continued in his letter to Overton. "You know the confidence I once had in that gentleman. However, of *him* I desire not now to speak; but I have a right to believe that most of the troubles, vexations and difficulties I have had to encounter, since my arrival in this City, have been occasioned by his friends. But for the present let this suffice."[15]

This naming of Calhoun as possibly involved in the President's "vexations and difficulties" placed a different cast on these fast-developing events. Jackson's concern over Calhoun's relationship to his administration had been growing for the past several months. For one thing, he had heard that the Vice President had had a hand in the composition of the nullification resolutions passed by the South Carolina legislature to protest the Tariff of Abominations. The south hated protective tariff legislation, as he well knew, but threatening nullification took opposition to federal law a little too far and that did not sit well with the President at all. For another, Calhoun had chosen to remain silent on the BUS question and had objected to the apportionment of the surplus revenue among the states after the national debt was paid. No doubt William B. Lewis, who disliked Calhoun, encouraged Jackson's sense of dissatisfaction with his Vice President. And the fact that Calhoun's wife, Floride, had refused to return a social call by the Eatons and was regarded by some as the leader of the "female contingent" intent on humiliating and ostracizing poor Peggy must have added to the President's growing annoyance with his supposed successor.

The situation worsened for Calhoun when Robert Y. Hayne of South Carolina and Daniel Webster of Massachusetts clashed on the Senate floor over the rights of the states, the nature of the Union, and the status of slavery. In a high-powered, emotional, yet closely argued speech Hayne articulated the Calhoun theory of nullification which advanced the right of a state to declare federal laws inoperative within its boundaries whenever such laws violated its interests and sovereignty. The rights of the south, Hayne protested, must at all times be respected, and any effort to jeopardize those rights would provoke an extreme reaction: nullification first, then secession if nullification failed to provide redress.[16]

Webster replied in a two-day speech. It reached a peak of high drama when he shook his finger at the Vice President, the author of nullification, and pronounced the Union a composition of people, not states. "I go for the Constitution as it is, and for the Union as it is," declared Webster. "It is, Sir, the people's Constitution, the people's government, made for the people, made by the people, and answerable to the people."[17]

Everyone presumed that Jackson would side with Hayne in defense of states' rights. Some of Duff Green's editorials in the *United States Telegraph* seemed to confirm this presumption until it was remembered that Green was Calhoun's kinsman and friend and that his first loyalty rested with the Vice President. If the debate had addressed itself exclusively to states' rights, most probably Jackson would have agreed with Hayne. But the argument drifted to nullification and secession and conceivably the breakup of the Union. That, Jackson could never espouse. He would rather "die in the last Ditch," as he once said, than "see the Union disunited."[18]

Because of the false presumptions propagated by Duff Green and his own abhorrence of disunion, Jackson could not remain silent. He could not give the impression that he sided with the theoretical views of Hayne and Calhoun. But how to disavow the doctrine? Fortunately, the problem resolved itself. For the past twenty years it had been the custom in Washington for Republicans in Congress to celebrate the birthday of Thomas Jefferson on April 13. Since Jackson was regarded as the "great restorer and exemplifier of Jeffersonian principles"[19] he was expected to attend and participate in the approaching celebration. And if he attended, then the Vice President, cabinet, and all the congressional panjandrums would also participate. Suddenly it occurred to Van Buren that the celebration might become the occasion for "some irregular and unauthorized proceedings" by the nullifiers and their friends, "which might menace the stability of the Union." The occasion might become a "stalking horse" to enlist additional congressional support for the pernicious doctrine of nullification.[20]

On the day of the celebration, the *United States Telegraph* published a program for the proceedings, and when Jackson saw the names of the principal participants he immediately concluded that the "celebration was to be a *nullification affair altogether.*"[21] That settled it. The moment had arrived for the President himself to put a stop to these shenanigans and make his own position absolutely clear not only to congressmen but to the American people.

Jackson immediately prepared three statements. Since he would surely be invited to offer a toast at the affair, he decided that that would be the moment to take his stand. He showed all three to Lewis, Donelson, and Van Buren and they agreed on the shortest one as the most "expressive." Jackson then placed the approved statement in his pocket and threw the other two into the fire.

The dinner was held at the Indian Queen Hotel. The celebrants sat at two parallel tables, with a cross table at the head. More than a hundred congressmen attended, along with the cabinet and other high-ranking government officials. The President arrived at five o'clock and stayed until ten. John Roane of Virginia officiated, assisted by a dozen other congressmen. Once the festivities began the guests eagerly anticipated the toasts to be drunk. Twenty-four of them were proposed, and all but six or seven mentioned Virginia and Jefferson and the great principles of states' rights for which both stood. Robert Y. Hayne, chairman of the Committee on Arrangements, spoke long and eloquently about how "great and glorious" victories had been won under the standard of states' rights. Then he proposed his toast: "The *Union* of the States, and the *Sovereignty* of the States."

Jackson fidgeted. Some of the toasts, he thought, bordered on sedition. He could not bear to "hear the dissolution of the Union spoken of lightly."[22]

Both Jackson and Calhoun were seated near the chair. Van Buren had been placed at the foot of the second table next to a presumed nullifier for safekeeping. Jackson picked up the list of regular toasts and wrote his own on the back of it. But as he wrote he inadvertently left out a single word.

The regular toasts concluded. The President was then asked to provide a volunteer. He rose.

"Our Union: *It must be preserved.*"

The words ricocheted around the room. "The veil was rent," recorded Van Buren, "—the incantations of the night were exposed to the light of day."[23]

Hayne jumped from his place and ran over to the President. He begged him to insert the word "federal" so that the toast could be reported as "Our federal Union." Since that was precisely the word Jackson had inadvertently omitted, he "cheerfully assented."[24]

The Vice President rose to offer the next toast.

"The Union," he said in a strong voice. "Next to our liberty, the most dear." Had he stopped with these words Calhoun would have shared some of Jackson's merit in terms of brevity and pungency. But he could not resist lecturing his audience for a few extra moments and in so doing dulled the edge of his thrusting words.

Next came the political master. Van Buren offered blessings on everyone. "Mutual forbearance and reciprocal concession," he purred. "Through their agency the Union was established. The patriotic spirit from which they emanated will forever sustain it."[25]

In all three toasts the keynote was "Union." Calhoun said it came next to liberty. But Webster, in his second reply to Hayne on the Senate floor, insisted that liberty and Union were inseparable—one not possible without the other. That was Jackson's opinion too. Liberty had always been uppermost in his thinking about government. But only through a strong Union—not a hyperactive government—could liberty be preserved and perpetuated.[26]

This brush with the extremist southern position totally alienated Jackson from his Vice President. It also severely damaged the relationship of the administration with its so-called mouthpiece, the *United States Telegraph.* At the same time Van Buren continued to gain ground. He now began urging Jackson to stand for reelection in 1832, something the General at first opposed.[27] It accorded with the Magician's desire to keep Old Hickory in place and stall Calhoun's ambitions for the succession—at least for another four years.

The ever-observant Amos Kendall watched the skillful New York operator work his magic. He had to express his admiration. "Van Buren glides along as smoothly as oil and as silently as a cat," he told Francis Blair. "If he is managing at all, it is so adroitly that nobody perceives it. He is evidently gaining from the indiscretions of Calhoun's friends. He has the entire confidence of the President and all his personal friends, while Calhoun is fast losing it."[28]

Not many days after the Jefferson birthday celebration a congressman from South Carolina came to the White House to pay his respects and take leave of the President before departing for his home. He asked Jackson if he had anything he wanted him to convey to his friends in South Carolina. "No, I believe not," came the immediate reply. But then the President remembered his toast and corrected himself. "Yes, I have; please give my compliments to my friends in your State, and say to them, that if a single drop of blood shall be shed there in opposition to the laws of the United States, I will hang the first man I can lay my hand on engaged in such treasonable conduct, upon the first tree I can reach."[29]

Between the Eaton affair, the nullification business, and the smooth footwork of the secretary of state, Vice President Calhoun was steadily losing his position of primacy with President Jackson. Over a period of five or six months a noose had begun winding itself around Calhoun's neck and it was slowly but inexorably squeezing the political life out of him. Then, without warning, the noose got a sudden and devastating tug. Three days after Jackson gave his memorable toast, John Forsyth, the governor of Georgia, wrote a letter to William H. Crawford. And that was the beginning of the end of John C. Calhoun as successor to President Andrew Jackson.

A conspiracy against Calhoun had been brewing for years. The cause of it went back to the time of Jackson's invasion of Florida and the efforts of some members of Monroe's cabinet, including Calhoun, to censure the General for his supposedly unauthorized seizure of the Spanish colony. Calhoun's opinions had never become public, but some men close to Old Hickory suspected him of "treachery." One of them was Sam Houston, who obtained a copy of a letter from Monroe to Calhoun, written September 9, 1818, which indicated that both men disapproved Jackson's action. Then, at the height of the 1828 presidential campaign, Van Buren sent James A. Hamilton to Nashville to make himself generally useful and help improve Van Buren's standing with the Hero. During this trip Hamilton also went to Georgia (ostensibly to see William H. Crawford to attempt a reconciliation between the Georgian and Jackson), where he met Governor John Forsyth who later wrote Hamilton a letter in which he explained that one of the sore points between Jackson and Crawford was the charge that he, Crawford, had proposed Jackson's punishment for the Florida invasion at a meeting of Monroe's cabinet. Crawford had denied the charge, said Forsyth. Rather it was Calhoun who had proposed the General's arrest and punishment.[30]

To avoid jeopardizing the election nothing was done about this letter. But any number of people knew of its existence, including Van Buren and William B. Lewis.[31] Not until the Eaton affair erupted in Washington did Lewis take it upon himself to apprise Jackson of the letter's existence. And he assured the President that it specifically accused Calhoun of favoring the General's arrest and punishment after the Florida invasion.

"You saw such a letter as *that*?" Jackson gasped. "Where is that letter?"

"In New York. . . . It is in the hands of Colonel Hamilton, and written by Governor Forsyth of Georgia."

"Then I want to see it," said the President.[32]

It took a while to bring the evidence directly before Jackson because Forsyth insisted first on getting Crawford's permission to release the information. In his reply to Forsyth's request, Crawford formally accused Calhoun of plotting Jackson's punishment for unauthorized behavior.[33]

On May 12, 1830, Crawford's letter was placed in Jackson's hands. The President immediately transmitted it to Calhoun and in his harshest tones requested an explanation. "The statements and facts" in this letter, said Jackson in his covering note, "being so different from what I had heretofore understood to be correct requires that it should be brought to your consideration."[34]

In sending his letter and Crawford's, Jackson deliberately provoked a rupture with his Vice President. And his reason was simple. He did it because Calhoun's nullification ideas generally alarmed and angered him, and he worried about the consequences if his Vice President succeeded him. By this time Jackson felt that Van Buren would be a better and safer presidential choice, so he had to jettison Calhoun. That is why his letter was a deliberate act of provocation. In demanding a response from Calhoun the President was initiating a break in their relationship. "The truth is," said an early Jackson biographer, "that before this affair began"—that is, at the moment the General demanded an explanation—"the President was, in his heart, totally estranged from Mr. Calhoun, and would have been glad of any pretext for breaking with him."[35]

Calhoun conveniently provided the pretext for an open rupture. In a fifty-two-page response dated May 25, he played right into Jackson's hands. And he did it gracelessly, which, of course, made the President's task of casting him out that much easier. The opening sentence set the tone for the entire document. "I cannot recognize the right on your part," said Calhoun, "to call into question my conduct." Hardly an auspicious way to avoid a quarrel, especially when directed to the President of the United States. And he continued in this vein. Did Jackson not have the wit to realize what was behind this sudden reappearance of Crawford into the political arena? "I should be blind not to see that this whole affair is a political manoeuvre," he went on, ". . . and that a blow was meditated against me." He would not say from which quarter the blow emanated, but two years before, a certain individual from New York approached him on this subject, which awakened his suspicions. There was a spectacular conspiracy at work, he protested, one aimed at his downfall; and although he did not name names, he was convinced and would soon share his conviction with the rest of the country that the prime mover of the plot was Martin Van Buren.[36]

When Jackson received Calhoun's letter his reaction was immediate. He told Lewis that he had been deceived by Calhoun, a man for whom he had shown only the "warmest friendship, and in whom he had reposed the most unbounded confidence." He felt betrayed. He felt dishonored.[37]

What added to Jackson's distress was the continuing "vexations" produced by the "Eaton malaria" and the resulting disrupted condition of his cabinet. Instead of standing behind him, he grumbled, the department heads conspired with Calhoun "to put Major Eaton out of the Cabinet, & disgrace me, and weaken my administration . . . [and] lessen my standing with the people, so that they would not again urge my reelection."[38]

"My reelection!" By the close of 1830 Jackson knew that he must run for a second term, strike Calhoun from the ticket, and flush away the disloyal and disruptive members of his cabinet. To pull this off without unduly agitating the American people would take enormous political skill and wisdom.

He started cautiously. But he soon identified all the major actions he must take. The first important step in the process was the decision to replace the *United States Telegraph* as the party mouthpiece with another newspaper. "The disposition which Gen. Green [the editor of the *Telegraph*] has exhibited to identify Gen. Jackson and his friends with the nullifiers of South Carolina," said Amos Kendall, "has excited anew their desire for another paper here."[39] To replace him Jackson's advisers recommended Francis P. Blair of Kentucky, whose experience as an editor of the *Argus of Western America,* slashing journalistic style, commitment to Jackson and the principles of reform, and close association with Amos Kendall and William T. Barry, the postmaster general, made him ideal. Blair was invited to come to Washington in time for the opening of Congress in December 1830. To help him find favor with Jackson, Amos Kendall gave him an outline of the program an administration paper must follow to satisfy the President. "The course a paper should pursue here is obvious. It must be for a thorough reform in the government." In addition it must be "opposed to the South Carolina nullifiers, in favor of a judicious Tariff and of National Internal Improvements or a distribution of the surplus revenue, for the payment of the national debt . . . against the U.S. Bank and in favor of leaving the states to manage their own affairs without other interference than the safety of the whole imperiously requires."[40]

Blair arrived in Washington on December 1 and everyone in the White House was struck speechless by his appearance. A walking cadaver, he presented himself looking disheveled and nonplussed. To top it off he had a large gash on the side of his head from a recent carriage accident.

He went immediately to see the President. Jackson studied him carefully. Mousy looking, hardly weighing more than a hundred pounds, Blair tried to look authoritative, but his appearance defeated the intent. The two men sat down and had a long conversation, but by the time it ended the President had completely forgotten about Blair's unprepossessing appearance. So immediate was the rapport struck between the two men that Jackson poured out all the troubles and frustrations he had suffered since the beginning of his administration. Blair responded with equal candor so that by the end of the interview the President was certain he had found the ideal penman to present him and his policies to the American public.[41]

Jackson insisted that Blair return for dinner. Naturally the little man accepted. But to his horror he discovered on his arrival in the East Room a great company of social dignitaries, all elegantly dressed. Blair had only one presentable coat, and that a frock coat. He was mortified when he entered the glittering room. He slunk into a corner, dreading the moment of Jackson's appearance. But when the President entered the room he immediately located Blair, walked over to him, and led him to a place of honor at the table at his own right hand. Blair was transfixed. His devotion and loyalty to Jackson from that moment never slackened.[42]

The first issue of the new *"Jackson paper"* appeared on Tuesday, December 7, 1830. It was a semiweekly and Blair called it *The Globe*. The first issue consisted of four sheets and announced at the outset that the editor's purpose was "to dedicate this paper to the discussion and maintenance of the principles which brought General Jackson into office." Blair then proclaimed the *Globe*'s basic philosophy: "The world is governed too much," he declared, and that motto was hoisted to the masthead. "We firmly believe that this Government will come to an end, if end it must, in wicked attempts to govern too much." Fortunately there was nothing to fear on that score as long as Andrew Jackson served as chief executive, the paper said.

Subscriptions poured into Blair's office from the moment of the announcement of the *Globe*'s inauguration, and within weeks the paper was a paying success as loyal Democrats signed on and canceled their subscriptions to the *Telegraph*.[43] Blair set up residence on Pennsylvania Avenue with his family and visited the White House practically every day to speak with the President and take direction. Everyone knew that Jackson dictated policy. Unlike the *Telegraph*, said Congressman Edward Everett, the *Globe* was *"his* paper."[44]

The founding of the *Globe* provided Jackson with the essential instrument he needed to secure absolute control of the Democratic party. It was a vital piece of organizational apparatus necessary for the permanent establishment of the party, and it added structural unity to bind Democrats closer to their leader. The journal aided Jackson not only in proclaiming his principles and policies but in securing discipline and loyalty among the party faithful.

Now Jackson was ready to take the next step in purging Calhoun and unifying his cabinet. Again, the Vice President assisted the operation. For reasons best known to himself Calhoun decided to publish the correspondence related to the Florida invasion, and that single desperate act wiped away whatever remained of the Jackson-Calhoun alliance. Perhaps the Vice President thought he could prove Van Buren's duplicity in the "conspiracy." Somehow he deceived himself into thinking that publication would improve his situation, otherwise he never would have committed such an incredible blunder. But the fact of the matter was that Jackson was pathologically sensitive about his actions in Florida and any publication of documents that failed to support all his claims about the adventure was guaranteed to invite a cataclysmic explosion. Calhoun's action, therefore, was sheer, inexplicable folly.

On February 17, 1831, a pamphlet containing the Jackson-Calhoun letters, along with a prefatory address, was published by Duff Green's *Telegraph*. Entitled "Correspondence between Gen. Andrew Jackson and John C. Calhoun . . . on the subject of the course of the latter, in the cabinet of Mr. Monroe, on the occurrences in the Seminole War," it included an explanation by Calhoun to the American people of his purpose in publishing the letters. "I have come before you . . . to give an account of my conduct . . . which has been called into question, and so erroneously represented." Anyone reading the pamphlet immediately concluded that it had two apparent purposes: to justify all that Calhoun had done in Monroe's cabinet; and to prove the existence of a plot to terminate Calhoun's political career, a plot concocted and supervised by Martin Van Buren. Although Van Buren's name was never specifically mentioned, no one missed the inference. Indeed Van Buren demanded that Green insert a notice in the February 25 issue of the *Telegraph* that he unequivocally denied involvement in the alleged plot. Any "assertion or insinuation" that he sought to prejudice Calhoun in the opinion of the President, he said, was "unfounded and unjust."[45]

The publication of the letters shook not only Washington but the entire country. What made it so reprehensible was that it held up the Jackson administration to public ridicule by revealing the scandal of the personal feuding that had been going on in the cabinet for the past two years. Calhoun revealed something that the public had not fully realized before. Now they knew, and it shocked and saddened them. Most Democrats agreed that Calhoun had argued his case quite convincingly, but they also agreed that he had done himself, the President, the party, and the country a distinct disservice. His "attack on the President," as it was frequently called, was uniformly condemned.[46]

It did not take long for the party line to come down from the White House. On February 21 the *Globe* carried an editorial in which Calhoun's pamphlet was termed "a firebrand wantonly thrown into the [Democratic] party. Mr. Calhoun will be held responsible for all the mischief which may follow." "War, open war, is now the cry," declared Amos Kendall. "Calhoun is a dead man," said another. The decision to read Calhoun and Duff Green out of the Democratic party came from Jackson himself. He pronounced the sentence by calling the Vice President's publication an act of self-destruction. "They have cut their own throats," he said, "and destroyed themselves in a shorter space of time than any two men I ever knew."[47]

Despite appearances, these events suited Jackson to perfection. Now he could get rid of Calhoun and his friends without appearing to be acting at the behest of Eaton and his wife. Naturally everyone believed that Van Buren had conjured up these phenomenal events. Only a magician of his skill and daring could produce such wonders.

Without Jackson intending it, Van Buren was being made to play the scapegoat, the villain of the piece. He knew that there would be a great deal of public sympathy for Jackson—and also for Calhoun, once the initial shock of what he had done wore off. Eventually, Van Buren knew, Calhoun would be seen as the benighted and innocent victim of a dastardly plot, conceived and executed by a master magician. "The offence charged against me," he later wrote, "was in every respect a heinous one. . . . It would have been difficult to conceive of a case better calculated to excite the unmeasured condemnation of all good citizens."[48]

To protect himself and his career, the New Yorker had to turn things around, and it only required a moment's thought for him to decide what he must do. He later convinced himself that his resignation from the cabinet was submitted to restore the General's "tranquility and comfort." Actually he did it for himself. And he had little choice.[49]

The only real hurdle now was the problem of explaining it to the President. It must not appear that he was deserting an administration in distress. After several bad starts, Van Buren finally got up the nerve to explain his situation to Jackson. It happened on a bright, sunny day when the two men were out horseback riding, as was their custom. The President said something about his hope that he would soon find some relief from his problems.

"General, there is but one thing can give you peace," responded Van Buren.

"What is that, Sir?"

"My resignation!"

The words jolted the old soldier. "Never, Sir!" he responded, "even you know little of Andrew Jackson if you suppose him capable of consenting to such a humiliation of his friend by his enemies."[50]

For four hours Van Buren argued with his chief, trying to "satisfy him that the course I had pointed out was perhaps the only safe one open to us." The next day, after a sleepless night, Jackson decided to let him go. He was "unusually formal and passionless" when Van Buren arrived at the White House.

"Mr. Van Buren," said Old Hickory, "I have made it a rule thro' life never to throw obstacles in the way of any man who, for reasons satisfactory to himself, desires to leave me, and I shall not make your case an exception."

The words struck Van Buren like a sledgehammer. This was precisely what he had feared. He jumped to his feet, swore his motives were selfless, and cried out that if only Jackson could peer into his heart and examine his "inmost thoughts" he would know the truth. "Now, Sir!" Van Buren declared, "Come what may, I shall not leave your Cabinet, [not until you say] you are satisfied that it is best for us to part. I shall not only stay with you, but . . . stay with pleasure."

Jackson seized Van Buren's hand. The little man had responded with all the melodrama and protestations of devotion the old man needed to hear. "You must forgive me, my friend," Jackson bawled, "I have been too hasty in my conclusions." Obviously he did not need convincing about the wisdom and necessity of Van Buren's resignation, especially if the little man expected to have any political future at all. What the President needed were assurances that Van Buren acted out of loyalty.

When Eaton heard about Van Buren's intention he reacted with intense embarrassment. "Why should you resign?" he said. "I am the man about whom all the trouble has been made and therefore the one who ought to resign." Later Van Buren swore that he never thought of inducing Eaton's resignation and there is every reason to believe him. Once the New Yorker resigned, the obvious thing for Eaton to do was follow suit. Their departure then lightened the burden of dismissing the other members of the cabinet.[51]

In the final discussions with the President, Eaton said he wished to submit his letter first, to which Van Buren cheerfully acceded. On April 7, 1831, Eaton tendered his resignation and gave as his reason his wish to retire to private life. On April 11 Van Buren followed as scheduled, but his letter alluded to the suspicions and charges brought against him and his desire to spare Jackson further distress from these unfounded accusations. The President responded graciously to both men, and on April 20, the *Globe* announced the resignations. That done, Jackson summoned Ingham and Branch—Berrien was out of town—and informed them what had happened. He spoke with them separately on April 18 and left it to them to decide on their own course of action.[52] But uncooperating Ingham had to be invited back for a second interview, at which time Jackson informed him flat out that he wanted his resignation. Both Berrien and Branch were dispatched with less trouble, and formal letters terminating their service were exchanged.[53]

The dissolution of the cabinet stunned the nation. In the history of the nation nothing like it had ever occurred before. No one ever dreamed it could happen. The American people had only a dim notion of the Eaton scandal and were totally unprepared for the shocking news of the mass resignations. "It produced a sensation." Forty years of orderly government suddenly disrupted by this "catastrophe." To many the cabinet purge seemed the equivalent of the fall of the government. It was a constitutional crisis of major proportions. Jackson, it appeared, had shaken the government as it had never been shaken before. "We live in an age of revolution," chortled Henry Clay as he pondered the political rewards for his party as a result of this debacle. "Who could have imagined such a cleansing of the Augean stable in Washington? a change, almost total, of the Cabinet."[54]

Although given more credit in arranging the cabinet dissolution than was his due, Van Buren did assist in the selection of the new cabinet. He himself consented to become minister to Great Britain. Jackson had insisted on it as a face-saving device both for himself and Van Buren. But almost everyone, including Henry Clay, acknowledged its suitability either to get him out of the country or to serve as his reward. Louis McLane of Delaware was brought home from London as U.S. minister and offered the Treasury post vacated by Ingham. In Van Buren's place, Edward Livingston was invited to head the State Department. To replace Eaton, the President wanted Hugh Lawson White, his original choice for the post. But White refused the offer. He said he lacked the necessary qualifications for the office and abhorred the idea of accepting political favors from a friend.[55] Jackson discussed the problem with Van Buren, Livingston, and Eaton, and since they understood the President's determination to remove the eastern Indian tribes beyond the Mississippi they recommended Lewis Cass. Big, burly, sad-faced, Cass enjoyed a very respectable reputation as territorial governor of Michigan for the past nineteen years. Van Buren liked him and told Jackson that he was "a most able administrator." Best of all was his soundness on the Indian question.[56]

To provide consideration for New England in the composition of the new cabinet, Jackson agreed to offer the Navy Department to Levi Woodbury, former governor and United States senator from New Hampshire and one of Van Buren's friends and supporters. A bit testy at times and a little temperamental, Woodbury proved an inspired choice. Decidedly above average in ability and intelligence, he brought a strong legal mind to the affairs of the administration and provided Jackson with the loyalty and dedication he so desperately needed.

Even shrewder was the choice of Roger Brooke Taney of Maryland for the office of attorney general. The President knew Taney and admired him both for his legal skills and his talent as a political organizer. An early Jackson supporter, Taney virtually ran the Democratic campaign in Maryland in 1828 as chairman of the Jackson Central Committee. A towering legal intellect, trained in Baltimore, he presently served as attorney general of his state and had earned a commendable reputation as scholar and politician. He was a Catholic, the brother-in-law of Francis Scott Key, and belonged to the landed aristocracy of southern Maryland. Scrawny, with bulging forehead, sharp nose, and a slightly protruding lower lip, Taney looked like a clerk on account of his nearsightedness (which caused him to squint) and a perpetual stoop.

The sole departmental officer to survive the purge was William T. Barry, the postmaster general, against whom only incompetence could be charged. He had proved his loyalty to the Jackson–Lewis–Van Buren team and was therefore retained. Since the Post Office head was not yet a regular member of the cabinet (but soon would be) an exception could be made in his case.

Jackson seemed pleased with his new cabinet and expressed hope that it would be united and harmonious. It was distinctly better than the first in terms of talent and loyalty, but it still lacked brilliance or any visible mark of particular distinction. Unfortunately the transition from the first to the second cabinet produced further unpleasantness, which again embarrassed the administration and endangered the program of reform. The Eaton scandal in all of its unholy glory tumbled into national view when, early in May, the *Telegraph* informed the rest of the country what had been common gossip in Washington for the last two years. Naturally, it implied that the dismissal of Ingham, Berrien, and Branch resulted from their moral rectitude in refusing to socialize with the notorious Peggy Eaton.

The withdrawal of Eaton from the cabinet and Washington society when he returned to Tennessee to campaign unsuccessfully for his old Senate seat had a beneficial effect on Jackson in that it restored his relationship with Andrew and Emily Donelson. Emily had been banished from the White House because of her behavior toward Peggy but returned with the Eatons' departure for Tennessee. Both Emily and Andrew acknowledged their own guilt in the unseemly affair. "After what has now passed," Donelson wrote his wife, ". . . I am almost as well satisfied that the view which Uncle takes is correct. If it seperates us from him as members of his family, we can only regret that it deprives us of repaying by our kind attentions to some extent, his munificent and tender care of us heretofore."[57]

Because of the "treachery" of Ingham, Branch, and Berrien, Jackson held fewer cabinet meetings and tended to look for counsel elsewhere. He sometimes turned to friends and relatives like Lewis, Donelson, Coffee, and Overton. He listened more and more to Martin Van Buren whose cautious wisdom, "loyalty and patriotism" Jackson had come to rely upon. After the cabinet breakup and the Magician's departure for London, probably no one succeeded Van Buren as principal adviser. As a rule Jackson took advice from the men whose thinking most nearly matched his own, and necessarily this shifted at times with different issues.

Following the dissolution of the cabinet Amos Kendall and Francis P. Blair began to emerge as important advisers to the President. And with their arrival into Jackson's inner circle the opposition began to talk about a "Kitchen Cabinet." According to those who invented and employed the term, there supposedly existed a group of aides outside the official cabinet with special talents at political manipulation who advised Jackson on running the government, distributing the patronage, and operating the Democratic party. Since they were not his official advisers, like cabinet officers (who were called the "parlor" cabinet), they were imagined as slipping into Jackson's study by way of the back stairs through the kitchen. Since advisers seemed to come and go during Jackson's eight years in office, neither the President's enemies nor future historians put a limit on the number or occupation of Kitchen members. They included editors, politicians, family and longtime friends, and even official cabinet officers.

As far as can be determined at present the first time the concept of the

"Kitchen Cabinet" appeared in a document was in December 1831 when Nicholas Biddle, president of the BUS, worried in a private communication that "the kitchen . . . predominate[s] over the Parlor" in advising the President.[58] Not until March did the term actually appear in print, however, when Senator George Poindexter of Mississippi, a sinister-looking profligate who abandoned Jackson for Calhoun and hated Van Buren, published an article in the *Telegraph* on March 27, 1832, which caught everyone's attention because of its use of the unusual term. "The President's press," he wrote, "edited under his own eye, by a 'pair of deserters from the Clay party,' [meaning Kendall and Blair] and a few others, familiarly known by the appellation of the 'Kitchen Cabinet,' is made the common reservoir of all the petty slanders which find a place in the most degraded prints of the Union."[59] With the publication of this piece the expression entered the nation's political vocabulary.

Actually the Kitchen Cabinet never existed—at least not in any of the ways described by the opposition. Granted Jackson received advice from a number of close friends who often helped him to clarify or sharpen his ideas, prepare statements and messages, and carry his decisions to a wide audience of politicians and the electorate. But there was no structure to the operation, no form. Membership in the group shifted from moment to moment and issue to issue. The only stable and permanent element in this unstructured affair was Jackson himself. All others came and went. Only he remained; only he decided who attended council meetings; only he determined the issues for discussion. His was the controlling influence.

Rarely, if ever, did Jackson ask his advisers to decide an issue. Invariably he came to a meeting—either "parlor" or "kitchen"—with a sense of his own direction. He set the problem before the group and heard their reaction, following which he made his decision. If a decision required a public statement in the form of a message, proclamation, order, or whatever, Jackson's private secretary, Andrew J. Donelson, usually prepared a draft. Frequently Kendall and Blair would have a hand in writing the draft. Most of Jackson's official documents bear the marks of half a dozen or more writers.

Because Jackson was so much the master of his own house the talk of Kitchen Cabinets and the "malign" influence of Van Buren, Blair, Kendall, Lewis et al. hardly troubled him. Before he left office Jackson had set up a wide network of advisers and consultants ranging from editors and cabinet officers to government officials, members of Congress, friends, and political leaders in the various sections of the country. Jackson was the center of this network, the cause and purpose of its existence. Small wonder, then, he came to dominate the political affairs of the nation. Small wonder he was able to alter the operation of government.

CHAPTER 16

Return to Reform

"THE PEOPLE EXPECT REFORM," said Jackson at the outset of his administration, "—they shall not be disappointed." It greatly troubled the President that he could not move the reform of the government along as fast as he initially intended, but he consoled himself with the knowledge that reform must be done *"Judiciously"* and upon *"principle"* to be effective and long-lasting.[1] His first intention had been to cut the size of the government. Indeed, his first cabinet had hardly been assembled when he directed them to begin a program of "retrenchment and economy," and to report directly to him on their progress.[2]

In initiating his program of "retrenchment and economy"—ultimately he called his entire program one of "reform retrenchment and economy"—Jackson proved to be a more than competent administrator. He not only devoted long hours to the preparation of "principles" for the guidance of his department heads but he met regularly with them and discussed their overall needs and problems. He delegated authority. He provided support. He kept careful watch over many operations of the executive office and paid particular attention to expenditures. He inspected the details of every appropriation authorized by Congress.

In order to inaugurate his program of "reform retrenchment and economy"—that is, rotation, debt reduction, alteration of the Bank of the United States, Indian removal, and the rest—Jackson obviously had to go to Congress and explain his program and invite their cooperation and support. His first opportunity to do this came in December 1829, when he was obliged by the Constitution to report to Congress on the state of the Union. In shaping this first message Jackson enlisted the aid of James A. Hamilton, son of Alexander Hamilton, as well as Amos Kendall, Donelson, and Lewis. The final draft of his message began with a review of foreign affairs, prefaced by the statement that the President would ask nothing that "is not clearly right" and "submit to nothing that is wrong." Jackson would repeat this slogan again and again throughout his eight years in office and it became a principle against which he measured the

This, one of the better likenesses of Jackson, was painted by Samuel L. Waldo within a few years of the Battle of New Orleans. *Courtesy of the Addison Gallery, Phillips Academy*

This miniature of Rachel Jackson, painted in oil on ivory by Louisa Catherine Strobel, was reputedly worn by Jackson over his heart after Rachel's death in 1828. *Courtesy of the Ladies' Hermitage Association*

General John Coffee, Jackson's friend, business partner, and military associate in the Creek War and at the Battle of New Orleans. This portrait hangs in the Hermitage. *Courtesy of the Ladies' Hermitage Association*

John Overton boarded with Jackson at the Donelson home, became Jackson's partner in land speculation, and served as a judge of the Superior Court of Tennessee following Jackson's resignation from the bench. *Courtesy of the Travellers' Rest Historic Site*

William Blount, land speculator and territorial governor, excercised an enormous influence on Jackson's early career. *Courtesy of the New York Public Library*

John Sevier, revolutionary war hero, Governor of Tennessee, and Jackson's rival for the post of Major General of the Tennessee militia. Their quarrel ended in a street brawl and politically split the state east and west. *Courtesy of the Library of Congress*

General Jackson quells a mutiny during the Creek War by threatening to shoot the first man who heads home. An engraving in Amos Kendall's biography of Jackson. *Courtesy of the Library of Congress*

Something of Jackson's commanding presence is conveyed in this portrait by Ralph E. W. Earl. The cape, hanging loosely from Jackson's shoulders, adds a touch of majesty. *Courtesy of the Ladies' Hermitage Association*

This pencil sketch of Jackson was drawn from life by Edward W. Clay in 1831. As the eyes and mouth indicate, the artist caught some of the physical pain Jackson constantly endured. *Courtesy of the National Portrait Gallery, Smithsonian Institution*

Nephew, ward, private secretary, and liaison with Congress, Andrew Jackson Donelson disappointed his uncle during the Eaton affair. At the height of their disagreement they communicated by letter (four in a single day), even though they resided under the same roof and ate at the same table. *Courtesy of the Ladies' Hermitage Association*

Political manager, neighbor, confidant, liaison with Congress, and White House resident, Major William Berkeley Lewis exercised considerable influence during Jackson's first administration. *Courtesy of the Tennessee State Library and Archives*

Margaret (Peggy) O'Neale Timberlake Eaton. This is one of the very few portraits extant. *Courtesy of the Library of Congress*

The mutual friendship and loyalty between John Henry Eaton and Jackson ultimately caused them both personal suffering and humiliation. *Courtesy of the Library of Congress*

No one encouraged Jackson more in his program of reform than Amos Kendall, Postmaster General, newspaper editor, fourth auditor, master propagandist, political organizer, and confidant-extraordinaire. *Courtesy of the Library of Congress*

Francis Preston Blair, distinguished editor of the Washington *Globe*, was called Preston by his friends, but Jackson called him "Bla-ar." *Courtesy of the Library of Congress*

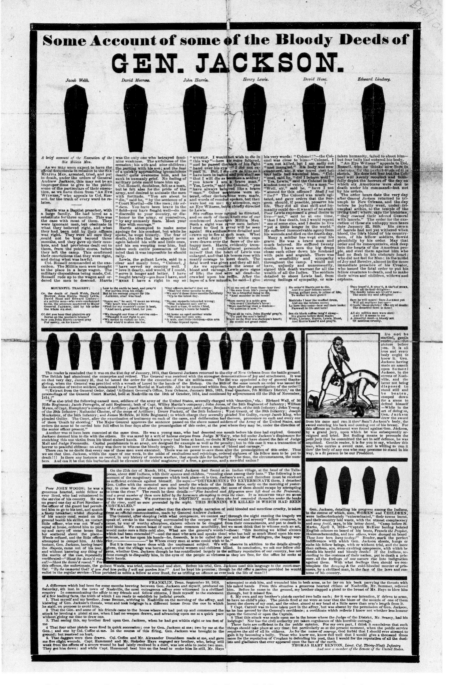

One of the most damaging propaganda broadsides to appear in the presidential campaign of 1828, the "Coffin Hand Bill" vividly recounted Jackson's execution of six military men during the Creek War. *Courtesy of the Library of Congress*

BORN TO COMMAND.

OF VETO MEMORY.

HAD I BEEN CONSULTED.

KING ANDREW THE FIRST.

No cartoon said as much about what happened to the presidency during Jackson's administration than "King Andrew the First," which appeared during the election of 1832. *Courtesy of the Library of Congress*

Bloated, grumpy, formally attired, and propped against a pillow, Jackson posed for this daguerreotype on April 15, 1845, just weeks before his death. *Courtesy of the Library of Congress*

Andrew Jackson, Jr., had one interest in life, as this picture indicates, and it ultimately killed him. The portrait is attributed to Ralph E. W. Earl. *Courtesy of the Ladies' Hermitage Association*

The "Great Father" and his Indian "children." On the wall can be seen a picture of Columbia standing triumphant over the prostrate form of Great Britain. *Courtesy of the William L. Clements Library*

Roger B. Taney. With the exception of Van Buren's election to the presidency, nothing gave Jackson greater pleasure than raising Taney to the position of Chief Justice of the United States. *Courtesy of the Library of Congress*

The elegant and aristocratic Nicholas Biddle, "Czar Nick" as the Jacksonians liked to call him—as drawn by J. B. Longacre—about the time that Biddle's bank came under presidential attack. *Courtesy of the National Portrait Gallery, Smithsonian Institution*

The learned and fastidiously dressed Edward Livingston, whom his friends and admirers called "Beau Ned." *Courtesy of the Library of Congress*

Louis McLane never learned the art of serving Jackson's needs in the cabinet; consequently his political career came to an abrupt end. *Courtesy of the Library of Congress*

Levi Woodbury, one of Jackson's more capable and industrious appointees to the cabinet. *Courtesy of the Library of Congress*

Benjamin F. Butler astounded Jackson by the speed with which he took control of the attorney general's office and mastered its duties and responsibilities. *Courtesy of the Library of Congress*

This print of the East Room (c. 1861) shows many of the furnishings installed during Jackson's administration. *Courtesy of the White House Collection*

success or failure of any negotiations involving foreign nations. The unsettled differences between the United States and Great Britain, France, and Spain were reviewed one by one in the message. What was needed from Great Britain was a show of amity and good will; from France a resolution of the just claims of American citizens for depredations upon their property committed during the Napoleonic Wars; and from Spain an indemnity for spoliations upon American commerce committed under Spanish authority. Denmark, too, owed American citizens for spoliations, but here negotiations had proceeded rapidly over the past year and there was hope that the matter could be settled in the immediate future.

Moving on, Jackson called for an amendment to the Constitution to prevent the election of a minority President, as occurred in 1825. "To the people belongs the right of electing their Chief Magistrate," insisted Jackson. Their choice must not be defeated either by the electoral college or the House of Representatives. *"The majority is to govern,"* he declared. "Let us, then . . . amend our system" so that the "fair expression of the will of the majority" will decide who serves as President. As the first expression of the new democracy, Jackson asked for the removal of *all* "intermediate" agencies in the election of the chief executive. He therefore asked for the abolition of the College of Electors and suggested that the presidential service be limited to a single term of four or six years.

Jackson went on to discuss rotation and how he hoped to reform and purify all the departments of government. He recommended tariff reform to eliminate the worst features of the Tariff of Abominations. He was especially anxious to extinguish the national debt and he therefore urged Congress to hold down appropriations. Once the debt had been liquidated, the resulting surplus could be distributed among the states for public works and education. He opposed government sponsorship of internal improvements as a violation of the Constitution, reminding the Congress that "this was intended to be a government of limited and specific, and not general, powers . . . and it is our duty to preserve for it the character intended by its framers."[3]

Jackson then took up the Indian question and offered a solution as to what to do with these Native Americans. "I suggest for your consideration the propriety of setting apart an ample district west of the Mississippi, and without the limits of any State or Territory now formed, to be guaranteed to the Indian tribes as long as they shall occupy it, each tribe having a distinct control over the portion designated for its use." There they may form their own government, he said. They will be subject to no other control from the United States except what is required to maintain peace on the frontier and between tribes. Given the past atrocities and the present continued greed of white men, Jackson declared, the only sane policy for a just government was to get the Indian to a place of safety, which he fervently believed existed west of the Mississippi River.

After next discussing the army and navy and the need to reform the judiciary, Jackson proceeded to drop a bombshell. At the very end of his message, in two short paragraphs, he announced his displeasure with the Bank of the United States. The charter of the Bank would expire in 1836, he reminded the Congress. Both the constitutionality and the expediency of the law creating the Bank have been questioned by the people, he said, and "it must be admitted by all that it has failed in the great end of establishing a uniform and sound currency."[4]

That last remark was shocking. It conveyed his conviction that the Bank was the most corrupting influence in American life. It was the opening shot in the long and tortuous history of the Bank War.

As the congressional session got under way one of the first legislative actions to provide the President with an opportunity to present a major statement of his reform intentions to the nation was a bill to extend the National Road from Maysville to Lexington, Kentucky. Begun in 1811 in Cumberland, Maryland, the National Road had been steadily extended westward over the years. This latest extension ran totally within the state of Kentucky and alarmed strict constructionists for fear that the federal government would be committed to small public works that were totally local in their purpose and usefulness. The debate over this Maysville Road, as it was called, lasted three days before winning passage in the House in late April 1830. Already apprehensive over its eventual passage in the Senate, Jackson had instructed his supporters to keep him informed of any congressional legislation that looked mischievous and in conflict with his stated objectives. "The people expected reform retrenchment and economy in the administration of this Government," he wrote. "This is the cry from Maine to Louisiana, and instead of these the great object of Congress, *it would seem,* is to make mine one of the most extravagant administrations since the commencement of the Government. This must not be; The Federal Constitution must be obeyed, State-rights preserved, our national debt *must be paid, direct taxes and loans avoided* and the Federal union preserved. These are the objects I have in view, regardless of all consequences, will carry into effect."[5]

When the bill passed the Senate the President was waiting for it. The measure, in his mind, totally contradicted his commitment to "reform retrenchment and economy" and what he felt the people expected of him as President. He could do no less than kill the bill with a veto.

The veto was dated May 27, 1830, and forwarded to the House of Representatives, where the bill originated. It caused extreme consternation among the friends of internal improvements, but to "true believers" of republicanism it "fell upon the ears," said John Randolph of Roanoke, "like the music of other days."[6] Friends of the bill claimed "that the *'hand of the magician'* was visible in every line of it."[7] True, much of the language is so stilted and circumlocutory that only Van Buren could have conjured it. Still, it was Jackson's message. In terms of doctrine and principle, the Maysville veto said exactly what Jackson wanted.

To start, the President challenged the bill's constitutionality. "I am not able to view it in any other light than as a measure of purely local character," he said. Moreover, the people have a right to expect that a "prudent system of expenditure" will characterize government spending "as will pay the debts of the Union and authorize the reduction of every tax to as low a point as . . . our national safety and independence will allow." When the debt is paid, he added, an accumulating surplus is expected to develop that may be distributed to the states for improvements. This is the soundest view of national policy, he insisted, and one which will provide many advantages to the government in the "elevation" of its character.

Another concern, the President revealed, is the question of whether a system of internal improvements ought to be commenced without a prior amendment to the Constitution explaining and defining the precise powers of the federal government. The veto stopped short of denying federal power over public works. It affirmed the right of Congress to appropriate money for purposes of defense and of national benefit, but that was all. "Sound principle" as well as political "prudence," said Van Buren, imposed this compromise on the President.[8]

Jackson took pride in the veto because it addressed some of the principal concerns of his administration. In the "Notes" he wrote for the veto message he touched on several of these concerns. Nothing in the Constitution, he jotted down, authorized the United States to become a member of a corporation created by a state—this referring to the Maysville, Washington, Paris, and Lexington Turnpike Road Company, incorporated by the Kentucky legislature and whose stock Congress contemplated buying. To permit the United States to become a member of this corporation "is corrupting and must destroy the purity of our govt.," he wrote. "it must be more injurious and destructive to the morales and Liberty of the people than the U. States Bank so much and so justly complained of."[9]

Again he expressed his concern for "Liberty"—again his concern for the "morales" of the people. The Maysville Road bill, like the BUS, jeopardized the "purity" of the government and threatened freedom. By becoming stockholders, Jackson said, whether stockholders of a road company or a bank, the United States government might "wield its power in your elections and all the interior concerns of the state, this would lead to consolidation and that would destroy the liberty of your country."[10]

Ultimately, Jackson decided that internal improvements exposed Congress to the temptation of making hasty appropriations. And this was "fatal to just legislation" and the "purity of public men." He therefore felt obliged to stand ready with his veto to turn back such legislation, especially when it showed no regard for the condition of the Treasury.

This first session of Congress in Jackson's first year in office provided ample opportunity for him to demonstrate the full meaning of his program of "reform retrenchment and economy." When the two houses adjourned on May 31, 1830, a pile of appropriation bills had been left behind for the presidential signature, and these bills drove Jackson into a genuine fit of anger. The amount appropriated reached nearly 1 million dollars. Think of it, he cried, a million dollars! Congress met on Saturday and Sunday morning to pass these bills, even though "they knew the Treasury was exhausted by former appropriations." Well, he would show them. He vetoed again and again. He had struck down the Maysville Road bill; now he scored a second veto with the Washington Turnpike bill. Next, for one of the first times in American history, he exercised the pocket veto—which permits the President to kill legislation by withholding his signature from a bill after Congress has adjourned. He annulled the appropriations for building lighthouses and beacons, dredging harbors, and other such improvements. He also killed a bill to purchase stock in the Louisville and Portland Canal Company. It was quite a massacre. But Jackson glowed. By these vetoes, he contended, he had provided "reform retrenchment and economy," just as he had promised.[11]

Of his many proposals to Congress in his first message the one that generated the most furor—and certainly Jackson was startled by such a vehement response—was Indian removal. Directed by the American Board of Commissions for Foreign Affairs, this storm of protest descended on both the Congress and the administration and sent cries of outrage reverberating through the House and Senate.

The policy of white Americans toward the Indians was a disgrace, right from the beginning. Sometimes the policy was benign, such as sharing educational advantages, but more often than not it was malevolent. From the beginning Americans drove the Indians from their midst, stole their lands, and, when necessary, murdered them. To many Americans, Indians were inferior and their culture a throwback to a darker age. The steady push of settlers west and south eventually cornered approximately 53,000 Cherokees, Creeks, Choctaws, and Chickasaws into 33 million acres in the southwestern section of the United States. Of these the Cherokees showed notable technological and material advances as a result of increased contact with traders, government agents, and missionaries. Naturally, there were some Americans—members of religious groups, like Quakers, for example—who strongly protested the inhuman treatment of Indians, especially when Jackson recommended transporting them beyond the Mississippi River.

Jackson's nationalism (a partial product of his expansionist ideas) and his states' rights philosophy (a product of his concern for individual liberty) merged to produce his Indian policy. Although devoted to limited government in Washington, the General nevertheless rejected any notion that jeopardized the safety of the United States. And as far as he was concerned the Indians living as tribes within the boundaries of the sovereign states constituted a distinct threat to the nation and must be expelled. Despite the howls of protest that erupted with his removal proposal he went right ahead and consulted with the Democratic leaders in Congress about the necessary strategies to maneuver a removal bill into law.[12]

The matter was appropriately sent to the respective committees on Indian affairs in the House and Senate, both of which favored the measure. Two Tennesseans, John Bell and Hugh Lawson White, headed these committees. As added protection, the administration looked to the House Speaker, Andrew Stevenson of Virginia, to break any tie votes and, as it turned out, he was required to do so on three separate occasions to save the removal bill from defeat.[13]

On February 22, 1830, the Senate committee reported the first bill, and two days later the House committee reported the second. As might be expected, given Jackson's interest and involvement, the two bills were remarkably alike. Fundamentally, they recommended establishing an area west of the Mississippi to be divided into enough districts to accommodate as many tribes as might choose to go west, and removing them there. The scheme also involved an exchange of land for all the tribes residing in the east. Both bills triggered heated debate over the constitutional and moral implications of the exchange and eventually questioned the President's unwarranted extension of executive power.

The Senate bill touched off several wild exchanges when it came up for debate on April 6. Senator Theodore Frelinghuysen of New Jersey led the opposition forces and spoke for three days, for a minimum of two hours each day. A deeply religious man, he was offended by the obvious intent of the bill's supporters. The Indians had a right to refuse to surrender their lands, he said. To threaten or harass them only invited violence and bloodshed. "We have crowded the tribes upon a few miserable acres of our Southern frontier: it is all that is left to them of their once boundless forests: and still, like the horse-leech, our insatiated cupidity cries, give! give! give!"[14]

Senator John Forsyth of Georgia responded with savage sectional rage. Frelinghuysen's "speech was plain enough," he said. "The Indians in New York, New England, Virginia etc etc are to be left to the tender mercies of those States, while the arm of the General Government is to be extended to protect the Choctaws, Chickasaws, Creeks and especially the Cherokees from the anticipated oppressions of Mississippi, Alabama and Georgia."[15]

Some senators asked for an amendment that would guarantee proper negotiations with the Indians in providing for removal, but this was rejected. Frelinghuysen also proposed that removal be delayed until Congress could determine whether the western lands were adequate to the needs of the Indians. Again this was rejected. Finally, on April 26, 1830, the bill came up for a final vote and passed by the count of 28 to 19 along fairly strict party lines.[16]

In the House of Representatives both the bill and President Jackson took a worse pounding. Removal came close to defeat because many members feared reprisals from religious groups in their districts if they voted for the bill. Serious debate on the measure began on May 15, when Henry R. Storrs of New York took dead aim on the White House and fired a powerful salvo. He accused Jackson of attempting to overthrow the constitutional securities of the states and their authority as well as assume the power of Congress to abrogate existing treaties in cases of necessity or war. "If these encroachments of the Executive Department," he said, "are not met and repelled in these halls, they will be resisted nowhere."[17]

Wilson Lumpkin of Georgia dismissed the arguments against the bill as simply an expression of party prejudice. What the Democrats were proposing, he contended, was the means of preserving the Indians against certain annihilation. Removal, he continued, was "their only hope of salvation." And thank God there was someone in the White House who understood this fact and wanted to act for the Indian's own good. "No man entertains kinder feelings toward the Indians than Andrew Jackson," he declared.[18]

During the debate a number of proposals were put forth that clearly indicated widespread concern over the fact that General Andrew Jackson was the man in charge of Indian removal. Perhaps Lumpkin believed in the President's kind feelings toward the Indians but other congressmen had their doubts. One Democratic representative from Pennsylvania, Joseph Hemphill, had many reservations. Like others, he was caught between his position as a loyal follower of the administration and as a representative from a district where many of his constituents opposed removal. Hemphill thought he could escape his dilemma by proposing a substitute bill in which removal would be postponed for a year in order to send out a commission to gather information about the land to which the Indians would be sent. A decent concern for humanity demanded nothing less, he said.[19] The vote on this substitute motion ended in a tie and was broken by the Speaker, who voted to kill it. Obviously the question of removal had strong opposition even among Democrats. For the bill to survive, the White House had to step in and take charge.

In intruding into the legislative process to get the bill he wanted, Jackson took several actions. First he delayed sending up his Maysville veto. If that veto had been announced at this time it would have killed removal on the spot. Next he pressured Democrats in the House for their support. They were told quite specifically that the President "staked the success of his administration upon this measure," that he wanted it passed, and that he would not accept a watered-down substitute.[20] His efforts paid off. Several members of the Pennsylvania and Massachusetts delegations succumbed to the White House pressure; thus when the bill

came up for a final vote it passed 102 to 97.[21] Jackson signed the measure
on May 28, 1830. The day following passage of this bill he sent up his
Maysville veto.

The Indian Removal Act of 1830 authorized Jackson to carry out the
policy outlined in his first message to Congress. He could exchange
unorganized public land in the trans-Mississippi west for Indian land in
the east. Those Indians who moved would be given perpetual title to their
new land as well as compensation for improvements on their old. The
cost of their removal would be absorbed by the federal government. They
would also be given assistance for their "support and subsistence" for the
first year after removal. An appropriation of $500,000 was authorized to
carry out these provisions.[22]

This monumental piece of legislation spelled the doom of the American Indian. It was harsh, arrogant, racist—and inevitable. It was too late
to acknowledge any rights for the Indians. They had long since been
abrogated.

Andrew Jackson has been saddled with a considerable portion of the
blame for the horror of removal. He makes an easy mark. But the criticism
is unfair if it distorts the role he actually played. His objective was not the
destruction of Indian life and culture. Quite the contrary. He believed
that removal was the Indian's only salvation against certain extinction.
The Indian problem posed a terrible dilemma and Jackson had little to
gain by attempting to resolve it. He could have imitated his predecessors
and done nothing. But that was not Andrew Jackson. He felt he had a
duty. And when removal was accomplished he felt he had done the
American people a great service. He felt he had followed the "dictates of
humanity" and saved the Indians from certain death.

Not that the President was motivated by concern for the Indians—their
language or customs, their culture, or anything else. Andrew Jackson was
motivated principally by two considerations: first, his concern for the
military safety of the United States, which dictated that Indians must not
occupy areas that might jeopardize the defense of this nation; and second, his commitment to the principle that all persons residing within
states are subject to the jurisdiction and laws of those states. Under no
circumstances did Indian tribes constitute sovereign entities when they
occupied territory within existing state boundaries.

The reaction of the American people to removal was predictable. Some
were outraged. Others seemed uncomfortable with it but agreed that it
had to be done. Probably a larger number of Americans favored removal
and applauded the President's action in settling the Indian problem once
and for all. In short, there was no overwhelming public outcry against it.

Jackson was extremely anxious to implement the Indian Removal Act
and he assigned commissioners to negotiate treaties with the principal
southern tribes as quickly as possible. The first such treaty was the Treaty
of Dancing Rabbit Creek, in which the Choctaw Nation agreed to evacu-

ate all their land in Mississippi and emigrate to an area west of the Arkansas Territory to what is now Oklahoma. The Indians ceded 10.5 million acres of land and promised to emigrate in stages: the first group in the fall of 1831, the second in 1832, and the last in 1833. Unfortunately the start of removal was delayed until late fall and produced avoidable horrors that resulted in many Choctaw deaths. The entire operation was marked by inefficiency, confusion, stupidity, and criminal disregard of the rights of human beings. It typified all too accurately the agony of Indian removal during the entire Jacksonian era.[23]

In October 1832 the Chickasaws also capitulated and, after considerable pressure, signed a removal treaty. But Jackson was less fortunate with the other southern tribes. The Cherokees and Creeks opted to sue in the courts and had retained William Wirt, a former U.S. attorney general, as counsel. When the case eventually reached the Supreme Court, Wirt argued that the Indians had a right to self-government as a foreign nation and that this right had long been recognized by the United States in its treaties with the Indians. Chief Justice John Marshall in the case *Cherokee Nation* v. *Georgia* handed down his opinion on March 18, 1831. He rejected Wirt's contention that the Cherokees constituted a sovereign nation. He also rejected Jackson's insistence that they were subject to state law. The Indians, he said, were "domestic dependent nations," subject to the United States as a ward to a guardian. They were not subject to individual states, he declared. Indian territory was in fact part of the United States.[24]

The Indians chose to regard the opinion as essentially favorable in that it commanded the United States to protect their rights and property. Meanwhile, Georgia passed legislation in late December 1830 prohibiting white men from entering Indian country after March 1, 1831, without a license from the state. This was clearly aimed at troublesome missionaries who encouraged the Indians to disregard state law. Samuel A. Worcester and Dr. Elizur Butler, two missionaries, defied the law; they were arrested and sentenced to four years imprisonment in a state penitentiary. They sued, and on appeal, in the case *Worcester* v. *Georgia,* the Supreme Court decided on March 3, 1832, that the Georgia law was unconstitutional. Marshall then issued a formal mandate two days later ordering the Georgia Superior Court to reverse its decision.[25]

It was later reported by Horace Greeley that Jackson's response to the Marshall decision was total defiance. "Well: John Marshall has made his decision: *now let him enforce it!*"[26] Greeley cited George N. Briggs, a representative from Massachusetts, as his source for the statement. The quotation certainly sounds like Jackson and many historians have chosen to believe that he said it. The fact is that Jackson did not say it because there was no reason for him to do so. There was nothing for him to enforce. Not until the court either summoned state officials before it for contempt or issued a writ of habeas corpus for the release of the two missionaries was there anything further to be done. Why, then, would Jackson refuse an action that no one asked him to take?

Even if Jackson did not use the exact words Greeley put into his mouth, even if no direct action was required at the moment, some historians have argued that the quotation represents in fact Jackson's true attitude. There is evidence that Jackson "sportively said in private conversation" that if summoned "to support the decree of the Court he will call on those who have brought about the decision to enforce it."[27] Actually nobody expected Jackson to enforce the decision, including the two missionaries, and therefore a lot of people simply assumed that the President would defy the court if pressured.

In the rush to show Jackson as bombastic and defiant, however, an important point is missed. What should be remembered is that Jackson reacted with extreme caution to this crisis because a precipitous act could have triggered a confrontation with Georgia. Prudence, not defiance, characterized his reaction to both the challenge of Georgia and later the threat of secession by South Carolina. As one historian has noted, Jackson deserves praise for his caution in dealing with potentially explosive issues and should not be condemned for his supposed defiance.[28]

Not much later a controversy with South Carolina over nullification developed. Jackson maneuvered carefully so that no action of his might induce Georgia to join South Carolina in the dispute. He therefore acted to isolate South Carolina in the dispute and force Georgia to back away from its position of confrontation. He needed to nudge Georgia into freeing the two missionaries. Consequently he moved swiftly to win removal of the Indians. His secretary of war worked quietly to convince the legal counsel for the missionaries and the friends of the Cherokees in Congress that the President would not budge from his position nor interfere in the operation of Georgia laws and that the best solution for everyone was for the Indians to remove. Meanwhile the Creeks capitulated, and the treaty of removal was ratified by the Senate in April 1832.[29]

Although Senator Theodore Frelinghuysen "prayed to God" that Georgia would peacefully acquiesce in the decision of the Supreme Court he soon concluded that the Cherokees must yield. Even Associate Justice John McLean, who wrote a concurring opinion in the *Worcester* case, counseled the Cherokee delegation in Washington to sign a removal treaty. Simultaneously, Jackson worked through mutual friends to talk Governor Wilson Lumpkin into pardoning the missionaries. Finally, when William Wirt agreed to make no further motion before the Supreme Court the governor capitulated and on January 14, 1833, ordered Worcester and Butler released from prison. The danger of confrontation passed.[30]

Ultimately, the Cherokees yielded to the President as well. On December 29, 1835, at New Echota, Georgia, a fraudulently contrived treaty was signed arranging an exchange of land. The Nation "agreed" to relinquish to the United States their rights and titles to all their lands east of the Mississippi River (approximately 8 million acres) and remove to the Indian Territory west of the Mississippi in return for which they would receive $5 million. Thus began one of the most disgraceful and heart-rending episodes in American history. The Cherokees were rounded up, herded into prison camps, and then sent west along what they came to call "The Trail of Tears." It has been estimated that some 18,000 Cherokees were removed, of whom 4,000 died as a result of their capture, detention, or westward journey. Jackson himself had retired from the presidency when the Cherokee exodus was set in motion. Still he shares much of the blame for his inhuman deed. He was so anxious to expel the red man from "civilized society" that he took little account of what his inflexible determination might cost in human life and suffering.

By the close of Jackson's first administration removal applied to all eastern Indians, not simply the southern tribes. After the Black Hawk War of 1832 Jackson responded to the demands of Americans in the northwest to send all Indians beyond the Mississippi. The Black Hawk War began when a hungry band of Sac and Fox Indians under the leadership of Chief Black Hawk recrossed the Mississippi River in the spring of 1832 to find food. People on the frontier panicked and Governor John Reynolds of Illinois called out the militia and appealed to Jackson for assistance. Federal troops were immediately dispatched under Generals Winfield Scott and Henry Atkinson. A short and bloody war ensued, largely instigated by drunken militiamen, and when it ended the northwestern tribes were so demoralized that they offered little resistance to Jackson's steady pressure for their removal. The result of the Black Hawk War, said the President in his fourth message to Congress, had been very "creditable to the troops" engaged in the action. "Severe as is the lesson to the Indians," he lectured, "it was rendered necessary by their unprovoked aggressions, and it is to be hoped that its impression will be permanent and salutary."[31]

A similar agony accompanied the removal of the Seminole Indians in Florida. It flashed into open warfare in late 1835 and raged until 1842 when the last battle was fought. The Seminoles were led by Chief Osceola until his capture through betrayal by the American commander of the federal troops. By the time this Second Seminole War ended nearly 4,000 Seminoles had been removed, $10 million spent, and 1,500 regular soldiers killed. The mortality among the Indians and volunteers cannot be calculated accurately.[32]

By the close of Jackson's eight years in office approximately 45,690 Indians had been relocated beyond the Mississippi River. According to the Indian Office, only about 9,000 Indians, mostly in the Old Northwest and New York, were without treaty stipulations requiring their removal when Jackson left office. The operation, of course, provided an empire. Jackson acquired for the United States approximately 100 million acres of land in exchange for about $68 million and 32 million acres of western land.[33]

The policy of Indian removal formed an important part of Jackson's overall program of limiting federal authority and supporting states' rights. Despite the accusation of increased executive authority, Jackson successfully buttressed state sovereignty and jurisdiction over all inhabitants within state boundaries. This is a government of the people, Jackson argued, and the President and Congress exercise jurisdiction over all *"the people of the union."* But "who are the people of the union?" he asked. Then, answering his own question, he said: "all those subject to the jurisdiction of the sovereign states, none else." Indians were also subject to the states, he insisted. They are subject "to the sovereign power of the state within whose sovereign limits they reside." An "absolute independence of the Indian tribes from state authority can never bear an intelligent investigation, and a quasi independence of state authority when located within its Territorial limits is *absurd.*"[34]

In addition to establishing the removal policy Jackson also reformed the bureaucracy handling Indian problems. Since 1824 a Bureau of Indian Affairs had supervised the government's relations with the Indians. By the time Jackson assumed the presidency the Bureau had become an "enormous quagmire" and the President determined to reorganize it. On June 30, 1834, Congress passed the necessary legislation establishing the Office of Indian Affairs under an Indian commissioner, and this administrative machinery remained in place well into the twentieth century. The Indian service was restructured into a more cohesive operation than had previously been the case. It regularized procedures that had been practiced as a matter of custom rather than law.[35]

The removal of the American Indian was one of the most significant and tragic acts of the Jackson administration. It was accomplished in total violation not only of American principles of justice and law but of Jackson's own strict code of honor. There can be no question that he believed he had acted in the best interest of the Indian, but to achieve his purpose countless men, women, and children suffered deprivation and death. Jackson's humanitarian concerns—and they were genuine—were unfortunately shot through with ethnocentrism and paternalism that allowed little regard or appreciation of Indian culture and civilization.

Andrew Jackson left office believing that thousands of Indians had found what he considered a safe haven west of the Mississippi River. He left believing he had saved the Indians from inevitable doom. And, considering the tribes which have survived to this day, perhaps he had.

CHAPTER 17

The Bank War Begins

ONE OF ANDREW JACKSON'S FEW FAMILY PLEASURES during his first administration—the banishment of the Donelsons had been an agony for him and only ended with the departure of the Eatons for Tennessee after the breakup of the first cabinet—was the marriage of his only son. The President was apprehensive at first. Andrew Jackson, Jr., was not as responsible as his father had a right to expect from this twenty-two-year-old man. Besides, he was constantly falling in love and then wanting to marry the girl, irrespective of her social and financial standing. But then at last young Andrew met an "accomplished, amiable, & handsome" young lady by the name of Sarah Yorke, and she proved a suitable match and brought many moments of joy and happiness to the old General for the remainder of his long life.

Sarah Yorke, the daughter of a wealthy merchant, lived in Philadelphia, where Andrew met her. As usual the young man was immediately smitten and proposed marriage, which she accepted without hesitation. Sometime around the middle of October 1831, Andrew informed his father of his plans and showed him one of Sarah's letters. Jackson, although wary—knowing his son's tendencies—offered no objection. "Your happiness will insure mine," he wrote Andrew, "for the few years which I can expect to live." After studying Sarah's letter and hearing his son enumerate her many wifely qualities, Jackson instructed Andrew to tell her "that you have my full and free consent that you be united in the holy bonds of matrimony; that I shall receive her as a daughter, and cherish her as my child." Privately, however, Jackson expressed some concern. The Yorke family fortune had not been "carefully attended to," he wrote, but "it was enough for me to know that he loved her, that she was respectable . . . and not one of the modern fashionables." Still, "I would have been better satisfied if he had married in a family I know."[1]

On November 20 Andrew, accompanied by Mary Eastin, left Washington to marry Sarah. The wedding took place in Philadelphia on November 24, 1831, and they honeymooned in the White House. Whatever doubts or fears Jackson initially entertained about the marriage quickly evaporated. Sarah became a comfort to him for the rest of his days, ministering to his needs and lavishing love and affection on him which he returned in abundance.

Jackson missed his son's wedding in order to attend to his many obligations in Washington. His new cabinet helped where they could but Jackson acknowledged certain deficiencies despite the restoration of harmony, and he openly expressed the wish that he could bring Van Buren back from England, where he was now serving as U.S. minister, and make him his Vice President. "I miss you, and Eaton, very much," he told the Magician. He respected his new secretary of state, Edward Livingston, for his legal and writing talents, but "he knows nothing of mankind" and therefore, according to Jackson, lacked judgment in assessing individuals.[2]

In some ways, Louis McLane, who had vacated the ministry in London for Van Buren, was the best of the new lot. As former chairman of the Ways and Means Committee in Congress for a number of years, and as a friend of Nicholas Biddle, president of the BUS, and the Barings of England, McLane thought he knew a great deal about finance. He and Jackson differed over the Bank of the United States, but it was "an honest difference of opinion," said the President, and one he felt would cause no problem.[3] Unfortunately, McLane did not respect the fact that the President would allow him to go just so far and no further. When he presumed to reach beyond his rightful limit, Jackson cut him down.[4]

Because he felt the BUS necessary for the well-being of the American people, McLane tried to get Jackson to change his mind about the Bank. He therefore worked out a plan which he thought would gain the President's approval. The central feature of his plan was the proposal to pay off the national debt before the end of Jackson's first term. The debt, at the moment, amounted to approximately $24 million and could be retired by applying $16 million of anticipated revenue plus $8 million to be realized from the sale of the government's stock in the BUS. The liquidation of the stock—to be sold directly to the BUS itself—was something Jackson wholeheartedly approved. Only one thing the secretary asked in return: that the President refrain from mentioning the Bank in his next annual message to Congress and allow McLane in his annual report to recommend recharter—the Bank's charter would expire in 1836—at the proper time. Otherwise, he said, his report might tempt the Ways and Means Committee to prepare a bill to recharter the BUS, and such a bill he could not oppose in good conscience.[5] Jackson agreed to these conditions after which McLane scooted off to Philadelphia to tell Biddle personally of his success in winning Old Hickory to his plan.

Biddle immediately thought that Jackson had withdrawn his objection to the Bank's present operation and he sighed with relief. However, he was unhappy that nothing would be said about the BUS in the next message, and at Biddle's suggestion the President agreed—without knowing the source of the suggestion—to allow the Congress to take whatever action it wished with respect to the Bank.

The National Republicans were worried over Jackson's apparent shift in policy when they read his 1831 annual message to Congress. They had expected to use his anti-Bank position in the coming presidential election to defeat him. They called a national convention of delegates to choose their candidates, and nearly 150 party members assembled in Baltimore between December 12 and 16, 1831. Eighteen states sent representatives and they unanimously nominated Henry Clay for president and John Sergeant of Pennsylvania as his running mate. However, this was not the first national nominating convention in American history. That distinction belongs to the Anti-Masonic party, the first third party, which met in Baltimore on September 26, 1831, and nominated William Wirt of Maryland and Amos Ellmaker of Pennsylvania. Ever since William Morgan's murder in 1826 the hostility against Masons had spread from New York into New England and the middle west. By the early 1830s elaborate party machinery existed in many states, complete with newspapers, local organizing committees, and such able leaders as Thurlow Weed and William H. Seward of New York, and Thaddeus Stevens of Pennsylvania. Many National Republicans had hoped to entice the Anti-Masons into joining them against that "arch mason," Andrew Jackson. But Henry Clay's membership in the Masonic fraternity killed any possibility of such a union.[6]

Once Clay nailed down his own nomination he was anxious to challenge Jackson over the Bank issue of recharter. He figured that no other issue offered him as much advantage in winning the election. That meant bringing the issue forcibly before the public, and nothing could achieve that goal faster than getting a recharter bill before Congress. He therefore went to Nicholas Biddle and urged him to request recharter, arguing that Jackson did not dare veto the bill before the election, for if he did he would surely lose the presidency. Since Biddle, in any event, must request recharter before Jackson's second term ended, Clay insisted that the bill stood a better chance for passage before the election than afterward. "The friends of the Bank," Clay informed Biddle, "expect the application to be made. The course of the President, in the event of the passage of the bill, seems to be a matter of doubt and speculation."[7]

Although Biddle hesitated at first, by the beginning of the new year he decided to go for recharter. More than anything else, he could not resist the demands of "our friends," Clay and Daniel Webster, who may have been urging him on for their own political purposes but whose support was crucial nonetheless. Still he was warned by pro-Bank senators that if he drove "the chief into a Corner he will veto the Bill."[8]

On January 6, 1832, a memorial for a renewal of the charter was formally submitted to Congress. Quite predictably, the radical anti-Bank advisers in the White House—such as Amos Kendall, Francis P. Blair, and Roger B. Taney—howled their dismay over the sudden appearance of the memorial to Congress. They assured Jackson that Biddle had converted an economic issue into a political one for Clay's benefit and thereby had presumed to intrude into the political process. Said Taney: "Now as I understand the application at the present time, it means in plain English this—the Bank says to the President, your next election is at hand—if you charter us, well—if not, beware of your power."[9]

Jackson did not need this trio to convince him of the Bank's treachery and malice. More than ever he was now certain that the Bank represented the most corrupting influence in American society and needed to be annihilated. He must slay this monster, not cage it. At first the President was willing to listen to possible schemes by which the Bank's charter would be altered to conform to his reservations and concerns. Not now. From the moment Biddle acted to force recharter prior to the 1832 election—a good four years before the present charter expired—Jackson determined to kill the beast.

But Biddle would be a worthy adversary. Scion of a distinguished and wealthy Philadelphia family, educated at Princeton where he was valedictorian of his class, Nicholas Biddle married an heiress, lived in a country estate where he indulged his taste for Grecian art objects, and was appointed to the board of directors of the BUS by James Monroe and because of his connections and marked business acumen was elevated to the presidency of the Bank in 1823. Articulate, bright, arrogant, vain, strong willed, energetic, with genuine intellectual and literary tastes, he was an aristocrat to his fingertips. He was five feet seven inches tall, strikingly handsome, and appeared more like a romantic poet or painter than a man of business and commerce. John Quincy Adams said he was a "man of eminent ability, of a highly cultivated mind, of an equable and placid temper, and in every other relation of life, of integrity irreproachable and unreproached."[10] Coming from the hypercritical Adams, that was high praise indeed.

To win reelection, therefore, Andrew Jackson faced a struggle with not one but two heavyweights: Henry Clay and Nicholas Biddle. And the presidential election year, 1832, started very badly for Jackson. First came the application for recharter, then he contracted influenza, finally his left arm started to act up again. The bullet fired by Jesse Benton in 1813 stayed in his arm for nearly twenty years and caused him periods of intense discomfort. By 1831 the bullet had worked itself downward in the inner side of his arm and stationed itself below the wound and less than an inch from the surface of the skin. It could be easily felt and moved. In April 1831 he thought of going to Philadelphia "to get the bullet cut out of his arm," and he "would have gone but for the political motives which he knew would be imputed."[11] Nine months later the pain intensified and disturbed his work schedule. Since it was so near the skin's surface his friends and family believed that it could be extracted quite easily and that its extraction would not only end the pain but have a beneficial effect on his general health. Old Hickory agreed, and so Dr. Harris of Philadelphia was summoned to perform the operation. The procedure was swift. No anesthesia was available, of course, so Jackson simply bared his arm, gritted his jaws, grasped his walking stick, and said, "go ahead." The surgeon made an incision, squeezed the arm, and out popped a "half ball" of the ordinary pistol size. The metal was "a good deal flattened by the contusion upon the bone and hackled somewhat on the edge." The wound was dressed and Jackson went right back to work. What awed everyone over the next three days was that the operation in no way interrupted his attention to business, notwithstanding his long bout with the flu.[12]

But of all the disappointments Jackson suffered in the opening weeks of the new year, none compared to what happened in the Senate on January 25. The nominations of Van Buren, McLane, and Livingston came up for confirmation early in January. Livingston and McLane went through without incident on January 12 and 13. But Van Buren got shot down. For two days the Magician's confirmation had been debated. Senator Henry Clay, in full cry, said he owed it to "the honor and character of the Government" to vote against confirmation. Daniel Webster also registered his opposition, but it remained for George Poindexter of Mississippi to stoop to personal abuse. Insinuations about Van Buren's sex life, along with references to his behavior toward Peggy Eaton, dribbled from his "polluted mouth." Stephen D. Miller of South Carolina took obvious pleasure in repeating some of the grossest innuendos. This prompted Alexander Buckner of Missouri to observe that "none but a liar—an infamous liar, would utter them."[13] For these two days the Senate chamber was turned into an arena of ferocious politicians tearing at each other to vent their anger over past injuries. Old wounds were picked raw. The friends of Vice President Calhoun pilloried Van Buren for intriguing his way into Jackson's affections. Van Buren's supporters responded in kind, charging the Vice President with deception and hypocrisy in the Seminole and Eaton controversies.

With rejection of the nomination a real possibility, and with so many senators aching for revenge over one wrong or another, the idea of "rewarding" Vice President Calhoun with the distinction and honor of defeating Van Buren's nomination occurred to both Democrats and National Republicans. If there were a tie in the Senate, Calhoun would cast the deciding vote—and what a spectacle that would make.

And so it happened. When the Senate was formally asked if it would consent to Van Buren's nomination as minister to Great Britain, 23 senators said yes and another 23 said no. All eyes turned to the Vice President. Calhoun's pleasure was palpable. Calmly and deliberately he cast the deciding vote and Van Buren's nomination was defeated.[14]

Minutes later Thomas Hart Benton overheard Calhoun talking with some of his friends about the defeat. The friends were expressing their fears that by their vote they had unwittingly elevated Van Buren to a higher office. Calhoun reassured them. "It will kill him, sir," he sneered, "kill him dead. He will never kick sir, never kick."[15]

Jackson was presiding at a dinner party when the Senate vote was taken. Adjournment of the upper house came well after six o'clock. Jackson was in rare form that evening and looked extraordinarily self-possessed. His long, narrow head, topped with thick graying hair which stood erect "as though impregnated with his defiant spirit," and his deeply furrowed brow and piercing blue eyes added to his commanding presence. Suddenly a messenger entered the room and whispered into his ear. The President's body stiffened, his eyes flashed their warning signal. He sprang from his chair.

"By the Eternal! I'll smash them!"[16]

Jackson's guests crowded to his side to learn the cause of this outburst. When they heard the devastating news they all commiserated with him. But he soon calmed down and started to calculate his advantages produced by the spite of Calhoun, Clay, and company. "The people," he later wrote to Van Buren, "will properly resent the insult offered to the Executive, and the injury intended to our foreign relations, in your rejection, by placing you in the chair of the very man whose casting vote rejected you." In his mind the negative vote was aimed directly at himself, to humiliate him before the electorate. Even so, he knew the people would rally to his side (as they always did, he said) and show their resentment to this outrage and indignity.[17]

For Van Buren, the rejection was the best thing that ever happened to him. It forever linked him to Jackson. His career, his fortune, his reputation were now all tied to Old Hickory, and if the old man continued to enjoy unbounded public affection so, too, would he. "Your course and the Presidents are now blended," wrote New York congressman Churchill C. Cambreleng; "we must strike while the iron is hot and weld it."[18]

Although Jackson was extremely anxious to have Van Buren at his side again, the Magician decided against returning home immediately lest it appear that he was in mad haste to climb to higher office. By touring Europe for a few months he could relax, enjoy himself, and conveniently miss the national nominating convention to be held in Baltimore by the Democrats in May. Of course Jackson knew who the party leaders would choose. Long ago he had decided that Van Buren would run with him on the ticket. "Jackson is rapped up in Van Buren," reported Senator William L. Marcy to the Albany Regency, and he will hear of no substitute for the ticket.[19]

The first Democratic national nominating convention met on May 21, 1832, at the Athenaeum, but because of the large number in attendance moved to the Universalist Church on St. Paul Street. Some 334 Democratic delegates assembled from every state but Missouri. In formulating convention rules the delegates decided to require a two-thirds vote for nomination of the Vice President. Presumably this rule would encourage unity within the party and provide the candidate with the appearance of solid support. On the second day the delegates reached the principal business of the convention. Without speeches or formal nominations they proceeded immediately to vote and on the first ballot nominated Van Buren. That this convention was summoned solely for the purpose of agreeing to a vice presidential candidate became obvious when it neglected to nominate Jackson for the presidency. The delegates simply "concurred" in the nominations the President had already received from many states. No platform was written, no address, no statement of principles. As for issues, who needed issues as long as Andrew Jackson sat in the White House?

At the moment, however, in Washington, two potentially lethal bills were slowly making their way through the legislative process in Congress, either of which could provide the issues which would convulse the nation. One was the bill to renew the charter of the Bank of the United States, and the other was a bill to revise the tariff schedule in order to rid it of the "abominations" passed in 1828.

Both issues came forward simultaneously in Congress. Henry Clay, in a speech running three days, proposed a new tariff schedule. He extolled his American System and insisted that it would benefit all sections of the Union. Never had he spoken so well, or so long. He was "in the prime of his prime," said one contemporary. His long exile from the Senate had provided him with renewed vigor. Now he was back, well rested, and in top condition.[20]

Jackson wanted a sharp cut in the tariff rates and through his Treasury secretary proposed a drop in the current 45 percent, to 27 percent overall. Naturally, the extremists on both sides of the issue rejected the proposal as too much or too little. Nullifiers and high-tariff advocates joined forces against the administration. After much haggling and maneuvering and the grumbling of some southerners the Tariff of 1832 passed on July 9, reduced revenues approximately $5 million, and lowered most rates to approximately 25 percent. But woolens, iron, and cottons retained their high protective schedules.

The President gladly signed the tariff bill on July 14, 1832. "The modified Tariff," he told John Coffee, "has killed the ultras, both tarifites and nullifiers, and in a few weeks that excitement that has been created by the united influence of the coalition of Calhoun Clay and Webster will cease to agitate the union." Although further mischief will be attempted, he predicted, "the virtue of the people" will dispel it.

The other potential bombshell to work its way through Congress in the spring of 1832 was the Bank bill. The anti-Bank organization slowly asserted itself in the spring of 1832 with Benton in the Senate, James

Knox Polk in the House, Blair commanding the *Globe,* and Kendall and Taney close at Jackson's side. Even Louis McLane deserted the Bank. The arrogance of the recharter demand in a bill that offered no compromise forced him to admit that the measure must be put down. Only Secretary of State Edward Livingston continued to argue for recharter but Jackson simply ignored him.

Nicholas Biddle reacted to the mounting campaign against his institution by rushing down to Washington to conduct the defense in person. He ordered petitions to be sent to Congress demanding renewal. He urged the Bank's retainers in Congress, like Daniel Webster, to deliver speeches that he could reprint and distribute around the country.

Jackson carefully observed—and Blair dutifully reported—Biddle's direct intrusion into the legislative process. The action proved all the President's fears and past warnings. Corruption, again generated by the BUS, reared its "hydra-head." Let anyone dare challenge the power and influence of the Bank and all the horrors commanded by this monster were loosed upon the land.

On June 11, 1832, despite the labored efforts of Thomas Hart Benton and the other Jackson leaders in Congress, the bill for recharter passed the Senate by a vote of 28 to 20. Almost a month later, on July 3, it rode triumphantly through the House by a count of 107 to 85. Solid support for the BUS came from the representatives from New England and the Middle Atlantic states with strong opposition from the south and almost divided reaction from the northwest and southwest. Biddle sighed with relief. "I congratulate our friends most cordially upon this most satisfactory result. Now for the President. My belief is that the President will veto the bill though this is not generally known or believed."[21]

There was no question that Jackson would veto. And he asked Kendall to begin the task of composition. Taney and Levi Woodbury also lent a hand, as did Andrew J. Donelson. Over all, the presence and will of Andrew Jackson predominated. What finally emerged was precisely what he wanted to say to Congress and the American people.[22]

Martin Van Buren returned to the United States from Europe on July 4, 1832, just in time to get down to Washington to see the President before the veto went forward. Jackson was anxious to see him. On the evening of Van Buren's first appearance at the White House after his return home he was startled to find his friend on a sickbed looking like "a spectre . . . but as always a hero in spirit." The President brightened when he saw the New Yorker. He reached out his hand in welcome. The Magician gushed a greeting. Then, holding Van Buren's hand in one of his own and passing the other through his long gray-white hair, he said: "The bank, Mr. Van Buren is trying to kill me, *but I will kill it!*"[23]

Signed and transmitted to Congress on July 10, 1832, the veto message hit the nation like a tornado. For it not only cited constitutional arguments against recharter—supposedly the *only* reason for resorting to a veto—but political, social, economic, and nationalistic reasons as well. The Bank of the United States, Jackson argued, enjoyed exclusive privileges conferred by the government which, for all intents and purposes, gave it a monopoly over foreign and domestic exchange. Government must never confer exclusive privileges on anyone or any institution, he asserted, for that creates inequity and leads ultimately to a deprivation of liberty. Investigation revealed, he said, that relatively few Americans owned stock in the BUS. It was "chiefly the richest class" who did, and yet they divided profits from investments of government funds generated from taxes on all the people. Some $8 million worth of shares belonged to foreigners, Jackson asserted. By this recharter, therefore, "the American Republic proposes virtually to make them a present of some millions of dollars." If the government must sell monopolies, he continued, "it is but justice and good policy . . . to confine our favors to our own fellow citizens, and let each in his turn enjoy an opportunity to profit by our bounty."[24]

Turning to the constitutional question, Jackson noted that the friends of the Bank had insisted that it had been settled by the Supreme Court in the case *McCulloch* v. *Maryland.* "To this conclusion," he declared, "I cannot assent." Both houses of Congress and the executive must decide for themselves what is or is not constitutional before taking any action on a bill, whether that action consists of voting for it by Congress or signing it by the President. "It is as much the duty of the House of Representatives, of the Senate, and of the President to decide upon the constitutionality of any bill or resolution which may be presented to them for passage or approval as it is of the supreme judges when it may be brought before them for judicial decision." What Jackson argued here, and argued in a way citizens in 1830 would understand, was the equality and independence of each branch of the federal government. A balance had been established by the Constitution among the three branches, and through the balance the liberty of the people was protected. To allow the Supreme Court total and final authority on constitutional interpretation skews the system. Just because the Court declares a bill constitutional does not mean that Congress *must* vote for such a bill when one is introduced, or that the President *must* sign it if, in their good judgment, they honestly believe the bill unconstitutional. "The authority of the Supreme Court," he averred, "must not, therefore, be permitted to control the Congress or the Executive when acting in their legislative capacities, but to have only such influence as the force of their reasoning may deserve." Since the matter of a national bank was subject to their action, Jackson simply claimed for the Congress and the executive the right to think and act as equal and independent members of the government.[25]

But the greatest devastation from this tornadolike veto came at the tail end of the message. It almost sounded like a call to class warfare. Certainly nothing like it had ever come from a President before—or ever would again.

It is to be regretted that the rich and powerful too often bend the acts of government to their selfish purposes. Distinctions in society will always exist under every just government. Equality of talents, of education, or of wealth can not be produced by human institutions. In the full enjoyment of the gifts of Heaven and the fruits of superior industry, economy, and virtue, every man is equally entitled to protection by law; but when the laws undertake to add to these natural and just advantages artificial distinctions, to grant titles, gratuities, and exclusive privileges, to make the rich richer and the potent more powerful, the humble members of society—the farmers, mechanics, and laborers—who have neither the time nor the means of securing like favors to themselves, have a right to complain of the injustice of their Government. There are no necessary evils in government. Its evils exist only in its abuses. If it would confine itself to equal protection, and, as Heaven does its rains, shower its favors alike on the high and the low, the rich and the poor, it would be an unqualified blessing. In the act before me there seems to be a wide and unnecessary departure from these just principles.[26]

Jackson then closed the message by placing his reliance on the American people. If they sustained him he would be "grateful and happy." More and more frequently Jackson spoke of his absolute confidence in the ability of the people to recognize the wisdom and moral worth of his actions. "In the difficulties which surround us and the dangers which threaten our institutions," he concluded, "let us firmly rely on that kind Providence which I am sure watches with peculiar care over the destinies of our Republic, and on the intelligence and wisdom of our countrymen. Through *His* abundant goodness and *their* patriotic devotion our liberty and Union will be preserved."[27]

So ended one of the strongest and most controversial presidential statements ever written. The friends of the Bank were utterly appalled by the tone and substance of the message, and some of its principles and arguments were later scored by historians and economists as "beneath contempt."[28] Nicholas Biddle likened it to "the fury of a chained panther biting the bars of his cage." It was, he said, "a manifesto of anarchy, such as Marat, or Robespierre might have issued to the mobs" during the French Revolution.[29] As an economic statement, totally unconcerned with the Bank's financial value to the nation, the message was and still is seriously flawed. But as propaganda it is a masterpiece.

Indeed, Jackson's Bank veto is the most important veto ever issued by a President. Its novel doctrines advanced the process already in train by which the presidency was transformed and strengthened. To begin with, Jackson accomplished something quite unprecedented by writing this veto. Previous Presidents had employed the veto a total of nine times. In forty years under the Constitution only nine acts of Congress had been struck down by the chief executive, and only three of these dealt with important issues. In every instance the President claimed that the offending legislation violated the Constitution. It was therefore generally accepted that a question of a bill's constitutionality was the only reason to apply a veto. Jackson disagreed. He believed that a President could kill a bill for any reason—political, social, economic, or whatever—when he felt it injured the nation and the people. The implications of such an interpretation were enormous. In effect it claimed for the President the right to participate in the legislative process. Jackson invaded the exclusive province of Congress. According to his view, Congress must now consider the President's wishes on all bills *before* enacting them, or risk a veto. It must defer to the will of the executive if it expects to legislate successfully. Jackson's interpretation of presidential prerogatives, therefore, essentially altered the relationship between the legislative and executive branches of government. The President now had a distinct edge. He was becoming the head of government, not simply an equal partner.

From the founding of the nation under the Constitution, the legislative branch was generally regarded as preeminent. In the minds of most, it was Congress, not the President, who embodied and secured representative government. The generation of Americans who fought the Revolution had been very suspicious of a strong chief executive. To them, executive power meant monarchical (and ultimately dictatorial) power. Thus, in dedicating themselves to the perpetuation of individual liberty they devised a system of government with a strong legislature elected by the people and in full control of the purse strings. Jackson changed that. Thenceforward the President could participate in the legislative process. Coupled with that was Jackson's total success in establishing the concept that he, as President, represented all the people. And he, as President, protected their liberty.

Critics were outraged by Jackson's claims. The editors of the Washington *National Intelligencer* later argued that the veto power "enabled the President . . . to usurp the legislative power." The question henceforth "is not what Congress will do," they jeered, "but what the President will permit."[30]

Jackson's veto message of 1832 also powerfully restated the philosophy of the minimized state. Centralized government endangered liberty, he said, and therefore it must never intrude in the normal operations of society. When it does interfere and assumes unwarranted power, such as creating a national bank, it produces "artificial" distinctions between classes and generates inequality and injustice.

The Bank War now shifted back to the Capitol. Congress had the option of accepting Jackson's decision or rejecting it by overriding his veto. No one doubted its intended course, and on July 11 Daniel Webster rose in the Senate to smite the President with the force of his eloquence and constitutional knowledge.

Again, mobs jammed the gallery to hear the "god-like Daniel," and he did not disappoint them. His words rose and fell with dramatic impact, the great head rolled to the rhythm of his cadences, and his right hand flashed through the air to punctuate his arguments. He was contemptuous of the President's constitutional arguments, outraged by his attitude toward the Supreme Court, and downright furious at his attempt to divest Congress of its full legislative authority. "According to the doctrines put forth by the President," intoned the glowering Webster, "although Congress may have passed a law, and although the Supreme Court may have pronounced it constitutional, yet it is, nevertheless, no law at all, if he, in his good pleasure, sees fit to deny it effect; in other words, to repeal or annul it." Webster's face darkened as his voice became more agitated. "Sir, no President and no public man ever before advanced such doctrines in the face of the nation. There never was a moment in which any President would have been tolerated in asserting such a claim to despotic power." Webster further contended that Jackson's bold assertion of his prerogatives was not confined to a simple statement of presidential preeminence over the other two branches of government. He went further. Jackson "claims for the President, not the power of approval, but the primary power of originating laws."[31]

Not exactly. What Old Hickory wanted to get across to Congress was his right to be a partner in the power of originating laws, a power that he argued was properly his by virtue of his veto authority.

Henry Clay agreed with Webster on every point. He called Jackson's action a "perversion of the veto power." The framers of the Constitution, he said, never intended it for "ordinary cases. It was designed for instances of precipitate legislation, in unguarded moments." It was to be used rarely, if ever, something all previous Presidents had understood. "We now hear quite frequently, in the progress of measures through Congress," he cried, "the statement that the President will veto them, urged as an objection to their passage!" Through the instrument of the veto, the President may effectively intrude into the legislative process and force his will upon Congress. This, he insisted, was "hardly reconcilable with the genius of representative government."[32]

The Democrats hooted at Clay's criticism. Thomas Hart Benton rose to reply. This big, powerful-looking man with an ego twice the size of his physique was every bit the match for Senators Webster and Clay. He called them the "duplicate Senators" and scolded them for faulting Jackson when the BUS, the most power-mad institution in the country, corrupted everything and everyone it touched.

Clay laughed at Benton. What a faker! He remembered back to 1813, he said, when Jackson and Benton were enemies and had engaged in a gunfight involving several other men, including Benton's brother, Jesse. And Benton dares to talk of disrespect and abuse. At least, taunted Clay, "I never had any personal rencontre with the President; I never complained of the President beating a brother of mine after he was prostrated and lying apparently lifeless." Nor, he continued, had he ever said that if Jackson were elected President, congressmen would have to protect themselves by carrying guns and knives.

"That's an atrocious calumny," cried Benton, springing to his feet.

"What," retorted Clay, "can you look me in the face, sir, and say that you never used that language?"

"I look," bellowed Benton, "and repeat that it is an atrocious calumny, and I will pin it on him who repeats it here."

Clay flushed with rage. "Then I declare before the Senate that you said to me the very words."

"False! False! False!" screamed Benton.

Other senators bolted to their feet, fearful the two men would attack each other. The chair gaveled for order and after a few moments the dignity of the Senate was restored.

"I apologize to the Senate," said Benton, "for the manner in which I have spoken—but not to the Senator from Kentucky."

Clay stood his ground. The thin line that marked his mouth slowly stretched into a smile. "To the Senate," he said, "I also offer an apology—to the Senator from Missouri, none!"[33]

Thus ended the great debate over Jackson's arbitrary seizure of legislative power and his illegal "experiments with the government and the Constitution." But despite the oratorical power of Webster and Clay, the Bank men could not muster a two-thirds vote to override Jackson's veto. The 22 to 19 tally fell far short of the needed vote. On July 16, 1832, both houses adjourned. Since there would be a presidential election in the fall, the members were terribly concerned about the effects of the Bank War in political terms. Jackson, in writing the veto as he did, laid the Bank issue squarely before the American people for decision. Never before had a chief executive taken a strong stand on an important issue, couched his position in provocative language, and challenged the electorate to unseat him if they did not approve. And the alternative was clear. Either Clay and the Bank—or Jackson and no Bank.

The decision rested with the American people.

CHAPTER 18

Jackson and the Union

THE PRESIDENTIAL ELECTION OF 1832 was one of the few times in American history that a major issue was submitted to the electorate for disposition. Normally, the American people do not decide issues directly. But Jackson insisted on a popular referendum. He so trusted the good judgment of the people and their devotion and affection for him, and he so despised the BUS as the worst of all corrupting agents in the country, that he believed the outcome a foregone conclusion. He reduced the contest to a simple morality struggle between good and evil, between an honest yeomanry and a decadent money power. Proud of his veto, certain of the triumph of goodness and decency, he made no particular effort to shape and direct this election. The mechanics of victory he left to others, such as Kendall, Blair, Lewis, Donelson, and a small army of politicians stationed around the country.

Amos Kendall served virtually throughout the campaign as national party chairman. A regular flow of correspondence and campaign propaganda to politicians in every state left his office each day. He urged organization; he encouraged the founding of newspapers; he prodded politicians to "proclaim" the message of Jacksonian reform. "You must try by an efficient organization and rousing the patriotic enthusiasm of the people," he told one party chieftain, "to counteract the power of money." "Have you an organization in your state?" he queried another. "Whether you have or not . . . send me a list of names of Jackson men good and true in every township of the state . . . to whom our friends may send political information. I beg you to do this *instantly.*"[1]

Francis Blair also proved to be a valuable campaigner during this election. Indeed, his newspaper kept up a steady barrage of uncommonly effective propaganda, some of it vicious but all of it effective. He and Kendall issued special *Extra Globes* during the campaign designed "to throw this paper into every neighborhood of the United States." They exhorted members of Congress "to assist in disseminating it among their constituents." "Extra *Globes,*" reported the Maine *Advocate*, "are sent in bundles by the Administration and its officers, into every town where a Jackson man can be found to distribute them."[2] The language and tone of the veto inspired much of the editorial comment. Instead of attacking Clay or Wirt (the candidates of the opposing parties) Democratic editors tended to single out the BUS (or Biddle) as the principal villain of this election. The *Globe* constantly referred to the Bank as a "monster," one with twenty-seven heads and a hundred hands.

Of course Nicholas Biddle did not sit mute in his office on Chestnut Street in Philadelphia and allow these outrageous statements against his Bank to go unchallenged. He poured thousands of dollars into a verbal assault on Jackson to defeat him. He paid for the reprinting of speeches by Clay, Webster, and anyone else who supported recharter. He even distributed 30,000 copies of the veto message because he considered it excellent propaganda for the Bank. "The U.S. Bank is in the field," wrote Senator William L. Marcy, "and I cannot but fear the effect of 50 or 100 thousand dollars expended in conducting the election in such a city as New York." Isaac Hill agreed. "The Bank is scattering its thousands here [New Hampshire] to affect us," he reported.[3]

Given Jackson's principal reason for attacking the Bank and Biddle's vigorous response, the editorial campaign against the "monster" soon widened to include broader questions of democracy and liberty. The struggle against the BUS was depicted as a struggle to preserve American liberty. "The Jackson cause," the editors chorused, "is the cause of democracy and the people, against a corrupt and abandoned aristocracy."[4]

As might be expected the National Republicans took a less exalted view of Jackson's presidential actions, especially his reform program. To all the propaganda about democracy and liberty, they countered with accusations of despotism and tyranny. "The spirit of Jacksonianism," insisted the Boston *Daily Advertiser and Patriot,* "is JACOBINISM. . . . Its Alpha is ANARCHY and its Omega DESPOTISM. It addresses itself to the worst passions of the least informed portion of the People." The Cincinnati *Daily Advertiser* said that Jackson had annulled "two houses of Congress, the Supreme Court and the Constitution of the United States." The "Constitution is gone!" moaned the Washington *National Intelligencer.* "It is a dead letter, and the will of a DICTATOR is the Supreme Law!"[5]

Jackson returned to his home in Tennessee during the summer of 1832 and therefore relied totally on Kendall and Blair to counteract the "lying" propaganda of the National Republicans. On his homeward journey he reportedly paid all his expenses in gold. "No more paper-money, you see, fellow-citizens," he remarked with each gold payment, "if I can only put down this Nicholas Biddle and his monster bank."[6] Gold, hardly the popular medium of exchange, was held up to the people as the safe and sound currency which Jackson and his administration hoped to restore to regular use. Unlike paper money, gold represented real value and true worth. It was the coin of honest men. Rag money, on the other hand, was the instrument of banks and swindlers to corrupt and cheat an innocent and virtuous public.

During his summer vacation at home only one issue necessitated his careful attention. He knew it posed a danger even before he left the capital. The Tariff of 1832, enacted during the closing moments of Congress, seemed certain to incite ambitious men into provoking trouble in the south. The President watched with deep concern as nullifiers in South Carolina announced their readiness to engage in some form of precipitate action. Reports out of that state of threatened civil strife sounded ominous. When someone said to Jackson that Calhoun "ought to be hung as a traitor to the liberties of the country" for proposing nullification, the President wholeheartedly agreed. Moreover, he said, if the nullifiers carried their threats into action he planned to march 10,000 volunteers into South Carolina to "crush and hang" the traitors. "These are and must be the feelings and sentiments of all honest men who love our happy country and who wish to hand down to their posterity the liberty we enjoy."[7]

The danger of overt action by the nullifiers became acute as the summer wore on. The tension, which mounted in cities like Charleston and produced armed mobs roaming the streets at night, won regular coverage in the newspapers and captured Jackson's daily attention.[8] Angry verbal exchanges in editorials of South Carolina newspapers provoked duels, bloody fistfights, and riots in early August and September. Then, when the President heard that an attempt had been made to bring about the disaffection of the army and naval officers in command at Charleston Harbor, he knew he must respond. Although he did not expect the events in the south to develop into a "desperate issue, yet it behooves us to be ready for any emergency," Jackson informed Levi Woodbury, the secretary of the navy. He therefore ordered several actions to be taken. The army and navy secretaries were ordered to cooperate in arranging the replacement of the officers and troops in Charleston "at any time it may be desireable." Let them "be relieved by a faithful detachment, and this carried into effect as early as possible at farthest, by the 20th of October." He then directed that General Winfield Scott supervise all preparations. He also directed that a naval squadron be readied at the Norfolk station to be deployed instantly "if we shall be required to use any." At the same time he opened up lines of communication to the "Unionists" in South Carolina—Joel R. Poinsett, Colonel William Drayton, James L. Petigru, the Richardsons, the Pringles, Judge David Johnson, and others—and urged them to provide him with quick and reliable information as events developed.[9]

Otherwise Jackson's summer was relatively peaceful. Democratic leaders around the country assured him of a great victory in the fall election and lauded his veto of the Bank bill "as a document worthy of the purest days of our Republic. It brings us back nearer to the original principles which pervaded, and the spirit which animated the fathers of our country, than anything which emanated from the Executive since the days of Jefferson."[10]

As these politicians perfected their organizations during the close of the election they continually adjusted their style and methods to conform to a changing social and economic system. They relied on cartoons, parades, barbecues, and other gimmicks to interest and amuse the electorate. They did not so much debase American politics as simply reflect the great revolutions taking place in almost every aspect of American life. The continuing development of the industrial revolution, the rapid economic growth of the 1830s, the revolution in transportation most recently advanced by the advent of railroads, the heightened mobility of the people as they raced across a continent, the apparent social mobility of classes as they raised their standard of living, the preoccupation with work, money, and "getting ahead"—all these shaped a new and modern American society to which politicians quite naturally responded in ways they thought appropriate.

Andrew Jackson symbolized that dynamic, explosive democracy. His popularity no longer rested solely on his past military accomplishments. By 1832 he was seen less as the "Hero of New Orleans" and more as the "man of the People." Said one politician: *"Democracy and Jackson."* They are one.[11]

Jackson returned to Washington on the evening of October 19 and he was immediately informed of the electoral defeat of the Union party in South Carolina. "You must be prepared to hear very shortly of a State Convention and an act of Nullification," Joel Poinsett advised him.[12] The President was also informed of the likelihood of an attack upon the federal forts in Charleston by the nullifiers. Straightaway, Jackson issued orders to the secretary of war.

Washington, October 29, 1832

Confidential

The Secretary of War will forthwith cause secrete and confidential orders to be Issued to the officers commanding the Forts in the harbour of charleston So Carolina to be vigilant to prevent a surprise in the night or by day, against any attempt to seize and occupy the Fts. by any Set of people under whatever pretext the Forts may be approached. Warn them that the attempt will be made, and the officers commanding will be responsible for the defence of the Forts and garrisons, against all intrigue or assault, and they are to defend them to the last extremity—permitting no armed force to approach either by night or day. *The attempt will be made to surprise the Forts and garrisons* by the militia, and must be guarded against with *vestal vigilence* and any attempt by force repelled with prompt and exemplary punishment.[13]

In addition to directing the preparations of the forts for possible attack, Jackson also turned his attention to the customhouse and post office. He authorized George Breathitt, brother of the governor of Kentucky, to journey to South Carolina, ostensibly as a Post Office inspector, to gather information about the reports of disloyalty and collusion within the revenue and postal service, "specifying the names of all officers so engaged." Breathitt was directed to consult with the Unionists in South Carolina as to the best direction for the government in counteracting the schemes of the nullifiers.[14]

It was during these November days of mounting crisis that Jackson learned he had won an overwhelming popular and electoral victory at the polls. He received 688,242 popular votes, while Clay took 473,462 and Wirt 101,051. The Hero won approximately 55 percent of the popular vote as against 37 percent for Clay and 8 percent for Wirt. In the electoral college Jackson garnered 219 votes against 49 for Clay and 7 for Wirt. Clay carried Massachusetts, Rhode Island, Connecticut, Delaware, Kentucky, and a majority of the Maryland vote, while Wirt won the single state of Vermont. Jackson swept all the rest except South Carolina, which gave its 11 votes to John Floyd of Virginia. In the vice presidential contest, Van Buren gained an easy victory by taking 189 votes to Sergeant's 49 and Ellmaker's 7. South Carolina awarded its 11 votes to Henry Lee of Massachusetts, while Pennsylvania gave 30 to its favorite son, William Wilkins.[15]

This election underscored something important about Jackson's relation to the American people. Clay had insisted on the Bank recharter as an issue with which to fight Old Hickory at the polls and it was as potent an issue as anyone could have desired. Still, the issue and the Bank's money were not powerful enough to unseat the General—or come anywhere near it. "The devotion to him is altogether personal, without reference to his course of policy," declared *Niles Weekly Register*.[16] "Who but General Jackson would have had the courage to veto the bill rechartering the Bank of the United States," asked one man, "and who but General Jackson could have withstood the overwhelming influence of that corrupt Aristocracy?"[17]

Indeed, the only real issue in the campaign seemed to be Jackson himself, and the people by their vote reaffirmed their trust and confidence in him. They felt secure in his leadership because he stood as the protector of their interests, their true representative. As one Ohio politician observed, the election was a triumph for "Jackson and Democracy."[18] If nothing else, the contest proved that one of Jackson's greatest assets was his ability to inspire the people to follow his lead, even when he frightened and worried them by raising such issues as the destruction of the Bank. "My opinion," said the defeated third-party candidate, William Wirt, "is that he may be President for life if he chooses."[19]

With Congress about to reconvene in December, with the situation in South Carolina growing worse, and with his new vote of confidence from the American people, Jackson briefly considered the formation of a new party in order to present a united front against the nullifiers. At various times he encouraged the leaders of the National Republican party to join him in his efforts to create a "moral force" in the country to combat the forces of disunion. Throughout the developing nullification controversy a number of National Republicans—in particular Daniel Webster—materially assisted the President in preserving the Union.

"It is my painful duty to state," the President informed Congress when it reconvened, that opposition to the revenue laws had risen to such a height as to threaten "if not to endanger the integrity of the Union." He hoped that a peaceful solution to the problem could be found through the prudence and patriotism of the people and officials of South Carolina. Should moderation and good sense fail, however, Jackson promised to return to Congress with suggestions for remedying the situation. In the meantime he suggested the gradual diminution of the tariff rates as one way to show goodwill on the part of the central government.[20]

What everyone knew at the time was that events had moved very rapidly in the past several weeks. On October 22, three days after Jackson's return to the capital from Tennessee, a special session of the South Carolina legislature met at the request of Governor James Hamilton, Jr. It subsequently called for a convention to meet in Columbia on November 19, 1832, to respond to the action of Congress in passing the Tariff of 1832. In turn, this convention, after it met, passed an Ordinance of Nullification on November 24, by a vote of 136 to 26, which declared the tariff laws of 1828 and 1832 "null, void, and no law, nor binding" upon South Carolina, its officers or citizens. After February 1, 1833, the Ordinance continued, "it shall not be lawful . . . to enforce the payment of duties . . . within the limits of this State." We are determined, the members said, to maintain this Ordinance "at every hazard" and "will not submit to the application of force . . . to reduce this State to obedience." If force is used, then the people of South Carolina "will thenceforth hold themselves absolved from all further obligation to maintain or preserve their political connexion with the people of the other States, and will forthwith proceed to organize a separate Government."[21]

News of the action of the Nullification Convention shot up to Washington and around the country with record speed. The defiance shocked and infuriated the President. As he prowled the corridors of the White House, he uttered all manner of savage threats, but at no time did he allow his feelings to color his judgment or influence his actions. In moments of crisis General Jackson exercised absolute control over his normally volatile emotions.

Joel Poinsett immediately reported on the proceedings of the Convention to the President. Fortunately, he said, Jackson's previous actions had prevented the seizure of military forts—Moultrie and Pinckney—in the Charleston harbor. He predicted that no violence was likely until February 1. After that date anything might happen.[22]

Jackson responded instantly. "I fully concur with you in your views of Nullification," he said. "It leads directly to civil war and bloodshed and deserves the execration of every friend of the country." He had taken additional "precautionary measures," he continued, and had directed General Winfield Scott to take command of the entire operation. "The Union must be preserved," Jackson reiterated, "and its laws duly executed." Poinsett was directed to tell the Unionists in South Carolina "that perpetuity is stamped upon the constitution by the blood of our Fathers." Nothing could dissolve the Union. Nothing. Constitutional amendment was the process provided to secure needed changes. For this reason a state may not secede, much less "hazard" the Union. "Nullification therefore means insurrection and war; and the other states have a right to put it down."[23]

Events in South Carolina began to move at a frightening clip toward confrontation with the federal government and possible civil war. The people of the state seemed to accept the Ordinance of Nullification with no perceptible concern. The Union party, though respectable in character, was overwhelmed in the fall elections by an "immense, an almost silencing majority," completely sympathetic to the nullifiers. Robert Y. Hayne resigned as United States senator and John C. Calhoun resigned as Vice President of the United States. Hayne was elected to succeed James Hamilton, Jr., as governor. A new legislature, composed mainly of nullifiers, elected Calhoun to take Hayne's seat in the United States Senate and then proceeded to pass the necessary legislation to carry the Ordinance into practical effect. For example, it authorized the governor to accept volunteers in case of invasion. Said Hayne in his inaugural address: "If the sacred soil of Carolina should be polluted by the footsteps of an invader . . . I trust in Almighty God that no son of hers[24] . . . will be found raising a parricidal arm against our common mother."[25]

South Carolina rang with a rebel yell. Blue cockades with a palmetto button at the center appeared everywhere, on "hats, bonnets and bosoms." Then events turned ominous, for medals were struck bearing the inscription: "John C. Calhoun, First President of the Southern Confederacy."[26]

The central question of the nullification controversy, raised by the tariff dispute, was whether the states had the right to declare federal law invalid within their boundaries (and, if necessary, to secede from the Union) in order to protect their rights. And Andrew Jackson had an absolutely clear answer to this question. It was simple and direct. It may not have been historically accurate, but he sincerely believed it to be so. The federal government, he said, was "based on a confederation of perpetual union" by an act of the people. A state may not invalidate federal law and may never secede. Moreover, the people, not the states, granted sovereignty to the federal government through the Constitution. They called the Union into existence, they created the federal government, and they granted federal power. These actions, he insisted, were taken by the people at conventions when they ratified the Constitution. And in ratifying the Constitution the people automatically amended their state constitutions to accord with the new arrangement.[27]

To enunciate his position Jackson decided to issue a presidential proclamation to the people of South Carolina. What he had in mind was a bold, forthright statement of what nullification entailed in terms of inevitable bloodshed and civil war. More than that, the proclamation was meant to generate a "moral force" in the country to counteract the forces of disunion; it was meant to reach out to all Americans—not simply South Carolinians—and rally them to the defense of the Union and the Constitution.

To assist him in the composition of this proclamation the President turned to his secretary of state, Edward Livingston. A plain-looking man, but not unattractive, with a prominent nose and expansive forehead, Livingston was a brilliant scholar of the law. Among his friends and admirers, he was known as Beau Ned because of the fastidiousness of his dress and the elegance of his manner. As a member of the cabinet, as a writer whose style frequently matched the grace and refinement of his bearing, and as one of the nation's outstanding constitutional minds, he could give the proclamation authority, grandeur, learning. But it must have fire. That above all.

Not that Livingston needed to provide the ideas for this proclamation. That the President would take care of himself. In fact Jackson closeted himself in his office and scribbled page after page of what he wanted said. Writing rapidly and with great emotion, he poured out his ideas about the Union, its preservation, and the rights of the states. His entire being vibrated with the intensity of his thought and conviction. After he had written fifteen or twenty pages, he was interrupted by a visitor who noted that three of the pages were still glistening with wet ink. "The warmth, the glow, the passion, the eloquence" of the proclamation shone bright on those still-moist sheets.[28]

Gathering these pages, Jackson presented them to Livingston and asked him to shape them into an authoritative and persuasive presidential paper. Meanwhile Jackson composed a conclusion to the proclamation and sent it to the secretary with the request that "it receive your best flight

of eloquence to strike to the heart." The document carried the full thrust
of his intent.

for the conclusion of the proclamation

Seduced as you have been, my fellow countrymen by the delusion theories and misrepresentation of ambitious, *deluded* & designing men, I call
upon you in the language of truth, and with the feelings of a Father to
retrace your steps. As you value liberty and the blessings of peace blot out
from the page of your history a record so fatal to their security as this
ordinance will become if it be obayed. Rally again under the banners of the
union whose obligations you in common with all your countrymen have,
with an appeal to heaven, sworn to support, and which must be indesoluble
as long as we are capable of enjoying freedom.

Recollect that the first act of resistance to the laws which have been
denounced as void by those who abuse your confidence and falsify your
hopes is Treason, and subjects you to all the pains and penalties that are
provided for the highest offence against your country. Can [you] . . . consent to become Traitors? Forbid it Heaven![29]

The proclamation, as finally composed by Livingston and amended and
approved by Jackson, was dated December 10, 1832, and published on
December 11. It is one of the most significant presidential documents in
American history and has been frequently compared to Lincoln's inaugural address. It contains the subtlety of language to make its legal and
constitutional arguments both impressive and persuasive. Yet it contains
enough Jacksonian passion to give it spirit and life. Much of the wording
and subtlety of expression should be credited to Livingston, but the ideas
about government and Union, the conviction of its sentiment, and the
weight of its thought belong to Jackson.

The proclamation opened by declaring the actions of the nullifying
convention to be aimed ultimately at the destruction of the Union. "I
consider, then, the power to annul a law of the United States, assumed
by one State, *incompatible with the existence of the Union, contradicted expressly
by the letter of the Constitution, unauthorized by its spirit, inconsistent with every
principle on which it was founded, and destructive of the great object for which it
was formed.*" The people of the United States, Jackson went on, formed
the Constitution, acting through their respective states. The Constitution
"forms a *government,* not a league," a government in which all the people
are represented and which operates directly on the people themselves,
not upon the states. A "single nation" having been formed, it follows that
the states do not "possess any right to secede."

Nor, the President continued, have the states retained their entire
sovereignty. They surrendered "essential parts of sovereignty" in
"becoming parts of a nation." The allegiance of their citizens was also
altered. It was transferred to the government of the United States. Their

citizens became American citizens and owed obedience to the Constitution and its laws.

The Union is older than the states, Jackson declared. Its political character commenced long before the adoption of the Constitution. "Under the royal Government we had no separate character; our opposition to its oppressions began as *united colonies*. We were the *United States* under the Confederation, and the name was perpetuated and the Union rendered more perfect by the Federal Constitution."[30]

Here, then, is Jackson's unique contribution to a more profound understanding and appreciation of the American experiment in democracy and constitutional government. He was the first American statesman to offer the doctrine of the Union as a perpetual entity. His arguments and conclusions provide a complete brief against the right of a state to secede. In terms of constitutional arguments, Jackson's statement is far greater than Daniel Webster's more famous reply to Hayne. Webster relied on a sentimental appeal, arguing for the Union "as a blessing to mankind." Jackson went beyond sentiment. He offered history and a dynamic new reading of constitutional law.[31]

Jackson's extraordinary understanding of what is meant by "the United States" did not arise from some profound intellectual exercise or a mastery of history and political science. Rather he simply knew as a fact, revealed by "common sense," that the people had called the Union into existence, and that only they could alter or dissolve it.

Having forcefully refuted the leading arguments of the nullifiers, Jackson concluded the proclamation with a direct appeal to the people of South Carolina. The mood changed dramatically. The tone darkened. The laws of the United States must be executed, he declared. "I have no discretionary power on the subject; my duty is emphatically pronounced in the Constitution." Let the truth be known as to what will happen if the laws are disobeyed.

> Those who told you that you might peaceably prevent their execution deceived you; they could not have been deceived themselves. . . . Their object is disunion. But be not deceived by names. Disunion by armed force is *treason*. Are you really ready to incur its guilt? If you are, on the heads of the instigators of the act be the dreadful consequences; on their heads be the dishonor, but on yours may fall the punishment. On your unhappy State will inevitably fall all the evils of the conflict you force upon the Government of your country. . . . I adjure you . . . to retrace your steps.[32]

Jackson never so much deserved the trust and confidence and love of the American people as he did at this moment. It was a superb state paper. Little in it needed improvement. Indeed, Abraham Lincoln later extracted from it the basic argument he needed to explain and justify his intended course of action to meet secession in 1861. The proclamation is a major statement in constitutional law. It came about only because

Jackson was a statesman of the first rank. And, as many Americans promptly acknowledged, they were fortunate to have him at the head of the government at this moment of crisis. "The dauntless spirit of resolution" presided over the nation in the person of General Andrew Jackson, protecting the Union and the people in his care.

CHAPTER 19

The Union Preserved

THE PUBLICATION OF THE PROCLAMATION produced cheers and welcome relief around the nation. Many who read it with fear and apprehension soon shed their anxiety over this clear and straightforward assertion of national supremacy. Even the opposition press approved. "The Presidents proclamation," wrote one National Republican, "gives great satisfaction to the liberal and patriotic of all parties, hereabouts. . . . May it accomplish its good ends."[1]

Jackson himself radiated contentment and goodwill. "I am assured by all the members of congress with whom I have conversed," he reported to the Unionists in South Carolina, "that I will be sustained by congress. If so, I will meet at the threshold, and have the leaders arrested and arraigned for treason."[2] Still, he knew the danger had not passed and he signaled an alert to his secretary of war, Lewis Cass. "We must be prepared for the crisis," he wrote. "The moment that we are informed that the Legislature of So Carolina has passed laws to carry her rebellious ordinance into effect which I expect tomorrow, we must be prepared to act." He wanted three divisions of artillery readied, each one "composed of nines, twelves, and Eighteen pounders." And he wanted assurances that troops could be moved within four days after such an order had been issued.[3]

But South Carolina did not plunge ahead and make good her threat of secession, in part for fear of giving the President a solid reason for military action. Moreover, the nullifiers observed how well the proclamation had been received throughout the nation. They already felt the effects of the "moral force" that had been generated. Nonetheless, the legislature did authorize Governor Hayne to call out the militia, accept volunteers, and, if necessary, to draft able-bodied men between the ages of eighteen and forty-five. It also appropriated $200,000 for arms. Hayne responded by asking for volunteers. He also began the process of raising and training an army.[4]

244

During the following weeks, Jackson attempted several things at once: he continued building his moral force throughout the country; he avoided any provocative acts (although his language was frequently provocative in private) that would create a head-on collision with the rebellious state; and he tried to create a volunteer force of Unionists in South Carolina as a counterweight to the nullifiers in case the use of military power became necessary.

More immediate to the resolution of the crisis was the need to revise the tariff by gradually diminishing its rates, as Jackson had requested in his State of the Union message to Congress. Louis McLane prepared such legislation and it was handed over to the chairman of the House Ways and Means Committee, Gulian C. Verplanck of New York, with a plea to move it as quickly as possible.

When finally written the Verplanck bill was then introduced into the House on January 8, 1833, the anniversary of the Battle of New Orleans, and it sliced duties in half. The reductions were scheduled over a two-year period and would approximate the duties of 1816 as amended in 1818. Although the bill did not completely fulfill Jackson's early promise of reform, it did address South Carolina's grievance by erasing previous wrongs. It constituted a gesture of friendship, a willingness to accept South Carolina's complaint and redress it. But to protectionists it seemed a clear surrender to the nullifiers. Even so, at virtually the same time, Jackson sternly warned the state against persisting in its defiance by asking Congress for authorization to deploy the military to put down armed rebellion. On January 16, 1833, he sent his "Force Bill" message to Congress which nullifiers subsequently called his "Bloody Bill" or "War Bill."

The Force Bill message was written with the aid of Louis McLane. It was a bold message, yet reasonable and even-tempered. No bluster clouded its content, no anger intruded. Jackson was intent on avoiding conflict, and most of his suggestions to Congress emphasized the need to *prevent* the use of force rather than the obligation to implement his authority to compel South Carolina to comply with the law. Again he repeated that if it came to conflict, South Carolina must strike the first blow.

The message began with the reminder that he had promised to notify Congress if the emergency worsened. He then narrated the events that had brought the country to its present crisis. In his opinion, said the President, the actions of South Carolina "are to be regarded as revolutionary in their character and tendency, and subversive of the supremacy of the laws and of the integrity of the Union." The right of the people of a single state, he said, to "absolve" themselves at will without the consent of the other states "and hazard the liberties and happiness of the millions composing the Union, cannot be acknowledged." Jackson did not deny the "natural right" of rebellion when all effort to redress op-pression had been exhausted. But all such effort had not been exhausted in the present instance, he insisted.[5]

Under the circumstances, then, the duty of the government was plain. The executive must execute the laws. Therefore the President asked that he be authorized to close any port of entry he deemed necessary and reestablish it at some other port or harbor. He also requested minor changes in the federal judiciary system in the area to protect United States property and jail lawbreaking nullifiers. Jackson took great pains to explain how this request involved preexisting laws, that he was simply asking for congressional approval to exercise these laws. His scheme proved devilishly clever. By moving the customs he would force the nullifiers to go to considerable trouble to carry out their threats. They would have to travel a distance and invade federal installations, thereby engaging in blatantly hostile acts against the government. In effect, the President had reduced considerably the likelihood of armed resistance to the laws. As one historian has noted, "Jackson had outmaneuvered his foes."[6]

With respect to possible military action, the President's message was relatively tame. No Jacksonian fire scorched its outer edges. If South Carolina resorts to force, he said, Congress need only make "a few modifications" of the law of 1792 as amended in 1795 for the President to call out the state militia and use federal troops and ships. Whenever he was officially informed that the execution of federal law had been resisted by force he had enough authority to respond to save the Union "from the maddness and folly" of the miscreants who dared to attack it.[7]

The message ended with a ringing rejection of secession at any time. And nullification was an abomination. Jackson labeled both pernicious. "The Constitution and the laws are supreme," he declared, "and the *Union indissoluble.*"[8] Some Americans at the time regarded secession as an intrinsic component of states' rights, and for them to surrender it would not only emasculate the states' rights philosophy but subvert individual liberty. Jackson divorced himself from these men with this message. He still retained his states' rights creed—indeed, he never abandoned it throughout his entire life—but it was totally shorn of any authority to tamper with the structure and integrity of the Union.

President Jackson marks an important break with the past. He is the first and only statesman of the early national period to deny publicly the right of secession. Secession was a doctrine no longer in keeping with a democratic society, no longer congenial to the idea of "a Federal Union founded upon the great principle of popular representation."[9] Whether at some point in time secession had any validity no longer mattered. It was a dead issue as far as Old Hickory was concerned, annihilated by the historical evolution of a democratic society.

Jackson not only insisted that the Union was indissoluble, but he argued that it had been formed by the sovereignty of the people, not the sovereignty of the states. It was not a confederation, not a banding together of individual states, but a permanent welding of the people.

Thus, by his words and deeds, Jackson continued to recast attitudes and perceptions of this nation and its operation. Republicanism was giving way to democracy, and Andrew Jackson was an important instrument in that change. Republicanism, with its emphasis on liberty, preached the need for strong states as a counterweight to the central government, but by the mid-1830s that philosophy could not accommodate the dynamics of an emerging industrial society. Protecting freedom in the modern world required a strong national government. Besides, the way to minimize the danger to individual rights was to fashion a government elected by all the people. In short, majority rule best protected freedom—not powerful states, and certainly not a hobbled or enfeebled central government.

The Force Bill message went down to Congress on January 16, only fifteen days before the February 1 deadline set by South Carolina. And political jockeying began immediately. "Now for my suspicions," reported Senator Silas Wright of New York to the Albany Regency. "They are that Messrs Webster, Clay and Calhoun are at this moment in the most perfect harmony of aims to make mischief." Wright was certain that Calhoun would never permit the use of military force in his state and therefore would accept some "arrangement" with Clay. The Verplanck bill would be killed, predicted Wright, at the same time that an alarm would be sounded in the Senate that the use of force was imminent. At that point Clay would step forward with a "peace offering" in the form of a substitute tariff which Calhoun would immediately pronounce "an acceptable offering to S. Carolina." Then both forces would "join to put down the war [Force] bill as they call it." Thus Clay and Calhoun would get credit for pacifying the south and preserving the Union, while Jackson would be "scored" for failing.[10]

Wright was not far off the mark as to the "arrangement" in progress. His only error was in thinking that Webster was part of it. Actually Webster took a very dim view of accommodating the South Carolinian, whose opinions on the Constitution and the Union he so heartily detested. His own nationalistic approach sharply conflicted with the nullifiers'. So when Clay and Calhoun got together to make their "arrangement"—which occurred shortly after Calhoun's arrival in Washington in early January to take his Senate seat—Webster stayed clear. In fact it was widely reported that, at the first opportunity, he would come out in the Congress in favor of Jackson's proclamation and speak very pointedly and forcefully in support of the President.

Given the conflicting views of Calhoun and Webster on the nature of the Union, a verbal brawl on the Senate floor could hardly have been avoided. It came in due course.

The Force Bill reached the Senate floor on January 28 and the excitement generated by the likely contest between the "giants" drew enormous crowds to the chamber. Finally, on February 15, the glowering, resentful, angry, and bitter South Carolinian rose to speak. (Actually he spoke briefly a number of times earlier, usually interrupting other speakers.) He stood at his desk, his gaunt figure hardly moving from his place. But his black, brilliant eyes roamed continuously around the room. He denounced the Force Bill as a declaration of war against his state in total violation of the Constitution. He attacked the manner of its presentation and once more tried to explain his tortuous theory of nullification.[11]

The godlike Daniel followed. And he spoke to the heart of a nation that no longer believed in limited government as a means of insuring liberty. A Union of people was his theme, and Webster gave it all the majesty of language that his great talent commanded. He made only one slip, in acknowledging that nullification might be justified if the Constitution was in fact a compact of states. Calhoun pounced on that admission and almost got the better of him. John Randolph, the addled former senator from Virginia, sat near Calhoun, and although he resented the South Carolinian and dismissed nullification as humbug, he was seen nodding his head in agreement as Calhoun spoke. A hat lying on a desk in front of him partially obscured Randolph's view of Webster. Suddenly his high, piercing voice could be heard throughout the chamber. "Take away that hat. I want to see Webster die, muscle by muscle."[12]

But it was not the Webster argument that was dying. Quite the contrary. Though he stumbled momentarily in the debate, Webster had the better of the argument as far as the rest of the country was concerned. President Jackson totally agreed with everything Webster said, and it gave Old Hickory great satisfaction to know that there was someone on the Senate floor—even though not of his party—who could defend the administration's argument and present a cogent case for the President's position. "Mr. Webster replied to Mr. Calhoun yesterday," he told Joel Poinsett, "and, it is said, demolished him. It is believed by more than one, that Mr. C. is in a state of dementation—his speech was a perfect failure; and Mr. Webster handled him as a child."[13]

The powerful debate ended on Wednesday, February 20, 1833, at ten in the evening when a final vote was taken in the Senate, despite Calhoun's efforts to force an adjournment. The nullifiers, almost to a man, stalked out of the chamber. Only John Tyler of Virginia remained to cast the single vote against the Force Bill. The final count was 32 to 1. Henry Clay and Thomas Hart Benton were among those not recorded.[14]

The full terms of what Silas Wright had called the "arrangement" between Clay and Calhoun soon became apparent in Congress as pressure mounted on both men to resolve the impass between those congressmen who were divided over the Verplanck tariff and Force bills. Clay quickly saw that the choice developing for the country was either civil war or a lower tariff. So he got together with Calhoun sometime in late January and offered to abandon the principle of protection and reduce duties gradually over a period of years to the revenue level, in exchange for which the South Carolinian pledged repeal of the Ordinance of Nullification. Although Clay's offer came nowhere near the breathtaking reductions of the Verplanck bill, Calhoun willingly accepted this "compromise" in order to acquire Clay's support in preventing Jackson from scourging South Carolina with fire and sword.[15]

Once the arrangement was accepted by both sides, Clay did not wait for the Verplanck bill to get to the Senate but immediately introduced his own "compromise" tariff. On February 9 he rose in the upper house and proposed a ten-year period of reductions which would be minuscule in the beginning of the period and then increase sharply toward the end. In effect he proposed that by the year 1842 the duties would stand at a uniform 20 percent *ad valorem* and remain at that level. During this period a truce could be declared against lowering or raising tariff rates.[16]

No sooner did the Kentuckian sit down than John C. Calhoun rose to inform the Senate that he approved Clay's bill and would support it. All true lovers of the Union should join him, he said. And with that fatuous remark the entire nation knew that Clay and Calhoun had reached an agreement to service one another's needs.

At this point Clay prevailed on his close friend in the House of Representatives, Robert Letcher, to move to strike out the Verplanck bill and substitute Clay's Senate bill. The move came so suddenly that the Jackson men were caught completely off guard. Then, before anyone realized what was happening, the substitute bill passed to a third reading. On the very next day, February 26, the Compromise Tariff of 1833, as it came to be called, passed the House by a vote of 119 to 85.[17] Jackson deserves a full measure of blame for this disaster. He was so preoccupied with winning passage of the Force Bill that he let everything else, including the tariff, go by the board.[18]

The sudden breakthrough in the House jolted the Senate into final action. On March 1, after Calhoun delivered another speech detailing his objections to tariff regulations but reaffirming his commitment to this compromise bill, the measure passed the Senate by the vote of 29 to 16.[19] On the same day, just a few hours earlier, the House moved to a showdown vote on the Force Bill, which had already received Senate approval on February 20. Jackson never let up in his insistence that the Force Bill be passed. Every day he met with representatives and hounded them about it, particularly after he had bungled the tariff reduction. The President wanted both measures—tariff bill and Force bill—delivered for his signature. He would not take one without the other. When the final vote was tabulated on March 1, the Jacksonians shouted their delight. By the count of 149 to 48 the Force Bill passed the House.[20]

What an unparalleled triumph, crowed Jackson. "I say unparalleled because it has not happened, according to my recollection, in the course of our legislation, that any measure, so violently contested as this has been, has been sustained by such a vote." It was very important to Jackson that the passage of the Force Bill precede the tariff because Congress thereby fully demonstrated "to the world that she was not to be deterred by a faction, which, if found in rebellion and treason, she was prepared to crush in an instant."[21]

On Saturday, March 2, 1833—the day after their passage—Jackson signed both bills, starting first (naturally) with the Force Bill. Two days later, March 4—which happened to be Inauguration Day—Duff Green in his *Telegraph* published the provisions of the Force Act in columns bordered in black for "the death of the Constitution." To many southerners it seemed as though the enactment of a "war bill" was a final act in the consolidation of power by the central government to suppress the states and the liberty of the American people.[22]

In point of fact the Force Act and Compromise Tariff ended nullification once and for all. Even South Carolina hotheads, like McDuffie and Barnwell Rhett, favored rescinding the Ordinance of Nullification. A convention was subsequently reconvened and the Ordinance repealed. But, in a symbolic gesture of defiance, the convention nullified the Force Act. "If this be no more than a swaggering conclusion of a blustering drama," commented the *Globe,* on March 28, "it will speedily be consigned to the contempt of an enlightened and patriotic public."

One factor compelling South Carolina's withdrawal from a stance of confrontation was the cool reception the doctrine of nullification received from other southern states. The Alabama legislature, for example, pronounced the doctrine "unsound in theory and dangerous in practice." Georgia said it was "mischievous," "rash and revolutionary." Mississippi lawmakers chided the South Carolinians for acting with "reckless precipitancy."[23] "Nullification is dead," declared Jackson. But "the next pretext will be the negro, or slavery question."[24]

Although the administration had stumbled its way through the congressional session of 1832–1833 and had witnessed the formation of the Clay-Calhoun alliance, the final events of this session in resolving the nullification controversy probably constituted Jackson's greatest victory as President. His policy—a combination of tariff reform and the Force Bill—was wise and practical. No other statesman at the time approached the solution of the crisis in quite the same way. They either plumped for one or the other. Clay and Calhoun (and Van Buren and Benton, it might be added) opposed the Force Bill and drove through their own tariff reform. But this tariff horrified a number of National Republicans, especially from the industrial states. Both Webster and John Quincy Adams disliked the Compromise Tariff and understood the political purposes it served. Of all the leading figures of the period, only Jackson had insisted on both measures as a combined package to solve the problem. And his "masterful statesmanship" played a crucial role in providing the final settlement that preserved the Union.[25]

CHAPTER 20

———————◁▷———————

"The Grand Triumphal Tour"

ON MAY 6, 1833, PRESIDENT ANDREW JACKSON, accompanied by some members of his cabinet and Major Donelson, embarked on a steamboat for Fredericksburg, Virginia, where the President was scheduled to lay the cornerstone of a monument in honor of the mother of George Washington. Then it happened. At Alexandria, where the steamboat made berth, Jackson retired to a cabin and had seated himself in a chair wedged between a long table and a bunk. He was reading a newspaper when he was interrupted by Robert B. Randolph, a former lieutenant in the navy, who had been dismissed for theft at Jackson's specific direction. Suddenly, Randolph "dashed his hand" into Jackson's face.[1]

"What Sir. What Sir," cried the President.[2]

A scuffle ensued and the table was overturned. Several of Randolph's friends, who had accompanied him aboard the vessel, seized the assailant and rushed him off the boat. Poor Jackson had been so trapped behind the table that he could not rise with ease, nor seize his cane in time to defend himself. "Had I been apprised that Randolph stood before me," he said, "I should have been prepared for him, and I could have defended myself. No villain has ever escaped me before; and he would not, had it not been for my confined situation."[3]

Eventually, Randolph was apprehended and brought to trial, but by that time Jackson had left office and had no wish to participate in the "villain's" prosecution. "I have to this old age complied with my mothers advice," he told Van Buren, "to 'indict no man for assault and battery or sue him for slander', and to fine or imprison Randolph would be no gratification, and not being prosecutor, nor having any agency in it I cannot enter a *noli prosequi.*" He had one request, however. If Randolph was found guilty, Jackson asked for a presidential pardon and the remission of any fine. This, he said, "would be the better mode to close this prosecution." It "might have a good effect upon society."[4]

That Andrew Jackson should be the first President to be criminally assaulted is very suggestive. For one thing it says something about Jackson himself, the kind of man he was and the emotional passions he aroused in some people. But for another, and far more important, it says something about the age. It was a sign—one ugly and frightening—that the country was undergoing disturbing changes in its character, mood, and behavior. In forty and more years of the presidency, nothing like this had happened before. Regrettably, assaulting Presidents became a terrible fact of American life. And the thing that Jackson dreaded the most came about, namely, the necessity of placing *"a military guard around the President."*[5]

Although the Randolph incident "vexed him a good deal," Jackson appeared in excellent spirits upon his return to Washington. The incident seemed to "put his blood in motion."[6] But something else roused his energies and warmed his mood. He had decided to make an extensive tour of New England with the hope of uniting the nation after the long agony of nullification. His purpose was obvious. He wanted to stimulate nationalistic sentiments for the Union among the electorate—to enhance the moral force in defense of the Union—and he knew that nothing set off demonstrations of patriotic feeling quicker than the living presence of the head of state as he moved among the people. In deciding to undertake this tour Old Hickory appreciated how much it might help to unite the nation, strengthen the bond of union, and overcome the anxiety created by the recent trauma.

In the early history of the United States, Jackson is one of the very few Presidents to take such a tour. Of the Presidents who preceded him, only George Washington and James Monroe traveled around the country. But only Jackson's tour established a warm rapport between the President and the people. President Washington was too remote and awesome to elicit more than respectful appreciation for his incalculable contribution to the nation's freedom, and the best that could be said about Monroe's tour is that it prompted one newspaperman to suggest that the President's arrival in Massachusetts marked the commencement of an "era of good feelings." But Jackson's caused an emotional debauch. The delight, the happiness, the pure joy shown by the people in seeing their President had never been expressed in quite the same way before. It was as though the people needed to shout and scream in order to expel from their minds all the anxiety for the Union that had festered within them for the past six months.

And how they did demonstrate! The parades, the banquets, the toasts and addresses, the streets lined with people, the windows crowded with joyous faces, the roofs alive with people, the thundering artillery to salute the Hero, the mobbing to shake the President's hand or touch him, the baby-kissing—all these occurred during Jackson's tour of New England in the late spring and early summer of 1833. It was one long, ecstatic ovation.[7]

The decision to make the tour came early in the new year. On February

5, 1833, a committee formed at a public meeting in Hartford, Connecticut, invited the President to visit New England and see for himself the cities, towns, churches, colleges, and industries of the region—in short, to inspect her "institutions of Republican Freedom" and mingle with a "virtuous people" to get to know them better.[8] On March 7, 1833, Jackson accepted, stating that he was anxious to view "the republican institutions which her sons have raised up with so much public spirit and success" and to savor "the satisfaction I should expect to derive from personal intercourse with the citizens themselves."[9] The final arrangements for the tour charted a course along the Atlantic seaboard with stops at all the major cities along the way. Jackson decided, by and large, to follow the route taken by President Monroe in 1818. He was to be accompanied by Major Donelson and Ralph Earl from his own household, along with Louis McLane and Lewis Cass. At New York the party would meet Martin Van Buren.

At nine o'clock on the morning of Thursday, June 6, 1833, the presidential party left the White House and headed for Baltimore. And the first day started with a grand adventure. For the first time in his life Jackson enjoyed the experience of a ride on a railroad train. At a point where the Washington Turnpike crossed the Baltimore and Ohio Railroad, about twelve miles outside Baltimore, the President boarded the train, or "Steam Carrs," as he called it, for the ride into town. And, "in a few minutes" he was whisked the twelve miles into Baltimore, arriving at half past two in the afternoon.[10] An immense crowd was waiting at the Three Tons Tavern on Brett Street to greet the Hero as he stepped from this new technological marvel of the modern age. Cheers rent the air again and again. Indeed, the President's three-day visit to Baltimore was the occasion for "an ear-splitting celebration."[11]

It so happened that while Jackson was visiting Baltimore, the great Indian chieftain Black Hawk also arrived in town on exactly the same day. A year before, the warrior had led his people, the Sac and Fox tribes, in a gallant but futile war against federal and state troops in northern Illinois. The war lasted only a few months and ended with the removal of the tribes across the Mississippi River. Black Hawk and some of his chiefs were "held as hostages for the future good conduct of the late hostile bands" and had been brought east and kept under heavy guard.[12] They were taken first to Washington and then to Fortress Monroe. After a month's confinement Black Hawk was released from prison and was now being paraded throughout the eastern states. The object of this tour was to demonstrate to him the superiority of American arms, to let him see with his own eyes the extent and power of the American nation and the utter futility of resisting removal of his people beyond the Mississippi River. Baltimore was Black Hawk's first stop and he was hauled before the President for final instructions before going forth to meet the American people.

He arrived at Jackson's hotel with a small entourage. The President ("Great Father" as he was called by the Indians) looked glum. He stared at the Indian chief and his demeanor grew stern. "Your conduct last year compelled me to send my warriors against you," the Great Father declared, "and your people were defeated, with great loss, and your men surrendered, to be kept until I should be satisfied that you would not try to do any more injury." Jackson then announced that he believed no further danger existed. The commanding generals on the frontier approved Black Hawk's return and the tribes had requested it. "Your chiefs," the Great Father continued, "have pledged themselves for your good conduct, and I have given directions, that you should be taken to your own country. . . . But if you again plunge your knives into the breasts of our people, I shall send a force, which will severely punish you for your cruelties. Bury the tomahawk and live in peace with the frontiers . . . and I pray the Great Spirit to give you a smooth path and fair sky to return."[13]

Chief Black Hawk stepped forward. He looked squarely at the President. He spoke softly but with great presence and dignity. *"My Father,"* he said, "my ears are open to your words. . . . I am glad to go back to my people. I want to see my family. . . . When I get back, I will remember your words. I won't go to war again. I will live in peace. I shall hold you by the hand."[14]

These words, as recorded by the American press, were undoubtedly doctored to reassure the reading public that the menace of Black Hawk had ended forever and that he would no longer disturb the peace. That evening both men attended a performance at the Front Street Theater, and it was difficult to decide which of the two commanded the greater interest and attention since many easterners had never seen a live Indian before, much less a great warrior such as Black Hawk. Throughout the rest of his tour he created quite a sensation.

On Saturday, June 8, Jackson and his party left Baltimore for Philadelphia. Along the way, at New Castle, the President noticed a banner stretched across the road bearing the words "The Union—It must be Preserved." The General studied it with pleasure. It showed that the American people understood the full purpose of his trip and approved.[15] At Philadelphia a crowd estimated at thirty thousand greeted their President with long-sustained cheers and huzzas. A barouche drawn by four white horses conveyed Jackson to the City Hotel, and the streets were so mobbed with people that a troop of cavalry was necessary to open a passageway. By this time the crowds bordered on frenzy.

During his brief stay in Philadelphia Jackson planned to visit the celebrated physician Dr. Philip Syng Physick to see if the good doctor could provide him with some relief from his constant pain and discomfort. The so-called "bleeding at the lungs" particularly distressed him. It went in cycles. Because the bullet fired by Charles Dickinson in 1806 lodged close to his heart it could not be removed. It subsequently formed an abscess which produced periodic flare-ups. There would be a period of repose during which the abscess remained stable or drained from his system without troubling him. But sometimes it would flare. A coughing spell or heavy smoking might trigger an attack. Then he would start hemorrhaging. Chills seized him. Soon he was drenched in sweat. Sometimes he collapsed. Finally, when the bleeding reduced the pressure on the abscess, he would slowly return to a "period of stability," although greatly weakened and several pounds thinner.[16]

After a brief and pleasant introduction, the President explained his symptoms to Dr. Physick, ending with a typical Jacksonian admonition. "Now, Doctor, I can do any thing you think proper to order, and bear as much as most men. There are only two things I can't give up: one is coffee, and the other is tobacco."[17]

The doctor was utterly captivated by his patient. For days afterward all he could talk about was Old Hickory. "He was so full of General Jackson, so penetrated with the gentleness, the frankness, the peculiar and indescribable charm of his demeanor, that he could talk of nothing else."[18]

As the most distinguished member of his profession in America at the time, Dr. Physick apparently understood the impossibility of achieving any lasting remedy or improvement in Jackson's condition, and so he simply encouraged him to keep up the good fight. "I have seen Doctor Phisic," the President informed his son, "who encourages me, and says my heart is not effected in any way, and the pain in the side can be removed by cupping."[19] He simply had to live with his condition as best he could.

On Monday, June 10, the President and his party set out for Independence Hall. A large crowd of invited guests was introduced to Jackson at a reception given by the mayor at the Hall, but soon a mob forced its way into the building. For two hours they surrounded him and shook his hand. The air was stifling. Someone had the good sense to open the windows but then a "ludicrous scene ensued." People began tumbling out of the windows, falling a distance of six feet. Some jumped, others dove, still others simply rolled out.[20]

Though exhausted, Jackson showed no sign of it. He flattered the ladies, as usual, shook the hands of their menfolk, patted the heads and cheeks of children, and even kissed babies. The scene horrified some. "The degeneracy of the age in taste, feelings, and principles," said one, was absolutely appalling. Jackson was led around by his party as though he were a wild beast on exhibition.[21] After the reception Jackson reviewed a military parade which lasted five hours. All the while he sat bolt upright in his saddle. It should have drained him, yet he retained enough strength to attend a military ball that evening. Clearly he was pushing himself and headed for another collapse.

The following morning he left by steamboat for New York, where preparations for his arrival had been going on for weeks. As the ship entered the Narrows the two forts nearby began firing a salute. Other ships of every size, shape, and description crowded the harbor. The landing of the presidential party took place at midafternoon, June 12, on the wharf at Castle Garden. General Jackson was received by the mayor and escorted to a "great saloon" which had been handsomely prepared for the occasion. Everywhere people assembled to catch sight of the President. "The wharves and housetops and vessels were covered with people." Troops were drawn up on the Battery. Some one hundred thousand people jammed the area.[22]

At that time Castle Garden was separated from the Battery by water. A wooden bridge connected them. Immediately after the official greeting, Jackson mounted a horse and led the procession across the bridge. He had just reached the other side, followed by one or two others, when the Battery side of the bridge collapsed. Dignitaries of every shape and age plunged into the water. Cabinet officers, presidential aides, governors, congressmen, mayors, and other celebrities tumbled into the shallow depths, all drenched, all frightened, and all struggling to regain solid ground. It was quite a sight. McLane escaped the dousing, but Cass, Donelson, and Levi Woodbury, the secretary of the navy, who had just joined the party, waded through four feet of water before clambering back to shore. Fortunately no one was seriously hurt, although dignities had been shattered and some sustained bruises and contusions.[23]

While the dignitaries scrambled out of the water to dry themselves and regain their composure, Jackson waited for the preparations to be completed for a parade up Broadway to city hall. Only a short time lapsed. When the signal was given, the dignitaries, still dripping wet, took their places in line, and off they all went in a grand march up lower Manhattan, Jackson on horseback leading the way.

From the Battery to City Hall Park, Broadway was one "solid mass of men, women, and children, who greeted their favorite with cheers, shouts, and waving of scarfs and handkerchiefs." The President doffed his tall hat, still draped with a "weeper" in memory of his beloved Rachel, as he gestured his thanks and greetings to the people on both sides of the street. People jammed every spot available—"a sea of waving and heaving and changing myriads." When the President reached city hall, he was formally greeted by Governor William L. Marcy and his staff. Then, standing on a platform fronting the park, the President received the marching salute of a corps of state militia. It was "truly a magnificent scene" and Jackson was deeply impressed. With "a quivering lip but a brightening eye," Old Hickory turned to Governor Marcy and said: *"Nullification will never take root* HERE."[24]

By this time the Vice President, Martin Van Buren, had joined the party, and when the city hall ceremonies concluded the two men headed for the American Hotel to rest. Jackson was subjecting himself to excessive physical punishment (which he realized) and he risked a complete breakdown.

"The Grand Triumphal Tour," as it was now called, next proceeded to New Haven and Hartford and then on to Pawtucket, Rhode Island, and Roxbury, Massachusetts. By the time the party arrived in Boston, Jackson was clearly in physical distress. Someone noticed that as he mounted his horse he fell forward upon the neck of the animal, as a tired old man would do. Then, like a shot, he bolted upright, sitting in the saddle in a stiff, soldierly fashion. It was the action of a determined man, but it was painful to witness. Over the weekend he continued to lose strength and on Monday, June 24, Jackson took to his bed. Then he began hemorrhaging. He had a cold, an abscess formed and ruptured.[25] A physician was immediately summoned, and the first thing he did was to bleed the President. When that procedure failed to gain results the good doctor bled his patient a second time.

After two days of rest, and after the doctor ceased his infernal bleeding, Jackson felt stronger. He willed himself to get out of bed. He was to receive an honorary degree of Doctor of Laws from Harvard University and nothing under heaven was going to prevent his appearance. John Quincy Adams, an overseer of the university, was appalled. As "an affectionate child of our Alma Mater," he wrote, he could not witness "her disgrace in conferring her highest literary honors upon a barbarian who could not write a sentence of grammar and hardly could spell his own name."[26] But Jackson was no illiterate frontiersman, much less a barbarian, even though his grammar and spelling lacked "refinement." He combined grace of manner with impressive intellectual power. And although he was indifferent to spelling he did, on occasion, write with eloquence and enormous stylistic skill.

It was a chilly and overcast day when Jackson received his degree from the hands of the president of Harvard University. The degree was conferred in Latin, and according to one humorous account the General responded: *"Ex post facto; e pluribus unum; sic semper tyrannis; quid pro quo,"* and not a scholar in the room could fault his grammar or knowledge of Latin. Actually, Jackson mumbled something in the vernacular, which nobody heard.

Major Jack Downing, the pseudonym for Seba Smith who was covering this "Grand Triumphal Tour" for local newspapers, later embellished the story about Jackson's use of Latin. After giving a speech at "Downingville," said Downing, the President was about to sit down when someone in the audience called out to him, "You must give them a little Latin, *Doctor.*" Whereupon Jackson replied, quick as lightning, "E pluribus unum, my friends, sine qua non!"[27]

From Cambridge, the presidential party headed for Charlestown, to view the Bunker Hill monument still under construction, as well as receive two cannonballs as mementos of the famous battle, and hear an address from Edward Everett. After that, Jackson moved on to Lynn, Marblehead, and Salem, but by this time the fatiguing journey was taking its toll and he could barely stand on his feet. A principal stopover occurred at Lowell, the famed manufacturing town where man-made canals generated the waterpower to drive over 200,000 spindles. Of greater renown was its army of factory girls, who lived and worked in town under conditions that seemed utopian for the time. They worked in the mills, boarded in homelike dormitories, and were supervised by concerned and watchful guardians.

Jackson's arrival in Lowell produced a parade in his honor that "exceeded all anticipation."[28] It was about three o'clock in the afternoon when he arrived. The military escort consisted of companies of artillery, riflemen, light infantry, and a procession of "young females" employed in the factories. "The women and girls were crazy to see us," reported Major Downing.[29] There were some five thousand of these young females, all under thirty and all dressed in snow-white dresses with sashes of different colors to designate their different manufacturing establishments. They were all hatless, their pretty faces shining up at Jackson as he passed. Each carried a parasol, most of which were green. They were massed four deep along the route and constituted a veritable *"mile of girls."* They waved their parasols at the President in graceful salute. When the President and his party arrived at the Merrimack Hotel they took a position on a platform and the whole procession of military and white-frocked young ladies passed in review before them.[30]

Although the mills had been closed down for the celebration of the President's arrival into town, at Jackson's request they were reopened. Their operation fascinated the old man. He asked dozens of questions and stared in amazement and wonder at their operation. He also inspected the town's fire-fighting equipment, which was regarded as the best in the country. The "immense power of the water wheels" attached to the equipment "was truly astonishing, covering the different buildings with water in a few minutes, by various pipes manned by the different engineers."[31]

Lowell dominated Jackson's thoughts long after he left the town. "What a country God has given us!" he kept repeating. He headed next for Portsmouth, New Hampshire, and then Concord. By this time he was exhausted and frequently faint as a result of the endless receptions, parades, and celebrations. He was also offended by the mounting politicking he had to contend with at each stop along the way. His health deteriorated badly. Fatigue wore him down. He seemed to some in mortal danger.[32]

All of a sudden he reached his decision. He would terminate the tour and return to Washington, and the reason given to the public was the obvious one of his poor health. The people in Maine, Vermont, and upstate New York, where stops had been scheduled, were all deeply disappointed by this sudden cancellation of the tour, but they were reminded that the President could no longer endure the steady drain on his strength. So Jackson turned around at Concord and returned through Lowell and Roxbury, avoiding Boston. He proceeded to Providence, where he caught a steamboat for New York, and from that point headed straight for Washington, arriving at ten o'clock on the morning of July 4. From Concord to Washington he traversed a distance of 474 miles in three days. Major Lewis was shocked at Jackson's appearance as he staggered into the White House. "I confess I was seriously alarmed at his feeble and emaciated appearance."[33]

The tour was a stunning political performance from start to finish, however. It accomplished everything Jackson desired. It stirred the patriotism of the nation, stimulated the notion of the Union as something perpetual, and raised the presidential office to new heights of popular esteem. For Jackson personally it strengthened his bond with the "ordinary citizens" of the nation. "Amid all these superfluous, and many of them silly, descriptions," commented the Richmond *Enquirer*, "we cannot fail to perceive that the president has been received with a cordiality of kindness, and a sincerity of respect, which bespeak the great popularity of the man and his administration."[34]

CHAPTER 21

Panic!

W HEN PRESIDENT JACKSON STAGGERED INTO HIS ROOM on the second floor of the White House he knew exactly what he must do to regain his strength and health. His chronic illnesses, extending back more than twenty years, had long trained him in the "art" of self-medication. The first thing he did was begin a regular regimen of hot baths, exercise (mostly horseback riding), and calomel. He also fasted a great deal but that resulted more from his poor appetite than a planned diet.[1]

Fortunately for Jackson's mental health his mind was constantly diverted from his physical discomfort by the needs and concerns of his office. Upon his return to Washington several items awaited executive action, the most important of which was the question of the removal of the government's deposits from the "Golden vaults of the Mammoth Bank."[2] He figured such action would hasten the monster's demise. He claimed that the people, by their vote in the presidential election, had registered their approval for its immediate destruction.

Although Jackson had concluded that the deposits must be removed, he refrained from ordering his new secretary of the Treasury, William J. Duane, to execute the order. His reluctance was wrongly seen by Duane as a recognition of the right of the Treasury secretary to decide the question himself. This was not Jackson's intention at all, but it was certainly one he unwittingly encouraged Duane to believe. Furthermore, Jackson did not wish to pull the government's funds out of the BUS in one fell swoop. Rather, as he explained to Duane, he preferred to withdraw the funds as the government needed them, until they were exhausted; meanwhile, new government revenues would be deposited in selected state banks.[3]

Soon after Jackson's return, Duane explained his opposition to removal to the President in a detailed letter dated July 10. The "arbitrary" act of replacing the BUS with state banks without the direction of Congress, he argued, was unwise and improper.[4] In any event he agreed to resign his office if he and the President could not agree upon a course

261

of action. A few days later Old Hickory made it clear to him that he wanted a substitute for the BUS prepared so that Congress might know the proper direction to take.[5]

Meanwhile the President sent Amos Kendall as a special agent to find state banks willing to accept the federal deposits when they became available and which were not fearful of facing the wrath of the BUS. Kendall went immediately to Baltimore, then Philadelphia and New York, before heading for Boston. Kendall claimed that he had two primary objectives in making the trip: first, to remove from Jackson's mind the doubt about state banks' being afraid or unwilling to become bankers for the government; and second, to ascertain the terms on which the banks would become the government's fiscal agents.[6] Actually he had a third purpose, and that was to find bankers who could qualify as loyal Jacksonians. To become one of the "selected banks"—or "pet" banks, as the opposition came to call them—it was essential that a prospective pet enjoy "friendly" relations with the Democrats.[7] And Kendall proved to be a most enthusiastic and zealous agent—exactly what Jackson wanted. He told Blair that four banks in Baltimore, another four in Philadelphia, and seven in New York had responded favorably to his invitation to assume the government's business. "We shall have a firm, zealous party," Kendall enthused, "and shall have put down the Bank forever."[8]

From the very beginning of his war against the Bank, Jackson understood his true object and goal. The nation was cursed with a Bank, he said, whose "corrupting influences" had fastened "monopoly and aristocracy on the constitution" and had made the government "an engine of oppression to the people instead of the agent of their will." Its annihilation would "restore to our institutions their primitive simplicity and purity." What Jackson planned to do, therefore, was to initiate removal immediately and then give "a full expose of the reasons that has induced it, and let, thro the Globe, be made unofficially, a statement of the causes and the facts that has induced it."[9]

By law, actual removal of the deposits belonged to the Treasury secretary, not the President. It was up to the secretary to issue the order and then notify Congress of his action. Whether he was obliged to follow the directions of Congress or the President when they conflicted, particularly on a fiscal matter over which Congress exercised absolute control, had never been tested.

At this point Kendall returned to Washington and submitted his report to Duane. He glowed with excitement over his success in finding seven banks who were prepared to serve as depositories for public funds on the government's terms. Considering the likelihood and danger of Biddle's retaliating against any institution cooperating with the government, this initial expedition was reasonably successful.

Duane forwarded Kendall's report to the President, but he privately characterized "the mission" as "abortive." He was being asked, he added, to "plunge the fiscal concerns of the country" into "chaos." Feeling this way and convinced that his standing as a member of the administration had been totally compromised, Duane decided that he would not remove the deposits. Nor would he resign. Since Congress had already declared its satisfaction with the BUS as the depository for government funds, and since the power of removal rested solely with him, he felt he must do what he thought proper for the good of the country.

That brought him to a head-on collision with the President, for Jackson was determined to go ahead with removal, with or without his secretary's consent. On September 20 the *Globe* announced in its columns that "the deposites of the public money will be changed from the bank of the U.S. to the state banks . . . in time to make the change by the 1st of October."

Duane was devastated when he read the statement. The President had gone ahead and issued a public declaration. The humiliation of it was more than he could bear. He immediately scratched out a statement and took it to Jackson.

"What is it?" asked the President.

"It respectfully and finally makes known my decision," replied Duane, "not to remove the deposites, or resign."

A flood of anger gripped the General. "But you said you would retire, if we could not finally agree."

"I indiscreetly said so, sir; but I am now compelled to take this course."[10]

Since the secretary would not obey him and would not resign, Jackson had only one recourse: dismissal. But that opened up a problem that all previous Presidents had deftly avoided, namely, the right of a President to dismiss a member of the executive branch whose appointment had been confirmed by the Senate. Since Congress created all cabinet positions and since appointment to them required confirmation, did that not suggest that dismissal also involved legislative concurrence? Some thought so. It seemed especially true of the Treasury secretary because of his handling of public funds, which Congress exclusively controlled. But no one had ever tested the question. No previous President had ever dismissed a cabinet officer. They simply got an offender to resign. In that way they avoided the constitutional question of the extent of the President's removal power.

Jackson was the first President to hit the problem head-on. He believed that all officials of the executive office fell totally and completely under his authority. They were to obey *him,* not the Congress. Here again Jackson established a new dimension of presidential power. He assumed total authority to remove all cabinet officers without notifying Congress, much less obtaining its consent. And this authority necessarily gave him increased power over the collection and distribution of public funds. Today the power of removal seems obvious. Not so in the early nineteenth century—not until Jackson decided it once and for all.

Jackson never for a moment doubted his right to remove any secretary if he refused to go quietly. When his interview with Duane ended he did not immediately dismiss him. He gave Duane another day or two to assess his situation. But when the secretary failed to come to his senses, Jackson sent him a curt letter in which he told Duane that "your further services as Secretary of the Treasury are no longer required."[11]

To replace Duane, the President chose Roger B. Taney, and it was done so expeditiously that "the business of the Treasury," said the General, "is progressing as tho Mr. Duane had never been born."[12] Taney immediately appointed Kendall as special agent for the removal of the deposits and together they prepared an order dated September 25, 1833, which officially announced the government's switch from national banking to deposit banking.[13] The order stated that commencing October 1 all future government deposits would be placed in selected state banks and that for operating expenses the government would draw on its remaining funds from the BUS until they were exhausted.

The "experiment" in deposit banking began with the seven institutions Kendall had selected on his summer tour. By the end of 1833, the original number had been increased to twenty-two. Over the next three years some ninety-odd banks were added to the system. By December 13, 1833, the public funds held by the BUS were practically drained away.

Taney's energy and skill in instituting deposit banking—all the while attending the business of the attorney general's office until a replacement could be found—commanded Jackson's unbounded admiration and respect. Taney was particularly careful in selecting the pets, for he realized that one miscalculation could ruin the entire system. He was totally committed to Jackson's reform program, and he threw himself diligently into the task of making this "experiment" in deposit banking a total success.[14]

The elevation of Taney necessitated finding a new attorney general, and, as usual, Jackson turned to Van Buren for advice. The Magician suggested Benjamin F. Butler, a member of the Albany Regency and Van Buren's longtime friend and former law partner. Butler was an excellent choice and combined superior legal skills with dedication and hard work. Although his appointment further weighted the cabinet toward the north and increased Van Buren's influence, it added needed strength to that body in terms of talent, loyalty, and commitment.

With his cabinet now complete and in reasonable harmony, Jackson was ready to complete his banking reform. Now if the monster would just lie still for the final blow. With "one million and a half of coin" to be used in case the beast put up a fight, the President felt confident and exhilarated. "We act solely on the defensive," he said with a straight face, "and I am ready with the screws to draw every tooth and then the stumps." If I am not mistaken, he went on, we will have "Mr Biddle and his Bank as quiet and harmless as a *lamb* in six weeks."[15]

Some lamb. The roar that echoed out of Philadelphia in the fall of 1833 sounded more like a raging tiger. Nicholas Biddle could hardly be expected to stand by without murmuring a sound while Andrew Jackson slaughtered his Bank. He had already begun to take defensive actions during the summer on hearing rumors that the deposits might be removed. He slowly reduced the Bank's lending operation. Then, when the signal was finally given to begin the shift to deposit banking, Biddle counterattacked. He initiated a general curtailment of loans throughout the entire banking system. He swelled the Bank's liquid assets by refusing to increase discounts, and he restricted discounted bills of exchange to eighty days. It marked the beginning of a bone-crushing struggle between a powerful financier and a determined and equally powerful politician. Biddle understood what he was about. He knew that if he brought enough pressure and agony to the money market, only then could he force the President to restore the deposits. He almost gloated. "This worthy President thinks that because he has scalped Indians and imprisoned Judges, he is to have his way with the Bank. He is mistaken."[16]

What made the situation all the more precarious was Jackson's ignorance of financial matters and his total lack of appreciation for the fiscal value of the BUS and its importance to the American economy. The Bank was interlaced with the economy. To damage it of necessity would devastate the financial and business communities. Moreover, the men associated with Jackson in this perilous "experiment" were equally ignorant. And a few of them were guilty of conflict of interest. Roger Taney, for example, had ties to the Union Bank of Maryland, and Reuben Whitney, one of Kendall's henchmen in the Treasury Department, to the Girard Bank in Philadelphia.[17] Fortunately, Taney was a man of integrity and was devoted to the success of deposit banking. He worked hard to overcome his fiscal limitations during the short period he served as secretary of the Treasury. He learned immediately that the system would never work without financial stability on the part of participating institutions and so he devoted his considerable talents and energies to achieving that end.[18]

But the storm unleashed by the order of the Treasury Department hit the administration with stunning force. The business community erupted with howls of complaint and condemned the order as endangering the entire economic fabric of the community. They labeled it a "naked, barefaced act of usurpation and mischief . . . a Proclamation of War."[19] But, if the outcry from the business community was severe, the political outcry was even worse. Jackson was again branded a tyrant, for "tyranny is a disregard of the law and the substitution of individual will for legal restraint."[20] Even Democrats bawled their fears and anxieties. Many of them had doubted the wisdom of the Bank War from the start. Still, they rallied behind Jackson over his Bank veto when Clay, Webster, and Biddle prematurely pushed for recharter. But removal!—that was something else. That endangered the very financial structure of the nation, and with it the American experiment in freedom and democracy. So total was the devastation to all but the staunchest Jacksonians that even Daniel Webster, who had slid away from many of his previous associates over nullification and nearly entered a political alliance with Old Hickory, eventually scrambled back into the opposition fold. Jackson's removal policy totally alienated him.[21]

Over the next several months Nicholas Biddle intensified the political and economic havoc that enveloped the country. He steadily increased the pressure of his squeeze. His curtailment of loans came with such suddenness that it pitched the country into an economic recession reminiscent of the Panic of 1819. By the opening of the new Congress in December 1833 a general cry of distress was beginning to be heard around the country. Every major city sustained a number of business losses; wages and prices sagged; workingmen were discharged. By the end of January 1834 the pressure was reported "as great as any community can bear." The distress among the merchants, said one, "is truly appalling."[22]

But the removal of the deposits provided Jackson with a number of important advantages. For one thing it strengthened his hand as party leader and head of the government. That he could take such a controversial issue and force its acceptance upon his party and the people measured the extent of his leadership and the force of his personality. To oppose removal meant opposing Jackson, and congressmen did so at their peril. Also, the people gravitated closer and closer to Jackson's position on the Bank issue because it had become infused with moral overtones, namely, the struggle of honest working people against evil aristocrats who were scheming to rob and exploit them. It must be remembered that whenever Jackson spoke to the people about the Bank they *always* heard these overtones—and responded just as he expected them to do. So removal strengthened the ideological stance of the Democrats. It provided them with an easy rhetoric that found great popular appeal. They could revile aristocrats, the money power, and foreign domination of finance with soaring indignation and righteous anger. They could load their accusations with enough moral outrage to frighten their opposition into virtual silence. Democrats became very adept at exciting the passions and prejudices of workers and farmers. They constantly identified themselves with the masses, claiming to protect them from a rapacious elite. They spoke of the people as good and wise and just, whose will must always be obeyed.

As the Panic of 1833–1834 intensified, delegations of businessmen visited Jackson in the White House to beg him to rescind the removal order. One such group of "great bankers and great merchants" brought a petition bearing six thousand signatures. They found Jackson seated at a desk with a long clay pipe in his mouth, the bowl of which rested on the table. Enormous clouds of smoke gushed from the blackened bowl.

"Now gentlemen, what is your pleasure with me?" the President asked.

The deputation came right to the point. They described their distress. They begged him to intervene and restore the deposits. They said that they feared insolvency.

"Insolvent do you say?" Jackson replied. "What do you come to me for, then? Go to Nicholas Biddle. We have no money here, gentlemen. Biddle has all the money. He has millions of specie in his vaults, at this moment, lying idle, and yet you come to me to save you from breaking. I tell you, gentlemen, it's all politics."

Jackson talked nonstop for fifteen minutes, excoriating Biddle and the Bank for the harm they had done the country and its institutions. Gradually he worked himself into a towering rage. He ranted; he paced the room; he gestured with wide sweeps of his arms; he pointed at the deputation and swore that his decision was irreversible and that he would never restore the deposits. Let there be no mistake on this point, he thundered, let it be understood distinctly and "explicitly that the name of Andrew Jackson would never be signed to a bill or resolution to place the Public money in the Bank of the United States or to renew the Charter of that Bank."

At length he paused. The harangue ended quietly. The deputation said nothing. They simply rose from their places and left the room.

When they had gone, Jackson broke into a broad grin. "Didn't I manage them well?" he laughed to the leader of the deputation who had been summoned back to the President's office. The visitor stared at his host. The old rascal had staged the tantrum. He was not one whit as angry as he pretended. He was an old hand at feigning anger in order to silence those who opposed him.

Other delegations beseeched him. To all he replied with the same tone and language. "In the name of God, sir! what do the people think to gain by sending their memorials here? If they send ten thousand of them, signed by all the men, women, children in the land, and bearing the names of all on the grave-stones, I will not relax a particle from my position."[23]

The stage was therefore set when Congress reconvened in December 1833, in what would be called the "Panic session," for what many observers predicted would be a monumental battle over the removal of the deposits. Without wasting a moment, Henry Clay rose to the occasion. His manner in debate was sly and insinuating at first, but as he built momentum it became sharp and biting. "Mr. Clay is captain and he trains his troops daily and constantly," wrote Senator Silas Wright, Jr., of New York. In the House the debate was just as vigorous and intense. The administration took a daily battering as the economic panic intensified around the country and petitions and memorials favoring the BUS swamped the Congress.[24]

It was during this "Panic session" that a new party—the Whig party—

emerged. The forces producing it had been in train for a number of years, but the pressures of the Bank War and Jackson's imperial presidency finally brought it into being during the late winter and early spring of 1834. National Republicans, Bank men, nullifiers, high-tariff advocates, friends of internal improvements, states' righters, and—most particularly—all those who abominated Jackson or his reforms slowly converged into a new political coalition that quite appropriately assumed the name "Whig." Derived from British politics, the name signified opposition to the monarchical party which advocated strong executive leadership. Also, the name was associated with the patriotic cause during the American Revolution. Perhaps Philip Hone, the New York merchant, first invoked the name to designate this new coalition.[25] But what gave the name wide currency was a speech delivered in the Senate on April 14, 1834, by Henry Clay. In using the term in his speech, Clay signaled its acceptance by the leadership of the anti-Jackson forces in Congress.

In terms of ideology, the Whig press declared that the new coalition represented the supremacy of representative government over dictatorial rule. The President had paralyzed the powers of Congress through an "extraordinary" exercise of the veto, they insisted. Never had there been such rapaciousness on the part of the executive to expand the authority of his office. The basic difference between the Democratic and Whig parties, they said, was that the former would rule by executive fiat, and the latter by legislative mandate.[26]

As for issues, the Whigs pretty much adopted Clay's American System for their program. By and large they favored a national bank, strong credit and currency facilities to assist the ongoing industrial revolution, and federally sponsored public works. Most them also advocated tariff protection, except southerners. As a group, Whigs tended to be socially conservative, economically venturesome, and politically hostile to "Jacksonian equalitarianism." For the most part they included industrialists, bankers, "go-ahead" businessmen, and conservative farmers from all sections.[27]

The realignment of parties during Jackson's administration generated a tremendous amount of political excitement, both in Washington and around the nation. "I have never known the country so generally and so deeply excited as they are upon the recent measures of the administration," wrote one man. "We have had," reported Representative Churchill C. Cambreleng to his friend Edward Livingston, "the most bitter and violent denunciations—with cries of ruin, panic and despair . . . [which] have succeeded in producing an excitement in the country which you have probably seldom seen even in times of embargo or of war."[28] During a period of approximately one hundred days a "phalanx of orators and speakers" in Congress daily excoriated the President and demanded his censure. At length, under Clay's guidance and insistence, a censure resolution was read on the Senate floor which was expected to "destroy whomsoever it struck—even General Jackson."²⁹ The resolution read as follows:

> *Resolved,* That the reasons assigned by the Secretary of the Treasury for the removal of the money of the United States deposited in the Bank of the United States and its branches, communicated to Congress on the 4th of December, 1833, are unsatisfactory and insufficient.
>
> That the President, in the late executive proceedings in relation to the public revenue, has assumed upon himself authority and power not conferred by the Constitution and laws, but in derogation of both.³⁰

After debating this resolution for months, after exploring all of the implications of Jackson's autocratic rule, the senators prepared to vote on the censure. The question was called. On March 28, 1834, by a vote of 26 to 20, the Senate passed the resolution of censure against the President of the United States. Earlier, on February 5, by a vote of 28 to 18, it rejected the reasons for the removal of the deposits given by Secretary Taney.

The censure, an unprecedented action by the Senate, was a savage blow to Jackson's pride. He reacted immediately. He had no intention of accepting this rebuke without a stiff, formal, and official reply and protest. So he set his new attorney general, Benjamin F. Butler, aided by Taney and Kendall, to work on a "Protest" message to be delivered to the Senate. Butler wrote the major portion of the message, but the ideas that informed the document emanated almost entirely from Jackson.³¹

The Protest message was dated April 15 and Jackson wasted no time at the very outset in registering his outrage. "Without notice, unheard and untried, I thus find myself charged . . . with the high crime of violating the laws and Constitution of my country." He then lectured the members about the divisions of powers under the Constitution, the rights of his office, and the necessity of a formal impeachment proceeding. The resolution of the Senate, he said, was wholly unauthorized by the Constitution. Without any action by the House, he had been found guilty of an impeachable offense. He defended his actions and claimed he had acted well within his constitutional rights.

Then Jackson made a remarkable assertion. He proclaimed that the President represents the American people and is responsible to them. No President had ever made such an assertion. No President assumed such a unique relationship with the electorate. When the words were spoken, the atmosphere in the Senate was palpable with excitement. Each word uttered sent shock waves around the chamber.

"The President is the direct representative of the American people," Jackson declared. Moreover, he is "responsible to them." That last statement was totally novel. It was a modern idea in keeping with the democratic spirit of the times, but it was certainly not one the Whigs could approve with their philosophy about legislative government constituting

the basis of republican rule. They insisted that the President was responsible to Congress. The opposition press agreed that Jackson's statement
about his rights and his relationship to the American people had "produced everywhere as great a sensation as within the hall of Congress."[32]

Without wasting a day, Daniel Webster rose in the Senate to deliver a
blistering attack on the President in answer to his "outrageous conten-
tions." "Again and again we hear it said," he rumbled in his magnificent
voice, "that the President is responsible to the American people! . . . For
whatever he does, he assumed accountability to the American people!
. . . [And] Connected, Sir, with the idea of this airy and unreal responsibility to the people is another sentiment, which of late we hear frequently
expressed; and that is, *that the President is the direct representative of the
American people.*" Webster's face darkened. "Now, Sir, this is not the
language of the Constitution. The Constitution no where calls him the
representative of the American people; still less their direct representative. . . . I hold this, Sir, to be a mere assumption, and dangerous assumption."[33]

Webster was followed by other senators, including Clay and Calhoun,
who denounced Jackson's presumption and assumption. Nevertheless,
the President's novel concept about representing the people found immediate acceptance with the electorate. Sighed Senator Leigh: "Until the
President developed the faculties of the Executive power, all men thought
it inferior to the legislature—he manifestly thinks it superior; and in his
hands the monarchical part of Government . . . has proved far stronger
than the representatives of the States." The President, not Congress, had
become the instrument of popular will.[34]

In introducing and ultimately winning acceptance of his interpretation
of presidential powers, Jackson liberated the chief executive from the
position of prime minister responsible only to Congress. With Jackson,
the chief executive no longer served simply as the head of a coordinate
branch of the government; no longer was he restricted in his actions by
what the Congress would allow him. Henceforth he could assert himself
as the spokesman of all the people and by the skillful use of his powers
force the legislature to follow his lead. This did not free him from the
political necessity of working with Congress to accomplish the public will,
but it did allow him to assume greater control of the government and to
dominate and direct public affairs.

All of which meant that Jackson saw himself as the head of the government, executing the popular will, and responsible only to the electorate.
He truly believed himself a servant of the people—and that, in the end,
is how the people saw him. They believed him "honest and patriotic; that
he was the friend of the *people,* battling for them against corruption and
extravagance, and opposed only by dishonest politicians. They loved him
as their friend."[35]

This mutual attitude of love and respect—amounting to a bond—

between a President and the electorate was something totally novel in American history. And out of this special relationship forged between Old Hickory and the American people a sense of mutual dependence and commitment emerged which changed the tone and style of the government to something publicists had started to call a democracy.

CHAPTER 22

The End of the Bank

ALTHOUGH JACKSON MAINTAINED AN AIR OF CALM throughout the verbal abuse he suffered during the Panic session of Congress, he did not sit still. He intruded his presence in the House and Senate at every opportunity. He asserted his leadership both as head of the government (a rank he accorded himself) and as head of the Democratic party. With the help of an enormous propaganda machine, which he directed through the columns of the *Globe,* and with the formidable support he enjoyed from the mass electorate, he commanded unassailable advantages which few congressmen could disregard or contest. What aided Jackson tremendously in his vigorous assertion of presidential power was the existence of an explosive political issue which he had raised and around which he had drawn very precise and impenetrable lines. He had decreed the destruction of the BUS. By removing the deposits he forced congressmen to come to terms with the issue and either join him in killing the monster or remove themselves from Democratic ranks. As the congressional session progressed and the economic suffering sharpened, Jackson's language became more explicit—and more colorful. "Were all the worshippers of the gold Calf to memorialize me and request a restoration of the Deposits," he told Van Buren, "I would cut my right hand from my body before I would do such an act. The golden calf may be worshipped by others but as for myself I serve the Lord."[1]

Because Jackson appreciated that pressure must be applied to Congress and that the most effective kind came from the country at large, he diligently undertook the task of mounting that pressure. Specifically, he called for mass meetings, caucuses, and conventions—all selected "by the people themselves and charged with their instructions" to express "popular" sentiments against the Bank. "Get up meetings and memorials," the President ordered the party leaders in the states, and "let the U.S. Bank turn its screws" to its everlasting shame.[2]

With congressmen, Jackson sometimes purred at them, and sometimes bared his claws. The Pennsylvania delegation, which reportedly led a

272

movement toward desertion from the Democratic fold, received a "fright-ful" mauling. "I am told," reported one Pennsylvania Whig, "that he absolutely rode with whip and spur over our delegation who were so overwhelmed that they had nothing to say for themselves."[3] One prob-lem that Jackson handled most expertly in Congress was the persistent rumor that the Bank War had been devised and plotted by New York politicians for the purpose of benefiting Wall Street financiers at the expense of their counterparts on Chestnut Street in Philadelphia. It was not enough for the administration to deny the rumors; the denial must come from the New Yorkers themselves—and from the very highest level. Consequently Jackson asked Van Buren to request Silas Wright, Jr., the Regency's most able spokesman in Congress, to deliver a speech in the Senate which would end the rumors once and for all. Coming from Wright, the repudiation would be seen as originating with Van Buren and bearing the approval of the Regency.[4]

As directed, Wright delivered the speech with his mentor perched in the chair of the presiding officer. As he spoke, other senators immediately sensed the significance of his speech, and several of them, including Webster, moved closer to Wright to catch each word. Among other things, Wright unequivocally repudiated the notion that a plot existed to make Wall Street the financial capital of the country. So well did he argue this point that Van Buren detected a definite change among both Whig and Democratic congressmen. "The current is now fast setting the other way," he told Theodore Sedgwick. "The successful effort of Mr. Wright to force out the true issue has given a right direction of public senti-ment."[5]

Shortly after Wright's speech, and just as several states began to re-spond to the President's urgings that they express their condemnation of Biddle's behavior, the tide of popular opinion on the issue turned irre-versibly away from the Bank and toward Jackson. For one thing, the economic panic began to ease. Also, the pets were holding their own, despite Biddle's determined efforts to drive them into bankruptcy.

The slow, steady cracking of opposition to the President's "experi-ment" with deposit banking finally widened into an unbreachable chasm when the pro-Bank governor of Pennsylvania, George Wolf, re-versed his position and denounced the BUS in his annual message to the state legislature on February 26, 1834. When a state bond issue failed to find subscribers, Wolf blamed the Bank and charged it with bringing "indiscriminate ruin" upon the community. The effect was devastating—and immediate. The state senate passed resolutions casti-gating the institution for its unconscionable actions; both United States senators stated publicly that, like Wolf, they were reversing themselves and would no longer support the Bank; and virtually the entire Pennsyl-vania delegation in the House abandoned the stricken institution. Most of these Pennsylvanians had decided that the financial distress of the past several months had not been caused by *a* national bank, but by *the* Bank of the United States.

The BUS was doomed. Deserted by its own state, the corporation was shunned and ostracized. Once Pennsylvania signaled its discontent, a yapping pack of opportunists pounced on the Bank and howled their demand for its immediate destruction. Andrew Jackson glowed. He immediately wrote to Wolf and expressed his appreciation and that of the country for "the exalted and truly patriotic stand you have taken in the defence of public liberty."[6]

The general reversal of attitudes within the business community about the culpability of the Bank in creating the present distress was reflected in the many newspapers that had previously defended the BUS. "There is by all accounts a great revulsion or rather awakening in public sentiment," claimed Van Buren. "The bankites are thunderstruck," noted Nathaniel Greene, editor of the Boston *Statesman,* "at this uprising of the people."[7]

The mounting public pressure, coupled with Jackson's firm leadership and resolve to kill the monster and make a go of deposit banking, awakened the Democrats in Congress to a sense of their actual and growing strength. Finally they effectively (not haphazardly as they had done in the past) organized themselves in the House, where they held a majority, to give Jackson the support he needed. Under the leadership of James Knox Polk, chairman of the Ways and Means Committee, the Democrats decided to test their strength and attempt a knockout blow that would end the Bank War once and for all by calling for a vote on a series of resolutions which had already been approved by Polk's committee. These resolutions were aimed at nullifying the action of the censure in the Senate by registering the House's total approval of the President's bank policy. On April 4, 1834, the questions were called. By a vote of 134 to 82, the House declared that the Bank of the United States "ought not to be rechartered." Then, by the count of 118 to 103, it agreed that the deposits "ought not to be restored." Next, by a vote of 117 to 105, it recommended that the state banks (the pets) be continued as the places of deposits for federal funds. And lastly, by the overwhelming vote of 175 to 42, the House authorized the selection of a committee to examine the BUS's affairs and investigate whether it had deliberately instigated the panic.[8]

That did it. That, in effect, ended all hope of the Bank's survival. It seemed only a matter of time before the Democrats would assemble enough evidence from an investigation to prove that Biddle had wantonly and irresponsibly brought economic havoc to the country in order to win recharter. Biddle's very ruthlessness killed the Bank, for he drove away prospective supporters and forced the Democrats to "an inflexible anti-Bank position."[9] He had convinced the public that he was an irresponsible and ungovernable force in American economic life. Even the business community eventually admitted that he had behaved improperly and by the spring of 1834 they forced him to ease the financial pressure.

"I have obtained a glorious triumph," Jackson crowed. If nothing else the votes in the House completely scuttled the efforts of the Senate to disgrace him by forcing a restoration of the deposits and a recharter of the Bank. Without the approval of the House, neither action by the Senate, with or without the intimidating tactic of a censure, could be enacted into law. "The overthrow of the opposition in the House of Representatives by the vote on the resolutions," wrote Jackson, ". . . was a triumphant one, and put to death, that mamouth of corruption and power, the Bank of the United States." The attorney general concurred. "The Bank is dead," Butler informed the Regency.[10]

Still, one more nail was hammered into the Bank's coffin—and the hammerer was Biddle himself. The investigating committee authorized by the House resolution arrived in Philadelphia armed with subpoena powers and anxious to examine all the Bank's books. The investigators found Biddle as truculent as ever. He refused permission to inspect the books or the correspondence with congressmen relating to personal loans from the BUS. And he steadfastly refused to testify before the committee. Back in Washington, after their futile and frustrating trip to Philadelphia, the committeemen demanded a citation for contempt, but many southern Democrats opposed this extreme action, and refused to cooperate. As Biddle bemusedly observed, it would be ironic if he went to prison "by the votes of members of Congress because I would not give up to their enemies their confidential letters." Although Biddle escaped a contempt citation, his outrageous defiance of the House only condemned him still further in the eyes of the American public. His latest action, commented William C. Rives, proved "to the people never again to give themselves such a master."[11]

Now that the Bank lay bleeding to death, Jackson prepared to move forward with his hard money and state deposit schemes in the expectation of providing a regulated, responsible banking system. On April 21, 1834, he proposed a series of measures that would provide a general reform of currency and banking. These proposals included the following: that the selection of pet banks be left to the secretary of the Treasury; that he be permitted to remove the deposits from any bank after submitting his reasons to Congress; that banks submit monthly reports of their condition; that the government have the right to examine the books and records of the pets; that gold be revalued to bring it to a parity with silver; and that the deposit banks be required to cease issuing notes under $5. Later, the prohibition against paper would be extended to all notes under twenty dollars. In this way the country would be restored to specie for its regular transactions and bank notes would serve commercial purposes only.[12]

The gold currency bill, or the Coinage Act of 1834, passed on June 28,

1834, with wide bipartisan support, and went into effect on July 31. It raised the ratio between gold and silver from 15.5 to 1 to 16 to 1. Silver was undervalued by this bill, but at least a gold eagle would pass at $10, a half-eagle at $5, and a quarter-eagle at $2.50. Unfortunately, the other proposals in Jackson's reform package took longer to enact and ultimately what Congress provided fell a long distance from what the President had requested. Instead of a banking system that could be regulated and controlled, a collection of unregulated banks holding more money than they could properly handle was allowed to mushroom all over the country. But one positive result was the tremendous infusion of capital into a rapidly expanding economy. A Deposit Act finally passed in June 1836 which Jackson signed "with a repugnance of feeling and recoil of judgment," and he only signed it because he believed it would enhance Van Buren's chances of election to the presidency in 1836.[13]

Before adjourning, the Senate managed to hand Jackson one more severe blow to his pride. On Tuesday, June 23, 1834, by a vote of 28 to 18, it rejected his nomination of Taney to be the secretary of the Treasury. Jackson was deeply offended by this action. He regarded it as a personal insult, directed at himself, and one in which he must somehow win retribution no matter how long it took or in what manner. But he was philosophic. "I have however the great consolation in the support of the great body of the people, and the pleasure to know that this corrupt majority cannot be gratified in the recharter of the Bank, its days are numbered."[14]

Jackson wasted no time in submitting another nomination, shrewdly calculating that the Senate had no stomach for rejecting a second name. He proposed Levi Woodbury, who desperately wanted the post and had Van Buren's active support. Balding, heavyset, and regularly plagued by presidential fever, Woodbury had a keen mind and strong administrative skills. He was tight-lipped and tactful and generally proved to be an excellent Treasury secretary—one of Jackson's more notable appointments. The nomination was confirmed immediately and unanimously on June 29. To replace Woodbury at the head of the Navy Department, Jackson again followed Van Buren's suggestion and selected Mahlon Dickerson of New Jersey. A former governor and senator, Dickerson was a "fussy" sort, frequently ill and overly testy at times. However, he had an outstanding record on the Bank and tariff issues and had repeatedly proved himself a loyal and dependable Jacksonian in Congress, obeying instructions from the White House to the letter. Unfortunately, he proved to be a careless and indolent administrator. His nomination stirred no opposition in the Senate, however, and he was confirmed the day after Jackson submitted it.

June 30 was the last day of the congressional session, and Thomas Hart Benton rose in the Senate and introduced a proposal to "expunge" from the record the resolution censuring Jackson's conduct. The other senators quickly rejected it, but Benton announced his determination to "expunge" no matter how many times he had to introduce it. During each session of Congress thereafter he called for its passage and it became one of the major points of violent argument between Democrats and Whigs.

Although Jackson suffered a few losses during this session of Congress, he exerted renewed leadership over the nation and the party by virtue of his triumph over the BUS, and he breathed new power and authority into the presidency. But far more important, the Bank War provided a powerful assist in moving the Republic further down the road to democracy. The war was constantly described by the Democratic press as an effort to stop the few from robbing the many. Quite simply, they said, it was a contest between democracy and aristocracy. Whatever the truth of this assertion, the American people came to believe that the destruction of the BUS did indeed constitute a momentous victory for majoritarian rule. And they saluted the President as their tribune and champion, one "honest and patriotic . . . battling for them against corruption. . . . They loved him as their friend" and they hailed him for having won a great victory for democracy.[15]

CHAPTER 23

———————⟨⟩———————

The Hermitage Fire

JACKSON'S PROBLEMS WITH THE CONGRESS, along with the recurring ill-nesses that plagued him throughout the spring and summer, were com-pounded in the fall when he received word from Tennessee that his beautiful home, the Hermitage, was in ruins as the result of a disastrous fire. It had occurred at four o'clock in the afternoon of Monday, October 13. His son, Andrew Jr., was absent in the fields at the time and Sarah rested in the house. Apparently the roof was ignited "by sparks or soot of the chimney" in the dining room and since a stiff northwest wind was blowing, the fire quickly spread. Within minutes several servants noticed the blaze and sounded the alarm. Two of them, Charles and Squire, attempted to get a ladder and climb to the roof but none could be found. Besides, "the roof was so steep which would have made it hard to get up to the fire."[1]

Joseph Reiff and William C. Hume, two carpenter-contractors who were constructing the Tulip Grove home nearby for Andrew J. Donelson, spotted the blaze and rushed to take charge of the efforts to extinguish the fire. They ordered the servants to save as much of the furniture in the house as possible. Most of the downstairs belongings were pulled clear, although many pieces of furniture were "broken and otherwise injured in getting it out." The upstairs furniture did not fare as well. Virtually all of it was partially damaged or destroyed and the losses included a consid-erable number of letters written by Rachel Jackson.[2]

Through determination and agility, Joseph Reiff managed to climb to the roof of the dining room, which extended as a wing from the house itself, where he directed the operations that finally put out the fire. He had the assistance of William Donelson's servants, who were working nearby, along with the laborers and hands who were building Tulip Grove. Fortunately they were all standing on the grounds outside the house when the roof fell in. No one was hurt.[3]

Robert Armstrong, Stockley Donelson, and Andrew each reported to Jackson on the disaster and all tried to minimize the extent of the damage to the house and its furnishings. All agreed that the walls of the house were sound and that the Hermitage could be rebuilt on its original site. "Some of the petition walls and arches over the window" needed work, said Stockley Donelson, "and some other repairing of the walls, all of which Mr. Austin can furnish brick to do by deferring the building of some of Maj Donelson back buildings. It can all be covered in before winter sets in, which it will be necessary to do, if the house is to be rebuilt in the same place etc; as the walls would be damaged by being exposed to the winter rains." Armstrong told Jackson that his papers, letter books, valuables, and most of the furniture had been saved. But he greatly underestimated the loss, although he did acknowledge that the upstairs wardrobe and large bedstead had been badly burned. The smoke damage was considerable, which no one recognized at first. Armstrong estimated that the house could be rebuilt for approximately $2,000 or $2,500 and he recommended that Jackson stick with the old site. Andrew thought it would take "3 or 4 & perhaps 5 thousand dollars to repair every loss—but I think not more than 3 or 4—that is to rebuilt it & furnish every thing again."[4]

Poor Sarah was distraught by the catastrophe. The family moved immediately to the Baldwin place at Hunter's Hill and Andrew reported that they were very comfortable. Within two days, a large work force set about preparing the house for renovation, at least until they had final word from Jackson as to whether they should rebuild on the old site or not. Three or four whipsaws were started and the workmen began to cover the house completely to protect it from further damage by the weather.

On October 23, the President learned of the fire. "The Lords will be done," he sighed. "It was he that gave me the means to build it, and he has the right to destroy it, and blessed be his name." Since neglect was imputed to no one and it appeared to be an accident, Jackson accepted his loss with Christian resignation. "I will have it rebuilt," he said. "Was it not on the site selected by my dear departed wife I would build it higher up the Hill, but I will have it repaired." His only worry concerned Sarah. "I am fearful that the fatigue & alarm may be injurious to our dear Sarahs health—let not the loss trouble you & her for one moment," he told his son.[5]

Since the walls and foundation of the Hermitage had been declared "safe & good," Jackson directed that they be "covered in before the heavy frosts & winter rains injure it" so that the house could be restored in the spring. Meanwhile he started to make plans for the rebuilding. He told his son he would arrange to have tin shipped up for the roof to cover a house eighty feet by forty-four. He wanted the windowsills made "of good hewn stone—if it can be got in time"—and he suggested hiring the workman who did Major Donelson's window and doorsills. He authorized Armstrong to draw on him for $1,500 to meet the initial expenses and he asked Andrew to "make a contract with some solvent & responsible workmen to undertake the whole job." He also asked for a detailed accounting of the loss of furniture and wondered about his wine cellar and Emily Donelson's china. With all the confusion and commotion, Jackson added, do not forget to harvest and house the cotton. "It becomes us now to act with oeconomy, and use industry to repair and regain the loss."[6]

Unfortunately, young Andrew was not the man to deal with emergencies or cope with financial and administrative problems. He much preferred to hunt and tipple. The serious matters of the farm bored him. Fortunately, Jackson had Colonel Robert Armstrong, postmaster at Nashville and a former comrade in the Creek War, to rely on to look after the repairs of the Hermitage. Armstrong reported on November 4 that in short order contracts would be let, repairs started, and the cost (with luck) kept around $2,500 to $3,000. Major Lewis, who had returned to Tennessee shortly after Jackson arrived back at the White House, also helped. He visited the Hermitage to inspect the damage and survey the operation of the farm. After consulting with Andrew and Armstrong, Major Lewis suggested to Jackson a number of alterations that would improve the style of the house and increase its size and the number of people it could accommodate. The President said he would have been content to restore the house to its former condition "but as I know I shall [not] be long on earth to enjoy its comforts in retirement," he left it to Andrew to exercise his own discretion about the proposed alterations, "provided it does not add too much to the expence of the repairs." All I want, he said, "is a good room to which I can retire if I am spared to live out my irksome term here, and I am sure I shall not want that room long."[7]

The Hermitage disaster was announced by the newspapers around the country and Jackson received many expressions of sympathy and offers of aid. A subscription, for example, was gotten up in New Orleans which would be offered to the country at large to raise a fund to rebuild the house, with no contribution larger than fifty cents so that *"every man"* who might wish to do so could tender Jackson "this complimentary mark of public gratitude." But the President rejected the offer. "I respect as I ought the feelings that dictated the generous feeling . . . but cannot accept the boon. I am able to rebuild it [myself]." He expressed the hope that the money already raised could be "applied to some charitable institution." Jackson was a proud man and he felt it improper for a President to take advantage of his position and popularity to feed on public generosity.

Because of Sarah's delicate health, the youth of her children—Rachel was born November 1, 1832, and Andrew III on April 4, 1834—as well as the difficulty of living at Hunter's Hill for the winter months, it was decided to send Sarah and the children to Washington to live with the President in the White House. Andrew would join them after the Hermitage had been covered for the winter and the cotton shipped to market. Major Lewis agreed to escort the family from Tennessee. The little family arrived at the White House at 11:30 P.M. on Wednesday, November 26. Rachel, whom the President always called his "little pet," flung herself into Jackson's outstretched arms when she spotted him. "Grandpa," she cried, "the great fire burnt my bonnet, and the big owl tryed to kill Poll [her parrot], but papa killed the owl." The old man hugged the child. "She is very sprightly," he boasted, "and the son is a beautiful and fine boy. I am happy they are safe with me."[8]

The contract for the rebuilding of the Hermitage was signed on January 1, 1835. Colonel Charles J. Love, a close friend and business associate for many years, helped supervise the preparation of the contract. Earlier, Jackson had called him in to participate in the negotiations and arrangements over the restoration. He told Jackson that they had "got the best bargain we could" for a price of $3,950, which did not include painting or decorating. It was further stipulated that the rebuilding would be completely finished by December 25, 1835.[9]

Work on the house began almost at once. And, as expected, problems arose immediately. Labor was scarce and it was difficult to secure enough hands to keep to the original schedule. In addition, changes were suggested to improve the appearance and size of the house. Lewis felt that the stories of the house should be made higher and Armstrong agreed. The size and arrangement of the windows were also altered to make them more decorative and in better proportion to the rest of the house. Jackson himself had a hand in some of the alterations. "I would reduce the roof somewhat," he instructed his son, "but not to make it too flat." He much admired the portico he had built for the White House, designed many years before by Benjamin Latrobe, as well as the Mount Vernon portico. This feature reflected the fashionable Greek revival style at the time with its temple-like columns and pure white color. This monumental portico style had a powerful influence on American architecture and it certainly excited the imagination of President Jackson. So he decided to add a colossal colonnade to his home in Tennessee, just like the one he had in Washington. To do this, the house itself was made taller—which is probably why he agreed to Lewis's suggestion—and this meant adding a "false" or "fake" front to the building in order to allow for columns big enough to provide the desired effect. It was all done so expertly that even today few people looking at the Hermitage realize that the front of the house is fake and serves merely as a setting for the columns.[10]

Because of the changes in design, the difficulty of obtaining sufficient laborers, and the normal delays in building operations, the Hermitage was not completed until the summer of 1836, approximately eighteen months after construction had started. The final accounting of the costs of the restoration was presented to Jackson by Colonel Armstrong on August 2, 1836. It came to $5,125 and included the changes made to the windows, the west wing, and kitchen, along with the addition of a full-length two-story (double) porch, front and back. To replace wardrobes, bedsteads, dressing bureaus, tables, chairs, rugs, drapes, and sundry other articles of furniture came to $2,303.77 and required purchases from seven Philadelphia merchants. And these expenses did not include personal items lost, such as little Rachel's bonnet. To replace these items, Sarah went on a shopping spree shortly after she arrived at the White House and ran up a $345.80 bill, all of which the President paid. In round numbers the cost of rebuilding and refurbishing the Hermitage totaled nearly $10,000 by the time everything was completed. But what arose from the ashes was majestic in size and appearance and totally appropriate to the manner, style, and presence of its master. As rebuilt, the Hermitage was and remains a beautiful house, fitting testimony to one of the grandest and most colossal figures to stride across American history.[11]

CHAPTER 24

Jacksonian Diplomacy

At the very start of his administration in 1829, when Jackson announced his intention of instituting reforms in the operation of government, he made it clear that his intention included foreign as well as domestic affairs. Shortly after his inauguration he called to the White House the various ministers representing foreign countries and told them that he had no designs on the safety of other nations and that his policy was simple and straightforward. It was a policy he later defined more precisely in his first message to Congress: "to ask nothing that is not clearly right, and to submit to nothing that is wrong." When they heard it, the American people applauded the sentiment. Throughout his New England tour his words constantly appeared in newspapers and on banners and signposts. Like his slogan "Our Federal Union, It Must Be Preserved," his admonition to the world that the rights of the United States must be respected stirred the patriotism of his countrymen.[1]

In terms of foreign affairs, Jackson's first administration was a smashing success. It began, in a sense, with the reopening of trade with the British West Indies that had been closed by Great Britain since the conclusion of the Revolutionary War. Repeated efforts to reopen the trade had failed; but Jackson was determined to succeed.

Louis McLane of Delaware was chosen to serve as minister to Great Britain and he proved an excellent choice. A former Radical Republican, he was described as "correct, conciliating and spirited," someone who "would give no insult, and he would receive none."[2] Early in June, 1829, McLane told Van Buren that if the United States would divorce itself from the errors of the Adams administration, which had bungled the West Indian business, the British might consider negotiating a treaty. In other words, the defeat of Adams by Jackson in 1828 might be viewed as a repudiation of the former President's unfortunate foreign policy and the British might then respond favorably to a friendly gesture and agree to commercial reciprocity.[3]

However risky it might seem, Jackson was quite prepared to repudiate his predecessor's foreign policy. He felt secure enough to move in a new direction, and what eventually emerged was an overall Jacksonian foreign policy that sought through practical—rather then formal—means to reconcile the differences that interrupted normal U.S. relations with other countries. Basic to his entire policy was Jackson's fierce desire to win global recognition for the independence, sovereignty, and rights of the United States, something not always accorded in the past. The departure by Van Buren (approved by the President) from the diplomacy of the past signified a willingness to accept any practical means to secure these ends. For example, Jackson was quite prepared to admit Adams's error in failing to respond to Parliament's offer in 1825 to grant American ships the same rights in the West Indies as the United States granted British ships in American waters. "Practical" diplomacy was what the Jackson administration chose to pursue.[4]

Not that Andrew Jackson would tamely accept any response—or, worse, no response—from foreign powers. If, by their conduct, they chose to see a nationalistic President in full cry, he could oblige them. On the other hand, if he must be conciliatory or accept certain peculiarities or special demands from foreign countries, he could also oblige. However, when conciliation and accommodation failed, then he was quite prepared to use the threat of force or some other equally intimidating tactic. With regard to Great Britain, he explained to Van Buren in a memorandum dated April 10, 1830, precisely what he meant.

> On the subject of our negotiation with great Britain, we ought to be prepared to act promptly in case of a failure. We have held out terms of reconciling our differences with that nation of the most Frank and fair terms. . . . These terms being rejected our national character and honor requires that we should now act with that promptness and energy due to our national character. Therefore let a communication be prepared for congress recommending a non intercourse law between the United States and Canady, and a sufficient number of Cutters [to enforce it]. . . . This adopted and carried into effect forthwith and in six months both Canady and the Westindia Islands will feel, and sorely feel, the effects of their folly in urging their Government to adhere to our exclusion from the West India trade.[5]

Put another way, the President was saying that Jacksonian diplomacy should be conducted along conciliatory lines, with a willingness to accept practical solutions to foreign problems, but always ready to act with "promptness and energy" to make foreign nations "sorely feel" the consequences of treating the United States with anything less than the respect and dignity due her.

In the case of the West Indian trade the British had in fact triggered the President's annoyance by long delays to McLane's gentle prodding. But McLane's persistence and mounting aggressiveness eventually paid off, especially when he reminded Lord Aberdeen, the British foreign secretary, that what was involved constituted more than trade. At stake was the future of American-British relations. And that produced the breakthrough, for Britain was extremely anxious to improve its relations with the United States.

McLane told several friends in Washington that if Congress would only show goodwill and move immediately to end American restrictions against British ships coming from the West Indies on a reciprocal basis, then perhaps the British might quit their stalling. Jackson himself contributed to the breakthrough by sending a message to Congress on May 26, 1830, stating that he expected to conclude the West Indian business successfully on the basis of reciprocity and requested permission to act independently after Congress adjourned.[6] The President had no authority to remove U.S. restrictions on his own, and so to avoid the necessity of calling a special session, he suggested the "propriety" of allowing him to end restrictions by proclamation once Britain agreed to permit American ships into the West Indies. Congress complied immediately with a bill passed on May 29 which approved reciprocity as the basis for an agreement.

Not much later the British responded. Aberdeen allowed that in view of the congressional action and the apparent repudiation by the American people of the Adams administration with its unacceptable demands regarding the West Indian trade, a pledge could now be given that Britain would remove all restrictions to trade relations between the United States and the British West Indies once Jackson implemented the law by his proclamation.[7]

McLane exulted. "I have the satisfaction to inform you," he wrote Levi Woodbury, among dozens of others, "that I have succeeded in my negotiations for the colonial trade! This government consents to restore to us the direct trade with her colonies upon the terms of my proposition." He did not fail to mention that "a good deal of labor & solicitude & perseverance" went into this "most happy result."[8]

Jackson received notification from McLane shortly after returning from a trip to Tennessee in 1830. He immediately issued his proclamation, dated October 5, 1830, by which American ports were opened to British vessels "upon the terms set forth in the said act."[9] A dispatch informed McLane of Jackson's action which was communicated to Aberdeen. Two days later, on November 5, 1830, the British lifted their restrictions.

It was a striking diplomatic triumph for the Jackson administration. A source of annoyance and discord stretching back over several decades had at last been cleared away. It was an important step in a growing sense of friendship between the two countries. Past hostility was giving way to mounting cordiality.

Nor was the West Indian trade the administration's only diplomatic success. Jackson's policy of giving no offense and suffering none included a belief that foreign nations responsible for damages to property belonging to American citizens should pay for them. During the fierce Napoleonic Wars of the early nineteenth century, Americans had suffered commercial losses at the hands not only of the French but also of smaller nations that had been obliged to enforce Napoleon's maritime decrees. American spoliation claims existed against France, Russia, Denmark, Portugal, the Netherlands, and the Kingdom of the Two Sicilies. Although previous administrations had sought a settlement of these claims, the complaints were rudely brushed aside. Now it was General Jackson's turn to settle the matter.

All his life Jackson had been taught that honest men paid their just debts. He believed that this principle also applied to nations. And he was not the man to be lightly turned away. The debts were legitimate obligations and Andrew Jackson wanted them paid. The President's persistence and determination to gain international recognition of United States' rights, along with a willingness to engage in endless discussions without tiring or giving up, and a disposition to compromise to resolve deadlocks, brought notable successes to several problem areas. A few of these successes were resolved through executive agreements, principally with Russia and Portugal, which accepted and paid the amounts negotiated.

Resolutions of other diplomatic problem areas were more complicated. These necessitated considerable diplomatic maneuvering. Jackson's first success with one of these came through negotiations with Denmark. According to some the total claims against that nation ran over two million dollars as of 1827. Denmark did not dispute the legitimacy of the claims, only the right of the United States to dispute the decisions of its prize courts once they were rendered. Henry Wheaton, the *chargé d'affaires* in Copenhagen and an outstanding international lawyer, argued persuasively that prize courts were designed to fix responsibility but when their judgments were unjust an aggrieved national had a right to protest. Wheaton persisted in his arguments and finally the Danish minister of foreign affairs, and the president of the chancery, accepted his position. They agreed to allow claims for the "seizure, detention, and condemnation or confiscations" of American vessels, cargoes, or property by Denmark in the years 1808–1811 and to pay a lump sum of $650,000. This figure represented total victory to Jackson. "We have obtained $150,000 more than our merchants had agreed to accept as full indemnity," he gloated to John Overton. "The sum to be paid being *$650,000* $500,000 having been offered by our merchants to have been recd in full." Jackson made no such boast when he reported the settlement to Congress. The convention was signed in Copenhagen on March 27, 1830, and submitted to the Senate for approval on May 27 with a presidential message that said in part: "The convention provides by compromise for the adjustment and payment of indemnities to no inconsiderable amount." The Senate willingly gave its consent.[10]

By the end of his first term in office, Jackson had gained a large measure of respect for American rights around the world, and he did it by his alert response to any action by a foreign power that bore the slightest semblance of contempt for American rights. The incident at the port of Quallah Battoo in Sumatra is a case in point.

On February 7, 1831, the American vessel *Friendship,* engaged in the pepper trade, was attacked and plundered by Sumatran natives. Specie, opium, stores, and instruments were taken. Jackson immediately dispatched the frigate *Potomac* to the scene with instructions to Captain John Downes to negotiate with the ruling king for restitution and indemnity. Failing that, Downes was authorized to take punitive action. But Downes exceeded his instructions by attacking the port of Quallah Battoo on February 6, 1832, and firing the town. Then he proceeded to negotiate and work out a peace agreement.[11] The President's response to the initial (and piratical) attack by the natives was perfectly appropriate. Unfortunately, his instructions to Downes to negotiate first were disregarded. Some Americans surpassed even Old Hickory in the intensity of their nationalism. But the *Globe* insisted that all Americans should be proud of what happened. "The Maylas on the other side of the globe were chastened in the name of Andrew Jackson and the American ensign became a safe passport among the remotest nations."[12]

Because of the incident in Sumatra, Jackson recognized the need for formal treaty agreements with Asiatic countries, and he therefore commissioned Edmund Roberts, a sea captain and merchant, as a special envoy to draw up commercial treaties with Cochin China (present-day Vietnam), Siam, Muscat, and Japan. By this action Jackson initiated diplomatic relations with nations of the Far East. Roberts failed with Cochin China because he refused to authorize an alteration of Jackson's letter of introduction to the emperor to permit a tone of supplication in the salutation.[13] This "breach of etiquette" doomed the mission. So he proceeded to Bangkok, where he enjoyed better results. On March 30, 1833, he concluded a Treaty of Amity and Commerce with the Siamese government. From there he went to Muscat and signed a treaty with that government on October 3, 1833. Both treaties opened these nations to American trade on a most-favored-nation basis, and they were ratified by the Senate in June 1834.[14] These were the first treaties between the United States and Far Eastern countries. What made the Muscat treaty especially valuable was the fact that the sultan of Muscat ruled the spice-rich island of Zanzibar off the east coast of Africa as well as the kingdom of Oman on the coast of Arabia.[15]

Jackson was so pleased with these results that in April 1835 he authorized Roberts to begin negotiations to open Japan to the West. He also authorized him to renew his attempts at a commercial treaty with Cochin China. Unfortunately, the envoy died at Macao on June 12, 1836, before reaching his destination. And although Roberts signed only two treaties with Asiatic countries, the information obtained about commercial advantages in the Orient later prompted a steady expansion of American trade in the Far East.[16]

Commercial treaties were also concluded with several South American countries. Colombia and Chile signed a series of treaties in 1831, 1832, and 1833 that extended reciprocal trade concessions to the United States. Indeed, when Jackson took office there were few commercial treaties with European and South American countries. By the close of his administration agreements had been concluded with Turkey, Russia, Morocco, Great Britain, Mexico, Colombia, Chile, Venezuela, the Peru-Bolivia Federation, Siam, and Muscat. This attention to improving commercial opportunities around the world provided another dimension to the economic expansion of America during the Age of Jackson.[17]

The Russian treaty was concluded by James Buchanan of Pennsylvania.[18] Through constant prodding, a certain amount of tact, and appeals to personal interests, Buchanan finally talked the Russians into agreeing to a treaty which he signed on December 18, 1832. This most-favored-nation treaty placed the ships, crews, and cargo of each nation on a basis of reciprocity, with each country receiving the same treatment it was accorded in its home port. This was the first such treaty the Russian government had ever signed.[19]

The Kingdom of the Two Sicilies proved more difficult. Several unsuccessful attempts had been made by previous administrations to obtain payment for losses by Americans in Naples during the Napoleonic Wars. In his third message to Congress, Jackson decided that the time had come to call a halt to U.S. forbearance. He promised to secure an indemnity and, to that end, he sent as his *chargé d'affaires* to Naples, the capital of the kingdom, John Nelson, a young Maryland supporter. The *chargé* soon discovered that the Neopolitan government had no intention of paying its debt and Nelson informed Jackson that only the use of naval force would pry the money out of the Neapolitans. The frigate *United States* arrived in Naples shortly thereafter. As Nelson predicted, the threat of force brought the government to its senses and on October 14, 1832, the Italians signed a treaty in which the debt was settled at 2,119,230 Neapolitan ducats, or approximately $1,755,450, to be paid in nine installments with an annual interest of 4 percent.

Still another diplomatic achievement came with the acceptance by Spain of a treaty that spelled out her obligations for indemnity to American citizens over claims from illegal seizures of ships during the South American wars of independence. The treaty, in which Spain agreed to pay $600,000, was signed in Madrid on February 17, 1834. This amount was less than half of what the United States originally demanded, but the civil strife of the Carlist wars had produced confusion and disorder in Spain, so the Jackson administration counted itself lucky to get even this much.

The continued success of Jacksonian diplomacy through three successive secretaries of state (Van Buren, Livingston, and McLane), in almost as many years, says something significant about the role played by the President. The foreign policy of the United States from 1829 to 1837 was Jackson's policy—just as it should have been. But if Jackson merits credit for the diplomatic successes of his administration, he also bears the blame for the disasters. And one came soon enough. It involved the spoliation claims against France, and the entire episode was so unfortunate that Roger B. Taney later called it "the most dangerous moment of Genl. Jackson's administration."[20]

After several years of intense negotiation, the United States minister to France, William C. Rives, finally won a treaty from the French on July 4, 1831, in which the United States would receive 25 million francs in six equal annual installments for damages sustained at sea by Americans because of Napoleon's Berlin and Milan Decrees. Ratifications were exchanged, but when the first installment came due the French Chamber of Deputies neglected to authorize payment and the draft issued by the secretary of the Treasury was refused. At this point Jackson sent Edward Livingston (who had just resigned as secretary of state) to France as his minister and instructed him to remind the French that Jackson was determined to bring about the "prompt and complete fulfilment" of the terms of the treaty.[21]

The President finally took formal notice of this disagreeable development in his fifth annual message to Congress, delivered on December 3, 1833. He began by expressing his deep regret that the terms of the treaty remained unfulfilled. A draft upon the French minister of finance had been drawn at Washington five days after the installment was payable at Paris. Not until that moment did Jackson realize that an *explicit* appropriation for the purpose was required from the Chamber of Deputies. He had received numerous assurances—most recently from the newly appointed American minister—that the appropriation would be forthcoming when the deputies met at their next session. "Should I be disappointed in the hope now entertained," Jackson concluded in this section of his message, "the subject will be again brought to the notice of Congress in such manner as the occasion may require."[22]

Not until January 13, 1834, did the appropriation bill come to the deputies and it was immediately sent into committee where it reposed like a corpse for two months. Then, on March 28, the Chamber agreed to consider the matter and after five days of intensive and often spirited argument, the motion to pay the indemnity was defeated by a vote of 176 to 168.[23]

Jackson was thunderstruck. He could not imagine a more stunning defeat, nor a more studied insult. The French had administered a savage blow and the President reacted with characteristic outrage. He even considered applying to Congress for authority to issue "Letters of Marque and Reprisal" which could easily have led to war between the two nations.

The rejection of the appropriation bill, of course, resulted from several causes. Some of the deputies thought the indemnity too high, that it would offend the French people and encourage other nations to demand restitution for alleged wrongs. Others, especially monarchists, hated the United States because of the American Revolution and its impact upon French life and thought. And still others, mainly republicans, disliked the king and his government and therefore seized any opportunity to embarrass it.[24]

Jackson's initial reaction, albeit couched in bluster, was to give the French a little time to reconsider and then wait to see how successful would be their government's declared intention to appeal to the next Chamber to make good on the terms of the treaty. He therefore informed the French minister in Washington, Louis Barbe Sérurier, that he would wait until the opening of the next Congress, at which time he would announce "the result of that appeal, and of his Majesty's efforts for its success."[25]

Jackson returned to the Hermitage during the summer of 1834 and waited out the time for the Chamber of Deputies to reassemble. He soon suffered a rude shock. Instead of taking up the matter during their summer session or holding a special session during the autumn, the French government informed the President that the indemnity question could not be brought to the Chamber of Deputies before Congress reconvened in December. Since Jackson had declared his intention of discussing the matter in his next message to Congress, the French government politely requested that he do it in such manner as to avoid anything unfriendly.[26]

Shortly after Jackson's return to Washington from Tennessee, the French minister, Louis Sérurier, was informed through the new secretary of state, John Forsyth, of the President's mounting irritation and was warned that Jackson was not the sort of President to sit quietly and indefinitely while France dawdled about honoring her commitment. After several more interviews with the secretary, the French minister felt compelled to inform his government that Jackson's message to Congress would likely be "very painful." The government of France could expect a very "hostile tone in the President's message."[27]

Sure enough. The sixth annual message to the Congress, dated December 1, 1834, opened almost immediately with a blast. "It becomes my unpleasant duty to inform you that [the] pacific and highly gratifying picture of our foreign relations does not include those with France at this time." The results of our long negotiations have been very frustrating, the President snorted. "Not only has the French government been thus wanting in the performance of the stipulations it has so solemnly entered into with the United States, but its omissions have been marked by circumstances which would seem to leave us without satisfactory evidences that such performance will certainly take place at a future period."[28] He continued:

It is my conviction that the United States ought to insist on a prompt execution of the treaty, and in case it be refused or longer delayed take redress into their own hands. After the delay on the part of France of a quarter of a century in acknowledging these claims by treaty, it is not to be tolerated that another quarter of a century is to be wasted in negotiating about the payment. The laws of nations provide a remedy for such occasions. It is a well-settled principle of the international code that where one nation owes another a liquidated debt which it refuses or neglects to pay the aggrieved party may seize on the property belonging to the other, its citizens or subjects, sufficient to pay the debt without giving just cause of war. This remedy has been repeatedly resorted to, and recently by France herself toward Portugal under circumstances less questionable.[29]

Seize French property! That produced a shock. And if France did not appropriate the money for the indemnity at the next session of the Chamber of Deputies, the message continued, it may be assumed that the treaty has been repudiated and therefore "prompt measures" by the Congress will be both "honorable and just" and have the "best effect upon our national character."

It was an incredible message and the French took immediate exception to it. The message caused "the greatest sensation," reported Livingston to Forsyth. The excitement in Paris "is at present very great."[30] Sérurier was ordered home and Livingston was offered his passports if he so desired. Although the French government had decided to go ahead and ask the Chamber for an appropriation to pay the indemnity, nevertheless it felt itself "wounded" by Jackson's groundless "imputations."

The news of Sérurier's recall hit the United States with devastating force. "A strong sensation" was felt in the House of Representatives, recorded John Quincy Adams in his diary, and many members wished to adjourn forthwith as a gesture of protest. A war hysteria of sorts gripped some parts of the country and a New York City contingent of national guardsmen offered their services to the President. But Jackson assured them "that the dangers of a rupture between us and our ancient ally . . . will soon pass away."[31]

An appropriations bill to indemnify the United States was finally introduced into the Chamber of Deputies by the minister of finance on January 15, 1835, and forwarded to the appropriate committee. On March 28 it was reported back with a report noting Jackson's message to Congress and suggesting that an acceptable explanation of his remarks ought to be demanded before France paid the indemnity. Debate on the measure began in earnest on April 9 and passed on April 18 by a vote of 289 to 137 with an amendment which required "that the money shall not be paid until the Government of France shall have received satisfactory explanations of the Message of the President of the Union dated the 2 Decr. last."[32]

Livingston was chagrined. The amendment, he told Forsyth, "I think will render the whole bill nugatory. . . . I shall therefore in obedience to your instructions ask for my passports." On May 5 he sailed from Le Havre for home aboard the USS *Constitution.* [33]

The news of the passage of the indemnity bill by the French Chamber of Deputies arrived in the United States on May 26. The first reaction was one long shout of thanksgiving. Once again the Jackson administration had triumphed and forced a European nation to pay its legitimate debt to this country. Then, this unexpected triumph was modified somewhat in the nation by the realization that an explanation of Jackson's message was required before the indemnity would be paid. This, said John Quincy Adams, "throws an awkward obstacle in the way of a final settlement." But most Americans thought it a face-saving device that really meant little. I hope, said William C. Rives, "that the silly condition" imposed by the French will not prove serious.[34] It remained for the White House to determine that question, and on May 29 the Washington *Globe* announced Jackson's reaction to the demand for an explanation. It was abrupt, rude, and needlessly aggressive—but it said exactly what the American people were thinking and saying. "France will get no apology," blared the *Globe,* "—nothing bearing even such a remote resemblance to one, that it can be palmed off upon the world as such by all the vaunting and gasconading of sputtering Frenchmen."

"No apology." That was Jackson's response to the French, and he meant it. "It is high time that this arrogance of France should be put down," the President wrote to Amos Kendall sometime later, "and the whole European world taught to know that we will not permit France or any, or *all* the European Governments to interfere with our domestic policy, or dictate to the President what language he shall use in his message to Congress." His message of 1834, he continued, did exactly what the Constitution required him to do, namely, communicate the condition of the Union to the Congress and what appropriate measures should be taken. "It would be disgraceful to explain or apologize to a foreign Government for any thing said in a message. it is the summit of arrogance in France, and insulting to us as an independent nation to ask it, and what no american will ever submit to."[35] Meanwhile, the French minister of foreign affairs, the Duc de Broglie, hoped to end the controversy by asking the President to indicate in some official way that he had never meant to assume "a menacing attitude toward France."[36]

In his next message to Congress, dated December 7, 1835, Jackson responded as best he could under the circumstances. After providing a brief recapitulation of what had transpired to date, he reviewed the behavior of the French and tried to justify his actions. Then he spoke the words that caught everyone's attention. "The conception that it was my intention to menace or insult the Government of France is as unfounded as the attempt to extort from the fears of that nation what her sense of justice may deny would be vain and ridiculous." He defended his message and denied that any nation had a right to question it. At this point he aimed his following words directly to the American people: "The honor of my country shall never be stained by an apology from me for the statement of truth and the performance of duty. . . . This determination will, I am confident, be approved by my constituents."[37]

Not only did the President's words start the process of resolving this dispute but events in Europe began to nudge things along at a quicker pace. The deteriorating political situation in Spain, the danger of another invasion of Belgium by Holland, the reluctance of Britain to interfere to halt the invasion, and especially the developing hostility of Russia toward France—all converged to prepare the French for an end to the controversy. Finally when Britain offered her good offices to help resolve matters both France and the United States accepted this friendly gesture. England encouraged the French to accept Jackson's newest message to Congress as the "explanation" they demanded. That done, they could then justify paying the indemnity. On February 15 the British notified the American government that the difficulties preventing payment had been removed and that the first installment of the indemnity would be forthcoming whenever demanded by the United States government.[38] Jackson immediately notified Congress on February 22 that the controversy had ended.[39]

The nation at large broke out in repeated shouts of praise for President Andrew Jackson. Even the Whigs found it difficult to deny him full credit for this achievement. Jackson himself was ecstatic. "I was shewn a letter yesterday," he wrote to Edward Livingston, "stating that I never stood so high in . . . Europe, and will now take our stand on a level with the greatest powers of Europe, and have a durable peace with all the world."[40] In his first message to Congress in 1829 he had said that "it is my settled purpose to ask nothing that is not clearly right and to submit to nothing that is wrong." But the motive underlying this "settled purpose" was to achieve the respect of the world. And this he did.

Still, he was faulted, then and later, for his strong-arm methods, in that his diplomacy consisted of the stick and the threat, of employing tactics and language that were far stronger than needed, thus endangering the peace and safety of the country. The criticism is well taken. But there were a number of extenuating circumstances, at least as far as the French controversy was concerned. First, the French acted very badly. They had agreed by treaty to pay the indemnity and then defaulted, not by accident but because they did not really want to pay the debt. Moreover, Livingston, who had an outstanding reputation at home and abroad as an intelligent and skillful lawyer as well as a Francophile, advised the use of strong measures. Jackson would have been foolish had he acted contrary to what his own minister, who was on the spot, advised him to do.

In any event, Jackson's handling of the controversy produced something that was very important for the United States. It increased European respect for America and strengthened the ties between the United States and Great Britain. It also reordered the relationship between France and the United States. France always presumed she could do whatever she pleased and get away with it because of her assistance in the American Revolution. Now she knew better, and that made for a healthier relationship.

But, in the long view of history, perhaps the most important result was Jackson's success in facing down European scorn[41] of the American experiment in liberty and forcing a recognition of American rights as a free and independent nation. In sum, then, Jackson proved extraordinarily successful in his conduct of foreign affairs, not simply because he won payment of financial obligations owed to this country, but because he raised the reputation of the United States throughout the world. Through a vigorous diplomatic policy that had specific and honorable goals to achieve, he advanced this nation's claim to the dignity and respect it rightfully deserved.

CHAPTER 25

Jacksonian Democracy

Along with his triumphs in the diplomatic field, President Jackson achieved something as unique as it was triumphant, namely, the elimination of the national debt! The last installment of the debt was paid in January 1835. It was one of the "reforms" for which Jackson had struggled over the last four years. It was an accomplishment for which he took justifiable pride.

For the nation as a whole, the obliteration of the national debt proclaimed the triumph of republicanism and the constitutional system. It was a mark of stupendous achievement, a badge of freedom, a symbol of success. It demonstrated the blessings of democracy to the entire world. Because the final payment of the debt nearly coincided with the anniversary of the Battle of New Orleans, the Democratic party felt it auspicious (and politically advantageous) to combine the two events into one great celebration. It was twenty years since Jackson had annihilated a British army and proved the might of American arms; now, in 1835, he had proved the vitality of American political institutions.

On January 8, 1835, a banquet of "extraordinary magnificence" was held at Brown's Hotel in Washington at 6:00 p.m. A dinner was provided "in the very best taste," and nearly 250 persons attended. The room was festooned with evergreens, a portrait of George Washington hung from one wall and a portrait of President Jackson from the opposite wall. Thomas Hart Benton presided, and assisting him were James K. Polk, Silas Wright, Jr., William R. King, and Isaac Hill, among others.

It was a glittering affair, but President Jackson declined to attend. The purpose of the occasion was to celebrate a historic moment and he did not wish to subvert it by his presence. He wanted no personal glorification. It was far more important that the nation celebrate its deliverance from "economic bondage." In that, and that alone, Andrew Jackson would have all the satisfaction and honor he needed.

In Jackson's place, Vice President Van Buren attended as distinguished guest. The entire cabinet also appeared, along with the Speaker of the

House, many members of Congress, and high-ranking officers of the army and navy.

The ceremonies began with a prayer by the chaplain of the Senate, the Reverend Mr. Hatch. Then Senator Benton rose to address the gathering and he quickly got to the point.

"The national debt," he exclaimed, *"is paid!"*

"Huzza!" roared the crowd.

"This month of January, 1835," Benton continued, "in the fifty-eighth year of the Republic, ANDREW JACKSON being President, the NATIONAL DEBT IS PAID! and the apparition, so long unseen on earth, a great nation without a national debt! stands revealed to the astonished vision of a wondering world!

"Gentlemen," Benton went on as he prepared to give his toast, "coming direct from my own bosom, will find its response in yours: President Jackson: May the evening of his days be as tranquil and as happy for himself as their meridian has been resplendent, glorious, and beneficent for his country."

Everyone in the room had risen as Benton began his salute to their great chief, and when he concluded they burst into a long round of applause.

It was the sort of thing that Jackson feared the occasion might become and why he chose to stay away. But the Democrats could not help themselves and they heaped lavish praise upon him as, one after another, they rose to offer a toast extolling Jackson's virtues as military hero and defender of the nation's liberty.

The President himself sent a toast to be read in his absence. It said nothing about his career or the eighth of January. It simply focused on the important event: the end of the national debt.

"The Payment of the Public Debt," he proclaimed. "Let us commemorate it as an event which gives us increased power as a nation, and reflects luster on our Federal Union, of whose justice, fidelity, and wisdom it is a glorious illustration."[1]

After dozens of other toasts, the evening ended with the singing of "The Altar of Liberty," a song especially written for the occasion. When it was all over, the Democrats shook hands and patted each other on the back in recognition of what they called one of the most "unique and glorious" events in the history of the United States.

Jackson deserved a great deal of credit for this extraordinary event. Not only had he long advocated this reform but he had conducted his administration as frugally as possible in order to achieve it. His efforts were aided and advanced, of course, by the economic vitality of the country, but he himself supervised congressional appropriations carefully, and regularly developed means to advance the date when the debt would be paid. And the achievement naturally added to his personal popularity and political strength. Ordinary citizens credited him with having run the government so efficiently and honestly that he had scored the spectacular feat of actually conducting the nation out of debt.

But if the new year began on a spectacular note it soon soured when Jackson was nearly killed in an assassination attempt. It was the first time a President had been attacked with intent to kill. Never before had an American citizen dared to approach the chief executive and seek to alter the course of history by pointing a loaded pistol at him and firing it.

The incident occurred on Friday, January 30, 1835, during the funeral of Representative Warren R. Davis of South Carolina in the House chamber. The rites concluded, the congregation, including the President, his cabinet, and members of both houses, proceeded to the east porch of the Capitol, the House members first, then the Senate, with the President following behind. Waiting at the entrance of the rotunda of the east portico stood a thirty-year-old man, his face hidden by a thick black beard. As the President reached the rotunda, the young man stepped up to him, drew a pocket pistol, and aimed it directly at Jackson's heart. He stood only two and a half yards away. He squeezed the trigger and an explosion rang out.

Jackson instantly reacted. Instead of ducking away, he lunged at his assailant, his walking cane raised high.

The young man dropped the pistol and produced a second gun which he had held ready-cocked in his left hand. He took dead aim at the President and pulled the trigger.

A second explosion thundered through the chamber. Jackson hesitated for a split second and then started forward again. The young man ducked away but was finally knocked down by Lieutenant Gedney of the navy. "The President pressed after him," wrote Senator John Tyler, who observed the incident up close, "until he saw he was secured."

In both instances the caps of the pistols had discharged but failed to ignite the powder in the barrel. The day was very damp, said Tyler, "a thick mist prevailing," and the pistols were loaded with the "finest powder. It is almost a miracle that they did not go off."[2]

The would-be assassin turned out to be one Richard Lawrence, an unemployed house painter. He was quickly hurried off to "civil authorities" and incarcerated. When the House sergeant-at-arms asked him why he attempted to assassinate the President, Lawrence replied that Jackson had murdered his father three years before. He also claimed to be the legitimate heir to the British throne and that Jackson had impeded his succession. "There is nothing but madness in all this," said John Tyler. Indeed. Lawrence was immediately brought to trial but on April 11, 1835, he was found not guilty because "he was under the influence of insanity."[3] He was committed to an asylum. Said one newspaper dolefully: "It is a sign of the times,"[4] a sign that something powerful and frightening was operating in the country which was changing its character and mood. The nation had come through forty years without such an experience. Six

Presidents had administered the country during periods of stress and calm, through war and peace. Still, nothing like this had ever happened before. Then, and later, some thought that the cause of this monstrous deed lay with the personality of Jackson himself, that he was just a little too strong, too controversial, too dominant a character, and therefore an inviting target for the demented in society. Recently there had been several threats against his life. Later there were more.

> Brower's Hotel, Philadelphia, July 4, 1835
>
> You damn'd old Scoundrel . . . I will cut your throat whilst you are sleeping. I wrote to you repeated Cautions, so look out or damn you I'll have you burnt at the Stake in the City of Washington.
>
> Your Master
> Junius Brutus Booth
>
> You know me! Look out![5]

No doubt the forceful personality of Jackson did indeed attract lunatics everywhere. But as some suspected at the time, a deeper and more troublesome factor may have been involved. American society itself was undoubtedly at fault. Since the beginning of the nineteenth century the American way of life had changed dramatically—sometimes for the better and sometimes for the worse. The industrial revolution, the transportation revolution, the increased migration westward, the steady rise of the standard of living, the increased momentum in the democratization of political institutions, and the social and economic mobility that visitors instantly noticed—all these had produced marvelous improvements in the quality of life in America. But they also produced hideous side effects. Poverty, urban crime and violence, blatant and vulgar materialism, the disparity of wealth and privilege spawned by the industrial revolution, racial and religious bigotry—these, too, increased. Social conditions fell to such a depth that reform movements had already begun. These were organized attempts to change and better American society, to combat materialism, to raise the quality of education, to advance the rights of women, to free the slaves, to ameliorate working conditions, to improve penal and mental institutions, and to establish temperance as a national virtue.[6] The assassination attempt, therefore, was only one more indication that something was terribly amiss with American life and needed attention and healing.

Immediately after the assassination attempt, Jackson himself was hurried to a carriage and sped to the White House. By the time he arrived in the mansion he had completely regained his composure. Martin Van Buren, who followed him to the White House and expected to witness an outpouring of Jacksonian wrath, was stupefied to find Old Hickory "sitting with one of Major Donelson's children on his lap and conversing with General Scott, himself apparently the least disturbed person in the room."[7]

But the near-horror of this incident was soon dispelled by a series of political victories that eventually brought great joy and satisfaction to the Jackson administration. When the chief justice of the United States, John Marshall, died on July 6, 1835, the President was determined to replace him with Roger Brooke Taney, who had been rejected by the Senate as secretary of the Treasury. The Senate had blocked a number of presidential appointments but over several months Jackson's political strength around the country grew with each new election. Connecticut, Illinois, and Louisiana each sent a new senator to the upper house and their loyalty to the party and the President proved unshakable. On December 28, 1835, Jackson formally nominated Taney as the chief justice and he was confirmed by a vote of 29 to 15 on March 15. Clay, Webster, and Calhoun voted "nay." Following this victory the President nominated and won confirmation of his appointment of Amos Kendall as postmaster general and accorded the post full cabinet standing.

Taney and Kendall were two of Jackson's best appointments. Kendall, especially, was helpful to the President in advancing his reform efforts and eventually winning passage of the Post Office Act of 1836 which went a long way toward modernizing and improving the postal service. But there was one incident involving the Post Office during Kendall's tenure that portended something truly frightening and dangerous. On July 29, 1835, a steamboat entered Charleston Harbor carrying a cargo of mail which included thousands of antislavery tracts sent by the American Anti-Slavery Society, founded in Philadelphia in 1833, and addressed to the city's most prominent citizens. Charleston's postmaster, Alfred Huger, locked up the tracts until he could get instructions from Kendall, but unfortunately word of the presence of these tracts quickly spread through Charleston and that evening a mob broke into the post office and seized them. The next evening, amid wild scenes of rejoicing, a bonfire on the Charleston parade grounds consumed the "incendiary" material, fed also by effigies of the nation's leading abolitionists, William Lloyd Garrison, Lewis and Arthur Tappan, Theodore Dwight Weld, and others.

Responding to Huger's urgent appeal for instructions, Kendall told him that the postmaster had no legal authority to exclude material from the mail on account of their "character or tendency." But, he said, "I am not prepared to direct you" to deliver the tracts. In effect Kendall threw the decision back at Huger and told him to do what he thought best.[8]

Kendall turned immediately to Jackson for direction. At the moment the President was relaxing at the Rip Raps in Virginia, his favorite vacation haunt. In response Jackson expressed sorrow that anyone in the country would attempt to stir up racial warfare in the south. But, he allowed, "we are the instruments of, and executors of the law; we have no power to prohibit anything from being transported in the mail that is authorized by law." The President was especially troubled by the recourse to violence in the seizure of the tracts. "This spirit of mob-law is

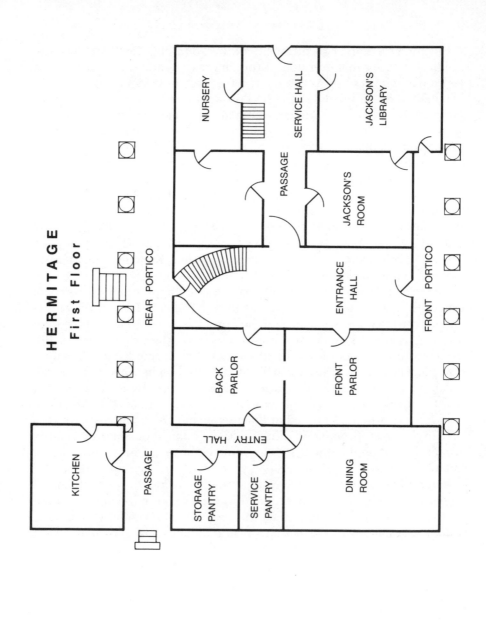

HERMITAGE
First Floor

NURSERY

SERVICE HALL

JACKSON'S LIBRARY

PASSAGE

JACKSON'S ROOM

REAR PORTICO

ENTRANCE HALL

FRONT PORTICO

BACK PARLOR

FRONT PARLOR

KITCHEN

PASSAGE

ENTRY HALL

STORAGE PANTRY

SERVICE PANTRY

DINING ROOM

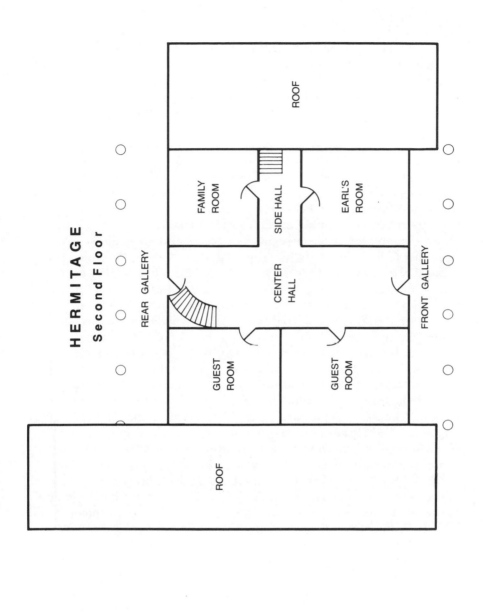

HERMITAGE
Second Floor

ROOF

REAR GALLERY

FAMILY ROOM

SIDE HALL

EARL'S ROOM

CENTER HALL

FRONT GALLERY

GUEST ROOM

GUEST ROOM

ROOF

becoming too common and must be checked," he declared, "or ere long it will become as great an evil as a servile war." However, until Congress passed the appropriate legislation to outlaw the delivery of abolitionist tracts to protect public safety, "we can do nothing more than direct that those inflamatory papers be delivered to none but who will demand them as subscribers."[9]

In his seventh message to Congress, delivered on December 7, 1835, the President asked for this necessary legislation, but Calhoun and other nullifiers objected. They wanted a law that forbade delivery of abolitionist tracts in any state or territory where local law forbade such material. What finally resulted was the Post Office Act of July 2, 1836, which forbade postmasters from detaining the delivery of mail under any circumstances. Unfortunately, southerners regularly violated this law and chose to believe that federal authority over the mail ceased at the reception point. What is also unfortunate is the fact that the President made no attempt to enforce compliance with this law, although in fairness it should be pointed out that his term of office ended shortly after the passage of the law and that during this period he was gravely ill and rarely left his sick room. Not until 1857 did the attorney general, Caleb Cushing, rule that a postmaster may refuse to deliver mail of an incendiary character but that it was up to the courts to decide what was and what was not incendiary. And although Jackson would not go to the courts for a ruling on abolitionist tracts and would not concede the right of the Supreme Court to have the last word on interpreting the Constitution, still that did not mean that Old Hickory was an enemy of the judiciary. He always recognized the right of the courts to settle any number of constitutional issues. Moreover, he would not sanction the demand of some Democrats to "reform" the lower courts by restricting their jurisdiction; nor would he allow the repeal of the Judiciary Act of 1789.[10] As to his failure to apply to the courts for a ruling on the abolitionist tracts, it must be remembered that application for judicial decision of political and private rights was not accepted procedure in the early nineteenth century.

In the final year of his presidency Jackson not only forced acceptance of two of his most important appointments to office and won passage of the reform Post Office Act, but he also completed his "experiment" in reforming the banking and currency system of the country. What brought the matter to a head was the existence of a mounting surplus. The lack of a national debt, the general prosperity of the country, and the strict economies practiced by the administration had produced an embarrassment of riches. At length the Democrats came up with a bill that attempted regulation of government deposits at the same time it called for the distribution of the surplus to the states in proportion to their representation in the House and Senate. The money, in excess of $5 million, would be distributed quarterly throughout 1837. Despite a number of reservations, Jackson signed the bill on June 23, 1836.

In another action to attack the problem of the speculative economic boom which had produced a flood of paper money around the country, Jackson decided to eliminate one of the leading causes of that speculation. The sale of land had reached fantastic proportions and hit a yearly total of $25 million by 1836. By the time Jackson decided to do something about it, the sales were running upward of $5 million a month.[11] He knew what to do but he also knew that Congress would strenuously object since he had in mind requiring gold and silver (specie) for payment in all land sales. So he waited until Congress adjourned and then issued his "Specie Circular" on July 11, 1836, forbidding the General Land Office from accepting paper for payment of public lands. It was another forceful (if underhanded) exercise of executive authority. It marked, said Senator Benton, "the foresight, the decision, and the invincible firmness of General Jackson."[12] It also showed a marked disregard for the will of the Congress. But Jackson felt justified. He knew that most congressmen were themselves deeply engaged in land speculation. They were not about to approve an order that would interfere with their own financial plundering.[13] So, motivated by the need to end the spiral of inflation, Jackson plunged ahead with his order and brought a jarring halt to the speculative land mania that had run out of control.

The Whigs erupted. The *National Intelligencer* denounced the circular "as a measure of the same arbitrary character as the removal of the public deposits in 1833, emanating from the imperious will of an irresponsible Magistrate, the execution of which will not only effectually cripple the deposit banks, but produce a derangement of all the business of the country."[14] Henry Clay faulted the circular as "a most ill-advised, illegal and pernicious measure"—just what a dictator might be expected to do. Frank Blair countered these attacks by declaring that only "the speculators and those who are the advocates of the *rag money* cry out against it."[15]

Jackson himself was supremely oblivious to the carping criticism and he turned his back on it by going home for a rest. He had not seen the Hermitage since the fire two years previously and he was anxious to inspect the completely renovated house.

He arrived at the Hermitage on the evening of August 4. He was totally exhausted from the long trip but when he saw his newly built mansion the weariness and exhaustion immediately slipped away. What he saw in the dim light was a beautiful and stately house rising majestically before him. It seemed to tower to an enormous height. A handsome portico supported by six fluted columns added a touch of elegance, but the double porch softened the look and made it appear like a comfortable plantation home. Two wings of a single story each, and projected forward a distance of ten feet, added approximately forty feet to the width of the original house. The left or west wing was the dining room, with a service pantry and a storage pantry behind it, and the right or east wing served as Jackson's study and library.[16]

The first floor of the house was divided by a large central hallway running the entire length of the building. At the far end of the hall a magnificent staircase swept upward in a flowing spiral to the second floor. The walls of the central hallway were covered with a wallpaper imported from Paris and, in four scenes, depicted the adventures of Telemachus on the island where Calypso lived while on journey in search of Ulysses. To the left of the hall were the front and back parlors separated by folding doors; to the right a passageway ran to an exit at the side of the house. Several bedrooms opened off the passageway. The General took the front bedroom; his son and daughter occupied the back bedroom, which had an adjoining nursery. Jackson's bedroom connected directly with his study next door. From this study Jackson had an exit built leading immediately to the front portico outside. The second floor was divided into four large guest rooms, one of which was reserved for the painter Ralph Earl.

Jackson enjoyed his brief sojourn at home. The house completely delighted him, and his neighbors and friends in Nashville provided a welcome-home reception on August 20. It was a great barbecue and dinner held in Nashville where the President circulated among his friends to shake hands and chat informally. A toast was given in his honor, after which Jackson responded with the following: "REPUBLICAN TENNESSEE:—Her motto, *'principles not men'*—She will never abandon her good old Jeffersonian Democratic Republican principles which she has so long maintained and practiced. . . ."[17]

In subsequent letters to friends Jackson repeated his reference to "good old jeffersonian Democratic republican principles," and claimed that they formed the basis of all his "reforms."[18] Historians generally have tended to deny that Jackson held any firm philosophy of government that guided his actions. They choose to believe that he was principally motivated by private animosities and deep-seated prejudices, by passion and pride. They do him a grave injustice. Actually Jackson not only subscribed to a definite philosophy of government but he imposed that philosophy on his party and because of it markedly hurried the democratizing process that had already begun.

To understand the thrust and direction of Jackson's political thinking it is necessary to remember the single, central event that shaped many of his ideas about government, to wit, the "stolen election" of 1825 when John Quincy Adams and Henry Clay entered a "corrupt bargain" and elevated Adams to the presidency in defiance of the popular will. To Jackson this was the ultimate corruption in a general Era of Corruption. It produced what became "the first principle" of Jacksonian Democracy, namely, *"the majority is to govern."*[19] This doctrine Jackson announced in his first message to Congress and he repeated it at every opportunity. The people govern, he said. Their will must be obeyed. Majority rule constitutes the only true meaning of liberty. All of which subverts the earlier notion of republicanism which did indeed provide for intermediate agencies to refine and alter the popular will when it was deemed necessary, such as occurred in 1825. The constant celebration of the people, therefore, was basic to Jacksonian Democracy. And it was this celebration throughout Jackson's administration that steadily advanced the march toward greater democracy in the United States.

At one point Jackson himself made a stab at defining Jacksonian Democracy and listed many of its identifying marks. If the "virtuous yeomanry of Tennessee," he wrote as he struggled with the definition, would simply ask political candidates a few basic questions, they could distinguish true Democrats from "Whiggs, nullies & blue light federalists"* by the answers they received. The people, Jackson continued, "ought to enquire of them, are you opposed to a national Bank—are you in favor of a strict construction of the federal and State constitution—are you in favor of rotation in office—do you subscribe to the republican rule that the people are the sovereign power, the officers their agents, and that upon all national or general subjects, as well as local, they have a right to instruct their agents & representatives, and they are bound to obey or resign—in short are they true republicans agreeable to the true Jeffersonian creed."[20]

Sovereign power resides with the people, declared Jackson, and that power applies to all national and local issues. Moreover, the people have a right to "instruct their agents & representatives" as to their will. It is not enough to say that once the people elect their representatives they have no further control of the governing process. For Jackson, they always retain control through the doctrine of instruction. He would take away from representatives the power or right to "correct" or alter or disregard the popular will.

Jackson would also deny the courts this power. But he made a distinction. He would allow the courts the right to review and interpret the *law* but he would not assign them ultimate authority in pronouncing "the true meaning of a doubtful clause of the Constitution" binding on all. The right to review and interpret the law may be "endured," he argued, "because it is subject to the control of the majority of the people." But pronouncing the true meaning of the Constitution was altogether objectionable because "it claims the right to bind" the states and the people with bonds that no one can loose except by amending the Constitution, a difficult process at best. To allow the Supreme Court the ultimate authority to interpret the Constitution perpetuates an aristocratic rather than a democratic system of government because four persons (five today) can dictate to a nation, with or without popular consent. And that

*Blue light Federalists supposedly signaled to the British fleet off the New England coast with blue lights during the War of 1812 to indicate a safe haven.

was intolerable. In a truly democratic state, he argued, the people ulti-mately decide the question of constitutionality. And they do it through the ballot box.[21]

In addition to preaching majoritarian rule as the first principle of Jacksonian Democracy, Old Hickory cited strict construction of the Con-stitution as an essential article of faith. He genuinely believed in limited government and the necessity of keeping government spending to an absolute minimum. He also included opposition to a national bank and rotation in office as part of his creed. Rotation in office was simply his way of stating that the operation of government must be open to all. No elitism. No official class. He himself did not always recruit from every social and economic class, but he insisted that democratizing the govern-ment be regarded as a cardinal doctrine of Jacksonianism.

Indeed, the General's views on holding office became even more demo-cratic as he grew older. He proceeded from the premise that all of-fices—whether appointed or elected—must ultimately fall under the ab-solute control of the people. Appointed offices should be rotated, preferably every four years. Elected offices must be filled *directly* by the people. In keeping with this principle, Jackson tried to abolish the Col-lege of Electors in the selection of the chief executive by proposing a constitutional amendment. In addition, he said the President should serve no more than a single term of either four or six years. Jackson advocated a single term in order to place the President beyond the reach of improper—"corrupting"—influences. Moreover, he believed that United States senators should be directly elected by the people. Also, their term should be limited to four years and they should be subject to removal. In Jackson's mind, the Senate was an elitist body of men com-mitted to the principles of aristocracy and totally unrepresentative of the American people. His thoughts on democratizing the Senate were con-veyed to the electorate in the editorial columns of the *Globe.* "We say, then, to the People of the United States, is it not worthy of consideration to provide an amendment to the Constitution, limiting the senatorial term to four years and making the office elective by the People of the several States?"[22]

Interestingly, Jackson would also require federal judges to stand for election, and presumably he would include the justices of the Supreme Court once the Constitution had been properly amended. And he would limit judicial terms to seven years but permit reelection. The historian George Bancroft interviewed Jackson on the subject and recorded some of the President's opinions. "He thinks every officer should in his turn pass before the people, for their approval or rejection," wrote Bancroft. "In England the judges should have independence to protect the people against the crown," said Jackson. But not in America. "Here the judges should not be independent of the people, but be appointed for not more than seven years. The people would always re-elect the good judges."[23]

Jacksonian Democracy, then, stretches the concept of democracy about as far as it can go and still remain workable. Obviously, Jackson himself was far ahead of his time—and maybe further than this country can ever achieve.

It should be noticed in reading Jackson's attempt at defining his brand of democracy that he said nothing about slavery, Indian removal, tariffs, or internal improvements. Jacksonian Democracy as such never represented a defense of slavery. Slavery was not a matter for government concern. The right of an individual to his private property without interference by the federal government was basic to the whole concept of freedom during this age. For the government to legislate abolition would strike at the very foundation of American principles and institutions, according to the Jacksonians.

To a large extent, therefore, the President and his friends equated all things in terms of the emerging democracy. Whenever they saw what might be interpreted as a conspiracy against majority rule they instantly raised their voices in protest and alarm. And they accused the Whigs of blaming every evil in the country on the rise of democracy. Edwin Croswell, editor of the Albany *Argus,* the mouthpiece of Van Buren's political machine, the Albany Regency, explained their thinking to George Bancroft. "The Tory leaders labor to convey the impression that the modern tendency to violence & to the disregard of the law," he wrote, "arises from too great an infusion of the democratic spirit, & from the character & example of the Executive. . . . It is important . . . that the public mind . . . should be disabused on the subject; & that the excesses of the day sh'd be traced to their true source,—the revolutionary speeches, sundry harangues, threatened assassinations, and defiance & violation of law, by the Bank & its party leaders & agents, of the Tory school, in & out of Congress, during the memorable Panic season."[24]

What has been truly extraordinary about the phenomenon that historians dubbed Jacksonian Democracy has been its attraction for both liberals and conservatives of every succeeding generation. It still fascinates and attracts them. Jacksonian Democracy contains elements of both ends of the American political spectrum: liberalism and conservatism. This fact probably results from the efforts of the Jacksonians themselves to retain the best of republicanism and yet meet the challenges and consequences of a new, industrial society. As such it has inspired much of the dynamic and dramatic events of the nineteenth and twentieth centuries in American history—Populism, Progressivism, the New and Fair Deals, and the programs of the New Frontier and Great Society to mention the most obvious.[25]

Because Jackson himself explained and demonstrated his brand of democracy everywhere he went—from the White House levees, to the huge receptions that welcomed him from town to town, to the chance encounters with individuals that occurred from time to time—he contributed significantly to the ever growing acceptance of his principles and political faith. For example, it was during his trip back to Washington from his sojourn in Tennessee when one of these "chance encounters" took place. A young man by the name of John Stetson Barry had just reached Frostburg, Maryland, where the National Road began, on his way to Wheeling. He had heard that President Jackson was in the neighborhood and to his surprise, on arriving at Frostburg, he found the General's carriage at the door of the local tavern. Barry and the other members of his coach entered the tavern and discovered the President "quietly seated in a chair & smoking a Dutchman's pipe 'of goodly length.' " As soon as he saw the party enter the room, Jackson "arose, shook hands with us, politely enquiring concerning our health." Everyone was amazed. The Hero appeared so unremarkable, so ordinary, so matter of fact. He just seemed like an "old gentleman," dressed plainly, greeting everyone courteously, and going about his business with no pretension or suggestion of self-importance. And he was the President of the United States!

Just at that moment a drunken Irishman staggered up to the President and demanded to be introduced. His conversation, recounted Barry in his diary, "excited no little laughter."

"Gineral, how old are ye?" demanded Paddy after the introductions had been completed.

Jackson showed no sign of offense or amusement. He answered as though the question was the most natural and proper in the world.

"If I live till the 18th of March next I shall be 70.*

"Gineral," Paddy persisted, "folks say you are a plaguy proud fellow, but I do not see as you are."

The group snickered its amusement. But again Jackson responded in a very straightforward manner.

"It is like a great many other things folks say of me," he replied, "there is no truth in it."

Just at that moment came the announcement that the stagecoach was ready to start and the group reluctantly departed, "leaving the paddy & the Gineral to their confab." But the idea of the President of the United States and a drunken laborer sitting in a public place and conversing informally struck the entire group as a sign of the uniqueness of American life and institutions, "a striking picture of *democracy.*" There could be no doubt that, in some remarkable and marvelous way, the average American, the "common man," had been admitted into the mainstream of the nation's political life.[26]

*Barry must have heard wrong. Jackson would be seventy on March 15, not the eighteenth.

CHAPTER 26

—————⟨======⟩—————

Texas

ONE OF ANDREW JACKSON'S MORE NOTABLE, and deeply felt, failures as President was his inability to bring Texas into the Union. He had long coveted Texas as an essential component of his dream of empire. He took the position that it was part of the Louisiana Territory and therefore had been legitimately acquired through purchase by the United States in 1803. The conclusion of the Transcontinental Treaty with Spain in 1819, which relinquished Texas in exchange for other territorial considerations, was something Jackson deplored and denounced. He blamed the loss of Texas on John Quincy Adams, the secretary of state in 1819, for having negotiated this "dismemberment" of the American empire.[1]

Once Mexico gained its independence from Spain (and Texas was recognized as part of Mexico) there were several attempts by the United States to acquire Texas—to "reannex" it, as Jackson said. Each effort failed for one reason or another, mostly Mexican unwillingness to part with the territory and American incompetence in negotiating the problem. Meanwhile Americans in increasing numbers—and with Mexican encouragement and approval—crossed the border and took up residence in Texas. For the next several years relations between the two countries deteriorated rapidly. The cupidity of the United States was blatant. Worse, the ministers sent as representatives of the United States lacked finesse, patience, understanding, or appreciation of Mexican character and national sense of honor. Undoubtedly, the worst one was Jackson's own appointee, Colonel Anthony Butler, a South Carolina–born Mississippian. The President nominated Butler on Van Buren's recommendation (Van Buren was responsible for a number of Jackson's maladroit appointments) and his own desire to select a minister who had firsthand knowledge of Texas.

Jackson's paramount objective with respect to Texas—indeed, his only objective—was its acquisition. He authorized Butler to offer $5 million for the territory and his minister tried one bribe or trick after another to wheedle, cajole, or entice the Mexicans into surrendering the province.

309

Nothing worked. All the while Mexican officials fumed over American arrogance and presumption. The Jackson administration was accused of fostering American emigration to Texas for the purpose of seizing it.

Perhaps it was always impossible to settle the Texas question amicably since Mexico objected so strenuously to dismemberment. Perhaps no one possessed the skill to bring about the acquisition of this valuable land. But certainly the Jackson administration botched the diplomacy necessary for any settlement, and the President himself deserves the blame. He should never have appointed Butler in the first place; then he should have replaced him early on, especially when he realized that his minister was a scoundrel who would stoop to any corrupt scheme to acquire Texas. Jackson's fumbling only increased Mexican suspicion and hostility. The Mexicans felt certain that the United States was encouraging filibustering expeditions in Texas, violating her own neutrality laws, and arming men to stir up revolution. It was a sorry diplomatic record and stands in marked contrast to the many diplomatic triumphs the Jackson administration achieved in Europe.

Jackson's mismanagement also discouraged the Texans. As his inability to purchase the province became clear, as the intention of the Mexican government to centralize control over all parts of the Republic also became obvious, thus diminishing Texan home rule, and as the grievances of the Texans elicited indifference and contempt by Mexican officials, a war party quickly emerged in Texas that won the active support of many Americans. The consequence was immediate. A war for independence flashed into the open in October 1835 and then reached a climax when the president of the Mexican Republic, General Antonio de Santa Anna, marched into Texas at the head of a 6,000-man army. Texas' independence was proclaimed on March 2, 1836. General Sam Houston assumed command of the Texan army and defeated Santa Anna at the Battle of San Jacinto on April 21, 1836. Santa Anna himself was captured and forced to sign a treaty (which was later repudiated) recognizing the independence of Texas.

The United States maintained an official position of neutrality during the hostilities in accordance with the Neutrality Act of 1818 but it was violated repeatedly, most notably when General Edmund Pendleton Gaines, commanding troops on the border, crossed the Sabine River in June 1836 and occupied Nacogdoches. The Mexican minister to the United States, Manuel Eduardo de Gorostiza, vociferously protested the invasion and demanded his passports. Relations between the two countries rapidly deteriorated. It reached a low point of sorts on June 28, 1836, when the secretary of the navy, Mahlon Dickerson, at a regular cabinet meeting, reported that he had received a message from Commodore Dallas describing the "indignities" which the American consul and residents at Tampico had suffered at the hands of the Mexican authorities. Moreover, these same authorities refused to permit American armed vessels in the vicinity to receive water or allow their officers to go ashore. Also, they threatened to put to death all Americans at Tampico in retaliation for the capture of Santa Anna by the Texans at San Jacinto.

The moment Dickerson finished his report the President "broke out in his most impassioned manner."

"Write immediately to Commodore Dallas," he barked, "& order him to *blockade* the harbour of Tampico, & to suffer nothing to enter till they allow him to land and obtain his supplies of water & communicate with the Consul, & if they touch the hair of the head of one of our citizens, tell him *to batter down & destroy their town & exterminate the inhabitants from the face of the earth!*"

The cabinet members sat looking at each other in a near state of shock. No one spoke.

Jackson turned to John Forsyth, the secretary of state. "Have you rec^d any information on this subject?"

Forsyth responded negatively.

"Then let the Secy of the Navy furnish you the papers," the President ordered, "& do you write immediately to Mr. Gorstiza informing him of the orders we have given to Commodore Dallas, & that we shall not permit a jot or tittle of the treaty to be violated, or a citizen of the United States to be injured without taking immediate redress."[2]

Although this incident did not (happily) produce the extermination of the inhabitants of Tampico, United States–Mexican relations continued to slide dangerously toward a violent confrontation. What hastened the slide was the behavior of the Texans. They were doing everything possible to gain American recognition of their independence, leading, they hoped, to eventual annexation. But the possible annexation of Texas had begun to trouble Jackson on a number of grounds. His sympathy and desire, along with his great friendship with Sam Houston, were well known. Without authorizing a single action, he was nonetheless suspected of aiding and abetting the Texas revolutionaries. Then abolitionists accused him of plotting to snatch Texas in order to swell the size of the slavocracy. But that was absurd. Jackson's passion for Texas had nothing to do with slavery. He wanted Texas for reasons of national security and national pride. Yet, what would the rest of the world think if he actively intervened and moved to advance the cause of Texas' separation from Mexico? What would they say? The United States could be accused of committing a dishonorable and brutal act of aggression, and not even Jackson could gainsay that. When Stephen F. Austin wrote the President an impassioned plea for assistance, shortly after the victory at San Jacinto, Jackson endorsed the back of it with the words: "The writer does not reflect that we have a treaty with Mexico, and our national faith is pledged to support it. The Texians [he invariably spelled the word with an *i*] before they took the step to declare themselves Independent, which has aroused and united all mexico against them ought to have pondered well, it was a rash and premature act, our nutrality must be faithfully maintained. A.J."³

And there were other considerations. The efforts of the abolitionists to exploit the issue to exacerbate feelings between the north and south was one. Slavery would become a ploy to undermine the democracy and win the restoration of aristocratic rule. The impact of this sectional rivalry over the issue on the upcoming presidential election was another consideration. Van Buren's election must not be jeopardized. Under no circumstances must a Whig succeed to the presidency. The democracy itself would suffer a terrible reversal if Van Buren were defeated. Finally, Jackson convinced himself that any gesture on his part toward recognition of Texas or its acquisition would lead to war with Mexico. So he did nothing. He left the matter in the hands of the Congress.

Meanwhile Sam Houston decided to free Santa Anna and send him under escort to Washington where he could talk with Jackson and possibly bring a resolution to the problem of recognition. Santa Anna's release also provided the advantage of getting rid of an embarrassing presence. Once out of Texas, Santa Anna was expected to keep Mexico in turmoil for years.

General Santa Anna arrived in the American capital on January 17, 1837. As soon as it could be arranged he went to see General Jackson. The two men provided a marked contrast. Jackson, still recovering from a recent hemorrhage attack, looked wan and pale. Not exactly feeble—for on such occasions he mustered great presence to impress visitors with the dignity of his office—but from time to time he needed support and he rested at every opportunity. Still his face and general appearance exuded great strength. Here was a powerful personality trapped inside a broken and feeble frame. Santa Anna, on the other hand, looked rested and relaxed despite his long trip. He thoroughly enjoyed the notoriety that accompanied his arrival in the capital. Depicted in the press as a terrifying and brutal monster, he delighted in showing himself off as a gracious and cultivated man of impeccable manners and dress. Swarthy, stolid looking, with heavy features, he still managed to appear elegant. A strong chin, a mouth slightly drooping, and black hair plastered across his head made him appear the very personification of Mexican pride and bearing.

The two men shook hands when they met in the White House on Thursday, January 19, 1837. "General Andrew Jackson greeted me warmly," Santa Anna recorded, "and honored me at a dinner attended by notables of all countries."⁴ After the official greeting and reception, the two generals met again the following day and sat down for a long and "free conversation." It was very informal. Jackson was dressed in his old calico robe, smoking his long-stemmed pipe. They talked mainly about the possibility of a treaty between their two countries which would permit an extension of the boundary of the United States to include Texas.

"If Mexico will recognize the independence of Texas," President Jackson said to his guest, "we will indemnify your country with six million pesos."

Santa Anna's eyes grew bright. A slight smile crossed his face. But then he grew cautious.

"To the Mexican Congress solely," he replied, "belongs the right to decide that question."[5]

This was Santa Anna's brief version of the interview. Jackson provided a different version and his account was recorded in a memorandum shortly after the interview. Furthermore, it is supported by an unsolicited letter written by Frank Blair a few years later.[6] According to Jackson, the Mexican general proposed the cession of Texas for a "fair considera-tion." Jackson countered by outlining a proposal by which the United States might extend her border to include Texas and northern California, in effect to run "the line of the U.States to the Rio grand—up that stream to latitude 38 north & then to the pacific including north California." As compensation he would offer $3½ million dollars. "But before we prom-ise anything," Jackson continued, "Genl Santana must say that he will use his influence to suspend hostilities."[7]

Blair, who was present during the entire interview, could never forget the conversation between the two generals—nor the "lecture" Jackson apparently gave Santa Anna. "No man ever gave another a better lesson of patriotism and public virtue than Santa Anna received from you," Blair wrote. "Not only in words, but in the example he saw before him of simplicity, probity and power."[8]

What was so instructive about the exchange between these two unlikely protagonists was the continuing desire of Jackson for Texas but only under the most legitimate and acceptable circumstances. It was very important to Jackson that the rest of the world see any exchange of territory as an honorable and proper transaction.

And so the interview between Jackson and Santa Anna ended on a polite but indefinite note. When the Mexican's stay in Washington ended after a round of farewell receptions, President Jackson provided him with a warship to take him to Vera Cruz. Santa Anna had nothing but praise for his host, and Old Hickory apparently thought the Mexican a very likable gentleman.[9]

Over the next several weeks Jackson moved closer toward recognition of Texas' independence. The obvious and passionate desire of the Tex-ans to be annexed coupled with the mounting evidence of support for such expansion by the American people weighed heavily on Jackson's mind. During the second week of February 1837—just weeks before the end of his administration—Jackson met with William Wharton and Me-mucan Hunt, the minister and special representative of the Republic of Texas, and in the course of their discussion the President suddenly and unexpectedly burst out with an emotional announcement of his desire for the immediate recognition of Texas' independence. The two men leapt at him. Would he act on this, they asked, and send a message to Congress and urge recognition?[10]

Jackson drooped. He slumped into his seat. The passion dissipated. No, he said, it was really up to Congress to decide, not the President. The two Texans just stared at him. They saw an old man of seventy, sick and seemingly too tired to hear the distant din of battle. Fortunately for this dying administration, the Congress responded to the cries for annexation heard around the country, and probably to their own secret desires. On February 28, the House of Representatives passed a series of resolutions appropriating the funds necessary for formal recognition and directed that an agent be sent to Texas by the President. The following day, on March 1, the Senate, by a vote of 23 to 19, recommended to the President the formal recognition of Texas.[11] Recognition was obviously not acquisition, but it was a start.

On Friday, March 3, the day before his administration would end, Jackson summoned Wharton and Hunt to the White House. On their arrival he announced to them that he had "consummated" the recognition of the Senate and the diplomatic appropriation bill of the House by nominating Alcée La Branche of Louisiana to be *chargé d'affaires* to the Republic of Texas. This nomination had already gone to the Senate. With Congress only hours away from adjournment, the three men waited up to see if the nomination would be acted upon. Near midnight word came that the Senate had confirmed La Branche as *chargé*.

Jackson graciously asked his guests to join him in a glass of wine. The three men stood, smiled at each other, and raised their glasses in a toast.

"Texas!"[12]

CHAPTER 27

———————————⟩⟨———————————

Life in the White House

WHEN ANDREW JACKSON, AS THE SEVENTH PRESIDENT of the United States, first moved into the White House on March 10, 1829, the mansion looked far different than it did when he left it. He completely altered its outward appearance. First of all there was no north portico in 1829, and without it the pediment looked naked. Second, the general appearance of the House can only be described as shabby. The mansion did not always get the attention it required to maintain its stately air. Inside, the East Room had never been decorated or completed. It was a big unpainted space, used mainly to accommodate overflow crowds at social gatherings, and therefore added to the general unfinished appearance of the House. And the residence had few modern comforts. No running water, for example. Two water closets were serviced by rainwater from tin cisterns built in the attic. All other water came from two wells situated in the breezeways between the House and the east and west wings.[1]

Jackson's most immediate problem was the daily operation of the mansion and here he relied on the Donelsons for their assistance. Emily Donelson served as surrogate First Lady, and despite her youth she proved very efficient. The actual management of the White House, however, first fell to Antoine Michel Giusta and his wife who had worked for President John Quincy Adams and stayed on during Jackson's first administration. There were twenty-four servants working for Giusta, according to the census of 1830, which was a very large number for the time. By 1833 the hired staff was reduced for financial reasons and the balance made up with slaves. According to a list of the President's servants prepared around 1833 or 1834, the White House staff consisted of the following: a house steward and housekeeper, a butler, a doorkeeper, an "odd man," a cook, an assistant cook, two sculleries, a housemaid, a staff maid, two laundry maids, two messengers, a valet, a coachman, and a footman.[2] This list did not include gardeners, stablemen, porters, and the like. The full staff for the House and grounds probably ran as high as ten additional employees.

When the family first moved into the White House in 1829, Jackson took the southwest corner of the second floor for his bedroom and a room at the other end of the corridor for his office. Across the hall from his bedroom, on the northwest side, the Donelsons occupied a suite of rooms for themselves and their small family. Donelson also had a small office on the northeast corner almost opposite Jackson's office. Between Donelson's office and bedroom, Major Lewis and Ralph Earl had their bedrooms.

The "Circular Green Room" on the second floor was probably used by Emily to receive callers and as a room where the ladies would congregate after dinner to talk and have coffee. Next to this circular room, on the southeast side, was the "audience room" where Jackson received petitioners, guests, and other callers. The next room, today's Lincoln Room, served as Jackson's office, which was also used for cabinet meetings. Here the President kept his books and papers. Maps decorated the walls. A rubber-faced oilcloth covered the floor. The window had silk curtains crowned with gilded-eagle cornices which Jackson had purchased. (Old Hickory always did like a touch of majesty to his surroundings!) The last room, at the corner, was a narrow chamber and contained one of the two White House water closets.[3]

To separate the office area on the second floor from the family quarters, Jackson installed glass doors. Thus, when official callers came to see the President they used the staircase off the entrance hall while the family used the grand staircase at the west end of the transverse hall. The servants used the small stairwell off the porter's room.

Jackson changed the interior and exterior design of the White House almost from the first moment he arrived. Indeed, the exterior design of the House was completed by Jackson. Within weeks of moving in, he commenced building the north portico and it was brought to completion in September, 1829. The north portico considerably altered and vastly improved the overall appearance of the White House. It added character and distinction to the building. It clothed what looked naked and provided just the right touch of grandeur. The portico is in the Greek Revival style that was so popular at the time and which Jackson himself copied in rebuilding the Hermitage after the fire in 1834. This colossal colonnade, ironically, heralded the arrival of the new democratic age to America.

Of paramount importance was the introduction by Jackson of running water into the mansion. In the spring of 1833 an engineer named Robert Leckie was assigned the task of piping water in iron pipes from Franklin Square directly into the White House. The work went quickly and was completed by the middle of May. A very elementary system, it used pumps, reservoirs, and fountains. But it provided water at only two or possibly three places in the mansion: the basement corridor; the butler's pantry; and possibly the kitchen. A brass cock or hydrant capped each pipe. Very soon thereafter—late 1833 or early 1834—a "bathing room" was installed to take advantage of this running water. The room had a hot bath, a cold bath, and a shower bath, and was equipped with large copper boilers for heating the water. The location of this room is uncertain, but most probably it was placed in the basement, if not the east wing.[4]

Other improvements included the grading of the south grounds and the marking of garden paths which were topped with gravel. More important, the north front of the White House grounds was refenced. Jackson wanted the configuration of the driveway and the gates at the north front radically altered. He directed the building of a parapet wall and iron railings. And he insisted that the gates and piers be moved wider apart than they had been. When completed the fence ran the entire length of the north facade and it framed the White House with a lacy though "orderly" line of black rails. The main gate was widened and the driveway leading to the north portico was fixed in its present position and laid over with gravel and edged with footpaths.[5]

Jackson also built a hothouse, probably on the ruins of Latrobe's Treasury fireproof vault. The fireproof was a single-story rectangular building that had been attached to the Treasury building and originally intended to connect the White House with the Treasury. Remodeled by Jackson, the hothouse, or orangery, as it was usually called, contained a tall central section for large plants and was flanked by glass-roofed wings that stretched out on either side. By 1836 this orangery was in full use. It was demolished in 1859.[6]

Of the White House's interior design, Jackson's most radical change occurred in the East Room. This was an immense room (80 feet by 40, and a ceiling 22 feet high) that had not been decorated. Architecturally, it had been completed in 1818. It had a frieze running all around, but nothing else. The plaster on the walls was unpainted; and the mantels were all temporary. Because of the size of the room—eighty by forty feet—it handled overflow crowds from the entrance and transverse halls when the mansion was opened for presidential levees on New Year's Day and the Fourth of July. Jackson turned over the task of decorating the room to Major Lewis, and Lewis decided to make the East Room not only modern but splendidly Jacksonian.[7]

Lewis demanded an air of thundering grandeur for the East Room, something he believed appropriate to the Hero of New Orleans. That meant gilt everywhere—and sumptuous color. There was a huge arched doorway leading into the room. Lewis wanted it decorated so that it literally became an "arch of triumph" through which President Jackson might enter ceremoniously from the hall to greet his adoring public. The mise-en-scène became a grand setting for the Old Hero. Indeed, as finally decorated, it was a magnificent and opulent room. The great arch was no longer an archway. It now blazed with gilded sun rays and twenty-four

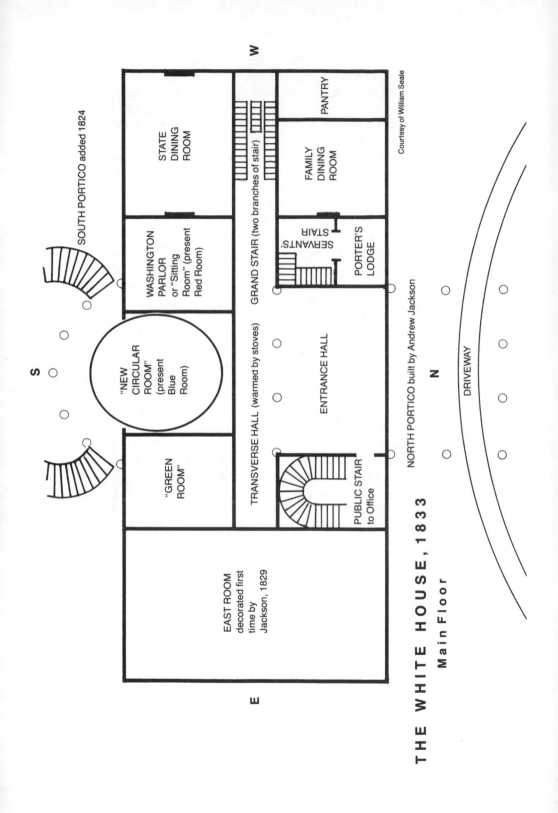

THE WHITE HOUSE, 1833
Main Floor

SOUTH PORTICO added 1824

STATE DINING ROOM

WASHINGTON PARLOR or "Sitting Room" (present Red Room)

"NEW CIRCULAR ROOM" (present Blue Room)

"GREEN ROOM"

EAST ROOM decorated first time by Jackson, 1829

GRAND STAIR (two branches of stair)

PANTRY

FAMILY DINING ROOM

SERVANTS' STAIR

PORTER'S LODGE

TRANSVERSE HALL (warmed by stoves)

ENTRANCE HALL

PUBLIC STAIR to Office

NORTH PORTICO built by Andrew Jackson

DRIVEWAY

Courtesy of William Seale

S

E

W

N

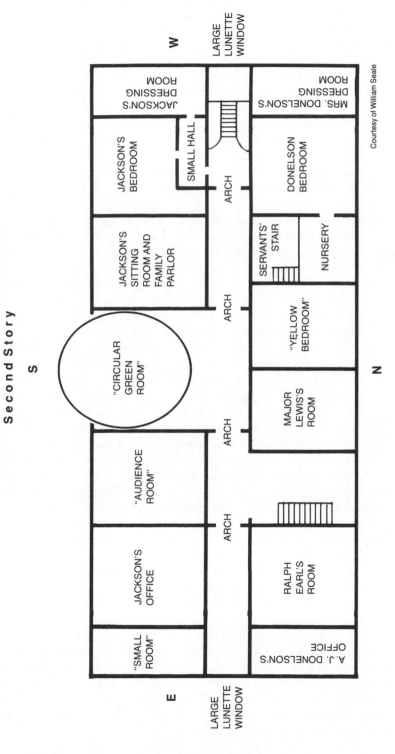

THE WHITE HOUSE, 1833
Second Story

S

W

N

E

LARGE LUNETTE WINDOW

LARGE LUNETTE WINDOW

JACKSON'S DRESSING ROOM

MRS. DONELSON'S DRESSING ROOM

JACKSON'S BEDROOM

SMALL HALL

DONELSON BEDROOM

ARCH

JACKSON'S SITTING ROOM AND FAMILY PARLOR

SERVANTS' STAIR

NURSERY

ARCH

"CIRCULAR GREEN ROOM"

"YELLOW BEDROOM"

"AUDIENCE ROOM"

MAJOR LEWIS'S ROOM

ARCH

ARCH

JACKSON'S OFFICE

RALPH EARL'S ROOM

"SMALL ROOM"

A. J. DONELSON'S OFFICE

Courtesy of William Seale

golden stars emblematic of the states. It seemed to some like the portal for a temple through which only a deity might pass.[8]

The room itself contained four fireplaces with mantels faced with "Egyptian" black marble. Three enormous sunflowers in plaster of paris were affixed to the ceiling and from them hung three immense chandeliers of gilded brass and cut glass. Each chandelier held eighteen oil burners and fonts with glass shades. On the walls were attached rows of matching sconces of "Bracket Lights" holding five oil lamps each, and heavily gilded globe and astral lamps were placed at every darkened and convenient spot around the room. A lemon-colored wallpaper provided a bright background and it was trimmed with cloth borders of blue velvet.[9]

A relatively new convenience appeared in the Jacksonian age which Lewis took immediate advantage of in decorating the East Room, namely, the furniture warehouse. Heretofore, for household furnishings, it had been necessary to shop at many places and frequently to have the artisans come to the White House and set up shop to provide all the necessary furnishings for any of the rooms. Now, thanks to "modern business methods," Lewis furnished the East Room by making one stop at the Philadelphia warehouse of Louis Veron, who stocked practically everything needed to decorate a house: lamps, tables, chairs, beds, sofas, curtains, stoves, carpets, washbowls, kitchen appliances, and so forth. A principal virtue in shopping at the warehouse was the amount of money that could be saved, for Jackson had made a great issue during his election campaign about the extravagances of the White House.

To commence the decorating, Lewis purchased from Veron a series of wide and high French plate mirrors in gilded frames and these were hung from the four walls of the East Room. Each was positioned directly opposite another, and the reflections carried the eye to an infinite distance. This effect was extremely popular in America throughout the nineteenth century. At the windows, silks of bright yellow and imperial blue were arranged in "luxuriant Grecian drapery," hanging from cornices topped by gilded eagles. The cornices themselves were decorated with a line of golden stars.

What furniture remained in the East Room from the days of James Monroe and John Quincy Adams was reupholstered or replaced with new furniture from the Veron warehouse. A mahogany table with black marble top was positioned under each chandelier. Lamps with glass globes, all held high by classical female figures, rested on the tables. Along the walls, pier tables were located which helped divide the lines of chairs and sofas scattered around the room. A 500-yard Brussels carpet in blue and yellow decorated the floor. This carpet alone cost $1,058.25. On crowded occasions, three "Imperial rugs" were laid to take the wear and tear of the mob. In deference to masculine need, twenty spittoons were strategically positioned around the room.

At night, with all the lamps lighted, the East Room dazzled the eye. The sheen of the curtains, the black marble against a yellow wallpaper, the many surfaces of gilt metal, and the explosion of sunbursts around the room combined into a handsome setting for the majestic presence of General Andrew Jackson. The martial boldness of the blues and yellows never appeared tawdry or overpowering. The light never glared. It shimmered in the watery glass of the chandeliers.[10] As certain White House rooms today represent particular Presidents—the Lincoln bedroom, for example—the East Room in the nineteenth century belonged to Andrew Jackson. Unfortunately, it is all gone, destroyed by a wrecking crew in 1950 when the interior of the mansion was completely rebuilt.

Submitted on November 25, 1829, the initial bill for the East Room furnishings, now preserved in the White House archives, came to $9,358.27. But Jackson also purchased mirrors, extra-cut lamp glasses, and other furniture for other rooms, particularly the Green Room and state dining room, and a $1,200 oilcloth for the transverse hall on the ground floor. He repapered his own bedroom, the public dining room, the private dining room, the sitting room, the Green Room, and the New Circular Room. He also bought a piano for $300.

In addition to the East Room furnishings, Jackson purchased a considerable amount of silver service, china, and cut glass. He also imported French porcelains and fine silks. The French sterling silver plate cost $4,308.82 and consisted of 36 spoons, 36 forks, 36 knives, 4 sweet-meat spoons, 2 sugar spoons, 48 tea and coffee spoons, 8 small spoons, and 2 mustard spoons. The service included 2 soup tureens, 4 vegetable dishes, 2 sauce boats and plates, 8 large and 12 small round plates and 6 oval plates, 2 baskets, 18 bottle stands, 12 skewers, 1 large and 1 small coffeepot, 1 cream jug, 1 fish knife, 8 double salts and 2 mustard stands, 36 tablespoons, 60 table knives with silver handles, 36 dessert knives with silver handles and blades, another 36 knives with silver handles and steel blades, 3 large carving knives and forks, 11 silver ladles, and 2 trunks to contain the whole. "Ordinary" kitchen utensils numbered between ten and fifteen dozen.

Jackson also purchased a 440-piece dinner set of French china, "made to order, with the American eagle." It cost $1,500 and included 32 round and 32 oval dishes, 6 dozen soup plates, 20 dozen flat plates, 4 long fish dishes, 12 vegetable dishes with covers, 8 sugar covers and plates, 6 pickle shells, 6 olive boats, and 4 octagonal salad bowls. In addition, the President bought a 412-piece dessert set for $1,000 which was made to order and designed in "blue and gold with eagle." Between the furniture, silver, china, cut glass, silks, and porcelains, Jackson spent approximately $45,000. For someone who constantly preached economy and retrenchment in government, he hardly practiced it himself when purchasing for the White House.

To some extent the amount of china and silver service purchased was necessitated by the size and number of Jackson's dinners and levees. The levees grew enormously during his administration because everyone in the city, especially visitors, wanted to see him and clasp his hand. Mobs crowded into the House whenever the levees were announced. "Some thousands had arrived there before us," reported one man, "of all ages and sexes and shades and colors and tongues and languages. There met the loud and whiskered representative of kingly legitimacy, with the plumed and painted untamed native of the western forest. The contrast was interesting and amusing." The company at Jackson's levees reminded one man of "Noah's ark—all sorts of animals, clean and unclean." Even the "rag-a-muffins of the city" gained entrance by climbing through the windows of the East Room.

In the midst of the mob, "tall and stately," stood the commanding figure of the venerable President. The guests approached him, took him by the hand, either bowed or curtsied, and spoke a greeting. Then they moved on to give place to others "to participate in the same privileges." Among the "dense mass of gazing and wondering spectators" were diplomats in their gold coats, officers in uniform, ladies in the latest finery, laborers, "rag-a-muffins," clerks, shopkeepers, and Indians "in war-dress and paint" with "plums" stuck in their hair. "Bonnets, feathers, uniforms and all, it was rather a gay assemblage," said one reporter.[11]

One of the most magnificent of these levees involved the celebrated "Jackson cheese." The idea of presenting President Jackson with a mammoth cheese originated with Colonel Thomas S. Meacham of Sandy Creek, Oswego County, New York, in the fall of 1835. He began on a modest scale—only a 500-pound cheddar—but the result looked too skimpy when he finished so he decided to increase its size. When he had finished, the monster weighed 1,400 pounds. It was four feet in diameter and two feet thick. The cheese was encircled by a "national belt," representing all the states, and on it were inscribed the words "Our Union, it must be preserved." A team of twenty-four gray horses drew the flag-draped wagon which bore the behemoth and carried it on the triumphant journey to Washington, where it was formally presented to President Jackson. Apparently, the President kept it in the vestibule of the White House where it was cured for nearly *two* years! Visitors must have gotten quite a start when they entered the mansion. Then, to get rid of it, Jackson directed that an invitation in the form of a public notice in the *Globe* be extended to all citizens to come to the White House between 1 and 3 p.m. on February 22—Washington's birthday—to sample the magnificent cheddar. It was one of the great levees of all time. The President, cabinet members, congressmen, diplomats, "the court, the fashion, the beauty of Washington," and, of course, "the People" (with a capital "P" as the *Globe* always wrote it) all attended. "All you heard was cheese; all you smelled was cheese." The carpets were slippery with cheese, pockets were filled with balls of the stuff, and the very air for half a mile around was permeated with the aroma of cheese. The mob demolished the cheddar within two hours and left only a few scraps to grace the presidential table.[12]

In addition to the levees, Jackson gave weekly dinners for department heads, congressmen, diplomats, and other distinguished guests. At first these dinners were rather ordinary, but once Jackson employed Joseph Boulanger, a Belgian chef, and once Emily Donelson, the First Lady, became more comfortable with her new role, the dinners became sumptuous. John R. Montgomery, a lawyer from Pennsylvania, recounted a formal dinner at the White House in 1834. The table, he said, "was very splendidly laid and illuminated." A large chandelier of thirty-two candles hung over the middle of it and all the piers and mantels glittered with numerous candles. "The first course was soup in the French style; then beef bouille, next wild turkey boned and dressed with brains; after that fish; then chicken cold and dressed white, interlaided with slices of tongue and garnished with dressed salad; then canvass back ducks and celery; afterwards partridges with sweet breads and last pheasants and old Virginia ham." For dessert, Montgomery reported jelly and small tarts in the Turkish style, blanche mode and kisses with dried fruits, preserves, ice cream and oranges and grapes. With the meal, sherry, port, Madeira, champagne, claret and Old Cherry were served. It was a gargantuan feast.[13]

Dinner guests invariably commented most favorably about the liquid refreshments served by the President. Indeed, Jackson began a true wine cellar at the White House. Racks for bottles and barrels were constructed along the walls of an area beneath the state dining room. This was the area that later became the map room where Franklin D. Roosevelt and Winston Churchill frequently met. The location was secured with heavy wooden bars during Old Hickory's tenure to keep out thieves. It stored hard liquor of many varieties, wine, and beer.

Obviously a touch of elegance—if not majesty—graced the presidential mansion during Jackson's residence. Still, he never forgot that the House belonged to the people and that he was their "steward."[14] To him this meant that anyone at virtually any hour could walk into the mansion to see the President and shake his hand. One foreign visitor was stunned to find no guard at the White House. A porter opened the front door when he knocked, a single servant ushered him into a large parlor, and Old Hickory interrupted what he was doing to greet the visitor and chat with him for a few minutes. "I need hardly say," wrote this particular foreigner, "that my reception seemed to me to be exactly what it ought to have been from the chief magistrate of such a republic, easy, unaffected, and unreserved, and at the same time not wanting in dignity."[15]

On one occasion, James Buchanan, just back from Russia, arranged to present a "Lady E from England" to the President. He attempted to engineer the meeting according to his experience with royalty. He called on Jackson an hour before the interview to give him a few pointers and found the President in old clothes, feet on his desk, enjoying his corncob pipe. Horrified, Buchanan reminded the General that his visitor was a woman of high rank and accustomed to all the "refinements" of good society.

Jackson favored Buchanan with one of his withering stares. "Jeemes Buchanan," he said, as he drew the pipe from his mouth, "when I went to school I read about a man that I was much interested in. He was a man who minded his own business and made a large fortune at it."

Buchanan withdrew as quickly as possible. He dreaded what would happen when "Lady E" arrived. A short time later he escorted the lady to the White House. "What was his surprise when Jackson descended to the coach in person, faultlessly arrayed, escorted the distinguished visitor to the House, and entertained her for an hour with such grace and courtesy that she declared she had never met a more elegant gentleman in all her travels."[16]

Both the high and the low approached the great democrat. Invariably, he was waylaid on his way to church. He attended the First Presbyterian church of Washington and rented pew no. 6, for which he paid $32.50 per annum.[17] His seat, noted one foreign traveler, was in "nowise distinguished from the others in the church. Nothing struck me more than seeing him mixing in the passage of the church with the rest of the congregation as a private individual, and conversing with such of them as he knew on going out, without the slightest official assumption." The President bowed to one and all, obviously "not an ungenteel man," wrote this commentator, "in manner and appearance."[18]

Naturally, the routine of the White House life centered on the President, but more particularly it centered on the condition of his health. If his health permitted he took daily horseback rides, and often he interrupted his daily schedule to take an afternoon walk accompanied by Ralph Earl. As his health declined over the years Jackson's excursions outside the White House became less frequent. At times he became a virtual recluse and often he spent an entire day in his bedroom or study to attend the demands of his office. He worked hard at being President. He was driven by an oppressive sense of duty. He rose early and went immediately to business. Even when ill he usually managed several hours of work. One of the President's secretaries, Nicholas Trist, remarked that Jackson exhibited an "utter defiance of bodily anguish. He would transact business with calmness and precision, when he was suffering the acutest pain, and when he was so pitiably feeble that signing his name threw him into a perspiration." Jackson performed his duties as chief executive with a degree of devotion and commitment that nearly consumed him. "He could not be kept from work," declared Trist in a fit of hyperbole. If too ill to "work with his hands, he wore himself out with thinking."[19]

In addition to the normal paperwork associated with his office, Jackson kept up a vast correspondence with officials, friends, family, politicians, and assorted citizens from all over the country. This effort required him to pen from ten to twenty letters every day. And sometimes these letters went on from four to eight to twelve pages of handwriting. The discipline required to write as much as he did was truly remarkable.

Each day the President saw many visitors, provided his health permitted. Some, like Blair, came daily to hear the presidential will. "From my daily habit of going to see you," Blair wrote him, "I am never easy till I pay a visit to your office."[20] The Kitchen Cabinet dropped in regularly. The "parlor" cabinet met the President every Tuesday, unless emergencies dictated more frequent meetings. Jackson also read a great deal: official documents for the most part, and correspondence. Like all good politicians, he read the newspapers, but few books. However, he did read from his wife's prayer book each day. Trist remembered going to the President's bedroom one night to get final instructions about the disposition of some letters and finding Jackson in his nightclothes but not yet in bed. The General was sitting at a little table with his wife's miniature before him, reading from Rachel's prayer book. The miniature was always worn "next to his heart, suspended round his neck by a strong, black cord," except in the evening when he removed it as he read his prayers. "The last thing he did every night, before lying down to rest," said Trist, "was to read in that book with that picture under his eyes."[21]

Life in the White House during Jackson's tenure more often than not revolved around the presence of many young children and babies. Jackson's grandchildren and the Donelson children formed the core to which were added other visiting youngsters from time to time. Parties were regularly given in their honor. An invitation to the little Woodburys, McLanes, Blairs, Macombs, Pleasantons, and others in the neighborhood summoned them to the White House to mark one occasion or another. One such invitation read:

> The children of President Jackson's family request you to join them on Christmas Day, at four o'clock P.M. in a frolic in the East Room.

> Washington, December 19

To this particular party a number of adults were also invited, including the Vice President; several foreign ministers; Mrs. James Madison, who brought along her grandniece, Addie Cutts; and Cora Livingston, the daughter of Edward Livingston. During the frolic such games as blind man's buff, puss-in-the-corner, and forfeits were played. Then, as a band struck up with the "President's March," the little guests marched into supper. Afterward, they had a snowball fight. The snowballs, made of cotton, were stacked on a table. A gilt gamecock, with head erect and wings outstretched, sat atop the mound. When the children had exhausted themselves they were lined up to take their leave. One by one they bowed or curtsied to the President. "Good night, General," they piped. The old soldier beamed. Dolley Madison, who stood by his side, exclaimed: "What a beautiful sight it is! It reminds me of the fairy procession in the 'Midsummer Night's Dream!' "[22]

Jackson also enjoyed entertainments. Apart from dinner parties and levees, most of the White House entertainments consisted of musicales. Celebrated artists, like visiting dignitaries, all came to see the Hero. Dancers, singers, actors, and painters sometimes mixed with heads of departments and diplomats at White House receptions. Jackson himself was not a man of the theater and rarely witnessed a stage performance. But touring companies invariably dropped by the White House to visit its distinguished occupant. And he treated them all with kindness, consideration, and respect. He was extremely paternalistic—to a fault. Whether they were children, women, artists, soldiers, friends, neighbors, family, or his country, Old Hickory assumed a personal responsibility for their safety and well-being. None complained. Indeed, it was part of his enduring appeal. Andrew Jackson was one of the few genuine heroes to grace the presidency. He was courageous and strong. And he was indomitable. The American people always believed that as long as General Andrew Jackson lived, the democracy was safe.

CHAPTER 28

———————<>———————

Farewell

O N SATURDAY EVENING, NOVEMBER 19, 1836, while working in his study on his last annual message to Congress, President Jackson was seized with a violent fit of coughing as the result of a bad cold. Then it happened. Suddenly he began hemorrhaging—and it was massive. Major Donelson was with him at the time and immediately summoned a physician. Following standard procedure, the doctor bled the President and then administered a preparation of salt. Miraculously, the hemorrhaging stopped. Virtually unconscious from the enormous loss of blood, Jackson was carried to his bed. Some of the servants began to wail that the end was near.

The next morning the President woke in great pain, particularly in his side where it was chronic. Then he started bleeding again, only not as profusely as the night before. When the doctor arrived, Jackson was "cupped and blistered" and for the remainder of the day he suffered excruciating pain. By evening, his condition was critical. So the doctor bled him again and drew "upwards of 60 ozs. blood." Which meant, Jackson later wrote, that "I lost in less than 48 hours, by the lancet and otherwise upwards of 70 ozs. of blood."[1]

By some incredible means, Jackson passed the crisis during the night of November 21. Later, the servants joked that he simply made up his mind to go on living and that was the end of it. Jackson himself had a different explanation. "A kind Providence, who holds our existence here in the hollow of his hand," decreed that he would survive. It was divine will.[2] But Jackson had come as close to death as that was possible and still pull through. For the next several days he just lay on his bed in a state of semi-consciousness. Once the doctor stopped bleeding him he began to regain his strength. But it was slow. For weeks he was very debilitated and listless. "Great care must be taken of him to prevent a return of the hemmoraghe," wrote Donelson, "and keep him free from cold, or it will be difficult for him to get thro the winter." But Jackson guarded himself well. He remained confined to his room for over two months. Between

327

the first seizure and the last day of his administration on March 4, 1837, Jackson left his bedroom and went downstairs a total of four times.[3]

Still, the final months of Jackson's term in office registered a definite upswing in his personal and political fortunes. First off, his health steadily, if slowly, improved. He returned to his duties, although he remained confined to his room. Then, he received the news he had been anticipating for months, namely, the election to the presidency of his friend and heir apparent, Martin Van Buren. Not until late November did it appear certain that the Little Magician had defeated the several Whig candidates running against him. Van Buren polled a total of 764,198 popular votes and 170 electoral votes representing 15 states. The combined Whig popular vote reached 736,147 with William Henry Harrison of Ohio taking 73 electoral votes, Hugh Lawson White of Tennessee receiving 26 electoral votes, and Daniel Webster 14 (Massachusetts) and Willie P. Mangum 11 (South Carolina).[4]

Unfortunately, the Democratic candidate for Vice President, Richard M. Johnson of Kentucky, did not receive a majority of electoral votes. Francis Granger of New York, William Smith, and John Tyler of Virginia took enough votes to send the election to the United States Senate where Johnson was subsequently elected on February 8, 1837, by a vote of 33 to 16.

Because of their many electoral successes around the country the Democrats in the Senate, led by Thomas Hart Benton, laid plans to bring about the passage of a resolution to "expunge" the censure of the President passed in 1834. Most Democrats agreed that the time had arrived to correct the record. "The people have called for it, in language not to be mistaken," wrote Chief Justice Roger B. Taney, "& justice demands that it should be done." Certainly, he said, it should be done before Jackson left the White House.[5]

So, on December 26, 1836, the third anniversary of the day on which Clay introduced the censure to the Senate, Benton offered the resolution to expunge it.

> *Resolved,* That the said resolve [of censure] be expunged from the journal; and, for that purpose, that the Secretary of the Senate, at such time as the Senate may appoint, shall bring the manuscript journal of the session 1833 '34 into the Senate, and, in the presence of the Senate, draw black lines round the said resolve, and write across the face thereof, in strong letters, the following words: "Expunged by order of the Senate, this ——— day of ———, in the year of our Lord 1837".[6]

The Whigs shouted their outrage. The great triumvirate—Clay, Calhoun, and Webster—each in turn spoke at length on the reasons for letting the censure stand. Calhoun reminded the senators that the Constitution requires that a journal be kept of their proceedings. How can it be kept, he said, if it is altered. "It does the very thing which the constitution declares shall not be done." Clay gave an emotionally charged address. "The decree has gone forth," he announced. "The deed is to be done—that foul deed which, like the blood-stained hands of the guilty Macbeth, all ocean's waters will never wash out." The censure is to be expunged on orders from the White House. "And when you have perpetrated it, go home to the people, and tell them what glorious honors you have achieved for our common country. Tell them that you have extinguished one of the brightest and purest lights that ever burnt at the altar of civil liberty. . . . Tell them that, henceforth, no matter what daring or outrageous act any President may perform, you have for ever hermetically sealed the mouth of the Senate. . . . And if the people do not pour out their indignation and imprecations, I have yet to learn the character of American freemen."[7]

Clay was good, and he knew it. It was a great misfortune that the country never received the full benefit of his magnificent talents. The presidency was forever denied him, and all on account of a "corrupt bargain" engineered to thwart the purpose and ambition of General Andrew Jackson.

Webster spoke last, but he was not as passionate as Clay or Calhoun, probably because he had suffered no personal griefs at the hands of Old Hickory. His protest, therefore, was brief and moderate, and he chose not to stand in the way of what he deemed inevitable.

Midnight approached. No one left the chamber, and it was packed. Tensions mounted. When Webster finished his remarks and sat down no one rose. There was a long silence. Finally, someone called the question. The presiding officer, King of Alabama, ordered a vote. Forty-three senators were present, five absent. In favor of Benton's resolution to expunge, 24; opposed, 19. Among those voting in favor were Benton, Buchanan, Grundy, Linn, Rives, Tallmadge, and Wright; those against, Calhoun, Clay, Crittenden, Webster, and Hugh Lawson White.

After the chair announced the results of the vote, Benton rose and asked that the order to expunge be executed. It was so ordered. And at that precise moment the Whigs walked out of the chamber to demonstrate their disapproval. Asbury Dickens, the secretary of the Senate, then took down the original manuscript journal of the Senate and opened it to the condemnatory sentence of March 28, 1834. As the secretary proceeded to draw a square of broad black lines around the censure and write the words of expunging, a storm of hisses and boos, groans and catcalls rose from the left wing of the circular gallery. They were right over the head of Senator Benton.

Benton sprang to his feet. "Bank ruffians! Bank ruffians!" he cried. "Seize them, sergeant-at-arms! . . . Let them be taken and brought to the bar of the Senate."

The ringleader was seized and that action intimidated the others. Once order was restored the process of expunging was performed in quiet. The secretary completed drawing the lines around the words of censure. Then across its face he wrote: "Expunged by order of the Senate, this 16th day of January, in the year of our Lord 1837."[8]

When the ceremony ended, Benton took the pen used by the secretary to expunge the journal and the next day sent his little son with it to Jackson. The old man was deeply touched. "I sincerely thank you for this precious *Pen,*" he wrote in return, "... and as this *pen* has been only used for this righteous act, so it shall be preserved with many other precious relics for further use, carefully kept by me during life, and shall by my last *will* and *testament* be bequeathed to you as its rightful heir—not only as its rightful heir, but as an evidence of my high regard, and exalted opinion of your talents, virtue and Patriotism."[9]

Jackson gave a "grand dinner" for the expungers and their wives shortly thereafter. He was still too weak from his recent illness to do more than greet these heroes and express his pleasure and gratitude over their action. Then he walked over to Benton, the "head-expunger," and led him to his own chair at the head of the table before withdrawing to his sickroom. The company celebrated for several hours.

And there were other bright moments in the waning days of Jackson's administration. On the morning of his last levee, a committee of citizens from New York presented him with a beautifully finished phaeton made from the timbers of the frigate *Constitution,* or, as it was more popularly called, "Old Ironsides." The General was delighted with this gift and accepted it with the "deepest sense of gratitude." The "live oak of 'Old Ironsides' of which it is composed," he said, will constantly remind me "of the glorious battles and the storms which that gallant vessel rode out in triumph. . . . As such I will take care that it will be preserved."[10]

But Jackson ended his presidency on a slightly discordant note by vetoing the attempt by Congress to rescind his Specie Circular, even though a majority of both houses were Democratic. The end of the session came on March 3, 1837, with everyone delighted to see it concluded. Brawling among themselves and frequently bickering with the chief executive, the senators and representatives walked away from their desks, which were still strewn with unfinished business and incomplete legislation.

Jackson's tenure also ended, but his record of achievement provided greater satisfaction. More than anything else, most commentators agreed that Andrew Jackson had created a new presidential style. To be sure, not everyone liked or admired his style, but they admitted its unique character. To his friends, the Jacksonian presidential style reflected and embodied the popular will, and this identification with the Democracy meant that the President could assume a more appropriate position in a modern society, namely, head of state and leader of the nation. Furthermore, to support the President in achieving his program and to help him implement his vision of the future, a party organization grounded in Jeffersonian republicanism had been established on a mass basis and committed to the doctrine that the people shall rule.

None of the previous Presidents acted upon, much less articulated, the notion that the President was elected by the people of the entire nation. Andrew Jackson established that contention. None previously claimed that the President was "more representative of the national will than the Congress." Old Hickory did. None argued superiority of a particular branch of the federal government. None tried to substitute his opinion for that of Congress, except where constitutionality was involved. Jackson did it regularly—or at least whenever he believed the public good required it. He is, therefore, the first modern President in American history, the first to conceive of himself as the head of a democracy.

There were many specifics to Jackson's accomplishments as President. He saved the Union and put down nullification. That above all was his crowning achievement. Almost as important was his unique success in paying off the national debt. As for "reform," Jackson did indeed— according to a recent study on the subject—provide the American people with one of the most honest and least corrupt administrations in the early history of this nation.[11]

Among his other accomplishments, Jackson also acquired an enormous territory from the Indians extending further than the combined states of Massachusetts, New Hampshire, Vermont, Connecticut, Rhode Island, New Jersey, and Delaware. Americans today may flinch at that achievement in view of the human suffering it involved among Indians, but Americans of the Jackson era recorded it with pride. More important, removal probably did in fact insure the survival of several southern tribes.

Jackson also hurled a corrupt national bank into oblivion, an action totally consistent with his democratic thinking and philosophy. Under Old Hickory a ten-year truce over the tariff was reached, and the sovereign status and national rights of the United States in foreign affairs improved during his tenure. Jackson's successful efforts at expanding American markets abroad through these negotiated treaties was a significant factor in the economic boom of the 1830s.

But there were failures, too. Jackson's appointments were generally wretched, although many of them, it should be noted, were the recommendations of Van Buren. Still, they were Jackson's responsibilities. However extraordinary his success at reform, he nonetheless appointed Samuel Swartwout (over Van Buren's objection), who stole more money than all the felons in his predecessor's administration put together. Also, Jackson did not always exercise effective leadership of the Congress and the nation—for example, his failure to win passage of the Verplanck tariff bill, his failure to prevent the election of a Whig as Speaker in 1834, and his fumbling efforts in the Texas question. Moreover, Jackson's inability to provide a better banking system to replace the BUS, his simplistic ideas about specie, and his arbitrary intrusion into land speculation did not serve his country well. And, most important of all, his ruthless determination to expel the Indians from their land blinded him to the infinite pain he inflicted upon a helpless people.

On balance, though, Andrew Jackson served the American people extremely well. He preserved the Union, strengthened the presidency, and advanced democracy. The people prospered, and they enjoyed peace and the respect of the entire world.

Jackson himself was not only conscious of his record as President and concerned about the ultimate judgment of history, but he wanted to explain to the American people, as his last official act as their representative, what he had been about during his eight years in office, and the principles that guided his actions. Like President George Washington, he proposed to issue a Farewell Address and had enlisted Chief Justice Taney in its composition. He wanted to emphasize "our *glorious Union*" and warn the nation that "ambitious and factious spirits," like the nullifiers and abolitionists, were ever ready to dissolve it and produce anarchy for their own selfish ends. Most particularly, he worried about sectionalism. Weak men, Jackson contended, will persuade themselves that their efforts at disruption are undertaken "in the cause of humanity and . . . the rights of the human race." But let them not be deceived, he wrote. "Everyone, upon sober reflection, will see that nothing but mischief can come from these improper assaults upon the feelings and rights of others."[12]

In writing this address, as long as Jackson and Taney kept to higher principles about the Union and the limits of federal power—two themes they developed at length—the address spoke nobly and interestingly. But, unfortunately, they chose to discuss the taxing power and finances and once those topics had been broached the discussion wandered off into paper currency, banks, monopolies, exclusive privileges and the like, about which the President had nothing particularly novel or worthwhile to say for this special occasion. Still, at one point, Jackson did manage to articulate his understanding of the meaning of the democracy that bore his name. And he tried to speak directly to the American people. The sovereignty of the country rests with you, he reminded them. "To you everyone placed in authority is ultimately responsible. It is always in your power to see that the wishes of the people are carried into faithful execution, and their will, when once made known, must sooner or later be obeyed." As long as the people remain "uncorrupted and incorruptible," as long as they remain watchful and jealous of their rights, the nation is safe, the government secure, "and the cause of freedom will continue to triumph over all its enemies."[13]

Here, then, was Jacksonian Democracy simply defined, here Jackson's legacy to the nation: the people are sovereign, their will is absolute; liberty survives only when defended by the virtuous.

He then went on in the address to discuss foreign affairs and insisted that preparedness was essential to an effective foreign policy. He tagged the navy as the country's first line of defense because of the nation's long Atlantic coastline.

Then he closed. The progress of the United States, Jackson said, had surpassed the most sanguine hopes of the Founding Fathers. The nation was prosperous, numerous, gaining in knowledge and all the useful arts, and had no longer any cause to fear danger from abroad. Its strength and power were well known throughout the civilized world.

> You have the highest of human trusts committed to your care. Providence has showered on this favored land blessings without number, and has chosen you as the guardians of freedom, to preserve it for the benefit of the human race. May He who holds in His hands the destinies of nations make you worthy of the favors He has bestowed and enable you, with pure hearts and pure hands and sleepless vigilance, to guard and defend to the end of time the great charge He has committed to your keeping. My own race is nearly run. . . . I thank God that my life has been spent in a land of liberty and that He has given me a heart to love my country with the affection of a son. And filled with gratitude for your constant and unwavering kindness, I bid you a last and affectionate farewell.[14]

It was a moving and fitting close, not only to this address but to an exciting, frequently turbulent, but always fascinating administration. Jackson signed the final page of the manuscript of this Farewell Address and sent it off to be printed and then forwarded to Congress and the press. He genuinely liked what Taney had written and hoped it might find a place alongside George Washington's Farewell Address as an inspiration for the American people. A few minutes after signing the document some friends came to visit and they drank some wine together. After a while Jackson set down his glass, lighted his long-stem pipe, took several puffs, and turned to watch the face of a tall, old-fashioned clock that stood in one corner. It was five minutes to midnight. Slowly, the minute hand moved toward twelve o'clock. Suddenly, the sharp, clear bell of the clock struck the hour. At that moment, Jackson turned to his friends and said: "Gentlemen, I am no longer President of the United States, but as good a citizen as any of you."[15]

After his company left him, the old man took down Rachel's Bible and read for a while. When his head began to ache he put the book aside and climbed into bed. The White House was dark and quiet. For all intents and purposes the presidency of Andrew Jackson was over.

The next morning, March 4, 1837, Inauguration Day, proved to be a bright and sparkling day. At noon the newly acquired phaeton stood gleaming in the sun at the entrance of the White House. Within moments the Old Hero descended from his bedroom, saluted the President-elect,

Martin Van Buren, who was waiting for him in the foyer, and together the two men took their places in the carriage and were driven to the Capitol for the swearing-in ceremonies.

An adoring crowd jammed the square on the east front of the Capitol and as the two men mounted the stairs of the portico "cheers of unanimous greeting rose from the surrounding people." Chief Justice Taney administered the oath, and Jackson had the "exquisite" pleasure of "witnessing the glorious scene of Mr Van Buren, once rejected by the Senate, sworn into office, by chief Justice Taney, also being rejected by the factious Senate."[16] When the ceremonies ended Old Hickory began to descend the steps and head for the phaeton waiting below. About halfway down he halted, possibly to steady himself. As he did so, the crowd exploded in a volley of "acclamations and cheers bursting from the heart and filling the air." They could no longer restrain themselves. It was, said Senator Benton, "the affection, gratitude, and admiration of the living age, saluting for the last time a great man."[17]

Jackson bowed once again. Uncovered, and with a look of "unaffected humility and thankfulness," he gestured in mute signs his deep appreciation for this demonstration of love and veneration. Benton choked up. "I was looking down from a side window," he wrote, "and felt an emotion which had never passed through me before." I have seen many inaugurations, he went on, but they all struck me as pageants, "empty and soulless." This one was different. This was real. "A man and the people"; he laying down power; they acknowledging for "unborn generations" a collective vote of thanks for lifting the nation to a new level of freedom and democracy.[18]

Jackson's career constituted one long, passionate trajectory through American politics and the American psyche. He was a unique figure, pragmatic, determined, clever, resourceful, larger-than-life and extremely popular. He was a politician who understood and respected the tradition of the past but who also knew when to step outside that tradition and act on his own. As one historian his noted, Andrew Jackson was both a harbinger of change and a representative of tradition.[19]

Without doubt his stepping down from office had a beneficial effect on American political life. It helped restore a more normal situation in political behavior; it helped revive the two-party system. And nowhere was the revival more apparent than in the south, where one party had ruled unopposed for more than a decade. Jackson was too grand a figure for normal politics. He cut too wide a swath across the political landscape. In many places, he and he alone had been the issue. Now that he was retiring to the Hermitage, a more usual political operation could emerge. According to a recent historian, a new political era began in 1836, and a genuine two-party system between opposing political groups committed to differing ideologies and issues commenced.[20]

By the time Jackson stepped into the waiting phaeton to carry him back to the White House he was totally exhausted. But, for the rest of his life, he remembered with tears in his eyes the affection poured out to him by the people on the occasion of his permanent retirement from public life.

CHAPTER 29

———————◇———————

Retirement

NOT UNTIL TUESDAY, MARCH 7, was the former President rested enough to begin the long journey back to the Hermitage. He was now almost seventy years of age, quite infirm, and rarely out of intense pain. For the trip home he was accompanied by his immediate family, son Andrew and his wife and their children, Ralph Earl, the painter and constant companion, and Dr. Thomas Lawson, an army physician whom Van Buren asked to accompany the ex-President. After many handshakes all around the Old Hero departed the White House for the last time. Van Buren escorted him to his carriage and accompanied him to the railroad depot. It was decided that the General should ride the railroad "for the sake of ease and comfort . . . until he reaches his private carriage which awaits him where the railroad connects with the macadamized National road." Before they separated Van Buren was overheard to promise to visit Jackson at the Hermitage. The old man nodded and smiled. Then he shook hands with the President and boarded the train.[1]

In slow and easy stages the Hero paraded across the countryside and everywhere he appeared crowds formed to cheer him and express their affection and esteem. The size of the crowds grew each day as word passed along his route that he was coming. There were receptions, dinners, parades, public gatherings. Some of these demonstrations staggered the old warrior. At Wheeling, several thousand people congregated at the dock to salute him and wish him "happiness thro life and a happy immortality." It was "one of the most numerous assemblages of my fellow citizens I have ever witnessed on any occasion," wrote Jackson, "—more numerous . . . than that at Washington on the 4th of March."[2]

At Cincinnati, where the triumphant Hero arrived on Saturday, March 18, at 5 P.M., another huge mob assembled. They came to see "the greatest man of the age, ANDREW JACKSON. They are the democracy," reported the Cincinnati *Republican* on March 20, "assembling for the last time, perhaps, to look upon, and take by the hand, the brave defender and protector of his country."

" 'Well done thou good and faithful servant,' " said the Louisville *Advertiser* on March 21, "has been echoed and re-echoed, from the Potomac to the Mississippi."

When Jackson reached Nashville at noon on Friday, March 24, "a vast assemblage of neighbors and fellow citizens gave a splendid and cordial public reception." They refused to be outdone by the receptions accorded their favorite son in other places. But closer to home he was met by a delegation of old men and boys in which he was told that "the children of his old soldiers and friends welcomed him home, and were ready to serve under his banner." And with that, General Andrew Jackson broke down. His entire body shook and tears streamed down his creased cheeks. "I could have stood all but this," he stammered, "it is too much, too much!"[3]

When the ex-President had regained his composure he returned to his carriage and rode the short distance to the Hermitage. Home at last—and for good. He sighed and coughed and felt strangely exhilarated. "I reached home on the 25th instant," he wrote to Van Buren, "somewhat improved in strength, but with a very bad cough. . . . The approbation I have recd. from the people on my return on the close of my official life, has been very gratifying to me. I have been every where cheered by my numerous democratic republican friends, and many of the repenting Whigs with a hearty welcome. . . . This is truly the patriots reward, and a source of great gratification to me, and will be my solace to the grave."[4]

During Jackson's prolonged absence in Washington his plantation had been managed by his son, Andrew Jr. But it is probably more correct to say that his son mismanaged the farm. The young man had no head for business, and the more the father reprimanded and warned him the more the son committed monumental errors of judgment. Either Andrew was stupid or he just did not care. Probably both. At times it almost appeared as though he resented his father's efforts to teach him how to survive in the modern world and the skills necessary to run a plantation.

Jackson had badgered his son for years about his poor business sense and his indolent habits. Young Andrew never seemed to complain or answer back. He offered excuses and then went right back to his old habits. At times he drove his father to distraction. And the situation did not improve after Andrew married Sarah Yorke on November 24, 1831, and began rearing a family. If anything, the situation got worse. He was regularly fleeced by greedy entrepreneurs who took advantage of his naiveté, and he had the dreadful habit of signing promissory notes for any friend who might ask his help. The General warned him repeatedly about his weaknesses. Hardly a year passed without a lecture.

> I have said before and now repeat—the world is not to be trusted. Many think you rich, and many you will find under false pretensions of friendship would involve you, if they can, strip you of your last shilling, and afterwards

laugh at your folly, and distress. Real charity always (when you have the means) relieve it, and providence will smile upon the act, provided it is done in the way pointed out by our saviour in his sermon on the mount which I beg you to read.[5]

But Andrew never learned, no matter how many times he was robbed. And he was one of those singular individuals who could smile through any adversity and reassure himself that the fault lay elsewhere. He was incompetent, lazy, weak, and unlucky. Worse, he developed a real drinking problem that got worse with the years. Apart from an occasional extramarital fling, he most enjoyed hunting. He wasted much of his life pursuing the sport and died prematurely in 1865 at the age of fifty-five when he accidentally shot himself in the hand while climbing a fence. He died of lockjaw.

The number of debts Andrew managed to accrue shocked and saddened his father, but the elder Jackson never repudiated or disavowed them. He always regarded them as responsibilities that he himself must pay if his son could not. It was a matter of family pride and honor. And by the time Jackson returned to the Hermitage in 1837 the problem of managing the plantation and the family's finances had been complicated by the onset of a grave national recession. A number of banks had failed by the time the ex-President began to study his plantation's accounts. Banks around the country were suspending specie payments. Runs on the banks in New York City alone had reached over $2 million.

The suspension of specie payments clearly signaled the start of a severe depression. If the Panic of 1837, as the dreadful debacle came to be called, had a point of origin it undoubtedly came on March 17, 1837, when one of the largest dealers in domestic exchanges, I. and L. Joseph of New York, went bankrupt. The immediate cause of this failure was the collapse of the New Orleans cotton market, and since the company had extensive dealings with banks, mercantile establishments, and commercial enterprises, the bankruptcy set off a chain reaction that dragged down hundreds of businesses. Foreign bankers and merchants liquidated their American holdings in an effort to escape involvement, but the economic collapse proved to be a worldwide phenomenon and everyone was eventually dragged into the maelstrom. For the next several months one bankruptcy followed another. The "happy and prosperous" country that Jackson had turned over to Van Buren seemed suddenly on the verge of total disaster.[6]

Angry critics, then and later, blamed it all on Andrew Jackson— specifically the excessive expansion of credit, currency, and marketable goods that occurred in the 1830s; the Bank War; the Deposit Act that encouraged states to a renewed program of improvements, especially in transportation; and the Specie Circular. But Jackson ascribed the panic conditions (especially the suspension of specie payments) to the greed of

wealthy capitalists, who had fattened themselves so rapidly during the last several years that they were now called "millionaires," a new term recently added to the American lexicon. The suspension of specie payments, argued Jackson, worked to the economic advantage of these millionaires. Paper gratified their gluttony, so they banished specie.

The Deposit Act of 1836 prohibited the government from depositing its funds in any bank that suspended specie payment, so when the banks suspended in the spring of 1837 the secretary of the Treasury was obliged by law to stop all payments of government money to these banks. This meant, in effect, that the Treasury became its own depository. Clearly, this situation could not continue and Van Buren finally decided to call a special session of Congress in September to address the crisis. Only three times previously had the Congress been summoned into special session, and all three had involved wartime emergencies. Jackson himself suggested divorcing the government from the banks. The thought was not original with him but had been proposed by several congressmen in the past and was finally adopted by the administration in what was called the Independent Treasury System. This system proposed to place government funds in repositories in Washington, New York, Boston, Philadelphia, Baltimore, and other cities, to be withdrawn as needed. Private banks would no longer have access to government money. The bond between government and banks would be forever severed.

Fortunately, the depression did not hit the agricultural areas of the country as hard as it did the commercial. Cotton, for example, still commanded a world market, and Jackson managed to grow enough of it during his first year home to get him through a very difficult time. Only his fragile health slowed him down, but it took a severe attack to immobilize him. One such occurred early in January 1838. For two nights and days, he reported on January 16, "I never closed my eyes, part of which my head was much affected, with occasional delirium." A month later he suffered another "hemorrhage equal to that I experienced at the City [Washington] in November, 1836." At one point he himself "despaired of surviving."[7]

For the first six months of 1838 Jackson hemorrhaged regularly and he endured debilitating headaches and a constant pain in his side. Sometimes a threatened hemorrhage was averted by "the application of the lancet and Cathartics"; most times they took their natural course and after the hemorrhage subsided he was freely bled. "I have a great difficulty of breathing," he told Blair in mid-summer, "and has lost by the lancet and cupping a great deal of blood within the last week." Surely he was a living phenomenon. He must have been to have survived such periodic and massive losses of blood.[8]

One happy event of 1838 occurred on July 15. It was a Sunday, and on that day General Andrew Jackson joined the Presbyterian Church. The act of joining had been in his mind for many years since both his wife and mother were members of the Presbyterian Church. Also, he had promised his wife to join but had postponed it because he felt that a public display of his religion would be regarded as hypocritical. He would be accused of joining the church *"for political effect."* So he put off this "public act" until he had retired "when no false imputations could be made that might be injurious to religion."[9]

He consulted the Reverend James Smith, who officiated at the Hermitage Church, which Jackson had built for Rachel in 1823, and admitted he felt more "identified" with the Presbyterian Church than with any other.[10] Smith discussed the matter with the Reverend Dr. John Todd Edgar, pastor of the First Presbyterian Church of Nashville, who apparently had been angling to get Jackson to join the church for some time. Then one Sunday during one of his many visits to the Hermitage Church, Edgar preached on the interposition of Providence in human affairs—a matter of irrefutable truth in Jackson's private canon—and seeing the old gentleman come alive to his words, Edgar began sketching the career of a "hypothetical" man who had escaped the hazards of the wilderness, war, the attack of Indians, the invasion of his country, the vicissitudes of political strife, and the determination of an assassin. How can such a man pass through all these scenes unharmed, said the clergyman, and not see the protecting hand of Providence in his deliverance?

Jackson stirred in his pew. When the service ended he was deep in thought. He brooded all the way home and spent the greater part of the day and evening in meditation and prayer. Part of the time he conversed with Sarah, his daughter-in-law, about joining the church and together they knelt and prayed.

Dr. Edgar visited him shortly thereafter. Jackson told him of his experience and how he had undergone what might be called a "conversion." Thereupon he asked to be admitted to the church along with his daughter-in-law.

Edgar questioned him about his conversion. Most of the answers met an approving nod of the head. Finally Edgar asked the most important question of all.

"General, there is one more question which it is my duty to ask you. Can you forgive all your enemies?"

The question came as a shock. For a moment the General stood silent. The two men stared at each other.

Jackson breathed deeply. His eyes glittered. "My political enemies," he said at last, "I can freely forgive; but as for those who abused me when I was serving my country in the field, and those who attacked me for serving my country—Doctor, that is a different case."

Edgar rejected the argument. There was no difference, he replied. Christians must forgive all. This was absolute. Without a general amnesty for all his enemies, Andrew Jackson could not join the church.

The stricken man sighed. There was a "considerable pause." Then

Jackson spoke again. Upon reflection, he began, he thought he could forgive all who had injured him, even those who reviled him for his services to his country on the battlefield. He was at long last prepared to grant amnesty to all the scoundrels and poltroons who had ever crossed his path.

Edgar smiled his approval. He left the room to inform Sarah. A moment later the woman rushed into the room and embraced the old man. There was a flood of tears and the two remained locked in each other's arms for many moments.[11]

All of which makes a pretty story. It is essentially Edgar's story, told many years later, and no doubt elaborately embroidered for special effect. Whatever the truth, on Sunday, July 15, 1838, the Hermitage Church was jammed with parishioners when the happy event occurred. Servants standing outside the church pressed their faces against the glass of the windows. The regular Sabbath services commenced, and at their conclusion General Andrew Jackson rose in his place to announce that he desired to join the church. He further declared his belief in its doctrines, and he resolved to obey its precepts. Also requesting admission were his daughter-in-law and a "beloved niece."[12] And so Andrew Jackson was formally admitted into the Presbyterian Church and received communion. "To see this aged veteran, whose head had stood erect in battle, and through scenes of fearful bearing, bending that head in humble and adoring reverence at the table of his divine Master, while tears of penitence and joy, trickled down his careworn cheeks, was indeed a spectacle of most intense moral interest."[13]

For the remainder of his life General Jackson conducted himself as a true believer. It was a faith more uniquely his own than anyone might recognize in the Presbyterian Church—he could never accept the notion of an "elect" chosen by God, for example, because it offended his democratic soul—but it would have been most uncharacteristic of him had he submitted totally to all the precise teachings of his church. Still he attended services regularly—as regularly as his health allowed—and he read a portion of the Bible each day, along with biblical commentaries and the hymn book. Before he died he read through "Scott's Bible" twice. Each night he read prayers in the presence of his family and servants, and sometimes he offered short homilies of his own.[14] A delightful if apocryphal story has it that after Andrew Jackson died one of his slaves was asked if he thought the General had gone to heaven. The man thought for a moment and replied, "If General Jackson wants to go to Heaven who's to stop him?"

CHAPTER 30

The Silver Jubilee

THROUGHOUT JACKSON'S RETIREMENT, LASTING nine years, he kept in active communication with his friends in Washington and tried on all important issues to intrude his presence and make his opinions known to the party and the nation. He offered his recommendations and advice to the President, members of the cabinet, congressmen, and Frank Blair, editor of the *Globe.* He took a keen interest in all events and at times provided a formidable voice when his passion for the safety of the Union was stirred. In moments of crisis he seemed to find renewed strength and vigor. He wrote to politicians in all sections of the country, urging their support of the Democratic program and warning of ills that would befall them all if the Whigs were brought to power.

But the American people surprised General Jackson by administering a crushing electoral defeat to the Democrats in the presidential election of 1840. Nearly two and a half million voters went to the polls, attracted by the excitement of the so-called Log Cabin campaign as well as their agitation over economic conditions. This electoral turnout jumped from 57.8 percent in 1836 to 80.2 percent in 1840. When all these votes were counted, the Whig candidate, William Henry Harrison, took 52.9 percent of them, or 1,275,612, while Van Buren captured 46.8 percent, or 1,130,-033. Harrison won 19 states for 234 electoral votes, and Van Buren took 7 states for a total of 60 votes.[1] What made the Democratic defeat so devastating was the length and breadth and depth of the Whig victory. Not only did the Whigs win states in every section of the country and win every large state except Virginia, but they also captured the Congress. Presumably the Whigs could now govern the nation and dismantle all of Jackson's reform programs.

The Hero was devastated. "Corruption, bribery and fraud has been extended over the whole Union," he wailed. "The democracy of the United States has been shamefully beaten," he told Van Buren, *"but I trust, not conquered."* Yet, as always, he reaffirmed his faith in the virtue of "the unbought people of this Union." The ultimate triumph of democracy, he said, depends on "the virtue of the great working class" who will resist being "ruled by the combined mony power of England and The Federalists of this Union." They will drive this "corrupt" pack back to "their native dunghills."[2]

Jackson's only really happy experience during 1840 was attending the twenty-fifth anniversary of the Battle of New Orleans on January 8. This "silver jubilee" meant a great deal to the old soldier and he later gave thanks that he had lived to see it happen. He really thought—and hoped—that the anniversary would rank with the Fourth of July as a national holiday, and he always noted whether suitable celebrations were conducted in Washington to acknowledge the importance of the event.

He set out for New Orleans with Major Donelson[3] on Christmas Eve and stopped off along the way at Vicksburg to accept the honors accorded him by the state of Mississippi. On the final leg of his voyage his ship was convoyed by four steamboats which were crowded with soldiers and a motley assortment of his fellow citizens. The convoy arrived at New Orleans with "cannons firing and colors streaming" on Wednesday morning, January 8. Thirty thousand spectators, according to one report, jammed the levee and the streets leading to it, and when the "gallant old chief" stepped foot upon the shore at 10 A.M., they exploded in a "chorus of enthusiastic cheers." All hats came flying off and were "waved vigorously at the General." Those without hats waved handkerchiefs. "Huzza! Huzza! Huzza!" they cried. "JACKSON! JACKSON! JACKSON!" It was "Vox Populi, vox dei," enthused one reporter, "and none can prevail against it."[4]

The mayor came forward and welcomed the Hero in a handsome address that could scarcely be heard. Jackson stood perfectly still throughout the address. Several spectators later reported that "the old General looks somewhat the worse for age, but is still remarkably active and hearty for one of his years." Then a procession formed. Old Hickory was led to a barouche, drawn by four white horses, and the "Legion and Washington Battalion" positioned itself around the open carriage. But the people themselves joined the escort as it moved slowly along Canal Street to the statehouse. The balconies, windows, doors, and rooftops of houses were crammed with spectators who waved at the General and called his name. It was a stupendous outpouring of affection and gratitude. "Truly, he was a spectacle worthy of the veneration of the people, who owed so much to him."[5]

The procession proceeded down Canal to Chartres Street into the Place d'Armes where the volunteers, cavalry, and infantry stood at attention on three sides of the square. Jackson received their salute as he passed before each line. Then he entered the cathedral, where a "Te Deum" was sung and the abbé delivered a "thrilling oration," first in English and then in French.

Following the services in the cathedral it was intended to march the Old Hero to the battleground to lay the cornerstone of a monument to commemorate the victory, "but the fatigue of the day was too much even for the iron frame of Old Hickory, enfeebled as it had been by sickness, and broken by the hardships of war." He begged off, and no one could complain. Instead he retired to the apartment prepared for him at the French Exchange on St. Louis Street. As his carriage moved again through the streets the mob pressed closer to get a better look at him. Never had there been "so grand a moral spectacle presented in America," said one, "as that of thirty or forty thousand people being almost willing to risk their lives merely to get a look at the brave old General."[6]

That evening Jackson attended the St. Charles Theater where there were further festivities, closing with the entire audience of two thousand singing "Hail Columbia" in honor of their Hero. Twice the General rose in his place to "acknowledge the enthusiastic cheering of the multitude." "I can remember Gen. Washington's arrival in Philadelphia in 1798, I saw Lafayette here in 1825, I have beheld many exhibitions of the kind," wrote one observer, "but never one like that of last Wednesday." Indeed, partisan and foe both agreed that this celebration marked a "supreme" moment in American history.[7]

So ended the commemoration of the silver jubilee of the Battle of New Orleans. But it took a physical toll. The totally exhausted Hero staggered homeward as soon as he mustered his strength. Some wondered if he would make it. But he reached Nashville safely on Saturday, February 1, and the following day he returned to the Hermitage.

Without question, by 1840, Andrew Jackson had achieved a new status with the American people. He had always been a symbol—a symbol of the enduring strength of a free people—but now he seemed more like a luminous fixture of a glorious past. Somehow the greatness of America evolved because Andrew Jackson lived. American democracy, as it had developed over the past few decades, appeared to many as nothing more than Jackson's lengthened shadow.

Long before he died Old Hickory was a legend, and his home virtually a shrine. More and more visitors came like pilgrims to see him. No one visited Nashville without driving out to pay their respects to General Jackson. On one occasion, Dr. William A. Shaw visited the tired and sick old man. He positively idolized the Hero. They got to talking about world politics and what the future held. At one point Jackson predicted with remarkable prescience that Russia would become the "great eastern rival of the United States of America, rising *pari passu* with her." He anticipated no further trouble with Great Britain, despite the long history of enmity that had once existed between the two countries. "The next great war we have will be with Russia," Jackson predicted.

And what will be the result, Shaw asked.

"We will beat them, sir," Jackson responded; "we can whip all Europe with United States soldiers. Give me a thousand Tennesseans, and I'll whip any other thousand men on the globe!"

Jackson reminisced the night away talking with Shaw, and as he did so, he grew more and more dreamy. Then, all of a sudden, he paused and turned to Shaw as though he had thought of something quite unique. When he finally spoke again he quoted Shakespeare. "There is a tide in the affairs of men," he said, "which, taken at the flood, leads on to fortune."

Shaw just listened.

Then, as though he understood these words for the first time, Jackson murmured: "That's true, sir, I've proved it during my whole life."[8]

CHAPTER 31

―――――◇―――――

"We Must Regain Texas"

PRESIDENT WILLIAM HENRY HARRISON had been in office hardly a month when he caught a bad cold, ate and drank to excess in order to combat it, and succumbed to pneumonia. He was the first President to die in office. The day following his death, John Tyler, a staunch states'-righter from Virginia and a former Democrat, succeeded to the presidency and both parties waited anxiously to see whether his policies would take a Whig or Democratic configuration.[1]

Andrew Jackson could barely disguise his delight when he learned of Harrison's demise. Predictably, he read Harrison's untimely death as a happy omen for the Republic. He praised "providence" for saving the nation from Whig misrule. "A kind and overuling providence has interfered to prolong our glorious Union and happy republican system which Genl. Harrison and his cabinet was preparing to destroy under the dictation of the profligate demagogue, Henry Clay." Jackson was sure that they planned to increase the debt, raise the tariff, and revive a national bank. All of which, Old Hickory said, "by the death of Harrison is blown sky high." The democracy has been spared, he exulted. *The Lord ruleth, let our nation rejoice.*"[2]

Henry Clay did indeed expect to direct legislation along anti-Jacksonian lines and readily convinced the Congress to pass another bank bill on August 6, 1841. Tyler waited the full ten days permitted by the Constitution before he acted, and then he vetoed the bill on August 16. The Democrats cheered. "It will do Old Hickory's heart good when he hears of the Veto," wrote one man. Another burst out: "Egad, he [Tyler] has found one of old Jackson's pens and it wouldn't write any way but plain and straitforward."[3]

Tyler followed with several more vetoes of Clay-inspired legislation and these vetoes worked marvelously for the Democrats because they split the Whig party from top to bottom. The entire cabinet, with the exception of the secretary of state, Daniel Webster, who was involved in negotiating a boundary treaty with the British, resigned. On the day

Congress adjourned, a large body of Whig congressmen issued an address that read Tyler out of the Whig party. All of which Jackson received with intense satisfaction. "Federalism with its cooneries and modern Whigeries is down forever," he wrote, "and our republican system will long endure."[4]

Another event that delighted the old soldier was the effort of his friends in Congress to reimburse him for the fine imposed on him in New Orleans by Judge Dominick Hall in 1815. Led by the senator from Missouri, Dr. Lewis F. Linn, a bill was introduced to restore to the General the $1,000 fine plus interest and costs. This, said Senator Benton, was "by way of expunging that sentence from the judicial records of the country."[5]

The introduction of the Linn proposal in the Senate touched off a partisan free-for-all between Whigs and Democrats that went on for two years. But over time opposition to reimbursement steadily diminished and finally the bill passed the House on January 8, 1844, the anniversary of the Battle of New Orleans, by a vote of 158 to 28. The selection of this date was prearranged by C. J. Ingersoll of Pennsylvania (who replaced Linn as leader in the drive for restitution upon Linn's sudden death), Silas Wright, Jr., and Thomas Hart Benton. The Senate approved the bill on February 10 by a vote of 30 to 16. Jackson, of course, felt very gratified, he said, by the justice "to which I was entitled by wiping from my memory that unjust imputation bestowed upon it by a wicked & corrupt Judge." But above all else, he felt grateful to the American people. "The democracy has produced this Justice to me," he wrote.[6] On Tuesday evening, February 27, 1844, Jackson received a check from the treasurer of the United States for $2,732.90, representing the principal and interest which had accrued since 1815.

What made the passage of the bill possible was the recovery of the Democratic party in the 1842 fall elections. This recovery truly buoyed Jackson's spirits and he repeatedly expressed the hope that he might live long enough to see his party recapture the presidency. But the strong likelihood that Jackson's days were numbered—something the old man himself had been anticipating for decades at least—prompted Frank Blair to query him about his will, particularly the disposition of his papers. At length Jackson agreed to place the entire corpus of his papers in Blair's safekeeping and he drew up a new will dated September 1, 1842. In it the General said that he desired to be buried next to his "dear departed wife" in the vault prepared in the garden of the Hermitage. He wanted all his just debts paid out of his estate—and he named a $6,000 debt owed to General Plauché and a $10,000 debt due Blair and his partner John C. Rives. He bequeathed the Hermitage to his son, along with all his slaves except for two boys whom he gave to his grandsons and four female slaves whom he left to Sarah. This last bequest recognized Sarah's "great kindness to me on all occasions, and particularly when I have been sick, and greatly debilitated she has watched over me with great kindness."[7]

Not a single slave did Jackson free, not even his own manservant, George. True, manumission was incredibly difficult in Tennessee by the 1840s; but for a man who cared so deeply about freedom he had no conception that it might apply to black people. In that respect he resembled most of his contemporaries.

His other bequests involved some of his prized possessions. To Andrew J. Donelson he left the elegant sword given him by the state of Tennessee, and to his grandnephew, Andrew J. Coffee, he gave the sword presented by the rifle company of New Orleans. Another sword presented by the citizens of Philadelphia went to his grandson and namesake. The gold box presented by New York and the large silver vase given by the ladies of Charleston, South Carolina, were left in trust to be awarded to patriots who displayed great valor in defending the country in the event that war was declared against some foreign enemy. The final article disposed of the pistols given him by General Lafayette. These pistols had been presented to Lafayette by General Washington and Colonel William Robertson, and Jackson now bequeathed them to Lafayette's son. In conclusion, he named his son as executor.[8]

Although thoughts of death almost daily intruded into his thinking during the final years of Jackson's life, he was summoned back to active participation in the nation's affairs when he was invited to assist in achieving the immediate annexation of Texas by the United States.[9] "The safety of the republic being the supreme law," Jackson wrote at this time, "and Texas having offered us the key to the safety of our country from all foreign intrigues and diplomacy, I say accept the key . . . and bolt the door at once."[10]

Andrew Jackson always insisted that Texas belonged to the United States by virtue of the Louisiana Treaty of 1803 and had been shamelessly surrendered by John Quincy Adams in the Florida Treaty. He also declared that if Great Britain allied herself with Texas—which already seemed in train—she could then move "an army from canady, along our western frontier," march through Arkansas and Louisiana, capture New Orleans, "excite the negroes to insurrection," "arouse the Indians on our west to war," and "throw our whole west into flames that would cost oceans of blood & hundreds of millions of money to quench, & reclaim. . . . Texas must be ours; our safety requires it." And, with the passage of time, Jackson became more shrill and chauvinistic. "We must regain Texas," he exploded at Major Lewis, *"peacefully if we can, forcibly if we must."*[11]

The Tyler administration was especially anxious to effect annexation. Adding Texas to the Union not only accorded with Tyler's own personal desire and that of his new secretary of state, John C. Calhoun,[12] but it was seen as a political triumph of such dimensions as to guarantee Tyler's reelection. But therein lay the danger. Because Van Buren Democrats worried that immediate annexation could eliminate their candidate from the presidential race, some of them opposed bringing Texas into the Union at this time. Consequently, the Tyler administration saw only one solution to the problem: enlist the venerable Hero of New Orleans in the cause for annexation.

The task of approaching Old Hickory was assigned to Robert J. Walker, senator from Mississippi. A wisp of a man, weighing hardly 100 pounds, Walker breathed expansionism as a holy cause. As such he made an ideal go-between. "I write you confidentially and in haste," was the opening sentence of Walker's letter to Jackson. "I think the annexation of Texas depends *on you.*" And this could be your "crowning act."[13]

Jackson could hardly resist such a summons and so he began writing letters to his old friend General Sam Houston, president of the Texas Republic, along with congressmen and politicians around the country, urging them to support the movement toward annexation. Not only Texas; he wanted to take Oregon and California as well! It was his old dream of empire.

> The important question, the Oregon and annexation of Texas, are now all important to the security and the future peace and prosperity of our union, and I hope there are a sufficient number of pure american democrats to carry into effect the annexation of Texas, and extending our laws over Oregon. No temporising policy or all is lost . . . *Oragon,* and Texas which was ours, *and must be* ours, or the safty of the south and west is put in Jeopardy.[14]

As for California, there could be no doubt of its attraction to the British, according to Jackson. "Need I call your attention to the situation of the United States," he lectured Walker, "England in possession of Texas, or in strict allience offensive & defensive, and contending for California."[15]

On April 12, 1844, a treaty of annexation was signed by the representatives of Texas and the United States. Almost immediately, President Tyler conveyed the news to Jackson. "For the part my dear Sir, that you have taken in this great matter," wrote Tyler, "you have only added another claim to the gratitude of the country."[16] Although Jackson had actually played only a very small part in getting the treaty signed, his role was nonetheless important. His influence, on both sides, carried enormous weight.

But the Senate balked at ratifying the treaty because the secretary of state, John C. Calhoun, foolishly stated in public that the principal reason for annexation was to safeguard the institution of slavery. Then, on April 27, 1844, Henry Clay published a letter written in Raleigh, North Carolina, opposing the acquisition of Texas. He regarded annexation as dangerous to the country in that it might trigger a war with Mexico, excite passions over slavery within the Union, and prove financially disastrous because the Texas debt of approximately $10 million would have to be assumed by the United States.

The very day that Clay's letter appeared in the Washington *National Intelligencer,* a similar letter opposing annexation by Martin Van Buren appeared in the *Globe.* Since both men were the intended presidential candidates of their respective parties, it can be assumed that the two men hoped to avoid making Texas an issue in the election and therefore had come to a prior understanding about Texas and agreed to declare their opposition to its annexation.[17]

Jackson shuddered when he read Van Buren's letter. "I have shed tears of regret," he admitted. "I would to god I had been at Mr. V. B. elbow when he closed his letter. I would have brought to his view *the proper conclusion.*"[18] Straightaway, Jackson wrote to Van Buren and frankly told him that in view of his annexation position "it was impossible to elect him." It was very painful for Jackson to write these words; still, he felt he must speak the truth.[19] But if Van Buren could not be elected, who could the Democrats nominate to run in his place? Jackson thought he knew. "The candidate for the first office," he said, "should be an annexation man, and from the Southwest."[20] No one else. Thus, James Knox Polk of Tennessee became his ultimate choice, a man who had been one of Jackson's oldest and staunchest supporters.[21] To anyone who had watched the course of political events over the last few years it had become increasingly obvious that Van Buren could not hold the party together, that his nomination in 1844 would drive away several segments of the Democratic organization, especially in the south and west. Jackson knew this. He also believed that Polk could unite the democracy. Polk stood for all the principles and reforms Old Hickory had sought to advance during his eight years in office. He also advocated annexation. And he came from the southwest. All of which determined Jackson to summon Polk to the Hermitage for an interview.

Standing before the old chief, Polk sputtered a protest when he heard what was being proposed. He had never aspired so high, he said. He would have been content with the vice presidency. "In all probability the attempt to place me in the first position would be utterly abortive," he added. Still, one never knew. Lightning might strike. In reporting this conversation at the Hermitage with one of his managers scheduled to attend the Democratic nominating convention in Baltimore, Polk conceded that in the "confusion which will prevail" there was "no telling what may occur."[22] Following his conversation with Old Hickory, the cautious Polk placed himself in the hands of his friends at the convention. "They can use my name in any way they may think proper," he wrote.[23]

In the meantime the Whig party held its nominating convention on May 1, four days after the publication of Clay's Raleigh letter, and nominated the Kentuckian despite his opposition to annexation. It nominated him by acclamation. As his running mate, the convention chose Senator Theodore Frelinghuysen of New Jersey.

The Democrats met on May 27. Through the astute maneuvering of Robert J. Walker the two-thirds rule was invoked. First adopted in 1832, this rule required approval of two-thirds of the delegates for any candidate to win nomination. Its adoption at the 1844 convention proved disastrous to the friends of Van Buren, for they had a clear majority of delegates but lacked two-thirds. On the ninth ballot the convention gave the nomination to Polk and chose George Dallas of Pennsylvania as his running mate. A "platform" proposed by Walker to the resolutions committee was also adopted. Among other things taken from the canon of Jacksonian Democracy about banks, tariffs, debts, and internal improvements, it also called for the "reoccupation of Oregon and the reannexation of Texas at the earliest practicable period."[24]

Jackson was overjoyed when he heard the good news. He sincerely regretted the necessity of dumping Van Buren but he justified it by insisting that the good of the country required it. He was especially happy over the resolution calling for Texas and Oregon. Once Texas is absorbed into the country, he wrote, and "our laws extended over Orragon," then "the perpetuation of our glorious Union" will be "as firm as the Rocky mountains, and put to rest the vexing question of abolitionism, the dangerous rock to our Union, and put at defiance all combined Europe, if combined to invade us."[25]

Polk demonstrated uncommon good sense in guiding his presidential campaign. For one thing he made excellent use of Jackson in getting him to talk Tyler into retirement. After several assurances from Old Hickory about how he would be treated in the future by the Democratic party, the lame duck President agreed to withdraw from the race.[26] Throughout the summer and fall Jackson also took an active part in promoting Polk's candidacy. He wrote vigorous letters to all sections of the country, most of which went straight into the newspapers.[27] He also wrote to Sam Houston and urged him to hold out against any European pressure to enter an alliance that would guarantee Texas' independence.

The election proved to be extremely close. A third candidate was put forward by the Liberty party, formed to bring about the abolition of slavery. This party named James G. Birney to head the ticket and he undoubtedly attracted votes away from Clay in crucial states. Polk won by a count of 170 electoral votes to 105. But the popular vote was much closer—1,337,243 to 1,299,062.[28] "A mere *Tom Tit*" has triumphed over the "old Eagle," snorted John Quincy Adams. "The partial associations of Native Americans, Irish Catholics, abolition societies, liberty party, the Pope of Rome, the Democracy of the sword, and the dotage of a ruffian [Jackson] are sealing the fate of this nation, which nothing less than the interposition of Omnipotence can save."[29]

Indeed, most observers saw the election as a victory of an "adventurous democracy" over the "respectable classes," a victory of workers, farmers, slave owners, the foreign-born, and the partisans of Texas. "Nothing can withstand the Democracy of this Country," complained a New York stock-broker. It had advanced too far and too long under the direction of that "ruffian" in the Hermitage.[30]

The splendid news of Polk's victory arrived at the Hermitage with the booming of cannon in Nashville on November 15. "I thank my god," the old man declared, "that the Republic is safe & that he has permitted me to live to see it, & rejoice." In letter after letter for the next several weeks Jackson repeated the phrase: "The Republic is safe." He had lived to witness Clay's third attempt and third defeat at winning the presidency and with him the defeat of Whiggery and "coonery" and aristocracy.[31]

The effort Jackson expended to win Polk's election was tremendous—and important. But again he paid a heavy price for it. He forced himself to write each day, which meant he had to be propped up in bed. He hemorrhaged a great deal and suffered from chills and fever. Between "the lancet to correct the first, and calomel to check the second, I am greatly debilitated," he said. He complained almost daily of "shortness of breath" and found that a few steps down the corridor from his room left him panting and close to fainting. No longer could he leave the house; no longer had he sufficient breath to walk each evening to the gravesite of his beloved Rachel. Soon after the election he was confined totally to his own room.[32]

Jackson knew he was dying and yet he could not let go. Regaining Texas was his single concern. He could not rest easy until he knew that the issue had been satisfactorily resolved. Once Congress reconvened in December, the General charged after its members with demands that they pass a joint resolution for immediate annexation and thereby execute the will of the people as mandated by Polk's election. "Remember, the word reannex," he wrote to his nephew, Andrew J. Donelson, who was now the American *chargé* to Texas, "this hold forth," namely, the right of the United States to Texas under the Louisiana Purchase of 1803. As for the Florida Treaty which renounced Texas, that was a "nullity, not having the approbation of France and the citizens of Louisia," no matter what "that old scamp, J. Q. Adams," says about it.[33]

Early in the congressional session a joint resolution was introduced for immediate annexation. This resolution required only a simple majority in both houses. The House took up the resolution first, and, after a lively debate, passed it on January 25, 1845. On February 27 an amended compromise was introduced into the Senate by Walker and barely squeezed through by a vote of 27 to 25, followed by House approval the next day. Tyler signed the resolution on March 1, 1845, just three days before he was scheduled to leave office.

What a "happy result," cried Blair in a letter to Jackson written moments after the House agreed to the amended measure. "I congratulate you, Dear General, on the success of the great question which you put in action."

Ten days later the feeble voice in the Hermitage replied: "I not only rejoice, but congratulate my beloved country Texas is reannexed, and the safety, prosperity, and the greatest interest of the whole Union is secured by this . . . great and important national act."[34]

CHAPTER 32

"We Will All Meet in Heaven"

BEFORE PRESIDENT-ELECT POLK LEFT for his inauguration in Washington he had several interviews with Jackson at the Hermitage. The last one took place on January 30, 1845, and during their conversations they discussed a number of mutual concerns, including Polk's intended cabinet. After the visitor left for Washington the two men continued to correspond right down to Jackson's final illness and death. Indeed, the old man's health worsened dramatically during the early spring of 1845. "My disease has assumed an alarming type of dropsy," Old Hickory wrote to Polk, "how soon this with my other combined afflictions may take me off, that all-wise god . . . only knows. I am ready to submit to his will with calm resignation."[1] He also submitted with resignation to the continued deterioration of his financial health. "Poverty stares us in the face," he admitted. The price of cotton had continued very low, so low in fact that "it yields at present nothing to the grower." He had raised a bountiful crop at the Hermitage but it brought only $1,300 on the market. Worse, a flood destroyed half the crop at the 1,186-acre plantation he had bought in 1838 in Mississippi for $23,713.80. The wood at this plantation was worth "an immense fortune," according to Jackson, and if Andrew had only "obayed my advice, and attended to the wood instead of pushing the cotton," they would have cleared themselves of debt.[2] The General reluctantly concluded that he must sell the Mississippi property. But once again Frank Blair came to his rescue. "Now, my Dear General," Blair wrote, "you must not permit such matters to afflict you while I have means to prevent it." Whatever Jackson needed, he said, he would raise.[3]

When this letter arrived at the Hermitage Jackson was working with Sarah on their accounts. He read the letter to her and both of them burst into tears. The Hero poured out his thanks to Blair "for this deinterested offer of such liberality and friendship." He reckoned that if he could have $7,000 it would "consolidate our whole debts." He swore he would repay all that he owed. "Mr. A. Jackson jnr has pledged himself that he will not create another debt, of one dollar untill he is clear of his present incumbrances."[4]

Under the circumstances it can be imagined how distressed Jackson must have been when his son brought him a report that Polk intended to replace the *Globe* as the administration's newspaper organ. He immediately wrote to Polk condemning the action. His letter was so vehement that Polk probably burned it. Still Polk did not relent and Blair was forced to sell out. On April 14, 1845, Blair and his partner, John C. Rives, publicly announced their departure. "How loathsome it is to me to see an old friend laid aside," Jackson moaned, "principles of Justice to friendship forgotten, and all for the sake of *policy.*" He snapped at Polk, at the same time sounding a warning. "My dear friend the movement was hasty and as I think badly advised and I pray my god that it may not result in injury to the perfect unity of the democracy."[5]

The closing down of the *Globe* meant that Jackson lost his public defender. He was very jealous of his reputation and quick to take offense over any criticism, and Blair had always been prompt in defending him against all critics. Now the newspaper was gone. And the old man sorrowed. In the future who would defend him against the scamps who might try to defame him? Who would guard his reputation?

He knew he had only a few months to live and yet he concerned himself over his stature in history. He was mindful of his rank among the founders of the country. Since the beginning of the year the shortness of breath had become so acute that he thought at times he would suffocate. Early in April his feet and legs swelled. Then his hands and abdomen. He looked awful. "It may be," he wrote, "that my life ends in dropsy, all means hitherto used to stay the swelling has now failed to check it. I am fully prepared to say the Lord's will be done."[6]

While he still drew breath, however labored, the Old Hero kept up a lively interest in the running of his plantation and the running of the nation. He wrote letters practically every day in his own hand, and there was no loss of intellectual vitality or strength. His handwriting showed few signs of physical difficulty. Although his body deteriorated rapidly, Jackson still willed to live. Isaac Hill was one of the General's last visitors "from back East." He was appalled by what he saw. A bloated shell stared up at him. "If it were any other man," Hill wrote, "I could scarcely suppose he would live a week." Dozens of other visitors came regularly to see Old Hickory in these final months of his life. They wanted the privilege of boasting that they had seen Andrew Jackson face to face before he died. On May 29, for example, a crowd of thirty trooped through his bedroom. "All were admitted," wrote one observer, "from the humblest to the most renowned, to take the venerable chieftain by the hand and bid him farewell."[7]

The General radiated graciousness, although he could barely hold his head up. The swelling of his body practically immobilized him. "Sir," the dying man croaked to one visitor, "I am in the hands of a merciful God. I have full confidence in his goodness and mercy. . . . The Bible is true. . . . I have tried to conform to its spirit as near as possible. Upon that sacred volume I rest my hope for eternal salvation, through the merits and blood of our blessed Lord and Saviour, Jesus Christ."[8]

As the days passed in late spring 1845 Jackson's bloated condition worsened. "I am a blubber of water," he said. The swelling now extended to his face and his suffering was quite acute. He could not lie down. Indeed he had not been able to lie down for the past several months. He had to be propped up with pillows in his bed at night and in his armchair during the day.[9] Each morning the family was surprised that he had survived another night. During the day he usually dressed in an old-style snuff-colored coat with a high stiff collar, presidential and dignified to the end. A coverlet was thrown over him from chest to toe and a servant boy stood nearby, fanning him to keep off flies and other insects. There was "a look of death" about him, reported visitors. His once falcon eye seemed "sunken and rayless," his countenance "languid and insignificant."[10]

Sarah Jackson or her widowed sister, Marion Adams, who lived with the family since her husband's death, constantly attended the dying man during the day. His granddaughter, Rachel, who was now twelve years of age, visited him frequently. Sometimes Jackson's strength seemed to return and he would talk at length about Texas or Oregon or political conditions within the country.

On Sunday, June 1, 1845, the General asked his family to invite the Reverend Mr. Lapshy and Dr. Curry to visit him after services. When the clerics arrived Jackson talked with them at length upon "religious subjects." He was "calm & resigned and said that he was ready to go whenever his divine master thought fit to take him, that he suffered a great deal of bodily pain, but the Lords will be done." The clergymen gave him Holy Communion. It was a "solemn scene," recorded his son.[11]

The Hero closed his eyes for a long moment after receiving Communion. When at last he opened them again he stared at his visitors most intently. "When I have suffered sufficiently," he said very slowly and deliberately, "the Lord will then take me to himself—but what are all my suffering compared to those of the blessed Saviour, who died upon that cursed tree for me, mine are nothing." With that Old Hickory began praying. The Hero of New Orleans, the terror of Indians, Spaniards, British soldiers, politicians, and other assorted "villains," lay on his deathbed praying with fervor and deep conviction. From that moment on, said his son, Andrew Jackson never again mentioned his suffering, "not a murmur was ever heard from him—all was borne with amazing fortitude—he spent much of his time in secret prayer, as was evident from the movements of his lips & hands."[12]

Not that his suffering escaped the attention of his family. They watched every movement he made and quickly responded to any sign of distress. In fact the very next day he began to swell alarmingly and his physician, Dr. John H. Esselman, was summoned immediately from Nashville. An operation was performed, Jackson was "tapped," and "much of the water was taken from his abdomen."[13] This provided immediate relief but totally prostrated the poor man. Still, as he said, he was used to this. Indeed, the number of surgical procedures performed on Jackson during his lifetime approaches the astronomical.

That night his suffering was very great. An anodyne was administered to help him sleep but it had little effect. Early the next morning Doctors Robertson and Waters arrived from Nashville to consult with Esselman, who had remained the night, and they agreed that nothing more should be done except to "conform to the General's temporary wants."[14] The next several days Old Hickory seemed to rally and he said he felt "pretty comfortable." He talked about his funeral arrangements and declared that he desired a simple burial and that he did not want any dirt thrown on his coffin. He wrote to the President, after which he broke out in a cold clammy sweat, evidence "of death approaching." Jackson talked very little after that. He seemed to know that the end was very near.[15]

On Sunday, June 8, a bright, hot day, Jackson's servants, George and Dick, had just propped him in his armchair when Dr. Esselman entered his room to check on his condition. "I immediately perceived that the hand of death was upon him," recorded the doctor. He summoned the family and Andrew then dispatched a servant to fetch Major Lewis. Shortly thereafter, "nature seemed to give way & the general fainted."

"He is gone," announced Dr. Esselman.[16]

The family stared at the figure for a moment, murmured a prayer, and then moved him back to his bed. But the old warrior still had life in him. Slowly he opened his eyes. He spoke, and the sound of his voice startled everyone in the room. He asked to see his grandchildren. Quickly they were hurried into the room and everyone crowded around his bed.

Jackson turned first to Sarah and thanked her for all her kindness, especially during his long illness. Next he said farewell to Marion Adams and after her, his adopted son. Finally he said good-bye to his grandchildren and then the children of Mrs. Adams. One by one he took them by the hand, kissed them, and blessed them. He told them that they had good parents and that they must all be obedient children. They must all "keep holy the Sabboth day and read the New Testament."[17]

Still alert, his mind incredibly clear, he noticed that two children were missing, a grandson and one of Mrs. Adams's sons. When told that they were attending Sunday school he asked that they be summoned. When they arrived in his bedroom Jackson kissed and blessed them.

By this time most of his servants had either gathered in the room or congregated at the windows. With such an audience, all in tears, he could not resist lecturing them, both family and servants. He delivered, said Dr.

Esselman, "one of the most impressive lectures on the subject of religion that I have ever heard." He spoke "with calmness, with strength, and, indeed, with animation." He confessed his implicit faith in the Christian religion, the hope of salvation as revealed in the Bible, his great anxiety that they should all "look to Christ as their only Saviour." Then he turned to his servants. They must do their duty, he declared. "As much was expected of them according to their duties," he said, "as from whites." They "must try and meet him in heaven."[18]

Major Lewis arrived about 2 P.M. The dying man smiled. "Major," he croaked, "I am glad to see you. You had like to have been too late." He gave Lewis messages for Houston, Blair, Benton, and others. He sent them his farewell. After that he lapsed into a long silence.[19]

At four o'clock the General appeared to be sinking rapidly. His son approached the bed and took the old man's hand. "Father," he whispered, "how do you feel,—do you know me."

The figure stirred. "Know you—yes," came the reply. "I would know you all, if I could but see—bring my spectacles."

His eyeglasses were adjusted to his head.

"Where is my Daughter & Marion," he asked. When he saw them he spoke again. "God will take care of you for me. I am my God's. I belong to him, I go but a short time before you, and I want to meet you all in heaven, both white & black."[20]

Everyone in the room burst into tears. The servants standing outside on the porch also cried out and wrung their hands. Jackson seemed startled by the sobbing.

"What is the matter with my Dear Children," he said, "have I alarmed you? Oh, do not cry—be good children & we will all meet in heaven."[21]

Those were Jackson's last words. He fixed his eyes on his granddaughter, Rachel, as though "invoking the blessings of heaven to rest upon her." His breathing was so gentle that it was difficult to know whether he was still alive. Major Lewis supported his head to help him breathe. At six o'clock, after "one slight convulsion," General Andrew Jackson, the seventh President of the United States, expired, aged seventy-eight years, two months, and twenty-four days. The long years of suffering had ended. "Thus died the greatest and best man of the age, or, perhaps of any age," said Dr. Esselman.[22]

It has long been assumed that the immediate cause of Jackson's death was heart failure as evidenced by dropsy. But recently medical experts have suggested that his death resulted from nephrotic kidneys caused by amyloidosis. This disease usually follows many years of infection. Certainly Jackson suffered a massive edema of the entire body during his last illness which, according to medical science, is not usual in congestive heart failure—at least not when the patient has suffered intermittent fluid retention over such a long period of time as Jackson did. Perhaps no single cause of death can ever be assigned. Jackson suffered from so many illnesses—respiratory and gastrointestinal—that after a long and valiant struggle his body simply gave out. It could no longer respond to his sovereign will.[23]

Immediately upon Jackson's death the news of it shot out across the countryside. No name was mentioned. "The Old Hero, the Old Roman, the Old Lion, the Great Captain is dead"—and everyone knew who that was.[24] Literally moments after the warrior expired, General Sam Houston and his young son arrived at the Hermitage to receive a final blessing. "He was there in time to grasp the hand of his friend, but it was cold in death." He fell to his knees, sobbing, and buried his face on Jackson's breast. After a moment Houston composed himself and drew the boy to his side. "My son," he said, "try to remember that you have looked upon the face of Andrew Jackson."[25]

Early Tuesday morning every conceivable vehicle in the neighborhood was pressed into service to carry the mourners to the Hermitage to attend the funeral service. Over two hundred carriages drove onto the grounds, to say nothing of the horses, and they filled the yard in front of the house and the surrounding woods. Something like three thousand people attended the service.[26] At eleven o'clock the Reverend Dr. Edgar took a position on the front porch next to the parlor and preached the eulogy. The servants, standing nearby in groups of fifteen and twenty, wept silently.

After the eulogy, hymns were sung while the coffin with a silver plate in the form of a shield bearing the name "ANDREW JACKSON" was placed in a second one of lead and the top carefully soldered. Then Jackson's remains were slowly carried to the mausoleum in the garden and laid beside his wife's, as he had directed. At the bottom of the vault, four feet below the level of the ground, a slab of limestone was placed over the coffin and inscribed with the words: "GENERAL ANDREW JACKSON."[27]

Edgar intoned the words of Psalm Ninety as the grave was closed. Three volleys of musket, fired by the Nashville Blues in uniform, concluded the service. Off in the distance could be heard the firing of minute guns and the mournful tolling of church bells.

An inventory of Jackson's personal estate was executed on August 4, 1845, and revealed the following: a large mansion (the Hermitage) with household furnishings, many of priceless value, on property of approximately 1,000 acres; 50 acres of cedar timber in Wilson County; a Mississippi plantation consisting of 2,700 acres; 110 slaves at the Hermitage and another 51 on the Mississippi plantation, for a total of 161 slaves, "large and small"; 50 horses, some of which were extremely valuable; 400 hogs, 180 sheep, and 100 cattle.[28] It was an enormous and valuable estate but within a few years his wayward son had dissipated all of it.

To the country at large Jackson left a unique legacy that can still (and probably always will) trigger disputes among historians. That he was colorful, volatile, larger-than-life, no one will dispute. That he loved his country with a passion and tried to serve it honorably in his own peculiar and particular way is also indisputable. Whatever he did, he stamped it with his own special style and grace. The offices he held, the years he lived, the people he influenced were all markedly changed by this extraordinary man. He altered the history of this nation, and profoundly assisted its rise to greatness. More than most Presidents he symbolized for his own time the strength and power and perpetuity of American democracy. And yet, as Herman Melville pointed out, he was picked up from the common clay and thundered higher than a throne.[29] He proved for all time the reality and splendor of the American dream.

Notes

Abbreviations and Short Titles Used in the Notes

Adams, *Memoirs*	Charles Francis Adams, ed., *Memoirs of John Quincy Adams* (Philadelphia, 1874–1877), 12 volumes.
AJ	Andrew Jackson
Benton, *Thirty Years View*	Thomas Hart Benton, *Thirty Years View* (New York, 1865), 2 volumes.
Calhoun Papers	W. Edwin Hamphill et al., eds., *The Papers of John C. Calhoun* (Columbia, S.C., 1963–), 15 volumes.
Jackson, *Correspondence*	John Spencer Bassett, ed., *The Correspondence of Andrew Jackson* (Washington, D.C., 1926–1933), 6 volumes.
JPP	Jackson Papers Project, Hermitage, Tennessee
JRDF	John R. Delafield Foundation, New York, N.Y.
Kendall, *Jackson*	Amos Kendall, *The Life of General Andrew Jackson* (New York, 1844).
LC	Library of Congress
NYPL	New York Public Library
Parton, *Jackson*	James Parton, *Life of Andrew Jackson* (Boston, 1866), 3 volumes.
Remini, *Jackson*	Robert V. Remini, *Andrew Jackson and the Course of American Empire, 1767–1821* (New York, 1977); *Andrew Jackson and the Course of American Freedom, 1822–1832* (New York, 1981); *Andrew Jackson and the Course of American Democracy, 1832–1845* (New York, 1984).

Richardson, *Messages and Papers*	J. D. Richardson, *Compilation of Messages and Papers of the Presidents* (Washington, D.C., 1908), 20 volumes.
THS	Tennessee Historical Society
Van Buren, *Autobiography*	John C. Fitzpatrick, ed., *Autobiography of Martin Van Buren* (Washington, D.C., 1920).
Webster Papers	Charles M. Wiltse et al., eds., *The Papers of Daniel Webster* (Hanover, N.H., 1974–), 5 volumes.

Chapter 1: Boy from the Waxhaw District

1. Alexander Walker, *Jackson and New Orleans* (New York, 1856), p. 327; James Parton, *Life of Andrew Jackson* (New York, 1860), II, 207.

2. Sir Harry Smith, *The Autobiography of Lieutenant General Sir Harry Smith* (London, 1902), I, 236; "A Contemporary Account of the Battle of New Orleans by a Soldier in the Ranks," *The Louisiana Historical Quarterly* (January 1926), IX, 11.

3. John Reid and John Henry Eaton, *The Life of Andrew Jackson* (University, Ala., 1974, reprint), p. 339; Parton, *Jackson,* II, 197.

4. Parton, *Jackson,* II, 197. For a British account of this action see John Henry Cooke, *A Narrative . . . of the Attack on New Orleans in 1814 and 1815* (London, 1835), pp. 234–35. See also John Buchan, *The History of the Royal Scots Fusiliers, 1678–1918* (London, 1925); John S. Cooper, *Rough Notes of Seven Campaigns in Portugal, Spain, France and America During the Years 1808–15* (Carlisle, 1914); Benson E. Hill, *Recollections of an Artillery Officer . . .* (London, 1836); and William Surtees, *Twenty Five Years in the Rifle Brigade* (London, 1833).

5. General Lambert to Lord Bathurst, January 10, 1815, in A. Lacarriere Latour, *Historical Memoir of the War in West Florida and Louisiana* (Philadelphia, 1816), p. cli.

6. John Reid to Abram Maury, January 9, 1815, Reid Papers, LC.

7. Raleigh (North Carolina) *Star,* February 10, 1815; *Niles' Weekly Register,* February 25, 1815; Walker, *Jackson and New Orleans,* p. 341; "A Contemporary Account of the Battle of New Orleans by a Soldier in the Ranks," p. 14.

8. Parton, *Jackson,* II, 208–209.

9. Lambert to Bathurst, January 10, 1815, in Latour, *Historical Memoir,* p. clii; Lambert to Bathurst, January 28, 1815, Public Record Office, London, War Office 1/141; A. P. Hayne to AJ, January 13, 1815, in John Brannan, ed., *Official Letters of the Military and Naval Officers of the United States During the War with Great Britain in the Years 1812, '13, '14 and '15* (Washington, 1823), p. 459.

10. *Niles' Weekly Register,* February 18, 1815.

11. Ibid.

12. William Graham Sumner, *Andrew Jackson* (Boston, 1882), p. 51.

13. Parton, *Jackson,* I, 49.

14. Although several gravestones in the churchyard today go back to the eighteenth century none belong to the Jacksons. In the twentieth century the people of Lancaster erected a gravestone for the father out of regard for his son.

15. A long-standing controversy exists about the birthplace of President Jackson: whether it was North or South Carolina. Jackson himself always believed it was South Carolina, and Elmer Don Herd, Jr., in his book *Andrew Jackson, South Carolinian* (Lancaster, S.C., 1963) provides convincing evidence to support this belief.

16. Remini, *Jackson,* I, 6; Tracy M. Kegley, "James White Stephenson: Teacher of Andrew Jackson," *Tennessee Historical Quarterly* (March 1948), VII, 38–51.

17. AJ to A. J. Donelson, March 21, 1822, Jackson Papers, LC.

18. Parton, *Jackson,* I, 64.

19. Ibid.

20. Ibid.

21. Ibid., p. 68.

22. Kendall, *Jackson,* p. 14.

23. Ibid., p. 25.

24. Parton, *Jackson,* I, 89.

25. Jackson to Kendall, January 9, 1844, Jackson Papers, LC.

26. Jackson to Willie Blount, January 4, 1813, Jackson Papers, LC.

27. Remini, *Jackson,* I, 27–28.

28. Ibid., pp. 28–29.

29. Parton, *Jackson,* I, 104–105.

30. Ibid., pp. 106–109.

31. Ibid., p. 109.

32. Ibid., p. 114.

33. Parton, *Jackson,* I, 113.

34. Ibid., p. 112.

35. Court Record, State of North Carolina, November 12, 1787, in Jackson, *Correspondence,* I, 4.

36. S. G. Heiskell, *Andrew Jackson and Early Tennessee History* (Nashville, 1918), p. 294. Recognizance Bond, October 28, 1787, private collection, copy JPP.

Chapter 2: Frontiersman and Lawyer

1. John Allison, *Dropped Stitches in Tennessee History* (Nashville, 1897), p. 10; bill of sale, November 17, 1788, Washington County Court Minutes, 1788–1793, copy JPP.

2. Jackson to Avery, August 12, 1788, copy JPP.

3. Parton, *Jackson,* I, 122–123.

4. Statement of John Overton to Robert Coleman Foster, May 8, 1827, in *United States Telegraph,* June 22, 1827.

5. Parton, *Jackson,* I, 133.

6. Parton, *Jackson,* I, 168–169.

7. John Downing to John H. Eaton, December 20, 1826, Dickinson Papers, THS. See also James Breckenridge to ———, April 8, 1827, and Humphrey Marshall to Henry Banker, June 1, 1827, Dickinson Papers, THS.

8. Kendall, *Jackson,* p. 90.

9. Records of Davidson County, copy JPP.

10. James McLaughlin to Amos Kendall, March 13, 1843, Jackson Papers, LC.

11. J.G.M. Ramsey, *Annals of Tennessee to the End of the Eighteenth Century* (Charleston, 1953), p. 484; McLaughlin to Kendall, March 13, 1843, Jackson Papers, LC.

12. A. W. Putnam, *History of Middle Tennessee* (Nashville, 1859), p. 318.

13. Arthur P. Whitaker, *The Spanish American Frontier* (Gloucester, 1962), p. 92.

14. Ibid., pp. 102–103.

15. Ibid., p. 113.

16. William Blount to John Gray Blount, June 26, 1790, in Alice B. Keith and William H. Masterson, eds., *The John Gray Blount Papers* (Raleigh, 1959), II, 67.

17. Blount to Robertson, October 17, 1792, in *American Historical Magazine* (January 1897), II, 82.

18. The appointment papers and license from Blount to practice law are in the Jackson Papers, LC; Blount to Robertson, October 28, 1792, in *American Historical Magazine* (July 1896), III, 280.

19. *United States Telegraph*, June 22, 1827.

20. When Jackson ran for the presidency in the election of 1828 the Nashville Central Committee put together a statement concerning the circumstances of Jackson's marriage, and this statement was widely published throughout the United States. See, for example, the *United States Telegraph*, June 22, 1827.

21. William W. Hening, *The Statutes at Large . . . of Virginia* (Philadelphia, 1823), XII, 227.

22. *United States Telegraph*, June 22, 1827.

23. The Jackson Papers Project conducted an extensive search for any record or mention of the marriage in Natchez and Jackson, Mississippi; Baton Rouge and New Orleans, Louisiana; and, of course, Washington, D.C.—without success. Various archives in Georgia and Tennessee as well as archives in Seville, Madrid, and Simancas, Spain, were also searched without success.

24. *United States Telegraph*, June 22, 1827.

25. For further information about the difficulties of the marriage and the theories advanced concerning where and when it took place, see Remini, *Jackson*, I, 60–67.

26. In a letter to Jackson dated April 15, 1791, George Cochran in Natchez speaks of "your friendly retreat at Bayou Pierre." Jackson Papers, LC.

27. Divorce Decree, Mercer County, Kentucky Court of Quarter Sessions Book, 1792–1796, copy JPP.

28. See his letter to Robert Hays, January 9, 1791, Jackson Papers, LC.

29. Marriage License, Miscellaneous Jackson Papers, Harvard University Library.

30. Copies of the *Gazette* are held by the JPP.

31. Oath of Loyalty before Carlos de Grand-Pre and Antonio Solar, January 12, 1790, Cuba, legajos 2362, Archivo General de Indias, Seville, Spain.

32. Cochran to Jackson, November 3, 1790, Jackson Papers, LC.

33. These letters can be found in the Jackson Papers, LC.

34. Davidson County, Wills and Inventories, I, 166–167, 176, 196–201.

35. Lewis to Cadwalader, April 1, June 12, 1827, Ford Collection, NYPL.

Chapter 3: Congressman Jackson

1. Jackson to John McKee, May 16, 1794, in Jackson, *Correspondence*, I, 12–13.

2. Ramsey, *Annals of Tennessee*, p. 648.

3. Ibid.

4. Ibid.

5. *Journal of the Proceedings of the Tennessee Constitutional Convention . . .* (Knoxville, 1852), passim.

6. Ibid.; Jackson to James Bronaugh, August 27, 1822, quoted in Herbert J. Doherty, Jr., "Andrew Jackson's Cronies in Florida's Territorial Politics," *Florida Historical Quarterly* (July 1955), XXXIV, 23.

7. John D. Barnhart, "The Tennessee Constitution of 1796," *Journal of Southern History* (November 1943), IX, 532–548, 654.

8. Mark Mitchell to Jackson [October ?] 12, 1795, Hurja Collection, THS.

9. AJ to Macon, October 4, 1795, in Jackson, *Correspondence*, I, 17–18.

10. Thomas Abernethy, *From Frontier to Plantation in Tennessee* (Chapel Hill, 1932), pp. 165–166.

11. AJ to John McKee, January 30, 1793, in Jackson, *Correspondence*, I, 12.

12. Overton to Jackson, March 10, 1796, Jackson Papers, LC.

13. Remini, *Jackson*, I, 86ff.

14. Jackson to Overton, June 9, 1795, Claybrooke and Overton Papers, THS.

15. Account Book, Ladies' Hermitage Association, Hermitage, Tennessee.

16. The Allison Transaction, no date, Jackson Papers, LC.

17. Ibid.

18. Jackson to Overton, June 9, 1795, Claybrooke and Overton Papers, THS.

19. Ibid.

20. Meeker, Cochran and Co. to Jackson, August 22, 1795, John B. Evans and Co. to Jackson, January 14, 1796, Jackson Papers, LC.

21. See Jackson's Memorandum, Allison Affair, July 15, 1801, Jackson Papers, LC.

22. Davidson County Wills and Inventories, II, 40.

23. Davidson County and Knox County Deed Books C and D, pp. 492–496, 454–456, and North Carolina Land Grant Book, vol. 88, p. 328, copies JPP.

24. See Blount's note, June 11, 1796, Jackson Papers, LC.

25. Allison to Jackson, May 13, 1795 in *Jackson* v. *Andrew Erwin et al.*, Case Record, copy JPP.

26. Jackson to Rachel, May 9, 1796, Provine Papers, Tennessee State Library. This is a copy; the original could not be found. Clearly Jackson's punctuation, spelling, and sentence structure have been edited here.

27. Parton, *Jackson*, I, 196.

28. See Jackson's account with Watson, December 3, 1796, Jackson Papers, LC.

29. Parton, *Jackson*, I, 196.

30. *Annals of Congress*, 4th Congress, 2nd session, p. 1668.

31. AJ to Robert Hays, December 16, 1796, Jackson Papers, LC; AJ to Overton, February 24, 1797, Hurja Collection, THS.

32. See letters of Macon and Tazewell and Steven Mason of Virginia in the Jackson Papers, LC; Remini, *Jackson*, I, 94.

33. AJ to Sevier, January 18, 1797, Jackson Papers, LC.

34. *Annals of Congress*, 4th Congress, 2nd session, p. 1738.

35. Ibid., pp. 1742, 2155.

36. Sevier to AJ, May 8, 1797, and AJ to Sevier, May 8, 1797, in Jackson, *Correspondence*, I, 31–33.

37. Such is implied in John Caffery to AJ, April, 1797, Jackson Papers, LC.

38. Sevier to AJ, May 11, 1797 and AJ to Sevier, May 10, 1797, in Jackson, *Correspondence*, I, 36, 35.

39. William H. Masterson, *William Blount* (Baton Rouge, 1954), p. 311.

40. AJ to Willie Blount, February 21, 1798, and December 15, 1797, particularly the "P.S." Blount Collection, LC.

41. Blount to John Gray Blount, November 7, 1797, in *Blount Papers*, III, 174–175.

42. See his letters to Cocke for November 9, 1797, and June 25, 1798, Jackson Papers, LC.

43. AJ to Robert Hays, November 2, 1797, Jackson Papers, LC.

44. Parton, *Jackson,* I, 219.

45. AJ to Overton, February 3, 23, 1798, Murdock Collection, THS.

46. Parton, *Jackson,* I, 242.

47. See Remini, *Jackson,* I, 110–111 for details.

48. Kendall, *Jackson,* p. 101, says that Jackson believed someone else could serve the people of Tennessee better.

Chapter 4: The Duel

1. The commission is located in the Jackson Papers, Tennessee State Library, and the notice of election on a joint ballot by both houses of the legislature is in the William Blount Papers, Tennessee State Library.

2. Parton, *Jackson,* I, 227; see also Kendall, *Jackson,* p. 107.

3. Copies of these decisions are located in the JPP.

4. Parton, *Jackson,* I, 228–229. A slightly different account is contained in James A. McLaughlin to Amos Kendall, January 3, 1843, Jackson Papers, LC. See also Kendall, *Jackson,* pp. 102–103.

5. "Early Connection with Masonry," in Jackson, *Correspondence,* I, 59.

6. For details of the conspiracy see Remini, *Jackson,* I, 117–118.

7. AJ to Sevier, March 27, 1802, Jackson Papers, LC.

8. Commission of Andrew Jackson as Major General of Tennessee, Jackson Papers, LC.

9. Carl S. Driver, *John Sevier, Pioneer of the Old Southwest* (Chapel Hill, 1932), p. 146; W. R. Garrett and A. V. Goodpasture, *History of Tennessee* (Nashville, 1900), p. 147.

10. Driver, *John Sevier,* pp. 145–146.

11. Jackson claims that Sevier knew he had nothing but a cane while he, Sevier, was armed with a cutlass. See AJ to Sevier, October 3, 1803, in Jackson, *Correspondence,* I, 71.

12. Parton, *Jackson,* I, 164.

13. AJ to Sevier, October 2, 1803, in Jackson, *Correspondence,* I, 71.

14. Sevier to AJ, October 3, 1803, Miscellaneous Papers, THS.

15. AJ to Sevier, October 3, 1803, in Jackson, *Correspondence,* I, 71.

16. AJ to Sevier, October 9, 1803, Jackson Papers, LC. With all this dallying it is possible that neither man really wanted to risk his life and career on a duel but that both wished to stigmatize the other with a refusal to fight. It should be pointed out that Sevier had eighteen children.

17. Sevier to AJ, October 10, 1803, Sevier Papers, THS.

18. Many of the details of the fight are taken from the affidavit of Andrew Green, October 23, 1803, in *American Historical Magazine,* V, 208. Parton, *Jackson,* I, 234–235, gives a slightly different version of the fight.

19. Jackson's General Order to the Militia as to Spanish Threats, August 7, 1803, in Jackson, *Correspondence,* I, 68.

20. AJ to Jefferson, August 4, 1804, in ibid.

21. For Jackson's efforts to win the governorship see Remini, *Jackson,* I, 127–129.

22. This is the reason given by his friend and biographer, Amos Kendall, *Jackson,* p. 103.

23. For details of these negotiations see ibid., pp. 129–130, and James Jackson to AJ, September 21, 1805, Jackson Papers, LC. The Jackson quote

comes from AJ to James Jackson, August 25, 1819, in Jackson, *Correspondence*, II, 428.

24. Remini, *Jackson*, I, 130–131; AJ to James Jackson, August 25, 1819, in Jackson, *Correspondence*, II, 428.

25. Deed, and AJ to Overton, July 21, 1813, Bedford County Deed Book E, pp. 95–96, copy JPP.

26. Bedford County Deed Book AAA, pp. 362–365, copy JPP.

27. On the Clover Bottom store see Coffee Papers, THS.

28. For this information see the Jackson Papers, LC; the Farm Journal, 1829, at the Hermitage; and Arda Walker, "Andrew Jackson: Planter," *East Tennessee Historical Society Publications*, no. 15 (1943), p. 30.

29. AJ to Andrew Jr., July 4, 1829, in Jackson, *Correspondence*, IV, 49–50.

30. See Jackson's affidavit, January 3, 1801, in Jackson, *Correspondence*, I, 57.

31. There is a long history to this duel, the details of which can be traced in Remini, *Jackson*, I, 136ff.

32. There is simply no real evidence to support this interpretation of the duel. The friends of Jackson simply preferred to believe this more defensible reason for killing Dickinson.

33. The Duel with Dickinson: The Card that Provoked the Challenge, in Jackson, *Correspondence*, I, 142–143.

34. AJ to Dickinson, May 23, 1806, in Jackson, *Correspondence*, I, 143–144.

35. Parton, *Jackson*, I, 299.

36. Kendall, *Jackson*, p. 117.

Chapter 5: Old Hickory

1. Parton, *Jackson*, I, 311.

2. Ibid., p. 316.

3. AJ to C. Claiborne, November 12, 1806, in Jackson, *Correspondence*, I, 153.

4. Order to the Militia, October 4, 1806, in ibid., I, 150.

5. AJ to Winchester, October 4, 1806, Jackson Papers, LC.

6. *Impartial Review*, October 4, 8, November 22, 29, 1806.

7. AJ to Daniel Smith, November 12, 1806, Jackson Papers, LC.

8. Remini, *Jackson*, I, 146.

9. AJ to Jefferson, November 12, 1806, in Jackson, *Correspondence*, I, 156.

10. Jefferson to AJ, December 3, 1806, Jefferson Papers, LC.

11. Dumas Malone, *Jefferson the President: Second Term, 1805–1809* (Boston, 1974), p. 247.

12. AJ to Dearborn, January 4, 1807, Jackson Papers, LC.

13. AJ to W. P. Anderson, June 16, 1807, in Jackson, *Correspondence*, I, 181.

14. Thomas P. Abernethy, *The Burr Conspiracy* (New York, 1954), p. 240. Jackson describes the trial in a letter to Thomas Bayly, June 27, 1807, Jackson Papers, Huntington Library.

15. AJ to Smith, November 28, 1807, Jackson Papers, LC.

16. Thomas Hart Benton, *Thirty Years View* (New York, 1854), I, 736.

17. AJ to Daniel Smith, November 28, 1807, Jackson Papers, LC.

18. This is as Jackson remembered it. See AJ to Andrew, Jr., December 1, 1844, copy JPP.

19. List of taxable property, January 1, 1812, Jackson Papers, LC.

20. AJ to George Colbert, June 5, 1812, Jackson Papers, LC.

21. Eustis to Blount, October 21, 1812, in Jackson, *Correspondence*, I, 240, note 5.

22. AJ to Blount, November 11, 1812, in ibid., pp. 238–239.

23. Parton, *Jackson*, I, 368.

24. Blount to AJ, December 31, 1812; AJ to [Blount], January 4, 1813, Jackson Papers, LC.

25. AJ to Eustis, January 7, 1813, quoted in Parton, *Jackson*, I, 372.

26. Wilkinson to AJ, January 22, 25, February 22, March 1, 8, 1813; AJ to Wilkinson, February 16, 20, March 1, 8, 15, 1813, Jackson Papers, LC.

27. Wilkinson to AJ, March 8, 16, 1813, Jackson Papers, LC; Parton, *Jackson*, I, 380.

28. AJ to Armstrong, March 15, 1813, Jackson Papers, LC.

29. AJ to Rachel, March 15, 1813, Jackson Papers, LC.

30. Parton, *Jackson*, I, 382.

31. Ibid., pp. 384, 486.

32. Ibid.

Chapter 6: The Creek War

1. Carroll to A. J. Donelson, October 4, 1824, in Jackson, *Correspondence*, I, 311, note 1.

2. Statement of AJ and Armstrong, August 23, 1813, Jackson Papers, LC; letter of William Carroll dated October 24, 1824, printed in the Knoxville *Register*, copy JPP; Parton, *Jackson*, I, 388.

3. Benton to AJ, July 25, 1813, in Jackson, *Correspondence*, 1, 312–313.

4. For further details of the quarrel see Remini, *Jackson*, I, 183ff.

5. Parton, *Jackson*, I, 392.

6. Certificate of James Sitler, September 5, 1813, in Jackson, *Correspondence*, I, 317.

7. Benton's Account of the Duel with Jackson, September 10, 1813, in ibid., p. 318.

8. Quoted in Parton, *Jackson*, I, 395.

9. The best account of the Creek War is Frank Lawrence Owsley, Jr., *Struggle for the Gulf Borderlands: The Creek War and the Battle of New Orleans, 1812–1815* (Gainesville, 1981). See pp. 6–41 for background.

10. Albert J. Pickett, *History of Alabama . . .* (Charleston, 1851), II, 275; H. S. Halbert and T. H. Hall, *The Creek War of 1813 and 1814* (University, Ala., 1969, reprint), pp. 79–80.

11. Blount to AJ, September 24, 1813, in Brannan, ed., *Official Letters,* p. 215; Blount to AJ, September 25, 1813, Jackson Papers, LC.

12. Reid and Eaton, *Jackson,* p. 33.

13. AJ to Leroy Pope, October 31, 1813, in Jackson, *Correspondence*, I, 339; J. Lyon to AJ, October 27, 1813, Jackson Papers, LC.

14. See AJ to Pope, October 31, 1813, in Jackson, *Correspondence*, I, 339, and AJ to Coffee, September 29, 1813, de Coppet Collection, Princeton University Library.

15. AJ to Coffee, September 25, 1813, Jackson Papers, LC.

16. Davy Crockett, *Life of Davy Crockett* (New York, 1854), p. 75.

17. Coffee to AJ, November 4, 1813, in Thomas H. Palmer, ed., *The Historical Register of the United States* (Washington, 1816), I, 333–335; John Reid to Nathan Reid, November 21, 1813, Reid Papers, LC; AJ to Blount, November, 4, 1813, Jackson Papers, LC.

18. Parton, *Jackson*, I, 439; AJ to Rachel, November 4, 1813, Miscellaneous Jackson Papers, Harvard University Library; and December 29, 1813, Jackson Papers, LC.

19. Reid and Eaton, *Jackson*, p. 56.

20. AJ to Blount, November 11, 1813, in Brannan, *Official Letters*, p. 265; Coffee to John Donelson, November 12, 1813, in *American Historical Magazine* (April 1901), VI, 176; John Reid to Nathan Reid, December 24, 1814, John Reid Papers, LC.

21. AJ to Blount, November 15, 1813, and AJ to Thomas Pinckney, December 3, 1813, Jackson Papers, LC.

22. Address of Officers, Jackson Papers, LC; Reid and Eaton, *Jackson*, p. 63; AJ to Rachel, December 9, 1813, Jackson Papers, LC.

23. Reid and Eaton, *Jackson*, pp. 68–71; Kendall, *Jackson*, pp. 216–217.

24. Reid and Eaton, *Jackson*, p. 84.

25. AJ to Rachel, December 14, 1813, in Jackson, *Correspondence*, I, 391–392.

26. Reid and Eaton, *Jackson*, p. 85; AJ to Rachel, December 29, 1813, Jackson Papers, Huntington Library.

27. Coffee to AJ, December 20, 1813, Jackson Papers, LC.

28. Blount to AJ, December 7, 1813, Jackson Papers, LC; Blount to AJ, December 22, 1813, in *American State Papers, Military Affairs*, III, 698.

29. AJ to Coffee, December 31, 1813, Jackson, *Correspondence*, I, 431.

30. Blount to Armstrong, January 5, 1814, in *American State Papers, Military Affairs*, III, 698.

31. Reid and Eaton, *Jackson*, p. 128.

32. Ibid., p. 129.

33. AJ to Thomas Pinckney, January 29, 1814, in Jackson, *Correspondence*, I, 448–501.

34. Ibid.

35. Reid and Eaton, *Jackson*, p. 136.

36. Parton, *Jackson*, I, 508.

37. General Order, March 12, 1814, in Jackson, *Correspondence*, I, 479.

38. AJ to Pinckney, March 14, 1814, Jackson Papers, LC; Halbert and Hall, *Creek War*, pp. 246–247.

39. Reid and Eaton, *Jackson*, p. 149.

40. AJ to Blount, March 31, 1814, in Jackson, *Correspondence*, I, 490; AJ to John Armstrong, April 2, 1814, National Archives.

41. AJ to Pinckney, March 28, 1814, in Jackson, *Correspondence*, I, 488–489.

42. AJ to Blount, March 31, 1814, in ibid., p. 491; AJ to Blount, April 1, 1814, Jackson Papers, LC; Reid to Elizabeth Reid, April 1, 1814, Reid to Nathan Reid, April 5, 1814, Reid Papers, LC; Coffee to AJ, April 1, 1814, Jackson Papers, LC.

43. AJ to Rachel, April 1, 1814, in Jackson, *Correspondence*, I, 493.

44. AJ to Blount, March 31, 1814, in Jackson, *Correspondence*, I, 491–492; Coffee to Mary Coffee, April 1, 184, Coffee Papers, THS.

45. The principal chief of the Upper Creeks from the towns of Oakfuskee, New Youka, Oakchays, Hillabee, Eufala, and the Fish Ponds assembled at the Bend was the prophet Monahee, but Menewa had charge of the defense.

46. Reid and Eaton, *Jackson*, p. 165; Anne Royall, *Letters from Alabama* (Washington, 1830), pp. 91–92.

47. Angie Debo, *The Road to Disappearance* (Norman, Okla., 1967), p. 82.

48. AJ to Blount, April 18, 1814, Jackson, *Correspondence*, I, 503.

49. AJ to Rachel, September 22, 1814, Jackson Papers, Huntington Library.

50. Treaty of Fort Jackson, in *American State Papers, Indian Affairs*, I, 826–827.

51. Kendall, *Jackson*, p. 89.

52. Reid and Eaton, *Jackson*, pp. 190–191.

53. AJ to Rachel, August 10, 1814, private collection, copy JPP; terms of the treaty can be found in *American State Papers, Indian Affairs,* I, 826–827.

Chapter 7: The Battle of New Orleans

1. AJ to Rachel, August 5, 1814, Jackson Papers, Huntington Library.

2. AJ to Armstrong, July 18, 1814, quoted in Reid and Eaton, *Jackson,* pp. 196–197.

3. AJ to Manrique, August 24, 1814, Jackson Papers, LC.

4. Reginald Horsman, *The War of 1812* (New York, 1969), p. 227; Frank L. Owsley, Jr., "Role of the South in the British Grand Strategy in the War of 1812," *Tennessee Historical Quarterly* (Spring 1972), XXXI, 29–30.

5. Gonzalez Manrique to Ruiz Apodaca, December 6, 1814, Cuba, legajos 1795, Archivo General de Indias, Seville, Spain.

6. AJ to Gonzalez Manrique, August 30, 1814; Gonzalez Manrique to Ruiz Apodaca, September 10, December 6, 1814; Cuba, legajos 1795, Archivo General de Indias, Seville, Spain.

7. AJ to Monroe, October 26, 1814, in Jackson, *Correspondence,* II, 82–83.

8. AJ to Gonzalez Manrique, November 6, 1814, Cuba, legajos 1795, Archivo General de Indias, Seville, Spain.

9. AJ to Monroe, November 14, 1814, in Jackson, *Correspondence,* II, 99.

10. Reid and Eaton, *Jackson,* p. 235.

11. AJ to Gonzalez Manrique, November 9, 1814, Cuba, legajos 1795, Archivo General de Indias, Seville, Spain.

12. AJ to Rachel, November 15, 1814, Miscellaneous Jackson Papers, Harvard University Library; AJ to Rachel, November 17, 1814, Jackson Papers, Missouri Historical Society.

13. They left November 27–28, and word of their departure reached Secretary Monroe through intelligence from Cuba. Monroe relayed this information directly to Jackson and warned him that the "attacks on other parts of our Union, is about to terminate in a final blow against New Orleans." Monroe to AJ, December 10, 1814, in Jackson, *Correspondence,* II, 110.

14. Louise Livingston Hunt, *Memoir of Mrs. Edward Livingston with Letters Hitherto Unpublished* (New York, 1886), pp. 53–54.

15. Parton, *Jackson,* II, 31.

16. Jane L. DeGrummond, *The Baratarians and the Battle of New Orleans* (Baton Rouge, 1961), pp. 7–9, 37–48.

17. AJ to Monroe, December 10, 1814, AJ to Coffee, December 11, 1814, in Jackson, *Correspondence,* II, 111–113; Latour, *Historical Memoir,* p. 72.

18. AJ to Claiborne, September 21, 1814, Jackson Papers, LC.

19. AJ to W. Allen, December 23, 1814, Jackson Papers, LC.

20. Horsman, *War of 1812,* pp. 238–239; Owsley, *Struggle for the Gulf Borderlands,* p. 139.

21. For all intents and purposes it also terminated sea access to Mobile, a potentially serious setback. See AJ to Winchester, December 16, 1814, and AJ to Coffee, December 17, 1814, Jackson Papers, LC.

22. AJ to Coffee, December 16, 1814, Coffee to AJ, December 17, 1814, Jackson Papers, LC.

23. Charles Gayarre, *History of Louisiana* (New York, 1866), IV, 419.

24. Ibid.

25. DeGrummond, *Baratarians,* pp. 75–76, 85–86.

26. Walker, *Jackson and New Orleans,* p. 150.

27. Vincent Nolte, *Fifty Years in Both Hemispheres* (New York, 1854), pp. 209–210.

28. AJ to Monroe, December 27, 1814, in Jackson, *Correspondence,* II, 127; Latour, *Historical Memoir,* pp. 102–103; Report of Killed, Wounded and Missing. . . . December 23 and 25, 1814, Jackson Papers, LC.

29. Latour, *Historical Memoir,* p. 112. See also Reid to Abram Maury, December 25, 1814, Reid Papers, LC.

30. Reid to Nathan Reid, December 30, 1814, Reid Papers, LC.

31. Walker, *Jackson and New Orleans,* p. 256; Reid to Elizabeth Reid, February 10, 1815, Reid Papers, LC.

32. AJ to Monroe, January 2, 1815, Jackson Papers, LC.

33. Latour, *Historical Memoir,* p. lix.

34. AJ to Monroe, February 13, 1815, Jackson Papers, LC, in which Jackson said he had no more than 3,000 men on the left bank, of whom 600 were regulars.

35. Lambert to Lord Bathurst, January 10, 1815, in Latour, *Historical Memoir,* p. cl; Horsman, *War of 1812,* pp. 245–246.

36. Robin Reilly, *The British at the Gates* (New York, 1974), pp. 295–296. See also DeGrummond, *Baratarians,* p. 131. The Forty-Fourth Regiment was led by a particularly incompetent officer, Lieutenant Colonel, The Honorable Thomas Mullens, third son of Lord Ventry.

37. Reid and Eaton, *Jackson,* p. 339.

38. Lambert to Lord Bathurst, January 10, 1815, in Latour, *Historical Memoir,* p. cli.

39. Reid to Abram Maury, January 9, 1815, Reid Papers, LC.

40. Coffee to John Donelson, January 25, 1815, *American Historical Magazine* (April 1901), VI, 186.

41. Lambert to Lord Bathurst, January 10, 1815, in Latour, *Historical Memoir,* p. cli; Parton, *Jackson,* II, 207; Walker, *Jackson and New Orleans,* p. 332.

42. Howell Tatum, "Major Howell Tatum's Journal," in John S. Bassett, ed., *Smith College Studies in History* (1920–1922), VII, 126.

43. Walker, *Jackson and New Orleans,* p. 353.

44. A. P. Hayne to AJ, January 13, 1815, in Brannan, *Official Letters,* p. 459. The casualty reports in the Jackson Papers, LC, state that the action on December 23, 1814, saw 26 killed, 115 wounded, and 72 missing; on December 28, 7 killed and 8 wounded; on January 1, 11 killed and 23 wounded. The total for the four actions on both sides of the river totaled 55 killed, 185 wounded, and 93 missing. For the British losses see Lambert to Bathurst, January 10, 1815, in Latour, *Historical Memoir,* p. clii; Lambert to Bathurst, January 28, 1815, Public Record Office, War Office 1/141.

Chapter 8: Indian Removal

1. AJ to Monroe, January 19, 1815, Jackson Papers, LC; Abbé Dubourg to AJ, no date, in Jackson, *Correspondence,* II, p. 150, note 1.

2. Latour, *Historical Memoir,* pp. 197–198.

3. Ibid., pp. 199–200.

4. Ibid.; Parton, *Jackson,* II, 273.

5. Brannan, *Official Letters,* p. 468.

6. Washington *National Intelligencer,* February 7, 1815.

7. February 14, 1815.

8. John Binns, *Autobiography,* quoted in Parton, *Jackson,* II, 248.

9. Monroe to AJ, February 5, 1815, in Jackson, *Correspondence,* II, 158.

10. AJ to Robert Hays, February 9, 1815, Jackson Papers, LC.

11. For an extended discussion of this point see Remini, *Jackson*, I, pp. 298–307.

12. AJ to Arbuckle, March 5, 1815, Jackson Papers, LC.

13. Statement in Jackson Papers, LC.

14. Nolte, *Fifty Years*, p. 238; Rachel to Robert Hays, March 5, 1815, Jackson Papers, LC; Reid to Elizabeth Reid, February 22, 1815, Reid Papers, LC.

15. Reid to Sophie Reid, April 20, 1815, Reid Papers, LC.

16. Parton, *Jackson*, II, 329.

17. AJ to Crawford, June 10, 1816, in *American State Papers, Indian Affairs*, II, 110.

18. AJ to Monroe, March 4, 1817, Monroe Papers, NYPL.

19. Ibid.

20. Jackson, Meriwether, and Franklin to Crawford, September 20, 1816, in *American State Papers, Indian Affairs*, II, 105; Grace S. Woodward, *The Cherokees* (Norman, 1963), p. 135.

21. Arrell M. Gibson, *The Chickasaws* (Norman, 1971), p. 105.

22. *American State Papers, Indian Affairs*, II, 95.

23. AJ to George Graham, December 21, 1816, in ibid., II, 123.

24. George Graham to AJ, January 13, 1817, in ibid., II, 140.

25. Graham to AJ, May 16, 1817, in ibid., II, 143.

26. For details of these negotiations see Remini, *Jackson*, I, pp. 333–335.

27. Treaty with Cherokees, July 8, 1817, in *American State Papers, Indian Affairs*, II, 130.

28. See Reginald Horsman, "American Indian Policy and the Origins of Manifest Destiny," in Francis Paul Prucha, ed., *The Indians in American History* (New York, 1971); Wilber R. Jacobs, *Dispossessing the American Indians* (New York, 1972); and Bernard Sheehan, *Seeds of Extinction* (Chapel Hill, 1973).

29. AJ to Coffee, July 13, 1817, Coffee Papers, THS; Commissioners to Graham, July 8, 1817, in *American State Papers, Indian Affairs*, II, 140–147; AJ to John C. Calhoun, September 2, 1820, Jackson Papers, LC.

30. Adams, *Memoirs*, IV, 238; AJ to Calhoun, June 19, 1820, in *Calhoun Papers*, V, 196.

31. Journal of the Convention, 1820, Jackson Papers, LC.

32. Ibid.; newspaper quoted in Arthur H. DeRosier, Jr., *The Removal of the Choctaw Indians* (Knoxville, 1970), p. 67; Doak's Stand Treaty, in *American State Papers, Indian Affairs*, II, 225.

Chapter 9: The First Seminole War

1. Calhoun to AJ, December 29, 1817, Jackson Papers, LC.

2. Monroe to AJ, December 14, 1816, in Jackson, *Correspondence*, II, 266.

3. AJ to Zuniga, April 23, 1816, in ibid., p. 241.

4. Zuniga to AJ, May 26, 1816, Jackson Papers, LC.

5. Edwin C. McReynolds, *The Seminoles* (Norman, 1957), p. 77.

6. Gaines to AJ, November 21, 1817, in *American State Papers, Military Affairs*, I, 686; James W. Silver, *Edmund Pendleton Gaines, Frontier General* (Baton Rouge, 1949), p. 63.

7. Calhoun to Gaines, December 16, 1817, in *American State Papers, Military Affairs*, I, 689.

8. Calhoun to AJ, December 26, 1817, in ibid.

9. AJ to Monroe, January 6, 1818, Monroe Papers, NYPL.

10. Rhea to AJ, January 12, 1818, in Jackson, *Correspondence*, II, 348.

11. Monroe to AJ, December 28, 1817, Monroe Papers, NYPL.

12. Samuel Flagg Bemis, *John Quincy Adams and the Foundations of American Foreign Policy* (New York, 1950), p. 314.

13. AJ to Captain McKeever, March, 1818, in Parton, *Jackson,* II, 447.

14. Hubert B. Fuller, *The Purchase of Florida* (Gainesville, 1964), p. 247.

15. AJ to Calhoun, February 10, 26, March 25, 1818, in *American State Papers, Military Affairs,* I, 697, 698–699.

16. AJ to Calhoun, March 25, 1818, in ibid., I, 698.

17. AJ to Calhoun, April 8, 1818, in Jackson, *Correspondence,* II, 358–359.

18. AJ to Rachel, April 8, 1818, in ibid., p. 358.

19. AJ to Rachel, April 10, 1818, Miscellaneous Jackson Papers, Harvard University Library.

20. AJ to Calhoun, April 20, 1818, in *American State Papers, Military Affairs,* I, 700–701.

21. Arbuthnot to John Arbuthnot, April 2, 1818, in ibid., p. 722.

22. AJ to Calhoun, May 5, 1818, in ibid., p. 702.

23. The court later changed its mind and rescinded the death penalty and substituted fifty lashes on the bare back and confinement with ball and chain to hard labor for twelve months, but Jackson reimposed the original penalty.

24. *American State Papers, Foreign Affairs,* IV, 595.

25. AJ to Calhoun, May 5, 1818, in Jackson, *Correspondence,* II, 367.

26. AJ to Calhoun, May 19, 1818, in *Calhoun Papers,* III, 547.

27. AJ to Calhoun, May 5, 1818, in Jackson, *Correspondence,* II, 367.

28. Masot to AJ, May 24, 1818, in *Calhoun Papers,* II, 372–373.

29. Parton, *Jackson,* II, 492–493.

30. Proclamation, May 29, 1818, in Jackson, *Correspondence,* II, 374–375.

31. AJ to Monroe, June 2, 1818, Monroe Papers, NYPL.

32. Harry Ammon, *James Monroe: The Quest for National Identity* (New York, 1971), pp. 417–425.

33. Adams, *Memoirs,* IV, 103–107; Ammon, *Monroe,* p. 421.

34. Adams, *Memoirs,* IV, 108–114.

35. Onís to Adams, July 8, 1818, in *American State Papers, Foreign Affairs,* IV, 496–497.

36. Adams to Onís, July 23, 1818, in ibid., 497–499.

37. AJ to A. J. Donelson, January 31, 1819, in Jackson, *Correspondence,* II, 408. March 4 marked the end of the short session of Congress.

38. *Annals of Congress,* 15th Congress, 2nd session, pp. 631–655.

39. AJ to Lewis, January 25, 30, 1819, Jackson-Lewis Papers, NYPL.

40. Ibid.

41. *Annals of Congress,* 15th Congress, 2nd session, pp. 1136–1138; 515–530, 583–1138, carries the full debate.

42. Adams, *Memoirs,* IV, 243.

43. Parton, *Jackson,* II, 557–558, 565, 566; Franklin (Tennessee) *Gazette,* July 17, 1818.

44. Philip C. Brooks, *Diplomacy and the Borderlands* (New York, 1970), p. 100; Charles C. Griffin, *The United States and the Disruption of the Spanish Empire* (New York, 1968), p. 169; George Dangerfield, *Era of Good Feelings* (New York, 1951), p. 146.

45. Bemis, *Adams,* pp. 318–319, which translates a letter of Onís to José Pizarro, the Spanish foreign minister, July 18, 1818. Ratification of the treaty took several years because of Spanish procrastination. Not until 1821 did it go into effect.

46. *National Intelligencer,* April 7, 1821.

Chapter 10: Governor Jackson

1. AJ to Donelson, no date, Jackson Papers, LC.
2. Monroe to AJ, January 24, 1821, Jackson Papers, LC.
3. AJ to Monroe, February 11, 1821, Monroe Papers, NYPL.
4. Rachel to Mrs. Eliza Kingsley, April 27, 1821, in Parton, *Jackson*, II, 595–596.
5. For a discussion of the wrangle see Remini, *Jackson*, I, 404–406. The correspondence between Jackson and Callava can be found in *American State Papers, Foreign Affairs*, IV, 759–761.
6. AJ to Adams, July 18, 1821, in ibid., 764–765; AJ to W.G.D. Worthington, July 26, 1821, Jackson Papers, LC; Parton, *Jackson*, II, 604.
7. AJ to Dr. James C. Bronaugh, June 9, 1821, in Jackson, *Correspondence*, III, 65.
8. See various proclamations in the Jackson Papers, LC; *The Territorial Papers of the United States*, Clarence E. Carter, ed. (Washington, 1936–), XII, 150; and *American State Papers, Miscellaneous*, II, 900, 907. See also Herbert J. Doherty, Jr., "The Governorship of Andrew Jackson," *Florida Historical Quarterly* (July 1954), XXXIII, 3ff.
9. Doherty, "Governorship of Andrew Jackson," p. 25.
10. For these various ordinances see Carter, ed., *Territorial Papers*, XXII, 156–157, footnote 4; Doherty, "Governorship of Andrew Jackson," p. 12; *American State Papers, Miscellaneous*, II, 905–907.
11. Rachel to Mrs. Eliza Kingsley, July 23, 1821, in Parton, *Jackson*, II, 604.
12. *American State Papers, Miscellaneous*, II, 849–875.
13. Ibid., pp. 811–812.
14. *American State Papers, Foreign Affairs*, IV, 770; Parton, *Jackson*, II, 631. Minutes of the examination of Callava, August 22, 1821, can be found in *American State Papers, Foreign Affairs*, IV, 783.
15. *American State Papers, Miscellaneous*, II, 809.
16. AJ to Adams, August 26, 1821, in ibid., II, 801.
17. Adams to deAnduaga, April 15, 1822, in *American State Papers, Foreign Affairs*, IV, 802–807.
18. Doherty, "Governorship of Andrew Jackson," pp. 13ff.; Herbert J. Doherty, *Richard Keith Call: Southern Unionist* (Gainesville, 1961), p. 20.
19. AJ to Adams, November 22, 1821, in Jackson, *Correspondence*, III, 139.
20. AJ to Bronaugh, August 27, 1822, quoted in Doherty, "Andrew Jackson's Cronies in Florida Territorial Politics," *Florida Historical Quarterly* (July 1955), XXXIV, 23.
21. See the Jackson-Monroe exchanges in Jackson, *Correspondence*, III, 122ff.
22. AJ to Monroe, October 5, 1821, in ibid., III, 123.
23. Pensacola *Floridian*, October 8, 1821, reprinted in *Niles' Weekly Register*, November 10, 1821.

Chapter 11: An Era of Corruption

1. AJ to James Gadsden, May 2, 1822, in Jackson, *Correspondence*, III, 161; John B. Moses and Wilbur Cross, *Presidential Courage* (New York, 1980), pp. 36–66.
2. Lyncoya's obituary notice, *United States Telegraph*, July 3, 1828.
3. Rachel to John Donelson, August 25, 1821, Miscellaneous Jackson Papers, THS.
4. Henry Wise, *Seven Decades of the Union* (Philadelphia, 1881), pp. 98–99.
5. Ibid., p. 113.

6. Ibid., pp. 80, 100–101.

7. Ibid., pp. 102–103.

8. Nathan Sargent, *Public Men and Events* (Philadelphia, 1875), I, 36.

9. August 6, 1822.

10. September 4, 1822.

11. J. D. Steele, Manuscript Journal, 1820–1829, Huntington Library.

12. "Memorandoms," [1822], Jackson Papers, LC.

13. Details of the so-called corruption of the Monroe administration can be found in Remini, *Jackson*, II, 12–38.

14. Not all historians are willing to accept the idea that the so-called Era of Good Feelings, as the years of the Monroe administration are usually referred to, was an Era of Corruption. But Richard L. McCormick, in a paper he read before the American Historical Association in San Francisco in December 1983 and entitled "Political Corruption in the Young Republic," finds sufficient evidence to support Jackson's fears and concerns.

15. See his "memorandoms" in the Jackson Papers, LC.

16. Baltimore *Federal Republican*, August 26, 1822.

17. Bronaugh to AJ, February 8, 1822, in Jackson, *Correspondence*, III, 148.

18. For further details on these points see Remini, *Jackson*, II, 29ff.

19. AJ to Coffee, February 10, March 25, 8, 1825, Coffee Papers, THS; AJ to Donelson, August 6, 1822, Donelson Papers, LC.

20. AJ to James Buchanan, June 25, 1825, Buchanan Papers, Historical Society of Pennsylvania, Philadelphia.

21. AJ to James W. Lanier, May 15 [?], 1824, in Jackson, *Correspondence*, III, 253.

22. AJ to James K. Polk, December 4, 1826, Polk Papers, LC; AJ to Francis Preston, January 27, 1824, Jackson Papers, Huntington Library; AJ to William S. Fulton, July 4, 1824, in Jackson, *Correspondence*, III, 139.

23. AJ to Donelson, February 12, 1824, Donelson Papers, LC.

24. AJ to Donelson, April 17, 1824, Donelson Papers, LC.

25. This is how Jackson later remembered the arguments to induce him to run. AJ to [John C. McLemore?], December 25, 1830, Miscellaneous Jackson Papers, New York Historical Society.

26. AJ to Dr. Bronaugh, July 18, 1822, Jackson Papers, LC.

27. AJ to Donelson, August 6, 1822, Donelson Papers, LC. Grundy's letter to Jackson, dated July 27, 1822, can be found in Jackson, *Correspondence*, III, 163–164.

28. For the details of the maneuvering by the Overton clique see Remini, *Jackson*, II, 39–53.

29. *Niles' Weekly Register*, August 24, 1822.

30. Again, for details of their maneuvering see Remini, *Jackson*, II, 51–53.

31. AJ to Coffee, October 5, 1823, Coffee Papers, THS.

32. Lewis to Lewis Cass, no date, possibly 1844 or 1845, Jackson-Lewis Papers, NYPL.

33. *Letters of Wyoming, to the People of the United States, on the Presidential Election, and in Favour of Andrew Jackson* (Philadelphia, 1824), pp. 10, 11, 24, 93, 94.

34. Ibid., pp. 11, 12, 14.

35. William Allen Butler, *Martin Van Buren* (New York, 1862), pp. 24–25.

36. Parton, *Jackson*, III, 48.

37. Van Buren to Benjamin F. Butler, February 15, 1824, Van Buren Papers, LC; Stephen Van Rensselaer to Solomon Van Rensselaer, February 15, 1824, in Mrs. Catharina V. R. Bonney, *A Legacy of Historical Gleanings* (Albany, 1875), p. 410.

38. AJ to Coffee, February 15, 1824, Coffee Papers, THS.

39. AJ to Donelson, March 6, 1824, Donelson Papers, LC.

40. AJ to Donelson, March 19, 1824, Donelson papers, LC; AJ to Coffee, June 18, 1824, Coffee Papers, THS.

41. The best discussion of this election is James F. Hopkins, "Election of 1824," in *History of American Presidential Elections,* Arthur M. Schlesinger, Jr., Fred L. Israel, and William P. Hansen, eds. (New York, 1971), I, 349–381.

42. AJ to Lewis, January 25, 30, 1819, Jackson-Lewis Papers, NYPL.

43. AJ to Lewis, December 27, 1824, Jackson Papers, Massachusetts Historical Society.

44. AJ to Coffee, January 10, 1825, Coffee Papers, THS.

45. Dangerfield, *Era of Good Feelings,* p. 338; *Niles' Weekly Register,* August 18, 1827.

46. Adams, *Memoirs,* VI, 464–465.

47. Hayne to J. V. Grimke, January 28, 1825, Miscellaneous Hayne Papers, New York Historical Society.

48. Van Buren, *Autobiography,* 199–200.

49. McLane to Mrs. McLane, February 6, 1825, McLane Papers, LC.

50. There is a delightful story Van Buren tells in his *Autobiography* (p. 151) about how the state went over to Adams, which is given full coverage in Remini, *Jackson,* II, 92–96.

51. Bemis, *Adams,* pp. 42–43. It is Bemis who called it a "diplomatic junket."

52. For details of Scott's action see Remini, *Jackson,* II, 94.

53. AJ to Coffee, February 19, 1825, Coffee Papers, THS.

54. AJ to Overton, February 10, 1825, Overton Papers, THS.

55. AJ to Lewis, February 14, 1825, in Jackson, *Correspondence,* III, 276; AJ to Lewis, February 10, 1825, Jackson-Lewis Papers, NYPL.

Chapter 12: "Jackson and Reform"

1. Henry Lee to AJ, September 17, 1828, Donelson Papers, LC; George Bibb to Felix Grundy, no date, Grundy Papers, North Carolina State Library.

2. Calhoun to AJ, June 4, 1826, in *Calhoun Papers,* X, 110.

3. See, for example, Robert J. Trumbull, *The Crisis or Essays on Usurpations of the Federal Government,* passim, originally published in the Charleston *Mercury* and later reprinted in pamphlet form in 1827, a copy in Jackson's personal library in the Hermitage, vol. XI, no. 8.

4. Lee to AJ, September 17, 1828, Donelson Papers, LC. See also Calhoun to AJ, June 4, 1826, in *Calhoun Papers,* X, 110–111.

5. Rufus King to John King, February 27, 1825, King Papers, New York Historical Society.

6. T. Bradley to Gulian C. Verplanck, November 13, 1827, Verplanck Papers, New York Historical Society.

7. *Register of Debates,* 19th Congress, 1st session, pp. 401–403; Benton, *Thirty Years View,* I, 70–77, contains details of the duel.

8. Richardson, *Messages and Papers,* II, 866–968, 872, 879, 882.

9. Edward P. Gaines to AJ, [1826], Jackson Papers, LC.

10. AJ to John Branch, March 3, 1828, Branch Family Papers, Southern Historical Collection, Chapel Hill.

11. Macon to B. Yancey, December 8, 1825, in Edwin M. Wilson, *The Congressional Career of Nathaniel Macon* (Chapel Hill, 1900), p. 76.

12. See especially Van Buren's letter to Thomas Ritchie, January 13, 1827, Van Buren Papers, LC.

13. Ibid. These are not the words Van Buren actually spoke to Calhoun. They are what he wrote to Ritchie in his letter of January 13, 1827. It is assumed that the arguments to both men were similar.

14. "We united heart and hand to promote the election of General Jackson," Van Buren recorded in his *Autobiography*, p. 514.

15. AJ to Amos Kendall, September 4, 1827, Jackson-Kendall papers, LC; AJ to Edward Livingston, December 6, 1827, Livingston Papers.

16. For Jackson's monetary views, pro and con, see Bray Hammond, *Banks and Politics in America* (Princeton, 1957); Arthur M. Schlesinger, Jr., *The Age of Jackson* (Boston, 1946); and John M. McFaul, *The Politics of Jacksonian Finance* (Ithaca, N.Y., 1972).

17. AJ to Colonel John D. Terrill, July 29, 1826, in Jackson, *Correspondence*, III, 308–309.

18. For details of this election, particularly the charges and countercharges leveled by the two parties, see Robert V. Remini, *The Election of Andrew Jackson* (New York, 1963).

19. For this statement see the *United States Telegraph*, June 22, 1827.

20. AJ to Houston, December 15, 1827, Jackson Papers, LC.

21. Remini, *Election of Jackson*, pp. 117–119. This work includes many more details of the 1828 election.

22. AJ to Green, August 13, 1827, Jackson Papers, LC.

23. *National Journal*, February 27, March 10, 22, 31, July 24, 1827, and *National Intelligencer*, March 13, 20, 1827.

24. W. T. Barry to Alfred Balch, November 19, 1827, Jackson Papers, LC.

25. AJ to Branch, June 24, 1828, Jackson Papers, LC.

26. Clinton to Atwater, February 29, 1828, Jackson Papers, LC; *United States Telegraph*, January 24, 1828.

27. Atwater to AJ, September 30, 1827, Jackson Papers, LC.

28. John Miller to John W. Taylor, February 8, 1828, Taylor Papers, New York Historical Society; Parton, *Jackson*, III, 144; *National Journal*, May 24, 1828.

29. For the newest study of anti-Masonry see William P. Vaughn, *The Antimasonic Party in the United States, 1826–1843* (Lexington, 1983).

30. Nicholas Trist to Donelson, October 19, 1828, Donelson Papers, LC.

31. For a discussion of all the maneuvering involved in the passage of this bill, see Remini, "Martin Van Buren and the Tariff of Abominations," *American Historical Review*, LXVIII, no. 4 (July 1958), 914–916.

32. October 20, 1828.

33. Schlesinger and Israel, eds., *History of American Presidential Elections*, I, 492.

34. H. Shaw to Clay, January 9, 1829, Clay papers, LC; *Niles' Weekly Register*, December 6, 1828; Edward Everett to A. H. Everett, December 2, 1828, Everett Papers, Massachusetts Historical Society.

35. New York *American*, November 9, 1827.

36. Parton, *Jackson*, III, 153; *United States Telegraph*, July 3, 1828.

37. Wise, *Seven Decades of the Union*, pp. 113–114; Bassett, *Jackson*, p. 406, footnote 1; Parton, *Jackson*, III, 154–155; Francis Preston to AJ, December 5, 1828, in Jackson, *Correspondence*, III, 452, footnote 2.

38. Parton, *Jackson*, III, 157.

39. Ibid., p. 156; Marquis James, *The Life of Andrew Jackson* (New York, 1938), p. 478.

40. Parton, *Jackson*, III, 158.

41. AJ to Coffee, January 17, 1829, Coffee Papers, THS; AJ to Jean Plauche, December 27, 1828, Jackson Papers, LC.

Chapter 13: The First People's Inaugural

1. Frances M. Trollope, *Domestic Manners of the Americans* (New York, 1949), I, 125.

2. *United States Telegraph,* January 28, 1829.

3. Alfred Mordecai to Ellen Mordecai, February 11, 1829, in Sarah Agnes Wallace, ed., "Opening Days of Jackson's Presidency as Seen in Private Letters," *Tennessee Historical Quarterly* (1950), IX, 368.

4. AJ to Van Buren, February 14, 1829, Van Buren Papers, LC; Kendall to Blair, March 7, 1829, Blair-Lee Papers, Princeton University Library.

5. Ibid.; James Hamilton to Van Buren, February 1929, Van Buren Papers, LC; W. A. Ingham, *Samuel D. Ingham* (Philadelphia, 1910), pp. 6–10; Kim T. Phillips, "The Pennsylvania Origins of the Jackson Movement," *Political Science Quarterly* (1976), XCI, 489–508.

6. AJ to Rachel, February 27, 1824, Charles Norton Owen Collection, Glencoe, Ill.

7. Kendall to Blair, March 7, 1829, Blair-Lee Papers, Princeton University Library; Louis McLane to James A. Bayard, February 19, 1829, Bayard Papers, LC.

8. Eaton to AJ, December 7, 1828, Hurja Collection, Tennessee State Library.

9. McLane to Van Buren, February 19, 1829, Van Buren Papers, LC; Kendall to Blair, March 7, 1829, Blair-Lee Papers, Princeton University Library; James A. Hamilton, *Reminiscences* (New York, 1869), p. 102.

10. Kendall to Blair, March 7, 1829, Blair-Lee Papers, Princeton University Library; Memorandum in Jackson's handwriting, [December 9, 1828], in Jackson, *Correspondence,* III, 451–452.

11. Kendall to Blair, February 3, 1829, Blair-Lee Papers, Princeton University Library.

12. Kendall, *Autobiography* (Boston, 1872), pp. 287–288.

13. "Rough Draft" of the First Inaugural Address, Jackson Papers, LC.

14. Richardson, *Messages and Papers,* II, 1000–1001.

15. Webster to Mrs. E. Webster, February 19, 1829, in Webster, *Private Correspondence* (Boston, 1857), I, 470.

16. Parton, *Jackson,* III, 169.

17. New York *Evening Post,* March 10, 1829.

18. *United States Gazette* (Philadelphia), March 6, 1829.

19. *United States Telegraph,* March 5, 1829.

20. *United States Gazette,* March 8, 1829.

21. Gaillard Hunt, ed., *The First Forty Years of Washington Society* (New York, 1906), p. 293; Parton, *Jackson,* III, 170.

22. Hunt, ed., *First Forty Years,* p. 291.

23. Boston *Statesman,* March 12, 1829.

24. Hunt, ed., *First Forty Years,* p. 291; Salmon P. Chase, manuscript diary, March 4, 1829, Chase Papers, LC; Richardson, *Messages and Papers,* II, 999–1001; Hamilton to Van Buren, March 5, 1829, Van Buren Papers, LC.

25. Hamilton to Van Buren, March 5, 1829, Van Buren Papers, LC.

26. Hunt, *First Forty Years,* p. 291.

27. *Argus of Western America,* March 18, 1829.

28. Hunt, *First Forty Years,* p. 291.

29. Joseph Story to Mrs. Story, March 7, 1829, William W. Story, *Life and Letters of Joseph Story* (Boston, 1851), I, 563.

30. Hamilton to Van Buren, March 5, 1829, Van Buren Papers, LC.

31. Hunt, *First Forty Years,* p. 284.

32. Ibid., p. 295.

33. Hamilton to Van Buren, March 5, 1829, Van Buren Papers, LC.

34. Hunt, *First Forty Years,* p. 297.

35. *Argus of Western America,* March 18, 1829.

Chapter 14: The Reform Begins

1. *Report of the Commission on the Renovation of the Executive Mansion* (Washington, D.C., 1952), p. 30.

2. Parton, *Jackson,* III, 180; Pauline Wilcox Burke, *Emily Donelson of Tennessee* (Richmond, Va., 1941), I, 173.

3. "Outline of principles," February 23, 1829, Jackson Papers, LC; Memorandum Book of A. Jackson commencing April, 1829, Jackson Papers, LC; See also Albert Somit, "Andrew Jackson as Administrative Reformer," *Tennessee Historical Quarterly* (1954), XIII, 204–233.

4. Parton, *Jackson,* III, 220.

5. Richardson, *Messages and Papers,* II, 1011–1012.

6. For details see Remini, *Jackson,* II, 186ff.

7. Benton, *Thirty Years View,* I, 737.

8. Ibid., p. 738.

9. Van Buren, *Autobiography,* p. 232.

10. See Max M. Mintz, "The Political Ideas of Martin Van Buren," *New York History* (1949), XXX, 422–448. There are two excellent biographies of Van Buren recently published: John Niven, *Martin Van Buren: The Romantic Age of American Politics* (New York, 1983), and Donald B. Cole, *Martin Van Buren and the American Political System* (Princeton, 1984).

11. Van Buren to Jesse Hoyt, April 13, 1829, in William L. Mackenzie, *Life and Times of Martin Van Buren* (Boston, 1846), p. 216.

12. Van Buren to AJ, April 23, 1829, Van Buren Papers, LC; AJ to Van Buren, April 24, 1829, in Van Buren, *Autobiography,* p. 265; AJ to Blair, January 5, 1839, Jackson Papers, LC; Van Buren, *Autobiography,* p. 269.

13. Jackson's Private Memorandum Book, and "Notes," May 1830, Jackson Papers, LC; AJ to Van Buren, May 15, 1830, Van Buren Papers, LC.

Chapter 15: Political Upheaval

1. Parton, *Jackson,* III, 287.

2. Ely to AJ, March 18, 1829, in Parton, *Jackson,* III, 186.

3. AJ to Stiles, March 23, 1829, in ibid., pp. 188–189.

4. Ibid.; Benton, *Thirty Years View,* I, 738.

5. "Narrative by General Jackson," in Parton, *Jackson,* III, 197–199.

6. Ibid.

7. Ibid., p. 204.

8. Ibid., p. 205.

9. Emily Donelson to Mary Coffee, March 27, 1829, in Burke, *Emily Donelson of Tennessee,* I, 178.

10. Van Buren, *Autobiography,* p. 350.

11. Ibid., p. 352.

12. Ibid., pp. 353–354; Levi Woodbury to Elizabeth Woodbury, December 24, 1829, Woodbury Papers, LC.

13. Memorandum, [January 1830], Jackson Papers, LC.

14. AJ to John McLemore, September 22, December 25, 1829, Miscellaneous Jackson Papers, New York Historical Society.

15. AJ to Overton, December 31, 1829, in Jackson, *Correspondence,* IV, 108–109.

16. *Register of Debates,* 21st Congress, 1st session, pp. 31–35, 35–41, 43–80.

17. Ibid., p. 77. A new and excellent biography of Webster is Maurice G. Baxter, *One and Inseparable: Daniel Webster and the Union* (Cambridge, 1984).

18. AJ to Claiborne, November 12, 1806, in Jackson, *Correspondence,* I, 153.

19. Parton, *Jackson,* III, 282.

20. Van Buren, *Autobiography,* p. 413.

21. Ibid.

22. *United States Telegraph,* April 15, 17, 20, 23, 1830; Kendall to Blair, April 25, 1830, Blair-Lee Papers, Princeton University Library.

23. Van Buren, *Autobiography,* p. 415.

24. Ibid.

25. *United States Telegraph,* April 15, 17, 20, 23, 1830.

26. *Register of Debates,* 21st Congress, 1st session, p. 80.

27. Richard Pollard to William C. Rives, June 10, 1830, Rives Papers, LC.

28. Kendall to Blair, April 25, 1830, Blair-Lee Papers, Princeton University Library.

29. Parton, *Jackson,* III, 284–285.

30. "Narrative by Major William B. Lewis," in Parton, *Jackson,* III, 320.

31. Ibid. Lewis visited New York in 1828 and Hamilton showed him the letter.

32. Ibid., pp. 323–324.

33. Crawford to Forsyth, April 30, 1830, in *Works of John C. Calhoun,* Richard K. Crallé, ed. (New York, 1851–1856), VI, 30.

34. AJ to Calhoun, May 13, 1830, in Jackson, *Correspondence,* IV, 136.

35. Parton, *Jackson,* III, 333.

36. Calhoun to AJ, May 25, 1830, in *United States Telegraph,* February 17, 21, 23, 26, 1831.

37. "Narrative of Major William B. Lewis," in Parton, *Jackson,* III, 326.

38. AJ to Donelson, December 25, 1830, Miscellaneous Jackson Papers, New York Historical Society.

39. Kendall to Francis P. Blair, October 2, 1830, Blair-Lee Papers, Princeton University Library.

40. Ibid.

41. Lewis to Overton, January 13, 1831, Overton Papers, THS.

42. Blair to Van Buren, December 9, 1858, Van Buren Papers, LC.

43. George Crawford to Blair, March 27, 1831, Blair-Lee Papers, Princeton University Library.

44. Everett to Alexander Everett, January 23, 1831, Everett Papers, Massachusetts Historical Society.

45. The complete work can be found in the *Telegraph,* February 17, 21, 23, 26, 1831.

46. Williams to Van Buren, March 22, 1831, Van Buren Papers, LC; Parton, *Jackson,* III, 345; AJ to Charles J. Love, March 7, 1831, in Jackson, *Correspondence,* IV, 246.

47. Kendall to Gideon Welles, March 19, 1831, Welles Papers, LC; AJ to Love, March 7, 1831, in Jackson, *Correspondence,* IV, 246.

48. Van Buren, *Autobiography,* p. 384.

49. Ibid., p. 402.

50. Ibid., p. 403.

51. Ibid., pp. 403–407.

52. Memorandum, April 18, 1831, in Jackson's handwriting, Jackson Papers, LC.

53. These letters can be found in Jackson, *Correspondence,* IV, 266, 295.

54. Parton, *Jackson,* III, 359; John Tyler to Littleton W. Tazewell, May 8, 1831, in Lyon G. Tyler, *The Letters and Times of the Tylers* (Richmond, 1884–1896), I, 422; Clay to Francis Brooke, May 1, 1831, in Calvin Colton, ed., *Private Correspondence of Henry Clay* (New York, 1857), p. 299.

55. White to AJ, April 20, 1831, in Jackson, *Correspondence,* IV, 267.

56. Van Buren to AJ, July 16, 1831, Van Buren Papers, LC.

57. Donelson to Emily, June 16, 1831, Donelson Papers, LC.

58. Biddle to Robert M. Gibbes, December 31, 1831, Biddle Papers, LC.

59. An article signed "Veritas" (undoubtedly Poindexter) appeared in the *Telegraph* on March 13 and referred to the "Kitchen Cabinet" in defending Poindexter's vote against the nomination of Van Buren as minister to Great Britain. Two days later the Richmond *Enquirer* mentioned the Kitchen Cabinet.

Chapter 16: Return to Reform

1. AJ to Van Buren, March 31, 1829, Van Buren Papers, LC.

2. "Outline of principles submitted to the Heads of Department," February 23, 1829, Jackson Papers, LC.

3. Richardson, *Messages and Papers,* II, 1006ff.

4. Ibid., p. 1025.

5. AJ to Van Buren, May 15, 1830, in Van Buren, *Autobiography,* p. 322.

6. Ibid., p. 326.

7. Ibid.

8. Ibid., p. 327; Richardson, *Messages and Papers,* II, 1046–1055. Over the next several years Jackson became more hostile to internal improvements, further narrowing the permissible area for federal involvement. He also gradually abandoned his ideas about the distribution of the surplus. See his sixth message to Congress, December 1, 1834, and his eighth, December 5, 1836, in ibid., II, 1340–1341, 1464–1465.

9. "Notes—The Maysville road bill," Jackson papers, LC.

10. Ibid.

11. Ibid.; AJ to Coffee, May 31, 1830, Coffee Papers, AJ to Overton, May 13, 1830, Overton Papers, THS; Richardson, *Messages and Papers,* II, 1165.

12. Governmental aspects of Indian-white relations are treated extensively in Francis Paul Prucha, *The Great Father* (Lincoln, 1984), 2 vols.; Reginald Horsman, *Expansion and American Indian Policy, 1783–1812* (East Lansing, Mich., 1967); and Wilcomb E. Washburn, *Red Man's Land/White Man's Law* (New York, 1971).

13. *Register of Debates,* 21st Congress, 1st session, pp. 1124–1125.

14. Ibid., pp. 310–311.

15. Ibid., p. 325.

16. Ibid., p. 383.

17. Ibid., pp. 1001–1002.

18. Ibid., pp. 1021–1024.

19. Ibid., pp. 1132–1133.

20. Van Buren, *Autobiography,* p. 289.

21. *Register of Debates,* 21st Congress, 1st session, pp. 1145–1146.

22. U.S. *Statutes,* IV, 411–412.

23. DeRosier, *Removal of the Choctaw Indians,* pp. 122, 128; Remini, *Jackson,* II, 270ff.

24. Report of the Cherokee case against Georgia can be found in 5 *Peters* 1ff.

25. 6 *Peters* 515.

26. Horace Greeley, *The American Conflict: A History of the Great Rebellion in the United States* . . . (Hartford, 1865), I, 106.

27. Charles J. Johnson to [?], March 23, 1832, David Campbell Papers, Duke University Library.

28. Richard P. Longaker, "Andrew Jackson and the Judiciary," *Political Science Quarterly* (1956), LXXI, 350.

29. Technically it was not a removal treaty but a clever scheme to get the Creeks to relinquish their land in return for a pledge that it would be allotted to the chiefs and headmen. The Creeks, after a show of resistance, were forcibly removed.

30. Van Buren to AJ, December 22, 1832, Van Buren Papers, LC; Benjamin F. Butler to Wilson Lumpkin, December 17, 1832, Gratz Collection, Historical Society of Pennsylvania; Martin R. Cain, "William Wirt against Andrew Jackson: Reflection of an Era," *Mid-America* (1965), XLVII, 113ff.

31. Richardson, *Messages and Papers*, II, 1166. For the Black Hawk War see Cecil Eby, *"That Disgraceful Affair": The Black Hawk War* (New York, 1973); Ellen M. Whitney, comp. and ed., *The Black Hawk War: 1831–1832*, 2 vols. (Springfield, Ill., 1970–1975).

32. See John K. Mahon, *History of the Second Seminole War, 1835–1842* (Gainesville, 1967), pp. 214–218.

33. Ronald N. Satz, *American Indian Policy in the Jacksonian Era* (Lincoln, 1975), 97, 115, note 1. From 1789 to 1838, approximately 81,282 Indians were removed beyond the Mississippi River. *House Documents*, 25th Congress, 3rd session, no. 347.

34. AJ to secretary of war, [1831], Jackson Papers, LC.

35. Satz, *American Indian Policy*, p. 152.

Chapter 17: The Bank War Begins

1. AJ to AJ, Jr., October, 27, 1831, in Jackson, *Correspondence*, IV, 365; AJ to Coffee, November 20, 1831, Coffee Papers, THS.

2. AJ to Van Buren, December 6, 17, 1831, Van Buren Papers, LC.

3. Ibid.

4. Roger B. Taney, "Roger B. Taney's 'Bank War Manuscript,' " Carl B. Swisher, ed., *Maryland Historical Magazine* (1958), LIII, 125.

5. John A. Munroe, *Louis McLane: Federalist and Jacksonian* (New Brunswick, 1973), p. 307.

6. *Niles' Weekly Register*, October 1, 1831; Harriet H. Weed, ed., *Autobiography of Thurlow Weed* (Boston, 1883), p. 389; Remini, *Andrew Jackson and the Bank War* (New York, 1967), pp. 90–91.

7. Clay to Biddle, December 15, 1831, Biddle Papers, LC.

8. Samuel Smith to William Rives, January 3, 1832, quoted in Munroe, *McLane*, p. 321.

9. Taney to Ellicott, January 25, 1832, Taney Papers, LC.

10. Quoted in Walter B. Smith, *Economic Aspects of the Second Bank of the United States* (Cambridge, Mass., 1953), p. 14.

11. Blair to Mrs. Benjamin Gratz, April 20, 1831, in Clay, "Two Years with Old Hickory," *Atlantic Monthly* (1887), LX, 193.

12. Parton, *Jackson*, III, 415; Donelson to Coffee, January 16, 1832, Donelson Papers, LC.

13. *Register of Debates,* 22nd Congress, 1st session, p. 1341.

14. Ibid., p. 1324.

15. Benton, *Thirty Years View,* I, 219.

16. Henry Wikoff, *Reminiscences of an Idler* (New York, 1880), pp. 29–31.

17. AJ to Van Buren, February 12, 1832, Van Buren Papers, LC.

18. Cambreleng to Van Buren, February 13, 1832, Van Buren Papers, LC.

19. Marcy to Azariah C. Flagg, February 6, [1832], Flagg Papers, NYPL.

20. Parton, *Jackson,* III, 451. Clay's speech can be found in *Register of Debates,* 22nd Congress, 1st session, pp. 462ff.

21. Biddle to Cadwalader, July 3, 1832, Biddle papers, LC.

22. Taney, "Roger B. Taney's 'Bank War Manuscript,' " pp. 226–227.

23. Van Buren, *Autobiography,* p. 625.

24. Richardson, *Messages and Papers,* II, 1139–1140, 1143–1144.

25. Ibid., pp. 1144–1145.

26. Ibid., p. 1153.

27. Ibid., p. 1154.

28. Ralph C. H. Catterall, *The Second Bank of the United States* (Chicago, 1903), p. 239.

29. Biddle to Clay, August 1, 1832, Biddle Papers, LC.

30. *National Intelligencer,* November 22, 1834.

31. Daniel Webster, *Works of Daniel Webster* (Boston, 1864), III, 434, 446, 438, 447.

32. Henry Clay, *The Works of Henry Clay,* Calvin Colton, ed. (New York, 1904), VII, 524.

33. William N. Chambers, *Old Bullion Benton: Senator from the New West* (Boston, 1956), pp. 184–186; Ben Perley Poore, *Perley's Reminiscences* (Philadelphia, 1886), I, 144.

Chapter 18: Jackson and the Union

1. Kendall to [?], July 25, 1832, Kendall Papers, New York Historical Society; Kendall to Welles, September 12, 1831, Welles Papers, LC; Jackson memorandum, July 1832, Jackson Papers, LC; Jackson to Lewis, August 18, 1832, Jackson-Lewis Papers, NYPL.

2. *Niles' Weekly Register,* March 14, 1832; Remini, "Election of 1832," in Arthur M. Schlesinger, Jr., Fred L. Israel, and William P. Hansen, eds., *History of American Presidential Elections* (New York, 1971), I, 510.

3. Marcy to Hoyt, October 1, 1832, William L. Mackenzie, *Lives of Benjamin F. Butler and Jesse Hoyt* (Boston, 1845), p. 113; Hill to Hoyt, October 15, 1832, in Mackenzie, *Life and Times of Martin Van Buren,* p. 239.

4. *Globe,* September 5, 1832; see also reprints in the *Globe* from other Democratic newspapers, September 8, 15, 22, October 3, 6, 17, 20, 1832.

5. *National Intelligencer,* September 6, 1832.

6. Parton, *Jackson,* III, 420.

7. AJ to Van Buren, August 30, 1832, Van Buren Papers, LC.

8. William W. Freehling, *Prelude to Civil War: The Nullification Controversy in South Carolina, 1816–1836* (New York, 1965), p. 253.

9. AJ to Woodbury, September 11, 1832, in Jackson, *Correspondence,* IV, 474–475; AJ to Donelson, August 30, September 17, 1832, Donelson Papers, LC; Freehling, *Prelude to Civil War,* p. 239ff.; AJ to Lewis, August 23, 1832, in New York *Times,* January 11, 1875.

10. Quoted in Remini, "Election of 1832," p. 509.

11. George Dallas to Edward Livingston, May 30, 1831, Livingston Papers, JRDF.

12. Poinsett to AJ, October 16, 1832, Jackson Papers, LC.

13. AJ to Lewis Cass, October 29, 1832, in Jackson, *Correspondence*, IV, 483.

14. AJ to Donelson, October 10, 1832, Donelson Papers, LC; AJ to Breathitt, November 7, 1832, in Jackson, *Correspondence*, IV, 484–485.

15. Svend Petersen, *A Statistical History of the American Presidential Elections* (New York, 1963), pp. 20–21.

16. April 21, 1832.

17. George Blair to Willie P. Mangum, December 8, 1832, in Henry T. Shanks, ed., *The Papers of Willie Persons Mangum* (Raleigh, 1950–1956), I, 588.

18. J. H. Kirth to Azariah C. Flagg, October 13, 1832, Flagg Papers, NYPL.

19. Wirt to John T. Lomax, November 15, 1832, in John P. Kennedy, *Memoirs of the Life of William Wirt, Attorney-General of the United States* (Philadelphia, 1849), II, 331.

20. Richardson, *Messages and Papers*, II, 1161–1162.

21. *State Papers on Nullification* (Boston, 1834), pp. 29–31.

22. Poinsett to AJ, November 24, 25, 29, 1832, Jackson Papers, LC.

23. AJ to Poinsett, December 2, 1832, Poinsett Papers, Historical Society of Pennsylvania, Philadelphia.

24. This may be a reference to Jackson, who was born in South Carolina.

25. Parton, *Jackson*, III, 458–459.

26. Ibid., p. 459.

27. Private Memorandum of A. Jackson, Jackson Papers, LC.

28. AJ to Livingston, December 4, 1832, Livingston Papers, JRDF; Parton, *Jackson*, III, 466.

29. AJ to Livingston, December 4, 1832, Livingston Papers, JRDF.

30. Richardson, *Messages and Papers*, II, 1203–1213.

31. My argument about Jackson and the perpetuity of the Union follows closely the analysis of Kenneth M. Stampp, *The Imperiled Union: Essays on the Background of the Civil War* (New York, 1980), pp. 33–34. For a new and extremely insightful study of the crisis, see Richard E. Ellis, *The Union at Risk: Jacksonian Democracy, States' Rights and the Nullification Crisis* (New York, 1987).

32. Richardson, *Messages and Papers*, II, 1217.

Chapter 19: The Union Preserved

1. Richard Rush to Edward Livingston, December 18, 19, 1832, Livingston Papers, JRDF. There were of course criticisms, especially among strong advocates of states' rights, north as well as south.

2. AJ to Poinsett, December 9, 1832, Poinsett Papers, Historical Society of Pennsylvania, Philadelphia.

3. AJ to Cass, December 17, 1832, in Jackson, *Correspondence*, IV, 502.

4. James O'Hanlon to AJ, December 20, 1832, Jackson Papers, LC; Freehling, *Prelude to Civil War*, p. 275.

5. Richardson, *Messages and Papers*, II, 1183–1184.

6. Ibid., pp. 1192–1193; Freehling, *Prelude to Civil War*, p. 285.

7. Richardson, *Messages and Papers*, II, 1194.

8. Ibid., p. 1195.

9. Ibid., p. 1194.

10. Wright to Flagg, January 14, February 2, 1833, Flagg Papers, NYPL.

11. *Register of Debates*, 22nd Congress, 2nd session, pp. 519–553.

12. Ibid., pp. 553–587; Benjamin F. Perry, *Reminiscences of Public Men* (Philadelphia, 1883), p. 45.

13. AJ to Poinsett, February 17, 1833, Poinsett Papers, Historical Society of Pennsylvania, Philadelphia.

14. *Register of Debates,* 22nd Congress, 2nd session, p. 688.

15. Clay to Francis Brooke, January 17, 1833, in Colton, ed., *Works of Henry Clay,* V, 347; Cambreleng to Van Buren, February 5, 1833, Van Buren Papers, LC; Charles Wiltse, *John C. Calhoun, Nullifier* (New York, 1949), 184–185.

16. *Register of Debates,* 22nd Congress, 2nd session, pp. 462–478.

17. *Register of Debates,* 22nd Congress, 2nd session, pp. 697–701, 715–716.

18. T. J. Randolph to William C. Rives, February 20, 1833, Rives Papers, LC.

19. *Register of Debates,* 22nd Congress, 2nd session, pp. 694–716.

20. Ibid., p. 1903.

21. AJ to Poinsett, March 6, 1833, Poinsett Papers, Historical Society of Pennsylvania, Philadelphia.

22. Nathaniel Macon to Van Buren, March 2, 1833, Van Buren Papers, LC. Calhoun said the Force Bill was an act to "repeal the Constitution." Calhoun to William C. Preston, no date, in *Calhoun Papers,* XII, 37.

23. *State Papers on Nullification,* pp. 230, 274.

24. AJ to Coffee, April 9, 1833, Coffee Papers, Tennessee Historical Society; AJ to Reverend Andrew J. Crawford, May 1, 1833, in Jackson, *Correspondence,* V, 72.

25. Freehling, *Prelude to Civil War,* p. 293.

Chapter 20: "The Grand Triumphal Tour"

1. AJ to Coffee, May 11, 1833, Coffee Family Papers, LC.

2. Donelson to Coffee, May 14, 1833, Donelson Papers, LC.

3. Memorandum, May, 1833, Notes on Lt. Randolph's conduct, in Jackson's handwriting, Jackson Papers, LC.

4. AJ to Van Buren, December 4, 1838, Van Buren Papers, LC.

5. AJ to Van Buren, May 19, 1833, Van Buren Papers, LC.

6. John Campbell to David Campbell, May 12, 1833, Campbell Papers, Duke University Library.

7. Donelson to Emily Donelson, June 22, 1833, Donelson Papers, LC.

8. *Globe,* March 15, 1833.

9. *Niles' Weekly Register,* April 6, 1833.

10. AJ to Andrew Jr., June 6, 1833, Jackson Papers, LC; *Globe,* June 8, 1833.

11. Manuscript Journal of a young Irishman touring the United States, May 27–November 15, 1833, Huntington Library.

12. *Globe,* April 24, 1833.

13. *Niles' Weekly Register,* June 15, 1833.

14. Ibid.

15. *Globe,* June 12, 14, 1833.

16. Moses and Cross, *Presidential Courage,* p. 40.

17. Parton, *Jackson,* III, 489.

18. Ibid.

19. Cupping is the method of drawing blood to the surface of the skin by creating a vacuum with a cup at the point where the cup is applied. AJ to Andrew Jr., June 10, 1833, in Jackson, *Correspondence,* V, 109.

20. *National Intelligencer,* June 20, 1833.

21. Ibid., June 18, 22, 1833; *United States Telegraph,* June 14, 1833.

22. Allan Nevins, ed., *The Diary of Philip Hone, 1828–1851* (New York, 1927), I, 94–95.

23. Fletcher Green, "On Tour with President Andrew Jackson," *New England Quarterly* (1963), XXXVI, 218.

24. New York *Standard,* June 13, 14, 1833; New York *American,* June 13, 15, 18, 1833.

25. Donelson to Emily Donelson, June 24, 1833, Donelson Papers, LC.

26. Adams, *Memoirs,* VIII, 546.

27. Parton, *Jackson,* III, 492.

28. *Niles' Weekly Register,* July 6, 1833.

29. Portland *Courier,* June 20, 1833.

30. *Niles' Weekly Register,* July 6, 1833.

31. Ibid.

32. William B. Lewis to Edward Livingston, November 18, 1833, Livingston Papers, JRDF.

33. Ibid.

34. *Niles' Weekly Register,* July 22, 1833.

Chapter 21: Panic!

1. AJ to Donelson, August 5, 1833, Donelson Papers, LC.

2. *Globe,* September 8, 1832.

3. AJ to Duane, June 26, 1833, in Jackson, *Correspondence,* V, 112. Livingston resigned as secretary of state to become minister to France. Louis McLane then resigned as Treasury chief to take over the State Department.

4. Duane to AJ, July 10, 1833, Jackson Papers, LC.

5. William J. Duane, *Narrative and Correspondence Concerning the Removal of the Deposites and Occurrences Connected Therewith* (Philadelphia, 1838), p. 57.

6. Kendall to Duane, July 28, August 10, 27, 1833, National Archives; Treasury Department Report, July 23, 1833; Reports of Amos Kendall, Including Correspondence with Banks, National Archives.

7. Kendall to John M. Niles, October 2, 1833, Niles Papers, Connecticut Historical Society, Hartford.

8. Kendall had some trouble along the way, however. A few banks refused to offer security. "Those not offering security where others do offer," he wrote, "will, I think, be thrown out of competition." Kendall to Thomas Ellicott [?], August 3, 1833, Taney Papers, LC.

9. AJ to Van Buren, September 8, 1833, Van Buren Papers, LC.

10. Duane, *Narrative and Correspondence,* p. 100.

11. Ibid., pp. 101–103.

12. AJ to Van Buren, September 23, 1833, Van Buren Papers, LC.

13. Levi Woodbury also assisted in the preparation of the order. Taney to Woodbury, September 25, 1833, Woodbury Papers, LC.

14. AJ to Van Buren, September 26, and Van Buren to AJ, September 28, 1833, Van Buren Papers, LC.

15. AJ to Van Buren, November 19, 1833, Van Buren Papers, LC.

16. Biddle to Joseph Hopkinson, February 21, 1834, Biddle Papers, LC.

17. Taney to Ellicott, October 23, December 13, 1833, Taney Papers, LC; John M. McFaul, *The Politics of Jacksonian Finance* (Ithaca, 1972), p. 60.

18. Taney to Ellicott, September 28, 1833, Taney Papers, LC.

19. *National Intelligencer,* October 2, 1833.

20. Ibid., September 21, October 2, 4, 16, November 2, 1833.

21. Webster to Stephen White, December 21, 27, 1833, in *Webster Papers,* III, 289, 296–297.

22. John Tyler to Mrs. Tyler, February 17, 1834, in Tyler, *Letters and Times,* I, 485; Jacob Barker to Van Buren, February 25, and Jesse Hoyt to Van Buren, January 29, 1834, Van Buren Papers, LC; Levi Lincoln to Webster, January 11, 1834, in *Webster Papers,* III, 308–309.

23. Parton, *Jackson,* III, 549–550, 553; C. W. Lawrence to George Newbold, February 9, 1834, Newbold Papers, New York Historical Society.

24. Wright to Flagg, December 11, 1833, Flagg Papers, NYPL.

25. Hone, *Diary,* I, xii, II, 629.

26. *National Intelligencer,* March 18, 1834. For party ideology see Daniel Walker Howe, ed., *The American Whigs: An Anthology* (New York, 1973), and *The Political Culture of the American Whigs* (Chicago, 1979).

27. Glyndon G. Van Deusen, *The Jacksonian Era, 1828–1848* (New York, 1959), pp. 96–97.

28. A. Rencher to Charles Fisher, February 11, 1834, Fisher Family Papers, Southern Historical Collection, University of North Carolina, Chapel Hill; Cambreleng to Livingston, March 16, 1834, Livingston Papers, JRDF.

29. Benton, *Thirty Years View,* I, 424.

30. Ibid., 423.

31. AJ to Kendall, April [1834?], de Coppet Collection, Princeton University Library.

32. *National Intelligencer,* May 6, 1834.

33. Daniel Webster, *The Writings and Speeches of Daniel Webster* (Boston, 1903), VII, 139, 143, 144, 145, 147.

34. *Register of Debates,* 23rd Congress, 1st session, pp. 1394–1395, 1397–1398, 1375. For a recent study of Webster, Clay and Calhoun see Merrill D. Peterson, *The Great Triumvirate* (New York, 1987).

35. Sargent, *Public Men and Events,* I, 347.

Chapter 22: The End of the Bank

1. AJ to Van Buren, January 3, 1834, Van Buren Papers, LC.

2. AJ to Tilghman A. Howard, August 20, 1833, in Jackson, *Correspondence,* V, 166.

3. Joseph Hopkinson to Biddle, February 11, 1834, Biddle Papers, LC; R. H. Wilde to Gulian C. Verplanck, February 22, 1834, Verplanck Papers, New York Historical Society.

4. Some even thought it originated with Amos Kendall. Silas M. Stilwell to Biddle, February 1, 1834, Biddle Papers, LC.

5. Van Buren to Sedgwick, March 20, 1834, Sedgwick Papers, Massachusetts Historical Society.

6. AJ to Wolf, February 1834, in Jackson, *Correspondence,* V, 243.

7. Van Buren to David E. Evans, February 13, 1834, Woodbury Papers, LC; Greene to Levi Woodbury, March 14, 1834, Woodbury Papers, LC.

8. *Register of Debates,* 23rd Congress, 1st session, pp. 3474–3477.

9. Charles G. Sellers, Jr., *James K. Polk, Jacksonian* (Princeton, 1957), p. 222.

10. AJ to Coffee, April 6, 1834, Coffee Papers, THS; AJ to Andrew, Jr., April 6, 1834, Jackson Papers, LC; Butler to Olcott, June 19, 1834, Olcott Papers, Columbia University Library.

11. Sellers, *Polk,* I, 222; Biddle to J. G. Watmouth, May 2, May 10, 1834, Biddle Papers, LC; Rives to Woodbury, May 26, 1834, Woodbury Papers, LC.

12. These measures were contained in a report submitted to the House Ways and Means Committee by Secretary Taney. *House Committee Reports,* 23rd Congress, 1st session, no. 422.

13. Benton, *Thirty Years View,* I, 657–658; Frank Gatell, "Spoils of the Bank War," in *American Historical Review,* LXX, 36.

14. AJ to Edward Livingston, June 27, 1834, Livingston Papers, JRDF.

15. Sargent, *Public Men and Events,* I, 347.

Chapter 23: The Hermitage Fire

1. Robert Armstrong to AJ, October 14, 1834, Donelson to AJ, October 14, 1834, in Jackson, *Correspondence,* V, 295–296; Andrew Jr. to Hutchings, November 20, 1834, Hutchings Papers, Dyas Collection, THS.

2. AJ to Harriet Butler, June 24, 1837, C. Norton Owen Collection, Glencoe, Ill.

3. Stockley Donelson to AJ, October 14, 1834, in Jackson, *Correspondence,* V, 296.

4. Stockley Donelson to AJ, October 14, 1834, Armstrong to AJ, October 14, 1834, in Jackson, *Correspondence,* V, 295–297; Andrew Jr. to Hutchings, November 20, 1834, Hutchings Papers, Dyas Collection, THS.

5. AJ to Andrew Jr., October 23, 25, 1834, Jackson Papers, LC.

6. Ibid.

7. AJ to Andrew Jr., November 12, 1834, Jackson Papers, LC; AJ to Andrew Jr., December 7, 1834, Jackson Papers, Huntington Library.

8. AJ to Andrew Jr., November 19, 26, 27, 1834, Jackson Papers, LC.

9. Love to AJ, January 28, 1835, and Memorandum of Agreement for Rebuilding the Hermitage, January 1, 1835, in Jackson, *Correspondence,* V, 315–317, 322–323.

10. AJ to Andrew Jr., October 30, 1834, Jackson Papers, LC.

11. Estimates for Rebuilding the Hermitage, August 2, 1836, in Jackson, *Correspondence,* V, 414–415; itemized list of expenses, December, 1834, Jackson Papers, LC; AJ to Andrew Jr., March 29, 1836, Jackson Papers, LC.

Chapter 24: Jacksonian Diplomacy

1. Jackson's address to the foreign ministers, April 6, 1829, U.S. Presidents, A. Jackson Papers, NYPL; Richardson, *Messages and Papers,* II, 1006.

2. Quoted in Munroe, *McLane,* p. 256.

3. Ibid., pp. 262–263.

4. The best and most complete statement of Jackson's foreign policy is John M. Belohlavek, *"Let the Eagle Soar!" The Foreign Policy of Andrew Jackson* (Lincoln and London, 1985).

5. Memorandum, April 10, 1830, Jackson Papers, LC.

6. Richardson, *Messages and Papers,* II, 1043.

7. Munroe, *McLane,* p. 278.

8. McLane to Woodbury, August 30, 1830, Woodbury Papers, LC.

9. Richardson, *Messages and Papers,* II, 1061–1062.

10. AJ to Overton, May 27, 1830, Overton Papers, THS; Richardson, *Messages and Papers,* II, 1068, 1044.

11. *American State Papers, Naval Affairs,* IV, 154ff.; John M. Belohlavek, "Andrew Jackson and the Malaysian Pirates: A Question of Diplomacy and Politics," *Tennessee Historical Quarterly* (1977), XXXVI, 19, 21, 22, 23.

12. July 11, 1832.

13. Roberts to Livingston, May 10, 1833, Edmund Roberts Papers, LC; Edmund Roberts, *Embassy to the Eastern Courts of Cochin-China, Siam, and Muscat* (New York, 1837), pp. 210–216.

14. Hunter Miller, ed., *Treaties and Other International Acts of the United States of America* (Washington, D.C., 1933), III, 755–758, 796–798.

15. H. M. Neiditch, "The Origins and Development of Andrew Jackson's Foreign Policy," Doctoral dissertation, Cambridge University, 1977, pp. 210ff.

16. Livingston to Roberts, June 6, 1832, Roberts Papers, LC; William B. Hatcher, *Edward Livingston: Jeffersonian Republican and Jacksonian Democrat* (Baton Rouge, 1940), p. 403.

17. The economic impulse of the Jackson administration is strongly emphasized by Belohlavek's study of Jackson's foreign policy, *"Let the Eagle Soar!"*

18. John Randolph of Roanoke was Jackson's first appointee to the Russian mission and it was a disaster. Randolph stayed at his post for a very brief period and then returned home—because of alleged illness—without so much as a by-your-leave.

19. Joseph C. Baylen, "James Buchanan's 'Calm of Despotism,'" *Pennsylvania Magazine of Biography and History* (1953), LXXVII, 296ff.

20. Taney to Van Buren, April 9, 1860, Van Buren Papers, LC.

21. McLane to Livingston, June 3, July 25, August 6, 1833. Livingston Papers, JRDF.

22. Richardson, *Messages and Papers*, II, 1239–1240, 1241.

23. Livingston to McLane, October 13, 1833, Livingston Papers, JRDF.

24. Richard A. McLemore, *Franco-American Relations* (University, La., 1941), pp. 112–113; George M. Gibbs to Van Buren, April 2, 1834, Van Buren Papers, LC.

25. McLane to Sérurier, June 27, 1834, in McLemore, *Franco-American Relations*, p. 120.

26. Comte de Rigny to Livingston, July 31, 1834, Livingston Papers, JRDF.

27. Sérurier to Rigny, November 29, 1834, in McLemore, *Franco-American Relations*, p. 128.

28. Richardson, *Messages and Papers*, II, 1321–1322.

29. Ibid., p. 1325.

30. Livingston to Forsyth, January 11, 1835, and Livingston to AJ, January 16, 1835, Livingston Papers, JRDF.

31. Adams, *Memoirs*, IX, 207; AJ to Rodney Church, April 27, 1835, Jackson Papers, LC.

32. McLemore, *Franco-American Relations*, pp. 151–152; Hatcher, *Livingston*, p. 443; Livingston to Forsyth, April 19, 1835, Livingston Papers, JRDF.

33. Livingston to Forsyth, April 19, 1835, Livingston to the Duc de Broglie, April 25, 1835, Livingston Papers, JRDF.

34. Adams, *Memoirs*, IX, 238; Rives to Van Buren, June 2, 1835, Van Buren Papers, LC.

35. AJ to Kendall, October 31, 1835, in Jackson, *Correspondence*, V, 374–375.

36. Broglie's note to his representative in Washington was later published in the *National Intelligencer*, January 22, 1836.

37. Richardson, *Messages and Papers*, II, 1367ff., 1379.

38. McLemore, *Franco-American Relations*, pp. 184, 187; Bankhead to Forsyth, February 15, 1836, in Richardson, *Messages and Papers*, II, 1440.

39. Richardson, *Messages and Papers*, pp. 1435, 1436.

40. AJ to Livingston, February 27, 1836, Livingston Papers, JRDF.

41. This point is discussed and analyzed in Livingston to AJ, June 23, 1834, Jackson Papers, LC.

Chapter 25: Jacksonian Democracy

1. A full account of the celebration can be found in the *Globe,* January 14, 1835.

2. Tyler to Robert Tyler, January 31, 1835, Miscellaneous Papers, Huntington Library.

3. Ibid.; Francis Scott Key to Roger B. Taney, January 30, 1835, Miscellaneous Key Papers, LC.; *Globe,* February 3, 4, April 13, 1835.

4. New York *Evening Post,* February 4, 1835.

5. "Booth" to AJ, July 4, 1835, in Jackson, *Correspondence,* V, 355.

6. For social reform in the Jacksonian era see Alice Felt Tyler, *Freedom's Ferment* (Minneapolis, 1944).

7. Van Buren, *Autobiography,* p. 353.

8. Kendall to Huger, August 4, 1835, in *Niles' Weekly Register,* August 22, 1835.

9. AJ to Kendall, August 7, 9, 1835, in Jackson, *Correspondence,* V, 360.

10. Kermit L. Hall, *The Politics of Justice: Lower Federal Judicial Selection and the Second Party System, 1829–1861* (Lincoln and London, 1986), p. 3ff.

11. *Globe,* June 22, 1836.

12. Benton, *Thirty Years View,* II, 676.

13. Ibid., p. 678.

14. July 14, 15, 1836.

15. *Globe,* October 12, 1836.

16. AJ to Kendall, August 5, 1836, A. G. Mitten Collection, Indiana Historical Society, Indianapolis.

17. Nashville, *National Banner,* August 26, 1836, copy JPP.

18. AJ to Blair, August 22, 1836, Jackson Papers, LC.

19. Richardson, *Messages and Papers,* II, 1011.

20. AJ to Donelson, May 12, 1835, Donelson Papers, LC.

21. These views, written by Blair, were expressed in the *Globe,* July 27, 1832, but they clearly carry Jackson's imprimature. The two men discussed them at the time the Bank veto was written. In that veto message Jackson had said: "The Congress, the Executive, and the Court must each for itself be guided by its own opinion of the Constitution."

22. *Globe,* April 1, 1834.

23. Manuscript Ledger, George Bancroft Papers, Massachusetts Historical Society.

24. Croswell to Bancroft, August 13, Bancroft Papers, Massachusetts Historical Society.

25. On this point see Robert V. Remini, *The Legacy of Andrew Jackson* (Baton Rouge, 1988), pp. 38–39, 43–44, and Harry L. Watson, "Old Hickory's Democracy," in the *Wilson Quarterly* (Autumn, 1985), pp. 132, 133.

26. John Stetson Barry, Manuscript Diary, Chicago Historical Society; Alfred Mordecai to Ellen Mordecai, March 4, 1830, Mordecai Papers, LC.

Chapter 26: Texas

1. For more details see Remini, *Jackson,* I, pp. 341ff.

2. Benjamin F. Butler to his wife, Harriet Butler, June 29, 1836, Butler Papers, New York State Library.

3. Austin to AJ, April 15, 1836 with endorsement, Jackson Papers, LC.

4. Ann Fears Crawford, ed., *The Eagle: The Autobiography of Santa Anna* (Austin, 1967), p. 187; *Globe,* January 21, 1837.

5. Blair to Jackson, August 28, 1839, Jackson Papers, LC; Santa Anna, *Autobiography,* p. 57.

6. Blair to AJ, August 28, 1839, Jackson Papers, LC.

7. Memorandum, no date, Jackson Papers, LC.

8. Blair to AJ, August 28, 1839, Jackson Papers, LC.

9. Santa Anna, *Autobiography,* p. 57.

10. Wharton and Hunt to AJ, February 8, 1837, in *Diplomatic Correspondence of the United States, American Historical Association, Annual Report* (Washington, 1907), I, 197.

11. *Congressional Globe,* 24th Congress, 2nd session, pp. 213, 219.

12. Wharton and Hunt to J. Pinckney Henderson, March 5, 1837, in *Diplomatic Correspondence,* p. 201.

Chapter 27: Life in the White House

1. William Seale, *The President's House: A History* (Washington, 1986), I, 198.

2. Statement, "White House Household," Jackson Papers, LC.

3. Seale, *The President's House,* I, 183–184.

4. Ibid., pp. 199–200.

5. Ibid., pp. 202–203.

6. Ibid., pp. 206–207.

7. Ibid., p. 185.

8. Ibid., p. 187.

9. Ibid., p. 186.

10. Ibid., pp. 186–187.

11. *Report of the House Committee on Expenditures on the Public Buildings,* April 1, 1842, pp. 5ff. For an announcement and description of the levees, see *Globe,* December 31, 1834, and newspaper accounts in Esther Singleton, *The Story of the White House* (New York, 1907), I, 214–227.

12. *Globe,* February 22, 1837; *National Intelligencer,* February 22, 1837; *Niles' Weekly Register,* February 25, 1837. "Register of the names of Citizens and amounts contributed" for the Jackson cheese, New York State Library, copy JPP.

13. Montgomery to Letitia A. Montgomery, February 20, 1834, in New York *Times,* February 21, 1935, copy JPP. A report on Jackson's earlier dinner parties can be found in David Campbell to Mary Campbell, May 21, 1829, Campbell Papers, Duke University Library.

14. Jessie Benton Fremont, *Souvenirs of My Time* (Boston, 1887), p. 98.

15. James Stuart, *Three Years in North America* (Edinburgh, 1833), II, 44–45.

16. Statement, Donelson Papers, LC, copy JPP.

17. Receipt, Jackson Papers, LC.

18. Stuart, *Three Years in North America,* II, 42, 43.

19. Parton, *Jackson,* III, 612.

20. Blair to AJ, July 30, 1836, Jackson Papers, LC.

21. Parton, *Jackson,* III, 602.

22. Anne H. Wharton, *Social Life in the Early Republic* (New York, 1902), pp. 264–266.

Chapter 28: Farewell

1. Donelson to Emily Donelson, November 20, 21, 1836; AJ to Mary Polk, December 22, 1836, private collection, copy JPP; AJ to Mausel White, December 2, 1836, in Jackson, *Correspondence,* V, 440.

2. AJ to Emily Donelson, November 27, 1836, in Jackson, *Correspondence,* V, 439.

3. Donelson to Emily Donelson, November 27, 1836, Donelson Papers, LC; AJ to Trist, March 2, 1837, Trist Papers, LC.

4. Petersen, *American Presidential Elections,* pp. 22–24.

5. Taney to AJ, December 8, 1836, Jackson Papers, LC.

6. Benton, *Thirty Years View,* I, 718, 719.

7. Ibid., pp. 728, 729.

8. Poore, *Perley's Reminiscences,* I, 142; Wise, *Seven Decades of the Union,* p. 143.

9. AJ to Benton, January 17, 1837, Jackson Papers, LC.

10. *Globe,* February 25, 1837.

11. Professor David Hackett Fischer was kind enough to share with me some of his conclusions about corruption within the administrations of the early Presidents. Much of his work is based on quantitative evidence. His study, soon to be published, is entitled: *Corruption: Rhythms of Renewal and Decay in American History.*

12. AJ to Taney, October 13, 1836, Jackson Papers, LC; the Farewell Address can be found in Richardson, *Messages and Papers,* II, 1511ff. For these quoted passages see pp. 1516, 1517.

13. Ibid., p. 1525.

14. Ibid., p. 1527.

15. Ben Perley Poore, Boston *Budget,* in *New York Times,* May 16, 1886, copy JPP.

16. *Globe,* March 8, 1837.

17. Benton, *Thirty Years View,* I, 735.

18. Ibid.

19. Hall, *The Politics of Justice,* p. 26.

20. Joel Silbey, "Election of 1836," in Schlesinger et al., eds., *History of American Presidential Elections,* I, 598.

Chapter 29: Retirement

1. *Globe,* March 9, 1837.

2. AJ to Donelson, March 19, 1837, Jackson Papers, Ladies' Hermitage Association; AJ to William Noland, March 11, 1837, Miscellaneous Collection, Colonial Williamsburg Foundation, copy JPP.

3. Nashville *Union,* March 25, 1837, copy JPP; *Globe,* April 10, 1837; Parton, *Jackson,* III, 630.

4. AJ to Van Buren, March 30, 1837, Van Buren Papers, LC.

5. AJ to Andrew Jr., November 16, 1833, Jackson Papers, LC.

6. On the panic, see Reginald C. McGrane, *The Panic of 1837* (Chicago, 1924); Samuel Resneck, "The Social History of an American Depression, 1837–1843," *American Historical Review* (1935), XL, 662–687; and Peter Temin, *The Jacksonian Economy* (New York, 1969).

7. AJ to Blair, February 26, 1838; AJ to Colonel Robert Armstrong, January 9, 1838, Jackson Papers, LC.

8. AJ to Blair, August 9, 15, 1838, Jackson Papers, LC.

9. AJ to William P. Lawrence, August 24, 1838, in Jackson, *Correspondence,* V, 565.

10. Reverend James Smith to Reverend Finis Ewing [1838], Ewing Papers, THS.

11. Parton, *Jackson*, III, 647. For a different account of the reasons that took Jackson into the church see Remini, *Jackson*, III, 444–447.

12. Nashville *Whig*, July 20, 1838, copy JPP.

13. Ibid.

14. Parton, *Jackson*, III, 648.

Chapter 30: The Silver Jubilee

1. Petersen, *American Presidential Elections*, pp. 18–27.

2. AJ to Van Buren, November 24, 1840, Van Buren Papers, LC; AJ to Kendall, January 2, 1841, in Jackson, *Correspondence*, VI, 88.

3. Ordinarily Jackson would have traveled with Ralph Earl to New Orleans, but Earl died suddenly on September 16, 1838.

4. *Globe*, January 20, 22, 1840; *Niles' Weekly Register*, February 1, 1840; Nashville *Union*, January 22, 1840, copy JPP.

5. *Niles' Weekly Register*, February 1, 8, 1840; Nashville *Union*, January 22, 1840, copy JPP.

6. *Globe*, January 22, 1840.

7. *Niles' Weekly Register*, February 1, 8, 1840; *Globe*, January 20, 30, 1840; Nashville *Union*, January 22, 1840, copy JPP.

8. Quoted in Parton, *Jackson*, III, 634.

Chapter 31: "We Must Regain Texas"

1. Blair to AJ, April 4, 1841, Jackson Papers, LC.

2. AJ to Blair, April 19, 1841, Jackson Papers, LC.

3. Dabney S. Carr to AJ, August 18, 1841, in Jackson, *Correspondence*, VI, 119.

4. AJ to Van Buren, November 25, 1841, Van Buren Papers, LC.

5. Benton to AJ, March 10, 1842, Jackson Papers, LC.

6. AJ to William B. Lewis, January 18, 1844, Jackson-Lewis Papers, NYPL; AJ to Blair, January 19, February 24, 1844, Jackson Papers, LC.

7. AJ's will, September 1, 1842, private collection, copy JPP.

8. Ibid. Other minor bequests like walking canes, a sword, and dueling pistols were made in a subsequent will dated June 7, 1843, in Jackson, *Correspondence*, VI, 220–223.

9. AJ to Lewis, February 27, March 11, 1844, Jackson-Lewis Papers, NYPL.

10. AJ to Blair [1844], Jackson Papers, LC.

11. AJ to Blair, March 5, 1844; AJ to Kendall, April 12, 1844, Jackson Papers, LC; AJ to Aaron V. Brown, February 9, 1843, in Jackson, *Correspondence*, VI, 201–202; AJ to Lewis, February 27, March 11, 1844, Jackson-Lewis Papers, NYPL.

12. After completing the negotiations for the Webster-Ashburton Treaty, Webster resigned and was replaced by Abel P. Upshur, who was accidentally killed in an explosion aboard the USS *Princeton*.

13. Walker to AJ, January 10, 1844, Jackson Papers, LC.

14. AJ to Walker, March 11, 1844, Jackson Papers, Chicago Historical Society; AJ to Blair, March 5, July 12, 1844, Jackson Papers, LC.

15. AJ to Walker, March 11, 1844, Jackson Papers, Chicago Historical Society.

16. Tyler to AJ, April 18, 1844, in Jackson, *Correspondence*, VI, 279.

17. Rodman W. Paul, *Rift in the Democracy* (Philadelphia, 1951), p. 38.

18. AJ to Blair, May 11, 1844, Jackson Papers, LC.

19. That Jackson wrote this letter is confirmed in AJ to Blair, May 11, 1844, Jackson Papers, LC. However, the letter to Van Buren itself is missing from the Van Buren Papers, LC, which tends to support the suspicion that some of Jackson's letters in the Van Buren collection may have been destroyed by Van Buren after Jackson's death.

20. Polk to Cave Johnson, May 4, 14, 1844, copy in the Polk Papers Project.

21. Tyler was out of the question and many Democrats could not abide Calhoun. Benton opposed annexation and that eliminated him. Silas Wright would have made an excellent choice but he was fanatically loyal to his friend and chief, Martin Van Buren.

22. Polk to Cave Johnson, May 3, 1844, copy in the Polk Papers Project, Vanderbilt University.

23. Ibid.

24. Charles Sellers, "Election of 1844," in Schlesinger et al., eds., *History of American Presidential Elections*, I, 772–774.

25. AJ to Blair, June 7, 25, 1844, Jackson Papers, LC.

26. See Remini, *Jackson*, III, 504–505, for details.

27. Sellers, *Polk*, p. 139.

28. Sellers, "Election of 1844," p. 861. Birney took 62,300 popular and no electoral votes.

29. Adams, *Memoirs*, XII, 103, 110.

30. Quoted in Sellers, *Polk*, II, 158.

31. AJ to Kendall, November 23, 1844, Jackson Papers, LC.

32. AJ to Blair, October 17, 1844, Jackson Papers, LC; AJ to Van Buren, February 10, 1845, Van Buren Papers, LC.

33. AJ to Donelson, December 11, 1844, in Jackson, *Correspondence*, VI, 338.

34. Blair to AJ, February 28, 1845, AJ to Blair, March 10, 1845, Jackson Papers, LC.

Chapter 32: "We Will All Meet in Heaven"

1. AJ to Polk, April 11, 1845, Jackson Papers, LC.

2. AJ to Donelson [1845], Donelson Papers, LC; AJ to Lewis, February 12, 1845, Jackson-Lewis Papers, NYPL.

3. Blair to AJ, February 12, 1845, Jackson Papers, LC.

4. AJ to Blair, March 3, 1845, Jackson Papers, LC.

5. AJ to Van Buren, February 10, 1845, Van Buren Papers, LC; AJ to Polk, April 11, 1845, Polk Papers, LC.

6. AJ to Blair, April 9, 1845, Jackson Papers, LC.

7. Letter of Hill to the *New Hampshire Patriot*, April 4, 1845, copy JPP; Diary of William Tyack, May 28–June 3, 1845, in Memphis *Commercial Appeal*, July 11, 1845, copy JPP.

8. Diary of Tyack, in Memphis *Commercial Appeal*, July 11, 1845, copy JPP.

9. AJ to Donelson, May 24, 1845, Donelson Papers, LC.

10. *Niles' Weekly Register*, July 5, 1845.

11. Andrew to A.O.P. Nicholson, June 17, 1845, Miscellaneous Jackson Papers, New York Historical Society.

12. Ibid.

13. Ibid.; Esselman to Blair, June 9, 1845, in *Niles' Weekly Register*, July 5, 1845.

14. Esselman to Blair, June 9, 1845, in *Niles' Weekly Register*, July 5, 1845.

15. Andrew to Nicholson, June 17, 1845, Miscellaneous Jackson Papers, New York Historical Society.

16. Ibid.; Esselman to Blair, June 9, 1845, in *Niles' Weekly Register*, July 5, 1845.

17. Andrew to Nicholson, June 17, 1845, Miscellaneous Jackson Papers, New York Historical Society.

18. Esselman to Blair, June 9, 1845, in *Niles' Weekly Register*, July 5, 1845; Elizabeth Donelson's pencil notations on the reverse side of Andrew J. Donelson to Elizabeth Donelson, May 20, 1845, Donelson Papers, LC.

19. Parton, *Jackson*, III, 678.

20. Andrew to Nicholson, June 17, 1845, Miscellaneous Jackson Papers, NYHS. Jackson's statement is attested to by several other witnesses, including Dr. Esselman and Elizabeth Donelson. It was repeated in many newspaper accounts. Obviously, it had a profound effect on these witnesses.

21. Ibid.

22. Esselman to Blair, June 9, 1845, in *Niles' Weekly Register*, July 5, 1845; Elizabeth Donelson's notations, Donelson Papers, LC; Andrew to Blair, June 10, 1845, Jackson Papers, LC.

23. Moses 'and Cross, *Presidential Courage*, p. 66.

24. Journal and Letterbook of William Frierson Cooper, June 10, 1845, Cooper Family Papers, Tennessee State Library.

25. Clarksville (Tennessee) *Jeffersonian*, June 21, 1845, copy JPP; Parton, *Jackson*, III, 786.

26. Nashville *Union*, June 12, 1845, copy JPP.

27. On July 15, 1976, in the presence of representatives of the Ladies' Hermitage Association, the top cover of Jackson's grave was removed, but the slab below ground level was not disturbed. What was observed is reported here. For other details of the funeral service, see Nashville *Union*, June 12, 1845, copy JPP.

28. Inventory of Estate presented in Davidson County Court by Andrew Jackson, Jr., executor, Wills and Inventories, XIII, 307, Davidson County, Tennessee, copy JPP; Account Book and Slave Register, 1845–1877, Hermitage, The Western Reserve Historical Society, Cleveland, Ohio, copy JPP.

29. Herman Melville, *Moby Dick* (New York, 1851), the concluding section of chap. 26.

Bibliography

For the most part this book was researched from a wide variety of surviving manuscript sources, the largest single collection of which can be found in the Library of Congress. This is the Andrew Jackson Papers, given in part to the Library by the Blair family, and it consists of roughly 22,500 items (mostly correspondence) which are kept in 269 volumes and 58 containers. The military papers occupy 14 volumes and the map division of the Library has 11 additional items dealing with Jackson's military operations along the Gulf Coast. John McDonough in his *Index to the Andrew Jackson Papers* (Washington, D.C., 1967) narrates the strange history of the collection, and how the papers were dispersed and later reassembled. A large number of Jackson letters are to be found in the Van Buren, Polk, and Blair Family papers which are also located in the Library of Congress.

The Tennessee Historical Society in Nashville is the next-best repository of Jackson documents. Over 10,000 pieces of documentary material dealing with Jackson and other early Tennessee leaders are located in this library. In addition, the Tennessee State Library and Archives in Nashville has 1,500 Jackson items. And the Ladies' Hermitage Association keeps a considerable collection of original Jackson documents, including his farm journal, account book, and personal library.

Some 450 Jackson letters and miscellaneous material, many of which are fragments of letters that Harriet C. Owsley cleverly matched with fragments in the collection in the Library of Congress, can be found in the Chicago Historical Society. Another very valuable collection of Jackson correspondence with William B. Lewis, consisting of 254 items, and sometimes called the Ford Collection or Jackson-Lewis Papers, is located in the New York Public Library. Both the Andre de Coppet Collection in the Princeton University Library and the Pierpont Morgan Library in New York City also contain important Jackson materials.

The Alabama Department of Archives and History at Montgomery possess some 200 items relating to Jackson's career in East Florida. The Bibliotheca Parsoniana in New Orleans contains material relating to the Battle of New Orleans. The William Clements Library at the University of Michigan has 33 Jackson letters; the Duke University Library, 47, and it has recently purchased many more; the Missouri Historical Society, 40; the New York Historical Society, 21; and the Thomas Gilcrease Institute of American History and Art in Tulsa, 10.

The Archivo General de Indias in Seville, Spain, houses a rich collection of documentary material related to Jackson, including many letters written by or to the General. These items tend to be scattered in the collection, but Cuba, legajos # 1795, proved the most valuable. The Archivo General de Simancas and the

Archivo Historico Nacional in Madrid, along with the Public Record Office in London, also yielded valuable documents.

The National Archives contains an enormous collection of manuscript documents dealing with virtually all aspects of Jackson's administration as well as his early military career. Records of the War Department, Letters of the Secretary Relating to Military Affairs, and Letters Sent to the President by the Secretary are most important, as are the Appointment Papers, Diplomatic Dispatches and Instructions, Domestic Letters, and Notes to Foreign Legations in the State Department archives. For the Indians, Record Group 75 of the Records of the Bureau of Indian Affairs was extremely valuable.

Copies of all or most of the manuscripts cited above have been collected by the Jackson Papers Project which was initially housed at the Hermitage outside Nashville, Tennessee, but in the summer of 1987 moved to the University of Tennessee at Knoxville. Two volumes of the Jackson papers have been published by the project in a letterpress edition covering the years 1770–1813. In addition the entire collection, consisting in 1987 of approximately 60,000 items, has been microfilmed in 39 reels and issued with a *Guide and Index to the Microfilm Editions* (Wilmington, 1987) prepared by Harold Moser, the director of the project.

In researching the life of Andrew Jackson it was of course necessary to consult the manuscript collections of many other individuals of the period, both friends and enemies, most of whom are mentioned in this book. A listing of all these collections is not possible here but it can be found in *Andrew Jackson and the Course of American Democracy*, the third volume of my more detailed biography of Jackson.

Of secondary sources the most exciting, most readable, and most valuable in understanding both Old Hickory and his era is without question *The Age of Jackson*, by Arthur M. Schlesinger, Jr. This is a modern classic, one of the very few landmark historical studies written in our time. Like any imperishable work it has been subject to repeated critical attack but the more it is probed and analyzed the more it sustains its primacy among Jacksonian studies. Schlesinger caught the spirit and meaning of the age and conveyed it to his readers in all the majesty and eloquence of language that is so typical of his writing. Unlike most historical works *The Age of Jackson* will surely survive the test of time.

Another classic work is Alexis de Tocqueville's *Democracy in America*, one of the major statements about American life in the nineteenth century. It too has been faulted and criticized but it continues to have a profound impact on the thinking of Americans about their past.

In many ways the best biography of the Hero is still the three-volume *Life of Andrew Jackson* by James Parton, published in 1861. However, some modern readers prefer the two-volume study by Marquis James which is extremely well written but one-dimensional in its interpretation of the Old Hero.

For other modern studies of the various personalities and issues discussed in this book I would refer the reader to the footnotes and to the bibliography appended to the final volume of my older, three-volume, Jackson biography cited above.

Index

Aberdeen, George Gordon, 4th Earl of, 285
abolition, 298–299, 302
Adair, General John, 100
Adams, John, 40
Adams, John Quincy Adams: as secretary of state, 114; defends AJ, 124, 134; AJ's opinion of, 126, 258, 309, 352; negotiates Transcontinental Treaty, 124, 127–128; characteristics, 152; presidential candidate, 145ff; early career, 151–152; elected President, 154; offers state department to Clay, 155; annual message, 159–160; refuses to attend AJ's inauguration, 177; opinion of Biddle, 223; and compromise tariff, 251; foreign policy of, 284, 285; on Clay, 351; mentioned, 291, 292, 315, 320
Adams, Marion, 356, 357, 358
Adams-Onís Treaty, 127–128, 129, 309
Advertiser, Louisville, 337
Advocate, Maine, 233–234
Alabama, 250
Alabama River, 87
Albany Regency, 148, 165, 225, 247, 264, 275, 307
Allegheny Mountains, 13, 55
Allison, David, appointed Blount's business manager, 21; relations with AJ, 33–34, 40, 49–50
Ambrister, Robert: described, 120; captured, 121; tried, 121; executed, 121, 373 note 23
Amelia Island, 119
American Anti-Slavery Society, 299
American Revolution: AJ's participation in, 8–9; mentioned, 7, 9, 10, 20, 294
American System, 151, 159
Ames, Fisher, 36
Anderson, Joseph, 21

Anderson, Captain Patten, 52
Anti-Masonic party, 22, 166–167
Apalachicola River, 117
Arbuckle, Colonel Mathew, 109
Arbuthnot, Alexander: described, 119; aids Indians, 119; captured, 121; tried, 121; executed, 119, 121; mentioned, 126
Argus, Albany, 165, 307
Argus of Western America, Kentucky, 164, 181, 200
Arkansas, 113, 348
Arkansas River, 113, 114, 128
Arkansas Territory, 216
Armstrong, John, 65
Armstrong, John W., 69
Armstrong, Robert, 278, 280
Ashe, Samuel, 12
Atlantic Ocean, 20
Atkinson, General Henry, 218
Austin, Stephen F., 311–312
Avery, Waightstill, 14–15

Baldwin, Abraham, 36
Baldwin, Henry, 139, 140, 173
Baltimore, 87, 254, 262, 339, 350
Baltimore and Ohio Railroad, 254
Bancroft, George, 306
Bank of the United States, Second: accused of fraud, 143; opposition to, 165, 175; AJ attacks, 210, 221ff; end of Bank, 274ff
Bank War, 220ff
Barataria Bay, 91
Baratarian pirates, 1, 91ff
Barry, John Stetson, 308
Barry, William: appointed postmaster general, 175; and Eaton scandal, 192ff; as administrator, 205
Batavia, N.Y., 166
Baton Rouge, 20, 24

Battery, N.Y., 257
Bayou Bienvenu, 93
Bayou Pierre, 24, 364 note 26
Bayou St. John, 90
Bean, Russell, 43–44, 75
Beard, Lewis, 12
Belgium, 293
Bell, John, 213
Bennett, James Gordon, 165
Benton, Jesse: quarrels with William
    Carroll, 68–69; gunfight with AJ,
    69–71, 223, 232
Benton, Thomas Hart: as AJ's aide, 60,
    64, 65; gunfight with AJ, 69–71, 162;
    leaves for Missouri, 71; reconciles
    with AJ, 71, 148; opinion of AJ, 187,
    334; and Van Buren's nomination,
    225; and Bank War, 226–227,
    231–232; appearance, 231; and Force
    Bill, 248, 250; moves to expunge
    censure, 276–277, 328–330; and the
    national debt, 295–297; and AJ's fine,
    347; AJ acknowledges, 358
Berlin and Milan decrees, 289
Berrien, John McPherson: appointed
    attorney general, 175; and Eaton
    scandal, 192ff; resigns as attorney
    general, 204
Bible: AJ's knowledge of, 6, 324, 341,
    356, 358
Biddle, Nicholas: and kitchen cabinet,
    206–207; and Bank War, 221ff,
    233–235; appearance, 223; early
    career, 223; characteristics, 223, 275;
    and election of 1832, 233–234; reacts
    to removal, 264–265, 266; loses
    public support, 273–274
Binns, John, 164
Birney, James, 351
Black Hawk, Chief, 218, 254–255
Black Hawk War, 218
blacks: and Battle of New Orleans, 1; in
    Tennessee, 30
Blair, Francis P.: supports AJ, 165;
    summoned to Washington, 200;
    founds Globe, 201; described,
    200–201; influence on AJ, 206; and
    Bank War, 222ff, 233–235; describes
    AJ, 313; as AJ's spokesman, 325, 342;
    receives AJ's papers, 347; and debt
    owed by AJ, 347; and Texas,
    352–353; loses Globe, 355
Blennerhassett, Harmon, 58
Blount, William: appointed territorial
    governor, 21; described, 21; political
    influence, 21–22, 32; appoints AJ
    attorney general, 21–22; opinion of
    AJ, 22; characteristics, 21; land
    speculations, 21; and Indians, 28;
    proposes statehood, 28; elected

Blount, William (cont'd)
    Senator, 32; expelled from Senate,
    39; dies, 45
Blount, Willie: elected governor, 62;
    asked to provide volunteers, 62;
    commissions AJ, 62–63; orders AJ to
    New Orleans, 64; orders AJ against
    Creeks, 72; levies new troops, 77–78;
    mentioned, 21
Boston, 258, 260, 262, 339
Boulanger, Joseph, 323
Bowlegs, Chief Billy, 120, 121
Brackenridge, Henry M., 132–133
Branch, John: appointed secretary of
    navy, 174; and Eaton scandal, 192ff;
    resigns as secretary, 204; mentioned,
    165
Breathitt, George, 237
Briggs, George N., 216
Broadway, New York City, 257
Broglie, Duc de, 292
Bronaugh, Dr. James C., 111, 132, 135
Brown, General Jacob, 111
Brown, Reverend Obadiah, 176
Brown's Hotel, 295
Buchanan, James: in election of 1824,
    152–153; characteristics, 152–153,
    323–324; minister to Russia, 288
Buckner, Alexander, 224
Bunker Hill, 258–259
Bureau of Indian Affairs, 219
Burr, Aaron: visits AJ, 55; early career,
    55; kills Hamilton, 55; appeal to
    westerners, 55; involves AJ in
    conspiracy, 56–60; arraigned, 58;
    reassures AJ, 58; deserts expedition,
    59; arrested, 59–60; tried, 60;
    defended by AJ, 59, 60
Butler, Colonel Anthony, 309, 310
Butler, Benjamin F.: appointed attorney
    general, 264; writes Protest message,
    269
Butler, Dr. Elizur, 216
Butler, Robert, 111, 131

Caffery, Mary, 190
Calhoun, Floride (Mrs. John C.), 194
Calhoun, John C.: War Hawk, 61;
    appointed secretary of war, 116;
    opinion of AJ, 116; authorizes
    invasion of Florida, 118; demands
    AJ's censure, 124; as presidential
    candidate, 145ff; elected vice
    president, 150; forms alliance with
    Van Buren, 161; and cabinet
    appointments, 173; sworn in as vice
    president, 178; and Eaton scandal,
    190ff; and nullification, 194ff; breaks
    with AJ, 198ff; defeats Van Buren's
    nomination as minister, 224–225;

Calhoun, John C. (cont'd)
  resigns as vice president, 239; elected
    to Senate, 239; alliance with Clay,
    247–249; described, 248; supports
    compromise tariff, 249; against
    expunging censure, 328–329; as
    secretary of state, 348–349
California, 20, 313, 349
Call, Richard Keith, 111, 133, 146
Callava, Colonel Jose: and transfer of
    Florida, 130–135; and controversy
    with AJ, 133–135
Cambreleng, Churchill C., 225, 268
Campbell, David, 21
Campbell, George W., 44, 50, 158
Campbell, Reverend John M.: and Eaton
    scandal, 191–192
Canada, 20, 61, 62, 87, 284, 348, 349
Carolina, USS, 95, 96, 97
Carr, Dabney S., 175
Carrickfergus, 4
Carroll, William: commands Tennessee
    troops at New Orleans, 2, 93; as AJ's
    deputy quartermaster, 64; quarrels
    with Jesse Benton, 68–69; in Creek
    War, 78; and Battle of New Orleans,
    93, 95, 99
Cass, Lewis: described, 205; appointed
    secretary of war, 205; tours with AJ,
    254, 257
Castle Garden, 257
Castlereagh, Viscount, Robert Stewart, 4
Cat Island, 92
Catawba Indians, 4, 5
Catawba River, 4, 5
Caucus of 1824, congressional, 142,
    148–149
Charleston, 7, 9, 235, 236, 299, 348
Chef Menteur, 90, 91, 99
Cherokee Indians: in Creek War, 81; and
    removal, 111, 113–114, 216–218
Cherokee Nation v. Georgia, 216–217
Chesapeake Bay, 87
Chickamauga Indians, 21
Chickasaw Indians: and removal, 111,
    112–113, 216
Chile, 288
Choctaw Indians: and Battle of New
    Orleans, 100; and removal, 111,
    114–115, 215–216
Churchill, Winston, 323
City Hall Park, 257
City Hotel (Nashville), 69, 70
Claiborne, William C. C.: elected to
    Congress, 39; appointed governor of
    Louisiana Territory, 49; and defense
    of New Orleans, 90, 92
Clay, Henry: and Burr Conspiracy, 58;
    War Hawk, 61–62; attacks AJ, 126;
    described, 126, 151, 267; as

Clay, Henry (cont'd)
    presidential candidate, 145ff; early
    career, 151; opinion of AJ, 151;
    supports Adams, 151–152; accused of
    corrupt bargain, 153–154, 155;
    named secretary of state, 155; and
    duel with Randolph, 159; AJ's
    opinion of, 126, 163, 346; and
    cabinet purge, 204; nominated for
    president, 222, 349; defeated, 237,
    352; and Bank War, 222ff; forms
    alliance with Calhoun, 247–249; and
    Force bill, 248; proposes compromise
    tariff, 249; attacks removal of
    deposits, 267–268; and Specie
    Circular, 303; against expunging
    censure, 328–329; introduces new
    bank bill, 346; opposes annexation,
    349–350
Clinton, De Witt, 166
Clover Bottom, 51, 56, 58
Coalition, the Adams-Clay: formation,
    151–152
Cochin China, 287
Cochran, George, 25, 26
Cochran, Vice Admiral Sir Alexander:
    recommends Gulf invasion, 87ff;
    begins invasion, 89
Cockburn, Sir George, 87
Cocke, Major General John, 72, 73, 75,
    77
Cocke, William, 32, 39
Coffee, John: forms partnership with AJ,
    51; commands cavalry, 64; described,
    64; assists AJ in gunfight with Bentons,
    69–71; in Creek War, 73–83; and
    Battle of New Orleans, 89ff; and
    Indian removal, 112–113, 114
Coffin Hand Bill, 163–164
Coinage Act of 1834, 275–276
Colombia, South America, 288
Colorado River, 127
Columbian Observer, Philadelphia, 146
Compromise Tariff of 1833, 249–250
Congress, U.S.: organizes Southwest
    Territory, 21; AJ member of, 33–38,
    39–41; declares war, 61; investigates
    First Seminole War, 125–127; AJ's
    relations with, 183ff, 233ff, 272ff;
    votes on censure resolution, 269
Congressional caucus of 1824, 148–149
Connecticut, 108
Constitution, U.S.: AJ on, 228, 239ff, 246
Constitutional Convention (Tennessee),
    29–32
Constitution, USS, 330
Conway, George, 38, 45
Cook, Daniel Pope, 154
Cook, Peter B., 121
Coosa River, 73, 80, 81, 87

Copenhagen, 286
Coppinger, Don José, 131
Cornwallis, Charles, First Marquis, 9
Corrupt bargain charge, 153–155, 304
Crawford, James, 4, 6
Crawford, Jane Hutchinson, 5, 9
Crawford, Thomas (AJ's cousin), 8, 9
Crawford, William H.: and Indians,
    111–112; AJ's opinion of, 116;
    demands AJ's censure, 124; as
    presidential candidate, 142–143,
    146ff; suffers stroke, 150; and
    Seminole controversy, 198–199
Creek Indians: attack settlers, 71; and
    Creek War, 72–85; in Florida, 85,
    117; and removal, 216, 217, 382 note
    29; mentioned, 21, 111
Creek War, 71–85
Crockett, Davy, 73
Croswell, Edwin, 165, 307
Cuba, 124, 131
Cumberland College, 137
Cumberland River, 13, 16, 27, 33, 34, 58,
    65
Cumberland Road, 210, 336
Curry, Dr., 356
Cushing, Caleb, 302
Cutts, Adele, 325
Cypress Land Company, 113

Daily Advertiser and Patriot, Boston, 234
Dallas, Commodore, 310, 311
Dallas, George, 351
Daquin, Major Jean, 92, 100
Davie, Colonel William Richardson, 8
Davis, Warren R., 297
Dearborn, Henry, 59, 62
Declaration of Independence, 7
Democracy, 186, 234–235, 236, 237, 242,
    247; AJ's views on, 135–136, 176
Democratic party: formation of, 157,
    159ff; and nominating convention,
    225–226; and election of 1828, 158ff;
    election of 1832, 222ff, 233–235, 237;
    and Bank War, 266ff; and election of
    1836, 328; and election of 1840, 342;
    and election of 1844, 350–352
Democratic Press, Philadelphia, 164
Denmark, 209, 286
Deposit Act of 1836, 276, 338, 339
Detroit, 62
Dickens, Asbury, 329
Dickerson, Mahlon, 276, 310–311
Dickinson, Charles: duel with AJ, 52–54,
    162, 255–256
Donelson, Alexander, 78
Donelson, Andrew Jackson: as AJ's ward,
    61; aide to AJ, 111, 327; early career,
    138; serves as AJ's secretary, 172,
    183–184; and Eaton scandal, 190ff;

Donelson, Andrew Jackson (cont'd)
    and Bank War, 227; accompanies AJ
    on tour, 252, 254, 343–345; builds
    home, 278; receives AJ's sword, 348;
    serves as chargé, 348, 352
Donelson, Elizabeth, 61
Donelson, Emily, 172, 183–184, 191, 192,
    206, 315–316, 323
Donelson, John, 111
Donelson, Colonel John (AJ's
    father-in-law): settles Nashville, 13,
    16; murdered, 16; estate inventoried,
    25
Donelson, Mary, 51
Donelson, Rachel Stockley (AJ's
    mother-in-law), 17
Donelson, Samuel, 17, 33, 111
Donelson, Severn, 61
Donelson, Stockley, 278, 279
Donelson, William, 278
Downes, Captain John, 287
Downing, Major Jack, 258, 259
Drayton, William, 235
Duane, William J.: appointed secretary of
    the Treasury, 261; opposes AJ on
    removal of funds, 261ff; dismissed,
    263
Dubourg, Abbé Louis William, 105, 106,
    108
Duck River, 19, 49

Earl, Ralph, 183–184, 254, 316, 324, 336
East Room, 315, 317, 320–321
Eastin, Mary, 172, 183, 220
Eaton, John: completes AJ's biography,
    64; aide to AJ, 111; member of junto,
    145; writes campaign material,
    146–147; and election of 1828, 158,
    163; appointed secretary of war,
    173–174; marries, 174; and scandal
    over marriage, 190ff; resigns as
    secretary of war, 204
Eaton, Margaret (Peggy) O'Neal
    Timberlake: described, 173;
    characteristics, 173–174; and scandal
    over marriage, 190ff
Edgar, Dr. John Todd, 340–341, 359
Education, 209
Election of 1824, 150ff
Election of 1828, 158ff, 168–169
Election of 1832, 222ff, 233–235, 237
Election of 1836, 328
Election of 1840, 342
Election of 1844, 350–352
Ellmaker, Amos, 222, 237
Ely, Reverend Ezra Stiles, 191–192
Emuckfaw Creek, 78, 80–81
England. See Great Britain
English Turn, 90
Enotachopco Creek, 79

Enquirer, Richmond, 161, 164, 260
Era of Corruption, 141ff, 186, 304, 375 note 14
Era of Good Feelings, 142, 186, 253, 375 note 14
Ervin, Joseph, 52–53
Erwin, Andrew, 50–51, 145
Escambia, 131
Esselman, Dr. John H., 357, 358
Evans, John B. and Co., 33, 34
Everett, Edward, 168, 201, 258–259
Expansion: AJ on, 56–60, 62, 119, 127, 309–314; mentioned, 109

Federal Republican, Baltimore, 141
Federalist party, 32, 142, 143–144, 157, 343, 347
Fielding, Henry, 159
Fitzhugh, William H., 161
Flint River, 117
Florida: under Spanish rule, 20; AJ's desire for, 56, 62, 65, 116; U.S. desire for, 61, 116ff; AJ plans to invade, 72; invaded, 116ff; ceded to U.S., 128; transferred to U.S., 131; and government, 131ff; and controversy over AJ's seizure, 190ff
Floyd, John, 237
Forbes and Co., 132
Force Bill, 245–250
Forsyth, John: and Seminole controversy, 198–199; supports Indian removal, 213; as secretary of state, 290–293; and Texas, 311
Fort, Captain John, 57, 58
Fort Barrancas, 88
Fort Deposit, 73, 79
Fort Gadsden, 122
Fort Jackson, 83–84, 87
Fort Mims, 71–72
Fort Moultrie, 239
Fort Pinckney, 239
Fort St. John, 90
Fort St. Leon, 90
Fort St. Philip, 89
Fort Scott, 117, 119, 120
Fort Strother, 73, 74, 77, 79
Fowltown, 117
France: sells Louisiana, 48–49; AJ's policy toward as President, 189, 209; and spoliation controversy, 286, 289–294
Francis, Chief Josiah (Hidlis Hadjo), 86, 119, 120
Franklin, state of, 13
Franklin, Jesse, 112
Franklin Park, Washington, D.C., 183
Franklin Square, Washington, D.C., 316
Frelinghuysen, Theodore, 213, 217, 351
French Broad River, 13
French Revolution, 229

Fromentin, Eligius: described, 132; and quarrel with AJ, 132–134

Gadsby's Hotel, 178, 181
Gadsden, James, 111, 122
Gaines, Edmund P.: assumes command at New Orleans, 110; invades Florida, 117; invades Texas, 310
Gallatin, Albert: describes AJ, 35, 36; nominated for vice president, 149
Galvestown, 119
Garrison, William Lloyd, 299
Gazette, Cincinnati, 163
Gazette, Kentucky, 25
Gazette, Knoxville, 45, 46, 47
Georgia: and Indian removal, 216–218
Ghent, Belgium, 96, 108
Gibbs, General Sir Samuel, 100, 101, 102
Girard Bank, Philadelphia, 265
Giusta, Antoine Michel, 315
Glasgow, University of, 4
Globe, Washington: founded, 201; political philosophy of, 201; in Bank War, 227, 233–235, 263; as instrument of propaganda, 272; mentioned, 204, 250, 292, 306, 322, 342, 350, 355
Gorostiza, Manuel Eduardo de, 310, 311
Granger, Francis, 328
Great Britain: and American Revolution, 7ff; and West Indies, 31, 36, 283–285; and War of 1812, 1–3, 61ff; and frontier, 20; U.S. declares war against, 61; reasons for war, 61; invasion plans, 87ff; AJ's policy toward as President, 189, 209, 283–285; and West Indian treaty, 283–285; and Texas, 348
Greeley, Horace, 216, 217
Green, Duff: buys newspaper, 164; announces cabinet nominations, 175; defends nullification, 195; breaks with AJ, 200, 202; and tariff, 250
Green, Colonel Thomas, 24
Green, Thomas Marston, 24
Greene, Nathaniel, 165, 175, 176, 274
Griswold, Roger, 36
Grundy, Felix: as War Hawk, 61; welcomes AJ, 111; member of junto, 145; and election of 1828, 158
Guide to Archival Materials (Baton Rouge), 24
Gulf of Mexico, 20, 87, 112

Hall, Dominick A.: AJ's opinion of, 347; dispute with AJ, 109–110, 162, 347
Hall, Captain William, 64, 75
Hamilton, Alexander, 55, 143, 157, 208
Hamilton, James A., 198, 208
Hamilton, James, Jr., 179, 180, 181, 238
Hammond, Charles, 163

Hanging Rock, Battle of, 8
Hardeman, Thomas, 29
Harper, Robert Goodloe, 36
Harrison, Daniel, 44
Harrison, General William Henry:
    candidate for President, 328; elected
    President, 342; dies, 346; mentioned,
    62
Harrodsburgh, Kentucky, 24
Hartford, 254
Hartford Convention, 108, 142
Harvard University, 258
Havana, 105, 131
Hayne, Arthur P., 89
Hayne, Robert Y.: and election of 1824,
    153; debates Webster, 195; and
    Jefferson birthday celebration,
    196–197; in nullification controversy,
    239, 244
Hays, Robert, 22, 25
Hays, Stockley, 69, 70
Heiskell, Dr. Henry Lee, 170
Hemphill, Joseph, 214
Hermitage: acquired by AJ, 51; early
    buildings erected by AJ, 55;
    expanded, 61; described, 139,
    303–304; burns, 278–279; rebuilt,
    281–282; costs of repair, 282–283; AJ
    returns to, 336–337; bequeathed to
    son, 359
Hill, Isaac, 164, 165, 175, 176, 234, 295,
    355
Himollemico (Creek Chief), 120
Hinds, Colonel Thomas, 93, 102
Hogg, Dr. Samuel, 170
Holland, 293
Holston River, 13
Holy Ground, 81
Hone, Philip, 268
Horseshoe Bend, Battle of, 78ff
Houston, Sam: in Creek War, 82; aide to
    AJ, 111; appearance, 149; and
    election of 1828, 158, 163; and
    Seminole controversy, 190, 198; in
    Texas, 310; sends Santa Anna to AJ,
    312; AJ appeals to, 349; at AJ's
    death, 358, 359
Huger, Alfred, 299
Hull, General William, 62
Hume, William C., 278
Humphries, Dr. William, 5
Hunt, Memucan, 313
Hunter's Hill, 27, 34, 51, 279
Hutchings, Andrew Jackson, 61, 130,
    137–138
Hutchings, John, 51
Huygens, Madame, 193

Illinois, 154
Independence Hall, 256

Independent Treasury System, 339
Indian Queen Hotel, 196
Indian removal: AJ on, 112ff, 175, 189,
    212ff; number of Indians removed,
    218, 382 note 33
Indian Removal Bill: introduced, 213;
    debate over, 213–215; provisions of,
    215
Indians: attack settlers, 15–16, 28; AJ's
    early involvement with, 15–16, 19–20.
    See also individual tribes.
Ingersoll, C. J., 347
Ingham, Samuel D.: appointed secretary
    of the Treasury, 173; and Eaton
    scandal, 192ff; resigns as secretary,
    204
Innerarity, John, 132, 133
Internal improvements: AJ on, 160, 161,
    209ff, 307, 381 note 8; mentioned,
    159
Ireland, 4

Jackson, Andrew (AJ's father): early life,
    4; migrates to America, 4; settles in
    Waxhaw District, 4–5; dies, 5, 362
    note 14
Jackson, Andrew:
—Early Life and Education: family
    background, 4–5; born, 5, 362 note
    15; mother's hopes for, 5; early
    education, 5, 10; educational
    deficiencies, 5–6; orphaned, 6, 7; in
    American Revolution, 8–9, 64;
    wounded, 8; captured, 8; imprisoned
    at Camden, 8; contracts small pox,
    8–9; exchanged, 8; resides with
    Crawfords, 9–10; returns to
    Waxhaws, 10
—Law Student and Frontier Lawyer:
    studies law, 10–12; high jinks as
    student, 10–11; admitted to bar, 12;
    arrested, 12; appointed public
    prosecutor, 12, 19; migrates west,
    12–13; purchases first slave, 14; duel
    with Avery, 14–15; journeys to
    Nashville, 15–16; boards with
    Donelsons, 17; quarrels with
    Robards, 18; moves to Mansker's
    station, 18; love for Rachel, 18,
    26–27, 34–35, 325, 352; relations
    with Blount, 21–22; appointed judge
    advocate, 22; assists Rachel's flight to
    Natchez, 22–23; marries Rachel, 24,
    364 note 23; remarries Rachel, 24;
    establishes home, 27, 34, 51, 55
—Congressman and Judge: attitude
    toward Indians, 28, 30, 31, 37, 111ff;
    favors statehood, 29; and
    constitutional convention, 29–32;
    elected to House of Representatives,

Jackson, Andrew *(cont'd)*
32; career in House, 33–37; arrives in Philadelphia, 33; and Allison affair, 33–34, 41; quarrels with Sevier, 38–39, 44ff, 50–51, 366 note 16; elected to Senate, 39; career in Senate, 40–41; resigns Senate seat, 41, 366 note 48; elected judge, 42; judicial career, 42–44; resigns as judge, 49, 51; organizes freemasons, 44

—Military Career: elected major general, 45; and Louisiana, 49; duels Dickinson, 52–54; involved in Burr Conspiracy, 55–60; informs Jefferson of conspiracy, 58; at Burr's trial, 59; and War of 1812, 62ff; ordered to New Orleans, 64; dismissed, 64; returns to Nashville, 65–67; and gunfight with Bentons, 68–71; ordered against the Creeks, 72; conducts Creek War, 72–85; adopts Indian child, 73; subdues mutiny, 74–77; receives rank in U.S. Army, 84; commands seventh district, 84; moves to Mobile, 87; invades Florida, 88; captures Pensacola, 88; arrives in New Orleans, 89–90; summons Rachel to New Orleans, 89; establishes headquarters, 91; invokes martial law, 93; and defends New Orleans, 91ff; repels British attack, 1–3, 98ff; defeats British, 1–4, 100ff; casualties, 3, 104, 371 note 44; meaning of victory, 3–4, 104, 108–109; returns to the city for victory celebration, 105–106, 108; and silver jubilee of victory, 343–345; named hero, 106; lifts martial law, 109; commands southern army, 111; salary of, 111, 130; appointed Indian commissioner, 112; concludes Indian treaty, 112ff; ordered to subdue Seminoles, 118; conducts First Seminole War, 119ff; conduct criticized, 125–127; appointed Governor of Florida, 129–130; resigns from army, 130; tenure as governor, 130ff; quarrels as governor, 130ff; resigns as governor, 135

—Political Career: builds Hermitage church, 138; accepts presidential nomination, 145–146; elected to Senate, 146; career in Senate, 146ff; and election of 1824, 150ff; resigns from Senate, 158; renominated for presidency, 158; directs presidential campaign, 158ff; elected President, 168–169; forms cabinet, 172ff; writes

Jackson, Andrew *(cont'd)*
inaugural address, 176–177; outlines reforms program, 176–177, 189, 200

—As President, First Term: begins administration, 183ff; living arrangements in White House, 183–184; redecorates White House, 183, 315ff; and rotation of office, 184ff; and Eaton scandal, 190ff; and nullification, 194–195; at Jefferson birthday celebration, 196–197; gives toast, 197; breaks with Calhoun, 198–203; seeks reelection, 199–200; purges cabinet, 201–202; forms Kitchen Cabinet, 206–207; and foreign relations, 208–209, 283–294; proposes constitutional amendment, 209; proposes Indian removal, 209, 212ff; and War against the Bank of the United States, 210, 221ff; and Maysville veto, 210–212; undergoes operation to remove bullet, 223–224; reaction to Van Buren's defeat in the Senate, 225; vetoes Bank bill, 227ff; and election of 1832, 222ff; reelected President, 237

—As President, Second Term: and nullification controversy, 235–243, 244ff; assaulted, 252–253; tours New England, 253ff; orders removal of government's deposits in BUS, 261ff; and presidential power, 227ff, 268ff, 272, 303, 330ff; censured by Senate, 269; protests censure, 269–271; learns of Hermitage fire, 279; rebuilds Hermitage, 280–282; and foreign policy, 283–294; and national debt, 176, 189, 209, 221, 295–297; attacked, 297–298; and abolitionist tracts, 299, 302; issues Specie Circular, 303; and Texas, 309–314; and life in the White House, 315–326; suffers physical collapse, 327–328; censure expunged, 328–330; accomplishments as President, 330–332; failures as President, 331–333

—Retirement: retires as President, 334–335; returns to Hermitage, 336–337; joins Presbyterian church, 339–341; attends silver jubilee of military victory, 343–345; restitution of fine by Congress, 347; writes will, 347–348; and acquisition of Texas, 348–353; supports Polk for the presidency, 350; quarrels with Polk, 354; and closing down of the *Globe*, 355; final illness, 355ff; dies, 358; causes of death, 358–359; buried at Hermitage, 359

Jackson, Andrew *(cont'd)*
—AJ as: administrator, 208ff; bully, 6, 7,
133; businessman, 33–34, 40, 49–52,
60, 337ff, 354–355; expansionist,
56–60, 62, 119, 127, 309–314;
gentleman, 14, 15, 17, 56; hero, 4,
66ff, 106ff, 326; as Indian fighter,
15–16, 19–20, 71ff; military general,
60ff, 71ff, 86ff, 118ff; protector, 6, 26,
61, 191–192; slaveowner, 51–52, 60,
347–348; statesman, 135–136, 217,
239–243, 249–251, 293–294, 330ff;
symbol, 236, 344–345, 360
—Characteristics: anger, 5, 6–7, 11, 14,
40, 68, 133, 267; feigned anger, 11,
267; ambition, 10, 12, 14, 15, 22;
appearance, 7, 11, 17, 35, 40, 89, 90,
149, 172, 314, 322, 324, 336–337,
343–344; arrogance, 122; athletic
interests, 7; caution, 11, 15, 150, 162,
217; charisma, 11, 90–91, 253ff;
conservatism, 11–12, 29–30, 144–145,
162, 176, 189, 209; courage, 6, 42,
67, 89, 237, 326; cruelty, 52, 80;
fondness for dancing, 7, 10–11;
fondness for horses, 7, 10; fondness
for horseracing, 52–53; generosity,
51; gentleness, 256; graciousness, 56,
90–91, 256, 323, 324, 355; health
problems, 84, 89, 135, 137ff, 154,
255–256, 261, 312, 327–328, 339,
352, 355ff; hostility, 6; integrity, 42;
intellectual power, 6, 187, 239–240,
258, 355; leadership, 11, 16, 63ff,
75ff, 86ff, 119ff, 207, 266ff; loyalty,
39, 59, 191–192; mischievousness, 6,
9–11; nationalism, 9, 56, 212, 284,
344–345; nicknames, 1, 4, 67, 85,
106; patriotism, 9, 136, 313;
perseverence, 67, 128, 265;
popularity, 3–4, 45, 67, 68, 84–85,
108, 127, 136, 181, 237, 253ff, 277;
pride, 60, 77, 79, 105; prudence,
11–12, 217; sense of duty, 64, 324;
sense of honor, 14–15; temper, 26,
68, 163; treatment of slaves, 51–52;
vindictiveness, 51, 86, 121; wildness,
9, 10–11, 26; will power, 66–67, 80,
84, 128, 137, 258
—AJ's Opinion of: Adams, John Q., 126,
309, 352; BUS, 189, 228ff; British,
87ff; Burr, Aaron, 56; Calhoun, John
C., 126–127, 194; Clay, Henry, 126,
163, 346; Crawford, William H., 116,
126, 142; Eaton, John H., 173;
election of 1824–1825, 155;
Jefferson, Thomas, 49, 59–60;
Missouri Compromise, 129; Monroe,
James, 126; Napoleon, 122; Spanish,
49, 56; Van Buren, Martin, 148, 187,

Jackson, Andrew *(cont'd)*
194; Wilkinson, General James,
57–60, 65
—Opinion of AJ by Others: 187, 256,
258, 313, 334, 351
—AJ's Views on: banks, 51, 145, 160,
162, 261, 275; blacks, 92;
Constitution, 228ff, 239ff, 246, 304ff;
democracy, 135–136, 176, 209, 304ff;
332–333; government, 29–30, 36–37,
144–145, 176, 209, 263ff, 304ff;
Indians, 111ff, 162; Indian removal,
114–115, 177, 189, 205, 209, 212ff,
307; internal improvements, 160,
161, 209ff, 307, 381 note 8; money,
51, 162, 176, 234–235, 275, 303;
national debt, 176, 189, 209, 221,
295–297; nullification, 194, 246;
religion, 140, 325, 327, 339–341;
secession, 246; slavery, 307; states'
rights, 31–32, 209, 212–213, 216,
219, 245–247, 305; Supreme Court,
228ff, 306–307; tariffs, 161, 176, 189,
226; Union, 239–243, 246
Jackson, Andrew, Jr. (AJ's adopted son):
born, 61; adopted, 61; AJ wishes to
see, 89; accompanies AJ to Florida,
130; attends college, 137–138;
accompanies AJ to Washington, 172;
marries, 220–221; character, 220,
280, 337–338, 354–355; and
Hermitage fire, 278ff; returns with AJ
to Hermitage, 336; dies, 338;
dissipates inheritance, 359–360
Jackson, Andrew III (AJ's grandson), 280
Jackson, Elizabeth Hutchinson (AJ's
mother): migrates to America, 4;
settles in Waxhaw District, 4–5; gives
birth to AJ, 5; moves in with
Crawfords, 5; hopes for AJ, 5, 6;
character, 5, 6, 9; tends
Revolutionary wounded, 8; wins sons'
release from prison, 8–9; nurses AJ to
health, 9; travels to Charleston, 9;
dies, 9
Jackson, Hugh (AJ's brother): migrates to
America, 4; dies, 8
Jackson, Rachel Donelson Robards (AJ's
wife): early life, 16; marries Robards,
16; leaves husband, 17; reconciled,
17; accused of adultery, 23–24; flees
to Natchez, 23; divorced, 24; marries
AJ, 24; influence on AJ, 26–27, 132,
140–141, 339–340; AJ's love for, 18,
26–27, 34–35, 325, 352; resents AJ's
absences, 39, 42; manages plantation,
51; nurses AJ to health, 71; during
Creek War, 84; summoned by AJ to
New Orleans, 89; reaches New
Orleans, 110; opinion of New

Jackson, Rachel *(cont'd)*
Orleans, 130; and AJ's election as
President, 169; illness and death,
169–170
Jackson, Rachel (AJ's granddaughter):
born, 280; visits AJ, 281–282, 358
Jackson, Robert (AJ's brother): migrates
to America, 4; in Revolution, 8;
captured, 8; imprisoned at Camden,
8; contracts small pox, 8; dies, 9
Jackson, Sarah Yorke (AJ's
daughter-in-law): marries, 220–221,
337; kindness to AJ, 220, 221, 354;
and Hermitage fire, 279, 280–281,
282; returns to Hermitage with AJ,
336; joins Presbyterian church,
340–341; in AJ's will, 347–348; and
AJ's final hours, 357, 358
Jacksonian Democracy, 156, 304ff, 332
Jamaica, 87, 89
Japan, 287
Jay, John, 31
Jay Treaty, 36
Jefferson, Thomas: and Republican
ideology, 36, 143–144, 157;
description of AJ, 40; as President,
48–49, 55; purchases Louisiana, 48;
popularity in west, 49; alerts western
command to conspiracy, 58–59; and
Indian removal, 114; birthday
celebration, 195–196
Jennings, Dr. O., 139, 140
Johnson, Richard M., 61, 328
Johnston, Littleton, 68
Jones, Lieutenant Thomas Ap Catesby,
91, 92
Jonesborough, 14, 19, 42
Joseph, I. and J. Co., 338
Jouett, Major John, 23
Judiciary Act of 1789, 302

Keane, General John, 93, 100, 101, 102,
103, 104
Kendall, Amos: early career, 164–165;
supports AJ, 164; characteristics,
175–176; appointment to Treasury,
176; opinion of AJ, 187; opinion of
Van Buren, 197; and Seminole
controversy, 202; influence on AJ,
206, 208; and Bank War, 223ff; and
election of 1832, 233–235; appointed
special Treasury agent, 262, 264;
selects pet banks, 262, 264, 386 note
8; helps write Protest message, 269;
appointed Postmaster General, 299;
and abolitionist tracts, 299, 302
Kerr, Dr. David, 106
Key, Francis Scott, 178, 205
King, William, 122, 295, 329
King's Mountain, Battle of, 13

Kingdom of the Two Sicilies, 286, 288
Kitchen Cabinet, 206–207, 325, 381 note
59
Knoxville, 13, 29, 32, 42ff
Krudener, Baron, 193

LaBranche, Alcée, 314
Lacoste, Pierre, 92, 100
Lafayette, Marquis de, 344, 348
Lafitte, Dominique, 91
Lafitte, Jean, 91
Lafitte, Pierre, 91
Lake Borgne, 90, 92
Lake Champlain, 87
Lake Pontchartrain, 90, 91
Lambert, General John, 99, 100, 102, 105
Lancaster District, South Carolina, 4, 5
Lapshy, Reverend, 356
Latrobe, Benjamin, 183, 281
Latrobe's Treasury Fireproof, 317
Lawrence, Richard, 297
Lawson, Dr. Thomas, 336
Leckie, Robert, 316
Lee, Henry, 158, 172, 237
Leigh, Benjamin, 270
Letcher, Robert, 249
Letters of Wyoming, 146–147
Lewis, Joel, 29
Lewis, William B.: and AJ's marriage, 26;
serves under AJ, 63–64; in Creek
War, 75; member of junto, 145–146;
and election of 1828, 158;
accompanies AJ to Washington, 172;
appointed to Treasury, 184; and
Seminole controversy, 190, 198–199;
and Hermitage fire, 280, 281;
decorates East Room, 317–321; final
moments with AJ, 357, 358;
mentioned, 126, 170, 187, 206, 208,
260, 316, 348
Liberty, 144, 145, 147ff, 155, 157–158,
161, 184–185, 197, 211, 234, 247
Liberty party, 351
Lincoln, Abraham, 241, 242
Linn, Dr. Lewis F., 347
Livingston, Cora, 325
Livingston, Edward: in Congress, 36; as
AJ's aide, 90; entertains AJ, 90–91;
appointed secretary of state, 205; AJ's
reservations about, 221; and BUS,
227; writes Proclamation, 240–243;
described, 240; characteristics, 240;
as minister to France, 289–293;
mentioned, 325
Livingston, Louise, 90
London, 105
Louailler, Louis, 109
Louisiana: under Spanish rule, 20;
purchased, 48–49; mentioned, 84,
348

Louisiana, USS, 96, 97
Louisiana Purchase, 127, 129, 309, 348, 352
Love, Charles J., 281
Lowell, Massachusetts, 259
Lumpkin, Wilson, 214, 217
Lyncoya (AJ's Indian son): found on battlefield, 73; adopted by AJ, 73; AJ's hopes for, 137–138; dies, 169

Macao, 287
Macarté House, 97
Macon, Nathaniel: influence on AJ, 31, 36, 37, 49; conservative views of, 37; mentioned, 149, 160
Madison, Dolley, 325, 326
Madison, James: supports AJ, 36, 37; AJ offends, 60; goaded to war, 62; party leader, 142–144
Madrid, 127, 288
Mangum, Willie P., 328
Manrique, Don Matteo Gonzales: threatened by AJ, 86–87; surrenders to AJ, 88
Mansker, Kasper, 18
Marcy, William L., 185, 225, 234, 257
Marshall, John: and Burr trial, 59, 60; swears AJ in as President, 179; and Indian removal cases, 216–218; dies, 299
Maryland, 205, 210
Masons, 44
Masot, Colonel José, 122
Mathews, General George, 119
Maysville veto, 210–212
McCamie, George, 4
McCay, Spruce, 10–12, 14
McCulloch v. *Maryland,* 228
McCulloch, Robert, 10
McDuffie, George, 250
McGillivray, Alexander, 71
McKeever, Captain Isaac, 120
McLane, Louis: and election of 1824, 154; as minister to Great Britain, 205, 221, 283–285; appointed secretary of Treasury, 205; and BUS, 221–222; and nullification, 245; tours with AJ, 254, 257; characteristics, 283; serves as secretary of state, 289; mentioned, 174
McLean, John, 175, 217
McNairy, John: meets AJ, 10; elected judge, 12; offers post to AJ, 12; migrates west, 12–13, 16; appointed federal judge, 21; attends constitutional convention, 29
McQueen, Chief Peter, 86, 119, 120
Meacham, Colonel Thomas S., 322
Meeker, Cochran and Co., 33, 34
Melville, Herman, 360

Menewa (Chief Great Warrior), 82–83, 369 note 45
Meriwether, General David, 112
Mero District, 13, 19, 22
Mexico: AJ's desire for, 57–58, 116; and Texas, 309ff, 349–350
Michigan, 205
Miller, Pleasant M., 146
Miller, Stephen D., 224
Míro, Esteban, 13, 21
Mississippi, 114, 250
Mississippi River: controlled by Spain, 20, 39; invasion route by British, 87ff
Mississippi Territory, 71, 84
Missouri, 129, 154
Missouri Compromise: AJ's opinion of, 129
Missouri River, 127
Mobile, 65, 66, 72, 87ff
Monahee, Chief, 369 note 45
Monroe, James: and invasion of Florida, 88, 118–119; and invasion of Louisiana, 99, 370 note 13; congratulates AJ on victory, 109, 116; nominated for President, 116; as President, 112, 114; appoints AJ governor of Florida, 129–130; treatment of AJ, 135; tours New England, 253, 254
Montgomery, Major Lemuel P., 82
Morgan, General David, 97, 103
Morgan, William, 166, 222
Morgantown, North Carolina, 13
Morocco, 288
Mount Vernon, 281
Muhlenberg, Frederick, 36
Muscat, 287, 288
Muscle Shoals, 51, 113

Nacogdoches, 310
Napoleon: sells Louisiana, 48–49; captured, 87; AJ's opinion of, 122
Nashville: settled, 13; AJ arrives in, 16; appearance, 16–17; reception for AJ, 111, 136, 304, 337; mentioned, 27, 42
Nashville Central Committee: and AJ's marriage, 23; and campaign of 1828, 158ff, 364 note 20; mentioned, 190
Nashville Junto, 145, 146
Natchez, 20, 23, 25, 27, 64
National debt, 295–297; AJ on, 176, 189, 209, 221, 295–297
National Hotel, 172
National Intelligencer, Washington, 148, 230, 234, 303, 350
National Republican party, 165, 222, 238, 244, 250–251
National Road, 210, 336
Neamathla (Seminole Chief), 117

Negro Fort, 116–117, 120, 122
Nelson, John, 288
Neutrality Act of 1818, 310
New Orleans: conspiracy involving, 57; defense of, 63, 64, 89ff; and silver jubilee, 343–345; mentioned, 20, 348
New Orleans, Battle of: principal actions, 1–3, 98ff; casualties, 3, 104, 371 note 44; meaning of victory, 3–4, 104, 108–109; reported, 3, 4; and silver jubilee, 343–345
New York, 87, 256–257, 262, 339
Niagara River, 166
Niles, Hezekiah, 168
Niles' Weekly Register, 108, 237
Noah, Mordecai M., 176
Nolichucky River, 13
North Carolina: forms Mero District, 13; ratifies Constitution, 20–21; cedes western territory, 21; and land fraud, 44ff
Northwest Ordinance, 28
Nullification: defined, 195; nullification controversy, 194, 235ff, 244ff

Office of Indian Affairs, 219
Ohio River, 65
Oklahoma, 216
Old Nashville Inn, 69, 70
O'Neal, William, 146
Onís, Don Luis de, 124
Oregon, 349, 351, 356
Osage Boundary, 113
Osceola, Chief, 218
Overton, John: meets AJ, 17; gives account of AJ's marriage, 23–26; congratulates AJ on election, 32; business relations with AJ, 33–34, 40, 49–50; described, 139–140; member of Nashville junto, 145; and election of 1828, 158; mentioned, 194, 206
Overton, General Thomas, 53

Pacific Ocean, 20, 128
Pakenham, Lieutenant General Sir Edward Michael: assumes command of invasion, 97; early career, 97; main assault, 1–3, 101–103; killed, 2, 102, 105
Panic of 1819, 143, 144
Panic of 1833–1834, 166–267
Panic of 1837, 338–339
Patriot, New Hampshire, 165
Patterson, Commodore Daniel T., 90, 97, 100, 103
Pea Island, 92
Pensacola, 65, 66, 122, 124, 132
Percy, Sir William, 88
Perdido River, 131
Petigru, James L., 235

Philadelphia, 7, 33, 34, 35, 127, 255–256, 299, 344, 348
Physick, Dr. Philip Syng, 255–256
Pinckney, General Thomas, 79, 81
Pirates, 1, 91ff
Plains of Gentilly, 90
Plauché, Jean, 100, 347
Plowboy, 52
Poindexter, George, 207, 224
Poinsett, Joel, 235, 236, 239
Polk, James Knox: and Bank War, 225–226, 274; AJ supports, 350; elected President, 351; meets with AJ, 354; angers AJ, 355
Poplar Grove, 27
Porter, David, 177
Porter, Peter B., 61
Portsmouth, New Hampshire, 259
Portugal, 286
Post Office Act of 1836, 299, 302
Potomac River, 159
Presbyterian church: AJ's affiliation with, 6, 324; AJ joins, 339–341
Pryor, Norton, 49, 50

Quakers, 212
Quallah Battoo, 287
Quebec, 62, 87

Racism, 299
Radicals, 147–148, 151, 159, 160, 175
Randolph, John: influence on AJ, 49; attacks Clay and Adams, 159; and Maysville veto, 210; and tariff, 248; appointed minister, 389 note 18
Randolph, Robert B., 252–253
Randolph, Mrs. Thomas Mann, 193
Red River, 128
Red Sticks. *See* Creek Indians
Reid, John: serves as AJ's aide, 64, 110; writes biography of AJ, 64; in Creek War, 75ff; and Battle of New Orleans, 99
Reiff, Joseph, 278
Removal of Indians. *See* Indian removal and particular tribes
Republican, Cincinnati, 336
Republican party, 36, 55, 142, 146ff
Republicanism, 143–144, 146ff, 155–156, 157, 161, 166, 168, 247
Review, Nashville, 53
Reynolds, John, 218
Rhea, John, 44, 118
Rhett, Barnwell, 250
Rice, Joel, 33
Richmond, 59
Richmond Junto, 161
Rigolets, 90, 92
Rip Raps, 299
Ritchie, Thomas, 161, 165, 175

Rives, John, 347, 355
Rives, William C., 275, 289, 292
Roane, Archibald: appointed attorney general, 21; elected governor, 45; votes for AJ as general, 45; and Sevier, 45ff
Roane, John, 196
Robards, Lewis: marries Rachel Donelson, 16; separates from wife, 17; reconciled with wife, 17; quarrels with AJ, 18; character, 17–18; accused of adultery, 18; deserts wife, 18; sues for divorce, 23–24; charges Rachel with adultery and desertion, 23–24; obtains divorce, 24; motives for delaying divorce, 24
Roberts, Edmund, 287
Robertson, James: explores western Tennessee, 13; appointed general, 21; political influence, 22; attends constitutional convention, 29; as mediator, 38–39; mentioned, 20
Robertson, William, 348
Rodriguez Canal, 96ff, 105
Roosevelt, Franklin D., 323
Ross, Sir Robert, 97
Ross, Colonel George, 100
Rotation of office, 185ff
Rowan House, 10
Russia, 286, 288, 293, 323, 344

Sabine River, 128
Sac and Fox Indians, 218
St. Augustine, 65, 124, 131, 132
St. Charles Theater, 344
St. Johns, 131–132
St. Marks, 120, 132
Salisbury, North Carolina, 10, 12
San Jacinto, Battle of, 310
Santa Anna, General Antonio de: invades Texas, 310; defeated, 310; captured, 310, 311; meets AJ, 312–313; returns to Mexico, 313; described, 312
Santa Fe, 57
Savannah, 7
Scotch-Irish, 4, 104
Scott, John, 154–155
Scott, General Winfield, 218, 239, 298
Searcy, Bennett, 12–13, 16
Sedgwick, Theodore, 273
Seminole controversy, 190ff
Seminole Indians: attack settlers, 117ff; and First Seminole War, 117ff; and Second Seminole War, 218; and removal, 218
Seminole War, First, 117ff
Seminole War, Second, 218
Sergeant, John, 222, 237
Sérurier, Louis Barbe, 290, 291

Sevier, John: early career, 13, 20, 37; appointed general, 21; elected governor, 32, 48; quarrels with AJ, 38–39, 44ff, 366 note 16; charged with fraud, 44ff; in Congress, 72
Seward, William H., 222
Shakespeare, William, 345
Shaw, Dr. William A., 344
Short Description of Tennessee Government, 30
Siam, 287, 288
Sitler, James, 70
Slavery, 51–52, 92, 129, 298–299, 302, 312
Smith, Daniel, 21, 30, 59
Smith, Reverend James, 340
Smith, Mrs. Margaret Bayard, 178, 179, 180, 181
Smith, William, 328
Sousa, Domingo, 133
South Carolina: and nullification, 217, 235ff, 244ff
Southwest Territory, 21
Spain: presence in southwest, 20, 39; and Louisiana, 48–49; and conspiracy, 56–60; and AJ's policy toward as President, 209, 288
Specie Circular, 303, 330, 338
Spoils system. See Rotation of office
Stark, Colonel Robert, 22–23
Statesman, Boston, 274
Statesman, New York, 141
Stephenson, James White, 5
Stevens, Thaddeus, 167, 222
Stevenson, Andrew, 213
Stokes, Colonel John, 12
Stono Ferry, Battle of, 8
Storrs, Henry, 214
Story, Joseph, 180
Stuart, James, 34
Sumatra, 287
Sumter, Colonel Thomas, 8
Supreme Court, 212ff, 227ff, 302
Suwannee River, 120, 121, 131
Swartwout, Samuel, 188–189

Talbot's Hotel, 57
Talladega, 73–74, 79
Tallapoosa River, 78, 81
Tallushatchee, 73
Tampico, 310, 311
Taney, Roger Brooke: described, 205; appointed attorney general, 205; and Bank War, 222ff; appointed secretary of Treasury, 264; helps write Protest message, 269; nomination for Treasury secretary rejected by Senate, 276; named Chief Justice, 299; on expunging censure, 328; composes AJ's Farewell Address, 332–333;

Taney, Roger Brooke *(cont'd)*
swears Van Buren in as President, 334
Tappan, Arthur, 299
Tappan, Lewis, 299
Tariff of Abominations, 167, 194, 209
Tariff of 1832, 226
Tariff of 1833 (Compromise), 249–250
Tarleton, Lieutenant Colonel Banastre, 7, 8
Tazewell, Henry, 37
Tecumseh, 71
Tennessee: settled, 13; movement toward independence, 13; and constitutional convention, 29–30; admitted to Union, 32; named, 30; and Indians, 29; development of, 44
Tennessee River, 73, 112
Texas: under Spanish rule, 20, 127, 128; AJ's desire for, 116, 309ff, 331, 356; and war for independence, 310; seeks U.S. recognition, 311–314; annexed by U.S., 352–353
Thornton, Colonel Thomas, 93, 99–100, 103, 104
Timberlake, Lieutenant John, 173–174
Tom Jones, 159
Tombigbee River, 112
Tompkins, Daniel D., 143
Transcontinental Treaty, 127–128, 309
Transylvania University, 138
Treaty of Dancing Rabbit Creek, 215–216
Treaty of Doak's Stand, 114–115
Treaty of Fort Jackson, 84–85, 111, 117, 126
Treaty of Ghent, 96, 108, 111
Treaty of New Echota, 217–218
Trist, Nicholas, 324, 325
Truth's Advocate and Monthly Anti-Jackson Expositor, 163
Truxton, 52, 60
Turkey, 288
Twelve Mile Creek, 5
Tyler, John: votes against Force Bill, 248; and assassination attempt, 297; defeated for Vice President, 328; becomes President, 346; vetoes Bank bill, 346; and Texas, 348–350, 352; retires, 351

Union Bank of Maryland, 265
United States v. *Major General Andrew Jackson,* 110
United States Telegraph: established, 164; mentioned, 168, 178, 195, 196, 197, 200, 201, 202, 206, 207, 250
Upshur, Abel P., 393 note 12

Van Buren, Martin: described, 148, 186; characteristics, 148, 186; nicknames,

Van Buren, Martin *(cont'd)*
148; friendship with AJ, 148, 187; leads Radicals in Congress, 148, 149, 153, 154, 160; joins AJ, 160–161; on party system, 160–161; forms alliance, 161; leads Democrats, 167; elected governor, 173; appointed secretary of state, 173; as secretary, 186–188; opinion of AJ, 187; and Eaton scandal, 190ff; resigns as secretary of state, 203–204; appointed minister to Great Britain, 204; and Maysville veto, 210–211; importance to AJ, 221; nomination as minister defeated in Senate, 224–225; nominated for Vice President, 226; and Force Bill, 250; tours with AJ, 254, 257; and national debt, 295; and AJ's appointments, 309; election as President, 312, 328; inaugurated, 334; promises to visit AJ, 336; calls special session of Congress, 339; defeated for reelection, 342; opposes annexation of Texas, 350
Vaughan, Sir Charles, 193
Venezuela, 288
Vera Cruz, 313
Veron, Louis, 320
Verplanck, Gulian C., 245, 247, 249, 331
Vicar of Wakefield, 6
Vidal, Mercedes, 133
Villeré, Major Gabriel, 93–94
Villeré, General Jacques, 93
Virginia, 299

Walker, Robert J., 349, 351, 352
Wall Street, 273
Wallace, Sir William, 6
War Hawks, 61–62
War of 1812, 61ff
Washington, D.C.: invaded by British, 87, 108; corruption in, 141ff
Washington, George: appoints Blount governor, 21; signs admission for Tennessee, 32; delivers Farewell Address, 36; AJ votes against, 36, 162; mentioned, 143, 172, 252, 253, 295, 332, 333, 344, 348
Washington Assembly Rooms, 181
Watauga River, 13
Waters, Dr., 357
Watson, Charles C., 35
Watson, Thomas, 51
Waxhaw Creek, 4
Waxhaw District, 4, 7ff
Weatherford, William (Chief Red Eagle): leads attack on Fort Mims, 71; conducts Creek War, 71–85; surrenders to AJ, 83–84

Webster, Daniel: and election of
    1824–1825, 154; debates Hayne, 195,
    242; views of Constitution, 195; and
    Bank War, 222ff; opposes Van
    Buren's nomination as minister, 224;
    supports AJ on nullification, 238,
    247–248, 266; and Compromise
    Tariff, 251; opposes AJ's Bank policy,
    266; attacks AJ, 270; candidate for
    President, 328; against expunging
    censure, 328–329; as secretary of
    state, 346, 393 note 12
Weed, Thurlow, 167, 222
Weehawken, New Jersey, 55
Weld, Theodore Dwight, 299
Welles, Gideon, 175, 176
Wellington, Duke of, Arthur Wellesley, 97
West Indies, 189, 283–285
West Point, 127, 138
Wharton, William, 313
Wheaton, Henry, 286
Whig, Nashville, 67
Whig party: origins of, 267–268; ideology,
    268; split, 346–347; mentioned, 303,
    328, 331, 350–351
White, Andrew, 47
White, Hugh Lawson: appeals to
    Congress, 37; and election of 1828,
    158; refuses appointment by AJ,
    173–174, 205; candidate for
    President, 328; votes against AJ, 329
White, Joseph, 9
White House: and AJ's inauguration,
    180ff; AJ's alterations of, 183, 315ff;
    mentioned, 281, 298
Whiteside, Jenkin, 44

Whitney, Reuben, 265
Wilderness Trace, 13
Wilkins, William, 237
Wilkinson, General James: in Louisiana,
    49; AJ's hatred of, 57–60, 65; as
    agent for Spanish, 57–58; informs
    Jefferson of conspiracy, 58–59; and
    War of 1812, 62–63, 65–66; AJ
    ordered to serve under, 63; orders AJ
    to halt advance, 65
Williams, Colonel John, 79, 81
Williams, John, 12, 145, 146
Winchester, James, 45, 56, 62, 89
Wirt, William: as attorney general, 124;
    defends Cherokees, 216, 217;
    nomination for President, 222;
    defeated, 237
Wolf, George, 273, 274
Wood, Molly, 10–11
Woodbury, Levi: described, 205, 276;
    appointed secretary of navy, 205; and
    Bank War, 227; and nullification
    controversy, 235; tours with AJ, 257;
    appointed secretary of Treasury, 276;
    characteristics, 276
Woods, John, 79–80
Worcester, Samuel A., 216
Worcester v. *Georgia,* 216–218
Wright, Silas, Jr., 247, 248–249, 267, 273,
    295, 347, 394 note 21

Yankee Doodle, 1, 106
Yorktown, 9

Zanzibar, 287
Zuniga, Mauricio de, 117